Quality Assurance and Certification in Ecotourism

Ecotourism Book Series

General Editor: David B. Weaver, Professor of Tourism Management, George Mason University, Virginia, USA.

Ecotourism, or nature-based tourism that is managed to be learning-oriented as well as environmentally and socioculturally sustainable, has emerged in the past 20 years as one of the most important sectors within the global tourism industry. The purpose of this Series is to provide diverse stakeholders (e.g. academics, graduate and senior undergraduate students, practitioners, protected area managers, government and non-governmental organizations) with state-of-the-art and scientifically sound strategic knowledge about all facets of ecotourism, including external environments that influence its development. Contributions adopt a holistic, critical and interdisciplinary approach that combines relevant theory and practice while placing case studies from specific destinations into an international context. The Series supports the development and diffusion of financially viable ecotourism that fulfils the objective of environmental, sociocultural and economic sustainability at both the local and global scale.

Titles available:

1. *Nature-based Tourism, Environment and Land Management*
   Edited by R. Buckley, C. Pickering and D. Weaver
2. *Environmental Impacts of Ecotourism*
   Edited by R. Buckley
3. *Indigenous Ecotourism: Sustainable Development and Management*
   H. Zeppel
4. *Ecotourism in Scandinavia: Lessons in Theory and Practice*
   Edited by S. Gössling and J. Hultman
5. *Quality Assurance and Certification in Ecotourism*
   Edited by R. Black and A. Crabtree

QUALITY ASSURANCE AND CERTIFICATION IN ECOTOURISM

Edited by

Rosemary Black

School of Environmental Sciences
Charles Sturt University
Albury, NSW
Australia

and

Alice Crabtree

Ecotourism Consultant
Cairns, Queensland
Australia

www.cabi.org

CABI is a trading name of CAB International

CABI Head Office
Nosworthy Way
Wallingford
Oxfordshire OX10 8DE
UK

Tel: +44 (0)1491 832111
Fax: +44 (0)1491 833508
E-mail: cabi@cabi.org
Web site: www.cabi.org

CABI North American Office
875 Massachusetts Avenue
7th Floor
Cambridge, MA 02139
USA

Tel: +1 617 395 4056
Fax: +1 617 354 6875
E-mail: cabi-nao@cabi.org

A catalogue record for this volume is available from the British Library, London, UK.

Library of Congress Cataloging-in-Publication Data

Quality assurance and certification in ecotourism / edited by Rosemary Black and Alice Crabtree.
p. cm. – (Ecotourism book series)
Includes bibliographical references and index.
ISBN-13: 978-1-84593-237-4 (alk. paper)
ISBN-10: 1-84593-237-4 (alk. paper)
1. Ecotourism--Quality control. 2. Ecotourism--Certification. I. Black, Rosemary, 1955- II. Crabtree, Alice. III. Title. IV. Series.

G156.5.E26Q83 2006
910.68′4–dc22

2006033312

ISBN: 978 1 84593 237 4

Typeset by AMA DataSet, Preston, UK.
Printed and bound in the UK by Biddles Ltd, King's Lynn.

Contents

CONCLUSION

Contributors

Rosemary Black

Dr Rosemary Black is a Senior Lecturer at Charles Sturt University. She teaches in the fields of heritage interpretation, interpretive guiding, ecotourism and outdoor education and is Course Coordinator of the Bachelor of Applied Sciences (Adventure Ecotourism). Prior to entering academia she worked as park ranger in New South Wales and a tour leader for World Expeditions, mainly in Nepal, Australia, India and Fiji. She has published over 18 refereed journal articles and book chapters and edited a book on Australian heritage interpretation and tour guiding. Her PhD focused on professional certification of tour guides in the Australian ecotourism industry. Her research interests are evaluation of interpretation, professionalism in tour guiding and social aspects of natural resource management, including gender issues and environmental education. School of Environmental Sciences, Charles Sturt University, PO Box 789, Albury, NSW 2640 (rblack@csu.edu.au).

Zoë Chafe

Zoë Chafe is a Staff Researcher at the Worldwatch Institute, an independent research organization based in Washington, DC. Previously, Zoë worked with the Centre on Ecotourism and Sustainable Development, a joint project of Stanford University and the Institute for Policy Studies, where her research focused on consumer demand for responsible tourism. She speaks

on tourism issues frequently, and has authored articles on responsible tourism and air travel in several international publications, including Worldwatch's annual facts and trends guide, *Vital Signs*. In 2005, Zoë served on the North American delegation to UN Environment Programme discussions on tourism and the environment. She holds a degree in Human Biology, with honours, from Stanford University. Worldwatch Institute, 1776 Massachusetts Ave, NW, Suite 800, Washington, DC 20036, USA (zchafe@worldwatch.org).

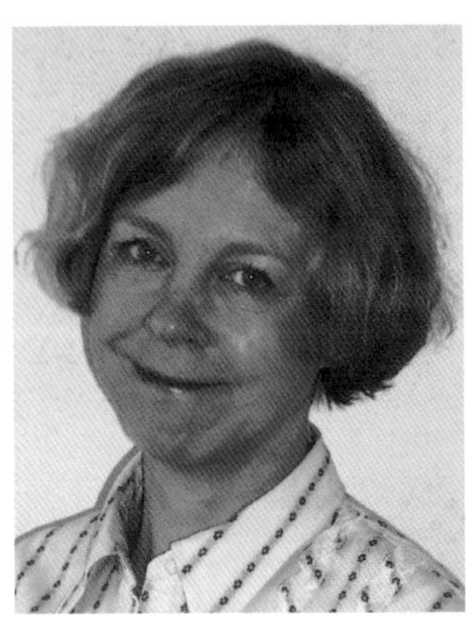

Sue Clark

Sue Clark is Visiting Lecturer in Tourism Planning at the Glion Institute of Higher Education (GIHE) in Switzerland. She has taught tourism at academic institutions in the UK, the USA and The Netherlands. She has had 25 years' experience working in the public and private sectors of the tourism industry and has a long-standing interest in nature and heritage tourism. After being on the Advisory Council of PAN Parks since 1999, she took the post of Senior Tourism and Marketing Adviser in summer 2004, with responsibility for the development of the PAN Parks project and for the establishment of tourism products. In cooperation with GIHE in 2004 she undertook a Training Needs Analysis of all current PAN Parks national parks staff and those involved in tourism around each park. Maaskantje 40, 5271 XG, St Michielsgestel, The Netherlands (clarkd@worldonline.nl).

Alice Crabtree

Dr Alice Crabtree is an independent ecotourism consultant. She was until recently Director (Asia-Pacific) for The International Ecotourism Society (TIES) and ran their Asia Pacific Office from Cairns. She was a founding member of Ecotourism Australia (EA) and served on its Executive, as well as playing a key role in the development of the world's first ecotourism-specific certification programme, NEAP and its sister programme, EcoGuides. Alice was also one of the principal authors of the International Ecotourism Standard (IES), an international programme developed for Green Globe. Alice is currently Chair of the Respect Our Culture Technical Advisory Committee (run by Aboriginal Tourism Australia) and continues to serve on the Sustainable Tourism Stewardship Council's Advisory Group. She has both taught and written extensively on tourism – with particular emphasis on ecotourism development in developing countries, nature guiding and interpretation, certification and accreditation issues with a focus on standards development for the ecotourism industry in Australia and Asia. Her current work focus is on AID work in China using community-based ecotourism as an alternative livelihood option for poverty alleviation in rural, ethnic minority areas and using ecotourism for conservation/biodiversity initiatives in coastal areas. PO Box 372, Trinity Beach, Qld 4879, Australia (crabtree@austarnet.com.au or acr26934@bigpond.com.au).

Megan Epler Wood

Megan Epler Wood is the principal of Epler Wood International, which has performed strategic market, business and project analysis in ecotourism and sustainable tourism for the World Bank/International Finance Corporation, USAID and private clients in the USA, Peru, Ecuador, Sri Lanka and Cambodia and on an international level. The firm publishes EplerWood Report at www.eplerwood.com with widely referenced original articles on monitoring, standards and consumer demand. Epler Wood founded the International Ecotourism Society (TIES) in 1990 and was its Executive Director and subsequently President from 1991 to 2002. She led the ecotourism workshop programme for the George Washington University from 1995 to 2000. EplerWood International, 369 South Union Street, Burlington, VT 05401, USA (megan@eplerwood.com).

Xavier Font

Xavier Font is Principal Lecturer in Tourism Management at Leeds Metropolitan University and member of the PAN Parks Advisory Council. He has degrees in tourism management and marketing from the Universities of Girona (Spain) and Surrey (UK). Formerly he lectured at Buckinghamshire Chilterns University College and was Project Officer for an EU project on forest tourism. His research focuses on standard setting and certification of sustainable tourism and hospitality. He has co-authored and co-edited four books and published in a variety of academic journals, including recent papers in *Annals of Tourism Research, Tourism Management, Journal of Sustainable Tourism* and *Corporate Social Responsibility and Environmental Management*. In the last 5 years he has undertaken research and consultancy for UNEP, WTO, EC, Ford Foundation, Travel Foundation, Foreign and Commonwealth Office and WWF International, Germany and The Netherlands. Tourism, Hospitality and Events School, Leeds Metropolitan University, Leeds, UK (x.font@lmu.ac.uk).

Carol Goodstein

Carol Goodstein is the Editor/Writer for the Rainforest Alliance, an international conservation organization. Prior to joining the Alliance, she was an editor at the Brooklyn Botanic Garden, where she contributed chapters on biodiversity to the *Gardener's Desk Reference*. Her freelance articles on travel and the environment have appeared in publications including *Nature Conservancy, Audubon, E, Elle, Newsweek International* and the *Amicus Journal*. She has worked as a consultant for a variety of clients including the National Park Service, the World Wildlife Fund and Fenton Communications. Goodstein holds a BA from Bard College and an MA from Boston University's School of Public Communication. Rainforest Alliance, PO Box 11029–1000, San Jose, Costa Rica (cgoodstein@ra.org).

Jill Grant

Jill Grant was the Executive Director of Green Globe Asia Pacific during late 2003 and 2004, where she was responsible for the development of partnerships with state and local government, the tourism industry and non-governmental organizations to encourage the adoption of sustainable practices and continuous improvement in the tourism industry. She has a background in agriculture, environmental science and education and over 15 years' policy and programme development experience in government, with a particular emphasis on sustainable development, tourism and environment industry development. As co-author of the National Ecotourism Strategy (1994), Manager of the National Ecotourism Program and the environmental aspects of the Regional Tourism Program, Jill developed a strong understanding of the key business and policy issues affecting the delivery of sustainable tourism activities. C/o Energy and Environment Division, Department of Industry, Tourism and Resources, GPO Box 9839, Canberra, ACT 2601, Australia (Jill.Grant@industry.gov.au).

Herbert Hamele

Herbert Hamele has been working for 20 years in the field of sustainable tourism development in Europe. In the 1980s he carried out a range of studies and model projects related to youth travel and German consumers' demand for sustainable tourism. In 1993 he founded and now chairs the European Network for Sustainable Tourism Development ECOTRANS, a registered not-for-profit association. He specializes in the development, monitoring, research, networking and dissemination of voluntary initiatives and best practice examples (www.ecotip.org) for sustainable tourism, with a special focus on ecolabels, awards and self-committed initiatives worldwide. ECOTRANS e.V., Futterstr. 17–19, D-66111 Saarbrücken, Germany (herbert.hamele@ecotrans.de).

James Higham

James Higham is an Associate Professor at the Department of Tourism, University of Otago, New Zealand. He teaches and researches in the areas of tourism impacts and evaluation, ecotourism business operations, wilderness management and the management of tourist engagements with wildlife populations. He was the recipient of a major government research grant (1999–2001) which explored the environmental values of visitors to ecotourism businesses in New Zealand. In 2002 he was the recipient of an Antarctica New Zealand scholarship, which included an extended visit to the Ross Sea region to explore the management of tourism in New Zealand's Antarctic dependency. Department of Tourism, School of Business, University of Otago, PO Box 56, Dunedin, New Zealand (jhigham@business.otago.ac.nz).

Colin Ingram

Colin Ingram is the Manager of the Park Policy and Services Branch within the Department of Environment and Conservation, Western Australia. Colin has worked in the protected area management field for over 20 years, initially as a Ranger in the NSW National Parks and Wildlife Service and over the past 10 years coordinating recreation and tourism policy, social research, community involvement programmes and the management of tourism operations and developments in Western Australian protected areas. Colin has

been an active member of national (Australian) working groups and task forces on issues including tourism accreditation, heritage tourism, protected area management and protected area research. He is the WA Chair of the WA Network of the Sustainable Tourism Cooperative Research Centre and Deputy Chair of FACET (Forum Advocating Cultural and EcoTourism). C/o Department of Conservation and Land Management, Locked Bag 104, Bentley Delivery Centre, WA 6983, Australia (colini@calm.wa.gov.au).

Jon Kohl

After serving in the US Peace Corps in Costa Rica and getting his Master's at the Yale University School of Forestry, Jon worked for 6½ years with a conservation NGO, RARE, in Mesoamerica. He managed the Nature Guide Training Program and later founded the Public Use Planning Program. Jon co-wrote the guide training manual and also wrote the public use manual. Since leaving RARE in 2004, he has been consulting in conservation, ecotourism, training and interpretation. His recent interest is the application of systems thinking to learning, project design and world view change. Apdo 12-2250, Tres Rios, Cartago, Costa Rica (jkohl@jonkohl.com).

Naut Kusters

Naut Kusters was educated in social forestry and has worked since 1992 as a project manager and consultant in rural tourism and ecotourism. Naut is the director of the European Centre for Eco and Agro Tourism (ECEAT), which is an international association promoting sustainable tourism in Europe's rural areas with branches in more than 15 countries. ECEAT maintains a marketing network of more than 2000 small-scale environmentally friendly accommodations (www.eceat.org). The association is one of the initiators of VISIT, the European Association of Tourism Ecolabels (www.yourvisit.info) and the Tour Link initiative, linking European tour operators with certified products. ECEAT – Projects, Postbox 10899, 1001 EW Amsterdam, The Netherlands (N.kusters@eceat.nl).

Gemma McGrath

Gemma McGrath, who is half-Spanish and half-Irish, studied French and Hispanic Studies at the University of Liverpool, and spent a year living in Peru. After graduating in the early 1990s, she worked as an overland tour leader in Latin America. She later took a Master's degree in tourism management at the University of Surrey and wrote her dissertation on developing ecotourism in Costa Rica. Her research interests lie in interpretation and service quality issues, especially in developing areas. Her doctoral thesis focused on the importance of developing the tour guide's role at archaeological sites in Peru. She is a Senior Lecturer and the Course Director of the International Tourism and Travel Communication BA. London College of Communication, University of the Arts, Elephant and Castle, London SE1 6SB, UK (g.mcgrath@lcc.arts.ac.uk).

Peter Mason

Dr Peter Mason is Professor of Tourism Management at the University of Luton. His early research concentrated on tourism development and impacts; more recently he has focused on tourism planning and management. He is known for his work on education and regulation in tourism and particularly for the first academic study that discussed and critiqued tourism codes of conduct. This was published by the Department of Geography, University of Plymouth, UK, and appeared later in a revised form in *Progress in Tourism and Hospitality Research*. In addition to work on codes of conduct, he is currently involved in researching and writing about visitor management, tour guiding and interpretation issues in tourism. Department of Tourism, Leisure and Human Resource Managment, University of Bedforshire, Park Square, Luton, LU1 3JU, UK (peter.mason@luton.ac.uk).

Hitesh Mehta

Hitesh Mehta is a Landscape Architect, Architect and Environmental Planner and works at Edward D. Stone Jr and Associates in Florida. He is one of

the world's leading authorities and researchers on ecotourism physical planning, in particular the landscape and architectural aspects of ecolodges. He is the main editor of the *International Ecolodge Guidelines* and authored chapters on Site Planning and Architectural Design and is currently writing a book on Best Practice Ecolodges. He sits on the Board of TIES and Advisory Board of BIOSFERA (Brazilian Environmental Society) and Japan Ecolodge Association. Hitesh has consulted on the design of many ecolodges in Rwanda, Uganda, Kenya, the Democratic Republic of Congo, Egypt, Australia, Panama, India, Madagascar, Turks and Caicos Islands, Sri Lanka and the USA. EDSA, 1512 E. Broward Blvd, Suite 110, Fort Lauderdale, FL 33301, USA (hmehta@edsaplan.com).

Cathy Parsons

Cathy is an environmental management consultant who was until recently the Chief Executive Officer of Green Globe Asia Pacific Pty Ltd. She was responsible for all aspects relating to the development and delivery of the Green Globe programme. Prior to taking up the position with Green Globe Asia Pacific, she worked as a Senior Executive in the Australian government for over 15 years. During this time she was responsible for dealing with a range of tourism and environmental issues. As former manager of the Regional and Environmental Tourism Branch in the Department of Tourism during the 1990s, she managed tourism programmes to assist the industry in developing products and services. She was a key player in developing the Australian National Ecotourism Accreditation Program and supporting the development of certification programmes for other tourism industry sectors. RMB 2001, Bungendore Road, The Ridgeway, NSW 2620, Australia (cparsons@netspeed.com.net).

Abigail Rome

Abigail Rome is an independent consultant working in ecotourism, sustainable tourism and conservation. She conducts research on a variety of related subjects (including ecotourism and sustainable tourism certification and community-based tourism), writes reports and articles for the general public, offers workshops and training, and organizes and leads occasional ecotours. While her focus is on Latin America, Abi has travelled and written

about tourism around the world. She has a Master's degree in plant ecology from Duke University (North Carolina) and spent 10 years working in protected areas management, first in the eastern USA and then in South America. Tierra Vista Consulting, 605 Ray Drive, Silver Spring, MD 20910, USA (abirome@earthlink.net).

Tara Rowe

Tara Rowe studied her Bachelor of Tourism Management at the University of New Brunswick, Canada. Acknowledging that life is about the journey, Tara integrates travel and learning as a way of life. In 2004 Tara completed a Master's in Tourism at the University of Otago, New Zealand. Her research interests include codes of ethics, sustainability, nature-based tourism and environmental certification.

Tara is now working in the area of sustainable product development for a regional economic development agency in Northland, New Zealand. Her key focus is to create a synergy for the region's natural, cultural and heritage values, and to successfully progress tourism through strategic planning. Department of Tourism, School of Business, University of Otago, PO Box 56, Dunedin, New Zealand (tara.northland@xtra.co.nz).

Ronald Sanabria

Ronald Sanabria, Director, Sustainable Tourism, Rainforest Alliance: Ronald has a *licenciatura* in Industrial Engineering from the University of Costa Rica (UCR) with a Master's in Sustainable International Development from Brandeis University. He began working in quality assurance, environmental management systems and other certification-related projects in 1992, including projects in tourism companies in Costa Rica. Ronald is the Rainforest Alliance's representative to the Sustainable Tourism Stewardship Council initiative.

Additionally, Ronald is part of the Rainforest Alliance's team currently providing services as the secretariat of the Sustainable Tourism Certification Network of the Americas, a regional platform of certification programmes aimed at sharing information and raising awareness about sustainable tourism. Ronald teaches at the UCR's Engineering Faculty. Director, Sustainable Tourism, Rainforest Alliance, PO Box 11029 –1000, San Jose, Costa Rica (rsanabria@ra.org).

Jennifer Seif

Jennifer Seif is the National Coordinator of Fair Trade in Tourism South Africa (FTTSA), a non-profit initiative that certifies tourist products in South Africa for compliance with 'fair trade' principles and criteria. Jennifer holds qualifications in development economics (Georgetown University), history (Boston University), social anthropology (University of Chicago) and business management (University of South Africa), and has twice been recognized by Ashoka as an expert in non-profit resource mobilization. She is currently completing a doctorate at the University of Pretoria, focusing on the marketing of tourism certification schemes. Fair Trade in Tourism South Africa, PO Box 11536, Hatfield 0028, South Africa (jennifer@fairtourismsa.org.za).

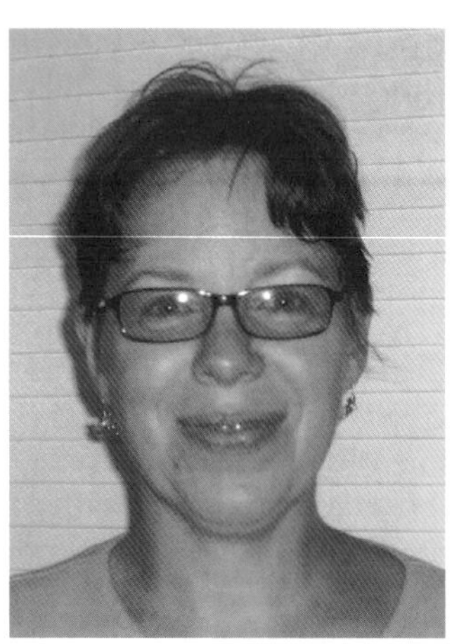

Elizabeth Skinner

For the past 20 years, Elizabeth Skinner has worked extensively in the field of certification, small business and community development and management. As a staff member of the Rainforest Alliance she managed its Agricultural Certification Program (ECO-O.K. Certification) and was Managing Director of its SmartWood Program. With SmartWood she researched sustainable certification business models for non-profits. Her other research and conservation work has included looking at cocoa and certification, medicinal plants and rainforest conservation, and ecotourism and certification. She holds an MSc in Community Development and Applied Economics from the University of Vermont and a BA from Barnard College, Columbia University. 8 School Street, Essex Junction, VT 05452, USA (skislo@verizon.net).

Anna Spenceley

Dr Anna Spenceley is a researcher and consultant specializing in sustainable tourism. In particular she works on nature-based, pro-poor, fair and responsible tourism, and trans-frontier conservation areas across Africa. She is a research fellow with the Transboundary Protected Areas Research Initiative, which is a partnership between the BMW Chair for Sustainability (University of the Witwatersrand), the Centre for the Integrated Study of the Human Dimensions of Global Change (Carnegie Mellon University) and the IUCN. International Centre for Responsible Tourism, c/o Institute of Natural Resources, PO Box 100396, Scottsville 3209, South Africa (annaspenceley@hotmail.com).

Rik Thwaites

Dr Rik Thwaites is a senior lecturer in Ecotourism at Charles Sturt University, Australia. Rik trained as a geologist and worked as a glaciologist, photographer and environmental consultant before undertaking a PhD on social, cultural, economic and policy factors influencing landscape management in northern China. His research interests include ecotourism as a tool for sustainable development, particularly in small and indigenous communities, and the nexus between communities, protected areas and tourism. Rik was an assessor for the Nature and Ecotourism Accreditation Program (NEAP) from 2000 to 2004, contributing to the development of the Green Globe International Ecotourism Standard and EcoCertification (NEAP version 3). School of Environmental and Information Sciences, Charles Sturt University, PO Box 789, Albury, NSW 2640, Australia (rthwaites@csu.edu.au).

Stuart Toplis

Dr Stuart Toplis has considerable travel and tourism industry experience (20 years), particularly in the areas of regional, ecotourism and sustainable tourism and was recently conferred the degree of Doctor of Philosophy, specializing in sustainable tourism. He has also been a committee member of Ecotourism Australia and the National Chairman of Assessors for the Eco Certification Program (2001–2004). During his career Stuart has been involved in a number of important and innovative areas in the Australian ecotourism industry, such as undertaking pioneering research into the employment potential of the industry and playing a major part in the development and continued redevelopment of the National Ecotourism Accreditation Program (Eco Certification Program). Industry Development Consultant, Tourism Victoria, GPO Box 2219T, Melbourne, Vic 3001, Australia (stuart.toplis@tourism.vic.gov.au).

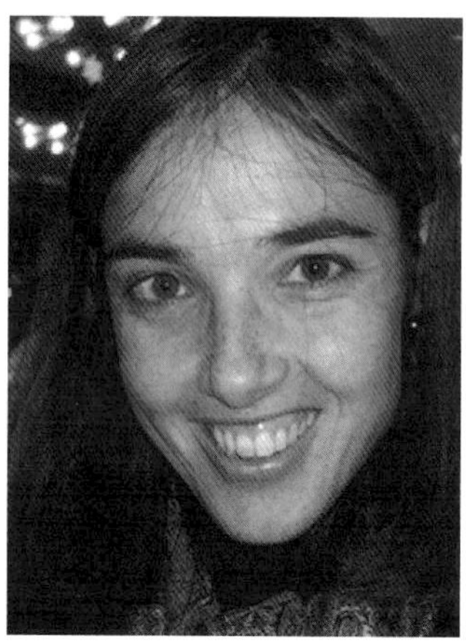

Louise Twining-Ward

Dr Louise Twining-Ward is a sustainable tourism advisor specializing in indicators and monitoring systems. She is Adjunct Lecturer at New York University, Course Designer for the University of the South Pacific and Visiting Fellow at the University of Surrey, where she gained her PhD in Tourism. Her work is mostly based in the South Pacific, where she lived and worked for 8 years. She is co-author of the book *Monitoring for a Sustainable Tourism Transition* (CABI) and a Member of the Board of Directors of the International Ecotourism Society. 369 Sterling Place, Brooklyn, NY 11238, USA (louisetw@verizon.net).

Gabor Vereczi

Gabor Vereczi has been a Programme Officer in the Sustainable Development section of the Tourism Department of the World Tourism Organization since 2000. He graduated at the Agricultural University of Gödöllö, Hungary, and later undertook postgraduate studies at the University of Minnesota, where he gained extensive experience in the fields of ecotourism, conservation, community development, environmental education and interpretation. Prior to his current position he worked as a lecturer in the Tourism Department of the Kodolányi János University College, Hungary, specializing in ecotourism, rural tourism, environmental economy and management. During this period he was involved in a consultancy coordinating regional tourism development programmes in Hungary, and for the Sustainable Tourism Indicators Workshop organized by WTO in Mexico. At the WTO he has coordinated projects in sustainable tourism indicators, voluntary initiatives and sustainability certification for tourism, compilations of good practice, climate change and tourism, sustainable tourism in coastal zones and natural and cultural sites, and community-based tourism, as well as activities during the International Year of Ecotourism 2002. World

Tourism Organization, Sustainable Development of Tourism Department, Capitán Haya, 42, 28020 Madrid, Spain (env@world-tourism.org).

Luis A. Vivanco

Luis A. Vivanco is Assistant Professor of Anthropology and Director of the Latin American Studies Program at the University of Vermont. He holds a PhD in Cultural Anthropology from Princeton University (1999). Since the early 1990s, he has conducted ethnographic research on the cultural and political dimensions of environmentalism and ecotourism in Costa Rica and southern Mexico. He is the author of the forthcoming book *Green Encounters: Shaping and Contesting Environmentalism in Rural Costa Rica*. He is also an Advisory Council member of Indigenous Tourism Rights International, and has lately been conducting research on the potentials and pitfalls of indigenous involvement in tourism certification programmes. 509 Williams Hall, Department of Anthropology, University of Vermont, Burlington, VT 05405, USA (lvivanco@uvm.edu).

Foreword

DAVID WEAVER

University of South Carolina, USA

At the dawn of its third decade as a formal construct, ecotourism is facing a crisis of credibility. Ironically, this crisis has arisen in large part due to the consensus that has been recently been reached as to the core criteria of ecotourism. One of these criteria, the imperative of ecological, economic and socio-cultural sustainability, is a noble burden that is unique to ecotourism, while another, the facilitation of effective visitor learning experiences, is only slightly less daunting. In both cases, it is not clear that the self-proclaimed ecotourism sector has lived up to these lofty expectations, besieged as it has been by the problem of 'greenwashing' as well as by well-intended attempts to expand its parameters into the minefield of mass tourism. This foray along the path of 'soft' ecotourism may well be necessary to confer on the sector the economies of scale necessary for the much-vaunted 'incentive effect' to be realized (that is, for ecotourism to generate enough revenue to justify the preservation of the relatively undisturbed habitat that is its main venue), but it also creates enormous challenges for meeting the sustainability criterion in particular. There is, after all, a very fine line between mass ecotourism and conventional mass tourism.

To address this crisis, it is essential that all products purporting to fall under the ecotourism banner be subject to quality assurance mechanisms that provide a reasonable guarantee of compliance with core criteria. While the design and implementation of such mechanisms, and in particular those based on the principle of certification, should therefore be a top priority for all ecotourism stakeholders, its accomplishment has been impeded by the incipient and diffuse knowledge base that informs this topic. This volume, however, is seminal in that it provides stakeholders with a synthesis of 'what is' and 'what ought to be' with respect to the issue of quality assurance in ecotourism. Rosemary Black and Alice Crabtree have succeeded in assembling an impressive array of experts from academia, industry, government and the non-profit sector who offer diverse theoretical and practical perspectives on the topic, thereby providing a foundation from which a credible ecotourism sector can emerge. I applaud their effort.

Foreword

MARTHA HONEY*

On 2 November 2005, in the ornate top-floor reception room at the US State Department overlooking Washington's granite monuments and Potomac River, a remarkable ceremony took place. US Secretary of State Condoleezza Rice gave the 2005 Award for Corporate Excellence to Lapa Rios, a 16-room ecolodge nestled in a private rainforest reserve in Costa Rica. Secretary Rice described Lapa Rios as 'a model of environmental stewardship and enlightened corporate leadership' and praised its American owners, Karen and John Lewis, for understanding 'that the best way to do well, is to do good'.

In accepting the honour and the trophy Karen Lewis graciously thanked the lodge's staff and explained, 'The Award validates not only our 15-year effort but also the concept of ecotourism. It verifies that ecotourism, when built on sound environmental and social principles, can be a successful business.' Indeed, ecotourism had never before received such high-level praise from the US government.

Somehow the 'good news' of ecotourism had percolated upwards, from the Osa Peninsula to the US Embassy in San Jose, to the top echelons in Washington. It seems ironic that the US government chose to honour ecotourism in Costa Rica rather than here in the USA. But the reality is that, in the USA, ecotourism is just beginning to take root and grow quickly, in part built on lessons learnt from Costa Rica and other countries around the world. In 2005, TIES sponsored the first conference on ecotourism in the USA. In 2007, we are sponsoring the second conference on North American ecotourism, focused on the USA and Canada.

* Martha Honey, PhD, is Executive Director of the Center on Ecotourism and Sustainable Development (CESD) and former Executive Director of the International Ecotourism Society (TIES), both based in Washington, DC. Over the last decade, she has written and lectured widely on ecotourism and certification.

Fortunately, as this volume demonstrates, ecotourism is widespread elsewhere, and Lapa Rios is one of many fine examples of ecotourism making a difference in the host community and the environment. Editors Rosemary Black and Alice Crabtree have brought together leading specialists from around the world and across a range of disciplines to offer a rich and textured assessment of the efforts to set quality standards for ecotourism through a range of tools, including awards, codes of conduct, indicators, certification and accreditation.

Setting quality standards for the tourism industry is complex. Tourism is not only the world's largest industry, but also one of the most diverse and dispersed. It operates in virtually every country, some 90% of tourism businesses are small or medium-sized, and it covers a wide variety of activities and enterprises. This presents considerable challenges for setting standards. As chapters in this volume illustrate, certification and other standard-setting mechanisms cover a range of occupations and businesses, including accommodation, destinations, tour operators, guides and other professionals, and protected areas. And, as other chapters detail, ecotourism also involves a range of stakeholders. These include practitioners with businesses and travel associations and academics and other professionals, officials and experts with parks and protected areas, NGOs, the UN, government agencies, international aid and development organizations, the media and public relations firms; and the list goes on.

The history of standard setting for ecotourism is relatively recent. While Mobil, Michelin, AAA and other tourism certification programmes that measure price and service date from the introduction of the automobile in the early 20th century, most 'green' certification programmes started in the wake of the 1992 Rio Earth Summit, the seminal UN meeting on the environment. The first international gathering of ecotourism and sustainable tourism certification programmes took place in November 2000 when 45 participants from 20 countries gathered at the Mohonk Mountain House (probably the oldest 'ecolodge' in the USA), outside New York City. This meeting produced the Mohonk Declaration, a framework document of fundamental principles necessary for all legitimate sustainable and ecotourism certification programmes. The Rainforest Alliance then spearheaded a 2-year feasibility study and global consultation, which resulted in a plan to create a global accreditation body, the Sustainable Tourism Stewardship Council (STSC). In October 2005, another meeting of key certification programmes, held in Rio de Janeiro, moved the STSC a step closer to creation, with the formation of an advisory council. Most importantly, the United Nations' International Year of Ecotourism in 2002, which included some eight regional forums and the World Ecotourism Summit in Quebec, signalled that ecotourism had taken on global importance and gave it further impetus in efforts to set standards to measure environmental and sociocultural impacts.

These are the public milestones marking, as did the State Department's Corporate Excellence award, the accomplishments of ecotourism. Parallel with this is the growing consumer demand for environmentally and socially responsible travel as well as a growth in efforts to 'green' some of the more mainstream sectors of the tourism industry. Today there are some 80 certification programmes functioning or in development, dozens of 'green' awards programmes, hundreds of codes of conduct, and a range of other mechanisms for measuring and rewarding ecotourism. As this volume illuminates, quality assurance initiatives and standards including certification have largely grown from the ground up, country by country and sector by sector. There are many little-known stories and unsung heroes; there are also numerous debates, conflicting assessments, failed programmes and ideas, and areas where more research and fieldwork is needed. This collection of essays honours and examines our progress so far, traces how far we have come, and outlines the debates and the challenges ahead.

While we have much to celebrate, the reality can also be sobering. Take, for instance, the issue of how Lapa Rios was selected for the State Department Award. It was almost certainly due to a personal recommendation by some guest and, ironically, not to the fact that Lapa Rios had recently earned the highest rating – five green leaves – in Costa Rica's national CST (Certification for Sustainable Tourism) programme. (Only one other hotel – Finca Rosa Blanca – has also received this top level.) Sadly, while CST's standard is strong, its marketing has been poor. There has been very little publicity for those lodges that become certified and few guests go to Lapa Rios because they know it has achieved five green leaves. In fact, today most sustainable tourism certification programmes suffer from wholly inadequate marketing programmes, and addressing this is but one of the challenges for building truly effective certification programmes.

Despite the challenges, this volume confirms there is much to celebrate. Today ecotourism and nature tourism are growing three times faster than the tourism industry as a whole, according to the UN's World Tourism Organization. Further, ecotourism has proved an effective tool for sustainable development: ecotourists, for instance, put many times more into the local economy than do cruise passengers – 14 times more in Belize, 23 times more in Costa Rica – while their social and environmental impacts are less. As we prepare to mark another milestone – the fifth anniversary since the International Year of Ecotourism – this volume is an important resource that benchmarks both the accomplishments and the challenges of ecotourism.

Preface

Book Rationale

It is already claimed that tourism is the world's largest industry, and predictions suggest that the industry will double over the next decade. Part of this growth includes a substantial increase in nature-based tourism and ecotourism, although this 'sector' is still relatively small and generally considered special interest. None the less, the huge growth in tourism indicates that increasing numbers of people are seeking travel experiences, and whether or not the experiences are nature-based or have an ecotourism focus it is inevitable that there are increasing impacts on the host destination. These impacts can be positive, with money being generated in local economies, benefits for local communities, greater understanding and respect for cultural differences and perhaps stimulating incentives or even finance for conservation initiatives. However, tourism impacts can also be negative, with environmental degradation, cultural commoditization and playground effects (prostitution, gambling, recreational drugs) all too common. These two faces of tourism – the Jekyll and Hyde, the positive and negative – mean there are avid supporters both for and against tourism.

This is where ecotourism comes to the fore – as a force within the industry that, in its very essence, aims to minimize tourism's negative impacts whilst maximizing tourism's positive impacts. Of course, this alone doesn't define ecotourism, but it does provide a major *raison d'être* for this volume. Genuine or quality ecotourism can provide a shining light, a good example, an influence that may help ensure that the huge, all-pervading tourism industry acts more responsibly and becomes more sustainable. We hope that in discussing some of the elements that make up quality ecotourism we can provide lessons that are not restricted to this sector of the industry alone.

It is, perhaps, unfair to suggest that mainstream tourism needs ecotourism to pave the way to a more sustainable industry. In the last 10 years there have been many initiatives by the tourism industry as a whole that have attempted to promote or integrate the values of sustainability. This is one of the reasons why chapters were solicited from individuals or programmes that were not necessarily ecotourism-specific, but had expertise on or fulfilled one or more of the component principles that make up ecotourism.

A wide range of international authors with different backgrounds and experience has contributed to this volume. We attempted to get a diversity of stakeholders' perspectives, including voices from those often not considered or heard. Some of the stories come from direct experience and on other occasions we used intermediaries (for example, we used consumer demand studies to represent the consumer, and an academic with significant hands-on experience to represent indigenous peoples and discuss their specific challenges). We aimed to present case studies that would help illustrate how various stakeholders or programmes attempt to ensure quality ecotourism. We hoped to at least introduce, if not marry, some of the contrasting theoretical and practical (industry) points of view.

The chapters in this volume inevitably reflect some personal understanding or interpretation of what ecotourism is, could be or should be. Some of the chapters focus on programmes or initiatives that will never be considered 'ecotourism', but were included because they illustrate attempts to achieve quality in one or more of the essential component principles of ecotourism (e.g. fair trade). This has inevitably led to a book with a diversity of views, which, in some cases, are discordant. In a field where there are still debates and arguments over the definition of or even the existence of genuine ecotourism, this was to be expected.

We hope this volume will add to a better understanding of ecotourism, with the dimension of quality and associated quality assurance tools to monitor, measure and assure genuine ecotourism – helping to ensure that the potential of ecotourism is realized.

Overview of Chapters

This volume has been organized to take the reader from a general introduction of the topic, quality in ecotourism, through to some of the various quality assurance tools or mechanisms that have been developed and applied, supported by a range of case studies. The initial chapters have been arranged to move the reader through the spectrum of tools, from what are perceived to be the least rigorous and effective (awards of excellence and codes of conduct) to more formal, credible and effective methods (certification and accreditation), with a brief foray into using indicators to measure and monitor effectiveness. The second theme dominating the arrangement of chapters is an attempt to explore different ecotourism stakeholders' perspectives.

The introductory chapter sets the context for the book by exploring the concepts of ecotourism, quality in tourism and finally quality in ecotourism. Part One of the book considers the spectrum of quality assurance tools that have been developed and applied in the ecotourism industry to address and improve quality. A range of measures exist, varying in their degree of effectiveness and their advantages and disadvantages. Each of the chapters in Part One provides a detailed analysis of a particular tool. Chapter 3 focuses on tourism awards for excellence in tourism, with Stuart Toplis examining the rationale behind quality and environmental awards, their roles and whether or not they are effective. Chapter 4 by Peter Mason looks at the effectiveness of tourism codes of conduct and provides a summary of their aims and rationale by presenting examples of visitor, host and industry codes. The next two chapters introduce certification, with Chapter 5 by Carol Goodstein considering some of the issues surrounding the development and implementation of an area- or ecosystem-specific programme called SmartVoyager, based in the Galapagos Islands. This is followed by Cathy Parsons and Jill Grant's chapter (Chapter 6), which looks at Green Globe, a global programme that seeks to achieve environmental, social and cultural improvements at the global, national and local levels. The last two chapters in this section look at indicators as tools to benchmark, monitor and perhaps even encourage quality ecotourism. Gabor Vereczi's chapter (Chapter 7) is based on the work of the United Nations World Tourism Organization and considers the use of sustainability indicators as essential tools to encourage, plan and monitor quality ecotourism for both destinations and ecotourism operations. His chapter is complemented by one by Louise Twining-Ward (Chapter 8), which discusses the different approaches to sustainable tourism indicators and monitoring and, using the case study of the Samoa Sustainable Tourism Indicator Project, demonstrates how an 'adaptive indicator approach' can work in practice.

Part Two of the book looks at a range of ecotourism stakeholders' perspectives – with an emphasis in one way or another on various industry certification programmes. Following an introductory chapter (Chapter 9), there are two chapters that focus on consumers and market demand for quality in ecotourism. Chapter 10 by Xavier Font and Megan Epler Wood explores, through a review of green consumer behaviour, sustainable tourism demand and the limited evidence available on market research for certification, an argument that certification is a supply-driven initiative, not a market-led approach. This chapter is followed by an analysis of consumer demand, based on the findings of a range of recent consumer studies and surveys, by Zoë Chafe (in Chapter 11). The community perspective is explored in the following three chapters. First, Abigail Rome, drawing mainly on examples from South America, examines the tourism perspectives of community members who have chosen to engage either in community-based tourism or in ecotourism partnerships. In Chapter 13 Luis A. Vivanco looks at the prospects and dilemmas of certifying indigenous tourism. In his chapter he evaluates the current indigenous involvement in and attitudes towards ecotourism and tourism certification programmes and considers some of the major opportunities and dilemmas certification initiatives bring to indigenous peoples. The next chapter (Chapter 14) takes us to another continent, Africa, where Jennifer Seif and Anna Spenceley look at the Fair Trade in Tourism certification system, which recognizes and rewards tourism establishments in South Africa that are committed to fair trade.

The following two chapters explore protected area managers' perspectives and explore innovations and partnerships with protected area managers that benefit the ecotourism industry and programme managers. Chapter 15 is by Colin Ingram, who uses Western Australia as a case study to explore the issues surrounding the use and application of various tourism certification programmes in the context of protected areas. This chapter is followed by one by Xavier Font and Sue Clark (Chapter 16), which discusses the Protected Area Network (PAN) of Parks, a programme that aims to create a network of European wilderness protected areas with a reliable trademark that guarantees nature protection, and some of the issues surrounding its development and implementation.

The next three chapters explore ecotour guide issues. The first, by Rosemary Black (Chapter 17), discusses the range of quality assurance mechanisms used in tour guiding, with a specific focus on professional certification. Her discussion is illustrated with two case studies, the Savannah Guides and the Australian EcoGuide Certification Program. The benefits of tour guide training as another quality assurance mechanism are discussed, in relation to a Central American-based tour guide training programme called RARE, by Jon Kohl (Chapter 18). He argues that an expanded definition of a guide's quality should include conservation success, but this is only achievable if ecotourism programme managers and operators use systems thinking. Chapter 19 by Gemma McGrath considers the value and roles of tour guides in the cultural site of Cusco, Peru, and the importance of training to improve tour guide performance.

The tour guiding chapters are followed by the perspectives of other players in the tourism industry, including those of tourism operators, an architect involved in designing and planning ecolodges and a former certification programme assessor. Chapter 20 by Tara Rowe and James Higham explores the awareness and perceptions of New Zealand ecotourism operators of environmental certification schemes. This chapter is followed by one authored by ecolodge architect Hitesh Mehta (Chapter 21), who reviews four different existing ecotourism certification programmes that include criteria for ecotourism accommodation and concludes by suggesting the need for an internationally recognized certification programme specifically for ecolodges. The following chapter by Rik Thwaites (Chapter 22) provides an insight into the Australian EcoCertification Program, focusing on the realities of developing and implementing an ecotourism-specific programme. The final chapter (Chapter 23) in this section, by Herbert Hamele, Naut Kusters, Ronald Sanabria and Elizabeth Skinner, uses the case studies of the Sustainable Tourism Network of the Americas and the VISIT network in Europe to argue the need for the consolidation of regional networks of certification programmes to fast-track sustainable tourism development and benefits.

The final concluding chapter (Chapter 24), by Alice Crabtree and Rosemary Black, draws together the key issues arising out of the discussions and debates presented in the book and looks to the future of quality in ecotourism both in theory and in practice.

All the chapters in this volume have successfully completed a double-blind refereeing process. Prior to acceptance, each manuscript passed through at least two critical reviews and corresponding revisions.

Acknowledgements

We would like to acknowledge the support we received from many individuals and organizations without which this volume would not have been completed. First and foremost, we would like to thank all the contributors for writing, revising and submitting their chapters for inclusion in this volume. Their support and faith in us as editors are welcomed and greatly appreciated.

Our sincerest thanks and gratitude go to the reviewers, who generously gave their time and expertise to provide feedback and comments for the authors and who have enhanced the quality of the chapters. The reviewers were Rosemary Black, Russell Boswell, Alice Crabtree, Maureen Cunningham, Penny Davidson, Stephen Edwards, Xavier Font, James Higham, Jean Pierre Issaverdis, Kreg Lindberg, Neil Lipscombe, Joanne Miller, Lindy McAllister, Simon McArthur, Greg Ringer, Abigail Rome, Amanda Stronza, Stuart Toplis, Bob Toth, David Weaver, Carolyn Wild and Heather Zeppel. Thanks also to Amos Bien, Allan Curtis and Louise Twining-Ward for their help and support.

The idea for this volume came from Professor David Weaver, who, as Series Editor, approached us to coordinate and edit this volume. We would like to thank him for giving us this opportunity to put together a book that presents a unique look at issues of quality in ecotourism, which we feel is currently missing from the ecotourism literature, and extending ourselves into the realm of book editing and publishing, which has been an exciting and challenging journey! We also thank him and Martha Honey for writing their respective Forewords.

The support of Charles Sturt University, where Rosemary works as a Senior Lecturer in the School of Environmental Sciences, is appreciated throughout the 3-year process, with some financial support and plenty of encouragement from fellow colleagues. The International Ecotourism Society, for which Alice formerly worked, has been supportive of the project and has facilitated the book's progress through allowing some synergies between this and other projects to develop.

We both wish to thank our families, friends and colleagues for their continued support and patience for the many hours we spent on the book. Alice would particularly like to thank her husband Colin and children Rebecca and Ben for stolen hours.

Finally, we would like to express our sincere thanks for the support and encouragement of Rebecca Stubbs, Nigel Farrar and Tracy Ehrlich from CABI.

Rosemary Black and Alice Crabtree
Albury and Cairns, 2007

Uniting Conservation, Communities and Sustainable Travel

TIES Organizational Description

Founded in 1990, The International Ecotourism Society (TIES) is the oldest and largest ecotourism organization in the world dedicated to disseminating information about ecotourism and sustainable tourism. It currently has members in nearly 100 countries. The organization's membership includes local and regional tour operators, lodge owners and managers, academics, consultants, conservation professionals and organizations, governments, architects, general development experts, NGOs, the media, students and travellers. TIES is part of a global consortium working to promote best practices for sustainable development and to assist small and community-based tourism projects. As a non-profit and non-governmental organization, TIES is unique in its efforts to provide environmental, economic and social guidelines and standards, training, technical assistance, research and publications to foster sound ecotourism development.

Abbreviations

AAA	Automobile Association of America
ABC	Affiliate/Awareness, Benchmarked, Certified (Green Globe)
ABTA	Association of British Travel Agents
ABTO	Association of Belgium Tour Operators
ACE	Adventure, Cultural and Ecotourism
ACF	Australian Conservation Foundation
ACT	Australian Capital Territory
ACTUAR	Asociación Costarricense de Turismo Rural Comunitario
ANTARAC	Australian National Training Authority (Research Advisory Council)
ANVR	The General Dutch Association of Travel Agencies
APEC	Asia Pacific Economic Cooperation
APPA	Appreciative Participatory Planning and Action methodology
ASACODE	Asociación San Migueleña de Conservación y Desarrollo
ASTOI	Associazione Tour Operator Italiani
ATAA	Australian Tourism Accreditation Authority
ATIA	Australian Tourism Industry Association
ATON	Australian Tourism Operators Network
ATTA	Australian Tourism and Travel Association
BBTAP	Better Business Tourism Certification Program
BEE	black economic empowerment
BEST	Business Enterprises for Sustainable Travel
BIOSFERA	Brazilian Environmental Society
BMP	business management practices
BSAC	British Sub Aqua Club
BTR	Bureau of Tourism Research (Australia)

CALM	Conservation and Land Management (Western Australia)
C&D	Conservación y Desarrollo
CAPAS	America Protected Areas System
CAS	complex adaptive systems
CAST	Caribbean Alliance for Sustainable Tourism
CBET	community-based ecotourism
CBT	community-based tourism
CBTEs	community-based tourism enterprises
CEC	Commission for Environmental Cooperation
CESD	Center on Ecotourism and Sustainable Development
CFCs	chlorofluorocarbons
CI	Conservation International
CMP	Conservation Measures Partnership
CPI	Consumer Price Index
CRC	Cooperative Research Centre
CREM	Consultancy and Research for Environmental Management
CSD	Commission on Sustainable Development
CSR	Corporate Social Responsibility
CST	Certification for Sustainable Tourism
CSTP	Certification for Sustainable Tourism in Peru
DFD	designing for deconstruction
DITR	Department of Industry, Tourism and Resources (Australia)
DoC	Department of Conservation (New Zealand)
DoT	Commonwealth Department of Tourism (Australia)
DTIE	UNEP Division of Technology, Industry and Economics
EA	Ecotourism Australia
EAA	Ecotourism Association of Australia
EC	European Commission
ECEAT	European Centre for Eco and Agro Tourism
ECO-CAMPING	ECOCAMPING Association
ECO-O.K.	Rainforest Alliance Agricultural Certification Program
ECOTEL	environmentally sensitive hotels certification programme
ECOTRANS	European Network for Sustainable Tourism Development
EEV	Ecologic Enterprise Ventures, Inc.
E for E	England for Excellence
EFQM	European Foundation on Quality Management
EFTGA	European Federation of Tourist Guides Associations
EGACP	EcoGuide Australia Certification Program
EMS	environmental management system
EP	environmental plan
EPA	Environmental Protection Agency
EU	European Union
EUROPARC	European Federation of Parks
FACET	Forum Advocating Cultural and EcoTourism (Western Australia)

FEMATOUR	Feasibility and Market Study for a European Ecolabel for Tourist Accommodations
FIF	Forschungsinstitut für Freizeit und Tourismus
FINAE	the Ecuadorian Achuar Federation
FIT	free independent traveller
FLO	Fairtrade Labelling Organization
FOS	Foundations of Success
FTO	UK Federation of Tour Operators
FTT	fair trade in tourism
FTTSA	Fair Trade in Tourism South Africa
GDP	gross domestic product
GG	Green Globe
GIHE	Glion Institute of Higher Education (Switzerland)
GOA	Guiding Organizations Australia
Green Stars	Australian accommodation star rating programme
IAATO	International Association of Antarctic Tour Operators
IAC	International Advisory Council
IATA	International Association of Travel Agents
IATG	Institute of Australian Tourist Guides Inc.
ICOMOS	International Council on Monuments and Sites
ICOMOS-ENAME	Charter for the Interpretation of Heritage Sites
ICT	Costa Rica Tourism Institute
IDB	Inter-American Development Bank
IES	International Ecotourism Standard (Green Globe)
IFOAM	International Federation of Organic Agricultural Movements
IGTOA	International Galapagos Tour Operators Association
IHEI	International Hotels Environment Initiative
ILO	International Labour Organization
INC	Institute of National Culture (Peru)
ISO	International Organization for Standardization
ITOA	Inbound Tour Organization of Australia
ITRI	Indigenous Tourism Rights International
IUCN	International Union for the Conservation of Nature
IYE	International Year of Ecotourism
LAC	Limits of Acceptable Change
LOHAS	lifestyles of health and sustainability
M&E	monitoring and evaluation
MBNQA	Malcom Baldridge National Quality Award (America)
MCTT	Mehloding ('green pastures') Community Tourism Trust
MIF	Multilateral Investment Fund
MINCETUR	Ministry of Tourism (Peru)
MORI	Market and Opinion Research International
MOU	Memorandum of Understanding
NaHHA	Native Hawaiian Hospitality Association

NCVER	National Centre for Vocational Education Research (Australia)
NEAP	National Ecotourism Accreditation Program (sometimes known as NEAP I)
NEAP	Nature and Ecotourism Accreditation Program (sometimes known as NEAP II)
NEAT	Nature, Ecotourism and Adventure Tourism
NEF	New Economics Foundation
NES	National Ecotourism Strategy (Australia)
NGO	non-governmental organization
NGTP	Nature Guide Training Program (Costa Rica)
NOLS	National Outdoor Leadership School
NSW	New South Wales (Australia)
NT	Northern Territory (Australia)
NTAP	National Tourism Accreditation Program (Australia)
NTIA	National Travel Industry Awards (Australia)
NTO	National Tourism Operations
OPEC	Organization of the Petroleum Exporting Countries
PAN	Protected Area Network
PASTILLE	Promoting Action for Sustainability through Indicators at the Local Level in Europe
PATA	Pacific Asia Travel Association
PCTS	Programa de Certificação em Turismo Sustentável
PEI	Prince Edward Island
PPT	pro-poor tourism
PROARCA	Programa Ambiental Regional para Centroamérica
PSA	Proudly South African
QAAP	Quality Assurance Accreditation Program
QTC	Quality Tourism for the Caribbean
QTS	quality tourism standards
RA	Rainforest Alliance
RARE	RARE Center for Tropical Conservation
READ	Rural Education and Development
RMA	Resource Management Act (New Zealand)
ROC	Respecting Our Culture Certification Programme
SA	South Australia
SARS	severe acute respiratory syndrome
SICGAL	System of Inspection and Quarantine for Galapagos
SKOANZ	Sea Kayak Operators Association of New Zealand
SMEs	small and medium-size enterprises
SMMEs	small, medium and micro-enterprises
SNV	a Dutch international development organization
SOLAS	International Convention for Safety of Life at Sea
SPPS	Statistical Package for Social Research
SPTO	South Pacific Tourism Organization
STA	Samoa Tourism Authority

STCRC	Sustainable Tourism Cooperative Research Centre (Australia)
STEP	Sustainable Tourism Eco-certification Program (USA)
STO	state tourism organization
STSC	Sustainable Tourism Stewardship Council
TAA	Tourism Accreditation Australia
TAAL	Tourism Accreditation Australia Limited
TAPAF	Tourism and Protected Areas Forum (Australia)
TCA	Tourism Council Australia
TCAWA	Tourism Council of Australia, Western Australia
TCWA	Tourism Council of Western Australia
TEP	Tourism Enterprise Programme (South Africa)
TIANZ	Tourism Industry Association of New Zealand
TIES	The International Ecotourism Society
TNZ	Tourism New Zealand
TOMM	Tourism Optimization Management Model
TQ	Tourism Queensland
TQM	total quality management
TUI	Touristik Union International, The Netherlands
UCR	University of Costa Rica
UK	United Kingdom
UN	United Nations
UNCSD-7	seventh session of the United Nations Commission on Sustainable Development
UNDP	United Nations Development Programme
UNEP	United Nations Environment Programme
UNESCO	United Nations Educational, Scientific and Cultural Organization
UNWTO	United Nations World Tourism Organization
USA	United States of America
USAID	US Agency for International Development
VISIT	Voluntary Initiatives for Sustainable Tourism
VTAB	Victorian Tourism Accreditation Board
VTOA	Victorian Tour Operators Association (Australia)
WA	Western Australia
WATC	Western Australian Tourism Commission
WHS	World Heritage Site
WTO	World Tourism Organization
WTTC	World Travel and Tourism Council
WTTRC	World Travel and Tourism Research Council
WWF	World Wide Fund for Nature (in USA and Canada: World Wildlife Fund)

1 Setting the Context: Quality in Ecotourism

Rosemary Black[1] and Alice Crabtree[2]

[1]*Charles Sturt University, Albury, NSW, Australia;* [2]*Ecotourism Consultant, Cairns, Queensland, Australia*

Introduction

Tourism is recognized as a global industry and known to be a significant contributor to economies and employment throughout the developed and the developing world (Weaver, 1998; Hawkins and Lamoureux, 2001). There were 760 million international arrivals recorded in 2004, accounting for almost US$622 billion of receipts (WTO, 2006). If the size of the tourism industry is not impressive enough, the fact that the 2004 figures represented a growth rate of 25% in 10 years certainly is. Predicted growth rates remain high – the United Nations World Tourism Organization estimates that by the end of 2020 there will be 1.6 billion international tourist arrivals worldwide (double the current level), spending over US$2 trillion (WTO, 2006). Globally arrivals are predicted to grow at an average of 4.3%; however, the strongest relative growth is predicted in the developing world. Of course, international travel is only one aspect of tourism, and domestic tourism can be equally important to many countries in terms of both volume and income generated (UNEP and WTO, 2005). Domestic tourism is predicted to grow strongly, even spectacularly, in developing nations such as India and China, where an emerging middle class has more disposable income.

The World Travel and Tourism Council's (WTTC) figures provide similar estimates of both tourism growth, with predictions of 4.2% per annum between 2007 and 2016 (WTTC, 2006), and current expenditure. If all the indirect economic effects of the tourism sector are taken into account, it represents US$4218 of GDP – 10.4% of the global GDP. Tourism is a major source of employment, with an estimated 234 million jobs within the tourism economy – about 8.7% of total global employment (i.e. 1 in every 11.5 jobs) in 2006 (WTTC, 2006).

With these facts it is undeniable that tourism is a major contributor to economic activity and a significant generator of employment. These are often touted as reasons to embrace tourism, and the massive growth in this industry does provide opportunities for spreading prosperity. However, tourism is not necessarily a benign, smokeless industry – it can, and often does, have major negative impacts on the natural and built environments and on the well-being and culture of host communities. This may include, but is certainly not limited to, aspects such as degradation of the physical environment, pollution, competition for scarce resources, disturbance to wildlife and landscapes, cultural commoditization and trivialization, displacement of host communities and introduction of undesirable activities. Conversely, tourism's positive impacts are not necessarily confined just to economic benefits and employment – it provides opportunities for visitors (and hosts) to celebrate cultural and natural heritage and can build constituencies for conservation, reduce threats to biodiversity, improve provision of services for remote communities and perhaps even be a force for inter-cultural understanding and peace. Tourism has the potential to provide many benefits, but this potential is only realized if tourism is carefully managed to ensure that negative impacts are kept to a minimum and positive impacts are maximized. This is a definition, if you so desire, of sustainable tourism – tourism that is based on the principles of sustainable development.

Sustainable development, with its definition firmly rooted in the report of the World Commission on Environment and Development (1987) (the Brundtland Report), is based on the principles of sound management of the world's resources, and on equity in the ways those resources are used and in the way in which the benefits so obtained are distributed. Although definitions of the concept of 'sustainable development' have evolved and been refined with Agenda 21 (the Action Plan from the UN Conference on Environment and Development in Rio, 1992) and the outputs from the World Summit on Sustainable Development (Johannesburg, 2002), the three pillars of economic, sociocultural and environmental sustainability remain at the core. Sustainable tourism is thus not a niche market segment, but an 'ideal' that balances the environmental, economic and sociocultural aspects to guarantee long-term sustainability that can (and many say should) apply to all forms of tourism in all types of destinations – including both the mass tourism and special interest segments (UNEP and WTO, 2005). For tourism to be considered sustainable it has to ensure that its operations not only do not jeopardize essential ecological processes but also help conserve natural resources, are viable economic enterprises that provide fair returns to all stakeholders and respect the sociocultural authenticity of the host communities.

The terms 'sustainable tourism' and 'ecotourism' are often used interchangeably, and this leads to confusion. Of course, ecotourism fully embraces the principles of sustainability, and genuine ecotourism should probably not just incorporate but exemplify sustainability, but ecotourism is certainly much more than just sustainable tourism. However, trying to find a perfect definition for ecotourism is impossible, with no consensus currently existing about the precise meaning of the term. However, there appears to be a continued level of interest in ecotourism and there has been an explosion and blossoming of academic literature on the subject in the last decade (see Honey, 1999; Wearing and Neil, 1999; Weaver, 2001a; Fennell, 2003; Fennell and Dowling, 2003). Despite this wealth of material, there is still considerable ongoing discussion and debate regarding interpretation and operationalization of the term (Blamey, 2001; Orams, 2001; Fennell, 2003).

It has been suggested that the plethora of definitions reflects the relative immaturity of this sector of the tourism industry (Weaver, 2001b), with individuals able to interpret notions of ecotourism as it best suits them. Unfortunately, this often appears to be the case, with the term often hijacked to take advantage of a mainstreaming of 'green' attitudes. The term ecotourism tends to be generously applied to a wide range of products and services, some of which meet the basic tenets of ecotourism, but all too many of which do not. This has inevitably resulted in confusion among both consumers and other stakeholders. Cynicism that the term is just a marketing gimmick that dresses up inferior product to increase market share (see Wight, 1993) has meant that many have abandoned the label to avoid the stigma of being perceived as 'greenwashing'. Somewhat ironically, attempts to solve the problem are sometimes made through coining new terms for tourism that still display the root characteristics and basic principles of ecotourism rather than taking steps to ensure credibility of the term.

Although ecotourism may be 'rare, often misdefined, and usually imperfect, it is still in its infancy, not on its deathbed' (Honey, 1999: 25). This volume does not aim to add to the debate and discussion surrounding the semantics of definitions. None the less, we do need to explore and highlight the key principles and basic tenets present in most definitions of ecotourism to help us find out what genuine and 'quality' ecotourism should be.

Definitions of Ecotourism

Ceballos-Lascuráin (1987) is credited with first using the term 'ecotourism'. While his definition and others (e.g. Boo, 1990) emphasize the nature-based experience, subsequent definitions have sought to emphasize the principles associated with the concept of sustainable development (Wallace and Pierce, 1996; Blamey, 2001; Fennell, 2001, 2003). Fennell's (2003) analysis of 15 definitions of ecotourism presented over the last 15 years demonstrates that definitions have emphasized different aspects of nature, relationships with local people, conservation and preservation. These could be construed as different 'versions' of ecotourism. For example, the Australian Ecotourism Strategy defines ecotourism as:

> nature-based tourism that involves education and interpretation of the natural environment and is managed to be ecologically sustainable. This definition recognises that the natural environment includes cultural components and that ecological sustainability involves an appropriate return to the local community and long-term conservation of the resource.
>
> (Commonwealth of Australia, 1994: 3)

This contrasts with one of the most frequently quoted definitions that considers ecotourism more simply as 'responsible travel to natural areas that conserves the environment and improves the welfare of local people' (Ecotourism Society, 1991). Once this statement is expanded the meaning and intent become clearer, but it perhaps exaggerates even further a different emphasis:

> This means that those who implement and participate in ecotourism activities should follow the following principles:
> - Minimize impact
> - Build environmental and cultural awareness and respect
> - Provide positive experiences for both visitors and hosts
> - Provide direct financial benefits for conservation
> - Provide financial benefits and empowerment for local people
> - Raise sensitivity to host countries' political, environmental, and social climate
> - Support international human rights and labour agreements
>
> (The International Ecotourism Society, 2006)

In trying to get to the underlying principles that govern what ecotourism is or is not, it is possibly simpler to look at individual components where the majority of definitions show consensus. Perhaps one of the most obvious dimensions of ecotourism emphasized in most, especially early, definitions (see Valentine, 1992) is that it is nature-based. Despite this, ecotourism should not be confused with or interchanged with nature or nature-based tourism (which it all too frequently is). Nature tourism is any form of tourism that relies primarily on natural environments for its attractions and/or setting. Ecotourism is generally acknowledged as a subset of nature tourism, as are substantial portions of the adventure tourism sector or the 3S (sun, sea and surf) sector (Weaver, 2001a). The differentiating points here are many, but certainly key is the fact that adventure and 3S tourism are not necessarily sustainable and are rarely learning-centred.

The widespread consensus that ecotourism is nature-based seems a simple enough precept, but even here there is considerable debate (see Blamey, 2001). What exactly constitutes nature-based? Is an environment modified by humans able to qualify? If not, how do you reconcile vast wilderness areas in Australia that have been altered over thousand of years by fire-stick farming or 'virgin' rainforests that have been altered by indigenous hunters and gatherers? At the other end of the scale, would a tourism product based in a largely urban environment that had a nature focus (e.g. a visitors centre for a World Heritage Site) qualify? If this visitors centre had been positioned thus to avoid damage to areas of high conservation significance, does this change your opinion? What about a zoo or wildlife park? If this zoo sensitively displayed endemic species in a natural (if captive) environment and provided education that allowed people to leave with a greater understanding and appreciation of native fauna, would this qualify?

The provision of education and/or interpretation and the concept of learning/understanding is, according to most definitions, another crucial tenet of ecotourism (Ham, 2001; Edwards *et al.*, 2003). This understanding may be through non-personal methods such as brochures or displays, but more commonly includes face-to-face mediation through a guide. These educational experiences satisfy the visitors' desire for information, but this is not a need unique to ecotourism. What seems to differentiate interpretation as part of ecotourism experiences is that education is skewed to attempting to provide a greater understanding and appreciation of the natural environment and processes that results in increased environmental care and responsibility. This may occur through influencing the visitors' attitude or even behaviour. The educational component of ecotourism thus does not just serve information needs, but helps to minimize environmental impacts and create a more informed and pro-conservation society (Blamey, 2001). Rather ironically, the more dedicated the ecotourist and the 'harder' the ecotourism experience (see 'hard' and 'soft' ecotourism later in this section), the more likely it is that you are simply preaching to the converted and not effecting change.

A third important principle of ecotourism is 'sustainability'. We have already discussed the fact that ecotourism needs to fully embrace and possibly exemplify sustainability. The two sustainability principles that are commonly associated with definitions of ecotourism are the need for return to local communities (and by default local economies) and returns for the environment through support for conservation. For example, the definition of ecotourism provided in the Australian National Ecotourism Strategy recognizes that the natural environment includes cultural components and that ecologically sustainable involves appropriate returns to the local community and long-term conservation of the resource (Allcock *et al.*, 1994: 3). Economic sustainability is usually provided in the form of both direct and indirect benefits of employment, diversification, foreign exchange earnings and even infrastructure development. Environmental sustainability is enhanced through better resource conservation, as well as cash or in-kind participation for conservation and biodiversity protection. However, some suggest that ecotourism should simply minimize its footprint through preventing, as far as possible, the negative effects of tourism. We argue that this is not enough and that quality ecotourism has to maximize the positive impacts of tourism and actively contribute to enhancing the environment.

This 'enhancement' is usually through visitors' involvement in conservation of the natural environment, although increasingly ecotourism is portrayed as a development tool that will help poverty alleviation, especially in developing countries or amongst indigenous communities with little to sell apart from their natural and cultural resources. It is indisputable that the long-term viability of the ecotourism industry is intrinsically reliant on maintaining the natural environment on which the industry depends, and, whilst respecting and being sensitive to the sociocultural environment and providing fair economic return to local communities is undoubtedly important, they are not the main focus of ecotourism. There are a distinct overlap and union between ecotourism and more people-oriented sectors such as fair trade and pro-poor tourism, but also fundamental differences. It is hoped that our examination of some of these overlaps (see Chapter 14 on Fair Trade) will enable exchange of best practice for both sectors to be considered.

While this and other reviews (see Blamey, 2001; Weaver, 2001b; Fennell, 2003) of ecotourism definitions continue to reveal a lack of consensus on the precise interpretation of ecotourism and a somewhat 'fuzzy' delineation of the exact bounds of basic principles, it is hoped that the intent or essence of ecotourism can be extracted from the sum of the core components. These are as follows. Ecotourism:

- Has a natural area focus.
- Is environmentally sustainable.
- Has some component of interpretation or education.
- Provides returns to the environment.
- Provides returns to local communities.
- Is culturally sensitive.

Identifying these key principles of ecotourism is a crucial step in the process of commencing our exploration of quality in ecotourism. However, as the reader will discover, some of the quality tools and mechanisms discussed in this volume attempt to address quality in all the principles of ecotourism, while other cases or discussions revolve around examples or programmes that are by no means ecotourism but serve as useful examples to emphasize a specific ecotourism element or principle.

Ecotourism Segmentation

To add to the difficulty of trying to define what quality ecotourism is, it is necessary not only to explore what the core principles that define ecotourism are, but also to consider the spectrum of products or activities that could be considered as ecotourism. This has obvious implications in operationalizing the term (as most ecotourism certification programmes have discovered), and also leads on to some interesting philosophical debate.

Not surprisingly, ecotourism, like any tourism sector can, and does, include a wide spectrum of different sectors, be it accommodation, tours, attractions, travel, retail or a myriad of support elements. Ecotourism activities show an enormous variety in products – the 'boutique' ecolodge or tented safari, trekking with indigenous people in the desert, a 2-hour whale watching trip or a lazy stroll down a boardwalk. Attempts to rationalize, or at least classify, the diversity of the ecotourism product are often made by separating ecotourism into 'soft' and 'hard' ecotourism (Laarman and Durst, 1987; Orams, 2001; Weaver, 2001a, b).

These terms refer to two dimensions – the ecotourist's degree of interest/expertise in the natural attraction and the level of challenge/physical difficulty involved in the activity. For example, a 'hard-core' ecotourist might be a passionate birdwatcher who is willing to live with few comforts in order to get the best chance to observe a new bird. Hard ecotourism may involve an immersion experience where visitors are totally removed from their home comforts and environmental bubble, perhaps living with and as the host communities/indigenous peoples do. On the other hand, it might include a physically challenging activity such as an extended bush trek, snow camping or sea kayaking. When an activity includes an adventure sport such as scuba-diving, skiing or mountaineering, this is used as a 'vehicle' to observe wildlife or 'feel' the landscape rather than being the main focus of the experience.

Hard ecotourism usually occurs over extended periods of time. In contrast, a 'soft' ecotourist, while still interested in the natural attraction, tends to have a more superficial and often highly mediated experience. These types of ecotourists are less likely and willing to experience discomfort and/or physical challenges as part of the experience (Orams, 2001; Weaver, 2001a). Hard ecotourists usually participate in extended, specialized ecotours (Orams, 2001), while soft ecotourists tend to engage in a short experience as part of a more multipurpose and multidimensional travel experience.

The hard–soft dichotomy is a useful construct that differentiates products and segments; however, it does not adequately account for differences in actual sustainability outcomes. A recent analysis by Weaver (2005) of the core criteria of ecotourism suggests two 'ideal types' based on the level of sustainability outcomes. The first type, 'minimalist' ecotourism, occurs when the focus is on a charismatic element (e.g. a dolphin), the educational message is shallow and a status quo approach is adopted towards sustainability; this is the manifestation of ecotourism that is most likely to mutate into something less benign, as it meets three key criteria only 'minimally'. In contrast, 'comprehensive' ecotourism is ecosystem- and deep learning-focused and oriented towards the enhancement of sustainability. Weaver (2005) argues that contemporary ecotourism is generally unable to fulfil the potential to achieve meaningful environmental and sociocultural sustainability and, of more concern, is capable of mutating into less benign forms of tourism.

The diversity of ecotourism experiences raises another hurdle when trying to define quality ecotourism experiences. How do we compare quality when legitimate expressions of ecotourism can be so fundamentally different? Should soft ecotourism be excluded from consideration as it may not necessarily exemplify environmental sustainability or has relatively superficial interpretation, or returns to the environment and local communities are restricted to minimizing harm, rather than maximizing benefits, and so are less than perfect? Or should hard ecotourism be ignored because it involves 'such a small number of participants as to render it almost irrelevant in terms of economic impacts' (Weaver, 2001a: 2).

We have already commented on the problems of hard ecotourism perhaps having a negligible environmental impact as a result of 'preaching to the converted', but there is also a paradox in the tendency for ecotourism to be slanted towards elitism. Hard ecotourism often requires physical fitness, often the domain of the young or at the very least the healthy. Extended trips, often to exotic locales and remote destinations, are frequently expensive, and hence there is a tendency for ecotourism to skew towards the wealthy. Highly specialized information often provided by ecotourism may also mean a bias towards more highly educated customers. These facts about the demographics of ecotourists are well known (see Wight, 2001) – but what are the results? There is some disquiet and perhaps a loss of credibility when a form of tourism that proclaims social sustainability has such an inclination against equity of access and contradiction of social justice. This is perhaps best expressed in the uneasy tendency for ecotourism to often tend towards high cost, low volume. The smaller volume still provides the same economic returns but environmental impacts are usually reduced – but could it and should it still be considered quality ecotourism? There are certainly valid arguments that suggest that small size should not necessarily automatically be considered to be more environmentally sustainable, but this remains a common perception. On the other hand, whilst soft ecotourism might be more accessible, there is a clear and present danger that it becomes so mainstreamed, and the principles are so diluted by its multidimensional nature that the potential positive impacts of ecotourism become negligible. Trying to isolate and delineate individual aspects of ecotourism may confuse and hinder the intent to determine what makes up quality ecotourism.

Quality in Tourism

Let's look instead at what constitutes quality in tourism. Most people's perceptions of 'quality' equate relatively simply to 'luxury', be it the size of the bed, the softness of the towels, the extras such as bathrobes and cosmetics, or the number and type of facilities such as restaurants, spas, swimming pools and gyms. Some of the earliest certification programmes in tourism, such as the AAA and Michelin guidebooks, rated this type of quality, along with service and price, in the well-known 'star' ratings (Honey and Rome, 2001).

Many people think they have an intuitive understanding of the term 'quality', and yet even they find it surprisingly difficult to define (Price, 1994; Reeves and Bednar, 1994; European Commission, 1999). According to Gilbert and Joshi (1992), the problem lies in the fact that quality has traditionally been used as an adjective (e.g. as in a quality product) to imply a high degree of excellence or as an associated distinguishing attribute. Quality can thus have very many different meanings, depending on the organization or customer using the term (Crosby, 1979; Deming, 1982; Feigenbaum, 1983). The quality management literature clearly suggests that the customer and his or her satisfaction should be the basis for measuring and improving quality. As such, quality exists only to the extent to which a product or service meets the expectations or requirements of the customer (Oakland, 1994; Weiermair, 1997).

It is certainly accepted that quality in tourism is equally as vexing and difficult to define as ecotourism (Toplis, 2000; Williams and Buswell, 2003). Quality is not an easy concept (Hjalager, 2001), simply because quality may be a product of or apply to a tourist destination, a region or nation, or simply an individual tourism business. Toplis (2000) suggests that the range of product and service categories, the complex nature of the overall tourist experience and the largely unpredictable and ever-changing preferences and attitudes of tourists are to blame.

Again, we have to accept that there is a plethora of meanings associated with the concept of quality tourism and perhaps that it is a relatively ambiguous classificatory term used by tourists to describe their construction of a tourist experience: 'This term may mean excellence, a matching of expectations to lived experience, a perception of getting value for one's money, or however the individual tourist chooses to define it' (Jennings and Weiler, 2005: 59). A discussion of the challenges of defining quality tourism experiences and the multiple interpretations and meanings can be found in Jennings and Polovitz Nickerson (2006). According to La Lopa and Marecki (1999), quality tourism may therefore be simply defined as a customer determination and it depends upon the tourist's actual experience with a tourism product or service, measured against his or her expectations.

However, the World Tourism Organization's work on quality in tourism is guided by an understanding of quality being the result of a process that implies the satisfaction of all the legitimate product and service needs, requirements and expectations of the consumer, at an acceptable price, and conformity with the underlying quality determinants such as safety and security, hygiene, accessibility, transparency, authenticity and harmony of the tourism activity concerned with its human and natural environment (Toplis, 2000).

Quality is considered a critical factor in the success of destinations and tourism businesses and many agencies have identified quality and its improvement as a key strategic objective. For example, the World Tourism Organization (2006) has a programme, 'Quality in Tourism Development', that deals with specific measures to improve the design and supply of tourism products and services. Improved quality, and hence satisfaction of visitors, will help result in increased competitiveness for tourism businesses and destinations. Governments are also showing increasing interest in the quality issues as Westernized economies shift from a manufacturing to a service base (Toplis, 2000). Ensuring that quality tourism products are delivered means that governments can attract international investment and market share, vital when tourism is becoming such a globally competetive industry (World Travel and Tourism Council, 2005).

The interest in raising the quality of tourism as a whole (and, implicitly or explicitly, the quantity) has been fuelled by a number of factors, including changes to the business environment, a growing sophistication of consumers, an increasingly competitive environment within which enterprises operate and more differentiated markets. At the same time, we have also seen a general shift away from just measuring success through profit to recognizing that other factors are important, such as the benefits to the environment, economy and society – as evidenced by a triple bottom line. These mirror the previously mentioned pillars of sustainable development and indicate the importance of sustainability as a component of quality. Trends indicate that corporate social responsibility (CSR) is becoming more common and almost mandatory in many industries (Overseas Development Institute, 2003; Ward, 2004), although still relatively poorly applied in tourism (see World Bank, 2006).

Consumers now have increased choice and expect to have products and services of a higher than minimum standard. As Camison (1996: 193) states, 'the key change in tourists' behaviour, connected to customer satisfaction criteria has been the swing in their preferences, more and more towards products with better quality/price ratio'. It may be that choice is becoming less focused on price and needs other sources of advantage in this highly competitive market (Tourism Victoria, 2000). The advent of value-adding to tourism product through ensuring quality by such means as using highly qualified guides, providing gourmet products, ensuring authenticity and appealing to environmentalism has huge potential for the ecotourism market.

Quality in Ecotourism

For the purposes of this volume we are considering quality ecotourism to mean tourism that has distilled the sum of all the key principles of a natural area focus, environmental sustainability, interpretation/education, returns to local community and cultural sensitivity such that the negative impacts of tourism are minimized and the positive impacts are maximized.

Exploring what makes up quality in ecotourism is important because it is clear that ecotourism is not a panacea that always guarantees that the environment is protected, economic activity is supported and local communities are equitably rewarded. Ecotourism is clearly a complex concept, and its manifestations or operationalization does not remain static.

Ecotourism, or best attempts at ecotourism, are often embraced in early stages of development because there are few apparent negative impacts and there appear to be positive benefits for the local community and environment. Unfortunately, ecotourism often mutates as a result of its own success – for, no matter the best of intentions, once the economic juggernaut starts rolling, controlling tourism is extremely difficult (for example, Amboseli National Park in Kenya). The spectre of ecotourism being the catalyst and paving the way for mainstream, mass tourism that has less regard for the natural and sociocultural environment occurs again and again. This is not a problem restricted to the ecotourism sector of the tourism industry – it is well known that tourism often carries the seed of its own destruction (Butler, 1980). Despite, or possibly because of, the major economic role tourism can have (Lindberg, 2001; Leiper, 2004), it has the capacity to degrade or destroy the very natural and cultural resources that it relies upon, with the popularity of a destination leading to adverse environmental, social and cultural impacts (Buckley, 2001; Wearing, 2001; Leiper, 2004).

Although much of the mainstream tourism industry relies on the same draw cards of the natural environment and local communities, in ecotourism the relationship with the natural environment and local community is a fundamental and essential link. The potential for the very worst of the negative impacts of tourism and the very best of the positive impacts appears to come to a head in the particularly fragile or sensitive natural or cultural environments that ecotourism tends to gravitate towards. Although this does not mean that ecotourism only occurs in protected areas, there appears to be an incipient disdain and almost contempt for ecotourism that uses areas of lower conservation significance or rehabilitated land. Most ecotourism occurs within areas of high conservation significance and unfortunately is relatively rare outside these areas. This may be a reluctance to go to supposedly inferior, lesser 'quality' environments, or even equating less meaningful experiences with an environment that may not be entirely authentic. Again, isolating individual aspects of ecotourism tenets can be detrimental; for the reality that conservation is significantly enhanced through efforts towards rehabilitation and destructive effects of ecotourism are significantly ameliorated by using degraded, rather than pristine, sites is apparent.

It could be argued that all these complexities in examining or providing a definitive interpretation of ecotourism are a reflection that it is nothing more than a mythical beast – something to aspire to, but clearly difficult to actually observe, and perhaps just a dream. Unlike mainstream, mass tourism, ecotourism promises far more than just a good time – it promises a better and greener world with proclaimed benefits for both the environment and the community. Successful application of all the concepts and ideals of ecotourism may be difficult, but it does not mean that striving for quality ecotourism should be abandoned or that the concept itself is flawed.

Perhaps the difficulties merely reflect the immaturity of the industry, although there is clear evidence of ecotourism coming of age with a recent and increasing focus on delivering genuine, high-quality ecotourism products with commendable performance, using a range of quality assurance tools (Manidis Roberts Consultants, 1994; Issaverdis, 1998, 2001; Toplis, 2000) and increasing professionalism (Black, 2002). The quality assurance tools include codes of conduct, awards of excellence, certification and professional certification and will be explored in more detail in Chapter 2 and Part One of this volume.

Summary

Ecotourism is generally considered to be a rapidly expanding sector of the tourism industry and, although there is still considerable debate over its precise constituents, there is little doubt that this level of interest is generated by a range of stakeholders who see ecotourism's potential.

While ecotourism and sustainable certification programmes have been comprehensively addressed in the literature (Font and Buckley, 2001; Honey and Rome, 2001; Honey, 2002; WTO, 2002), there have been few critical reviews of other quality assurance tools and initiatives in the ecotourism literature nor has there been a more general discussion of issues of quality in ecotourism. Much of the academic, and even grey, literature simply describes a range of programmes and best practice guidelines, promotes the benefits of such techniques and provides case studies on best practice companies and schemes. To date there has been little critical analysis of the challenges and opportunities associated with planning, developing and implementing quality in ecotourism, which we try to address in Part One of this volume. The extensive interest in ecotourism has not been reflected in any substantial critical review and appraisal of the various tools and initiatives for developing quality ecotourism products. There is continued ignorance and abuse of what could or should be considered quality ecotourism. So, in Part Two of the book we aim to present a range of ecotourism stakeholders' perspectives on quality in ecotourism, with a particular focus on certification programmes.

The reality is that it is difficult to define quality. This is because there is a somewhat intangible notion of exactly what a quality ecotourism product is, furter confused by the different perceptions of primary consumers (tourists) and secondary consumers (primary stakeholders such as local communities or protected area managers). The situation is further muddied because expectations are always changing.

None the less, we hope this collection of ideas and issues will constructively add to the debate and development of better ecotourism.

References

Allcock, A., Jones, B., Lane, S. and Grant, J. (1994) *National Ecotourism Strategy.* Commonwealth Department of Tourism, Australian Government Publishing Service, Canberra.

Black, R.S. (2002) Towards a model for tour guide certification: an analysis of the Australian Ecoguide Program. Unpublished doctoral thesis, Department of Management, Monash University, Melbourne.

Blamey, R.K. (2001) Principles of ecotourism. In: Weaver, D. (ed.) *The Encyclopedia of Ecotourism.* CAB International, Wallingford, UK, pp. 5–22.

Boo, E. (1990) *Ecotourism: the Potentials and the Pitfalls*, Vols 1 and 2. Worldwide Fund for Nature, Washington, DC.

Buckley, R. (2001) Environmental impacts. In: Weaver, D.B. (ed.) *The Encyclopedia of Ecotourism.* CAB International, Wallingford, UK, pp. 379–394.

Butler, R.W. (1980) The concept of a tourist area cycle of evolution: implications for management of resources. *Canadian Geographer* 24, 5–12.

Camison, C. (1996) Total quality management in hospitality: an application of the EFQM model. *Tourism Management* 17(3), 191–201.

Ceballos-Lascuráin, H. (1987) The future of ecotourism. *Mexico Journal*, January, 13–14.

Commonwealth of Australia (1994) *National Ecotourism Strategy.* Australian Government Printing Service, Canberra, ACT.

Crosby, P.B. (1979) *Quality is Free.* McGraw-Hill, New York.

Deming, W.E. (1982) *Quality, Productivity and Competitive Position.* MIT Press, Cambridge, Massachusetts.

Ecotourism Society (1991) *Ecotourism Society Newsletter* 1(1), Spring.

Edwards, S., McLaughlin, W.J. and Ham, S.H. (2003) A regional look at ecotourism policy in the Americas. In: Fennell, D. and Dowling, R. (eds) *Ecotourism: Policy and Strategy Issues.* CAB International, Wallingford, UK, pp. 293–307.

European Commission (1999) *Towards Quality Rural Tourism: Integrated Quality Management (IQM) of Rural Tourist Destinations.* EU Tourism Unit, Luxembourg.

Feigenbaum, A.V. (1983) *Total Quality Control.* McGraw-Hill, New York.

Fennell, D.A. (2001) A content analysis of ecotourism definitions. *Current Issues in Tourism* 4(5), 403–421.

Fennell, D.A. (2003) *Ecotourism*, 2nd edn. Routledge, London, UK.

Fennell, D.A. and Dowling, R.K. (2003) *Ecotourism Policy and Planning.* CAB International, Wallingford, UK.

Font, X. and Buckley, R.C. (2001) *Tourism Ecolabelling: Certification and Promotion of Sustainable Management.* CAB International, Wallingford, UK.

Gilbert, D. and Joshi, I. (1992) Strategic marketing planning and the hotel industry. *International Journal of Hospitality Management* 9(1), 47–52.

Ham, S.H. (2001) *Recommendations for USAID Involvement in Ecotourism Activities in Bolivia. Consultant's Final Report.* International Resources Group, Washington, DC, and US Agency for International Development, La Paz, Bolivia.

Hawkins, D.E. and Lamoureux, K. (2001) Global growth and magnitude in tourism. In: Weaver, D. (ed.) *The Encyclopedia of Ecotourism.* CAB International, Wallingford, UK, pp. 63–72.

Hjalager, A. (2001) Quality in tourism through the empowerment of tourists. *Managing Service Quality* 11(4), 287–295.

Honey, M. (1999) *Ecotourism and Sustainable Development: Who Owns Paradise?* Island Press, Washington, DC.

Honey, M. (ed.) (2002) *Ecotourism and Certification: Setting Standards in Practice.* Island Press, Washington, DC.

Honey, M. and Rome, A. (2001) *Protecting Paradise: Certification Programs for Sustainable Tourism and Ecotourism.* Institute of Policy Studies, New York.

Issaverdis, J.P. (1998) Tourism industry accreditation – a comparative critique of developments in Australia. Master of Business in Tourism Development, Victoria University, Melbourne, Victoria.

Issaverdis, J.P. (2001) The pursuit of excellence: benchmarking, accreditation, best practice and auditing. In: Weaver, D. (ed.) *The Encyclopedia of Ecotourism.* CAB International, Wallingford, UK, pp. 549–563.

Jennings, G. and Polovitz Nickerson, N. (2006) *Quality Tourism Experiences.* Elsevier Butterworth-Heinemann, Oxford, UK.

Jennings, G. and Weiler, B. (2005) Mediating meaning: perspectives on brokering quality tourist experiences. In: Jennings, G. and Nickerson, N. (eds) *Quality Tourism Experiences.* Elsevier, Boston, pp. 109–147.

Laarman, J.G. and Durst, P.B. (1987) *Nature Travel and Tropical Forests.* FREI Working Paper Series, Southeastern Center for Forest Economics Research, North Carolina State University, Raleigh, North Carolina.

La Lopa, J.M. and Marecki, R.F. (1999) The critical role of quality in the tourism system. *Quality Progress* 32(8), August, 37–41.

Leiper, N. (2004) *Tourism Management*, 3rd edn. Pearson Hospitality Press, Sydney, Australia.

Lindberg, K. (2001) Economic impacts. In: Weaver, D.B. (ed.) *The Encyclopedia of Ecotourism.* CAB International, Wallingford, UK, pp. 363–378.

Manidis Roberts Consultants (1994) *An Investigation into a National Ecotourism Accreditation Scheme.* Commonwealth Department of Tourism, Canberra, ACT.

Oakland, J. (1994) Total quality management. In: Lock, D. (ed.) *Gower Handbook of Quality Management*, 2nd edn. Gower Publishing, Aldershot, UK, pp. 10–27.

Orams, M.B. (2001) Types of ecotourism. In: Weaver, D. (ed.) *The Encyclopedia of Ecotourism.* CAB International, Wallingford, UK, pp. 23–36.

Overseas Development Institute (2003) *Public Sector Roles in Strengthening Corporate Social Responsibility: A Diagnostic Framework and Options Appraisal Tool.* World Bank, New York.

Price, F. (1994) The quality concept and objectives. In: Lock, D. (ed.) *Gower Handbook of Quality Management*, 2nd edn. Gower Publishing, Aldershot, UK, pp. 3–9.

Reeves, C.A. and Bednar, D.A. (1994) Defining quality: alternatives and implications. *Academy of Management Review* 19(3), 419–445.

The International Ecotourism Society (2006) *The Ecotourism Society Newsletter* 1, no. 1 (Spring 1991). Available at: http://www.ecotourism.org (2 April 2006).

Toplis, S. (2000) Evaluating the effectiveness of the Australian Tourism Awards in promoting ecological sustainability to the Australian tourism industry: a Victorian perspective. Doctoral thesis, Department of Hospitality, Tourism and Leisure, RMIT University, Melbourne, Victoria.

Tourism Victoria (2000) *Nature-based Tourism: Directions and Opportunities for Victoria 2000–2003.* Tourism Victoria, Melbourne.

United Nations Environment Programme (UNEP) and the World Tourism Organization (WTO) (2005) *Making Tourism More Sustainable: A Guide for Policy Makers.* UNEP, Paris.

United Nations Environment Programme Industry and Environment (1995) *Environmental Codes of Conduct for Tourism.* United Nations Environment Programme Industry and Environment, Paris.

Valentine, P.S. (1992) Review: nature-based tourism. In: Weiler, B. and Hall, C.M. (eds) *Special Interest Tourism.* Belhaven Press, London, pp. 105–128.

Wallace, G.N. and Pierce, S.M. (1996) An evaluation of ecotourism in Amazonas, Brazil. *Annals of Tourism Research* 23(4), 843–873.

Ward, H. (2004) *Public Sector Roles in Strengthening Corporate Social Responsibility: Taking Stock.* World Bank and International Finance Corporation, New York.

Wearing, S. (2001) Exploring socio-cultural impacts on local communities. In: Weaver, D.B. (ed.) *The Encyclopedia of Ecotourism.* CAB International, Wallingford, UK, pp. 395–410.

Wearing, S. and Neil, J. (1999) *Ecotourism: Impacts, Potentials and Possibilities.* Butterworth and Heinemann, Oxford, UK.

Weaver, D.B. (1998) *Ecotourism in the Less Developed World.* CAB International, Wallingford, UK.

Weaver, D.B. (ed.) (2001a) *The Encyclopedia of Ecotourism.* CAB International, Wallingford, UK.

Weaver, D.B. (2001b) *Ecotourism.* John Wiley and Sons Australia, Milton, Queensland, Australia.

Weaver, D. (2005) Comprehensive and minimalist dimensions of ecotourism. *Annals of Tourism Research* 32(2), 439–455.

Weiermair, K. (1997) On the concept and definition of quality in tourism. In: Keller, P. (ed.) *Quality Management in Tourism.* AIEST, St Gallen.

Weiler, B. and Ham, S.H. (2001) Tour guides and interpretation. In: Weaver, D. (ed.) *The Encyclopedia of Ecotourism.* CAB International, Wallingford, UK, pp. 549–563.

Whelan, T. (1991) Ecotourism and its role in sustainable development. In: Whelan, T. (ed.) *Nature Tourism: Managing for the Environment.* Island Press, Washington, DC, pp. 3–22.

Wight, P. (1993) Sustainable tourism: balancing economic, environmental and social goals within an ethical framework. *Journal of Tourism Studies* 4, 54–66.

Wight, P. (2001) Ecotourists: not a homogenous market segment. In: Weaver, D.B. (ed.) *The Encyclopedia of Ecotourism.* CAB International, Wallingford, UK, pp. 37–72.

Williams, C. and Buswell, J. (2003) *Service Quality in Leisure and Tourism.* CAB International, Wallingford, UK.

World Bank (2006) E-forum. Available at: http://www.devcomm-congress.org/worldbank/forumwb/forum_topics.asp?FID=21 (25 June 2006).

World Commission on Environment and Development (WCED) (1987) *Our Common Future.* Oxford University Press, Oxford.

World Tourism Organization (WTO) (2002) *Voluntary Initiatives for Sustainable Tourism.* World Tourism Organization, Madrid, Spain.

World Tourism Organization (WTO) (2006) Tourism Facts and Figures. Available at: http://www.world-tourism.org/facts/eng/vision.htm (10 April 2006).

World Tourism Organization (WTO) and United Nations Environmental Programme (UNEP) (2001) *International Year of Ecotourism 2002.* WTO and UNEP.

World Travel and Tourism Council (WTTC) (2006) *Executive Summary: Travel and Tourism Climbing to New Heights.* The 2006 Travel and Tourism Economic Research, World Travel and Tourism Council, London.

2 Achieving Quality in Ecotourism: Tools in the Toolbox

Rosemary Black[1] and Alice Crabtree[2]

[1]*Charles Sturt University, Albury, NSW, Australia;* [2]*Ecotourism Consultant, Cairns, Queensland, Australia*

Introduction

This chapter sets the context for Part One of the book by introducing the spectrum of quality assurance tools that have been developed and applied in the ecotourism industry to address and improve quality. Specifically the chapter looks at awards of excellence, codes of conduct, certification and accreditation, and monitoring and evaluation. The latter part of the chapter provides a more detailed overview of certification programmes. This emphasis on certification reflects the benefits of this approach over other voluntary initiatives, such as awards and codes, and the increasing number of programmes throughout the world. Each of the chapters in Part One provides a detailed analysis of a particular quality assurance tool.

What is commonly known, labelled and marketed as ecotourism is often not, and unfortunately there are no restrictions that govern the use of the term. Misuse of the term ecotourism may arise out of ignorance – a lack of awareness of the weight of the principles and ideology that the term carries with it – but deliberate misrepresentation and abuse of the term also appear common.

Ignorance may hopefully be rectified by better education and raising awareness among the broader tourism industry. However, of more concern is the trend to ecotourism 'lite' (Honey, 2002). This trend involves minimal, cosmetic and usually cost-saving actions that are proclaimed as 'helping to save the world' to appeal to the green market. Few, if any, of the necessary and fundamental reforms in environmental or social practices are embraced or implemented. An example is the request by some hotels to reuse towels that are now common in accommodation facilities from Britain to Barbados, where the greatest savings are to the operator's laundry bills. Another trend of concern is 'greenwashing' (Wight, 1993; Weaver, 2001; Honey, 2002), where operations or projects claim ecotourism credentials, but are just using

 Quality Assurance and Certification in Ecotourism (eds R. Black and A. Crabtree)

green terminology to cover up poor or mediocre practices and policies and to convey an image of being environmentally friendly. All this presumes that 'green sells', and the abuse of the term ecotourism becomes a mere marketing ploy. Whatever the cause, abuse of the term tarnishes the reputation of ecotourism.

The misuse and abuse of the term ecotourism have resulted in confusion, misunderstanding and disenchantment with the whole concept, not just the name, among many ecotourism stakeholders (Burns, 1997). This situation impedes the ability for genuine, quality ecotourism to deliver on its promises – delivering quality experiences for the clients, but also positive returns for the host community, host environment and host enterprises. The promotion and delivery of products that are not ecotourism need addressing to create and establish legitimacy and credibility for the term and the practice of genuine ecotourism. One way to ensure that this occurs is for products and services to meet the key principles of ecotourism, as outlined in Chapter 1. To achieve this situation it is necessary to have a clear and unambiguous understanding of the key principles of ecotourism, as well as the quality assurance tools and initiatives designed to help deliver more consistent, quality ecotourism products.

Quality Assurance Initiatives in Ecotourism: Tools in the Toolbox

In the last 10 to 15 years there has been a proliferation in policy, instruments, quality assurance tools and other mechanisms to ensure better sustainable tourism and ecotourism (Font and Buckley, 2001; Honey, 2002; WTO, 2002; Fennell and Dowling, 2003; UNEP and WTO, 2005). This growth in quality assurance tools has mirrored, with a slight lag, the growth of ecotourism itself.

Most people will be familiar with regulatory tools – mandatory requirements that are enshrined in law and have to be complied with. Legislation, regulation, licensing and permits are interrelated and set out requirements that are both compulsory and enforceable, and often lead to sanctions and penalties if they are not met. Legislation provides the authority to enforce requirements, which are defined and elaborated by regulations. Licensing is the process of checking compliance with legislation and regulations, and conveys a permission to operate (UNEP and WTO, 2007). Explicitly, the purpose of licensing is to protect the public from incompetent practitioners. For example, the process may require an individual or tourism business to have a licence, or a permit to operate or conduct an activity and/or enter/practise in a particular location such as a national park. It is necessary to ensure that mandatory and/or legislative requirements do not act as barriers to business, and that they act mainly to restrict operations to those that meet a minimum acceptable standard. Thus, they mainly serve to protect the public from incompetent practice. Minimal standards, whilst necessary and important, do not demonstrate a quest or aim for best practice or quality.

The focus of this volume is on quality ecotourism, and, despite the necessary and important role that regulation, policy and other government initiatives play in complementing and supporting ecotourism planning and delivery, these initiatives will not be discussed in any detail. The focus instead is on the spectrum of voluntary initiatives that may be used to promote and support quality ecotourism. Voluntary initiatives are not compulsory, which means that the initiator is not obliged by law to propose or run the initiative and the target groups are not obliged to conform/apply; therefore voluntary initiatives do not restrict trade or operation. Thus, these tools can demand best practice rather than accepting a minimum standard. Voluntary initiatives must as a minimum meet, but preferably exceed, regulatory compliance. They often indicate practices for which there is no legislation or regulatory control.

Voluntary tools include initiatives such as prizes and awards of excellence, codes of conduct or practice, environmental management systems, best practice guidelines, self-commitments and self-declarations, professional certification programmes for individuals such as tour guides, certification and accreditation programmes, as well as less well-known initiatives such as sustainable tourism charters in New Zealand (Enterprise Northland, 2005). The tools and their operating characteristics are often depicted on a quality continuum (Manidis Roberts Consultants, 1994; Issaverdis, 1998, 2001; Black, 2002), which ranges from relatively weak measures that serve mainly to raise awareness, to stronger and more credible measures that demand formal quality system components, such as benchmarking, performance indicators and auditing.

The spectrum of quality assurance tools that will be examined in Part Two of this volume follows this continuum from awards through codes of conduct to certification and accreditation programmes. Sustainability indicators have also been discussed in two chapters because they are a useful tool for monitoring and evaluating quality initiatives for ecotourism.

The following discussion briefly introduces some of the quality assurance tools used in the ecotourism industry that are illustrated in more detail using case studies in the subsequent chapters. Moving from the relatively weak tools to the stronger and more credible tools we introduce awards, codes of conduct, certification and accreditation and finally monitoring and evaluation.

Awards of Excellence

At one end of the quality continuum spectrum are awards – a reward that is generally solicited or applied for. Even within this category there is considerable variation in credibility, relating to the rigour of the selection process and whether or not there are performance indicators (see Chapter 3 in this volume); however, it is rare for on-site assessment or verification to take place. The award winner usually gains a seal of approval – in effect a logo that is often used for marketing purposes. Awards fulfil an important purpose by providing an incentive for good performance and service and celebrating excellence.

How successful the award is at promoting the product/business depends upon how well known and respected the award is. The credibility of the award depends on the integrity of the application and selection procedure, with some awards almost evolving into a type of ecolabel remarkably similar to certification, with stringent application criteria and attempts to verify claims – a type of conformity assessment (e.g. David Bellamy Awards for Conservation). As discussed in Chapter 3 of this volume, there are some concerns that awards depend in part, not on how good the business or product is, but on how good an application is submitted.

Codes of Conduct

Codes of conduct or codes of practice were one of the earliest voluntary initiatives developed to address quality issues in tourism. They provide information that aims to influence behaviour of tourists or tourism enterprise operators by providing guidelines or rules of appropriate behaviour. The voluntary nature of codes of conduct means that there are rarely any checks on compliance. Codes have certainly been criticized because they are often vague and have been proclaimed as a type of self-regulation and yet have no penalties for non-compliance, and so they are often considered the weakest form of quality control (Weaver, 2001). Codes are explored in more detail in Chapter 4 of this volume, and as with awards there is great diversity. However, evidence suggests that codes can influence tourists' and tourism enterprise operators' behaviour and practices (see Stonehouse, 2001; Chapter 3 in this volume). Certainly codes addressing tourism and child prostitution have resulted in raising global awareness of serious social problems and have stimulated national and international legislation (WTO, 2002).

Codes often declare a self-commitment to ecological sustainability or ethical tourism and, even without enforcement, place a strong moral commitment to comply. As with awards, there may be tendencies to mutate into more formal and enforceable standards, with the development of some form of conformity assessment. Many codes try to boost credibility and commitment by integrating a requirement to sign a declaration that commits the individual or enterprise to compliance (e.g. the former Tourism Council of Australia Code of Conduct). The implication of this requirement is that non-compliance may lead to public exposure. The associated reputational risk provides additional pressure to ensure the compliance of codes. Unfortunately, codes, as well as industry-led certification, are perceived by some (Mason and Mowforth, 1996; Chapter 4 in this volume) with a degree of concern, as simply a pragmatic way that government regulation can be staved off, despite only having voluntary and unenforceable rules for which there are no formal consequences for non-compliance.

Certification and Accreditation

The terms certification and accreditation are sometimes used interchangeably, particularly in Australia, Asia and New Zealand (Honey, 2002), and yet they represent two quite different and separate quality mechanisms with different processes and implications. Certification is a voluntary procedure that sets, assesses, monitors and gives written assurance that a business, product, process, service or management system conforms to a specific requirement. A marketable logo (sometimes called an ecolabel) is given to those that conform or meet the criteria, with the standard at least meeting, but generally being above, any regulatory requirements. Most importantly, certification measures compliance through both initial assessment and subsequent audits (i.e. it monitors and polices). Certification endorses skilled expertise or best practice rather than regulating for a minimum acceptable standard.

Accreditation, in contrast, is defined here as the procedure by which an authoritative body formally recognizes that a certifier or certification programme is competent to carry out specific tasks (i.e. it certifies the certifiers or demonstrates that they are doing their job correctly). The development of a global accreditation body for sustainable and ecotourism certification programmes has been under consideration since the Ecotourism and Sustainable Tourism Certification Workshop held at Mohonk, USA, in 2000. Certification experts from 20 countries that had created, run or evaluated tourism certification programmes, including most of the leading global, regional, national and sub-national programmes, formulated a set of basic principles and components that should be part of any sound sustainable and ecotourism certification programme (this is known as the Mohonk Agreement – see Honey, 2002), and workshop participants approved a proposal by Rainforest Alliance to investigate the feasibility of a Sustainable Tourism Stewardship Council (Rainforest Alliance, 2001; see Chapter 23 in this volume).

Monitoring and Evaluation

To assess whether quality ecotourism is being achieved either through the quality assurance tools examined in this volume or through other initiatives such as sustainable tourism charters, government policy and legislation, there needs to be some meaningful method of evaluating whether the underlying principles of ecotourism are being achieved and performance monitored. Monitoring instruments and related procedures such as benchmarking, reporting, indicators, assessment or auditing are vital components of any quality system. The credibility of any quality tool often hinges on these components, as the lack of monitoring or enforcing of standards may result in fraud. Some of these monitoring instruments are used as stand-alone tools, although many are also standard components of certification programmes.

Benchmarking is the process of comparing performances and processes within an industry to assess relative position against either a set industry standard or against those that are 'best in class'. Best practice should be drawn from benchmarking processes and identifies leaders in the field or leading practices. One of the most well known of the sustainable tourism certification programmes, Green Globe (see Chapter 6 in this volume), uses benchmarking indicators on a set number of criteria to provide an assessment of comparative performance.

All credible certification programmes use conformity assessment to check compliance, with the most reliable programmes insisting on regular on-site verification by trained third-party assessors. Details of this process and some of the challenges these processes present are evident from a number of chapters in this volume (see Chapters 6, 14, 22) that cover various different types of certification programmes.

Indicators are information sets or measurements that are selected to be used on a regular basis to measure changes that are of importance, for example changes in the ecosystem. Well-selected indicators provide early warning of changes that may need addressing, and as such are of importance to planning and management processes. Indicators are discussed in more depth in Chapters 7 and 8 in this volume.

Summary

The long-term viability, competitiveness and economic and environmental sustainability of the ecotourism industry are reliant on two important factors. The first is maintaining and enhancing the unique natural and cultural environments on which the industry depends (Issaverdis, 1998; Toplis, 2000). The second is increasing the professionalism of the industry. Ecotourism appears to have emerged from its infant stage into an increasingly mature, but perhaps still adolescent, industry. A number of trends indicate the coming of age and increasing sophistication of the ecotourism industry: first, a growing consensus on ecotourism's core principles (see Chapter 1 in this volume); second, an increasing number of recognized best practices for the ecotourism industry (see chapters in Part One of this volume); and, third, genuine attempts to set appropriate and relevant guidelines and benchmarks. Finally, the ecotourism industry is showing evidence of increasing professionalism as well as the development of a spectrum of specific quality assurance tools and instruments to ensure that ecotourism standards are clearly defined, set, measured and met.

References

Black, R.S. (2002) Towards a model for tour guide certification: an analysis of the Australian EcoGuide Program. Doctoral thesis, Department of Management, Monash University, Melbourne, Victoria, Australia.

Burns, J. (1997) Ecotourism: what's in a word? Confusion for a start. . . . *Travelweek* 869: 33.

Enterprise Northland (2005) Available at: http://www.enterprisenorthland.co.nz/projects/activate/sustainable_tourism_project.htm (accessed 15 January 2006).

Fennell, D.A. and Dowling, R.K. (2003) Ecotourism policy and planning: stakeholders, management and governance. In: Fennell, D.A. and Dowling, R.K. (eds) *Ecotourism Policy and Planning*. CAB International, Wallingford, UK, pp. 331–344.

Font, X. and Buckley, R.C. (2001) *Tourism Ecolabelling: Certification and Promotion of Sustainable Management*. CAB International, Wallingford, UK.

Honey, M. (ed.) (2002) *Ecotourism and Certification: Setting Standards in Practice*. Island Press, Washington, DC.

Issaverdis, J.P. (1998) *Tourism Industry Accreditation – A Comparative Critique of Developments in Australia*. Victoria University, Melbourne.

Issaverdis, J.P. (2001) The pursuit of excellence: benchmarking, accreditation, best practice and auditing. In: Weaver, D. (ed.) *The Encyclopedia of Ecotourism*. CAB International, Wallingford, UK, pp. 579–594.

Manidis Roberts Consultants (1994) *An Investigation into a National Ecotourism Accreditation Scheme*. Commonwealth Department of Tourism, Canberra.

Mason, P. and Mowforth, M. (1996) Codes of conduct in tourism. *Progress in Tourism and Hospitality Research* 2(2), 152–163.

Rainforest Alliance (2001) *A Proposal from the Rainforest Alliance as Coordinator of the Feasibility Study, Organizational Blueprint and Implementation Plan for a Global Sustainable Tourism Stewardship Council (STSC): An Accreditation Body for Sustainable Tourism Certifiers*. Rainforest Alliance, New York.

Stonehouse, B. (2001) Polar environments. In: Weaver, D. (ed.) *The Encyclopedia of Ecotourism*. CAB International, Wallingford, UK, pp. 219–234.

Toplis, S.C. (2000) The perceived effectiveness of the Australian tourism awards in promoting improvements in quality and ecological sustainability to the Australian tourism industry: a Victorian perspective. Unpublished PhD thesis, RMIT University.

UNEP and WTO (2007) *Making Tourism More Sustainable: A Guide for Policy Makers*. UNEP, Paris, France.

Weaver, D. (2001) *Ecotourism*. John Wiley and Sons Australia, Milton, Queensland.

Wight, P. (1993) Ecotourism: ethics or eco-sell? *Journal of Travel Research* 31(3), 3–9.

WTO (2002) *Voluntary Initiatives for Sustainable Tourism: Worldwide Inventory and Comparative Analysis of 104 Eco-labels, Awards and Self-commitments*. WTO, Madrid, Spain.

3 Green and Gold? Awards for Excellence in Australian Tourism: Promoting Quality and Sustainability to the Tourism Industry

Stuart Toplis

Tourism Victoria, Victoria, Australia

Chapter Profile

In Australian tourism, and no doubt throughout the international tourism industry, there is heightened concern by government agencies and industry associations for the quality of services offered and the need to conserve and enhance the natural and cultural environments the industry inherently depends upon. Tourism Awards for Excellence are regarded by many tourism industry stakeholders as a key mechanism in achieving industry-wide improvements in quality and they devote a considerable amount of resources to sponsor and conduct this phenomenon. The question, however, is whether the resources put into these awards produce any serious results in achieving their stated purpose: first, promoting improvements in quality through high-profile recognition and rewarding of excellence across all tourism industry sectors, including ecotourism, and, second, promoting improvements in ecological sustainability in the Australian tourism industry. In essence, awards may redefine the meaning of quality, in this context, to incorporate a sustainability dimension.

This chapter examines separately the rationale behind the introduction of these two forms of awards, their roles and whether they have been effective in achieving these roles, from an Australian perspective. It also discusses the similarities between the two constructs and the recent trend towards the convergence of quality and sustainability within the awards context.

Introduction: Importance of Tourism and its Challenges

Australia is positioned on the edge of the fastest-growing tourism region in the world – East Asia and the Pacific. As a result, the tourism industry has emerged as an increasingly important sector of the Australian economy in terms of employment, growth and exports. In 2000/01, tourism generated 4.7% or AU$31.8 billion of GDP and accounted for 551,000 jobs in Australia or 6% of total employment. Tourism employment grew faster than total employment. The last decade has seen international tourism become a major contributor to the Australian economy, in terms of both employment and foreign exchange (Commonwealth Department of Industry, Tourism and Resources, 2002a). Yet, despite this growth and the increasing significance of the industry to the Australian economy, tourism is facing a number of issues over the next 10 years compounded by recent catastrophes such as the terrorist attack on 11 September, the Iraq War and severe acute respiratory syndrome (SARS). These issues include seasonality and global competitiveness, transport and infrastructure growth, destination development and visitor experience, satisfaction, behaviour and stakeholder awareness (Valles, 2001) and are forcing the continuous adaptability of the world tourism industry.

At a national level, the Commonwealth Department of Industry, Tourism and Resources (2003b) has identified that the prime challenges for the tourism industry are investment attraction, the adequacy of Australia's current transport modes to disperse tourists around the country, the need for skilled, innovative staff and managers, the low rate of domestic tourism growth, the increasingly competitive global market, changes in consumer tastes and strengthening the capacity for businesses to manage risk.

Improving Quality and Ecological Sustainability in Tourism

Central to addressing the aforementioned issues are two primary challenges that are consistently receiving priority recognition in the tourism industry, namely the need for improving quality and ecological sustainability. These challenges are due to the heightened concern by government agencies and industry associations about the quality of services offered and the need to enhance the natural and cultural environments on which the industry inherently depends. The World Tourism Organization's work programme clearly focuses on the improvements in ecological sustainability and quality in the international tourism industry (WTO, 2003).

The European Commission (2003) recognizes that the satisfaction of tourists' demands and the protection of the environment are essential to the success of tourism in member states, stating that:

> The central challenge for European tourism, its businesses and destinations, is to ensure that it respects the limits of its resource base, and of those resources' capacity to regenerate, while being commercially successful through a competitive quality development that takes into account diverging developments in the various types of tourism, and creating wide societal and environmental benefits.
>
> (European Commission, 2003: p. 6)

In Australia, the Commonwealth Department of Industry, Tourism and Resources (2002) maintains that if the industry is to remain competitive it will need to continually improve the quality of product and service to grow its tourism market and ensure that the tourism industry does not over-exploit the resources and communities on which it is based. This is particularly true for the country's burgeoning ecotourism sector, whose very survival depends on the safeguarding of natural and cultural amenities that attract tourists in the first place. Research clearly establishes that international and domestic visitors regard the country's clean, unspoilt natural environment as a primary motivator for a visit to Australia. However, ecotourism, in its strictest sense, can only account for a small proportion of the Australian tourism market and, as a result, there is a crucial need for the mainstream tourism industry to meet the sustainability challenge.

In New Zealand the Tourism Industry Association of New Zealand (2000) argues that the two challenges are interrelated and interdependent and presented a 'star chart' to illustrate the linkages and relationships that must be managed to ensure sustainable development (Fig. 3.1). In essence, it advises that, if businesses don't deliver value to customers, tourism development cannot be sustainable. Similarly, if host communities object to more visitors, tourism cannot be sustainable. And, if a value is not placed on the environment, the sustainability of a key asset is put at risk. The importance of quality is also recognized in the British Government's 1999 strategy for the development of tourism, *Tomorrow's Tourism,* as a central issue for

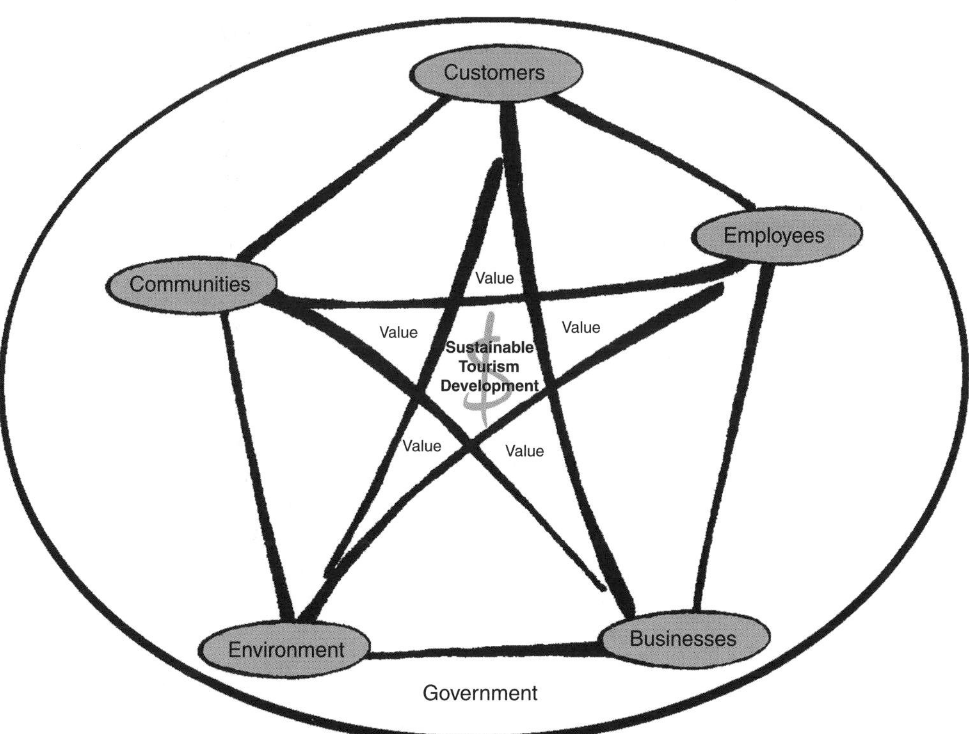

Fig. 3.1. Framework for Sustainable Tourism (from Tourism Industry Association of New Zealand, 2000: 8).

sustainable tourism in England (UK Department of Culture, Media and Sport, 1999).

Awards for Excellence in Tourism

Central to improving quality and ecological sustainability in the tourism industry are tourism enterprises, which are responsible for delivering a wide variety of tourism goods and services and recognized as a core component of tourism. This recognition is reflected in the considerable resources devoted by the tourism industry, both public and private sector, to mechanisms targeted at these enterprises, with the intent of promoting improvements in the quality and ecological sustainability of the industry. These mechanisms include self-regulatory techniques such as accreditation/certification, codes of conduct and awards for excellence. It is the latter that are the focus of this chapter.

Awards for excellence exist in most facets of society, from local literary awards to world-famous cinema awards such as the Academy Awards. Despite the great variance in their geographical scope and profile, these phenomena share a common purpose – to reward and recognize excellence within their sphere of influence. The tourism industry is no exception, with a number of awards for excellence covering most spectra of the industry, including the ecotourism sector. While these awards can be categorized in a number of different ways, such as geographically, by industry sector or by target audience, there appear to be two main forms of awards that manifest in the tourism industry, namely quality or environmental awards for excellence.

Quality awards for excellence in tourism

In terms of the tourism and travel industry, quality awards for excellence are part of a plethora of awards for excellence programmes covering most spectra of this diverse industry. A review of these awards revealed that some of the programmes have been in existence for several years, while others have been recently introduced. Some relate to specific sectors while others are much broader in their scope (Toplis, 2004). In all circumstances they are recognized as the highest accolade in the tourism industry and are awarded on a competitive basis. Yet, even though the awards purport to command a high profile in the industry, this is not demonstrated in tourism literature, which pays relatively little attention to the concept of quality awards for excellence (Toplis, 2004). The published literature available in this field is restricted to the marketing of the various awards such as 'Calls for Entry' and 'Event' programmes. To conceptualize awards for excellence in tourism one must therefore refer to the literature on the general quality awards in industry, but in the context that there are some fundamental differences between the types of awards.

In terms of the quality awards in industry generally, a number are bestowed each year around the world to individual organizations. An analysis of a collection of these awards revealed that each award is managed by a different organization, whether government, industry association or non-governmental body, each using its own judging criteria. Further, the awards ostensibly command a high profile in their own country and sometimes around the world, share common principles and have been given credibility through high-level government and industry support (Toplis, 2004). Nevertheless, a review of the literature has found that research into quality awards is also limited (Garvin, 1991; Øvretveit, 1993; Gilmour and Driva, 1994; Steventon, 1994; Bohoris, 1995; Ghobadian and Woo, 1996; Laszlo, 1996; Tummala and Tang, 1996; Kristensen and Juhl, 1999; Tan, 2002). This situation is possibly due to the strict confidentiality rules applied to most quality awards.

With the trend towards economic globalization and the concurrent increase in international trade, quality awards for excellence are regarded as an important initiative to assist businesses in improving their competitive edge on a worldwide scale by raising quality standards (Laszlo, 1996). The reason for the introduction of quality awards for excellence by governments, non-governmental agencies and industry associations appears to be threefold: first, to elevate quality standards and expectations within individual organizations; second, to facilitate communication and sharing among and within organizations of all types based upon common understanding of key quality requirements; and, finally, to raise the profile of the quality movement (Hunt, 1993).

From an individual enterprise's viewpoint, the purpose of awards according to Øvretveit 'is to assess past quality excellence and whether the enterprise is doing what quality experts believe has to be done to ensure and improve quality continually in the future' (1993: 80). Yet, based on the review, the purpose of quality awards for excellence appears to be more far-reaching. For instance, when the Australian Quality Awards (now known as the Australian Business Excellence Awards) were established in 1988, the Awards were regarded as a unique piece of intellectual property that was clearly destined to become not only the pinnacle of achievement in quality, but the foundation and framework on which the modern Australian quality movement was to be built (Sprouster, 1994). According to Gummesson (1993: 53), quality awards 'have gained the unofficial character of national standards'.

It can be established that quality awards for excellence in tourism have been introduced predominantly by industry associations and governments, not only to raise standards of excellence within individual tourism businesses but also to raise the profile of the industry in general. The 'England for Excellence Awards', for instance, were created in 1988 by the English Tourist Board not only with the intention of raising the profile of the Board and tourism in England but also as an integral part of the Board's drive to raise standards in England's tourism industry (S. Mills, personal communication, 1995). Like the general quality awards in industry, it appears that the various awards were introduced in response to increased global competition in the tourism marketplace. This is reflected in a statement by the New Zealand

Tourism Board concerning its national awards programme: 'they are about giving the industry the vision, tools and encouragement to attain higher standards to ensure New Zealand stands among the best in the world' (1999: 5).

There are a number of roles awards can play in achieving or promoting quality improvements. Awards have been established to recognize and reward the efforts of individual companies in the area of quality management and improvement (Belharz, 1994). For instance, the original purpose of the Canada Award for Excellence was to celebrate and recognize as role models organizations that have obtained world-class successes through quality management (Laszlo, 1997).

Tangible benefits to award winners include recognition, with rewards ranging from preferential marketing programmes to exclusive logo usage. One benefit to the winners of government-supported awards is that these awards represent government certification of product quality (Wisner and Eakins, 1994). The European Quality Award carries considerable prestige with the promotion of the Award, together with the opportunity to use the Award logo in corporate literature. This clearly establishes the winner as one of the members of the most successful companies in Europe (Hunt, 1993).

The raising of standards is meant to be achieved through the incentive of high-profile recognition of excellence. As the English Tourist Board (now VisitBritain) advocates, 'Quality and service are the watchwords of the tourism industry. At the English Tourist Board, we believe your dedication to the pursuit of excellence should be recognised – as well as given the credit it deserves' (1995b). This high-profile recognition of excellence that recipients of tourism awards receive, such as preferential promotional opportunities or the right to use the Awards logo in the promotion of business, is regarded as holding a number of competitive advantages such as national media exposure (English Tourist Board, 1995b).

Looking beyond tourism once more, the promotion of the award winners is an important signal to customers and employees and may also generate interest in total quality among other companies. As Berry and Parasuraman state, 'having winners to shower praise and tribute in the presence of peers showcases service leadership. They become lighthouses of change' (1991: 109). The Australian Quality Awards (now the Australian Business Excellence Awards), for example, provided five levels of recognition: (i) commitment; (ii) achievement; (iii) commendation; (iv) award; and (v) prize (Australian Quality Council (AQC), 1997). In doing so, it is inferred that awards assist enterprises to measure the progressive improvement in their practices with clear 'milestones' along the path of achievement (Australian Quality Council, 1998). And here lies the second role of the awards: as a framework for self-evaluation and continuous improvements for award applicants.

The award criteria not only are designed to serve as a reliable basis for making awards by external assessors, but also permit a diagnosis of the applicant's overall quality management even if the company is not successful in winning an award. In essence, the criteria enable self-evaluation, which in turn supposedly leads to continuous improvements. This is a notion identified by the Australian Quality Council: 'they are equally useful for self assessment by an organisation to identify its strengths and its opportunities for improvement of operations and results' (AQC, 1997). For instance, Berry and Parasuraman (1991) believe that companies seeking awards such as the American Malcolm Baldridge National Quality Award (MBNQA) benefit because the application process offers a framework for thinking about quality, identifies weaknesses and energizes the organization. Even though only a few companies can win an award each year, the self-evaluation criteria create a quality progress profile. Alternatively, Zink *et al.* (1997) argue that applying for an award is not the most important step in improving quality but rather it is a means of going public with one's commitment to quality management. Internally, the whole process should be based on a regular self-assessment, matching the organization against a model for business excellence, provided by quality awards such as the European Quality Award and MBNQA. Crucial to this self-evaluation and continuous improvement process is the formal feedback given to applicants by quality award administrators. For instance, in the case of the Australian Business Excellence Awards and MBNQA, all awards applicants receive a written feedback summary of their strengths and the areas that need improvement in their quality management (USA National Institute of Standards and Technology (NIST), 1996).

Quality awards are often regarded as providing a powerful incentive for organizations outside the application process to strive for continuous improvement, with the award criteria offering useful guidelines for companies wishing to implement a programme of continuous quality improvement (Codling, 1994). This is particularly true for the MBNQA application guidelines, which include detailed selection criteria. Non-applicants are further assisted and encouraged in their continuous improvement efforts through a comprehensive programme of sharing the practices and experiences of those receiving recognition in the various award programmes (NIST, 1996). Indeed, MBNQA award winners are compelled by law to share their knowledge, and that they have done so without suffering competitively has led other companies to follow suit (Garvin, 1991). In its desire to improve the competitiveness of tourism in destinations, the European Commission identified the Quality Award Criteria Framework that was developed by the European Foundation on Quality Management (EFQM) as the model and basis on which to improve the performance of destinations in Europe (Go and Govers, 2000).

Quality award recipients are also considered to be a valuable source of information for benchmarking by organizations, thereby serving as leading indicators of best practice (Camp, 1995). As Kristensen and Juhl state, 'Quality award models are operational benchmarking tools that can be used by companies in their internal educational programme and in their self-assessment process' (1999: 1). On the aggregate level it is also an obvious model for comparing best practice between countries.

It is also advocated that several national and regional quality awards have been established to promote quality and serve as perceived models of total quality management (TQM), a quality-oriented approach that consists of applying a selection of quality management mechanisms throughout an organization. According to Laszlo (1996), national quality award criteria are intended to provide impartial bases of comparison for the relative advances made in the application of TQM principles within various organizations. In fact, it is maintained that quality awards' assessments are the only comprehensive means available to date by which TQM initiatives can be thoroughly monitored and assessed, and that they provide any business with a competitive internal mechanism necessary to face the imposition of future barriers to trade in the form of technical or quality standards (Ghobadian and Woo, 1996). However, Bohoris (1995) reviewed and compared the three main national quality awards, and found that each model has its unique award system and set of examination criteria and differed from the others in terms of purpose, overall approach, underlying values and concepts represented in their frameworks, and their contributions to the practice of TQM.

In terms of quality assurance, quality awards are promoted as helping customers to decide how to assess and predict the quality of a service prior to purchase, particularly in services, where assessing quality is more difficult (Øvretveit, 1993). From a tourism perspective, 'quality awards for excellence', in particular the associated logo, are also regarded as providing the consumer with the confidence to purchase a particular tourism product. As emphasized by the New Zealand Tourism Board:

> when you travel around New Zealand, there are certain signs of excellence you can look for to ensure you're getting the best quality from your travel experience, regardless of your budget. The distinctive New Zealand Tourism Awards logo is a sure sign you will experience the best New Zealand's tourism industry has to offer.
>
> (1998: 32)

Despite the promoted importance of quality awards in transforming business, the evaluation of the various awards' effectiveness in achieving their aims is limited. Of all awards identified, the MBNQA has received the most attention in academic research. According to Garvin, the Award has become one of the most important catalysts for transforming American business:

> more than any other initiative, public or private, it has reshaped managers' thinking and behaviour. The Award not only codifies the principles of quality management in clear and accessible language. It also goes further: it provides companies with a comprehensive framework for assessing their progress toward the new paradigm of management and such commonly acknowledged goals as customer satisfaction and increased employee involvement.
>
> (1991: 80)

This is a finding supported by Sterett and Durkee (1993), who assert that the Award is generating a large amount of interest, making available detailed information and fostering changes in business practices for improved quality.

However, Garvin (1991) also highlights the other side of the MBNQA. Despite its popularity, the award has come under increasing scrutiny. Critics cite three major deficiencies: first, reports of enormous investment by companies intent on winning the award; second, Baldridge critics note that the award does not reflect outstanding quality; and, third, the poor sales and earnings growth of some past winners have led critics to question whether the award is in fact an accurate gauge of a company's competitiveness and profit potential. The latter notion is supported by Collier, who infers that quality awards do not ensure continuous marketplace success: 'no award system can guarantee success for ever' (1990: 60).

Munro-Faure and Munro-Faure (1994) identified further shortcomings of the Baldridge and other quality awards. They argue that companies shouldn't adopt the formal assessment criteria slavishly as a model for success. The award criteria should only be used as guidelines, which may be adapted to suit an individual organization, adding that the application for an award should be the result, not the aim, of any continuous improvement programme.

From an Australian perspective, a survey of previous Australian Business Excellence Award winners in 1993 found that most of the organizations felt that improved employee morale was the main benefit derived from winning the awards. Interestingly, of the 17 responses only six indicated measurable improvement areas (Gilmour and Driva, 1994). Furthermore, in 1993, 8000 organizations requested guidelines about the Australia Quality Award process, and how to make an application to be considered for an award. Of these, only 32 actually applied to go through the award evaluation process, suggesting that non-entrants may be using the criteria to assist in their overall quality improvement and planning activities (Beilharz, 1994). This highlights the self-evaluation and internal planning role of quality awards.

Whilst the publicly available academic literature on the evaluation of the effectiveness of the various quality awards in tourism is almost non-existent, it is apparent from the recent changes made to some awards that a degree of internal evaluation has occurred. For instance, the Travel Industry Association of America made significant changes to its awards programme, the Odyssey Awards, on the recommendation of a special task force. It was felt that the awards were becoming meaningless, and the number of award categories were reduced from over 20 sectoral categories to three general categories to reflect the much broader industry trends such as the significance of the environment and community to the industry's long-term sustainability (Kroel, personal communication, 1995).

In Australia, the National Travel Industry Awards also adjusted its categories to reflect the changing dynamics of the industry as it entered the new millennium. As the Awards Managing Director, Geoff Brooks, states, 'if the awards are to perpetuate, then we are going to have to constantly modernise the program to reflect changes in the industry and, where possible, to anticipate them. We have to evolve with the industry if you like' (cited in *Travelweek*, 1999: 1). The English Tourist Board (1999) reports that the England for Excellence Awards have been highly successful not only in highlighting some of the success stories of English tourism, but also in promoting healthy and friendly competition, and in turn helping raise standards throughout the industry. As Stephen Mills from the English Tourist Board stated:

> We have not carried out any systematic research into the effectiveness of Awards Schemes, such as England for Excellence. We know that such Schemes can attract significant publicity – both for the Awards bodies and also for the recipients. The England for Excellence scheme was introduced originally in 1988 with the twofold intention of raising the profile of the English Tourist Board and tourism in England and also encouraging (and rewarding) excellence in a variety of fields. The format and the range of awards has varied over the years, but we are continuing with the awards this year – the 10th anniversary. The industry likes them; they are quite high profile; and we have been able to find sponsors prepared to foot the quite high cost of administration.
>
> (S. Mills, personal communication, 1998)

By examining the available quality in tourism and general quality literature it has been possible to establish the conceptual framework from which awards for excellence, such as the Australian Tourism Awards, can be seen to operate. As previously highlighted, quality awards for excellence in tourism are regarded by many as integral to achieving excellence and best practice in the tourism industry and are also considered a valuable source of information for benchmarking. Some consider awards as being at the pinnacle of the mechanisms used to promote continuous improvements in quality, as demonstrated in Fig. 3.2. It is essentially a continuous improvement pyramid that distinguishes between and recognizes the progression a tourism operator must follow from minimum acceptable standards to excellence. In this model codes of conduct are seen as minimal acceptable

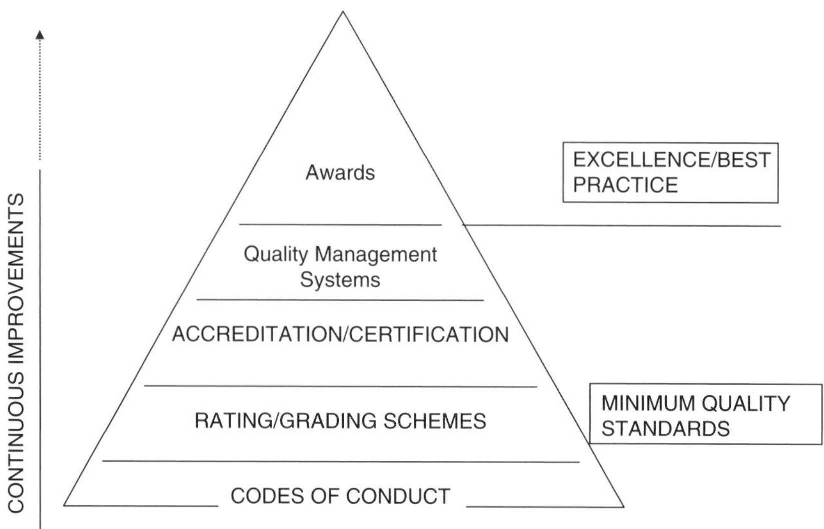

Fig. 3.2. Quality awards for excellence conceptual framework.

standards that an operator must commit to (through an affirmation programme) prior to becoming an accredited operator. On achieving accreditation, the operator becomes eligible to enter an award. Importantly, as reflected in the model, each year the criterion is made more stringent.

Environmental awards in tourism

In the last decade a number of dedicated environmental awards in tourism have been instigated by various organizations worldwide, predominantly by government agencies and industry associations, some in partnership with conservation groups, some international in coverage, others sector-specific. Hamele (1994) identified over 32 environmental awards in tourism worldwide, with many found in Germany. A more recent study undertaken in 2001 for the World Tourism Organization identified 17 environmental awards schemes related directly to tourism (WTO, 2002). At the same time, long-standing tourism awards have introduced environmental categories and general environmental awards, such as the Australian Banksia Environmental Awards, which now include tourism-related categories.

An analysis of 11 international environmental awards schemes by Toplis (2004) highlighted an apparent coincidence, with most of the awards established at a time when environmentalism was at its peak, in the early 1990s. For example, the Wales Tourism Awards 'Community/Environmental' category was established in 1992 to reflect growing public awareness of environmental issues and the increasing importance of sustainable tourism (Wales Tourist Board, 1995a). According to Stephen Mills of the English Tourist Board, the 'Green Tourism Award', later known as the Tourism and the Environment Award, was first introduced as part of the E for E (England for Excellence) scheme in 1990, 'the time when we first started work in earnest on tourism and the environment issues' (S. Mills, personal communication, 1998).

Whilst the various award schemes identified vary in scope and administration, the underlying philosophy for their establishment appears to be twofold: first, to promote environmental awareness through tourism and, second, to encourage environmental improvements in the tourism industry. For example, the purpose of the international Tourism for Tomorrow Awards is to promote environmental awareness in tourism and encourage an environmentally responsible approach to tourism management (Neale, 1998). Similarly, the European Prize for Tourism and the Environment was established to encourage environmental awareness and remind the tourism industry and tourists themselves about their duties towards world heritage (*Leisure Opportunities*, 1995).

Given the underlying rationale behind environmental awards in tourism, it is understandable that the target audience of these awards, in the main, is the general tourism industry. It is an approach demonstrated in the assessment criteria on which entrants are judged, which in most cases are closely aligned with the principles and practices of sustainable tourism.

Exceptions to this trend are the Pacific Asia Travel Association (PATA) Gold Award and the former Banksia Awards Ecotourism category award. These are promoted as having a broad focus but this is not translated to the assessment criteria, which indicate that their focus is prime facie ecotourism. On the other hand, the administrators of the Australian National Travel Industry Awards (NTIA) strongly emphasize that their Environmental Award is not an ecotourism award, 'although a specialist ecotourism operator could win it'.

Despite these differences the various awards identified share a number of common and interrelated roles for achieving their stated aims. First, it is apparent that the primary role of the various environmental awards for excellence in tourism in achieving their stated aims is to recognize and reward outstanding environmental practices of individuals, businesses and governments. For example, each year the winners of the Tourism for Tomorrow Awards are announced at a presentation dinner in London, hosted by Sir Colin Marshall, Chairman of British Airways, with renowned environmentalist David Bellamy presenting the awards. Since its inception, the event has been televised by the UK travel programme, 'Wish You Were Here . . .?', which is broadcast to over 14 million viewers (British Airways, 1996). It is maintained that this high-profile exposure provides the recipient with a competitive advantage. As consumer demand for 'greener' tourism increases, awards will prove to be a valuable marketing tool and method of public disclosure (UNEP IE, 1999).

This notion is reflected in comments made by Mike Dyer of the Couran Cove Resort, recipient of the National Tourism Industry Awards Environmental Award category, who stated that, in winning the award, 'it gave us a lot of confidence to go out into the market and make our claims – the acknowledgment that we had won the environmental award gave us credibility' (cited in *Travelweek*, 1999). In turn, by promoting healthy competition, it is argued that awards help raise environmental standards throughout the industry (English Tourist Board, 1995 b) and in doing so raise general industry standards by selecting projects and businesses demonstrating best practice and providing role models for the environmental improvements achieved by tourism businesses. Other operators, according to the World Travel and Tourism Council and International Hotel and Restaurant Association, 'are encouraged to follow suit and consider the environment in the everyday running of their businesses' (1999: 8).

Finally, according to the United Nations Environmental Program, 'awards are a way both of implementing codes of conduct and monitoring their effectiveness' (UNEP IE, 1999). For instance, the PATA Environment Award has gained further significance due to the development of the PATA Code for Environmentally Responsible Tourism adopted by PATA members at the PATA 1992 Conference in Hong Kong (PATA, 1992).

Effectiveness of the awards

Unfortunately, gauging the effectiveness of these awards schemes in achieving their aims is difficult, as the administrators of the various awards profiled have undertaken little research, combined with no scholarly attention having been given to this topic. As Stephen Mills from English Tourist Board stresses:

> Schemes such as E for E or the EU Tourism and the Environment Award benefit the few but encourage the many. Other types of schemes, such as Commendation schemes, or the Board's own Accommodation grading schemes, serve both to raise awareness within the industry, setting benchmarks to aspire to, and particularly to provide customer reassurance. Long term I suspect that grading schemes are of greater benefit, but the one off awards are fun for the industry and do get good publicity, particularly within the trade press.
>
> (S. Mills, personal communication, 1995)

Nevertheless British Airways found, as part of a study of the environmental attitudes and behaviour of its leisure customers, that the current awareness of the Tourism for Tomorrow Awards was low, demonstrating a weakness in the Awards' branding (Pembroke, 1996). This low level of awareness of the Awards was also apparent amongst Australian tourism enterprises (Toplis, 2004).

The Convergence of Quality and Sustainability in Awards for Excellence

It has emerged from the preceding discussion that, while quality and environmental awards for excellence in tourism have a different rationale for their instigation, the manner in which these two phenomena achieve their implied purposes is distinctly similar. The recognition and rewarding of excellence in a high profile manner, a framework for continuous improvements, benchmarking, consumer and industry awareness raising and consumer assurance are all common themes threaded throughout these two forms of awards (as presented in Table 3.1). Consequently such a set of circumstances presents the opportunity for the convergence of quality and environmental awards into one integrated awards programme. Indeed, key quality awards such as the MBNQA and the Australian quality awards introduced environmental questions into core criteria over 5 years ago and in doing so clearly recognized and acknowledged that these awards have a role, not only in promoting quality improvements, but also in encouraging the adoption of sustainable practices by industry.

Within the tourism industry, it is apparent from the available literature on quality and environmental awards programmes that there is limited recognition of the potential convergence of quality and sustainability. Nevertheless, the New Zealand Tourism Board (1998), in its support of initiatives to improve environmental efficiency in the tourism industry, fully recognizes environmental initiatives in its annual tourism awards.

The following section provides a case study of one of the most prestigious award schemes in Australia, which had formerly focused primarily

Table 3.1. Similarities between quality and environmental awards for excellence.

	Quality awards for excellence	Environmental awards for excellence
Rationale	To raise quality standards of the industry To raise profile of the industry	To raise environmental standards of the industry To raise awareness of environmental issues
Roles	High-profile recognition and rewarding of excellence Framework for self-evaluation Implementation of codes of conduct Benchmarking Models of TQM Consumer assurance	High-profile recognition and rewarding of excellence Implementation of codes of conduct Benchmarking Consumer assurance

on quality issues, but more recently has introduced aspects of ecological sustainability into its criteria.

Case Study 1: the Australian Tourism Awards for Excellence

The Australian Tourism Awards ('the Awards'), as one of a collection of tourism and travel-related awards for excellence conducted in Australia, are promoted by the industry as one of the most important events on the national tourism industry calendar.

Rationale for the Australian Tourism Awards

The Awards were established by the Australian Tourist Commission and the Department of Arts, Sports, Tourism and Territories in 1985 and subsequently transferred to the Australian Tourism Industry Association (ATIA) in 1989 until this organization, trading as Tourism Council Australia (TCA), was placed in voluntary administration in December 2000. The Awards are now administered through a joint agreement of each state/territory with the Australian Tourism Awards Management Group reporting to the Australian Standing Committee on Tourism.

The Awards were instigated at a time when Australia was experiencing significant growth in international tourism. According to Tolhurst (1993: 47), 'this rapid growth of Australian tourism meant the country was entering a more complex service environment with different client categories – from convention delegates to Asian language-speaking visitors – all demanding different service levels'. The Awards, it is maintained, were ostensibly conceived to act as a catalyst to encourage and recognize high standards of service and infrastructure to cope with the demands and expectations of the more sophisticated traveller, at a time when standards of service were questionable, with the parodied 'couldn't care less' attitude being widespread (Kurosawa, 1992). Furthermore, 20 years ago the Australian tourism industry had a major image problem. Successive Australian Commonwealth governments, and the public generally, did not regard tourism as particularly valuable or important in the national economy (Leiper, 1995). It is apparent, from the timing of their instigation and the comments of key industry players at the time, that the Awards were an integral part of a public relations campaign by groups representing tourism interests, such as the former ATIA, to gain recognition of tourism 'as an industry' by the community and by governments. As the then Federal Minister for Tourism, John Brown (1985: 24) stated, 'the Australian Tourism Awards were instituted last year to add prestige to an industry that has never been recognised as such by federal governments'.

The Australian Tourism Awards for Excellence are a national competition based on a federation structure. There is no direct entry to the Awards in any category. All entries must have won a state or territory award, except Category 27, 'Outstanding Contribution by an Individual', which is at the discretion of the national judging panel. Judging the Australian Tourism Awards is a national panel of judges drawn from key areas of the industry, as well as representatives of the major sponsors. For instance, in the state of Victoria, judges are selected by the Chief Executive Officer of Tourism Victoria on the basis of expertise and experience in the tourism industry.

The Awards are judged on a self-nominated written submission prepared by a tourism business in accordance with the published Guidelines for Entry. Submissions must contain a response to the general criteria as well as the category-specific criteria. There are limits on the size and format of the submission. The Awards are a competitive system with only one award winner per category, although in recent years finalists and merit certificates have been awarded. Whilst assessment is made primarily on the submission, entrants are also visited or contacted by a judge to review the product and to verify claims made in the submission.

The criteria and category guidelines for the Awards are set at a national level and coordinated by all states on behalf of Australian Tourism Awards Management Group. Entrants are assessed on a range of general criteria, including customer service, business development, staff training and contributions to tourism growth in their sector, as well as category-specific questions listed under 'Specific Criteria'. In 1985 the awards began with eight categories, increasing nearly twofold to 15 the next year and evolving to 28 award categories in 1997. All are promoted as reflecting industry trends and growth segments, as presented in Table 3.2. As of 2004 there still remain 28 award categories.

Table 3.2. Comparison of award categories 1985–1997.

1985 award categories	1997 award categories
International Accommodation	Major Tourist Attractions
National Accommodation	Significant Regional Attractions
Budget Accommodation	Major Festivals and Special Events
Tourist Attractions	Significant Regional Festivals and Special Events
Festivals	Environmental Tourism
Tourism Marketing	Heritage and Cultural Tourism
Tourist Services	Aboriginal and Torres Strait Islander Tourism
Restaurants and Catering	General Tourism Services
Tour Services and Transportation	Meetings Industry
Training and Education	Tourism Retailing
Resorts	Tour and Transport Operators – Major
Tourist Shops and Souvenirs	Tour and Transport Operators – Significant
Outstanding Achievements	Tourism Associations
Tourism Authorities	Tourism Marketing and Promotional Campaigns
	Media
	Industry Training – Private Sector
	Industry Education
	Tourism Restaurants
	Wineries
	Tourism Development Project
	Hosted Accommodation
	Motel/Hotel Budget Accommodation
	Unique Accommodation
	Camping and Caravan Parks
	Superior Accommodation
	Deluxe Accommodation
	Outstanding Contribution by an Individual Tourist Industry Employee

Importance of the Awards

Over the last 15 years, successive Australian governments have recognized the importance of and supported the Australian Tourism Awards as a key initiative to encourage standards of excellence in the tourism industry (Commonwealth Department of Tourism, 1992; Office of National Tourism, 1998). A recent Federal Government Green Paper on Tourism regards government support of the Awards' recognition of quality in the marketplace as a highly cost-effective approach to promoting improvements in quality in tourism, stating that:

> The Awards are a well established means of celebrating quality and best practice, with individual winners gaining recognition in the marketplace and accompanying commercial benefits. While the industry should have the primary responsibility for running and funding of such awards, government sponsorship may be justified to encourage excellence, particularly in those areas identified as priorities for industry development.
>
> (Commonwealth Department of Industry, Tourism and Resources, 2003)

In Victoria, Tourism Victoria considers that awards are an integral part of the process of encouraging and rewarding excellence in professionalism and standards (Tourism Victoria, 2002). Furthermore, each year a number of organizations, both public and private, show their support of the awards through sponsorship, which contributes towards the administration and presentation costs associated with the awards. For example, the Office of National Tourism provided a grant of AU$35,000 in 1997, and has done so for a number of years (Commonwealth Department of Industry, Tourism and Resources, 1998). Tourism Victoria contributes over AU$100,000 per annum, both financially and in-kind, to the administration of the Victorian Tourism Awards (Drayton, personal communication, 2003).

Shortcomings and impact of the Awards

In the early 1990s, the Australian Tourism Awards came under increasing criticism from within and outside the industry, with critics citing a number of major deficiencies. Some in the industry believed that those responsible for the Awards needed to rethink their whole structure. For example, it was argued that under the present structure the submissions requested for individual sections are almost beyond the capacity of small business, and therefore operators with the capacity to engage a professional service to compete have a great advantage. As asked by one industry critic, 'are the Awards to be given for actual achievements, or rather on the presentation of what the establishment says it offers and delivers?' The critic added 'that unless there is a real emphasis placed on actual performance and achievement in quality for the awards, I certainly have no intention of participating, or supporting the event, in future' (Forell, 1992: 23). Other criticisms included the high cost of entry, the manner in which the award system is conducted and, in an industry characterized by small business, the awards have a 'big-business' domination.

In 2001, a total of 104 entries were received for all Victorian Tourism Awards categories. Whilst there is no universal list of tourism operators in Victoria, some commentators suggest there are approximately 5000. It could then be implied that only 2% of the state's tourism industry entered for an award in 2001.

As presented in Fig. 3.3, a long-term trend analysis of the level of participation in the Victorian Tourism Awards indicates that, after a period of growth in the late 1990s, the number of entrants has been declining since the peak in 1999 of 169 entrants. Furthermore, the number of merit and finalist awards has fluctuated during this period, suggesting an inconsistency in the standard of businesses entering the awards during this time (Table 3.3).

In terms of evaluating the effectiveness of the Awards, after each of the Australian Tourism Awards ceremonies, the state and territory chairs and coordinators meet to review all categories. It has been noted earlier that categories have changed over time; however, no formal record of the reasons for those changes has been maintained (e.g. no formal resolutions or minutes of meetings) or are publicly available. It is understood that decisions about the Awards usually occur informally and relatively spontaneously during the post-national awards meeting of state award coordinators (Sullivan, personal communication, 1995). Despite a number of enquiries and correspondence between state awards coordinators throughout Australia, the author was

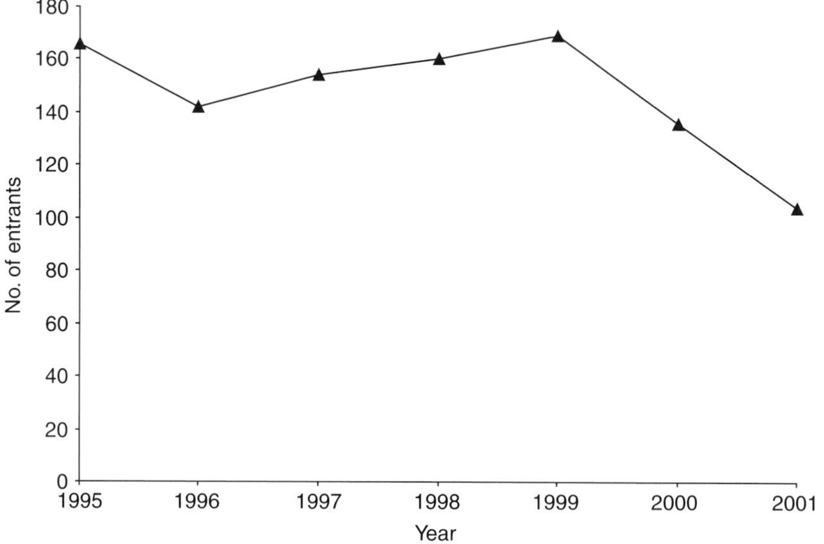

Fig. 3.3. Number of entrants – Victorian Tourism Awards 1995–2001.

Table 3.3. Merits and finalists – Victorian Tourism Awards 1995–2001 (from Tourism Victoria, 2002).

Year	Merits	% of total entrants	Finalists	% of total entrants	Combined total	% of total entrants
1995	17	10	28	17	45	27
1996	28	20	22	15	50	35
1997	24	16	30	19	54	35
1998	18	11	28	18	46	29
1999	9	5	28	17	37	22
2000	15	11	25	18	40	30
2001	10	10	12	12	22	21

unable to unearth any official and publicly available attempts at evaluating the effectiveness of the Australian Tourism Awards prior to 2001.

Toplis (2004) found that the Australian Tourism Awards, from a Victorian perspective, were not well understood by tourism enterprises, particularly small tourism businesses in regional areas. This limited understanding and associated apathy and cynicism regarding the Awards system has contributed to a noticeably low propensity to enter the Awards. Those tourism enterprises who did enter the Awards tended to be medium- and large-sized city-based businesses and they did so to raise the profile of their businesses in the marketplace. Toplis (2004) also found that those enterprises that choose to enter the Awards have a strong possibility of winning an award at the state level, and yet the purported competitive advantage of the Awards was not reflected in the findings.

In 2001, the Australian Standing Committee on Tourism initiated a review of the Australian Tourism Awards. A Steering Committee, representing the Awards stakeholders and the state tourism organizations, commissioned Ernst and Young to review the Awards' operational aspects in response to negative feedback from the industry and to stakeholders and to identify the optimal future management framework for the system. The review found broad industry dissatisfaction with many aspects of tourism award processes, including the cost/benefit of submissions, poor perceptions of its judging processes and other factors that reduce participation in the Awards programme. Despite this, there is strong support for the continuation of the Awards in an enhanced and simplified form. The industry stakeholder's willingness to contribute to this review process demonstrated their support for the Awards to be reformed and refined so that 'we are all singing from the same hymn book' in time for the 2002 awards (Ernst and Young, 2001).

The Australian Tourism Awards and sustainability

As established earlier in this chapter, awards for excellence in tourism can play an important role in promoting sustainability to the tourism industry. In terms of the Australian Tourism Awards, a review of the available promotional material, such as the 'Calls to Action' brochures, revealed no direct reference to sustainability. However, in 1998, the former Tourism Council Australia (TCA) relaunched its Code of Sustainable Practice and stated that 'signatories to the Code will be encouraged to participate in the TCA Tourism Awards in their respective States/Territories' (TCA, 1998). Hence the industry's former peak body and the then administrator of the Australian Tourism Awards' approach to achieving sustainable tourism viewed the Awards as playing a crucial role. This direction was further emphasized in a model presented in the publication.

Prior to 2002, one tourism award category, the Environmental Tourism Award, prime facie pertained to ecological sustainability and may therefore have the potential to act as a stimulus for adoption of ecologically sustainable tourism practices by entrants and the broader industry alike. However, the scope of this category was found to be limited to a handful of nature-based tourism businesses and consequently has a limited influence on changing industry-wide sustainable practices (Toplis, 2004).

In 2002, the administrators introduced a number of fundamental changes to the Awards. In the context of this discussion, a core question on ecological sustainability was introduced for all award categories and the ambiguous Environmental Tourism Award category was changed to accurately reflect its traditional nature-based focus. It is now referred to as the Ecotourism Award category and its criteria are consistent with the Nature and Ecotourism Accreditation Program (now known as the EcoCertification Program).

Conclusion

In conclusion, it has been demonstrated in this chapter that there are a number of awards for excellence targeted at the tourism industry, with the two key forms being quality and environmental awards for excellence. While the awards are promoted as the highest accolade in their respective areas of influence and share a number of similarities, they also share a common lack of critique, evaluation and academic attention.

Awards for excellence have the potential to become an important catalyst for transforming the Australian and world tourism industry, enabling it to meet the challenges of the new millennium. The awards not only codify the traditional principles of quality improvements but also have the ability to provide tourism businesses with a comprehensive framework for assessing their progress towards the new paradigm of quality, which includes environmental considerations. However, there is a danger that winning an award can become the goal rather than being the consequence of an organization's quality improvement process. The underlying value of awards lies in the discipline they inspire and not the award itself, a concept that is yet to be understood by many in the tourism industry. Their strength lies in their high profile, their weakness lies in their misunderstanding and narrow interpretation of quality.

References

Australian Quality Council (AQC) (1997) *Australian Quality Awards 1997 Fact Sheet.* Available at: http://www.ozemail.com.au/~bhead/aqafact.htm (5 July 1997).

Australian Quality Council (AQC) (1998) *Australian Quality Awards for Business Framework: A Framework for Business Improvement and Long Term Success.* AQC, St Leonards.

Beilharz, G.R. (1994) *Quality Management in Service Organizations.* Longman, Melbourne.

Berry, L.L. and Parasuraman, A. (1991) *Marketing Services: Competing through Time.* The Free Press, Don Mills.

Bohoris, G.A. (1995) A comparative assessment of some major quality awards. *International Journal of Quality and Reliability Management* 12(9), 30–43.

British Airways (1996) *Tourism for Tomorrow Awards Nomination Form.* British Airways, Harmondsworth, UK.

Brown, J. (1985) Say G'day and back one of our most vital products. *The Australian*, 20 November, 24.

Camp, R.C. (1995) *Business Process Benchmarking: Finding and Implementing Best Practice.* ASQC Quality Press, Milwaukee.

Codling, S. (1994) Benchmarking. In: Lock, D. (ed.) *Gower Handbook of Quality Management*, 2nd edn. Gower Publishing, Aldershot, UK, pp. 36–51.

Collier, D.A. (1990) The customer service and quality challenge. In: Clark, G. (ed.) *Managing Service Quality.* IFS, Kempston, pp. 53–60.

Commonwealth Department of Industry, Tourism and Resources (1998) *Annual Report 1997–98.* Commonwealth of Australia, Canberra.

Commonwealth Department of Industry, Tourism and Resources (2002) *The 10 Year Plan for Tourism: A Discussion Paper.* Commonwealth of Australia, Canberra.

Commonwealth Department of Industry, Tourism and Resources (2003a) *Corporate Plan 2003–2004.* Commonwealth of Australia, Canberra.

Commonwealth Department of Industry, Tourism and Resources (2003b) *A Medium to Long Term Strategy for Tourism: Green Paper.* Commonwealth of Australia, Canberra.

Commonwealth Department of Industry, Tourism and Resources (1992) *Tourism, Australia's Passport to Growth: A National Tourism Strategy.* Commonwealth of Australia, Canberra.

Edge, J. (1994) Quality improvement: lessons for management. In: Lock, D. (ed.) *Gower Handbook of Quality Management*, 2nd edn. Gower Publishing, Aldershot, UK, pp. 662–685.

English Tourist Board (1992) *The Green Light: A Guide to Sustainable Tourism.* ETB, London.

English Tourist Board (1995a) *Annual Report 1995.* English Tourist Board, London.

English Tourist Board (1995b) *The England for Excellence Awards 1995 Call for Entries.* English Tourist Board, London.

English Tourist Board (1999) *The 1998 England for Excellence Awards.* Available at: http://www.visitbritain.com.news/awards/eintro.htm 1 page (4 June 1999).

Ernst and Young (2001) *Review of the Australian Tourism Awards.* Ernst and Young, Sydney.

European Commission (2003) *Basic Orientations for Sustainability of European Tourism: Consultation Document.* EC Enterprise Directorate-General, Luxembourg.

Forell, C. (1992) Tourism awards 'need rethink'. *The Age*, 21 July, 23.

Garvin, D.A. (1991) How the Baldridge Award really works. *Harvard Business Review*, November–December, 80–93.

Ghobadian, A. and Woo, H.S. (1996) Characteristics, benefits and shortcomings of four quality awards. *International Journal of Quality and Reliability Management* 13(2), 10–44.

Gilmour, P. and Driva, H. (1994) The impact of winning the Australian Quality Award. *The Quality Magazine*, December, 18–19.

Go, F.M. and Govers, R. (2000) Integrated quality management for tourist destinations: a European perspective on achieving competitiveness. *Tourism Management* 21, 79–88.

Gummesson, E. (1993) *Quality Management in Service Organizations: An Interpretation of the Service Quality Phenomenon and a Synthesis of International Research.* ISQA, Stockholm.

Hamele, H. (1994) *The Book of Environmental Seals and Ecolabels: Environmental Awards in Tourism.* ECOTRANS, Saarbrucken.

Hunt, V.D. (1993) *Managing for Quality: Integrating Quality and Business Strategy*. Business One Irwin, Homewood.

Kristensen, K. and Juhl, H.J. (1999) Five years of quality awards in Denmark. *The TQM Magazine* 11(2), 1–4.

Kurosawa, S. (1992) A salute to excellence. *The Australian Magazine*, 17–18 October, 22.

Laszlo, G.P. (1996) Quality awards – recognition or model? *The TQM Magazine* 8(5), 14–18.

Laszlo, G.P. (1997) US and Canadian national quality awards: increased emphasis on business results. *The TQM Magazine* 9(5), 381–383.

Leiper, N. (1995) *Tourism Management*. TAFE Publications, Collingwood.

Leisure Opportunities (1995) Sustainable Tourism Competition. *Leisure Opportunities*, March, 2.

Main, J. (1991) Is the Baldrige overblown? *Fortune*, 1 July, 42–45.

Munro-Faure, L. and Munro-Faure, M. (1994) *TQM: A Primer for Implementation*. Pitman Publishing, London.

Neale, G. (1998) *The Green Travel Guide*. Earthscan, London.

New Zealand Tourism Board (1998) NZTB Strategy. Available at: http://www.nztb.govt.nz/nztb/strategy.html (16 August 1998).

New Zealand Tourism Board (1999) New Zealand Tourism Awards recognising excellence. Media Release July 1999. Available at: http://www.tourisminfo.govt.nz/documents/Media/Press/AwardsProfile.htm (21 September 1999).

Office of National Tourism (1997) *Today's Consumer, Tomorrow's Visitor: Keeping Pace with Tourism Trends*. DIST, Canberra.

Office of National Tourism (1998) *A Ticket to the 21st Century: National Action Plan*. DIST, Canberra.

Øvretveit, J.A. (1993) Auditing and awards for service quality. *International Journal of Service Industry Management* 4(2), 74–84.

Pacific Asia Travel Association (PATA) (1992) *PATA Code for Environmentally Responsible Tourism*. PATA, San Francisco, California.

Pembroke, K. (1996) The sustainable tourist: a benchmark survey of environmental priorities, awareness, attitudes and opinions, interest and preferences and behaviour of British Airways leisure customers. Summary report prepared for British Airways Environment Branch, unpublished.

Ross, J.E. and Omachonu, V.K. (1994) *Principles of Total Quality*. St Lucie Press, Delray Beach.

South Australian Tourism Commission (2002) *Corporate Plan 2002–2004*. SATC, Adelaide.

Sprouster, J. (1994) The national value of the Australian Quality Awards. *The Quality Magazine*, December, 2.

Sterett, W.K. and Durkee, D.C. (1993) The impact of the Baldridge Award. In: Sheuing, E.E. and Christopher, W.F. (eds) *Service Quality Handbook*. AMACOM, New York.

Steventon, D. (1994) Quality Awards – a means to end or an end in themselves? *The TQM Magazine* 6(5), 7–8.

Tan, K.C. (2002) A comparative study of 16 national quality awards. *The TQM Magazine* 14(3), 165–171.

Tolhurst, C. (1993) Tourist industry finds need to develop its own programs. *Australian Financial Review*, 23 November, 47.

Toplis, S.C. (2004) The perceived effectiveness of the Australian Tourism Awards in promoting improvements in quality and ecological sustainability to the Australian tourism industry: a Victorian perspective. Unpublished PhD thesis, RMIT University.

Tourism Council Australia (TCA) (1998) *Code of Sustainable Practice*. TCA, Sydney.

Tourism Industry Association of New Zealand (2000) *Tourism 2010: A Strategy for New Zealand Tourism.* TIA, Wellington.

Tourism Victoria (1998a) *Victorian Tourism Awards Call for Entries 1998.* Tourism Victoria, Melbourne.

Tourism Victoria (1998b) *1998 Ansett Australia Victorian Tourism Awards Programme.* Tourism Victoria, Melbourne.

Tourism Victoria (1998c) *1998 Ansett Australian Victorian Tourism Awards Judges Manual.* Tourism Victoria, Melbourne.

Tourism Victoria (2002) *Victoria's Tourism Industry Strategic Plan 2002–2006.* Tourism Victoria, Melbourne.

Travelweek (1999) Couran's Banksia award backs NTIA creditability. *Travelweek*, 23 June, 8.

Tummala, V.M.R. and Tang, C.L. (1996) Strategic quality management, Malcolm Baldrige and European quality awards and ISO 9000 certification. *International Journal of Quality and Reliability Management* 13(4), 8–38.

United Kingdom (UK) Department of Culture, Media and Sport (1999) *Tomorrow's Tourism: A Growth Industry for the New Millennium.* DCMS, London.

United Nations Environment Programme Industry and Environment (UNEP IE) (1995a) *Environmental Codes of Conduct for Tourism.* Technical report no. 29, UNEP IE, Paris.

United Nations Environment Programme Industry and Environment (UNEP IE) (1995b) Environmental management tools: facts and figures. *Industry and Environment* 18(2–3), April–September, 4–10.

United Nations Environment Programme Industry and Environment (UNEP IE) (1999) The UNEP Tour Operator Initiative on Sustainable Tourism Development. Available at: http://www.unepie.org/tourism/progress.html (18 August 1999).

United States of America (USA) National Institute of Standards and Technology (NIST) (1996) Malcolm Baldridge National Quality Award 1996 Fact Sheet. Available at: http://www.quality.nist.gov/qualfact.htm (2 January 1997).

Valles, D.M. (2001) *Final Report of Working Group C: Improving the Quality of Tourist Products.* European Commission, Brussels.

Wales Tourist Board (1995a) *Wales Tourism Awards 1995: Call for Entries.* WTB, Cardiff.

Wales Tourist Board (1995b) *Quest for Quality: The Wales Tourist Board's Quality Assurance Schemes for Accommodation.* WTB, Cardiff.

Wisner, J.D. and Eakins, S.G. (1994) A performance assessment of the US Baldrige Quality Award winners. *International Journal of Quality and Reliability Management* 11(2), 8–25.

World Tourism Organization (WTO) (2002) *Voluntary Initiatives for Sustainable Tourism: Worldwide Inventory and Comparative Analysis of 104 Eco-labels, Awards and Self-commitments.* WTO, Madrid.

World Tourism Organization (WTO) (2003) Tourism Market Trends 2000. Available at: http://www.world-tourism.org/market_research/facts&figures/market_trends/ita.htm (14 April 2003).

World Travel and Tourism Council and International Hotel and Restaurant Association (1999) Tourism and sustainable development: the global importance of tourism. Background paper prepared for the United Nations Department of Economic and Social Affairs, Commission on Sustainable Development, Seventh Session, 19–30 April 1999, New York.

Zink, K.J., Schmidt, A. and Voss, W. (1997) Total Quality 'down under': the Australian Quality Award – an innovative model for business excellence. *The TQM Magazine* 9(3), 54–66.

4 'No Better than a Band-Aid for a Bullet Wound!': the Effectiveness of Tourism Codes of Conduct

Peter Mason

University of Bedfordshire, Luton, UK

Chapter Profile

The chapter title is paraphrased from a review of an article on tourism codes of conduct that this author submitted to a journal in the early 1990s.[1] This comment and others from this not entirely constructive review are revealing in a number of ways. The review suggested that tourism codes are of little use and argued that codes are about cure; yet this chapter will argue that they are intended to be about prevention. Other comments in the review revealed the belief that codes are largely concerned with regulation, while this chapter argues that codes should be used as part of an education process. The chapter begins by attempting to define tourism codes and links them to tourism guidelines. This is followed by setting codes of conduct in a wider framework of ethics and morals. The main part of the chapter provides a summary of the aims of and rationale for tourism codes and presents examples of visitor, host and industry codes. The penultimate section raises several issues about codes of conduct and it is here that there is further discussion about their effectiveness. This is followed by a final section containing concluding remarks.

Introduction

Tourism codes of conduct have been used for a number of years as part of attempts to manage tourism. Tourism regulations, self-regulation, guidelines and codes of conduct are often linked in discussions about the impacts of tourism and its management, but there are important differences between these terms. A major difference is that, although each is concerned with regulating tourism, it is only actual regulations that are likely to have some form of legal status, while codes of conduct, codes of practice and guidelines tend to lack this status and are usually a form of voluntary self-regulation (Stonehouse, 1990).

There are very few legally backed regulations pertaining specifically to tourism (Mason, 2003) except those concerned largely with specific activities or sectors, such as the hospitality industry. Such regulations include laws on food hygiene and others with a specific sector focus, such as adventure tourism, on safety issues. Laws relating to exploitation of the environment and the need for conservation exist in many countries, but tend not to refer specifically to the effects of tourism and are generally targeted at locals rather than tourists. Therefore, there are virtually no laws concerned specifically with the impacts of tourism (Swarbrooke, 1999), and yet the detrimental consequences of tourism for the environment are a major reason for the emergence of ecotourism.

Hence, most attempts to regulate tourism impacts have been in the form of tourism codes of conduct and guidelines, and a variety of codes have been in existence since at least the early 1980s (Mason, 1997). Tourism codes and guidelines are frequently combined together but are not identical (Mason, 2003). Guidelines are usually based on well-considered precepts, indicating a course of action to be followed with the reasoning behind it, while codes of conduct provide sets of rules for behaving in certain circumstances (Stonehouse, 1990). Tourism codes are a form of voluntary self-regulation and ecotourism management frequently involves a number of voluntary strategies, including certification and models of best practice, as well as the use of codes of conduct (Dowling and Fennell, 2003). Codes usually indicate forms of appropriate (or indeed inappropriate) conduct and hence they can be set within the context of ethics.

Codes, Ethics and Morals

Tourism codes do not just involve the provision of information, but are concerned with the behaviour of tourists. As they frequently advocate desired behaviour and/or advise against undesirable conduct, they have an ethical dimension (Malloy and Fennell, 1998). Ethics is concerned with people making choices and acting in a reasonable manner (Fennell and Przeclawski, 2003) and is closely linked to morality where 'morality is taken to mean moral judgements, standards and rules of conduct' (Taylor, 1975). As Wilson (1990: 82) states, the major use of the term moral 'refers to a certain set of underlying predispositions, to the basic ecology as we may here briefly . . . put it, of human desires, emotions and deeds'.

Ethics has a long pedigree as a key element in major philosophies and, although there is insufficient space in this chapter to discuss details, many well-known philosophers and philosophies have made important contributions on ethics. In the classical era, for example, Socrates argued that 'virtue is knowledge' and Plato discussed the 'idea of the right'. Modern Western philosophy includes significant ideas on ethics, including the arguments of Kant, who referred to 'moral duty', meaning that the knowledge of one's duty is a major motivational factor in behaviour (Fennell and Przeclawski, 2003), and Nietzsche, who attempted to deconstruct ethics and morals by suggesting that there was no such thing as 'moral facts' but only 'moral interpretations' (Benn, 1998). The 20th-century philosophy of existentialism was very much concerned with the actions of individuals and placed ethics at the centre when suggesting that any human act is 'right or wrong' depending on the actor's free will and responsibility (Guignon, 1986).

Ethics has a number of key applications in the modern world. One of these relates to the behaviour of companies and commercial organizations. Much of this concern with 'corporate' ethical values and behaviour is directed at marketing (Fennell and Przeclawski, 2003). Underlying these corporate values are corporate ethical values (Hunt *et al.*, 1989), which help establish and maintain standards and influence courses of action. Hence, there is a close link between values, ethics and the moral judgements that people make.

Historically, tourism and ethics have not been closely linked. However, tourism appears to be a very appropriate candidate for ethical scrutiny (Fennell and Przeclawski, 2003). Tourism involves many different players representing different viewpoints; it has social, economic, political and environmental dimensions and has been noted for its ability to create a range of important impacts (Fennell and Przeclawski, 2003). As the major players in tourism have different value positions, there is the likelihood of conflict and the interaction between the players is likely to create a number of ethical dilemmas (Fennell, 2000). For example, inappropriate behaviour from one set of players not only may lead to impacts, but can influence the views and beliefs of other players about this first set of players.

These ethical dilemmas and conflicts are generally the result of the interaction of the main players in tourism, that is, the tourists themselves, inhabitants of visited local areas and what Fennell and Przeclawski (2003) refer to as the 'tourism brokers' and by this they mean, for example, members of the tourism industry such as tour guides, tour operators and hotel staff. Tourism codes of conduct have been created, largely, as a response to these ethical dilemmas and the perceived negative consequences of tourism and have usually been an attempt to generate more desirable and beneficial behaviour amongst the key players that minimizes conflict and helps reduce negative effects of tourism.

Aims, Objectives and the Nature of Tourism Codes

Aims, audience and authorship of codes

The use of tourism codes of conduct is a relatively recent phenomenon, although there are examples, such as the English Countryside Commission's Country Code, that date back to the 1960s (Mason and Mowforth, 1995). It is perhaps not surprising that tourism codes first began to emerge at a time, in the late 1960s and early 1970s, when mass tourism was growing, the supposed benefits of tourism were being questioned and a more critical perspective on its impacts was being adopted (see Jafari, 1981; Fennell, 1999).

From the late 1980s, codes were developed by governments, the private sector and concerned individuals, as well as by non-governmental organizations (NGOs). The main aim of these codes has been to influence attitudes and modify behaviour (Mason and Mowforth, 1996). They are usually part of a wider process involving attempts to regulate tourism and are often used in conjunction with guidelines.

A number of discrete target groups for tourism codes of conduct have been identified. These groups are as follows: visitors, the tourism industry and members of host communities (UNEP, 1995; Mason and Mowforth, 1996). The most significant target audience in terms of sheer number of codes is the visitor. The WTTRC (1995), for example, listed almost 80 visitor codes in use around the world in 1994 and it seems very likely that by 2007 this will have risen to several hundred. A number of codes have also been prepared for use by those directly involved in the tourist industry and there are also codes prepared for the use of host populations.

In addition to a variety of target audiences for codes of conduct there are a range of different authors. A significant number of codes have been written by concerned individuals and NGOs, while government bodies and the tourism industry itself have not been, until recently, very active in producing codes (Mason and Mowforth, 1996).

Perhaps strangely, given their apparent intention, codes frequently fail to specify either their broad aims or more specific objectives (Mason, 1994). Nevertheless UNEP, having conducted a survey of voluntary environmental tourism codes in the mid-1990s and received information on 30 codes used by countries and international associations, was able to deduce a number of specific objectives (UNEP, 1995). UNEP (1995: 8) produced, in summary form, five objectives of such codes, which are as follows:

- To serve as a catalyst for dialogue between government and other bodies involved in tourism.
- To create an awareness in government and industry of the need for sound environmental management.
- To heighten awareness amongst tourists of the need for appropriate behaviour.
- To make host populations aware of the need for environmental protection.
- To encourage cooperation between government agencies, host communities, industry and NGOs.

Codes attempt to regulate but also aim to educate their respective audience by providing information, advice and frequently instructions.

The message of tourism codes

It would appear from the UNEP summary of the aims of tourism codes that they are primarily concerned with environmental impacts and improving environmental management; however, the message of tourism codes is not just confined to environmental issues. A number of visitor codes, for example, make reference to sociocultural matters, such as respect for local religious beliefs, and the inclusion of sociocultural aspects had become the norm by the late 1990s (Mason *et al.*, 2000). Codes with industry as the audience frequently refer to the need for appropriate training and honest marketing of tourism products (Mason and Mowforth, 1996).

It is possible to categorize and group codes not just according to their message and audience, but also by whether they are deontological or teleological (Malloy and Fennell, 1998; Garrod and Fenell, 2004a). As Garrod and Fennell (2004a) indicated, deontological codes include ethical perspectives that are rules-based and assess 'rightness' and 'wrongness' on the basis of actions and duties. Teleological codes, in contrast, are those that advocate the type of good behaviour 'which produces the best consequences for the greatest number of people' (Garrod and Fennell, 2004a: 342). It is possible to illustrate the differences between deontological and teleological codes through the use of an example. A deontological code might contain an instructions such as 'Please do not feed the wildlife,' while a teleological code would contain the statement 'Please do not feed the wildlife, as this may lead to behavioural changes and growing dependency on humans as food providers.' In simple terms, unlike deontological codes, teleological codes provide an explanatory guideline to support the instruction in the code.

Visitor Codes

Until recently the great majority of codes were aimed specifically at the visitor. Such codes are usually location-specific. A good example concerned with a major region where ecotourism has become significant is the Himalayan Code. This code was devised, after consultation with indigenous groups, government representatives and external experts, by the UK NGO Tourism Concern (Mason and Mowforth, 1995). This code focuses on a number of environmental and cultural issues. As well as a set of instructions, the code also includes guidelines that support the instructions or advice on behaviour. For example, one of the five major environmental instructions stated: '*Limit deforestation* – make no open fires and discourage others from doing so on your behalf. When water is heated by scarce fire wood, use as little as possible. When possible choose accommodation that uses kerosene or fuel-efficient wood stoves' (Mason and Mowforth, 1995: 13). As all the instructions in the code, whether environmental or sociocultural in focus, are supported by a rationale, the Himalayan Code is a good example of a teleological code. However, frequently visitor codes are not accompanied by guidelines and therefore many, particularly early codes produced in the period up until the early 1990s, are deontological.

A large number of visitor codes are more locally oriented than the Himalayan Code and may contain a mixture of environmental and sociocultural messages. However, such codes may still be attempting to reach a wide range of visitors. The Ceredigan Marine Heritage Coast code (Wight, 2004) is one example. It is designed for the marine environment of the coast of Wales. Unusually, it covers not just land but extends into the sea. The code is shown in Box 4.1. The Ceredigan Marine Heritage Coast Code of Conduct clearly

Box 4.1. Ceredigan Marine Heritage Coast Code of Conduct (from Wight, 2004).

Boats
- Operate with care and attention to safety of occupants and other sea users

Dolphins
- Maintain a steady speed and course or slow down gradually
- Don't chase, manoeuvre erratically, turn towards or attempt to touch or feed

Seals
- Don't interfere with seals or pups on beach
- Control dogs and keep away from seals

Birds
- When sailing, keep 100 m out from cliffs in the breeding season
- Don't sail directly towards rafts of birds resting or feeding on the sea
- Avoid unnecessary noise close to cliffs

Fishing
- Don't discard tackle, take home for proper disposal

Jet skis
- Don't launch or operate in the area (Heritage Coast)

Divers
- Observe BSAC Code of Conduct

Beaches
- Take home all your litter
- Keep to by-laws
- Replace shore rocks you move to keep alive the animals that live underneath

focuses on a number of environmental issues and several different user groups including those on land and at sea. This code is very direct and except for the last statement lacks supporting guidelines. Hence, it can be viewed as largely deontological, rather than teleological.

In many parts of the world, particularly the USA and Canada, visitor codes tend to be tourism sector-specific and/or 'single focus' (Wight, 2004). One particular focus, which has become an important element of ecotourism experiences on several continents and has led to a proliferation of visitor codes, is whale watching (Garrod and Fennell, 2004b). By early 2000, there were many whale watching codes in existence and these were aimed at visitors at specific locations in Europe, North America, South America and the Pacific Rim. As Garrod and Fennell (2004a) reported, one of the major aspects of this proliferation of codes is the high degree of variability between codes in terms of message and approach, which may limit their effectiveness. This issue is discussed in more detail later in the chapter.

Combining codes to be more effective: experiences in Antarctica

It has been suggested that to be effective codes should be targeted at different user groups in the same location and should be used together (Valentine, 1992;

Mason and Mowforth, 1996). Antarctica has been described as the ultimate ecotourism destination (Bauer, 2001) and it provides a good example of how codes targeted at different audiences can be used together in an attempt to manage visitors. Here, it is codes for both visitors and operators that have been used at the same time. It is the unusual political and economic circumstances on the continent that enable a much clearer picture of the use and effectiveness of tourism codes than in most other parts of the world. Hence, experience derived from managing ecotourism in Antarctica has been used with its management in other important ecotourism locations (Mason and Legg, 1999).

Antarctica is unique in that it is not owned by any one country, is the continent dedicated to science, is managed through the Antarctic Treaty System and is almost in its entirety designated as a protected area. It is also the one part of the earth where tourism is a major economic activity, as almost all other forms of commercial activity are prohibited and it has almost no permanent resident population. Antarctica is also the only continent where it is possible to argue that currently all tourism can be classified as ecotourism (Bauer, 2001). Until the late 1990s tourism operations were managed almost entirely through self-regulation. This was largely possible because of the relatively small number of tourists – with approximately 10,000 per annum throughout the 1990s (Bauer, 2001) – and the arrangements between the tour operators who manage the vast majority of visits to the continent as almost all visiting tourists until the late 1990s reached Antarctica by cruise ship.

Tourists first came to Antarctica in significant numbers in the 1960s (Hall, 1992). One of the first operators to bring tourists was Lars-Eric Lindblad (Mason and Legg, 1999). Lindblad instilled a strong environmental ethic in visitors (Stonehouse and Crosbie, 1995) and this contributed to the practices adopted by the cruise ship staff who subsequently led visits to Antarctica. In 1991, the cruise ship operators joined together to form the International Association of Antarctic Tour Operators (IAATO). IAATO created an operator code of conduct for their own members and also devised visitor guidelines and visitor codes of conduct. The Lindblad approach, on which IAATO based its various guidelines, involves preparatory lectures aboard ship prior to arrival, by those with extensive experience of Antarctica (Mason and Legg, 1999). At these initial sessions, passengers receive copies of the guidelines and codes of conduct as well as Antarctica Treaty recommendations on tourism on the continent. The visitor code of conduct makes reference to potential and actual impacts on the environment, as well as plant and animal species, cultural heritage sites (primarily the huts of Antarctica explorers) and tourist safety. The guidelines accompanying the code provide the rationale for the specific instructions in the code.

As part of the Lindblad approach, cruise ship tourists are taken ashore by inflatable boat, in groups of ten to 15, and accompanied by a guide. Although free to wander, partly for safety reasons tourists are required to stay close to the landing point. Any transgression of codes of conduct/guidelines is met with an on-the-spot admonishment by the guide, and tourists can be sent back to the cruise ship. Debriefing sessions are held back on-board ship, as well as discussions concerning any issues and problems, and these usually involve attempts to reinforce the environmental ethic.

The use of codes of conduct appears to have been a successful way of managing tourists to the Antarctic for at least 25 years (Stonehouse and Crosbie, 1995). However, this may be due to the relatively small number of visitors and the fact that the great majority arrive under supervision from IAATO cruise ship staff. It also seems likely that many Antarctic tourists are very well informed prior to arrival, are aware of the likely consequences of their behaviour for the continent and in fact leave Antarctica as 'ambassadors' for the unique environment (Mason and Legg, 1999). In this way, they not only would appear to develop a conservation ethic that they subsequently apply to other protected areas, but also inspire responsible behaviour in future Antarctic tourists, although it may be difficult to assess this. Whether this form of self-regulation can continue to be successful, in the face of an overall growth of tourist numbers to Antarctica, increasing ship size and increasing diversity of language groups from the late 1990s onwards, remains to be seen.

Antarctic experiences applied to Arctic ecotourism

The experience gained from managing tourism in Antarctica has been used in the creation of the World Wide Fund for Nature (WWF) (Arctic) Arctic Tourism Project (Mason *et al.*, 2000). The Arctic and subarctic region shares many of the environmental features of the Antarctic and attracts similar types of ecotourists, although it is made up of sovereign space owned by several countries and, significantly, has many indigenous as well as transplanted communities. The WWF Arctic Tourism Project was established in February 1995 and aims to link tourism and conservation. This is an aim that is common, although not always stated overtly, in ecotourism projects. Over a period of 3 years, several Project meetings took place, involving ecotour operators, national and local government officials, local community representatives, NGO staff, Arctic scientists and Arctic tourism experts. These meetings have involved drafting of guidelines and codes of conduct. The final version of these documents appeared in 1997. They were published in a document by WWF Arctic that contained ten principles for Arctic tourism. These are as follows (WWF Arctic, 1997):

- Make tourism and conservation compatible.
- Support the preservation of wilderness and biodiversity.
- Use natural resources in a sustainable way.
- Minimize consumption, waste and pollution.
- Respect local cultures.
- Respect historic and scientific sites.
- Communities should benefit from tourism.
- Trained staff are the way to responsible tourism.
- Tourism should be educational.
- Follow safety rules.

The principles for Arctic tourism were accompanied by detailed guidelines. The document in which the principles appeared also contained a code of conduct for Arctic tourists and a separate code for Arctic tour operators (WWF Arctic, 1997). However, each of these codes was linked very closely to the ten principles. The document containing the principles and Arctic tourism codes was subsequently distributed to more than 5000 user groups, government bodies, NGOs and local communities in the Arctic (Mason *et al.*, 2000). Between 2000 and 2003 a number of pilot projects were established in a variety of Arctic locations, including Arctic Canada, Alaska, Northern Finland and on Svalbard, to trial the tourism codes. Not only was this an attempt to investigate how they might function in a real context, but also to monitor how various indigenous groups reacted to such codes. At the time of writing these pilot projects had just ended, and results had not yet been published.

Codes for Host Populations

There are several examples, particularly in developed countries and increasingly in the developing world, where local residents in a destination are now actively involved in the provision for tourism and also its planning and management. This followed a groundswell of opinion in the early 1990s in favour of such participation (Middleton and Hawkins, 1998).

One of the earliest communities to become actively involved in the planning for nature-based tourism in their area was Erschmatt in the Valais region of Switzerland (Mason and Mowforth, 1995). In the early 1980s, the community created the Pro Erschmatt Society, which developed guidelines and a code of conduct to provide information on the perceived local needs for tourism and to indicate to potential tourism developers their views. The code covered a number of economic and environmental as well as sociocultural aspects of tourism and was designed to manage tourism so that it brought maximum benefit to the local community (Krippendorf, 1987). The Pro Erschmatt Society code is particularly significant, as, being one of the first, it has influenced the development of several subsequent host codes (Mason and Mowforth, 1996). This code is shown in Box 4.2. The Pro Erschmatt Society code makes a number of strong statements and is clearly an aspirational list, but could be criticized for being unrealistic in its aims and this point is taken up late in the discussion of issues regarding the use of codes. Nevertheless, it does reveal a community concerned for the nature of tourism in its local area.

Codes for the Tourism Industry

There are far fewer codes aimed at the tourism industry than at other target groups, particularly in comparison with visitor codes. However, a number are in existence. The German organization Tourismus mit Einsicht (Tourism

Box 4.2. The Pro Erschmatt Society Code of Conduct (from Mason and Mowforth, 1996).

The Pro Erschmatt Society supports a healthy tourism adapted to local needs that meet the following criteria:

- It must benefit the population as a whole and not individual speculators
- It must not abuse the environment through speculation and thereby rob it of its recreational quality, but respect both the landscape and local architecture
- It must take into account future generations and be based on medium- and long-term solutions, rather than short-term ones
- It should allow the community to develop and should not impose a prohibitive infrastructural burden on it
- It should not involve speculation leading to rocketing land prices, which makes property too expensive for the local population
- It should not lead to a sell-out of our country
- It must not generate dead holiday villages, inhabited for only a few weeks in the year
- It must be based on autonomous local decision making
- It must create attractive jobs, take into account the local businesses and not waste land

with Insight) produced one of the first codes aimed at the tourism industry. This is shown in Box 4.3. As with the Pro Erschmatt code, the Tourismus mit Einsicht code can be seen as somewhat aspirational. However, it is clearly a teleological code that provides a set of statements supported by a brief rationale and is attempting to create a more honest, more responsible and hopefully more sustainable form of tourism (Mason and Mowforth, 1995).

The US-based International Ecotourism Society (TIES) has for a number of years produced codes of conduct for tour operators and other sectors of the tourism industry. In 1993, for the first time, the organization produced codes that targeted specific groups and individuals involved in tourism, as well as preparing codes to be used at different stages of tourism activity. These guidelines appeared in the document *The Ecotourism Guidelines for Nature Tour Operators*, which was distributed to various sectors of the US tourism industry. According to TIES, this publication not only provided the most comprehensive statement on what guidelines should be observed but how services should be delivered, the precise objectives and who should benefit from them (Epler Wood, 1993). Hence, for example, the Society has produced guidelines for operators for the pre-departure programme and principles for guiding tours, as well as guidelines for monitoring the effects of tourism (Ecotourism Society, 1993). The Ecotourism Society provided information and advice under several distinct headings in their guidelines, and these headings – 'guideline', 'objectives', 'techniques' and 'visitor benefits' – are used throughout all types of operator guidelines it has produced. An example to illustrate how these various headings are employed is shown in Box 4.4. The

Box 4.3. Tourismus mit Einsicht code for the travel business.

We, the travel business

1. We act as a business organized on commercial principles which tries to meet the travel needs of its clients while achieving reasonable economic results. We can reach this goal in the long run only if we succeed in making better use of the opportunities of travel and simultaneously reducing its dangers. We shall therefore promote forms of tourism that are economically productive, socially responsible and environment-friendly.

2. We see our clients as people who enjoy life and who want their holidays to be the 'most pleasurable weeks of the year'. We also know that there is an increasing number of interested, considerate and environment-conscious tourists. We shall try to respond to and encourage this trend without preaching to our guests.

3. We shall bear in mind the interests, independence and rights of the local population. We shall respect local laws, customs, traditions and cultural characteristics. We shall always remember that we as travel agents, and as tourists, are guests of the local population.

4. We want to collaborate as partners with the service industry and the host population in the tourist areas. We advocate fair business conditions that will bring the greatest possible benefit to all partners. We shall encourage active participation of the host population wherever possible.

5. Our efforts to improve travel should include a careful selection and continuous training of our staff at all levels as well as development and supervision of our services.

6. We want to provide our clients with expert and comprehensive information about all aspects of the country they want to visit through catalogues, travel information and guides. Our advertising must be not only attractive but honest and responsible. We shall try to avoid the usual superlatives and clichéd texts and pictures. Special emphasis will be placed on a respectful description of the population in the host areas. We shall desist from any advertising with erotic enticements.

7. Our guides and social directors will have a particular responsibility in promoting tourism with insight and understanding. We shall provide special, and continuous, training for personnel working in these areas.

8. We shall not organize travel trips or expeditions to ethnic groups who live apart from our Western civilization. We shall not promise our clients 'contact with untouched peoples' because we know that they are vulnerable and must be protected.

9. All our activities and those of our business partners will have to meet the same strict quality standard. We want to make our business partners aware of the fact that they too should contribute to an environment-conscious and socially responsible tourism.

10. We are prepared to formulate within our professional associations a set of principles encompassing the ethics of the tourist trade, which shall be binding for all members.

Box 4.4. The Ecotourism Society general principles for guiding tours (from Ecotourism Society, 1993).

Guideline
Prepare travellers for each encounter with local cultures and with native animals and plants.

Objectives
Pave the way for reciprocal sensitivity between cultures by teaching tourists to be unobtrusive while they are encountering environments and cultures.
Provide visitors with the opportunity to learn more about the social and political circumstances of the region being visited.
Provide visitors with the opportunity to learn more about local environmental problems and conservation efforts.

Techniques
Provide quality orientation and enough leaders to manage the group according to the sensitivity of the environment visited.
Give quality interpretation at all times; explain local cultures and describe natural history. Encourage interpretation with local people while overseeing contact to avoid cultural errors.
Conduct briefings before each stop, including behaviours to avoid, restricted practices and zones, special alerts for fragile and endangered species, specific distances to maintain with local wildlife and local regulations.
Use time on the road and in cities for educational discussions of all kinds including balanced discussions of local issues.

Visitor Benefits
Awareness of how to encounter cultures and environments with minimum negative impact.
Insight into natural history and the cultures and environments of the region, local values and concerns, and the need for conservation.
Insight into the visitor's own role and potential contribution to local conservation and sustainable economic development efforts.

International Ecotourism Society indicates that the guidelines they have produced are not meant to be threatening to the tourism industry, but should be viewed as a form of 'heavily researched road map that provides nature tour operators and lodges with the information they need to begin pursuing the full agenda of objectives' (listed in the publication) (Epler Wood, 1993: ii). In fact, these guidelines, which are teleological in that they provide a rationale for each of the statements/advisory comments, provide a message for tour operators on how their customers, the tourists, should benefit if the guidelines are observed by the industry.

Concluding this section of the chapter is a table that provides a summary of the main types of tourism codes, indicating the authorship, target audiences and major messages contained within the code content (see Table 4.1).

Table 4.1. Key elements of tourism codes of conduct (from Mason and Mowforth, 1996).

Types of codes	Authorship	Audience	Message
Visitor codes	Predominantly NGOs and concerned individuals, but also some government bodies such as Ministries of the Environment	Domestic visitors and international visitors, especially overseas visitors to developing countries	Minimize environmental and sociocultural damage to areas visited. Maximize economic benefits to host community. Encourage more equality in relationship between visitors and hosts. Promote more responsible and sustainable forms of tourism
Industry codes	Predominantly coordinating bodies such as NTOs and IATA, also government and to a lesser extent NGOs and concerned individuals and exceptionally tourism companies, e.g. Chateau Whistler Hotel Group	Tourism industry in general and some codes for specific sectors, such as the hotel industry	Appropriate training/ education for staff. Honest marketing of products. Develop awareness of environmental and sociocultural impacts of tourism. Promote more responsible and sustainable forms of tourism. Promote recycling
Host codes	Predominantly NGOs and concerned individuals, some host communities in both developed and developing countries, and a small number of host governments	Mainly host communities, especially in developing countries	Information and advice about visitors. Minimize environmental and sociocultural damage. Maximize economic benefits to host community. Encourage more equality in relationship between host and visitors. Advocate more democratic and participatory forms of tourism

Issues with the Use and Effectiveness of Tourism Codes

Although many tourism codes are impressive in terms of the range of issues they cover and in their depth of discussion and information, there are a number of significant problems with them. The following section attempts to address the claim made in the title that codes are 'no better than a Band-Aid for a bullet wound'.

Mason and Mowforth (1996) suggested four major problem areas with tourism codes. First, codes must be practised as intended, but, as UNEP (1995) indicated, most codes tend to be poorly implemented. An indication of whether codes are well implemented can be derived from monitoring. However, until very recently, the great majority of codes were not monitored, so it is very difficult to evaluate their effects (UNEP, 1995) and hence effectiveness. This is partly as a result of codes being predominantly voluntary. This requires those applying the codes to monitor usage, in the knowledge that there is no external agency checking up and there are clearly inherent problems with this. Curtin (2003), however, in relation to the use of codes in the management of whale watching in the internationally important destination of Kaikoura, New Zealand, indicated that occasional 'spot checks' and consumer power in the form of complaints can offset the problems of the inability to constantly monitor the use of codes. In this New Zealand context, the fact that the licensing body providing a permit for whale watching operators, the government Department of Conservation, is the same body involved in 'spot checks' may assist with effectiveness of the codes. Nevertheless, this is a relatively unusual situation and it would seem obvious that, unless a code is implemented, there is little chance of it achieving its desired impact.

Secondly, several codes may be found operating in the same location but they may be written by different authors and aimed at targets existing at different scales, from local to national or even international. This suggests a much greater need to coordinate codes and there is perhaps a related need to reduce variability between codes. This is particularly the case when there is concern about the accuracy of the message of the code, or the rationale or guideline underlying the message. This is not so much to do with ethical choices, i.e. whether certain behaviour is 'right' or 'wrong', but whether the code has been created with accurate scientific knowledge. For example, in relation to whale watching codes, Garrod and Fennell (2004a) indicated that there is a large variation in the content of various codes, which appears to be the result of a lack of precise knowledge. In relation to minimum approach distance to whales, there is no widespread agreement and, while some codes make recommendations on swimming with cetaceans, others indicate that it should be prohibited altogether (Garrod and Fennell, 2004a). This variability may not only cause confusion, but also provide users with an excuse to flout the suggested instructions.

Collaboration between groups can offset the problems of a lack of coordination. However, there are relatively few examples of collaboration in the design and creation of codes. Nevertheless, the example of the 'Code of Ethics and Guidelines for Sustainable Tourism in Canada' indicates the potential but also the practical problems of attempts at coordination and collaboration. In 1990, the Tourism Industry Association of Canada joined with the National Round Table on the Environment and the Economy to create a 'Code of Ethics and Guidelines for Sustainable Tourism' (Wight, 2001). This was aimed at tourists, but was directed at segments of the tourism industry, ministries involved with tourism and tourism associations (Font and Buckley, 2001). This code was unique at the time of its creation in that it covered not only environmental but also sociocultural factors, had guidelines to back it up, was meant to operate at different scales, was published in

English and French, and also included a comprehensive range of topics for each tourism aspect, including the tourist, the host community, marketing, conservation of natural resources, environmental protection and industry cooperation (Wight, 2001). However, this code suffered from the fact that it was only voluntary and consequently was less well disseminated and picked up than first hoped, particularly by the tourism industry (Wight, 2001). The code required cooperation between different tourism bodies, and the coordination was far from successful. As Wight indicated, instead of comprehensive codes a number of fragmented efforts at the sub-sector or destination level occurred and these were mainly in the form of visitor codes, such as those developed for whale watching in British Columbia but also the east coast of Canada.

The example of the 'Canadian Code of Ethics and Guidelines for Sustainable Tourism' suggests the importance of using codes aimed at different audiences simultaneously, but, as Valentine (1992) suggested, most codes are targeted at visitors. Hence, Valentine argued that in any given situation it is necessary to employ simultaneously a number of codes of conduct with different target audiences. For example, a code aimed at visitors should be used in conjunction with another aimed at operators, as a code for one group on its own would not be as effective. However, this may lead to a proliferation of codes, which could appear to contradict the argument for less variability in codes, but would nevertheless appear to further support the need for greater coordination between code authors. In some regions of the world, it would appear that the argument for targeting more than one code audience is being taken seriously. As discussed above, IAATO in Antarctica, WWF in the Arctic region and the International Ecotourism Society in the USA have produced codes for both tourists and tour operators and to date this would appear to be a more successful strategy than codes aimed at one target group only.

A third issue relating to the effectiveness of codes raised by Mason and Mowforth (1996) is that codes may be little more than clever marketing devices, rather than genuine attempts to promote more sustainable forms of tourism. Under such conditions, a code can be used in an attempt to persuade potential customers that an ecotour operator adheres to a set of environmental and/or sociocultural principles. The reality may be that the principles are not adhered to but are rather a cynical attempt to get a customer to part with their cash, believing they are buying an ethical/green tourism product – a process that the media has termed 'greenwashing'. In this way, codes can give a tourism company a level of credibility in the eyes of consumers that is entirely fallacious. It is likely to be extremely tempting for a company to claim they adhere to some form of environmental or sociocultural code. As Smith and Duffy (2003: 89) claimed, specifically within a tourism context, 'Put simply, codes of ethics improve a company's image, allow it to avoid scandal and improve its sales.' Hence, monitoring will be essential to ascertain if an ecotourism company does indeed follow the code it claims to espouse. However, as has already been stated, very little monitoring of the implementation and effectiveness of codes has taken place.

Even if codes of conduct are not deliberately created as marketing devices, they may be largely a set of aspirational statements that do little more than assuage the guilt of tourists about the potential (or real) negative effects of the tourism activity they are involved in. In terms of codes produced by the industry, or with industry as the target, they can be criticized on the grounds that they are more about 'egotourism' than ecotourism (see Wheeller, 1993): that is, they make the tourists feel happy about their holiday choice, but do no more to conserve the environment in which these tourists' experience takes place than a holiday not backed up by a code.

The fourth factor raised by Mason and Mowforth (1996) is that codes are voluntary and hence are a form of self-regulation. As such, they can do little more than exhort the target audience to respond to the requests/instructions contained within the code. Virtually no codes are backed up by actual legally binding documents, which, of course, limits their effectiveness. However, as Garrod and Fennell (2004a) reported, there are variations in the attitudes to whether codes should be backed up by external regulation or not. In their empirical study, they found that in relation to whale watching there were far more non-voluntary than voluntary codes developed in North America, while Europe developed far more voluntary than non-voluntary codes. This may be due to the fact that government was particularly active in creating codes in North America, while in Europe NGOs were more active in this area (Garrod and Fennell, 2004a).

The use of voluntary codes in relation to specialist ecotourism activities such as whale watching has become increasingly popular in the last decade or so (Garrod and Fennell, 2004a). Voluntary codes are relatively easy to introduce in a short space of time and can 'plug the regulatory gap' (Garrod and Fennell, 2004a: 339). However, evidence from a number of locations globally suggests that external regulation may be far more effective than self-regulation (Mason *et al.*, 2000). As Mason and Mowforth (1996) argued, the motivation for self-regulation by the industry is either the tourist industry wishing to appear to be acting responsibly in advance of imposed regulation to weaken the force of an imminent regulation, or an attempt to stave off external regulation entirely.

In terms of the effectiveness of codes, a further issue has been raised by Garrod and Fennell (2004a). This is what they term the 'ownership' of codes. By this they mean that voluntary codes are more likely to be 'owned', and hence, they claim, more effective, if the intended user groups have been allowed, or indeed encouraged, to participate in the creation of the content of the code. Unfortunately, Garrod and Fennell (2004a) found that the largest producer of whale watching codes in their study was not one of the major user groups, but in fact government. However, it is not just the content of a code that may give ownership to user groups, but also the tone and format (Mason *et al.*, 2000; Garrod and Fennell, 2004a). User groups may suggest, for example, that a code will be more effective if its contents are not just in the form of instructions but if the instructions are backed up with a rationale in the form of guidelines. In this instance, they would be supporting a teleological rather than a deontological code. Blangy and Epler Wood (1993) suggested that teleological codes are likely to be more effective than deontological codes, particularly if they are self-explanatory and positive and avoid prohibitive language. The WWF Arctic Tourism Project codes, discussed above, were developed through a process of negotiation and consensus building (see Mason *et al.*, 2000), which was intended to give 'ownership' to user groups. These codes contain largely positive statements supported by explanatory guidelines, and the process of the creation of the WWF Arctic Tourism codes was derived from that used in the creation of IAATO codes for use in Antarctica. However, many codes developed in the period from the late 1960s to the late 1980s were blatantly deontological with frequent use of advisory statements beginning with 'Don't', but failing to provide any supporting rationale for the statement. It is arguable whether such codes have been at all effective.

One further criticism of tourism codes' effectiveness can be raised. Although many users are likely to support instructions made in codes, there will also be some, probably a small minority, who will choose to deliberately ignore these. Human nature suggests that there are also those who will go further than ignoring a code's instruction and deliberately do the opposite. This may well be an issue with deontological codes that have statements beginning 'Don't'. For such people, there is a thrill in 'breaking the law' and they may take delight in tearing up a printed code that contains the instruction 'Do Not Litter' and dropping the remnants in the wilderness!

Conclusions

Codes of conduct and guidelines are part of the attempt to regulate ecotourism. However, codes of conduct and guidelines are not the same as regulations, as these usually have legal status while codes and guidelines are voluntary and a form of self-regulation. Codes of conduct have a range of authors, including governments, NGOs, industry representatives and concerned individuals. Codes are targeted at tourists, industry, government and host communities. The message of most codes involves statements, or more usually instructions, about environmental and cultural factors. Codes may be backed up with guidelines and as such can be classified as teleological; however, many codes lack supporting guidelines and are largely a set of instructions and these can be termed deontological.

There are several issues regarding the use and effectiveness of tourism codes. Few codes are monitored and there is a great variability among codes and a general lack of coordination. Codes can also be misused, and 'greenwashing' certainly occurs. For example, an unscrupulous operator can claim that it meets certain requirements of a code written by, say, an environmental group (with no evidence to support this) in an attempt to sell more holidays. 'Ownership' of codes is important in terms of their effectiveness. It has been claimed that codes that have been designed with the involvement of intended user groups, who thus feel ownership of content and tone, are likely to work better than those created by external bodies. However, many codes have been created without the participation of user groups. Codes of conduct also suffer from the fact that they are largely voluntary. Relying on the altruistic motives of those involved in tourism may be unrealistic, and this has led some commentators to conclude that external regulation is required to strengthen this form of voluntary self-regulation.

The use of codes in ecotourism management can provide an easy target for those who view such an approach as a very weak and ineffective form of regulation. However, it is possible to rebuff this belief as it can be argued that such criticism misses the point, as codes should be more about education than regulation and are concerned more with prevention than cure.

Note

[1] The revised article was, however, published in 1994.

References

Bauer, T. (2001) *Tourism in Antarctica*. Haworth Press, New York.

Benn, P. (1998) *Ethics*. McGill–Queens University Press, Montreal.

Blangy, I. and Epler Wood, M. (1993) Developing and implementing ecotourism guidelines for wildlands and neighbouring communities. In: Lindberg, K. and Hawkins, D. (eds) *Ecotourism: a Guide for Local Planners*. Ecotourism Society, North Bennington, Vermont.

Curtin, S. (2003) Whale watching in Kaikoura. *Journal of Ecotourism* 2(3), 173–195.

Dowling, R. and Fennell, D. (2003) The context of ecotourism policy and planning. In: Fennell, D. and Dowling, R. (eds) *Ecotourism Policy and Planning*. CAB International, Wallingford, UK, pp. 4–23.

Ecotourism Society (1993) *The Ecotourism Guidelines for Nature Tour Operators*. Ecotourism Society, North Bennington, Vermont.

Elper Wood, M. (1993) Introduction. In: *The Ecotourism Guidelines for Nature Tour Operators*. Ecotourism Society, North Bennington, Vermont.

Fennell, D. (1999) *Ecotourism: an Introduction*. Routledge, London.

Fennell, D. (2000) Tourism and applied ethics. *Tourism Recreation Research* 25, 59–69.

Fennell, D. and Przeclawski, K. (2003) Generating goodwill in tourism through effective stakeholder interactions. In: Singh, S., Timothy, D. and Dowling, R. (eds) *Tourism in Destination Communities*. CAB International, Wallingford, UK, pp. 135–151.

Font, X. and Buckley, R. (eds) (2001) *Tourism Ecolabelling*. CAB International, Wallingford, UK.

Garrod, B. and Fennell, D. (2004a) An analysis of whale watching codes of conduct. *Annals of Tourism Research* 31(2), 334–352.

Garrod, B. and Fennell, D. (2004b) Whale watching codes of conduct. In: Tourism State of the Art Conference Proceedings, University of Strathclyde (CD format).

Guignon, C. (1986) Existential ethics. In: Demarco, J. and Fox, R. (eds) *New Directions in Ethics*. Routledge and Kegan Paul, New York, pp. 73–91.

Hall, C.M. (1992) Tourism in Antarctica: activities, impacts and management. *Journal of Travel Research* 30(4), 2–9.

Hunt, S., Wood, V. and Chonko, L. (1989) Corporate ethical values and organisational commitment in marketing. *Journal of Marketing* 53, 79–90.

Jafari, J. (1981) Editors page. *Annals of Tourism Research* 8, 3–4.

Krippendorf, J. (1987) *The Holidaymakers*. Heinemann, London.

Malloy, D. and Fennell, D. (1998) Ecotourism and ethics. *Journal of Travel Research* 36, 47–56.

Mason, P. (1994) A visitor code for the Arctic? *Tourism Management* 15(2), 93–97.

Mason, P. (1997) Tourism codes of conduct in the Arctic and sub-Arctic region. *Journal of Sustainable Tourism* 5(2), 151–162.

Mason, P. (2003) *Tourism Impacts Planning and Management*. Butterworth Heinemann, Oxford.

Mason, P. and Legg, S. (1999) Tourism in Antarctica. *Pacific Tourism Review* 3(1), 71–84.

Mason, P. and Mowforth, M. (1995) *Codes of Conduct in Tourism.* Occasional Paper No1, Department of Geographical Sciences, University of Plymouth, UK.

Mason, P. and Mowforth, M. (1996) Codes of conduct in tourism. *Progress in Tourism and Hospitality Research* 2(2), 152–163.

Mason, P., Johnston, M. and Twynham, D. (2000) The WWF Arctic tourism project. *Journal of Sustainable Tourism* 8(4), 305–323.

Middleton, V. and Hawkins, R. (1998) *Sustainable Tourism: a Marketing Perspective.* Butterworth Heinemann, London.

Schwartz, S. (1994) Are there universal aspects in the content and structure of values? *Journal of Social Issues* 50, 19–45.

Schwartz, S. and Bilsky, W. (1990) Towards a theory of the universal content and structure of values. *Journal of Personality and Social Psychology* 58, 878–891.

Smith, M. and Duffy, R. (2003) *The Ethics of Tourism Development*. Routledge, London.

Stonehouse, B. (1990) A travellers code for Antarctic visitors. *Polar Record* 26(156), 56–58.

Stonehouse, B. and Crosbie, K. (1995) Tourism impacts and management in the Antarctic Peninsula. In: Hall, C.M. and Johnston, M.E. (eds) *Polar Tourism: Tourism in the Antarctic and Arctic Regions.* Wiley, Chichester, UK, pp. 217–233.

Swarbrooke, J. (1999) *Sustainable Tourism Management.* CAB International, Wallingford, UK.

Taylor, P. (1975) *Principles of Ethics: an Introduction*. Dickenson, Encino, California.

UNEP (1995) *Environmental Codes of Conduct in Tourism*. Technical Report 35, United Nations Environment Programme, Paris.

Valentine, P. (1992) Nature-based tourism. In: Weiler, B. and Hall, C.M. (eds) *Special Interest Tourism*. Belhaven, London, pp. 105–128.

Wheeller, B. (1993) Sustaining the ego? *Journal of Sustainable Tourism* 1(1), 21–29.

Wight, P. (2001) Environmental management tools in Canada. In: Font, X. and Buckley, R. (eds) *Tourism Ecolabelling*. CAB International, Wallingford, UK, pp. 141–164.

Wight, P. (2004) Practical management tools and approaches for resource protection and assessment. In: Diamantis, D. (ed.) *Ecotourism.* Thomson International, London, pp. 48–72.

Wilson, J. (1990) *A New Introduction to Moral Education*. Cassell, London.

WTTRC (1995) *World Travel and Tourism Research Council Database on Codes of Conduct for the Travel and Tourism Industry.* World Travel and Tourism Research Council, Oxford.

WWF Arctic (1997) *Linking Tourism and Conservation in the Arctic*. WWF Arctic Tourism Programme, Oslo.

5 SmartVoyager: Protecting the Galápagos Islands

CAROL GOODSTEIN

Rainforest Alliance, Costa Rica

The natural history of these islands is eminently curious, and well deserves attention.
(Charles Darwin, 1845, *The Voyage of the Beagle*)

Chapter Profile

SmartVoyager is a certification programme designed to minimize the environmental impacts of tour boat operations as well as improving conditions for workers, residents and tourists in the Galápagos Islands. Launched in 2000, it is based on 12 principles and has standards covering a range of environmental and social concerns, from potential sources of pollution, to procurement and supply management, living conditions and training for boat crew and guides.

Introduction

After 25 years, Galápagos Island native Rocío Martínez de Malo had finally stashed away enough savings to secure a loan and make a down payment on the *Daphne*, a 16-passenger tour boat. As a small boat owner, she found herself in the challenging position of competing with better-known companies who own larger boats and can afford to advertise. 'With just one boat, it has been difficult to spend money on promotion,' explains Martínez (R. Martínez de Malo, Galápagos, personal communication with R. Sanabria, 2003). Upon hearing about SmartVoyager, a programme that awards its green seal of approval to tour boat operations meeting a strict set of conservation standards, Martínez hoped that the certification would give her the attention she both needs and deserves.

Launched in May 2000 by the Ecuadorean conservation group Conservación y Desarollo (C&D), with the support of the Rainforest Alliance, an

(eds R. Black and A. Crabtree)

international non-profit organization based in New York, SmartVoyager is designed to minimize the environmental impacts of tour boat operations while improving conditions for workers, residents and tourists. The programme's standards cover potential sources of pollution, such as waste water and fuels; call for procurement and supply management guidelines that reduce the chances of introducing alien species into the fragile ecosystem; and require good living conditions and advanced training for boat crews and guides. Also under the programme, passengers must be able to appreciate the beauty of the islands and see wildlife close up – while leaving no trace of their visit.

The SmartVoyager approach is holistic and not limited to passenger comfort and safety, but incorporates good environmental and social performance, which adds to the overall quality and service that a tour boat is able to provide. The programme is based on a definition of ecotourism that combines elements of nature conservation, respect for local cultures, local community participation and benefits and education – a description accepted by organizations such as the International Ecotourism Society (TIES). SmartVoyager's goal is to transform the islands' tourism industry by training tour operators in sustainable procedures and verifying compliance with strict standards through monitoring and evaluation audits. Tour boat operations meeting the conservation standards receive the SmartVoyager certification seal.

While the programme was initially designed for large passenger boats holding more than 16 travellers, thanks to World Bank funding, in 2002 SmartVoyager was adapted to smaller boats such as the now-certified *Daphne*. As of July 2004, a total of nine SmartVoyager-certified boats were operating in the Galápagos Islands. Another four vessels were in the process of working towards certification and scheduled to receive their seals later in 2004 (M. Ferro, Ecuador, personal communication, 2004).

Why the Galápagos?

Known for their stunning beauty, plant and animal species found nowhere else on earth, for remarkable wealth of marine resources and as the birthplace of Charles Darwin's evolution theory, the Galápagos are an increasingly popular tourist destination. Comprised of 16 main islands scattered over some 6 million ha of ocean lying 970 km off Ecuador's coast, the islands are renowned for their unique animal and plant life, which, having evolved in virtual isolation, demonstrate a variety of adaptive patterns. As such, the Galápagos are the crown jewel of Ecuador's national park system and its most popular tourist destination.

Ecuador took official possession of the archipelago in 1832. Two designations as a wildlife sanctuary (1935 and 1959) and the eventual declaration of the Parque Nacional Galápagos in 1968 meant that inhabitants could live only in settlements designated as 'rural zones' on the islands of Santa Cruz, Isabela and San Cristobal. Now 95% of the archipelago is within the national park jurisdiction. Since the creation of a national park, the Galápagos were declared a UNESCO World Heritage Site. As result of that designation and because of its remarkable biodiversity, tourism in the Galápagos has been tightly controlled (Stewart, 2002).

Nevertheless, the number of visitors to the Galápagos has grown from 46,000 in 1994 to 60,000 in 2000 – a substantial increase in a country where tourism is the fourth largest industry, earning more than US$430 million in 2001 and employing more than 72,000 people (Hanna *et al.*, 2003). Because tourists contribute millions of dollars to Ecuador's treasury, tourism has provided a powerful incentive for the government to protect the islands. However, even as tourism plays a leading role in saving the islands, growth comes at a cost to the environment and local people. While most visitors to the Galápagos come to marvel benignly at the sea lions, seals, blue-footed boobies and giant tortoises, at the same time they are unwittingly contributing to the islands' demise. Water pollution, a lack of recycling systems, unsatisfactory working conditions and a scarcity of environmental education and training for workers, island residents and tourists are all impacting on the fragile island ecosystem.

Even though the archipelago and surrounding waters comprise the Galápagos National Park and Marine Reserve, the agency in charge of managing and protecting the Galápagos' natural resources and regulating the activities that take place within the park – including tourism and fishing – has not been effective and the islands continue to be cleared for farming and tourism-related development, and the waters overfished. When the Galápagos National Park was created in 1959, the population was just over 1000 individuals spread out over 13 islands. Since then, the population has burgeoned at an unsustainable annual rate of 6%. Because the Pacific waters off South America have been overfished, newcomers are drawn to the healthy fish populations in the protected national marine reserve. Illegal hunting poses a grave threat to the survival of giant tortoises and other wildlife species that once thrived in abundance. Policing the Galápagos National Park has been difficult because of the increasing population pressure, increased illegal fishing, increased development and corruption (Watson, 2004).

Still another grave threat to the Galápagos is the introduction of exotic species, which tourists and tour boats inadvertently bring to the islands. These exotic and often invasive species can disrupt the delicate web of island life, devastating native species and habitats.

While the Galápagos National Park has a very complex and comprehensive system for reducing environmental impacts from boats and tourists, in 1998 no effort was in place to encourage responsible environmental and social performance beyond the minimum required levels to foster continual improvements. With pressures stemming from tourism steadily mounting, Ecuador's government agencies, conservationists and tourism sector all began to recognize the need to implement management practices that would address challenges to the islands' ecosystems. Since regulatory measures and legislation were not resulting in positive change, a voluntary tool such as certification was deemed necessary. Certification was not seen as a way to reverse the negative impacts of tourism but to prevent, mitigate or eliminate the industry's negative environmental impacts (R. Sanabria, Costa Rica, personal communication, 2004).

Developing Guidelines

In 1998, the Ecuador-based not-for-profit C&D with the support of the Rainforest Alliance and a number of scientists and experts in tourism and certification issues collaborated on a 2-year multi-stakeholder planning process for the development of the environmental and social standards that became the basis for the SmartVoyager certification programme. SmartVoyager certification standards are based on 12 principles. Using the Rainforest Alliance's standards for agriculture and timber certification as a model, C&D worked with scientists, conservation experts, tour operators and others to conduct all initial research and set standards for the maintenance and operation of tour boats in the Galápagos. 'We tried to make the guidelines as practical as possible to avoid the problems of very academic or theoretical criteria that could frighten away boat operators,' explains C&D's Co-Director Jose Valdivieso (J. Valdivieso, Ecuador, personal communication, 2004). The standards they designed cover a host of environmental and social concerns: they protect against potential sources of pollution; set rules for the good management of docks, tour boats and the small craft that ferry passengers out to the boats; specify criteria for the procurement and management of supplies; and prevent opportunities for introducing alien plant and animal species. For local people and workers, these standards require good living conditions and advanced training for the boat crew and guides.

The Rainforest Alliance and C&D have worked together in Ecuador since 1993, on the certification of banana and coca plantations. Both the Rainforest Alliance and C&D belong to the Sustainable Agriculture Network, a coalition of conservation organizations in Latin America coordinated by the Rainforest Alliance. 'After establishing certification programs in timber and agriculture, tourism seemed like the next logical step,' explains Rainforest Alliance co-founder and board chair Daniel R. Katz. 'Recognizing the growth of tourism to the Galápagos and tourism's inherent potential as a conservation tool, we responded to our members' interest in responsible travel by becoming actively involved in the development of SmartVoyager' (D. Katz, New York, personal communication, 2004).

SmartVoyager became the first certification programme in Ecuador to unite tourism operators, scientists, ecologists, the government and other stakeholders to achieve minimal environmental impact by transforming the Galápagos tourism industry. SmartVoyager believes that the creation of viable, sustainable tourism initiatives that have credibility in the international environmental community will reduce pressure on areas rich in biodiversity. The economic benefits of tourism, if properly managed, are critical to sustainable development, and give the tourism industry the potential to be a great conservation ally (Sanabria, 2003).

SmartVoyager works to certify individual tour boats, rather than their associated companies. 'We focus on individual boats rather than an entire company to ensure that each vessel is complying with the standards,' explains Valdivieso (J. Valdivieso, Ecuador, personal communication, 2004).

Individual boats must be certified, rather than an entire company, because some companies might bring only one of their boats up to standard and then claim that the entire company meets the sustainable standards. The risk is greenwashing and abusing the certification by expanding its scope to the entire company when only one of its potentially multiple operations has gone through the certification process. This does, of course, cause limitations on the use of the seals and marketing when only part of a company's operations is certified. But it also encourages companies to ensure that their entire fleet meets the standards (R. Sanabria, Costa Rica, personal communication, 2004).

Among the many stakeholders who offered significant inputs to the development of the standards and who pledged to support the programme was the International Galápagos Tour Operators Association (IGTOA), a group of 33 North American travel wholesalers who provide the majority of package tours to the islands. Members voted at IGTOA's 1999 meeting to support the SmartVoyager certification programme because it met their own objectives. Shortly after its annual members' conference in June 2004, IGTOA reaffirmed its support for the SmartVoyager certification programme (IGTOA VOZ, 2004).

The Certification Process

Today, C&D is in charge of SmartVoyager's technical aspects, including evaluations, audits, continued research, guideline revision, quality control and local promotion and fundraising. The Rainforest Alliance, which supported the programme through initial promotion, fund-raising and the establishment of an international advisory committee, is now responsible for international outreach.

The certification process summarized and described in Box 5.1 is initiated by companies sending to C&D a basic, four-page application form. They are

Box 5.1. How does SmartVoyager work? (From SmartVoyager, 2002.)

To assure transparency, the following mechanisms have been established: certification standards are public documents available to any interested party on the Rainforest Alliance web site, and suggestions for improvements are welcomed (recommendations are collected throughout the year, formal revisions are conducted every 6 months); certification audits are performed by properly trained C&D auditors with a signed statement to ensure no conflict of interest; the certification is awarded by an international, independent certification committee; and public presentations and consultation meetings are conducted every time the auditors are on the islands. The following is an overview of the general steps that constitute SmartVoyager's certification process.

Application: Applicants should submit an application form to C&D. Once the company has presented the application form, it will receive the necessary documentation to continue with the certification process.

(*Continued*)

Box 5.1. (Continued).

Self-assessment: After the application has been submitted, the tour operator usually performs a self-assessment or internal review to determine its level of compliance with the standards.

Evaluation: In some cases, and as a complement to the self-assessment, the operator may request a short evaluation to decide whether or not an on-site assessment needs to be performed. If so, C&D assigns an assessor to perform this evaluation (pre-assessment). The client must cover the costs of the evaluation.

Audits: These on-site assessments involve visits to the vessels and the inland facilities to assess compliance with SmartVoyager standards, and are required for all operations. The scope and intensity of the assessment depend on the size and type of operation. The cost of the audit (mainly auditor's fee and travel expenses) is covered by the client.

Status Granting: After the necessary assessments have taken place and all documentation is presented to C&D, the audit report is sent to an international certification committee and a status rating is granted to the operation: (i) Approved: when the operation complies with at least 80% of the total SmartVoyager standards, there are no fatal flaws, and there is a commitment to assure continual improvement every year. Only when the operation is approved can a boat be certified. (ii) Denied: when the operation does not comply with SmartVoyager standards, and it is not expected that improvements will occur in the short run.

Certification Contract: Approved operations must enter into a certification contract for the use of the SmartVoyager™ certification mark.

Annual Renewal: Companies are required to submit annual reports on their certified operations. Annual programme fees must be paid for certified boats according to SmartVoyager's fee structure.

Annual Audits: All certified boats must be audited yearly to re-verify compliance with SmartVoyager standards and to revalidate their certificate. The scope and intensity of the audits depend on the size and type of operation. The client covers audit expenses.

Unannounced Visits: Besides yearly audits, SmartVoyager's staff and/or external observers may randomly visit certified companies.

Emergency Assessments: If serious violations of SmartVoyager standards occur or are suspected, C&D may perform emergency assessments of certified boats.

then assigned an auditor for the first inspection, a pre-audit that provides a quick diagnostic report of points of non-compliance with the guidelines. Necessary changes and investments may need to be undertaken, and timelines are set up for their completion. C&D then conducts a complete site audit with one auditor and one or two assistants in training. C&D staff members who conduct the audits are specifically trained to assess the certification standards. The programme is divided into 12 principles (see Box 5.2).

Box 5.2. SmartVoyager's certification standards are organized into 12 principles (from Sanabria, 2001).

Company Policy
The company must have a management policy that includes compliance with national legislation and international agreements as well as SmartVoyager standards.

Conservation of Natural Ecosystems
The tourist operation must support and promote conservation of the Galápagos National Park and the Marine Reserve.

Reduction of Negative Environmental Impacts
The tourist operation must prevent, mitigate and compensate for any environmental damage done to the Galápagos Islands and Marine Reserve.

Lowering the Risk of Introduction and Dispersal of Exotic Species
The tourist operation must prevent the introduction of species from the continent to the islands and the dispersal of species between islands.

Just and Proper Treatment of Workers
The tourist operation must elevate the socio-economic welfare and quality of life of workers and their families.

Employee Training
All personnel involved with the tourist operation must receive environmental education and training.

Community Relations and Local Welfare
The company must make a commitment to the welfare and socio-economic development of the Galápagos Islands community.

Strict Control of Use, Supply and Storage of Materials
Boat operators must plan and control the consumption, supply and storage of materials, taking into consideration the well-being of tourists, workers and local communities and the conservation of natural ecosystems.

Integrated Waste Management
Boats must follow a waste-management plan, including the reduction, reuse, recycling and adequate final treatment and disposal of all wastes.

Commitment on the Part of the Tourist
Tourists must be guided in their involvement in protecting natural resources and local cultures, tread lightly and collaborate with the island conservation programmes.

Safety
SmartVoyager is not a safety certification programme. However, certified boats must adhere to international safety standards and have all the appropriate licences and approvals.

Planning and Monitoring
Tourism operations must be planned, monitored and evaluated, taking into consideration technical, economic, social and environmental factors.

The complete set of standards is available online at: www.rainforest-alliance.org/tourism.cfm?id=smartvoyager

Each principle is comprised of criteria and some criteria also include indicators. In the final scoring only criteria, not indicators, are considered.

For an operation to become certified, it needs to have a final score of at least 80% compliance with no less than 50% compliance for each principle (see Box 5.1). The final analysis is sent to the certification committee, composed of a representative from C&D, at least two other members of SmartVoyager's International Advisory Committee and independent specialists on ecotourism, the Galápagos and conservation.

Seals of certification are awarded to boats that fulfil at least 80% of the criteria, provide a written commitment for continual improvement in subsequent years and prove an absence of 'fatal flaws' (see Box 5.3), which are generally accepted as detrimental practices (Stewart, 2002).

Box 5.3. Fatal flaws (from C&D, Ecuador, electronic communication, 2004).

A boat can be certified before achieving full compliance with 100% of the standards, but certain conditions must be met:

- The boat must meet enough of the standards to satisfy the certification committee and achieve a score of at least 800.
- The boat must show concrete evidence of improvements in all areas.
- The boat must have a social and environmental management plan that details the areas needing improvements and sets objectives for making the improvements. The plan must be approved by the auditors.
- The boat has no fatal flaws.

A boat can be decertified if:

- It does not make enough progress from one year to the next to satisfy the certification committee. (Certification is based on continual improvements.)
- A surprise audit shows serious *retrocesos* (backsliding).
- The boat suffers a fatal flaw.

Decertification is done through a process similar to certification. The programme has an open door to accept complaints from the public, tourists, workers, the government or any source. The programme documents all complaints – who made the complaint, how it was handled, the resolution, dates. The reporting of any fatal flaw or other serious violation of the standards triggers an emergency audit. The audit report is sent to a decertification committee for a decision.

The committee can decide to:

- Agree that the problem has been satisfactorily corrected.
- Issue a warning and call for another audit after a designated time period to see if the problem has been addressed. (These emergency audits might include outside experts – someone with special expertise in the problem.)
- Immediately decertify the boat.

All reports of fatal flaws are investigated to see if a full audit is necessary. The preliminary investigation can sometimes be done by telephone or email, but usually it is necessary to send an auditor to the boat.

(*Continued*)

Box 5.3. (Continued).

Fatal flaws include:

- A serious violation of a national law or international treaty.
- Allowing unauthorized tourist activity. This could include harassing wildlife, collecting flora or fauna, or major deviations from the park-authorized itinerary, such as allowing tourists to visit a restricted site.
- Serious, prolonged leakage of fuels or other contaminants. Any boat suffering a fuel spill would immediately be subject to an emergency audit.
- Any serious, unauthorized waste disposal, such as unapproved emptying of bilge or sewage tanks or throwing garbage overboard.
- Any serious breach of quarantine procedures, such as knowingly transporting supplies with a high possibility of contamination by foreign species. (SICGAL and the standards are the references.)
- Any serious discrimination or harassment of employees; forced or indentured labour; any violation of human rights. (ILO and the standards are the references.)
- Any grave safety violation. A boat without proper first-aid supplies is a fatal flaw. (The International Convention for the Safety of Life at Sea – SOLAS – and the SmartVoyager standards are the references.) The lack of an International Safety Management Code (ISM) valid certificate if required by law also constitutes a fatal flaw.
- Lack of an environmental and social management plan. The plan can be extensive or minimal, depending on the size of the boat, but a boat cannot be certified – or remain certified – if there is no active plan.

Once certified, the boats are subjected to annual audits and unannounced auditor visits on site, while the boats are in port but also at sea. Boat owners may pay directly for the audits but some audits are covered by grants and subsidies. There are no application fees, and annual renewal fees include auditing expenses. On top of these fees, the operations must cover the auditor's transportation and room and board. The first payment covers 2 years as an incentive for operations to join. Then recertification fees are paid on a yearly basis according to the scale shown in Table 5.1.

Initial Boats Sign On

C&D worked carefully to explain the goals and objectives of SmartVoyager through one-on-one meetings and group seminars with boat operators, which highlighted the importance of the voluntary mechanism and the benefits that best practice implementation brings to the business and the islands. After learning how the programme works, Ecoventura and Canodros, two Ecuadorean operators, expressed interest in becoming certified. C&D auditors visited the boats numerous times and prepared detailed reports on specific conditions that needed to be met in order for the boats to win

SmartVoyager certification. While both Ecoventura and Canodros were already in compliance with some of the standards established by the programme, the companies changed their practices to meet most of the other principles. Tourism operations are monitored and evaluated according to technical, economic, social and environmental factors.

'We have always tried to be responsible towards our working environment, the Galápagos Islands,' reflects Ecoventura director Santiago Dunn. 'Therefore we looked for a seal that made us become more strict with our environmental criteria – criteria that were even stricter that those requested by the local authorities. SmartVoyager met all of our requirements' (S. Dunn, Ecuador, personal communication, 2004).

During the first year of SmartVoyager's operations, which started in May 2000, five of the 20 large tour boats that travel through the Galápagos were certified by the programme as ecofriendly and socially responsible after being assessed by C&D auditors. All five made tangible changes (see Box 5.4), including the use of lead-free and TBT-free paint, the implementation of waste disposal systems, the production of fresh water with a desalinization

Table 5.1. SmartVoyager recertification fees (from C&D, Ecuador, electronic communication, 2004).

1.	Fewer than 20 passengers	US$1536
2.	From 20 to 60 passengers	US$3840
3.	From 60 to 100 passengers	US$7680

Box 5.4. Changes made to SmartVoyager-certified boats (from Stewart, 2002; A. Dueñas, Ecuador, personal communication, 2004; S. Dunn, Ecuador, personal communication, 2004).

The following are examples of changes that are implemented by SmartVoyager certified boats:

- Use of lead-free paint.
- Use of biodegradable soaps, detergents and shampoos.
- Implementation of a waste-disposal system, including recycling bins.
- Production of fresh water through the use of a desalinization plant, a method that purifies water with ozone and eliminates chlorine discharge into the ocean.
- Treatment of black and grey waste water under aerobic decomposition.
- Installation of light bulbs that do not attract insects to prevent the introduction of non-native species to the islands.
- Replacement of two-stroke outboard motors on dinghies with four-stroke engines, which are 70% quieter, emit virtually no fumes and use 50% less fuel.
- Guarantee of sanitary conditions – as well as a good quality of life – for all crew members.

plant on board, the careful management of fuels and improved conditions for workers.

In 2001, the SmartVoyager initiative was commended by UNESCO's World Heritage Committee: 'Given the nature of tourism visitation to the Galápagos, and the impacts of tourism on the fragile environment, and in light of the proposed Marine Reserve. It believes that consideration should be given to promoting similar schemes in other World Heritage sites' (UNESCO, 2001).

Adapting the Programme to Smaller Vessels

Of the 84 tour boats that ply the waters of the Galápagos, 12 are considered large, carrying 40 or more passengers, another 20 are medium-sized, carrying between 21 and 40 passengers, and 32 are small, carrying fewer than 21 passengers. The remaining number represent a variable portion of operators that fluctuates for several reasons including operations under repair, seasonal operations, boats that sink, invalid operation permits and operations that simply have stopped functioning (A. Dueñas, Ecuador, personal communication, 2004).

While SmartVoyager is a voluntary programme, open to all tourist vessels that wish to comply with the programme's regulations, the standards initially targeted medium- and large-scale operators. At first, small boat operators expressed little interest in becoming certified and did not participate in the development of the standards. 'They simply had scarce economic resources to implement the program,' surmises Mauricio Ferro, Co-Director of C&D, 'or it was not properly promoted at the beginning' (M. Ferro, Ecuador, personal communication, 2004).

Most of these small boats are individually owned and family-operated. As with most small enterprises, these operations have limited funds for upgrading equipment and little interest in changing procedures. The small boat operators all faced a considerable decline in tourism caused by a combination of the terrorist attacks on 11 September 2001 and the dollarization of Ecuador's economy, which has meant that, since 9 September 2002, the US dollar has been the country's sole legal tender. These small family-owned operations thought that, while certification might be worthwhile for large firms, the SmartVoyager standards were too complex and rigorous, and beyond their reach. However, they demonstrated a willingness and commitment to the SmartVoyager standards they could afford. These include security standards, waste management, signage, conservation support and sustainable labour practices, among others. What remained – and continue to be – more difficult are the more expensive elements of certification (Sanabria, 2003). For example, a significant expense to operators working to comply with SmartVoyager certification is the installation of desalinization systems, which are designed to avoid the consumption of scant freshwater resources.

Another cost incurred by meeting the standards is the need for the construction of warehouses on the mainland to provide proper food storage and prevent the introduction of invasive species to the islands. However, not all operators have the resources to build these warehouses. The desalinization facilities and the warehouses, along with the cost of installing four-stroke motors on the boats – which are also required by the programme – and a number of other factors, prevented more boats from becoming certified.

With financial support from the World Bank and in coordination with Ecuador's Ministry of the Environment, Tourism and Commerce, the Galápagos National Park, the Galápagos Chamber of Commerce, the Galápagos Shipowners Association and the Rainforest Alliance, C&D was able to test the feasibility of adapting SmartVoyager standards to small boats. Through an intensive outreach effort, small boat operators were made aware of the challenges and opportunities afforded by SmartVoyager certification and how they could participate in revising the standards. A cross-section of small boat operators determined that 93% of the original requirements were applicable to all boats, regardless of size. The remaining 7% of the requirements, which mainly deal with infrastructure, were revised so that they could be applied to small boats.

The outreach effort enabled the small boat operators to learn what standards were required, how to comply with these requirements and why the requirements were included in the standards. After this training, C&D auditors assessed 32 small boats. They found that, of those, 24 complied with all applicable requirements. So far, five of the small boats have been certified. Of the remaining 19, eight have the resources to upgrade equipment and can be certified after additional training and technical assistance in such areas as documenting their environmental policies and performing internal audits. Importantly, although these boats complied with most standards, they did not comply with those that require upgrading equipment, documenting their environmental policies and performing internal audits.

In 2004, Massachusetts-based Ecologic Enterprise Ventures, Inc. (EEV), an alternative, environmentally oriented venture capital firm, made available US$90,000 in fixed-asset financing for two small tour boat operators in the Galápagos: Daphne Cruises and Rolf Wittmer Turismo Galápagos. Loan proceeds financed capital improvements required by certification, including the purchase of eco-friendly four-stroke outboard engines, which significantly reduce contamination of the marine environment from petrol and outboard engine oil. It also translates directly to increased income, as fuel consumption savings of 50% create an important economic gain for local operators. These engines, along with purchase of on-board desalinization machines and other appropriate technologies, have helped to bring the two small boats into full compliance with the SmartVoyager certification standards.

The remaining small operators are stymied both by the need for technical assistance and by a lack of funds required to replace and upgrade equipment that does not comply with certification requirements: for example, air conditioners and refrigerators using CFCs, replacing two-stroke outboards with four-stroke models and noise abatement systems on propulsion and generator engines. If low-interest loans, matching grants or other instruments were made available, a large portion of the remaining small boats and many mid-size boats would be able implement these changes to improve their environmental performance. Efforts continue to enable boat operators to access funds for capital improvements.

The small boat certification initiative was completed in 14 months with an investment of less than US$66,000. As of July 2004, passengers travelling in boats certified by the SmartVoyager programme represent approximately 25% of all tourists sailing to and visiting the Galápagos Islands. Local auditors have been trained and most small operators now understand what they need to do to maintain biodiversity and protect the environment. One of the greatest accomplishments has been widespread acceptance that SmartVoyager standards are appropriate guidelines for improving performance and becoming environmentally and socially responsible. Designers of new boats are applying the standards in their design process. '*Sky Dancer* is one of the few boats whose construction involved a preliminary study of social and environmental impacts,' explains Santiago Dunn, owner of the boat.

> *Sky Dancer* was designed and built according to strict technical guidelines, which ensure minimum environmental impact, provide the utmost in safety conditions for tourists and crew and improve the quality of conditions for workers, as is stipulated by SmartVoyager principles and standards.
>
> (S. Dunn, Ecuador, personal communication, 2004)

Now that several boats are certified, peer pressure and competition are motivating boat operators to consider SmartVoyager certification. Owners of all sizes of boats are asking for training and technical assistance so that they too can comply with the standards and be certified. Ideally, boats of all sizes would be certified to ensure improved environmental and social performance. If funding for such assistance becomes available, a much larger portion of the fleet will be certified.

Spreading the Word

According to Stephen Edwards, a tourism specialist with the Washington DC-based non-profit Conservation International:

> The Galápagos Islands are particularly ideal for a tourism certification program because the tourism system in Galápagos is generally well organized, sophisticated and controlled. This provides for relatively easy access to operators and boats, and certification systems can potentially be aligned with the current itinerary system to reward extra levels of compliance . . . It is clear that tourists coming to the Galápagos are coming for a natural history experience, and Galápagos does not disappoint! However, it is not an inexpensive destination. This means that the market that is coming tends to be well-educated, a supporter of conservation, and therefore likely to demand a high-quality experience as well as to support conservation initiatives like certification.
>
> (S. Edwards, Ecuador, personal communication, 2004)

The SmartVoyager certification programme has been promoted throughout the international tourism industry, enhancing Ecuador's reputation and the competitiveness of its tourism sector. Other segments of Ecuador's tourism sector recognize the SmartVoyager programme as a model for their operations and of how to engage small enterprises in environmental initiatives. As Doris Welsh, IGTOA's Vice-President, explains:

> The SmartVoyager program has brought a tremendous amount of awareness of sustainable tourism to all the players within the tourism industry in Galápagos. For example, five years ago, you would never hear about pangas [dinghies] being equipped with four-stroke engines. Great strides have already been made. We realize this program could take several more years to fully develop, however. With so relatively few boats certified to date, the challenge still remains of getting the word out to tourists interested in visiting Galápagos on the merits choosing to book a trip to Galápagos on one of the SmartVoyager certified boats.
>
> (D. Welsh, Miami, Florida, personal communication, 2004)

Lessons Learned and Future Plans: Moving Towards Collaborative Sustainability

Throughout its development, those involved in SmartVoyager have learned that, in order to have a successful and sound ecotourism certification scheme, some general principles and elements must be implemented. These lessons are best summarized in the Mohonk Agreement (see Black and Crabtree, Chapter 2, this volume), which provides a framework developed at the conclusion of an international workshop convened by the Institute for Policy Studies in November 2000, with participation from 20 countries and representatives from most of the leading global, regional, national and sub-national sustainable tourism and ecotourism certification programmes.

The programme has taken the necessary steps to turn these lessons into strengths. The following factors have been essential in the development and future maintenance of the programme (Sanabria, 2001): proactively looking for international and governmental support, increasing communication efforts with different stakeholders (government, industry, other NGOs and local peoples), promptly clarifying misunderstandings and misperceptions, holding open discussions with all interested parties, networking with governmental and other non-governmental efforts, strengthening a participatory approach through public consultation and educating people about the benefits and challenges of certification.

The Galápagos National Park has begun to follow several SmartVoyager regulations, including the use of anti-insect light bulbs on vessels, the efficient handling of garbage and compliance with the International Safety Management code on 16 passenger boats.

Along with SmartVoyager's success, it is equally important to mention some difficulties faced by certification programmes. First, some programmes face unfavourable local political circumstances. For example, political realities preclude participatory processes, making it difficult, if not impossible, to hold discussions on sustainable tourism standards among stakeholders. In the case of the Galápagos, the programme needed to be sensitive to the fact that it needed to involve more than one company in the pilot phase and ensure representation from different regions (i.e. boat operators from continental Ecuador, the coasts and the highlands, as well as operators from the islands) to increase acceptance. Including boats of different sizes and a mix of local owners versus continental owners would have increased uptake from the beginning. Secondly, there are often insufficient funds to develop the programme in the initial stages. Thirdly, there is no international accreditation body for tourism certifiers to help guide the establishment of the programme and attest to its continued credibility. Fourthly, often there is a lack of understanding of what third-party, independent certification means, and how it could support industry, governmental, conservation and social well-being efforts. Finally, there is a need to develop creative financial mechanisms that would support small companies and give them the resources necessary to implement changes in their operations.

In 2005, a total of nine SmartVoyager-certified boats ply the waters of the Galápagos; an average of 9548 tourists per year sail aboard these boats; 150 local personnel are involved in the programme; and 400 employees have labour rights and medical services as a result of the commitment these operators have to social and environmental responsibility. C&D expects to certify 24 boats before the end of 2005 (M. Ferro, Ecuador, personal communication, 2004).

The Rainforest Alliance and C&D did not design SmartVoyager for market competitiveness, but considered it to be a conservation programme. Thus, the aim is not to limit the number of operations but rather to turn the Galápagos into a more responsible destination by having as many boats as possible enrolled in the programme. The competitive advantage lies in better use and consumption of resources and long-term sustainability of their businesses by having a protected environment in which to operate. Bad environmental conditions will eventually have a negative impact on business because the main attraction in the Galápagos is its natural assets (R. Sanabria, Costa Rica, personal communication, 2004).

By June 2004, SmartVoyager was in the process of developing its standard for terrestrial ecotourism accommodation services and it is actively participating in the Sustainable Tourism Certification Network of the Americas (see Chapter 23) to exchange views and develop a common understanding with peer programmes in the region.

References

Hanna, J., Toth, B., Quintero, J. and Valdivieso, J. (2003) Ecuador: fostering environmentally sustainable tourism and small business innovation and growth in the Galapagos. *En Brevé* 26, June.

IGTOA VOZ (2004) An e-Newsletter from the International Galapagos Tour Operators Association, June, Volume IV, Number 6. www.igtoa.org

Institute for Policy Studies (2000) Ecotourism and Sustainable Development, 'Mohonk Agreement'. Available at: www.ips-dc.org

Sanabria, R. (2001) Evolving ecotourism alliances conserve biodiversity in the Galápagos Islands. *Industry and Environment* (UNEP, Paris) 24(3–4), 33–36.

Sanabria, R. (2003) *SmartVoyager: Supporting Ecuador's Competitiveness Plan: A Pilot Certification Project for Small Boat Operators in the Galapagos Islands.* Rainforest Alliance, New York.

SmartVoyager (2002) *Get Certified.* SmartVoyager one-pager, Rainforest Alliance, New York.

Stewart, E. (2002) *SmartVoyager: Environmental and Social Certification Program of Tour Boats in the Galapagos.* Stanford Graduate School of Business, Berkeley, California.

UNESCO (2001) *Convention Concerning the Protection of the World Cultural and Natural Heritage.* World Heritage Committee 25th Session. UNESCO, Paris.

Watson, P. (2004) *Population Migration Threatens the Galapagos.* Sea Shepherd Organization, Friday Harbor, Washington.

6 Green Globe: a Global Environmental Certification Programme for Travel and Tourism

CATHY PARSONS[1] AND JILL GRANT[2]

[1]*Former CEO Green Globe Asia Pacific;* [2]*Department of Industry, Tourism and Resources, Canberra*

Chapter Profile

Green Globe is a global tourism certification programme that developed out of Agenda 21 and applies the principles of sustainable development to the travel and tourism industry. The programme seeks to achieve environmental, social and cultural improvements at a range of levels from global to local and encourages and facilitates compliance with national and regional legislation. The Green Globe programme is open to all travel and tourism industry sectors and sizes and types of operations, including companies and communities. The programme has five standards – Company, Community, Ecotourism, Design and Construct Standards and Precinct Planning and Design Standards – which provide comprehensive coverage of the tourism and travel industry. Tourism operations are encouraged to enter the programme at the benchmarking level. This chapter describes the development and implementation of the Green Globe programme, highlighting the lessons learnt along the way as well as the challenges and benefits of the programme.

Introduction

Green Globe, a global tourism certification programme, arose from the 1992 Agenda 21 document and its principles for sustainable development as they applied to travel and tourism. This landmark agreement was signed by 182 countries at the 1992 United Nations Earth Summit in Rio De Janeiro (United Nations, 1992a,b) and paved the way for concerted action by nations wishing to address the challenges and maximize the development opportunities the tourism industry offers. The Green Globe programme aims to provide the travel and tourism industry with a certification system that responds directly to the major environmental problems facing the planet, including the greenhouse effect, overuse of freshwater resources, destruction of biodiversity, production of solid and biological waste and social equity issues.

The programme seeks to achieve environmental, social and cultural improvements at the global, national and local levels and encourages and facilitates compliance with national and provincial legislation as required by agencies or authorities. It is also attractive to the tourism industry because it targets the achievement of significant cost savings through an integrated and systematic approach to reducing energy consumption, decreasing waste generation and lowering the use of potable water.

The Green Globe certification programme deals with the entire travel and tourism industry, and yet it has developed the flexibility to take into account the specific requirements of different sectors. Under the provisions of the Company Standard, all types of companies used by tourists and travellers can be certified, including administration offices, aerial cableways, airports, airlines, bus companies, hotels, car hire, cruise ships, farm stay, golf courses, exhibition halls, convention halls, vineyards/wineries, tour operators, tour wholesalers, marinas, railways, restaurants and trailer (caravan) parks. The launch of the International Ecotourism Standard in 2002 provided a specific programme for operators who meet the definition of ecotourism as set out in the Standard. This was followed by the release of a Community Standard in 2003 for tourism destinations, a Design and Construct Standard for new tourism infrastructure and a Precinct Planning and Design Standard (PPDS). With the availability of five different standards, the Green Globe programme provides comprehensive coverage.

The Green Globe programme aims to include the latest travel and tourism sustainability research and industry best practices through continual review and improvement. In responding to internal and external critiques, the programme has evolved from its inception in 1994 as a membership-committed programme to a process-oriented programme and finally to its current version as a performance, compliance, outcomes-based system. Utilizing its operational experience, the programme has created an upgraded certification programme backed by the research programme of the Australian-based Sustainable Tourism Cooperative Research Centre. In early 2003, Green Globe announced an enhanced system to streamline delivery and product development from the Asia Pacific headquarters in Canberra, Australia. The ABC (Affiliate/Awareness, Benchmarked, Certified) system was strengthened and successfully tested in key markets. The three levels are shown in Fig. 6.1.

The programme reflects and accommodates the World Tourism Organization's Global Code of Ethics and regional–national variants such as the Pacific Asia Travel Association – Asia Pacific Economic Cooperation (APEC) Code for Sustainable Tourism.

History of Green Globe

Since its inception, the programme has undergone two major stages of development. Its evolution was stimulated by its experience in field-testing the programme, by internal and external criticism and by the results of three

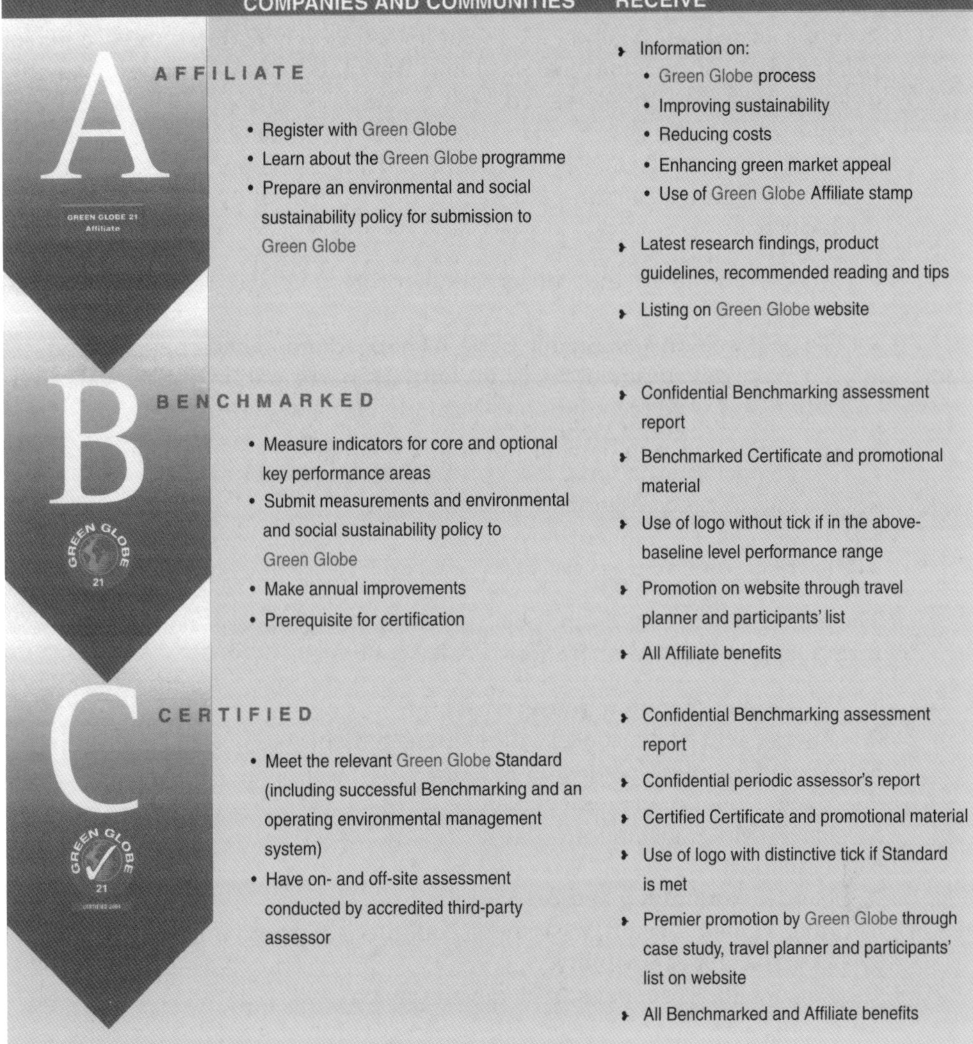

A – **Affiliate/Awareness** to kick-start sustainable and responsible travel practices;
B – **Benchmarked** to measure and improve environmental performance; and
C – **Certified** to ensure internationally recognized and audited quality levels.

Fig. 6.1. ABC of Green Globe.

United Nations forums (the 1992 Rio de Janeiro Earth Summit, the 1999 Commission on Sustainable Development meeting in New York and the 2002 World Summit in Johannesburg). At the 1992 Rio gathering, the Chair of the Earth Summit, Maurice Strong, stated that the tourism industry needed to consider seriously its relationship with the environment and establish a long-term framework for sustainable development. In response, the World Travel and Tourism Council (WTTC), World Tourism Organization (WTO) and the Earth Council joined together to apply the principles of Agenda 21

(United Nations, 1992a) to the tourism industry and to develop a programme of action. Agenda 21 (United Nations, 1992a) provided a set of principles for local, state, national and international action on sustainable development, and these related well to tourism activities. The result was *Agenda 21 for the Travel and Tourism Industry: Towards Environmentally Sustainable Development* (World Travel and Tourism Council, 1995).

This Agenda 21 action plan included a number of overall objectives for the industry:

- To contribute to the conservation, protection and restoration of the ecosystem.
- To be based on sustainable patterns of production and consumption.
- To make development decisions with the participation of the local population and with recognition of local identity and culture.
- To create employment for women and indigenous peoples.
- To respect international laws protecting the environment.
- To halt or reverse protectionism in trade.
- To develop systems to warn nations of natural disasters that could affect tourists/tourist areas (World Travel and Tourism Council, 1995).

The plan aimed to convert the objectives into specific targets, naming ten areas for travel and tourism operations to take concrete action:

1. Waste minimization, reuse, recycling.
2. Energy efficiency, conservation, management.
3. Management of freshwater resources.
4. Waste water management.
5. Hazardous substances.
6. Transport.
7. Land-use planning and management.
8. Involvement of staff, customers, communities in environmental issues.
9. Design for sustainability.
10. Partnerships for sustainable development.

In 1994, the World Travel and Tourism Council (WTTC), a London-based organization composed of chief executive officers of major tourism corporations, initiated Green Globe with the aim of providing guidance materials and support for industry members in undertaking activities to achieve sustainability outcomes in the Agenda 21 target areas. Green Globe was originally conceived as a membership-based programme, whereby travel and tourism companies joined and voluntarily implemented sustainable tourism practices based on Agenda 21 principles. A cross-section of companies (airlines, hotel chains, tour operators, travel agents) joined and the Green Globe programme quickly gained a considerable profile within the industry, particularly amongst the large international hotel chains.

In April 1999, the seventh session of the United Nations Commission on Sustainable Development (UNCSD-7) was focused on sustainable tourism. The Commission on Sustainable Development (CSD) is a high-level

United Nations body established to facilitate the implementation of sustainable development. The primary role of CSD is to monitor, review and coordinate implementation of Agenda 21 and the Johannesburg Plan of Implementation. CSD usually meets annually and considers specific themes. In 1999 themes included sustainable tourism and sustainable production and consumption, and the meeting concluded that, to achieve and maintain sustainable tourism, organizations needed to integrate the following fundamental processes:

- Build travel and tourism policies on Agenda 21 principles.
- Use voluntary mechanisms to regulate sustainable tourism, including certification industry codes.
- Raise awareness.
- Oppose illegal, abusive and exploitative tourism.
- Capacity building.
- Integrated planning.
- Research impacts on societies, cultures and environments.
- Develop and transfer technology.
- Assess leakage.
- Propose policies to enhance local and indigenous benefit.

Notably, self-regulation was identified at the UN meeting as one of the prime processes required for the achievement and maintenance of sustainable tourism. The Green Globe programme agreed with this approach and supported the view that if the industry did not 'green' itself then government-imposed legislation and regulation may force it to do so. As a result, the 'voluntary mechanism' was transformed into a more rigorous certification programme.

Following UNCSD-7, the Green Globe programme was restructured, securing direct investment from WTTC members, and became partners with the Sustainable Tourism Cooperative Research Centre (STCRC) in Australia to establish Green Globe Asia Pacific, which was headquartered in Australia. This restructuring was the key to the transformation of Green Globe into a credible worldwide certification programme backed by scientific research. The certification programme was based on International Organization for Standardization (ISO) standards and Agenda 21 principles, and incorporated recommendations from UNCSD-7. Central to this new approach was the introduction of independent verification of the achievements of an operation and hence its legitimate (or otherwise) credentials for certification. A two-logo process was established, whereby a tourism operation could use the logo without a 'tick' during its path towards certification and then could use the logo with a 'tick' once it had been certified by an independent third party.

After 1999, the system of independent assessment worked well, with certification being based on a rigorous process. Training schemes for auditing companies carrying out the on-site inspections reinforced this process; however, further improvements were needed. The Green Globe programme continued to receive some criticism (WWF, 2000) for allowing the logo to be used as soon as an operation was committed to undertaking the certification programme. It was argued by some critics that an operation could use the logo without actually acting in an environmentally or socially responsible manner. The programme was also criticized at this time for not incorporating the work of other tourism certification programmes into the Standard, and providing inadequate guidance for participants from some sectors of the industry.

In February 2000, the STCRC was delegated the task of enhancing the best features of the 1999 model in order to upgrade the programme. The revised model was to focus on an outcome approach to certification through a set of performance criteria, and the programme would 'benchmark' environmental performance and measure real environmental improvements on an annual basis. The new system targeted nine key environmental and social performance areas:

1. Greenhouse gas emissions.
2. Energy efficiency, conservation and management.
3. Air quality protection and noise control.
4. Freshwater resource management.
5. Wastewater management.
6. Waste minimization.
7. Improved social and cultural relations.
8. Land management.
9. Ecosystem conservation and management.

Benchmarking criteria were selected to work within a travel and tourism operating environment and to be relevant to key business and environment issues. Benchmarking criteria were developed for 25 company sectors, as well as Benchmarking indicators for ecotourism products, communities, and design and construction of tourism infrastructure.

In the criteria developed for hotels, for example, energy consumption – generally the biggest cost after labour – is one of the key performance areas. The indicator used is energy consumed per guest night (or area under roof). This ratio is then independently analysed by Earthcheck (a business established by STCRC to develop the Benchmarking database and prepare assessment reports) and 'Benchmarked' against a set of reference values that are applicable to sectors and locations throughout the world. The Transparency Documents that support this analysis are available from Green Globe and allow companies and other stakeholders to better understand the database that underpins the Benchmarking system. Details of how the measures work and how they are collected and recorded are provided by Green Globe. To be successfully Benchmarked, companies must be above a baseline level of performance for the key performance areas and they must maintain this performance annually. In most cases, companies improve their levels of performance above baseline in subsequent years. Their performance is shown in an annual assessment report, which illustrates how well the operation compares to the baseline and best practice and its previous year's results, where applicable. The Benchmarking formed the basis of the 2001 version of the Green Globe Company Standard and, over the past few years, minor modifications have been made.

The current version of the Green Globe Company Standard (STCRC, 2004a) sets out the requirements needed to meet a level of environmental and social management performance that produces the sustainable development outcomes sought by Agenda 21. The Standard recognizes continuous improvement for those participating in the programme. It aims to facilitate improvements in the local and global environmental quality, conservation of local heritage, improvement of local living conditions and contribution to the local economy. A 2007 version is currently being piloted and is expected to be fully implemented during 2007.

Green Globe Programme Delivery

The delivery of the Green Globe programme has a number of components, including product development, customer service and marketing, and its global delivery is now centralized at the Green Globe Asia Pacific office. Green Globe Asia Pacific is a joint venture between Green Globe Ltd (UK) and the Sustainable Tourism CRC (STCRC), based in Queensland, Australia. The STCRC derives from the Australian government programme established to boost collaborative links between industry, research organizations, educational institutions and relevant government agencies. The Sustainable Tourism CRC comprises 16 universities, major industry associations, all state and territory tourism departments and private industry partners.

STCRC's mandate is to 'deliver innovation to enhance the environmental, economic and social sustainability of tourism.' It was responsible for developing the upgraded Green Globe Company Standard and the new Benchmarking system. Through one of its business units, Earthcheck, it delivers the Benchmarking assessment reports to Green Globe customers.

In addition to its partnership with STCRC, the Green Globe programme has formed various industry alliances. For example, the Pacific Asia Travel Association (PATA) has endorsed the programme as part of its commitment to sustainable travel and tourism. The Caribbean Alliance for Sustainable Tourism markets the Green Globe programme in that region. The Green Key programme in the Nordic countries has previously worked closely with Green Globe, as has the Green Seal programme in the USA. The New Zealand Tourism Industry Association, Bali Greenery, the International Hotel and Restaurant Association, the China State Environmental Protection Agency, the West Virginia EPA, USA, and Ecotourism Australia (which jointly developed the International Ecotourism Standard with Green Globe) have had formal alliances with Green Globe. In forming partnerships with regional networks and other certification programmes, Green Globe is being proactive in initiating the process of building a global brand.

The programme receives feedback and advice on the content and quality of its programme. These include external referees contributing to the Benchmarking indicators, consultants including Sustainable Tourism

Services in Australia and PA Consulting, attendees of the Green Globe assessor training courses, and the 16-member Green Globe International Advisory Council (IAC), which comprises representatives from the travel industry, NGOs and international agencies. The full list of members is on the web site (www.greenglobe21.com/AboutUs.aspx – Management structure).

The Green Globe Company Standard

The Green Globe Company Standard (www.greenglobe21.com/AboutCompany.aspx) was established in April 2001 and subsequently updated in June 2004 and March 2007. It is the heart of the Green Globe scheme as it applies to almost any tourism-related business. It has evolved and improved through research, analysis, real experience and application. Initially it was a standard based on an ISO-style approach, involving an environmental policy and a 'tick the box' checklist. This process-based system had failings, as it could easily mean that a company achieved all requirements of the Standard, but could still be failing to achieve environmental outcomes. There needed to be a system based on real environmental achievements, a performance-based standard including critical processes such as the development of a policy and an environmental management system (EMS).

Green Globe's current standard provides tourism operations with a framework to 'benchmark' their environmental and social performance, achieve certification and continuously improve their performance. It also guides operations to achieve continual improvements in several environmental and social performance areas through the implementation of an environmental management system. The result is that the operation both improves its environmental and social performance and saves money through putting in place cost-saving practices and technologies.

The Company Standard is based on requirement criteria organized into six sections:

1. Policy.
2. Benchmarking.
3. Compliance.
4. Approach.
5. Performance.
6. Communication.

For operations (companies and communities) seeking Green Globe Benchmarking and Certification, senior management must write, adopt and promote an environmental and social sustainability policy. This policy commits the operation to making annual improvements in relevant Green Globe performance indicators (described below), as well as meeting relevant environmental legislation and regulations. It establishes a framework for regularly recording and measuring performance indicators and setting targets. It also commits the operation to giving special consideration to employment of local persons and use of local products and services. The Green Globe Company Standard provides a sustainable tourism programme that is applicable across the full spectrum of tourism activities and from which all tourism businesses, regardless of size or location, can benefit. Note that those businesses that meet the definition of 'Ecotourism' as defined in the Green Globe International Ecotourism Standard, and that choose to be certified against that Standard, are required to meet more rigorous criteria, including eight core principles (www.greenglobe21.com/AboutEcotourism.aspx). The Ecotourism Standard has a stronger emphasis on social and cultural aspects as well as requirements relating to responsible marketing, construction impacts, education and conservation.

The Company Standard's framework for Benchmarking environmental and social performance specifies that an operation will assess the significance of the positive and negative impacts of its activities, products and services in each of the key performance areas; establish targets to reduce negative and improve positive impacts; and monitor progress to ensure year-to-year improvement. Specific indicators for sectors help companies with their Benchmarking process. The Green Globe Benchmarking report is designed to ensure that operations achieve a minimum specified improvement in relevant performance areas.

The regulatory framework required under all Standards states that operations seeking Benchmarking must maintain an up-to-date register of relevant legislation, regulations and other requirements, as well as records of their compliance and, where compliance was not maintained, records of remedial action taken.

Development, implementation and maintenance of an environmental management system (EMS) are an integral part of the Standard. A senior executive in the operation seeking Benchmarking/Certification is to be responsible for the EMS's implementation, ensuring that staff receive training in the EMS. This executive should also assess the possible environmental impacts of planned, accidental and emergency situations and develop ways to mitigate negative impacts, as well as undertaking regular reviews of the EMS.

Finally, the Standard deals with stakeholder consultation and communication, stating that the operation will regularly communicate its environmental and social performance resulting from participation in Green Globe to customers and stakeholders and will determine the significance of its impacts through consultation with and feedback from stakeholders. It states that the operation should inform customers (i.e. tourists) about sensitive local customs, ways of life, natural areas and environmental issues and how best to contribute to the local economy.

The Green Globe System

The Green Globe programme is open to all travel and tourism industry sectors and sizes and types of operations, including companies and communities, which are referred to as 'operations' (this differs from the Green Globe International Ecotourism Standard, where it is only the 'products' that can be Benchmarked and Certified). Tourism operations can enter the programme at the Benchmarking level. Travel and tourism operators committing to Certification are automatically required to undertake Benchmarking. Affiliates are encouraged to move to Benchmarking or Certification after 12 months through the imposition of a significantly increased fee after the first 12 months and a requirement to prepare an environmental and social sustainability policy prior to renewal of their registration.

At each of the three levels, there is a clear protocol in place dictating the eligibility or otherwise of an operation's use of the Green Globe logo. For example, there is a distinction made between an operation's registration for Benchmarking or Certification and the successful Benchmarked or Certified status of an operation. The Green Globe logo may only be used after the successful completion of the entire certification process. A certificate is issued with a unique serial number, is year-dated and has an expiration date. To support applicants, Green Globe has developed a set of web-based materials for the three levels of the Green Globe programme.

The cost of enrolling in Green Globe ranges from US$150 for Affiliate companies up to nearly US$6000 for a community seeking Certification. Operations in any of the three levels are listed in a single 'Participants List' on the Green Globe web site.

A = Affiliates/Awareness

This is the introductory stage, which enables companies and communities to learn about Green Globe and raise their general environmental awareness. Through the requirement to develop an environmental and social sustainability policy, Affiliates are encouraged to think about their impact on the environment and what actions might be taken to reduce these impacts.

While any company or destination can remain as an Affiliate for longer than a year, Green Globe encourages them to enrol in the Benchmarking or Certification process and to take practical steps to improve their sustainability performance. Higher fees in the second year and regular reminders by Green Globe assist in the process of upgrading. Affiliates are provided with access to specific information on the Green Globe web site to assist them in moving to Benchmarking. This includes provision of case studies, green tips, product guidelines, sample policies and a Benchmarking User's Guide.

B = Benchmarking

This level is intended to measure real environmental performance of operations. Since it is applicable for operations worldwide, it provides an internationally comparable performance standard. Companies may opt either to just undertake Benchmarking or to combine it with advancing to the next level, Certification. Companies or communities that are successfully Benchmarked receive the Green Globe logo without the tick.

The programme has Benchmarking guides to assist operations in 25 different travel industry sectors, as well as for the Community, Ecotourism, Design and Construct Standards and Precinct Planning and Design Standards. Further guides are being developed for other sectors as demand dictates. These guides assist operations through the steps to achieve Benchmarking. They include key performance areas, indicators and measures specifically determined for each sector. The company guide can be applied to 25 different types of companies, ranging from accommodation and marinas to visitor centres and vineyards.

The Green Globe Community/Destination Standard provides communities with a framework to benchmark their environmental and social performance, to certify their performance and to continuously improve their performance. The Benchmarking User's Guide has been prepared to assist Communities with the process of Benchmarking and is available as part of the package of support material provided for communities that sign up for the programme.

The Green Globe International Ecotourism Standard (IES) and User's Guide were developed as a cooperative venture between Ecotourism Australia and the STCRC. The IES is based on Ecotourism Australia's EcoCertification Program, formerly known as the Nature and Ecotourism Accreditation Programme. The User's Guide is available to businesses that register one or more ecotourism products for Benchmarking.

The principal objective of the Green Globe Design and Construct Standard is to facilitate environmentally sustainable design and construction of travel and tourism infrastructure. It documents the requirements for facilitating and assessing the environmental, social and economic performance of the design. It is aimed at assisting developers to assess their performance, encourage continual improvement and improve profitability by reducing wastage and increasing eco-efficiency. The supporting handbook was designed to assist travel and tourism infrastructure developers seeking to participate in the Green Globe Design and Construct programme and undertake the Benchmarking and Certification process. The PPDS is aimed at measuring development issues and rewarding developers at the master planning stage.

Benchmarking and Certification of tourism operations

B = Benchmarking

The Benchmarking process relating to the Company Standard involves operations collecting, on an annual basis, measures of indicators for the nine key performance areas previously outlined. In addition to the core set of indicators for these key performance areas, Green Globe recommends that operations select optional indicators that are specific to their circumstances.

For instance, Kaikoura District Council in New Zealand has included an indicator relating to chemical spills as this is relevant to protecting marine life from truck accidents. Three Rivers Ecolodge in Dominica has used the proportion of renewable energy used as a percentage of total energy consumed as its optional indicator in its quest to reduce its reliance on fossil fuels. Green Globe works with operations to choose the best measures for their situation and has trained travel and tourism professionals to support this process. Operations may seek a recommendation from Green Globe as to the type of professional support required, or operations may utilize the web-based register directly.

STCRC has established an independent organization called Earthcheck, which has determined a baseline level of performance and best practice level of performance to illustrate where an operation's performance is placed within the industry. It allows comparison with industry best practice, and it allows improvements in performance to be tracked annually. The baseline is determined through a process whereby Earthcheck has developed a unique database from 240 countries containing extensive information on domestic and individual resource consumption, conservation and social activity. In large countries (the USA, Canada, Australia, France, Spain), subdivisions are introduced at a regional (e.g. state, province) level. This database provides the guidelines for the level of baseline and best practice for each country or province. Where information on a country (or province) does not currently exist, a neighbouring region with a similar geographical, climatic and economic profile is used as a proxy. Information has also been compiled on baseline and best practice for individual tourism sectors (e.g. hotels, restaurants, etc.) found in individual countries and provinces. The travel and tourism industry values are tagged to the average domestic and industrial consumption/production/activity of their region. In this way, baseline practice and best practice numbers are established for the Benchmarking indicators for each sector in each country or province. The benchmarks are available to registered Green Globe customers.

Whilst a key issue in defining environmental performance benchmarks is that they must reflect best practice to be credible, they must also be achievable by reflecting local conditions and the type of activity being certified. The benchmark for the amount of energy consumed per guest night per year, for instance, must be tailored to the climate in particular geographical areas. Similarly, benchmarks for purchasing local goods, hiring local people and using renewable energy sources will vary depending on the level of production, labour supply and skills and the availability and cost of alternative energy technologies in a particular country or region. The intention of Green Globe is not to discourage the industry by setting standards that only a few can achieve, but rather to encourage, through its services and support, widespread adoption of the principle of continuous improvements, which provide tangible benefits towards achieving a sustainable travel industry. The baseline level determined will be environmentally responsible. Green Globe provides information on its web site on the differences between an operation that has only been Benchmarked and one that has been Certified and provides premium marketing through the provision of case studies only to those businesses that have been Certified and are entitled to use the Green Globe logo with the tick.

Green Globe has recognized that greenhouse gas abatement is a major global environmental issue that transcends local and international boundaries and is particularly relevant to the tourism industry, which consumes significant amounts of fossil fuel through air travel. In response to this issue, the programme has developed high-profile international environmental performance currency to gauge and benchmark performance. Programme participants have been asked to concentrate on this area for improvement, with the major focus being reduced energy use per customer. Thus, greenhouse gas emission reductions can be measured collectively through:

- Reduction in energy use.
- Reduction in the primary consumption of raw materials.
- Reduction in the energy required for potable water transmission.
- Reduction in the use of energy required for water treatment and clean-up.
- Sequestration of carbon through habitat conservation.

This is achieved through Green Globe's current Benchmarking indicators. The Benchmarking software automatically calculates the greenhouse gas contributions in terms of the total number of CO_2 tonnes emitted annually.

The programme recognizes that the long-term solution to reducing greenhouse gas production by travel and tourism (and all other industries) is to tackle it at source by introducing more efficient, less non-renewable energy-intensive equipment and procedures. However, application of this 'cleaner production' or 'eco-efficiency' approach will take time. Additionally, many operations in the industry are already energy-efficient and/or further significant reductions in energy from fossil fuel sources may, for operational and commercial reasons, simply not be feasible.

Green Globe recognizes that an optional indicator may be carbon sequestration through habitat conservation. Under the Kyoto Protocol, the international treaty on greenhouse gas emissions, carbon sequestration has been designated as an acceptable mechanism to offset net carbon emissions. Growing forests naturally remove carbon dioxide (CO_2) from the atmosphere and convert the carbon into new tree biomass, resulting in carbon storage (sequestration) in both wood and soils. Under the Kyoto Protocol, companies can receive credit towards compliance by purchasing forests for conservation purposes. However, carbon sequestration will be credited only for trees planted after 1 January 1990.

For Green Globe participants, the issue is to evaluate the total amount of carbon dioxide generated through all the operation's activities and to offset as much as possible through purchasing land to protect natural tree growth. Involvement in carbon sequestration can be through large-scale national and international programmes, as well as by direct actions in promoting local tree-planting schemes.

C = Certification

This level requires a business to meet all aspects of the relevant Green Globe Standard. The Green Globe Company Standard was based on Agenda 21 and requires an ISO-style environmental management system. In focusing on sustainable travel and tourism, it provides strong support for the WTO's Global Code of Ethics and requires certifying companies to:

- Develop a sustainability policy.
- Benchmark environmental performance.
- Involve stakeholders.
- Be independently audited prior to certification.

Operations seeking full certification must be benchmarked above the baseline level of performance. This means that companies and communities have actually demonstrated a minimum standard of environmental performance prior to certification. When the operation considers it is ready for certification, it advises Green Globe, which in turn either provides names of accredited Green Globe assessors suitable for conducting a certification assessment or assigns the certification task to an accredited certification firm. Fees are based on a rate negotiated between the operation and the firm and are additional to the fee paid to Green Globe. Typically, an assessment of a small operation takes between 4 and 8 hours to complete. The assessor emails the completed certification assessment report to Green Globe and authorized Green Globe personnel approve (or otherwise) certification based on the advice of the assessor.

If the operation is approved, a formal certificate is presented and the operation may use the Green Globe Certification logo (with the tick). The logo must be updated and renewed each year, based on a successful environmental performance report.

Benchmarking and Certification for communities/destinations

Many communities are actively involved in and strongly affected by tourism activities and as a result are seeking recognition for their tourism management and environmental performance achievements. The Green Globe programme is encouraging the concept of certifying entire communities as sustainable tourism destinations and has launched a certification programme that specifically addresses the diverse range of issues involved in sustainable communities. Successful pilot studies were completed at Douglas and Redland Shires in Queensland, Australia, and Kaikoura in the South Island of New Zealand. There are now 11 communities throughout the world undertaking Benchmarking and Certification, including: Surf Coast Shire in Australia, Snaefellsnes in Iceland, the Bali Tourist Development Corporation in Indonesia and the Commonwealth of Dominica in the Caribbean.

Green Globe believes travel and tourism destinations are an appropriate scale for considering sustainable tourism management, planning and development. Effective planning generally occurs at the destination level, usually through local government, and new tourism products are developed within a destination's particular image and brand. Tourists choose holidays based on a destination's perceived attractions or experiences.

In keeping with the fundamental Green Globe principles, a destination will be required to demonstrate environmental performance according to the principles of Agenda 21. Upon certification, it must demonstrate continuous improvement. Beyond this, a Green Globe destination must encourage cooperation between the tourism industry, government departments, NGOs and communities at a local level. Local political, cultural and social conditions will be considered in order to create a realistic, achievable programme of action that is flexible enough to suit a location's various attributes. A key result of destination certification will be the increased involvement of the private sector in environmental action, which will, in turn, provide the opportunity for Green Globe and the destination to heighten community and consumer awareness through the destination brand.

Benchmarking and Certification for ecotourism products

The principal objectives of the Green Globe International Ecotourism Standard (IES) are: to assist operators of ecotourism products to protect and conserve natural and cultural heritage; to respect social and community values, contribute to an improved environment and improved ecotourism experiences; and to achieve better business through meeting responsible ecotourism performance standards.

The IES provides operators with a framework to benchmark their operations/ecotourism products in terms of environmental and social performance, to achieve certification and to continually improve their performance. The IES is designed around the key principles of ecotourism, which include the requirement for a natural area focus, interpretation and education, ecologically compatible infrastructure, contribution to conservation, benefiting local communities, cultural respect and sensitivity, customer satisfaction and responsible marketing.

Products that can be Benchmarked must be in the categories of accommodation, tours or attractions. The Benchmarking measures are similar to those for a Company, i.e. they need to address issues such as greenhouse gas emissions, energy and water consumption, waste and use of recycled paper and biodegradable products. As well as these measures, ecotourism products must be measured in terms of the proportion of trained customer service staff. This ensures that the operation maintains the highest standards in its day-to-day delivery of the product(s), and is made aware of the importance of its environment and the aims of ecotourism. Finally, it is vital that the operation, in benefiting from some of the world's most important natural resources, clearly demonstrates an ongoing commitment to conservation. This is measured through monetary investment and/or in-kind contribution (e.g. supply of labour or physical resources) to local conservation projects.

Benefits of Benchmarking and Certification

Many benefits of the Green Globe programme have been identified for companies and destinations involved in its environmental certification programme. First, Benchmarking and Certification facilitate a competitive advantage in an increasingly eco-conscious market. A number of studies (MORI, 1995, 1998, 1999; Travel Industry Association of America, 1997; English Tourism Council, 2002) have shown that a majority of travellers are inclined to support 'green' travel companies and pay more for the services of environmentally and socially conscious companies. Green Globe is promoting its Benchmarked and Certified companies on its web site and through media exposure, and encouraging Certified or Benchmarked companies to maximize awareness of their achievement. This is designed to help increase consumer awareness of the programme.

Secondly, the programme demonstrates improved environmental performance to the community, regulators, shareholders and employees, and to investors, who are increasingly looking for ethical standards. The certification process establishes quality performance. The Kandalama Hotel at Dambulla, Sri Lanka, for instance, was proud to be the first Green Globe Certified hotel in Asia and its on-ground environmental performance is very high. The Melia Bali Villa and Spa resort of Bali, Indonesia, has embarked on an ambitious series of actions to enhance its environmental and social performance. This resort advertises its Green Globe credentials throughout Europe and the Asia Pacific as part of its marketing campaign. Linus Bagley, former manager of the Binna Burra Lodge in Lamington National Park, Queensland, Australia, has stated that Green Globe Certification was the best step his company had taken in its overall aim to improve its environmental and social management performance. At the World Travel Market in November 2004, the Caribbean Alliance for Sustainable Tourism (CAST) released a brochure listing the 57 Certified operations and the 25 Benchmarked operations in the region, encouraging tourists planning a holiday in the Caribbean to look for the Green Globe logos. A booklet produced for promoting 'Naturally Jamaica' lists the 29 hotels and attractions that have been Green Globe Certified as examples of businesses that are committed to sustainable tourism development. The Rainforest Alliance has produced a similar catalogue, which lists all operations in the Americas that are Certified under a range of programmes (including Green Globe) and distributes this at major travel shows in Europe and the USA.

A third benefit of Benchmarking and Certification is the contribution to improvements in the efficiency of operations through the use of fewer resources. Savings are achieved through reduced energy consumption, reduced waste generation, reduced use of potable water and enhanced efficiency arising from treating such issues in an integrated, systematic manner. A recent survey of Green Globe operations in the Caribbean (CAST, 2001) found that 90% of operations saw a reduction in both water and electricity bills. In addition to these tangible savings, around two-thirds recognized increased staff motivation, almost half found that their business had received international exposure as a result of their Green Globe participation and most believed they had an effective management system in place as a result of the programme.

Fourthly, the Benchmarking and Certification process can help to improve staff commitment, increase productivity linked to clear environmental policies and programmes and improve knowledge and awareness of sustainability issues through targeted environmental training and on-the-job implementation. In addition, Green Globe offers the potential for improving relations between tourism operations and their local communities. Operations are actively encouraged to work with local communities through transparent and participatory consultation and communication activities, as well as incorporation of 'buy local' and 'employ local' strategies where feasible and appropriate.

Fifthly, the programme can be adopted by any tourism operation in any location and is available to mainstream operations as well as those already involved in ecotourism activities and thus knowledgeable about sustainable practices. The programme places environmental management within a consistent framework that can, theoretically at least, be used by any tourism business anywhere in the world to systematically monitor tourism environmental performance.

Sixthly, the programme can be especially useful in countries where tourism bodies or governments have established their own local certification programmes but seek to extend the marketing value of an international brand through an alliance with Green Globe. These alliances may also include quality assurance programmes. For example, in Australia, a cooperative arrangement between the organization that 'Star'-rates accommodation, the Australian Automobile Association (AAA Tourism), the STCRC and Green Globe, provides the mechanism for 'Green Stars' properties to be recognized as Green Globe Affiliates. This also provides a lead-in for these businesses to consider the benefits of moving to Benchmarking and Certification. In the first 6 months following the launch of the Green Stars programme, 60 properties sought a 'green' assessment, including the entire 'Sundowner' chain, with 14 properties around Australia. The Green Stars do not change the Star rating of a property but they do provide a special endorsement for achieving practical environmental standards, including energy efficiency, waste minimization and water management. The Green Stars assessment is carried out at the same time as the regular Star rating. Those successfully rated are automatically recognized as Green Globe Affiliates and provided with support material to assist them to measure energy and waste consumption. For a small additional fee, the property can request a Benchmarking report about these two measures. In this way, it is hoped that more properties will choose to advance to full Green Globe Benchmarking. Details of the Green Stars programme are on the AAA Tourism web site (www.aaatourism.com.au).

Finally, the system, as well as its flexible adaptation to various sectors, also retains its rigour. All certification organizations and environmental management organizations involved in assessing participants are required to undertake Green Globe training and to update their Green Globe qualifications every 3 years. Training systems and standards have been designed to match the requirements of the Green Globe Standards. Assessors are trained by

Green Globe and must either work for an accredited certification organization or be accredited as an individual. Independent checks of audits are conducted and Green Globe will not issue a Certification certificate unless it has been recommended by an accredited assessor. In using a network of facilitators and in operating training programmes globally, the initiatives help to build capacity for sustainable tourism. Green Globe also undertakes quality control checks of its process through spot checks of operations to ensure that the integrity of its Standard is maintained.

Future Directions

Tourism is one of the world's most rapidly growing industries, with the World Tourism Organization predicting a continued increase in numbers of around 3.6% per annum over the next 10 years. As a result, tourism can put pressure on scarce resources. Whilst governments can regulate to minimize environmental impacts from tourism development, in many parts of the world, the tourism industry needs to take responsibility for its own actions. Certification programmes such as Green Globe continue to evolve to meet the requirements of the industry for a simple and relatively low-cost system but at the same time being at the cutting edge to reflect changes in technology and consumer sentiment.

In the future the Green Globe programme aims to focus on raising general consumer awareness of the brand so that an increasingly environmentally conscious community can begin to demand that the tourism industry plays its role in minimizing environmental impacts. This is a major challenge in a world full of conflicting brands and huge marketing budgets. One strategy that Green Globe is currently implementing is the formation of strategic alliances with influential global organizations that support sustainability principles.

It also plans, with the backing of the STCRC, to develop enhanced and new products. A new set of measures specifically for ski resorts is already well advanced. It will also increase its focus on identifying communities and destinations that have a commitment to sustainable planning and the development of a sustainable tourism industry.

Finally, and perhaps most importantly, the Green Globe programme needs to continue its high level of service to its customers and ensure that they achieve maximum value for their participation in the programme. To assist in this process, it has developed a web site to help consumers identify Green Globe businesses and communities through a travel planner and potentially make online bookings.

Conclusion

Green Globe is an example of a global tourism certification programme that incorporates a suite of environmental and social performance measures that can be used extensively by the travel and tourism industry to improve environmental and social performance, and its Benchmarking and Certification levels and logos are providing a new and improved service for tourism. At a time when increasing numbers of global and regional codes for sustainable tourism and ethical tourism are being launched, Green Globe is an example of a certification programme that can assist tourism operations to achieve the highest standards of performance and is equally applicable to small companies as it is to large communities. As distinct from some other certification programmes, Green Globe, through its Benchmarking and Certification systems, ensures environmental performance accountability. Over the past 5 years, the programme has been adapted and enhanced to provide flexibility as well as rigour for an ever-changing tourism and travel industry. Many of these changes provide lessons for other certification programmes currently being implemented or developed.

References

Caribbean Alliance for Sustainable Tourism (CAST) (2001) *What Do These Hotels Have in Common?* CAST, San Juan, Puerto Rico.

Ecotourism Australia and Sustainable Tourism Cooperative Research Centre (2003) *Green Globe 21 International Ecotourism Standard.* Green Globe 21, Brisbane, Australia.

English Tourism Council (2002) *English Tourism Council Annual Survey.* English Tourism Council, UK.

Koeman, A., Worboys, G., De Lacy, T., Scott, A. and Lipman, G. (2002) In: Honey, M. (ed.) *Ecotourism and Certification – Setting Standards in Practice.* Island Press, Washington, DC.

Market and Opinion Research International (MORI) (1995) *Business and the Environment.* MORI, London.

Market and Opinion Research International (MORI) (1998) *Public Views on Travel and Environment.* MORI, London.

Market and Opinion Research International (MORI) (1999) *Business and the Environment: Attitudes and Behaviour of the General Public – Trends 1998–99.* MORI, London.

Sustainable Tourism Cooperative Research Centre (STCRC) (2003) *Green Globe 21 Community Standard for Travel and Tourism.* STCRC, Brisbane, Queensland, Australia.

Sustainable Tourism Cooperative Research Centre (STCRC) (2007) *Green Globe 21 Company Standard.* STCRC, Brisbane, Queensland, Australia.

Sustainable Tourism Cooperative Research Centre (STCRC) (2004b) *Green Globe 21 Design and Construct Standard.* STCRC, Brisbane, Queensland, Australia.

Sustainable Tourism CRC (2006) *Green Globe 21 Precinct Planning and Design Standard,* Brisbane, Queensland, Australia.

Tear Fund (2000) *Tourism – An Ethical Issue.* Market Research Report, IPSOS-RSL, Middlesex, UK.

Travel Industry Association of America (1997) *Survey Results.* Travel Industry Association of America, Washington, DC.

United Nations (1992a) *Agenda 21: The United Nations Program for Action from Rio.* United Nations, New York.

United Nations (1992b) *Proceedings of the United Nations Conference on Environment and Development – Rio Principles, Rio de Janeiro, 3–14 June 1992*. United Nations, New York.

World Travel and Tourism Council (WTTC) (1995) *Agenda 21 for the Travel and Tourism Industry: Towards Environmentally Sustainable Development*. WTTC, London.

World Wide Fund for Nature (WWF) (2000) *Tourism Certification, Synergy and WWF*. WWF, London, UK.

7 Sustainability Indicators for Ecotourism Destinations and Operations

GABOR VERECZI

United Nations World Tourism Organization, Madrid, Spain

Chapter Profile

This chapter considers the use of sustainability indicators to encourage, plan and monitor quality ecotourism for both destinations and ecotourism operations. Sustainability indicators are essential tools for the planning, management and monitoring of any tourism activities. However, application of indicators is especially important for ecotourism destinations, where tourism is often operated in a highly sensitive natural and cultural environment and which require more systematic control of environmental and socio-economic impacts.

The United Nations World Tourism Organization has been working in the field of sustainability indicators for the past decade and published a new guidebook on this topic in 2004. Based on information collected and research for this guidebook, this chapter details general consideration for the use of indicators, as well as specific applications for ecotourism destinations and operations.

Indicators can be developed for the following factors related to ecotourism destinations and operations: contribution to the conservation of the natural environment; relations with the local community, economic benefits, sociocultural impacts; information and interpretation; marketing and management of ecotourism; and safety for ecotourism activities.

Introduction – the Imperative of Sustainable Tourism

As a result of the rapid expansion of the tourism sector, traditional and emerging tourism destinations are facing increasing pressure on their natural, cultural and socio-economic environments. There is now strong recognition that uncontrolled growth in tourism aiming at short-term benefits results in significant negative impacts, harming the environment and societies and destroying the very resource on which tourism is built and thrives. On the contrary, when tourism is planned, developed and managed using

 Quality Assurance and Certification in Ecotourism (eds R. Black and A. Crabtree)

sustainable criteria, tangible benefits occur for local communities, society and the natural and cultural environments.

Host societies have become progressively aware of the problems of unsustainable tourism, and sustainability concerns are increasingly being addressed in national, regional and local tourism policies, strategies and plans. A survey conducted by WTO on the results of the International Year of Ecotourism 2002 (UN GA, 2003) demonstrates this trend, in which 94 countries reported on a wide variety of ecotourism activities linked with conservation and community development programmes, and half of the reporting countries elaborated comprehensive national or regional ecotourism policies and strategies. In addition, increasing numbers of tourists are now demanding higher environmental standards from tourism services, as well as a greater commitment of operators to local communities and economies. This trend was demonstrated, among others, in the WTO ecotourism market studies (WTO, 2002a) conducted in seven European and North American ecotourism-generating countries in 2002, through surveys with specialized tour operators and tourists.

Ecotourism activities tend to take place in highly sensitive and fragile natural and cultural environments, making it imperative that sustainability concerns are addressed adequately. According to the Quebec Declaration on Ecotourism (WTO, 2002b), ecotourism embraces the three pillars of sustainable tourism, addressing the economic, social and environmental impacts of tourism. It also embraces the following specific principles, which distinguish it from the wider concept of sustainable tourism:

- Contributes actively to the conservation of natural and cultural heritage.
- Includes local and indigenous communities in its planning, development and operation, and contributes to their well-being.
- Interprets the natural and cultural heritage of the destination to visitors.
- Lends itself better to independent travellers, as well as to organized tours for small-size groups.

To ensure that quality ecotourism is delivered it is essential that aspects of these specific principles are monitored effectively for tourism destinations in general and especially for ecotourism operations.

Sustainability Indicators in Tourism

Measuring the performance of the entire tourism sector, at the local, national or global level, or even that of particular tourism enterprises, has traditionally concentrated on its economic and financial dimensions, sometimes including its labour component. However, it is obvious that the development of tourism infrastructure and facilities, the influx of tourists and the type of activities undertaken by tourists have a much wider range of both positive and negative impacts. These may range from positive environmental effects, such as the protection and management of a natural area for tourism or the construction and operation of transport and accommodation facilities, to those of a sociocultural character, such as the cross-cultural exchanges that occur as a result of the interaction between tourists and the host population.

The current approach, therefore, is to identify and measure the entire range of impacts that tourism can have in a particular area or society, preferably in advance of any development. This is to guarantee that such development will be sustainable socially, culturally, economically and environmentally in the long run.

Decision makers thus need, and should demand, accurate information on the potential impacts of tourism development and operations on the environmental and sociocultural conditions of destinations. Furthermore, to effectively manage sustainable tourism development, decision makers also need information on the results of management actions taken to minimize negative impacts and maximize positive impacts of tourism. The essential tools for providing this information should be a set of carefully selected 'sustainability indicators' and they should be considered as fundamental building blocks for tourism planning, management and monitoring processes.

In the context of sustainable tourism development, sustainability indicators are information sets that are formally selected for regular use to measure changes in assets and issues that are key for the development and management of a given destination. Indicators are measures that are expressed in single numbers, percentages or ratios, qualitative descriptions or the existence/non-existence of certain elements concerning environmental, social and economic issues. They are signals of current issues, emerging situations or problems, the need or otherwise for action and the results of such actions.

Good sustainability indicators must be easy to understand, as well as economically and technically feasible to measure. Some of the benefits that are incurred from good indicators include:

- Clarification of sustainability issues and improved communication for stakeholder groups.
- Better decision making, which may lower risks and/or costs.
- Identification of emerging risks and/or conflict, thus allowing proactive mitigative actions (prevention).
- Identification of impacts, to allow for rapid corrective action.
- Performance measurement of the implementation of development plans and management actions, e.g. evaluating progress in the sustainable development of tourism.
- Reduced risk of planning mistakes, thus identifying limits and opportunities.
- Greater public accountability, e.g. providing credible information for the public and other tourism stakeholders that fosters trust.
- Constant monitoring can lead to continuous improvement.

An example of how indicators can help clarify issues, improve communication with stakeholders and provide greater public accountability is illustrated using the case study of Villa Gesell in Argentina (see Box 7.1).

Box 7.1. Indicators on the level of community participation in Villa Gesell, Argentina (from WTO, 2001a).

Villa Gesell is a small beach municipality in Argentina, with attractive coastal ecosystems. The destination served as a pilot study and host for a WTO regional workshop on sustainable tourism indicators in 2001, involving local stakeholder groups. In one of the workshop sessions a debate arose on the level of participation of the local community in tourism planning, and whether the local government made sufficient efforts to facilitate it. The opinions were largely divided, and for some participants the process was ample, while for others it was very limited. The situation was clarified when the representative of the Municipality of Villa Gesell presented the facts:

> The objective of the Municipal Government was to gain the opinion of at least 1500 residents about the strategic plan, in order to approve it. We did not achieve this desired participation level, but we obtained the opinion of about 800 persons during the three public forums organized and through the Internet. We made the plan accessible on the municipal web site for comments.

Well-defined indicators on the level of community participation in planning and management processes allow both evaluation of the efficiency of the process and demonstration of credibility to the community itself and the efforts made to gain consensus on local issues.

There are many different types of indicators, each with different uses for decision makers:

- Early warning indicators (e.g. decline in numbers of tourists who intend to return).
- Indicators of stresses on the system (e.g. water shortages or crime indices).
- Measures of the current state of the industry (e.g. occupancy rate, level of tourists' satisfaction).
- Measures of the impact of tourism development on the biophysical and socio-economic environments (e.g. indices of the level of deforestation, changes of consumption patterns and income levels in local communities).
- Measures of management efforts (e.g. clean-up cost of coastal contamination).
- Measures of management effect, results or performance (e.g. changed pollution levels, greater number of returning tourists).

These types of indicators can be expressed and portrayed in different ways, depending on a number of factors, such as the method of data and information gathering, the means of calculation, adequacy of the policy or sustainability issues in question and the technical capacities of managers to process the information, as well as the level of understanding of users. Indicators utilize either quantitative or qualitative measurements.

Quantitative measurements

- Raw data (e.g. number of tourists visiting a site/year/month, or volume of waste generated/month/week expressed in tonnes).
- Ratios, where one data set is related to another showing a relationship (e.g. the ratio of the number of tourists to local residents in the high season, showing whether tourists outnumber locals, and if so by how much).
- Percentage, where data are related to a total, a benchmark or an earlier measure (e.g. per cent of waste water receiving treatment, per cent of local population with educational degrees of different levels, per cent change in tourist arrivals and expenditures over last year).

Qualitative/normative measurements

- Category indices – which describe a state or level of attainment on a graded list (e.g. level of protection of natural areas according to the IUCN Index, grades in the scales of environmental certification systems).
- Normative indicators – related to the existence of certain elements of tourism management and operation (e.g. existence of a tourism development plan or a plan with tourism components at local, regional and national levels, questionnaires evaluating certification systems, for example, the existence of beach clean-up programmes, beach zoning, first-aid booths, pet control, etc.).
- Nominal indicators, which are in essence labels (e.g. existence/application of certification systems, which are normally based on a complex set of criteria and checklist, but, if the certified status is awarded to companies that comply with criteria, the label appears to users as a single nominal Yes/No indicator).
- Opinion-based indicators (e.g. level of tourists' satisfaction or level of satisfaction of local residents relative to tourism or specific elements). These measurements are normally based on questionnaires and may be expressed as numbers or percentages as above – where essentially qualitative data are quantified.

The level of understanding and monitoring skills of indicator users can influence the types of indicators applied in small communities, which might have limited capacities for measuring and using sophisticated indicators. An example of the capacity of communities to develop and apply indicators is illusrated in Box 7.2.

A Suggested Procedure for Indicator Development in Tourism Destinations

Indicators can be applied at different levels of tourism planning and management, from international and national levels to local destinations, and

Box 7.2. Gradual development of monitoring capacities: advancing towards more precise indicators (from WTO, 2004: Case study 6.13 India: Community Based Tourism in Corbett National Park Using Appreciative Participatory Planning and Action (APPA) Methodology).

A community-based tourism project in villages surrounding the Corbett National Park in India demonstrated that indicators were of great use to specify product development objectives and enhance the communities' understanding of tourism issues. In the initial stages of the project, communities were more comfortable with descriptive and qualitative indicators and with relative exercises, such as ranking, rather than using quantitative indicators. During the initial diagnosis and trend analysis the variation in levels of tourist arrivals or numbers of vehicles could be portrayed with ease, but the specification of exact numbers was more difficult as recording arrivals and movements required tools, time and resources. Capacities have been developed gradually to set more exact targets, maintain records and carry out participatory evaluation with more precise, quantifiable indicators to monitor tourism's impacts and performance. The following performance indicators were used for the project evaluation:

- Number of beneficiaries.
- Increase in earning and profit.
- Incentives for community-based tourism.
- Number of repeat visitors.
- Number of products for sale.
- Number of villagers trained.
- Number and extent of new skills acquired.
- Increase in awareness.
- Relations between community members.

down to specific tourist attractions and sites and individual tourism establishments or businesses. The information at the different levels is closely interrelated and the indicators feed into each other, as demonstrated in Box 7. 3.

At each tourism destination certain data and information exist that can serve as indicators if their relevance to sustainability issues is understood. The most commonly used and perhaps best understood indicators are economic factors, such as tourism revenues and expenditures, or baseline data and statistics, such as tourist arrivals, bed nights spent and accommodation capacities. Whilst these figures are conventionally used to measure the success of the tourism industry, they are also essential information to a number of different sustainability issues, and are often integrated into effective indicators. For instance, any information on tourist numbers is of use when trying to assess the levels of stress on a resource. For example, some of the environmental issues, such as water supply or waste, or social issues related to host communities can only be effectively understood when linked to tourist numbers, such as the water consumption per tourist or per room or the amount of waste produced by tourists in the peak season.

Box 7.3. A hierarchy of indicators: applications at different levels (from WTO, 2004: Indicators pilot study 1995, summarized in Manning *et al.*, 1997).

Indicators at many different scales are potentially relevant to the management of tourism in a destination. Here is one example with reference to Prince Edward Island (PEI) National Park and its peripheral community in the Atlantic region of Canada.

National:	per cent of visitors to Canada who visit PEI National Park.
Regional:	per cent of visitors to the Atlantic region who visit PEI National Park.
Local destination:	per cent of visitors to the Park region who stay overnight.
Site:	maximum number of visitors to the beach area on peak day.
Establishment:	per cent occupancy of accommodation in Park region.

Note that specific indicators when aggregated may be of use to higher-order jurisdictions to measure collective results (such as average occupancy at the regional level).

At the outset, it should to be recognized that different destinations have varying levels of tourism planning and regulation processes. In destinations where a tourism strategy and planning process are already in place, focusing on sustainability indicators can help improve data collection and potential sources, analysing and reporting processes, whereas, in destinations where a formal planning process has not been established, the indicators development procedure can be a catalyst. The procedure recommended in the WTO Guidebook (WTO, 2004) therefore contains some basic elements of tourism planning, specializing on indicators evaluation to select the most relevant and feasible ones. The main elements of this procedure are illustrated in Fig. 7.1.

The main criteria for selecting sustainability indicators in tourism are:

- **Relevance** of the indicator to the selected issue.
- **Feasibility** of obtaining and analysing the needed information.
- **Credibility** of the information and reliability for users of the data.
- **Clarity** and understandability to users.
- **Comparability** over time or between destinations or tourism operations.

However, the lack of users' technical capacities or cost implications often make it unfeasible to apply the desired indicator. While providing the necessary technical capacities and funds for the use of an indicator can be a development objective itself, it is important to use alternative or approximate measures in the meantime, to obtain at least some indications on the importance of the issue, even if it means limited accuracy. For example, the most precise way of evaluating the quality of potable water is through laboratory analysis. However, in remote parts of countries like Costa Rica, laboratory analysis is impossible due to the lack of such facilities and trained personnel. Prior to the government establishing these types of facilities, approximate indicators such as the frequency of illnesses registered in clinics caused by poor drinking water were used.

Research and Organization

A. Definition/delineation of the destination

B. Use of participatory processes

C. Identification of tourism assets and risks; situation analysis

D. Long-term vision for a destination

Indicators Development

1. Selection of priority issues and policy questions
2. Identification of desired indicators
3. Inventory of data sources
4. Indicators selection

Implementation of indicators

1. Evaluation of feasibility/implementation procedures
2. Data collection and analysis
3. Accountability and communication
4. Monitoring and evaluation of results

Fig. 7.1. Recommended procedure for indicators development (WTO, 2004).

Indicators in Policy-making and Certification Processes

Indicators are useful at the different stages of policy-making and planning processes, as well as tourism business management processes. For example, for delineating a tourism destination, or defining the scope of a tourism operation to monitor, managers have to consider existing data and information boundaries that will support indicators. In the initial diagnosis of a planning process, indicators provide information on actual conditions, then for the formulation of clear objectives and action plans and finally in the subsequent monitoring of impacts and advances. Throughout this process indicators can serve as communication tools, allowing a common understanding amongst stakeholders and greater accountability. Indicators may also serve to verify compliance with regulations, and their comprehensive application can allow benchmarking and comparison between tourism destinations and operations.

Indicators can form the basis of any quality assurance system or sustainability certification programme, considering that certification criteria are usually evaluated through indicators as part of the verification process. The World Tourism Organization has been actively involved in the field of voluntary initiatives and certification systems, recognizing them as important tools and self-regulatory mechanisms for sustainable tourism since the UN Commission on Sustainable Development meeting in 1999. After publishing the results of a comprehensive analysis of 104 voluntary initiatives (WTO, 2002c), WTO organized a series of regional conferences (WTO, 2003a, b, c) on sustainability certification, and produced a set of recommendations for governments (WTO, 2003d) on this issue.

The voluntary application of indicators by ecotourism operations, for regular monitoring and reporting purposes, can allow for more flexible adaptive management as an alternative to stringent regulation. Indicators can be used to reduce the conventional regulatory approach to managing issues and risk, permitting a more flexible and responsive management. Often ecotourism in sensitive areas presents risks of potential impacts that can create concerns among planners, conservationists or local communities. The response of regulating use (anticipate and prevent damage by zoning or limits to uses) may not always be needed and may reduce the benefits that the initiative was seeking to create. If there are robust and established indicators that are used to monitor areas of concern, this can delay, and even replace, the need for creating such regulation. Monitoring the areas most at risk and incorporating adaptive management measures to respond to monitoring, permit timely action if a problem begins to be detected. An example of this approach is described in Box 7.4.

Measuring Sustainability of Ecotourism Destinations and Operations

The Quebec Declaration on Ecotourism recommends, among other things, that integral and regular monitoring of ecotourism activities should be conducted. There was also a call for development of appropriate and relevant indicators for use by managers in governments and to monitor the effectiveness of sustainability certification programmes.

The most relevant indicators for ecotourism focus around measures that link to the principles of ecotourism, such as conservation of the natural and cultural environment, returns to local communities, the sociocultural impacts,

Box 7.4. Adaptive management through monitoring and reporting on environmental and social impacts (from WTO, 2004: Case study 6.21 Sydney Quarantine Station (Australia): Applying the Tourism Optimization Management Model (TOMM)).

The North Head Quarantine Station is a site of natural and historic significance, within the Sydney Harbour National Park, Australia. In 2000 the state government decided that the best way of securing the future of the site would be to lease it to a tourism operator, who would introduce a range of complementary economic uses. However, it was also deemed necessary for the operator to address some conservation and management concerns, many of which had been raised by the local community. These latter requirements were to be formulated as conditions of the planning permission and lease criteria; however, it became clear that the costs and limitations they would impose would render the project unviable.

An alternative adaptive management solution was adopted, dependent on a process of regular auditing and reporting. This involved constant, systematic monitoring, against agreed indicators of a range of social and environmental impacts, to check that agreed optimal conditions were being met. If impacts were found to be greater than the indicators, established management responses would come into force. For example, if the indicator was regular counting of bird breeding sites and this showed a decrease over time, then measures would be implemented to reduce noise, lighting and visitor movements. This model approach involves an annual environmental management report on the condition of the site and the sustainability of the operation.

Further information: http://www.q-station.com.au

or environmental management of ecotourism operations, as discussed in the following sections.

Conservation of the natural environment at ecotourism destinations and areas

The fact that ecotourism normally occurs in relatively undisturbed natural areas, which are particularly vulnerable to negative impacts by tourism activity, suggests that precautions need to be taken to manage tourism. Specially selected indicators can be used as effective management and monitoring tools for protected and other natural areas. Specific factors that would be of relevance here for indicator application include the following:

- Extent of protected area(s) – square km (classified by level of protection, according to IUCN categories).
- Biodiversity index of flora and fauna.
- Health of population of key species (counts, sightings).
- Tourism contribution to the maintenance of natural and ecotourism areas (e.g. revenue generated from entrance and concession fees, sales of products and services, donations and in-kind contributions).

- Tourism management capacity of the protected area or ecotourism site (staff assigned for the maintenance of tourism infrastructure and services, annual expenditure on management and control).
- Tourism infrastructure and its impact (e.g. extent of trail system, erosion in trails, accommodation capacity, transportation services and noise caused by them, vehicular congestion, visual impacts).
- Use levels (visitor numbers at specific sites).
- Existence of tourism management plan (e.g. designation and regulation of tourism use zones).

Relations with the local community, economic benefits, sociocultural impacts

An important part of ecotourism activities is experiencing the traditional lifestyles of communities living in natural areas. These small, traditional, often indigenous, communities are highly sensitive to the sociocultural impacts of tourism. As is mentioned in other chapters in this volume (see Chapters 12, 13, 14), the active participation and agreement of local communities in the management of ecotourism on a continuing basis are fundamental. The participation of communities in the defining indicators and monitoring processes is essential as tourism affects their daily lives and they are in the best position to evaluate impacts and decide the level of ecotourism activities that meets their expectations.

It is interesting to note, and no doubt obvious from other chapters in this volume, that criteria and indicators in certification systems currently largely focus on environmental impacts. This may be a function of the fact that environmental impacts are more tangible and easier to measure, but, in light of the fact that in ecotourism the sociocultural impacts can be significant, they also need to be effectively monitored. Most sociocultural and economic impacts on host communities are difficult to measure and tend to be relatively subjective. However, some examples of indicators for local community participation and benefits that might be considered are:

- Per cent of local products and services consumed by tourism.
- Employment of local residents in site management and tourism operations (numbers, income levels).
- Level of satisfaction of residents regarding tourism development in the area – particularly regarding natural systems.
- Level of assistance to local environmental awareness: number of local awareness-raising actions (courses, meetings, promotion of content in the curriculum of the local educational system).
- Existence of a participatory planning process in the community (frequency of community meetings and attendance rates).
- Level of collaboration between protected area authorities and local communities (number of forums, existence of joint committees).
- Alternative tourism programmes promoted or organized for communities adjacent to national parks, protected areas and other ecotourism

destinations (number and capacity, participation, tourist satisfaction with programmes).

- Access by locals to key sites (per cent of site freely accessible to public).

Measuring the economic impacts and benefits of tourism in communities can be a difficult task because of the sensitive sociocultural aspects, as demonstrated in the case study in Box 7.5.

Examples of indicators on sociocultural impacts of tourism can include:

- Ratio of tourists to locals (average and peak day).
- Per cent of residents changing from traditional occupations to tourism over previous year(s): men and women.
- Number or per cent of residents continuing with local dress, customs, language, music, cuisine, religion and cultural practices (e.g. change in number of local residents participating in traditional events).
- Increase/decrease in cultural activities or traditional events (e.g. per cent of locals attending traditional ceremonies).
- Residents' perception of impact on the community using a questionnaire.

Monitoring the quality of information and interpretation services provided for tourists is important for the success of ecotourism operations, as the knowledge on nature or culture gained by visitors through tours is a key value-added factor and distinguishes genuine ecotourism programmes. Professional interpretation services (e.g. guides, interpretation centres and trails) are essential parts of a quality ecotourism experience and contribute to nature conservation through awareness-raising. Poor information can lead to negative impacts on destinations, and poor interpretation can result in client dissatisfaction. Measuring the quality of information and interpretation services can be undertaken, for example, through feedback gained via guides,

Box 7.5. The challenge of monitoring household earnings resulting from ecotourism activities (from WTO, 2001b).

Monitoring of household earnings in rural communities can be difficult, as surveying direct indicators can be intrusive. Community members, especially women, are often reluctant to report their earnings because if they reveal their tourism earnings they often lose their control over these family resources. Other, indirect indicators that are in the public domain can be more suitable such as the number of bicycles, better housing and ability to send children to school.

Another option is to measure household income and other community indicators from the demand side. Surveys of tourist expenditure can reveal a great deal about community benefits without having to investigate household earnings in rural communities. It is possible to discover from tourists what they have been spending and where, and from this information to make good estimates of the amount of money flowing into local communities from tourism. Similarly, it is a relatively easy matter to identify from the tourism industry the amount of money that is being spent in the local community.

evaluation surveys on interpretive services, or more structured surveys of tourists' satisfaction. Interpretation activities can also be combined with monitoring flora and fauna to assist protected area managers in tracking populations of key species, as well as providing tourists with an opportunity to participate in conservation activities, for example, as in the Argentinian case study provided in Box 7.6.

To provide the expected benefits to conservation and community development, ecotourism has to be an economically viable activity; therefore evaluation of marketing activities is also important. A good knowledge of the ecotourism market (demand and offer) and evaluation of the effectiveness of marketing and promotion activites are also factors contributing to sustainability.

Ecotourism activities are often delivered in remote natural areas with specific conditions (e.g. rainforests, deserts, mountains) and involve physical activities (such as trekking, canoeing), necessitating the monitoring of safety of ecotourism activities. According to a study of factors central to sustainable ecotourism (Bassotti, 2003), safety of the activity is ranked second in importance by clients, after the protection of the environment. Indicators that respond to safety and security of ecotourism destinations and operations are therefore important.

Monitoring ecotourism operations

Ecotourism operations are usually expected to minimize negative impacts on the natural and sociocultural environment, and contribute to the conservation of natural areas. For this reason, activities are increasingly, but not exclusively, being organized by specialist tour operators for small groups. The level of sustainability depends on the operating practices and on the quality of the offered service. Indicators can help measure the achievement of an operator's own standards of operation, or benchmarked standards (as in a certification systems), and can assist in achieving control of impacts.

Box 7.6. Involving tourists and guides in data gathering (from WTO, 2004).

In Argentina, the Iguazu Natural Forest Reserve diversified its economic base to include the development of ecotourism. To assist with conservation and to plan the interpretive component of the tourist experience, more information was needed on the location and visibility of different animal species. Local tour guides and tourists were involved in the process themselves by receiving appropriate training and recording sightings on forms.

Although not scientifically rigorous, the process provided a picture of wildlife movement and changes in visitor perceptions over time. Involvement of local guides in the process increased the local community's knowledge and appreciation of the value and importance of fauna, ecologically and economically, and also added value to the visitors' experience.

Indicators relevant to operations can refer to all the above-mentioned areas, such as:

- Use and management of natural resources (existence of environmental management company policies, management of water, energy, waste, building materials).
- Contribution to nature conservation (in kind and cash contribution to the maintenance of natural areas, through paying concession and entrance fees to authorities managing those areas).
- Economic and social benefits provided for local communities (employment, use of locally produced supply, community outreach programmes).
- Quality of information and environmental interpretation provided for tourists, compliance with safety standards (preparedness, cases of incidents).

Conclusion

In many ways, ecotourism is a microcosm of all the issues of sustainable tourism, but focused in a more concentrated way on specific ecosystems and traditional cultures. Each ecotourism destination, site and operation has its own specific environmental, sociocultural and economic characteristics that require the definition of specific indicators to monitor impacts. In summary, responsible decision making has to be based on reliable information so that tourism managers can work with well-defined indicators. Besides supporting tourism planning and monitoring processes, indicators are also important tools of communication. Even at a local destination level, the complexity of stakeholder and interest groups cannot be overestimated, and all these groups need to understand the implications of tourism development and tourist activities. Indicators can provide them with the necessary information that supports their active involvement and commitment towards an urgent and unavoidable responsibility of public and private tourism managers to achieve a more sustainable tourism sector and to contribute more strongly to sustainable development.

Endnote: the World Tourism Organization's Indicators Initiative

Since 1992 WTO has been active in the effort to develop and implement indicators that help in the sustainable development of tourism at different destinations. A wide range of activities have been undertaken, including pilot studies, the publication of an initial indicators guide in 1996, and a series of regional workshops for capacity building. Based on a comprehensive year-long review of international experiences and with the involvement of around 60 experts, WTO has recently published a revised Guidebook on Indicators of Sustainable Development for Tourism Destinations (WTO, 2004). This new guidebook describes over 40 major sustainability issues, ranging from the management of natural resources (waste, water, energy), to development control, satisfaction of tourists and host communities, preservation of cultural heritage, seasonality, economic leakages and climate change. For each issue, indicators and measurement techniques are suggested, with practical information sources and examples. The publication also contains a procedure to develop destination-specific indicators and their use in tourism policy and planning processes, as well as applications in different destination types (e.g. coastal, urban, ecotourism, small communities). Numerous examples and 25 comprehensive case studies provide a wide range of experiences at the company, destination, national and regional levels from all continents.

References

Bassotti, G. (2003) Factores de calidad en ecoturismo, una visión práctica para su aplicación. *Estudios y Perspectivas en Turismo* (CIET, Buenos Aires) 12(1 and 2), 7–24.

Manning, T., Clifford, G., Dougherty, D. and Ernst, M. (1997) *What Tourism Managers Need to know: A Practical Guide to the Development and Use of Indicators of Sustainable Tourism.* WTO, Madrid.

United Nations General Assembly (UN GA) (2003) *Report Prepared by WTO: Outcomes of the International Year of Ecotourism 2002.* UN, Geneva.

WTO (2001a) *Final Report, Regional Workshop for South America on Sustainable Tourism Indicators, Villa Gesell, Argentina.* WTO, Madrid.

WTO (2001b) *Final Report of the Seminar on Planning, Development and Management of Ecotourism in Africa (Maputo, Mozambique, 5–6 March 2001).* WTO, Madrid. Available at: http://www.world-tourism.org/sustainable/IYE-Main-Menu.htm (see section on 'Events' and 'WTO Regional Ecotourism Conferences and Seminars').

WTO (2002a) *Ecotourism Market Study Series (Germany, Italy, France, United Kingdom, Spain, USA, Canada).* WTO, Madrid.

WTO (2002b) Quebec Declaration on Ecotourism. In: *Final Report of the World Ecotourism Summit (2002, Quebec City, Canada).* WTO, Madrid. Available at: http://www.world-tourism.org/sustainable/IYE/quebec/index.htm

WTO (2002c) *Voluntary Initiatives in Tourism: Worldwide Inventory and Comparative Analysis of 104 Eco-labels, Awards and Self-commitments.* WTO, Madrid.

WTO (2003a) *Final Report, WTO Regional Conference for the Americas on Sustainability Certification of Tourism Activities (Sauípe, Bahía, Brazil, 29–30 September 2003).* WTO, Madrid. Available at: http://www.world-tourism.org/sustainable/conf/cert-brasil/esp.htm

WTO (2003b) *Final Report, WTO Asia–Pacific Conference on Sustainability Certification of Tourism Activities (Kuala Lumpur, Malaysia, 11–13 December 2003).* WTO, Madrid. Available at: http://www.world-tourism.org/sustainable/conf/cert-malaysia/finalrep.htm

WTO (2003c) *Final Report, WTO Regional Conference for Europe on Public Private Partnerships for Sustainability Certification of Tourism Activities (Mariánské Lázne, Czech Republic, 17–20 October 2004).* WTO, Madrid. Available at: http://www.world-tourism.org/sustainable/conf/cert-czech/fin-rep.htm

WTO (2003d) *WTO Recommendations to Governments for Supporting and/or Establishing National Certification Systems for Sustainable Tourism.* WTO, Madrid. Available at: http://www.world-tourism.org/sustainable/doc/certification-gov-recomm.pdf

WTO (2004) *Indicators of Sustainable Development for Tourism Destinations – A Guidebook.* WTO, Madrid.

8 Adapting the Indicator Approach – Practical Applications in the South Pacific

Louise Twining-Ward

New York University, New York, USA

Chapter Profile

Monitoring using indicators is central to sustainable development policy and development and an integral component in many quality assurance and certification programmes. It provides the opportunity to assess the effectiveness of new policies and actions, identify the most successful and appropriate ones, and draw attention to problem areas so that appropriate management responses can be taken. However, current understanding of sustainable tourism indicators is still relatively weak and there are as yet few examples of successful long-term sustainable tourism monitoring programmes in practice. In view of new and alarming evidence of global change, there is a need to take stock of current indicator approaches and see how they can be adapted and refined in line with what is now known about the behaviour of tourism ecosystems, as well as the need to provide quality supply- and demand-side tourism experiences.

This chapter looks at the rationale for monitoring based on new ecosystem knowledge. Following a discussion of the different approaches to sustainable tourism indicators and monitoring, the case of the Samoa Sustainable Tourism Indicator Project is explained. This example demonstrates how an 'adaptive indicator approach' can work in practice, helping not only to develop sustainable tourism indicators but also to create more integrated and whole-systems approaches to monitoring. The implications of these findings for other quality assurance tools are then considered, using examples from projects recently developed for the South Pacific Tourism Organization.

Introduction

There is significant and increasing evidence to show that, over the last 50 years, humans have interacted with and altered the environment more than any other time during history in order to meet growing demands for food, fresh water, fuel and economic activities such as tourism (WGBU, 1997; NRC, 1999; GECP, 2001; Wilson, 2002; Reid *et al.*, 2005). There have undeniably been substantial net gains in human well-being and economic development over this period, but at growing costs in terms of ecosystem resilience (the ability of an ecosystem to recover following a crisis) and indigenous lifestyles. Changes and events that used to be of local significance such as civil unrest, economic downturn, hurricanes and forest fires, now often have global implications. It is in the context of the increased frequency and global relevance of ecosystem change that monitoring using sustainability indicators has become increasingly relevant.

Another reason for an increased focus on indicators and monitoring is improved understanding of the way in which ecosystems function. Ecosystems were formerly conceived as simple, stable systems which, if undisturbed by humans, would eventually reach an equilibrium state. However, now there is increasing evidence that most, if not all, ecosystems exhibit complex system behaviour. That is, 'they are more than the sum of their parts, they are structured in layers from the bottom up and have the ability to self-organise, change in form, co-operate or compete, resulting in multiple system changes of an unpredictable nature' (Miller and Twining-Ward, 2005).

Indicators are tools used to assess change in established variables on a regular basis and are essential to help us understand the changes that are taking place and react to them. The information provided by indicators can help managers to assess their actions and adapt and refine them as necessary. However, to date, most work in this area has been based on reductionist, linear views of tourism associated with identifying 'tourism impacts' and focused specifically on economic, environmental, social and cultural areas with very little crossover. If unrefined, this approach may lead to important omissions in our understanding of how tourism ecosystems work and crucial mistakes in our planning and management of tourism.

The third reason for the focus on indicators and monitoring is their relevance to quality assurance and certification. Quality is becoming an essential ingredient in many sustainable tourism programmes, recognizing that if customers are not satisfied it does not matter how much the business is environmentally, or socioculturally sustainable, it will not survive economically. The assessment of quality through certification mechanisms involves ongoing monitoring, improvements and re-monitoring. Indicators have therefore become part and parcel of nearly all quality assurance programmes and are likely to play an increasingly important role in the management and evaluation of ecotourism in the future.

This chapter starts by reviewing in more detail the rationale for the use of indicators and monitoring in the context of global change and revised approaches to the study of ecosystems, as well as their value to quality assurance systems. The issue of the design and management of sustainable tourism indicators is then examined. It is argued that in order to reach their full potential indicators need to be more reflective of the complex systems they are designed to monitor. That is, they should be trans-disciplinary, incorporate local knowledge and critical issues where possible, and be part of an integrated management response system that ensures that indicators lead to improved action. Following examples from the work of WTO and the Tourism Optimization Management Model (TOMM) in Australia, a case study of the development of a sustainable tourism indicator system in Samoa is presented in order to highlight how an adaptive indicator approach can work in practice. The commentary section of the chapter reviews the implications of these findings for other quality assurance tools such as tourism accreditation systems, and suggests how these can be enhanced by whole-systems analysis.

Rationale for New Approaches to Indicators and Monitoring

If indicators and monitoring systems are going to be useful to us in terms of contributing towards greater sustainability and higher quality in ecotourism, their design, monitoring and management need to reflect the way in which ecosystems function. This section looks at the rationale for approaching indicators and monitoring in a more integrated and whole-systems manner.

New ecosystem knowledge

Old-school ecology, based on the works of such scientists as Clements (1916), predicted that all ecosystems, if undisturbed by humans, would eventually reach a balanced self-perpetuating state of equilibrium. It was therefore the 'negative impacts' of humans on the ecosystem that needed to be addressed and where possible reversed, a concept that has become ingrained in tourism management and planning for decades. New ecology, led by scientists such as C.S. Holling, suggests that orthodox approaches to human–nature interactions, whilst not inherently wrong, provide only a partial explanation of ecosystem functions (Gunderson *et al.*, 1995). Holling (1978, 1986, 2001) found that periods of ecosystem stability were often interspersed with sudden, chance events, now called 'surprises', where human expectations in no way match reality. For example, he found that estimates of fish or wildlife population seldom ever conformed to real-life fluctuations, weather reports were consistently wrong and ecosystems seemed to regenerate haphazardly after a disturbance such as a volcanic eruption rather than returning to the previous stable state. These are now understood as characteristics of complex adaptive systems (CAS). CAS are more than the sum of their parts; they behave in a non-linear fashion (inputs are not always equal to outputs in time or space) and are characterized by 'surprise' behaviour when results differ qualitatively from expectations or when action produces a result the opposite of that which is intended (Holling, 1978, 1986, 2001; Farrell and Twining-Ward, 2004).

This cutting-edge work in ecology is now supported by innovative research in the field of global change science, which examines the changes in the earth system in relation to human–environment interaction (IGBP, 2001; Steffen *et al.*, 2004). The realization that human-induced change, such as acid rain and emission of greenhouse gases, and disasters, like Bhopal and Chernobyl, have transnational consequences has triggered the need to better understand human–nature interactions (Kates *et al.*, 2001). This has been given additional urgency with new evidence that non-linear changes in the earth system are the norm, not the exception (Steffen *et al.*, 2004) and are inherent characteristics of a CAS.

In a world of complex systems, monitoring is obviously a crucial tool for managers at all levels, enabling them to keep on top of change and react to it in a positive manner and before critical thresholds are reached. Box 8.1 provides an example of how monitoring using indicators has become crucial in the context of global change.

Another implication of this new knowledge for the current debate is in the design of indicators and monitoring systems. Even a superficial understanding of ecosystems drives home the need for whole-systems approaches to the development of indicators that appreciate the interconnectivity between social systems and ecosystem services, incorporate ongoing mechanisms for

Box 8.1. Monitoring the ozone hole (adapted from Steffen *et al.*, 2004: 14, 15, 19).

The most well-known abrupt change in the behaviour of the earth system that has already occurred is the formation of the ozone hole over Antarctica. The ozone hole was the unexpected result of the release of synthetic chemicals, chlorofluorocarbons (CFCs), used in aerosols and refrigerants (which were thought at the time to be environmentally harmless). Together with a number of other conditions, the provision of excess chlorine in the atmosphere from the CFCs triggered the abrupt change in the chemistry of the lower stratosphere and led to the formation of the ozone hole.

However, had it not been for close monitoring, the situation could well have become much more serious and widespread before it was noticed. Scientists with the British Antarctic Survey had routinely and consistently monitored the column of ozone concentration over Antarctic since the 1950s and thus observed the unexpected loss of the ozone in the southern high latitudes before the hole reached catastrophic proportions.

The global response to the ozone hole via the Montreal Protocol, which banned the use of ozone-deleting substances in 1987, was fast and effective. The quick response involved public perception that this environmental change was harmful to human health, scientific agreement on the agent and cause of the change and a technological solution (chemical substitutes) that did not require a change in societal behaviour. In this case, societal response was apparently sufficient to reverse the changes under way in the ozone layer. Other kinds of potential abrupt changes, however, may prove less amenable to such rapid and effective response, given the need for all three of the conditions above to be met.

review and improvement and processes to ensure that improved information leads to improved action.

Ecotourism and Sustainability

Over time, ecotourism, because of its reliance on the quality of the environment, has become one of the leading forces behind the movement towards greater sustainability across the tourism industry. As well as the leading lights, however, there have also been examples of 'greenwashing' and the use of ecotourism as little but marketing hype (Wheeller, 1994; Wight, 1995). In order to highlight bona fide ecotourism suppliers, improve the general standard of ecotourism products and protect vulnerable resources from deterioration associated with overuse, many types of quality assurance tools have been developed, including certification, accreditation, codes of conduct, triple- and quadruple-line reporting, along with other corporate social responsibility mechanisms. In virtually all of these processes (with the exception perhaps of codes of conduct) some sort of monitoring using indicators is an integral component.

Indicators enable ecotourism companies, tourism offices and NGOs to track their progress against defined targets or goals. When used on a local or regional basis, they can also provide a helpful source of comparison between different operations and enterprises and an inspiration for further management efforts in particular areas, such as community benefits or water conservation. The provision of information also improves transparency and demonstrates progress and professionalism. It enables firms to be on top of change taking place in the environment and adapt to it before it impacts the bottom line. Indicators provide information to help guide quality assurance programmes, helping to create linkages between seemingly remote global problems and day-to-day actions (Miller and Twining-Ward, 2005). MacGillivray (1997: 261) writes, 'The underlying assumption is that, given adequate information and the associations in which to do so, healthy, wealthy and wise citizens can participate in sustainable development'.

Despite their useful contribution in many fields, if indicators are to have any long-term practical value they also need to be able to influence policy. It is in this area that the contribution of indicators has yet to be fully explored. A 30-month study by PASTILLE (2002: 45) of four European cities concluded that 'sustainability indicators do not currently have much impact on decision making at municipal level'. Further, the New Economics Foundation (NEF, 2001) found, in its UK study, that 61% of all local authorities surveyed were using indicators of sustainability, but there was little evidence to support the thesis of indicators having led directly to a change in policy. Indeed, of the five benefits identified by NEF, their survey showed that indicators were helping to improve understanding about sustainability, were serving to track changes and were promoting partnership, but not having a direct effect on policy. The report notes that many managers appreciate the significance of the indicators but see the programmes as marginal, lacking buy-in from stakeholders and consequently unconnected with policy making (Miller and Twining-Ward, 2005).

Current Approaches to Sustainable Tourism Indicators

Work on sustainable tourism indicators at an international level is currently led by a group of dedicated individuals at the World Tourism Organization (UNWTO). The progress made by the organization over this time can be tracked by reviewing their three major indicator publications (WTO, 1993, 1996, 2004), discussed in Bakker and Twining-Ward (2005), and their most recent activities are reviewed in Chapter 7.

In the first report, entitled *Indicators for the Sustainable Management of Tourism* (WTO, 1993), the international task force focused primarily on indicators that would measure the impact of tourism on the natural and cultural environment. The indicators developed were divided into those intended for national use and those for local or 'hot spot' application and then tested for usefulness in five locations worldwide. The second report, *What Tourism Managers Need to Know: A Practical Guide to the Development and Use of Indicators of Sustainable Tourism*, emphasizes the use of 12 'demand-driven' core indicators developed for use in 'all destinations' (WTO, 1996). This booklet heightened awareness of sustainable tourism indicators but did not do justice to the complexity of indicator development or begin to explain how indicators are used to influence policy. The most recent addition to the WTO indicator publications, *Indicators of Sustainable Development for Tourism Destinations: A Guidebook* (WTO, 2004), is quite the opposite. This comprehensive new text expands the indicator knowledge base considerably, providing both the fundamental principles and the practice of establishing an indicator programme. Several hundred indicators and 25 in-depth case studies of their use are explained, along with detailed discussion of indicator development. This text clearly demonstrates that there is now increased interest, use and understanding of how indicators can be integrated into planning and decision-making processes in tourism businesses and destinations. However, there are still several areas that need addressing in the context of new approaches to global change, complex systems and quality assurance, such as:

- The need to acknowledge that indicator development is an ongoing rather than linear process.
- The need to search for more integrated whole-systems measures rather than simple statements (e.g. the existence of a tourism plan).
- The need to clarify the process of converting indicator results into improved management action rather than simply as a tool for international comparison.

Unfortunately, however, the emphasis of most sustainable tourism monitoring is still more on what to monitor than how to integrate the results of monitoring into a sustainable tourism plan of action, or remedial action. To be effective, indicators have to be viewed as a means, not an end, and to be integrated into existing management processes so that the results are actually used to improve sustainable tourism planning and development.

Some of the issues identified above have been addressed by the Tourism Optimization Management Model (TOMM), developed by Manidis Roberts Consultants (1997) to monitor and manage tourism development on Kangaroo Island in South Australia. TOMM provides an integrative and place-based approach to not only monitoring sustainable tourism development but also converting the monitoring results into effective management action. TOMM was developed as a variation on Limits of Acceptable Change (LAC) and designed to monitor and quantify the key economic, marketing, environmental, sociocultural and experiential benefits and impacts of tourism activity, assist in the assessment of emerging issues and provide alternative future management options (Manidis Roberts Consultants, 1997; Stankey, 1999). The project has been successful for a number of reasons, not least because the indicators were seen not as the end of the road but as a means to improve management action. In this way, the push to monitor was not just to collect information (which included indicators on the health of the economy, number and type of tourists, health of the environment, type of experience visitors were having and the health of the community) but to become a 'centre of excellence and inspirational leader in destination management' (Miller and Twining-Ward, 2005: 204). Over 60 indicators were considered to measure community-identified 'optimum conditions' and eventually just 17 selected for use, based on what were considered by the community to be 'optimum conditions'. The indicators included, for example:

- Number of seals at designated tourism sites.
- Annual variation between room nights sold between peak and low season.
- Number of traffic accidents involving non-residents per annum.

The indicators are relatively holistic and cross-sectorial and acceptable ranges were established to assist the interpretation of results. A particular strength of the programme, however, is the management response system. This allows for the information collected from the indicators to be compared with the optimal conditions so that, where variation occurs, action can be taken. The process is described in general terms as follows:

1. Define community values and determine indicators to measure these.
2. Develop a monitoring programme to measure indicators.
3. Collect information. Are we in an acceptable range?
4. If yes, continue monitoring. If no, initiate a management response, monitor the response and then continue monitoring.

The TOMM project is one of the earliest and longest-running sustainable tourism management and monitoring systems. Institutional and funding arrangements have, however, been an ongoing issue for the project, as has the sustainability of human resources. More detailed analysis of TOMM and the lessons learned is included in Miller and Twining-Ward (2005). Some of the technical recommendations made by the former and current project managers, Liz Jack and Toni Duka, are provided in Box 8.2.

Box 8.2. Lessons learned from TOMM (adapted from Miller and Twining-Ward, 2005).

- Ensure data are collected in an appropriate and consistent manner.
- Data are only of value if they can be applied and used by others. They cannot be the sole focus of the process even though agencies may see them this way.
- Communication of the findings in a format and language understood by the intended audience is essential.
- Review existing data collection systems to see how they can be applied; do not reinvent the wheel.
- Review indicators on a regular basis for relevance to both the destination and audience needs and integrate into existing information systems.
- Align indicators and data collection processes with other models, where applicable, so that a global comparative study may be possible.
- Ensure that the development of indicators meets the long-term needs of the community, not just funding agencies.
- Do not try to engage everyone at the same time. Identify target markets and work towards engaging the entire community in the long term.
- Work collaboratively and collectively with government and non-government agencies and community groups to ensure a mutually beneficial approach for all involved.

The following case study looks at how indicator development and sustainable tourism monitoring were developed for use in Samoa, an island in the South Pacific.

Sustainable Tourism Monitoring in Samoa

The Samoa Sustainable Tourism Indicator Project was developed by the author in collaboration with the Samoa Tourism Authority and an interdisciplinary project advisory committee, made up of a cross-section of private, public and non-profit sector representatives, between 1998 and 2000. The idea for the project came as a result of a review of tourism plans and policy documents from around the region. These documents revealed that many island states in the South Pacific, such as Samoa, Niue, Tonga and Fiji, have made public commitments to the sustainable development of their tourism sectors but have few tools available to assist them to identify what this might look like or how they will know if progress is being made towards their goals.

It was against this background that the author began working with the Samoa Tourism Authority (STA) to establish a project that would develop a practical and user-friendly monitoring system to assist Samoa in their transition towards sustainable tourism. The objectives of the project were to clarify what sustainable tourism meant in the country and identify areas of key concern, and then set appropriate indicators to monitor these key components.

The long-term vision was for the information supplied by the indicator monitoring to be used to help improve future planning and development strategies. In a similar way to the TOMM management response system, and based on a study of adaptive management (discussed later in this chapter), an implementation framework was designed for the Samoan system to help ensure that the indicators were just one part of an 'adaptive learning cycle', which involved monitoring and then revising management practice on the basis of the monitoring results before re-monitoring. A seven-stage research plan was developed for use in this study and is shown in Fig. 8.1.

The monitoring programme differs from other indicator development processes in three main ways. First, it was designed in a cyclical, rather than linear, manner. This meant that, instead of coming to a halt following the identification of indicators or implementation of the action strategies, reviewing and improving the monitoring system and then re-monitoring, the indicators were seen as integral components of the process. Secondly, it employed an 'adaptive, learning-based approach', whereby the activities to be undertaken during each phase of the work were defined as a result of the learning that took place in the previous phase. Thirdly, considerable emphasis was put on stakeholder participation during the project. As well as using lessons learned from previous studies and monitoring elsewhere, stakeholders were involved in the identification of key issues, which were eventually translated into a set of objectives and charter for sustainable tourism in the country (Twining-Ward, 2002). The issues of concern were enormously diverse and cross-cutting, including, for example:

- The degradation of land and coastal resources through deforestation for construction and other purposes, leading to the subsequent downstream

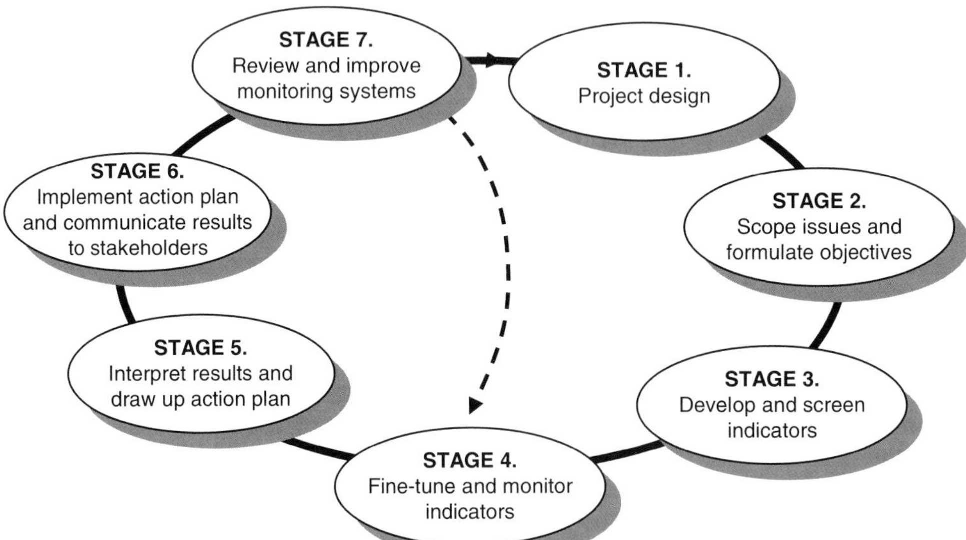

Fig. 8.1. Samoa's adaptive monitoring cycle (adapted from Twining-Ward and Butler, 2002).

effects such as increased runoff, soil erosion, siltation of lagoons and reduced fresh water supplies.

- An increase in non-biodegradable waste linked to the growing urban and tourist population and compounded by the lack of suitable landfill sites and difficulties of recycling on small islands.
- Lack of trade or professional training has restricted the ability of those living in rural areas to benefit effectively from tourism.
- Concern on behalf of village councils that the power vested in the village *matai* (chiefs) and respect between youth and elders are being challenged through changes in dress and behaviour codes.

As can be seen from the above examples, tourism could not be monitored in a vacuum but was inextricably linked to social, economic and environmental changes occurring in the country. Consequently the indicators also needed to be cross-cutting, monitoring areas where tourism interfaces with key sustainable development issues, as identified by local stakeholders. Examples of some of the selected indicators are provided here.

- Per cent of villages important to tourism participating in land and forest conservation programmes. This indicator aimed to show the linkages between conservation and ecotourism, identify the current status and monitor the trend with a view to encouraging positive trends.
- Per cent of tourist accommodation facilities composting or recycling their biodegradable wastes. Analysis of waste composition in landfills conducted by the Environment Department revealed a large proportion of biodegradable waste that could easily have been composted or reused as pig fodder.
- Per cent of full-time jobs in tourist accommodation facilities that are located in rural areas. This indicator aimed to show the linkages between tourism and rural employment directed at the issues of excessive rural–urban drift.
- Per cent of hotels and tour operators consistently providing visitors with information about village protocol. This indicator aimed to monitor and highlight the importance of encouraging culturally sensitive behaviour amongst tourists.

The emphasis of the indicators was on monitoring the interaction between tourism and identified critical quality of life and sustainability issues in the country and then working out how the indicator results were going to be used to create improved sustainability outcomes. Assisted by the example of TOMM and work in adaptive management and sustainability monitoring (principally Gunderson *et al.*, 1995; Meadows, 1998; Busch and Trexler, 2002), an adaptive, learning-based implementation framework was developed in Samoa to convert indicator results into management responses.

Acknowledging that indicators are unlikely to be perfect first time around and having the flexibility to expect and adapt to change were regarded as particularly important, especially given the unpredictable nature of complex tourism systems explained earlier. Situations change, stakeholders learn and new data become available over time, so the framework needs a frequent review, with indicators as a means to improved management, not an end in themselves. Sustainable tourism managers need to learn which are the driving (keystone) variables and how the system reacts to changes in stimuli, just as forest managers have learned the role of surprise events such as forest fire in the regeneration of woodlands. Over time, this knowledge can provide opportunities for creativity, when 'movers and shakers' may seize the moment and create new forms of entrepreneurial activity (for further discussion of this area see Russell and Faulkner, 1999).

Another important element of this project relevant to the current discussion is the implementation framework. Without a well-designed implementation framework in place to convert indicator information into tangible action, any indicator programme risks coming to a halt once the results of the monitoring activities have been published. In TOMM, the management response system is regarded as a critical component of the monitoring programme, alerting stakeholders to those indicators that are not performing within their acceptable range or to other potential issues that may merit additional monitoring (Jack and Duka, 2004). The implementation framework for the Samoa indicator project was developed to facilitate the move from results to action on a long-term basis, providing opportunities for stakeholder involvement and effective social learning. The framework shown in Fig. 8.2 illustrates how indicator results were evaluated against 'acceptable ranges' and those providing 'unacceptable' results were investigated in order to establish appropriate management responses and prioritize action strategies. Feedback from

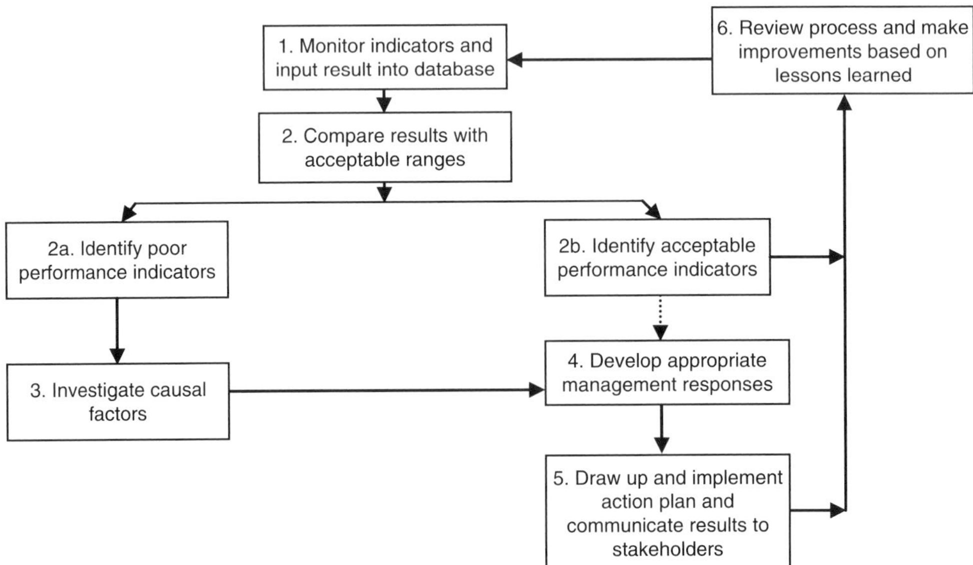

Fig. 8.2. Implementation framework for the Samoa sustainable tourism indicator project (from Twining-Ward, 2002).

those involved in the monitoring process was then used to improve the indicators for the next round of monitoring. The process is then repeated in a cyclical manner; the improved indicators are re-monitored with improved data collection methods, the results are analysed using revised acceptable ranges, and new management responses are developed, where appropriate, based on lessons learned from past experience.

Understanding the Adaptive Approach

Greater understanding of adaptive approaches to indicator development and monitoring can be gained through the study of 'adaptive management'. Adaptive management is about incorporating an ongoing process of experimentation, monitoring and revision as an ongoing social learning process (Parson and Clark, 1995). Adaptive managers are encouraged to monitor using carefully chosen indicators and learn from the results about how their particular system works and reacts to change. The idea is that this will enable them to build the resilience of their forest, hotel or marine park, make more informed decisions and address ecosystem issues before these become ecosystem crises. The development, design and use of indicators are an integral part of adaptive management, described by Borman *et al.* (1997) as 'learning to manage, managing to learn'. The strong emphasis adaptive management puts on engaging stakeholders and the progressive accumulation of knowledge helps make monitoring an ongoing learning and action-oriented process. It also assists in making the important connections between information collection and management action, the absence of which is a common failing of monitoring programmes.

The adaptive process demonstrates clearly how designing the indicators is only part of the job. The real challenge is in using the results to create positive sustainability outcomes within an adaptive learning cycle. The simple five-step adaptive management cycle is outlined by the British Columbia Ministry of Forests (2004).

1. Define the problem and identify the indicators.
2. Design a management plan to improve the quality and reliability of knowledge.
3. Implement the plan.
4. Monitor the results, measuring identified indicators to see how well the plan matched up with the objectives.
5. Evaluate the results and adjust the actions and objectives based on lessons learned.

The difference between this and the largely one-way WTO indicator development process is illustrated in Fig. 8.3.

Adaptive management has been endorsed by scholars involved in a wide range of areas, from global change to organizational behaviour. The Millennium Ecosystem Assessment, a 4-year study of the consequences of ecosystem change for human well-being, involving 2000 of the world's

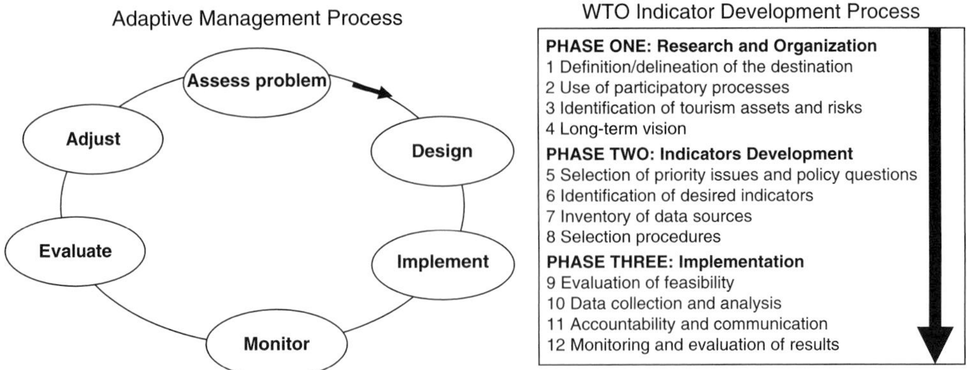

Fig. 8.3. Comparison of approaches (adapted from Miller and Twining-Ward, 2005).

top scientists, states that active adaptive management can be a particularly valuable tool for reducing uncertainty about ecosystem management (Reid *et al.*, 2005). Adaptive management has also been applied to sustainable tourism with some success (Holling and Chambers, 1973; Moser and Petersen, 1981; Manning, 1998; Rollins *et al.*, 1998; Reed, 1999; Twining-Ward, 2002), but further work is needed to overcome political and institutional barriers. Steinitz and Faris (2005: 46) explain:

> While an appreciation of adaptive management is standard fare for the scientific community, the task of implementing it assumes a remarkable level of institutional sophistication and a political process that operates much more efficiently, and with a longer-term outlook, than current political, public policy, and environmental management institutions in most of the world.

Managers are understandably reluctant to experiment when the potential benefits and costs are uncertain. Nevertheless, in the light of the Samoa project the benefits of adopting an 'adaptive approach' to indicators and monitoring is worth pursuing. What makes adaptive management particularly valuable in the development and use of sustainable tourism indicators is the emphasis it puts on monitoring not as an end in itself but as a means to more sustainable outcomes.

By consolidating lessons learned from investigation of adaptive management, the Samoa study as well as practical examples of tourism indicators in use demonstrated by the UNWTO, TOMM and others, it is appropriate to make some recommendations about how to create an adaptive approach to sustainable tourism indicators that addresses some of the constraints to sustainable tourism monitoring highlighted earlier. Five key recommendations are made here:

1. The need for multidisciplinary input, in particular the application of progress made from ecosystem monitoring.
2. The importance of adopting place-specific solutions, incorporating local knowledge bases and focusing on issues identified by local stakeholders.
3. The need for cross-cutting indicators that enhance our knowledge about the complex interactions between human and natural systems.

4. The value of flexible, learning-based approaches that develop over time and are adjusted and improved as new knowledge emerges.
5. The need to visualize the process as a means to achieve improved sustainable tourism outcomes, not as an end in itself, and to plan from the start of the process how the results of monitoring will be used to improve decision-making.

The following section looks at the wider application of these recommendations for the development of quality assurance programmes, using the example of work recently completed for the South Pacific Tourism Organization (SPTO).

Implications for Quality Assurance and Certification

In 2005, the SPTO embarked on several projects that aimed to enhance the quality and sustainability of tourism opportunities in its 12 member countries under the EU-funded Pacific Regional Integration Programme. One of these projects was the development of a regional accommodation classification scheme, designed to increase the quality and sustainability of tourism accommodation throughout the region, through the identification of verifiable standards and the design of a transparent process of assessment. Accommodation classification is the process by which accommodation establishments are broken down into categories and awarded grades according to the quality of their physical and/or service characteristics. The most common international approach to accommodation classification is 'star rating', used by travel agents worldwide to help match client needs with appropriate accommodation supply. Unfortunately, most star-rating schemes are heavily weighted in favour of consumer demand rather than sustainable tourism best practice. In many cases the criteria established for higher rating, such as changing towels twice a day, encourages unsustainable consumption. Other examples include giving more points to properties with 24-hour outside lighting, golf courses and large swimming pools, regardless of the sustainability of local power or water sources. As a result, in some areas star rating and certification programmes (such as Green Globe) may be in direct conflict with each other, one focusing on the extent of luxury and consumption (star rating) and the other the extent of conservation and protection.

In order to avoid this problem in the case of the SPTO project, a more integrated classification model was developed, based on examples of progressive accreditation and sustainability certification internationally and using the lessons learned from the Samoa Indicator Project. Examples of more integrated approaches to accommodation classification can be seen in the Caribbean, Central America, Maldives, Australia and New Zealand.

The Caribbean Hotel Association highlights the benefits of close links between hotel classification and environmental criteria and notes that governments such as Antigua, Barbados, Jamaica and St Lucia are not only incorporating environmental criteria into their hotel grading systems but also considering the effects of the development of the quality of life and social heritage of the affected communities (CAST, no date).

The Certification for Sustainable Tourism (CST) programme regulated by the Costa Rican National Accreditation Commission is designed to differentiate tourism sector businesses based on the degree to which they comply with a sustainable model of natural, cultural and social resource management. Four fundamental aspects are evaluated: the interaction between the company and its surrounding natural habitat; the management policies and the operational systems within the company; the interaction of the company with its clients; and the interaction of the company with the local communities. In each area a number of criteria have been established based on Agenda 21 and ISO 14001; these include waste reduction, reuse and recycling, energy efficiency, conservation and management, an environmentally sensitive purchasing policy, social and cultural development, hazardous waste disposal, company transportation and its effect on the environment, land-use planning and management, and environmental/historic site protection. The criteria are reviewed on an annual basis by a technical committee (further information from: www.turismo-sostenible.co.cr/EN/sobreCST/about-cst.shtml).

The Maldives Resort Classification was a joint project between the Ministry of Tourism of the Republic of Maldives and the WTO to develop a resort classification system as part of a national quality assurance programme. The scheme provides a more holistic approach to rating by assessing the resort in the context of its environment. It offers an addition of a 'plus' for environmental care, social responsibility and management philosophy and practices (WTO, 2004). Other countries are also beginning to follow this trend: the Australian AAA five-star scheme is linking to Green Globe, and Green Keys in Denmark plan to link to their new star rating (both Green Globe and Green Keys are sustainable tourism certification programmes). The New Zealand system, Qualmark, has also been leading the way in terms of cross-sectorial accreditation. As well as accrediting hotels using Qualmark, it is also available for cultural and nature experiences, coaches and rental cars, activity adventure tourism, and other types of operators. Businesses are assessed based on six core aspects (customer service, facilities and equipment, you and your staff, environmental and cultural impacts, general safety, overall business success) and the scheme is integrated with the Kiwihost customer experience training. A similar model has been developed for use in the Cook Islands (for further discussion see SPTO and TRC, 2005).

So, although at first sight star rating may seem totally unrelated to ecotourism, quality assurance and indicator programmes, there are many similarities and useful synergies that can be realized through the merging of a number of perspectives. Both mechanisms require the identification of criteria to measure, measurement processes and administrative structures that help to convert the results of the assessment into improved management practice. Table 8.1 provides an overview of how the adaptive indicator principles were integrated into the SPTO Accommodation Classification Project.

Table 8.1. How the adaptive indicator principles were applied.

Principle	Implementation	Evaluation
Multidisciplinary input	Interviews were conducted in five countries and a workshop held to identify the key issues to address and evaluate potential solutions. The workshop enabled the training of 'project champions' – a group of individuals who could encourage, monitor and inspire the implementation of the schemes. These included not only tourism operators and officials but also experts in public health, environmental management, education and consumer protection.	The incorporation of multidisciplinary expertise helped to develop and refine a system that appreciated the interaction between tourism operations and other sustainable development concerns, e.g. taking the emphasis off the guest room and on to aspects such as interaction with the local community and environmental hazard preparation.
Place-specific solutions	Stakeholders made it clear that national accommodation classification was a priority. This was made possible by devising a framework with four different levels of involvement, which countries could select according to their experience and preferences.	The scheme was flexible enough for national interpretation whilst at the same time allowing for enough commonality to make regional training and support possible. The idea of a national committee also provided opportunity for the inclusion of culturally specific criteria.
Cross-cutting indicators	The accommodation classification project was designed as a four-block framework in which the code of practice formed the foundation, ensuring a more whole-system approach combining sustainability and quality concerns.	Having a rating scheme that incorporates environment management, social issues and the relationship with the local community makes sustainability monitoring open to all rather than just those who can afford certification.
Flexible, learning-based approaches	Classification has conventionally been a 'mystery examination' for the hotelier. To change this around a more formative and nurturing approach to accommodation classification was recommended, involving hoteliers in self-assessments, peer review and support, providing them with helpful reports on what needs to be improved and following up on their progress with web-based support tools.	The project envisaged the assessor as a capacity builder rather than an 'inspector', in a similar way to the Qualmark scheme in New Zealand. This approach focused on helping properties to upgrade in ways that will improve customer satisfaction. The constraints to this approach are the current low level of experience of assessors in the region and the lack of transparency that has characterized classification to date; there are also concerns about conflicts of interest if assessors become independent advisers.

(*Continued*)

Table 8.1. (Continued).

Principle	Implementation	Evaluation
A means to greater sustainability	Integrating the code of practice into the accommodation classification process enabled much wider and more effective sustainability outcomes. Incorporating monitoring into the framework will allow for the creation of an adaptive feedback loop.	The value of the code of practice is in providing a common set of objectives from which other sustainability tools can be developed. Monitoring its use will provide useful information on how to improve it in the future.

Conclusion

This chapter has reviewed the rationale for indicator development and monitoring from a number of different perspectives, including new approaches to the study of ecosystems, global change and increasing use of verification tools in quality assurance and certification programmes. The result of this analysis provided the basis for an 'adaptive indicator approach' and five principles for the design and management of monitoring systems, which have also been shown to be applicable to other types of quality assurance programmes such as accommodation classification.

There is increasing evidence on an almost daily basis of the complexity of tourism ecosystems: the global fallout from 9/11, the 2004 South Asia tsunami, Hurricanes Katrina and Rita in the USA and the knock-on effects of airline mergers and bankruptcies. All these give weight to the timeless remark by biologist Garrett Hardin, 'we can never do merely one thing' (1968: 457). In a large, complex system with numerous feedback relationships, one can almost never anticipate the full consequences of any particular action. Accordingly, all our strategies, whether these are for indicator development, accommodation classification or ecotourism certification, must be adaptive and incorporate whole-systems approaches and we must learn, improve and refine our approaches over time.

Examples are provided here of how integrated and adaptive approaches can be used to improve indicator development and monitoring outcomes and also be applied to other types of quality assurance systems. If we start looking at these tools as a 'means' to improved sustainability outcomes, rather than as an 'end' in themselves, the commonalities emerge, synergies develop and breakthroughs are possible. The five adaptive indicator principles are highlighted: the need for **multidisciplinary input**; **place-specific solutions**; **cross-cutting indicators** that enhance our knowledge about the complex interactions between human and natural systems; **flexible, learning-based approaches**, which develop over time and are adjusted and improved as new knowledge emerges; and, most importantly, the process as a **means to achieve improved sustainable tourism outcomes** and not as an end in itself. Although these are not the only considerations that are important, they are a useful starting point and may be usefully applied to the range of quality assurance techniques discussed in this volume, whether these be for ecotourism or mainstream tourism.

Monitoring using indicators is crucial to virtually all sustainable development strategies as it provides the opportunity to assess the effectiveness of policies and actions, identify the most successful and appropriate ones, and draw attention to problem areas so that appropriate management responses can be made. It is even more crucial given that we now know tourism systems are complex, behave in a non-linear manner and are often subject to 'surprise' events. Managers need to be prepared, better informed and constantly experimenting, monitoring and improving their knowledge of the complex system they are dealing with if a transition towards more sustainable tourism is to be achieved any time in the near future.

Acknowledgements

The author would like to acknowledge the tireless support of Bryan Farrell and Graham Miller in the review of early drafts of this chapter, as well as the support of the Samoa Tourism Authority and the South Pacific Tourism Organization.

References

Bakker, M. and Twining-Ward, L. (2005) *The World Tourism Organization.* In: Miller, G.A. and Twining-Ward, L. *Monitoring for a Sustainable Tourism Transition.* CAB International, Wallingford, UK, pp. 177–200.

Borman, B.T., Tarrant, R.F., Martin, J.R., Gordon, J., Wagner, F.H., McIver, J., Wood, G., Reeves, G., Alegria, J., McIlwain, J., Cunningham, P.G., Verner, J., Brookes, M.H., Christensen, N., Friesema, P., Klein, K., Berg, J., Furnish, J. and Henshaw, J. (1997) *Adaptive Management: Common Ground where Managers, Scientists, and Citizens can Accelerate Learning to Achieve Ecosystem Sustainability.* Ecological Stewardship Books, World Resources Institute, Washington, DC.

British Columbia Ministry of Forests (2004) *Adaptive Management: Learning from our Forests.* Ministry of Forests, Victoria, BC.

Busch, D.E. and Trexler, J.C. (eds) (2002) *Monitoring Ecosystems: Interdisciplinary Approaches for Evaluating Eco-Regional Initiatives.* Island Press, Washington, DC.

Caribbean Action for Sustainable Tourism (CAST) *Trends in Hotel Certification and Rating Programs: Guidelines for the Caribbean.* CAST. Available at: www.cha-cast.com

Clements, F.E. (1916) *Plant Succession: An Analysis of the Development of Vegetation.* Carnegie Institution of Washington Publication 242, 512 pp.

Farrell, B.H. and Twining-Ward, L. (2004) Reconceptualizing Tourism. *Annals of Tourism Research* 31(2), 274–295.

GECP (2001) Earth science system: an integrated approach. *Environment* 43(8), 21–27.

Gunderson, L.H., Holling, C.S. and Light, S.S. (eds) (1995) *Barriers and Bridges to the Renewal of Ecosystems and Institutions.* Columbia University Press, New York.

Hardin, G. (1968) The tragedy of the commons. *Science* 162, 1243–1248.

Holling, C.S. (ed.) (1978) *Adaptive Environmental Assessment and Management.* John Wiley, New York.

Holling, C.S. (1986) The resilience of terrestrial ecosystems: local surprise and global change. In: Clark, W.C. and Munn, R.E. (eds) *Sustainable Development of the Biosphere.* International Institute for Applied Systems Analysis, Cambridge University Press, Cambridge, pp. 292–317.

Holling, C.S. (2001) Understanding the complexity of economic, ecological, and social systems. *Ecosystems* 4, 390–405.

Holling, C.S. and Chambers, A. (1973) Resource science: the nurture of an infant. *BioScience* 23(1), 13–20.

IGBP (2001) Global change and the Earth system: a planet under pressure. *IGBP Science* 4. Available at: http://www.igbp.kva.se//uploads/ESO_IGBP4.pdf

Jack, E. and Duka, T.J. (2004) Kangaroo Island tourism optimisation management model: it's easy for you you're an island. In: WTO (ed.) *Indicators for the Sustainable Development of Tourism Destinations: A Guidebook.* WTO, Madrid.

Kates, R.W., Clark, W.C., Corell, R., Hall, J.M., Jaeger, C.C., Lowe, I., McCarthy, J.J., Schellnhuber, H.J., Bolin, B., Dickson, N.M., Faucheux, S., Gallopín, G.C., Grübler, A., Huntley, B., Jäger, J., Jodha, N.S., Kasperson, R.E., Mabogunje, A., Matson, P., Mooney, H., Moore, B., O'Riordan, T. and Svedin, U. (2001) Environment and development: sustainability science. *Science* 292(5517), 641–642.

MacGillivray, A. (1997) Social development indicators. In: Moldan, B. and Bilharz, S. (eds) *Sustainability Indicators: Report of the Project on Indicators of Sustainable Development.* Wiley & Sons, Chichester, UK, pp. 256–263.

Manidis Roberts Consultants (1997) *Developing a Tourism Optimisation Management Model.* Manidis Roberts Consultants, Surrey Hills, UK.

Manning, E.W. (1998) *Governance for Tourism: Coping with Tourism in Impacted Destinations.* Centre for a Sustainable Future, Foundation for International Training, Toronto.

Meadows, D.H. (1998) *Indicators and Information Systems for Sustainable Development: A Report to the Balaton Group.* The Sustainability Institute, Hartland, Vermont.

Miller, G. and Twining-Ward, L. (2005) *Monitoring for a Sustainable Tourism Transition: the Challenge of Developing and Using Indicators.* CAB International, Oxford.

Moser, W. and Petersen, J. (1981) Limits to Obergürgl's growth: Alpine experience in environmental management. *Ambio* 10(2/3), 68–72.

New Economics Foundation (NEF) (2001) *Taking Flight: The Rapid Growth of Ethical Consumerism.* NEF, London.

NRC (1999) *Our Common Journey, a Transition Toward Sustainability.* National Academy Press, Washington, DC.

Parson, E.A. and Clark, W.C. (1995) Sustainable development as social learning: theoretical perspectives and practical challenges for the design of a research program. In: Gunderson, L.H., Holling, C.S. and Light, S.S. (eds) *Barriers and Bridges to the Renewal of Ecosystems and Institutions.* Columbia University Press, New York, pp. 428–460.

PASTILLE (2002) *Local Sustainability Indicator Sets in their Context.* FP5, European Union, Brussels.

Reed, M.G. (1999) Collaborative tourism planning as adaptive experiments in emergent tourism settings. *Journal of Sustainable Tourism* 7(3/4), 331–355.

Reid, W.V., Mooney, H.A., Cropper, A., Capistrano, D., Carpenter, S.R., Chopra, K., Dasgupta, P., Dietz, T., Duraiappah, A.K., Hassan, R., Kasperson, R., Leemans, R., May, R.M., McMichael, T.A., Pingali, P., Samper, C., Scholes, R., Watson, R.T., Zakri, A.H., Shidong, Z., Ash, N.J., Bennett, E., Kumar, P., Lee, M.J., Raudsepp-Hearne, C., Simons, H., Thonell, J. and Zurek, M.B. (2005) *Ecosystems and Human Wellbeing. Synthesis.* Report of the Millennium Ecosystem Assessment, Island Press, Washington, DC.

Rollins, R., Trotter, W. and Taylor, B. (1998) Adaptive management of recreation sites in the wildland–urban interface. *Journal of Applied Recreation Research* 23(2), 107–125.

Russell, R. and Faulkner, B. (1999) Movers and shakers: chaos makers in tourism development. *Tourism Management* 20, 411–423.

SPTO and TRC (2005) *Accommodation Classification Resource Kit.* SPTO, Suva. Available at: www.spto.org

Stankey, G.H. (1999) The recreation opportunity spectrum and the limits of acceptable change planning systems: a review of experiences and lessons. In: Aley, J., Burch, W.R., Conover, B. and Field, D. (eds) *Ecosystem Management: Adaptive Strategies for Natural Resource Organizations in the Twenty-first Century.* Taylor and Francis, Philadelphia, Pennsylvania, pp. 173–188.

Steffen, W., Andreae, M.O., Bolin, B., Cox, P.M., Crutzen, P.M., Cubasch, U., Held, H., Nakicenovic, N., Scholes, R., Talaue-McManus, L. and Turner, B.L., II (2004) The Achilles heels of the earth system. *Environment* 46(3), 8–20.

Steinitz, C. and Faris, R. (2005) Response to Bryan Farrell's commentary. *Environment* 40(1), 41.

Twining-Ward, L. (2002) Monitoring sustainable tourism development: a comprehensive, stakeholder-driven, adaptive approach. PhD thesis, University of Surrey, Guildford, UK.

Twining-Ward, L. and Butler, R. (2002) Implementing STD on a small island: development and use of sustainable tourism development indicators in Samoa. *Journal of Sustainable Tourism* 10(5), 363–387.

WGBU (1997) *World in Transition: The Research Challenge. Annual Report.* Springer, Berlin. Available at: http://www.wbgu.de/wbgu_jg1996_engl.pdf

Wheeller, B. (1994) Ecotourism: a ruse by any other name. In: Cooper, C.P. and Lockwood, A. (eds) *Progress in Tourism and Hospitality Research.* Vol. 6. John Wiley and Sons, Chichester, UK, pp. 3–11.

Wight, P.A. (1995) Environmentally responsible marketing of tourism. In: Cater, E. and Lowman, G. (eds) *Ecotourism: A Sustainable Option?* Royal Geographical Society in Association with John Wiley, Chichester, UK, pp. 39–55.

Wilson, E. (2002) *The Future of Life.* Alfred A. Knopf, New York.

WTO (1993) *Indicators for the Sustainable Management of Tourism.* International Institute for Sustainable Development, Winnipeg, Canada.

WTO (1996) *What Tourism Managers Need to Know: A Practical Guide to the Development and Use of Indicators of Sustainable Tourism.* WTO, Madrid.

WTO (2004) *Indicators of the Sustainable Development for Tourism Destinations: A Guidebook.* WTO, Madrid.

9 Stakeholders' Perspectives on Quality in Ecotourism

ROSEMARY BLACK[1] AND ALICE CRABTREE[2]

[1]*Charles Sturt University, Albury, NSW, Australia;* [2]*Ecotourism Consultant, Cairns, Queensland, Australia*

Introduction

This chapter sets the context for Part Two of the book by introducing the key stakeholders involved in ecotourism, and provides an overview of some of the major challenges faced by the ecotourism industry in addressing, developing and implementing quality ecotourism. Part Two of the book presents 14 chapters from a range of ecotourism stakeholders, including tourists, communities, protected area managers, ecotour guides and ecotourism industries. This part of the book explores a range of stakeholders' views on how best to pursue quality in ecotourism, or specific elements pertinent to ecotourism principles. Some of these stakeholders have not had a strong or, indeed, any voice in the ecotourism debate, and they bring refreshingly different perspectives to the discussion.

In contrast to mainstream tourism, where the range of stakeholders is relatively small and mainly restricted to those directly influenced by economic connections, the stakeholders involved in ecotourism are more diverse and eclectic. This diversity reflects the fact that ecotourism promises so much for so many – a vehicle for poverty alleviation, a spearhead for sustainable development, an education tool, a way to rejuvenate cultural traditions, and a means of supporting and financing conservation projects are just a few of the potential 'draws'. Broadly speaking, ecotourism stakeholders can include tourism enterprises, tourists (consumers), all levels of governments including protected area managers, non-governmental organizations (both tourism industry and those representing conservation and community interests) and development agencies. This diversity of stakeholders can be problematic when trying to assess whether quality ecotourism is achieved because different stakeholders often perceive or demand very different outcomes from their involvement (see Swarbrooke, 1999; Honey and Rome, 2001; Weaver, 2001; Epler Wood, 2002).

However, to be successful, it is important that ecotourism acknowledges the range of stakeholders' views and tries to meet and balance their different needs, demands and interests to ensure shared ownership. It is important to engage the full range of stakeholders when quality assurance tools are being developed, particularly where standards are involved. As discussed in Part One of this volume a spectrum of quality assurance tools exists, many of which are voluntary, and they include awards, codes of conduct and certification programmes. These initiatives are designed to help deliver more consistent, quality ecotourism products that better meet the ecotourism principles outlined in Chapter 1. Thus engagement with stakeholders requires clear two-way communication and appropriate participatory and consultative processes if standards are to succeed. This is partly because imposed standards remove the possibility of any sense of ownership and on-ground practical suggestions about how the standard might be met. A range of participatory processes involving consultation and decision making by communities can often lead to more innovative and productive partnerships (Swarbrooke, 1999) that result in genuine community involvement.

While we sought a range of stakeholders' perspectives for this volume we recognize that there are other important stakeholder groups we have not included, such as international funding agencies, national, regional and local governments and, to a lesser extent, conservation NGOs and certification programme managers. These groups obviously have a considerable interest in or involvement with planning for quality in more sustainable and ecotourism development.

We know international funding agencies have been a major source of start-up funding for many sustainable tourism certification programmes (Epler Wood, 2002) and while they are not directly represented in this volume they are mentioned in several chapters, including Chapter 23, which discusses consolidating regional networks of certification programmes. International funding agencies such as the World Bank, European Commission and Inter-American Development Bank have funded many ecotourism projects with loans and grants (Epler Wood, 2002), including initiatives such as the development of a proposed global accreditation body for sustainable tourism certification programmes, known as the Sustainable Tourism Stewardship Council (Rainforest Alliance, 2001, 2003). The development of credible quality assurance tools for ecotourism may well assist this sector to fund projects that are more likely to help alleviate poverty and be environmentally and socially sustainable.

The involvement of the public sector – local, regional and national governments – in ecotourism initiatives is also important and has been discussed in detail elsewhere (Buckley *et al.*, 2003; Fennell and Dowling, 2003). The public sector provides alternative tools to the voluntary initiatives. Specifically they consist of legislation and policy, funding and fiscal incentives, land-use planning, official standards and designation of conservation areas (Swarbrooke, 1999; Weaver, 2001). National governments can play an important leadership role (WTO, 2006), for example, by initiating and supporting the development of a national ecotourism strategy, as in the case of the

Australian Ecotourism Strategy (Commonwealth Department of Tourism, 1994). Regional and local governments also have an important role to play, being involved in developing and implementing ecotourism planning guidelines (Epler Wood, 2002). This stakeholder group and these alternative tools, such as government policy and regulations, are glimpsed in many of the different chapters, particularly in Chapters 15 and 16. A recent and detailed discussion of governments' potential role in encouraging sustainable tourism and ecotourism, and potential overlap and synergies with voluntary initiatives, can be found in the World Tourism Organization report (WTO, 2006).

Non-governmental organizations are another important group that have threads of their interests and issues woven through many of the chapters in this volume, although we have not obtained their views specifically as a stakeholder. The focus of most NGOs (such as WWF, Conservation International, The Nature Conservancy Council, Flora Fauna International) is on protecting biodiversity and the natural environment, and by default trying to ensure sustainable development for local communities. The fundamental demand for quality ecotourism to integrate conservation means that this group has a natural affinity with sustainable or ecotourism. This is reflected in many NGOs developing ecotourism initiatives and becoming increasingly involved in quality assurance measures. NGOs have initiated, developed and currently manage many quality assurance initiatives, such as codes of conduct, ecotourism certification programmes for tour operators and professional certification programmes for guides. We look at two examples of these, with Chapter 5 on the SmartVoyager programme for the Galápagos Island and Chapter 23 on regional networks presenting Rainforest Alliance's role in the Americas.

The stories of some of these stakeholders can be gleaned from some of the chapters in Part One of this volume, or have been covered by other authors; for example, the story of certification programme managers has been well covered by Font and Buckley (2001), Honey (2002) and the WTO (2002).

In Part Two of the book we hear the stories of five key stakeholder groupings:

1. Ecotourists (consumers).
2. Host communities, including indigenous communities.
3. Ecotour guides.
4. Ecotourism industry.
5. Protected area managers.

Ecotourists/Consumers

Tourists, as the consumers of the ecotourism product, are a major stakeholder in ecotourism. However, the diversity of consumers means there are multiple voices and no one voice can represent all ecotourists. We present two contrasting views in the following chapters, one by Xavier Font and

Megan Epler Wood, who present their views on current ecotourist/consumer research of what consumers think about quality in ecotourism and how they have responded to quality assurance initiatives. Their chapter is followed by Zoë Chafe's, which defines the current consumer demand that exists for ecotourism, sustainable tourism and/or responsible tourism, using the results of recent surveys and polls, and presents evidence that tourists are interested in purchasing ecotourism products.

Quality assurance initiatives can provide tourists with the opportunity to identify and select products and services that promote environmental, social and cultural concern and sensitivity or have a commitment to protecting the environment and respect the social, cultural, economic and political concerns of host countries and communities (Honey and Rome, 2001). However, to date, consumer recognition of and preferential choice for one of the most distinctive quality tools, certification, has been poor (Synergy, 2000; Font and Buckley, 2001; WTO, 2002, 2006). Despite the premise that 'green sells', surveys of consumers suggest that, while they may express concern for environmental issues, this is not translated into actual purchasing of green products (Martin, 1997; Weaver, 2001; Epler Wood, 2002, 2004). Many tourism enterprises complain that quality ecotourism initiatives such as certification do not translate into increased sales. Epler Wood (2004) refers to this as the 'green gap' and argues that the distance between consumers' intentions and their actions is wide. Epler Wood (2004) describes this disparity with results of a survey of ecotour operators in Ecuador, where she found that, although there was apparently genuine concern among tourists about environmental and social issues, fewer than 10% of the clients that booked ecotours requested information from operators on their eco-social standards. None the less, the many consumer surveys (see Chapter 11 in this volume) demonstrate that consumers' interest in green products represents a latent demand for quality ecotourism that has yet to be tapped. We hope you may draw on your own experience as a consumer of tourism products and review these contrasting chapters to come to your own conclusions, and possibly solutions on how to seek and gain consumers' voices to facilitate the sharing of power and decision making with consumers to ensure quality ecotourism experiences.

Host Communities

Traditionally most quality initiatives in ecotourism have concentrated on environmental components and the cost savings that can be obtained through eco-efficiencies. While ecotourism is most often associated with these environmental or 'green and brown' issues, recent trends suggest a move to more people-focused issues.

There has been a growing interest in harnessing tourism for poverty alleviation and the support and development of more community-based tourism projects. This movement has been supported by advocacy organizations like Tourism Concern, which has spurred greater emphasis on social and cultural issues. There is certainly an increasing recognition of the need for better consultation and more participatory community involvement in ecotourism.

As outlined in Chapter 1, one of the principles for ecotourism is providing returns for local communities. The benefits that ecotourism can provide include not only fundamentals such as direct and/or indirect employment and economic benefits, but also a number of other benefits. These might include increased viability of existing accommodation houses and restaurants, provision of additional revenue for local retail businesses and other services, an increase in the market for local products and greater community awareness of the value of local/indigenous culture and the natural environment (Wearing, 2001). Quality ecotourism also offers communities opportunities such as sponsorship packages, provision or upkeep of community infrastructure and training programmes.

In the context of ecotourism, a host community is a group of people in an ecotourism destination, usually permanent residents who have a common interest and bond in maintaining a high quality of life for themselves (Weaver, 2001). However, as Swarbrooke (1999) points out, while this definition suggests homogeneity, the reality is much more complex, with most local communities consisting of different interest groups and many voices, some of which may conflict. A diversity of voices presents challenges for ecotourism planners and developers; however, effective and genuine participatory processes are needed with local communities to achieve quality ecotourism.

Another of the challenges in relation to communities is to find better ways to integrate private, commercial tourism interests with community interests and needs. While traditionally communities have been reasonably well involved in influencing public-sector tourism planning and development control systems, it is suggested that communities play a more proactive role to maximize direct control between themselves and tourists (Swarbrooke, 1999; Weaver, 2001). Thus, host communities situated near ecotourism attractions or facilities may regard quality initiatives in ecotourism as a way of measuring and improving the environmental and sociocultural impacts of a tourism project that may directly or indirectly impact upon them, their culture and their lifestyle. In the case of certification, the process may involve assessing the financial benefits to both the country and the local community. For example, criteria may specify local ownership or local partners, local hiring of staff and use and promotion of locally made products. According to Honey and Rome (2001), quality assurance tools such as certification can facilitate increased local equity and also assist communities in negotiations with investors, developers and managers of tourism facilities.

We have attempted to present the voice of contrasting communities from different regions of the world (see Chapters 12, 13 and 14 in this volume). The demand quality ecotourism makes for better involvement of local communities and recognition of the rights and aspirations of indigenous people (Weaver, 2001) are particularly explored in Chapters 13 and 14 of this volume.

Ecotour Guides

'Ecotour guiding' is a relatively new term, which has followed ecotourism into the lexicon. Ecotour guides may be employed by ecotourism operators, adventure travel companies, natural resource management agencies (rangers), non-governmental organizations (NGOs), voluntary conservation organizations and educational institutions. Black (2002) defines an ecotour guide as someone employed on a paid or voluntary basis who conducts paying or non-paying tourists around an area or site of natural and/or cultural importance, utilizing the principles of ecotourism and interpretation. In other words, s/he communicates and interprets the significance of the environment, promotes minimal impact practices, ensures the sustainability of the natural and cultural environment, and hopefully motivates those tourists to consider their own lives in relation to larger ecological or cultural concerns.

In addition to being the personal 'face' of any organization, whether it is a natural resource management agency, tour operator or local conservation group, ecotour guides should role-model environmentally and culturally sensitive behaviour, as well as being responsible for leading and managing the group and generally for providing a safe and enjoyable experience for each visitor. Ecotour guides thus perform all the generic tour guiding roles of leader, educator, public relations representative, host and conduit (Cohen, 1985; Pond, 1993), but additionally play a key role in interpreting the environment and modelling appropriate behaviour such that a conservation ethic is generated.

Quality assurance initiatives such as ecotourism certification programmes may benefit guides with criteria that stipulate minimum guiding standards and/or qualifications and ratios of guides to consumers and may provide opportunities for training and professional development (see Crabtree and Black, 2000). All these measures contribute to high-quality guiding, which will ideally also translate to a better-quality experience for the consumer and hence greater customer satisfaction. Professional certification of individual ecotour guides is important not only because it awards qualifications but also because it may be used to benchmark existing guides' standards and highlight training needs (see Chapters 17, 18 and 19 in this volume; Crabtree and Black, 2000). Tour guides are usually employed by tour operators, though in many small tour operations the owner/operator is also the guide. In cases where a guide is employed, conflicts may arise between the guide and operator needs and motivations. All these issues bring a degree of complexity to the equation, but guides clearly play a pivotal role in the ecotourism experience and are at the interface between the consumer, the operator, the environment and the host community. Their importance in providing quality ecotourism has been largely ignored by the ecotourism industry, although there has been limited research in this area (see Weiler and Davis, 1993; Haig, 1997; Black, 1999, 2002; Ballantyne and Hughes, 2001; Welier and Ham, 2001; Armstrong and Weiler, 2002). We hope the three chapters that focus on guides in this volume might help address this gap.

Ecotourism Industry

The ecotourism industry is a complex phenomenon comprising a variety of different sectors in tourism and including players in both the private and public sector. We define the ecotourism industry as representing the sum of those commercial and industrial activities that produce goods and services that are wholly or mainly consumed by travellers participating in ecotourism (adapted from House of Representatives Select Committee on Tourism, 1978). The players may include, among others, outbound and inbound tour operators, travel agents, the travel media, tour guides, transportation carriers, hotels and restaurants, visitor attractions and tourist information centres. The scale and type of organizations may vary considerably from locally owned, one-person enterprises through to nationally owned chains that operate across the domestic market to large-scale, foreign-owned or controlled chains or corporations that are transnational in their operations. Ecotourism enterprises may deliver a diverse number of different products, ranging from tours and attractions to accommodation, from experiences lasting a few hours to multi-day trips, from small bed and breakfast establishments to large ecolodges. The diversity that makes up the ecotourism industry means that there is a huge variety in the number of potential elements that need to be considered when looking at quality.

This diversity has both benefits and challenges, for, while the mosaic of players within the industry can add richness to the ecotourism fabric, it can also lead to conflicts between the different players, who have competing interests. These players may also hold different views on what ecotourism is, or should be. The fuzzy boundaries and different manifestations of ecotourism are certainly one of the problems in attempting to define ecotourism and lead to many of the challenges in developing and implementing appropriate and relevant quality assurance initiatives.

Many commentators view commercial tourism enterprises negatively because, as businesses, they are perceived as focusing on commercial activities, profits and short-term gains. However, the tourism industry as a whole has increasingly embraced voluntary actions to increase environmental, sociocultural and long-term economic sustainability through a number of different initiatives. These include some of the tools and mechanisms already addressed in this volume, such as awards of excellence, codes of conduct and in some cases the development of ecotourism-specific certification programmes (e.g. NEAP). Industry associations have been involved in the development of a range of quality assurance initiatives, such as self-help guides and manuals (e.g. International Hotels Environment Initiative (TCA, 1998)), charters, networks and newsletters (e.g. Green Hotelier newsletter). A growing number of industry associations concerned with issues of tourism sustainability and ecotourism have been established, as well as existing associations setting up special working groups (e.g. PATA Sustainable Tourism Committee). Even the travel media, which are notoriously self-interested, have produced some outstanding projects, as demonstrated by the recent release of Code Green by Lonely Planet Guidebooks (Lorimer and Gelber, 2006).

Many feel that all this is too little, too late and that an industry embracing self-regulation with non-enforceable codes and guidelines is just a self-interested attempt to stave off stricter controls that governments might impose through regulation. This view is continued with the conviction that the industry does not, and will not, openly embrace corporate responsibility beyond that which returns a tangible financial profit. Certainly this view is compounded by the fact that most sustainable tourism and ecotourism quality assurance tools have a one-sided focus on environmental issues, particularly the use of energy, potable water and waste management. The reduction of energy and water consumption and minimization of waste may well limit consumption of scarce resources, but the resultant eco-efficiencies also result in considerable cost savings. These are estimated by WTO (2002) to be up to 20%.

Although there is an argument that 'the ends should not justify the means', the fact is that some of these initiatives are positive and beneficial, and result in better knowledge on how to apply sustainability principles, ensuring that there are wins for the environment, the local community and the economy. It may be that the tourism industry is not as bad as it has been painted, or perhaps it is simply waking up to the fact that becoming more environmentally and socially responsible and embracing the tenets of quality ecotourism simply translate to plain business sense.

We are not going to provide excuses for or answers to these conundrums, but hope that the stories from a range of industry sectors (albeit from three very different perspectives) in Chapters 20, 21 and 22 will speak for themselves and show whether the ecotourism industry can uniformly be tarred with the same brush. The perspectives of ecotourism operators on sustainable tourism initiatives in New Zealand, a region blessed with a 'green and clean' image and trying to live up to the successful marketing campaign of '100% pure', raise some interesting issues in Chapter 20. The author of Chapter 21, an ecolodge architect, reviews four different existing ecotourism certification programmes that include criteria for ecotourism accommodation and concludes by suggesting the need for an internationally recognized certification programme specifically for ecolodges. We also hear from arguably one of the most successful ecotourism certification programmes, the Australian EcoCertification Program (formerly known as NEAP), 'developed by industry for industry', through the eyes of a former programme assessor (Chapter 22) who was involved in delivering the programme. This chapter provides an insight into the development of the programme and identifies key changes introduced as a result of experience, the inbuilt demand for continuous improvement, internal politics and external pressure and forces.

Protected Area Managers' Perspectives

Protected areas are often the lifeblood for ecotourism. The very attributes for which they are gazetted – high natural scenic values, unique endemic flora and fauna, distinctive landscapes or landforms – are also the basic raw materials for ecotourism. Protected area managers' views on quality ecotourism are relevant not only because the areas they manage are the favoured location for ecotourism activities, but also because they present the park through their own ecotourism activities and events, such as education programmes and interpretation in visitor centres, brochures, signage or guided walks and talks with rangers.

Protected areas are 'honeypots', attracting tourism to their special or outstanding natural and cultural resources. It is not surprising, then, that many protected areas are coming under increasing pressure and experiencing negative impacts through sheer numbers of tourists (Wearing and Neil, 1999; Butler and Boyd, 2000; Weaver, 2001). Protected area managers face a difficult task in balancing the need for conservation of the resource with their secondary directive of allowing access and opportunities for recreation.

Despite these problems, tourism has been heralded not only as the bane, but also as the possible saviour of protected areas. With financial stringency and the general trend towards 'user pays' among protected area management agencies, ecotourism offers these agencies some exciting opportunities with its fundamental precept and promise of returns to conservation. Harnessing the potential of ecotourism to deliver significant benefits to conservation and protected areas does not rely on just collecting entrance fees. In-kind support through help with maintenance, feral animal and weed control, revegetation and regeneration projects and collaborative printing of brochures cover just a few of the mechanisms that can be increasingly seen around the world. Protected areas are also often forced through reduced budgets to rely more and more on tour operators to present the conservation values of the area to visitors. Evidence also suggests that protected areas are becoming increasingly dependent on tourism to generate operating revenue (Weaver, 2001; Fennell, 2003).

Protected area managers have a strong interest in quality ecotourism, particularly to ensure that their visitors minimize their negative impacts on the park, whilst maximizing their positive returns. In Australia, a number of protected area management agencies are using the quality assurance tool of EcoCertification as a tool for filtering or selecting appropriate tourism products and raising industry standards. Since 2004, the Great Barrier Reef Marine Park Authority has given extended permits of 15 years to appropriately certified tour operators, and Conservation and Land Management in Western Australia gives preferential access to operators who hold the 'Advanced Ecotourism' level of EcoCertification. The involvement of protected area managers in ensuring quality ecotourism is explored in more depth in Chapters 15 and 16. Chapter 15 presents the perspective of a protected area manager, who uses Western Australia as a case study to explore the issues surrounding the use and application of various tourism certification programmes in the context of protected areas. Chapter 16 discusses the Protected Area Network (PAN) of Parks, a programme that aims to create a network of European wilderness protected areas with a reliable trademark that this guarantees nature protection and some of the issues surrounding its development and implementation.

Summary

Ecotourism involves many stakeholders, often with differing interests and motivations and frequently looking for different outcomes from ecotourism. Any discussion of ecotourism and quality in ecotourism needs to recognize the range of stakeholders' views and try to meet and balance their individual needs, demands and interests.

Part Two of this volume presents a range of key stakeholders' perspectives, which that we hope will highlight some of the key issues and challenges faced by ecotourism stakeholders in addressing, developing and implementing quality in ecotourism.

References

Armstrong, E.K. and Weiler, B. (2002) Getting the message across: an analysis of messages delivered by tour operators in protected areas. *Journal of Ecotourism* 1(2 & 3), 104–121.

Ballantyne, R. and Hughes, K. (2001) Interpretation in ecotourism settings: investigating tour guides' perceptions of their role, responsibilities and training needs. *Journal of Tourism Studies* 12(2), 2–9.

Black, R.S. (1999) Ecotour guides: performing a vital role in the ecotourism experience. Paper presented at the World Ecotourism Conference, Kota Kinabalu, Malaysia.

Black, R.S. (2002) Towards a model for tour guide certification: an analysis of the Australian EcoGuide Program. Doctoral thesis, Department of Management, Monash University, Melbourne, Victoria, Australia.

Buckley, R., Pickering, C. and Weaver, D.B. (eds) (2003) *Nature-based Tourism, Environment and Land Management.* CAB International, Wallingford, UK.

Butler, R.W. and Boyd, S.W. (eds) (2000) *Tourism and National Parks: Issues and Implications.* John Wiley and Sons, Chichester, UK.

Cohen, E. (1985) The tourist guide: the origins, structure and dynamics of a role. *Annals of Tourism Research* 12, 5–29.

Commonwealth Department of Tourism (1994) *National Ecotourism Strategy.* Commonwealth of Australia, Canberra, Australia.

Crabtree, A. and Black, R.S. (2000) *EcoGuide Program Guide Workbook.* Ecotourism Association of Australia, Brisbane, Queensland.

Epler Wood, M. (2002) *Ecotourism: Principles, Practices and Policies for Sustainability.* United Nations Environment Programme, Paris, France.

Epler Wood, M. (2004) *The Epler Wood Report: The Green Market Gap.* EplerWood International, Burlington, Vermont.

Fennell, D. (2003) *Ecotourism.* Routledge, London, UK.

Fennell, D.A. and Dowling, R.K. (2003) Ecotourism policy and planning: stakeholders, management and governance. In: Fennell, D.A. and Dowling, R.K. (eds) *Ecotourism Policy and Planning.* CAB International, Wallingford, UK, pp. 331–344.

Font, X. and Buckley, R. (eds) (2001) *Tourism Ecolabelling: Certification and Promotion of Sustainable Management.* CAB International, Wallingford, UK.

Haig, I. (1997) Viewing nature: can a guide make a difference? Master of Arts thesis in Outdoor Education, Department of Outdoor Education, Griffith University, Brisbane, Queensland.

Honey, M. (ed.) (2002) *Ecotourism and Certification: Setting Standards in Practice.* Island Press, Washington, DC.

Honey, M. and Rome, A. (2001) *Protecting Paradise: Certification Programs for Sustainable Tourism and Ecotourism.* Institute of Policy Studies, Washington, DC.

House of Representatives Select Committee on Tourism (1978) *House of Representatives Select Committee on Tourism Final Report.* Australian Government Publishing Service, Canberra, ACT.

Lorimer, K. and Gelber, E. (2006) *Code Green: Experiences of a Lifetime.* Lonely Planet, Melbourne, Australia.

Martin, A. (1997) *Tourism, the Environment and Consumers.* MORI, London.

Pond, K. (1993) *The Professional Guide.* Van Nostrand Reinhold, New York.

Rainforest Alliance (2001) *A Proposal from the Rainforest Alliance as Coordinator of the Feasibility Study, Organizational Blueprint and Implementation Plan for a Global Sustainable Tourism Stewardship Council (STSC): An Accreditation Body for Sustainable Tourism Certifiers.* Rainforest Alliance, New York.

Rainforest Alliance (2003) *Sustainable Tourism Stewardship Council: Raising the Standards and Benefits of Sustainable Tourism and Ecotourism Certification.* Rainforest Alliance, New York.

Swarbrooke, J. (1999) *Sustainable Tourism Management.* CAB International, Wallingford, UK.

Synergy (2000) *Tourism Certification: An Analysis of Green Globe 21 and Other Tourism Certification Programs.* WWF–UK, London.

Tourism Council of Australia (TCA) (1998) *Being Green Keeps You Out of the Red: an Easy Guide to Environmental Action for Accommodation Providers and Tourist Attractions.* Tourism Council Australia and CRC Tourism in association with the Department of Industry, Science and Tourism and Environment Australia, Tourism Council Australia, Woolloomooloo, NSW.

Wearing, S. (2001) Exploring socio-cultural impacts on local communities. In: Weaver, D. (ed.) *The Encyclopedia of Ecotourism.* CAB International, Wallingford, UK, pp. 395–407.

Wearing, S. and Neil, J. (1999) *Ecotourism: Impacts, Potentials and Possibilities.* Butterworth Heinemann, Oxford, UK.

Weaver, D.B. (ed.) (2001) *The Encyclopedia of Ecotourism.* CAB International, Wallingford, UK.

Weiler, B. and Davis, D. (1993) An exploratory investigation into the roles of the nature-based tour leader. *Tourism Management,* April, 91–98.

Weiler, B. and Ham, S.H. (2001) Tour guides and interpretation. In: Weaver, D. (ed.) *Encyclopedia of Ecotourism.* CAB International, Wallingford, UK, pp. 549–563.

World Tourism Organization (WTO) (2002) *Voluntary Initiatives for Sustainable Tourism: Worldwide Inventory and Comparative Analysis of 104 Eco-labels, Awards and Self-commitments.* WTO, Madrid, Spain.

World Tourism Organization (WTO) (2006) *Making Tourism More Sustainable: A Guide for Policy Makers.* WTO, Madrid, Spain.

10 Sustainable Tourism Certification Marketing and its Contribution to SME Market Access

Xavier Font[1] and Megan Epler Wood[2]

[1]*Leeds Metropolitan University, Leeds, UK;* [2]*EplerWood International, Burlington, Vermont, USA*

Chapter Profile

The question of how well certification of sustainable tourism can contribute to building market access for business enterprises has important implications for how NGOs, donors and governments approach their support of sustainable tourism. Most literature to date has indicated that sustainable tourism certification has two benefits: first, improving the quality of management and services of companies and the sustainability of enterprises; and, second, improving the market for certified enterprises. Policy makers have supported certification projects with the understanding that both of these benefits were realistic outcomes of certification projects, without reliable research at hand to validate these views. This chapter investigates whether sustainable tourism certification has genuine market benefits. The authors conclude that, while certification may be a valid method to involve businesses in quality and sustainability oversight of their businesses, there is insufficient evidence to suggest that certification of sustainable tourism will have market benefits, and that such benefits should not be used to justify government, NGO or donor support of tourism certification.

Introduction

The certification of sustainable tourism and ecotourism has gained increasing support as a dual strategy to provide consumers and businesses with an objective source of quality and sustainability assurance information while also building market demand in the ecotourism and sustainable tourism marketplace. In this chapter the authors investigate if market drivers exist for certification or if quality and sustainability assurance alone may have to provide sufficient incentive for tourism providers to certify their products.

Increasingly policy makers are turning to certification as a market mechanism to promote sustainable production and consumption. The most recent such project is the 2003 Inter-American Development Bank (IDB) and

Multilateral Investment Fund (MIF) US$3 million grant to support the creation of the network for the Americas for sustainable tourism certification programmes. This project was justified in the donor memorandum as a mechanism for increasing the competitiveness and market access of sustainable tourism small and medium-sized enterprises in Central and South America (IDB and MIF, 2003). A similar European network, VISIT, received considerable funding from the EU, particularly for the Green travel market, with the specific claim that it would contribute to marketing certified businesses (H. Hamele, personal communication, 15 April 2005). In light of these developments, the authors sought to investigate, independently of any funded certification programme, if indeed there is a market-based argument for the creation of future initiatives to support certification of sustainable and ecotourism.

The purpose of this chapter is to consider whether certifying tourism businesses for sustainability will contribute to greater consumer interest and build the market for ecotourism and sustainable tourism. This chapter reviews the literature on green consumer behaviour and sustainable tourism demand and the limited works available on the market for certified sustainable tourism. The authors investigate key marketing challenges as presented in the literature in the green and sustainability marketplace with respect to positioning, branding, business-to-business promotion and distribution. In light of these challenges, the authors review to what extent tourism certification programmes are presently positioned in the marketplace and what obstacles to positioning exist. Finally, the authors investigate the existing theories behind effective niche marketing and how consumer loyalty is won, to discover if marketing theory supports the idea that certification of tourism can effectively be linked to effective marketing campaigns.

Green Consumer Behaviour

In the 1990s, there was tremendous interest in the potential of the green market in the USA for a wide variety of consumer goods. The 'green' market is loosely defined as the market for products that have been produced without damage to the environment. While there were significant data in the early 1990s to indicate that a growing number of consumers in North America were interested in buying green products (Cambridge Reports/Research International, 1992), however, there is increasing evidence that consumers who have strong opinions and attitudes about the importance of conserving the environment are not acting upon these values when purchasing products. By 2000, the market literature was increasingly indicating that environmental integrity of products is not a market driver.

Perhaps the most important psychographic surveys on this topic were performed by Roper, a leading American consumer research organization, performing the same survey on the marketability of green products twice, once in the early 1990s and once in the late 1990s. These statistically valid surveys revealed that the committed environmental consumer market share in the USA did not grow in the 1990s. It remained at just over 10% of the market, while the remaining 90% of consumers expressed less interest in environmental purchasing as the decade progressed. Fewer Americans sought environmental labels, recycled products and biodegradable cleansers, or avoided styrofoam and aerosols. This research suggests that, while consumers stated their intention to make environmental integrity a priority, in reality they prioritize price, brand recognition and word-of-mouth recommendations over concerns about environmental impact (Ackerstein and Lemon, 1999).

Except for a few prominent products, most products did not benefit from the 'ecolabelling' in the 1990s, according to an investigation into 'brand greening'. While academics and environmentalists continued to promote the 'green' market as one of the most rapidly growing markets in the USA and ecolabelling as a means to reach this market, the reality was different (Ackerstein and Lemon, 1999). For example, the LOHAS or 'lifestyles of health and sustainability' market emerged in the USA in the 1990s with highly optimistic projections for market reach. The LOHAS market includes organic foods, energy-efficient appliances, solar panels, alternative medicine, yoga tapes and ecotourism. The Natural Marketing Institute estimates that 68 million Americans, or one-third of the American adult population, qualify as LOHAS consumers, and yet the actual sales data indicate that there is a yawning gap between what consumers say they will buy in surveys and the actual sales data. While the Natural Marketing Institute study indicates that 40% of Americans say they have purchased organic food and beverages, only 2% of the US$600 billion food and beverage market comes from organic products (Cortese, 2003). Sustainable products market research expert Harvey Hartman stated in 2003 that consumer research 'mechanically ties consumer behaviour to consumer attitudes', and that 'we cannot quite shed the belief that consumers act merely on their convictions, despite the large and growing body of evidence to the contrary' (Hartman and Hartman Group, 2003: 44–45).

Sustainable Tourism and Ecotourism Demand

In 1997, the World Tourism Organization presented information to indicate that ecotourism accounts for 20% of the world tourism market. At that time, there were many highly publicized reports indicating that ecotourism was the fastest-growing tourism market in the world. Since that time the WTO has supported a number of studies into the size of the ecotourism market for the International Year of Ecotourism. The 2002 WTO report, which used statistically valid in-flight survey data from the US government, found that the ecotourism market in the US market is closer to 5% of the total number of travellers going overseas. This same study also demonstrated that there is little evidence that the ecotourism share of the overall travel trade was increasing rapidly between 1997 and 2001. The report states that on balance outbound US tourism did not grow rapidly, and there is little evidence that US travellers were the source of the often-cited ecotourism boom (WTO, 2002). Notably, a 2003 survey of successful ecolodge owners and regional ecotourism experts worldwide found that the US market was cited as the largest and most significant ecotourism market in the world (Epler Wood *et al.*, 2005).

These results seem to mirror what researchers have found about the green consumer market as a whole. While there was great optimism in the early 1990s, the reality was different. What fuelled these overestimates? A number of trends came into play. There were many surveys that looked at consumers' intentions, but few that tested consumers' purchasing habits. There were also certain countries that prospered greatly, leading to the conclusion that the prospects for the global market were greater than they were. Certain destinations were expanding at double-digit rates between 1986 and 1998 – e.g. Ecuador at 17%, Costa Rica 42%, Belize 25%, Botswana 19% and South Africa 108% per annum; however, these countries were known to be stable and had well-developed wildlife parks and reasonable infrastructure. It therefore became increasingly apparent in the 1990s that few countries could emulate these conditions. At the same time the ecotourism market seemed to be very 'hot' in certain countries, and yet there was little, if any, serious market survey work undertaken to look at inbound data at the destination level to confirm the exact nature of this trend. It was impossible to find psychosocial data in the 1990s in destination countries that looked at travellers' interests and attitudes, and there were no studies that looked at the 'green' values of the tourists arriving in these 'hot' ecotourism destinations. Traveller motivations were studied on a global level, but not on arrival or post-arrival in specific countries. This led to many optimistic conclusions about green motivation for travel without specific supporting data. However, there was one interest group that was expressing increasing scepticism. The ecotourism industry, lodge owners and tour operators were making it known to Epler Wood as president of the International Ecotourism Society that their clients were not mentioning any desire for 'green standards'.

In 2003, EplerWood International (Epler Wood, 2004) undertook a survey for the US Agency for International Development's (USAID) Proyecto Caiman in Ecuador with 25 reputable US-based ecotour operators working both on the mainland of Ecuador and in the Galápagos Islands. The operators surveyed were a highly representative sample of reputable companies operating in Ecuador that seek to meet environmental and social standards. The survey included a question to each owner on the eco-social concerns of their clients, and how this influenced product selection. There was a 48% response rate to these questions. Eco-social concern was defined as 'clients concerned about environmental and social impacts, and interested in a contribution to sustainable development'. Figure 10.1 reveals that, while 42% of tour operators' clients are perceived as being very eco-socially concerned, 50% exhibit a low concern for environmental and social impacts. Nearly 70% of tour operator clients express no concern or interest in eco-social issues when selecting their products, and only 8% expressed a specific interest when selecting their tour. These results confirm studies in the broader marketplace that, while there is

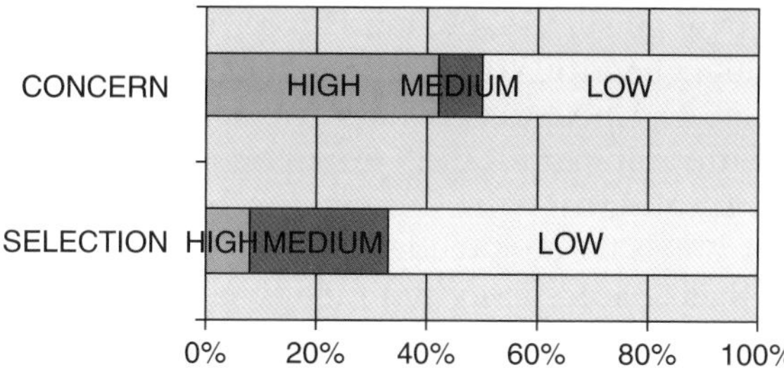

Fig. 10.1. Perceived eco-social concern and selection preferences for ecourism products by ecotour clients in Ecuador (from Epler Wood, 2004).

a genuine concern for environmental and social values in the ecotourism marketplace, less than 10% of the market booking ecotours with highly reputable ecotourism operators is requesting information from their operators on eco-social standards (Epler Wood *et al.*, 2005).

It would clearly be helpful if we could compare these results from US markets with the situation in Europe. However, in Europe, the research on the ecotourism market was greatly hindered by the fact that the market did not use the term 'ecotourism', particularly in the 1990s. The WTO studies on the ecotourism market in Europe were limited, underfunded and based on even smaller samples than the US WTO study referenced above and, according to Goodwin and Francis (2003: 272), although 'passive and uncritical tourists still outnumber active and enlightened ones' the balance is shifting. In the case of the UK, evidence (Goodwin and Francis, 2003: 272) suggests that there is a clear aspiration on the part of consumers to purchase and enjoy holidays that meet a range of responsible tourism criteria. However, the surveys 'record the views of respondents about how they would like to behave, and do not necessarily accurately forecast how consumers will actually behave when booking holidays' (Goodwin and Francis, 2003: 277–278). They confirmed that, according to tour operators, destination, price, services and departure dates remain the tourist's key decision-making criteria.

Market for Certified Sustainable Tourism

To date the market for certified sustainable tourism has not been intensively researched and there are no statistically valid studies the authors have been able to identify on this market. One of the reasons the authors have sought to write this chapter is because considerable investment in certification is being predicated on the thesis that certification will improve the competitiveness of businesses in the marketplace. We could find only anecdotal evidence that this is the case (see, for example, GG21, 2005, suggesting that 76% of enquiries to the Three Rivers ecolodge in Dominica stated that being Green Globe-certified influenced customer decision making). The fact that stronger evidence is lacking has been controversial and has caused disagreements in the sustainable tourism academic and practitioner community about the importance of having evidence that certification is a valid market tool.

In the late 1990s, over 60 sustainable tourism certification programmes were launched, but only a handful conducted market research to assess the demand for certification. The most current data available come from VISIT, a regional network of European certification programmes (see Chapter 23 in this volume), which indicates that most German tourists want environmental information about hotels to be included in tour operators' catalogues (ECOTRANS and FUR, 2003). A survey from the English Tourism Council, carried out during the planning of a certification programme, supported the introduction of certification/ accreditation with responses such as '84% of consumers said they would choose an attraction or accommodation provider that was part of a green accreditation scheme over one that was not, if such a scheme existed', and '58% state that the commitment to being environmentally friendly is important when selecting accommodation' (ETC, 2002). However, it could be argued that a more holistic approach to consumer purchasing patterns would not bring about the same answers based on the arguments laid out earlier in this chapter. Similarly a recent study from New Zealand asked whether consumers would be willing to purchase certified products. After defining what certification is meant to achieve, they found that tourists stated pro-certification values (Fairweather *et al.*, 2005).

In the absence of more robust certification demand data, other survey work is often quoted to support the introduction of standards. For example, research for the Association of British Travel Agents claims that 85% of people thought it was important that tourism should not damage the environment, 78% of people considered the provision of social/environmental information by their holiday company as important (ABTA, 2000) and more than 70% of tourists responded that they do not have sufficient environmental information about their holidays (Lübbert, 2001). The UK charity Tourism Concern surveyed readers of their magazine on ethical tourism to find that 96% of respondents who normally travelled independently said they felt that tourism should be fairer for destination communities (Tourism Concern, 2001).

These and other statistics appear to imply that there is a market for sustainable tourism products because these products are sustainable, and they have been used to justify the claim that certification is the right tool to prove this sustainability. Longitudinal data are not available to make comparisons, with the exception of two Tearfund-funded surveys in 1999 and 2001 done using the same methodology and questions showed an increase in this aspiration to purchase an 'ethical holiday' from 45% to 52% (Tearfund, 2002, quoted in Goodwin and Francis, 2003: 278), but this gives no indication on how the aspirations can be converted into sales. Conducting market research where consumers are asked to make alternative choices, using more powerful data analysis techniques, such as conjoint analysis, that replicate market conditions, would show how product attributes are prioritized. Better understanding of distribution channels and how these influence decision making would be necessary to discover if the consumers these studies reflect have more likelihood to purchase according to their ethics or not. A better understanding of the attributes that consumers actually use when making decisions, and the priority given to each attribute, is necessary.

Market Positioning

Weeden (2002: 142) has argued that responsible and ethical tourism 'can allow companies to compete on more than just price'. Many mindful tour operators and lodge owners believe that making their practices responsible helps position them in the market. Positioning is a highly important concept in market literature today because of the difficulty in distinguishing the attributes of products in the increasingly crowded global marketplace. The contention is that the certification of responsible practices effectively helps responsible tourism vendors to distinguish their approach – and thus gives them a unique market position. Of sites approved by the Certified Audubon Signature Sanctuary, 90% believe this status 'has or will have value in marketing and promotional efforts, with the remaining 10% indicating only that they don't know' (USGA, 2004). More specifically, 18% of respondents to the Green Globe membership survey indicated an increased media exposure since becoming a Green Globe participant, while '22 percent of our participants indicated that they have experienced an increase in green market appeal and 8 percent indicated that they have received more customers as a direct effect of being Green Globe Participants' (GG21, 2004). It would be important to look at the data that the industry is using in order to understand if customers are directly attributing purchases to Green Globe certification or to a variety of factors. Market positioning is difficult to properly assess, and it is rare that consumers have just one motivator to purchase a product.

One of the most frustrating aspects of positioning products in the tourism industry is that the consumer needs to be able to experience the difference. In surveys of tour operators and vendors, EplerWood International found that many businesses note that their clients become much more engaged and loyal as they begin to understand the significance of responsible practices during their travels (Epler Wood *et al.*, 2005). One of the problems with most of the certification schemes is that the difference is not obvious to the potential purchaser before travelling. UK operators who are using responsible tourism as part of their marketing are assuring the tourist purchasing the product that they will experience the difference. An increasing number of tour operators are using this marketing approach (UNEP, 2005). However, further research is required to validate this approach.

Ecotourism certification starts from the assumption that the sustainability message will be a unique selling proposition that will give certified products a competitive advantage through better product positioning. However, psychographic analysis has yet to be applied to the ecotourism field, such as the type that Roper Starch Worldwide performed in the 1990s on green consumers. Harvey Hartman points out that consumers are notoriously inconsistent in applying their values to purchasing, and that current market research fails to reflect on the many factors influencing decision making. He notes that there are core, mid-level and peripheral consumer markets in the ethical marketplace that all apply some level of ethical consideration, but that only the 'core' group responds to 'knowledge and authenticity factors' (Hartman and Hartman Group, 2003: 41). It is likely that it is this group that responds to certification as a marketing tool, but there is no statistically valid information available about the size of this core market for sustainable tourism and ecotourism. In the words of psychosocial market researcher Harvey Hartman, it would help researchers to understand 'which dimensions of a particular world are likely to have the most impact on a given consumer's buying decisions, and understanding what product attributes resonate with these dimensions' (Hartman and Hartman Group, 2003: 42).

Proponents of sustainable tourism and ecotourism certification suggest that consumer demand for certification will take time to build. According to Amos Bien of the International Ecotourism Society (TIES), 'Case after case has demonstrated that consumer demand develops long after a certification program is well established' (Bien, 2005: 16). His recent summary of research on marketing for sustainable tourism and ecotourism certification suggests that consumer demand takes between 8 and 15 years (sometimes as long as 20 years) to develop. Bien states that 'safety, quality and price needs must be satisfied before a consumer will consider other factors' (Bien, 2005: 17).

With the evidence that is presently available, it appears that certification can help incrementally with product positioning, and while some businesses perceive that it does they recognize that this benefit takes years to accrue. According to the TIES research (Bien, 2005), an 8–20-year cycle of investment would be required. With this in mind, the authors conclude that certification cannot provide product positioning to the degree necessary for businesses seeking to justify the investment in the traditional 3-year market planning cycle, or even a 5-year market planning cycle, while certification can play a role in product positioning in a much longer period of time, if businesses are willing to invest in this kind of long-term positioning approach. However, this positioning benefit would be viable only if the certification organizations working with businesses have long-term viability and the capability to co-market the certification brand. Early results from Costa Rica and Australia indicate that even the most well-thought-of certification programmes have not been organized to offer a market positioning benefit. Given the fact that neither of these programmes has gained international market attention, it is not surprising that more businesses are not becoming certified.

Branding

The main issue reported in the literature on challenges for certification marketing is that there are too many ecolabels, and that fewer, more recognizable labels would strengthen the brand (Font, 2001; Lübbert, 2001). With an average of only 50 certified products per ecolabel, the current impact on the market is minimal, and the brand/brands are largely unknown. Either through clustering groups of brands (e.g. VISIT initiative, Network of Americas) or through the expansion of current brands (e.g. Green Globe), we are seeing the development of some regional brands, as fast as the politics between certification programmes allows.

These types of strategies are well reported elsewhere in this volume (see Chapter 23), and yet it can be argued that all these brands will encounter financial challenges if they are to become sufficiently strong to be meaningful to their target markets (Font, 2005). After a period of development of bottom-up, locally based, capacity-building certification programmes, it appears that we are moving to a phase where larger brands may dominate and change the profile of this sector. Examples of this are the announcement of the European Ecolabel, mainly known for white goods but now also available for holiday accommodation with high environmental standards, and the new proposal for specific sustainable tourism standards from the International Organization for Standardization.

The current certification brands that do not have a strong foothold in the market will likely lose out when they come face to face with stronger, well-funded brands. Branding, however, is not sufficiently powerful to influence customer choice at present. A study of 100 consumers who booked with NEAP (now known as Ecocertification) operators in Australia indicated that not one consumer was aware of the company's certification and most were unaware of NEAP certification (Planeta.com, 2003). Further research is needed to determine evidence if the additional NEAP logo is converting additional clients. It is worth mentioning here that certification programmes often appear to be their own worst enemies. For example, the former Nature and Ecotourism Accreditation Programme in Australia has had three major name or brand changes in 9 years – and with each name change a change in logo,with up to nine different logos (the programme has three categories) in the marketplace for one programme. Yet even the stronger Green Globe brand has very low brand recognition according to a recent study in New Zealand (Fairweather *et al.*, 2005).

The argument here is that brand loyalty in tourism is low, because there is an increasing trend towards trying different destinations (particularly for long-haul holidays). The potential of an international tourist visiting the same long-haul destination, let alone using the same provider, is low. A challenge for sustainable tourism or ecotourism brand loyalty is whether, after having taken a holiday in, for example, a Green Globe certified hotel in Barbados, they will choose to look for a Green Globe hotel when they visit Fiji. There are three problems here: first is that the small number of certified firms severely restricts choice; the second is that the distribution channels for holidays do not make this type of choice easy; and, thirdly, the products within the brand are not homogeneous enough to be perceived as a brand. When we look at Green Globe-certified hotels around the world, there is a great diversity, with small and large, business and rural, budget and luxury. The only thing they have in common is caring about the environment.

The next challenge, and more profound, is not the number of brands, but the meaning the brand will have to the consumer. The issues raised in positioning have knock-on effects for branding. Certification is one form of a self-regulating industry and guarding customers against false claims. This, indeed, is one of the prime calls for the development of ecotourism certification programmes, and certainly it is a highly legitimate reason for promoting certification. Amos Bien comments, 'it is clear that unless a program is long-established, simply adding a certification logo to a business' advertising is not going to increase occupancy' (Bien, 2005: 17). However, he concludes, improved standards through compliance with recognized norms of best practice and cost savings can help justify the certification initiative. The bottom line is that ecotourism and sustainable tourism labels do not provide sufficient marketing power to attract consumers.

There are exceptions to this conclusion, when, for example, the product attribute being certified is exceedingly clear and visible to the consumer. With Blue Flag beaches, for example, the cleanliness of the beach and ocean water is being certified. The product attributes are clear and meaningful (certification means to the client, above all, that they are not swimming in contaminated water). There are sufficient beaches certified throughout Europe for tourists to now expect their holiday destination to have a Blue Flag, and ask themselves why if it does not. With environmental standards for accommodation, it is a different story. First, the difference between a hotel that consumes little water and energy and produces little waste (amongst other criteria) is not immediately obvious to the client. Secondly, for most clients it is not as meaningful as other product attributes such as location, overall quality, facilities and so on. Thirdly, there are plenty of hotels out there with the same standards, but not certified.

Distribution of Certified Products

The distribution/commercialization of certified products can take two avenues, targeting the consumer directly and working through distribution channels. Increasingly the travel industry is moving towards direct marketing to consumers via the Internet, but the importance of wholesalers and tour operators in the travel distribution chain, particularly in Europe, remains strong and certification's marketing benefits must be understood not only via direct marketing to the consumer, but also via wholesale distribution channels. According to Bien,

> certification programs' efforts to market directly to the consumer frequently fail, because there are 1) not enough certified products initially, 2) the cost of direct consumer marketing is extremely high, 3) unlike retailers, who market to consumers on a daily basis [*sic*] certification programs would have to pay the entire cost of a promotional program, 4) unlike retailers, certification programs are generally unskilled at primary consumer marketing.
>
> (Bien, 2005: 16)

The Certification for Sustainable Tourism (CST) programme in Costa Rica exemplifies some of the problems. It has been consistently referenced as a model for sustainable tourism certification programmes, and has been understood to be the model upon which other sustainable tourism certification programmes will be based – at least in the Americas, if not worldwide. Yet an independent study (Newton *et al.*, 2004) looked at how far the CST had progressed since its founding in 1996 and found that 5% of the tourism hotel businesses in Costa Rica had been certified by 2004. The investigators sought to understand why there had been limited participation and found many explanatory factors. In terms of the programme's effectiveness as a market tool for business, it was found that only 8% of the businesses reported that marketing benefits are an incentive to become certified by CST. Nearly half of the certified hotels do not advertise that they have been certified and the researchers found that very little advertising is done for certified hotels by the CST; furthermore, not all hotels that claimed they were certified could be found on the CST web site. Other relevant tourism organizations, such as the powerful and influential Chamber of Commerce for Tourism in Costa Rica, are not linked to the CST web site and little promotion is done of the CST web site by its own governmental sponsor, the Institute for Costa Rican Tourism. The CST web site does not allow the consumer to compare and contrast properties in a way that facilitates selection. With only 5% of hotels in the country participating, many properties that are involved with sustainable tourism management are not participating in the programme (Newton *et al.*, 2004). In short, the marketing programme for CST is not reaching the consumer.

This same study also reviewed the marketing outreach effectiveness of the ecotourism certification programme run by Ecotourism Australia. The conclusion was that 'One of the problems that CST and Ecotourism Australia have is a general lack of awareness for their certifications. Neither program has created a name for itself on the international market, which substantially limits both programs effectiveness' (Newton *et al.*, 2004: 26).

In general, certification programmes do little promotion of the certified companies because they perceive that getting involved in marketing companies conflicts with the task of evaluating standards, and also because they are often delivered by NGOs and government agencies that lack marketing experience and effectiveness. Leading NGO and donor-funded certification practitioners have suggested that reducing the number of certification programmes and consolidating lists of certified companies to larger, searchable databases would create the necessary economies of scale to make marketing the products directly to consumers via the Internet more feasible and presentable. The VISIT programme has sought to consolidate the information of over 1500 accommodation providers in Europe since 2002 (www.yourvisit.info). The Green Travel Market promotes a range of sustainable tourism products (www.greentravelmarket.info), where very few sales can be claimed because suppliers are certified as sustainable (Kusters, personal communication, 23 May 2005). A review of these web sites indicates they do not provide the depth and visual presentation that consumers (or tour operators searching for suppliers) shopping the Web expect, and this lack of competitiveness will probably inhibit the growth of this approach unless long-term funding is found to improve these web sites to more competitive standards and their competitiveness can be assured via their ability to attract a market. Rainforest Alliance has just published a catalogue of certified tourism businesses in the Americas and at the time of writing this chapter its effectiveness cannot be evaluated. Bien (2005) notes that certification programmes have to pay the entire cost of a promotional programme and that, unlike retailers, they are generally unskilled in primary consumer marketing.

Both Bien (2005) and UNEP (2005) have found that the real demand for certification is from large purchasers, such as wholesalers, governments or other intermediaries in the commercialization chain, not individual consumers. They note that many tour operators in Europe are implementing sustainability policies and are presently directly inspecting properties to ensure quality and sustainability. From this information Bien (2005) predicts that certification programmes may exert the most influence by providing certified product information for these buyers.

Legislation will soon require large tour operators in Europe to report on their corporate social responsibility strategies, and the resulting requirement for sustainable supply-chain management could drive wholesalers to require the purchase of socially and environmentally managed products. Committed tour companies have shown interest in working with certified products for this reason, even when they are not communicating information on certification to their clients (TOI, 2002, 2004; see also ECEAT, 2005, for a review of the EU-funded project Tourlink, linking tour operator supply chains and certification). In practice, these tour operators set their own standards in most cases, because certification labels are not available in all the destinations where the tour operator works (Font *et al.*, 2004). Furthermore, the task for certification programmes is to prove that the information they can provide for the buyers is reliable, not only on certification issues, but on quality of accommodation, food and service. It would be an enormous challenge for the existing certifiers to offer the larger wholesalers the information they require, which is why tour operators are using their own inspections at present. Most certification programmes do not link quality services to sustainability standards, and it is debatable whether they could add these demanding components to their programme.

Many of the benefits of sustainability standards are not visible to the consumer; tour operators are unlikely to highlight certified suppliers separately according to the labels on the market, thereby undermining the value of a certification label. This is indeed a catch-22. While dozens of tourism certification labels seek to become better recognized in the market, the key buyers – the wholesalers – are not highlighting the certified product they buy because: (i) the labels are not consistently available around the world, and (ii) they do not represent meaningful value added to the consumer. For one season only, TUI Netherlands, which sells mainstream sun–sea–sand holidays, had a separate section of their main summer sun brochure highlighting all the holidays with proven sustainability credentials (through TUI's own internal verification), but the bookings were so low that they changed their brochures after one season. Sustainability did not work as a selling proposition, and the tour operator had to change its strategy.

The suggestion, therefore, that certification can be an effective marketing tool via distribution channels has little supporting evidence. Certainly, wholesalers from Europe will be seeking to upgrade the sustainability of their supply chain in the near future, and this is good news indeed. If certification of tourism products could facilitate this drive for sustainability, it would be outstanding. But the evidence suggests that these wholesalers will have to rely on their own property inspections because: (i) there is no identifiable market incentive for them to pay certifiers to do the work for them because they are not highlighting certification labels in their own literature; (ii) certification programmes are likely to have great difficulties delivering all the quality and service information tour operators require; and (iii) certifiers are not likely to have the market competitiveness they need to deal with demanding international buyers in terms of providing updated, well-managed information online that can be easily accessed and used by their buyers – at least according to the study of CST (Bien, 2005), which has been represented throughout the NGO, government and donor worlds as a leading example of sustainable tourism certification programmes.

Alternative Approaches to Marketing Sustainable Tourism

Understanding the motivations of the market in the 21st century should be a fundamental part of designing future sustainable development projects, in all green business arenas. Declining demand for existing green products and a demand for convenience, taste and quality seem to override the consumer's conscience in all but a very small percentage of the market. It may well be that an emotional rush to save our planet made the sustainable development community assume that consumers would make green purchases to save the environment.

The effort to gain a better understanding of the green consumer has led market researchers to conclude that there is a hierarchy of seriousness within the market, from the core groups that value authenticity (identified as about 10% of the market by Roper) to the peripheral groups that are simply looking to have fun – a much larger group. Stanley Plog finds that 'venturers' are the target market for ecotourism, and they are defined by survey research as 'intellectually curious' individuals who seek to be 'immersed in destination experiences' (Plog, 2004: 63). They respond to market messages for destinations that are both 'unique and involving'. Hartman and Hartman Group (2003) suggest that buyers concerned about sustainability make judgements through 'subjective–experience orientations' rather than 'objective-truth' thinking.

The book *The Cultural Creatives* (Ray and Anderson, 2000), based on psychographic surveys of 100,000 Americans, suggests that consumers are seeking connections to traditional values that have been lost due to modern progress. Modern societies, according to psychographic market researcher Harvey Hartman, have been dominated by technological values since the mid-19th century, and, while hardly anyone complains about the material benefits, there is hunger for a deeper sense of connection to nature, family, elders and community. With this theory in mind, the ecotourism market needs to help travellers feel they can belong to a world where they can have experiences that transcend material values. The logic of this is that ecotourism and sustainable tourism marketing will need to adopt lifestyle marketing approaches. All the literature indicates that the *Cultural Creatives* market goes away on holiday for renewal. They want to feel they have had a real 'experience' that extends their bodies, minds and souls. King makes the point that 'life style marketing tends to focus on and confirm more of what the customer would like to see in and of themselves rather than on any physical properties of the product or service being promoted' (King, 2002: 106). He concludes that this requires that destination marketing organizations reinvent themselves, shifting the emphasis towards preparing customer-focused holiday experiences (King, 2002).

For the sustainable development of ecotourism to grow and offer real economic benefits to local people, it will have to market the essence of what it delivers – nature, interactivity, experiential style, healthfulness, connections with community traditions, and the life-enhancing educational value of products that appeal to an audience that wants to do a good thing for themselves and the planet. For example, the UK is a relatively mature originating market for many international destinations, the third biggest spender on international tourism after the USA and Germany (WTO, 2001). Significant market segments in the UK are seeking more experiential holidays. Travel is increasingly 'about experiences, fulfilment and rejuvenation', rather than about 'places and things'; the lifestyle market is of increasing importance (King, 2002).

Conclusions

This chapter reviewed the thesis that sustainable tourism certification provides greater market access for certified businesses, as has been maintained by major donors, NGOs and governments. The literature on green consumerism suggests that, in the early 1990s, the market for green products was growing rapidly and would be based on consumers' growing desire to have products that are authentically sustainable. However, by 2000, this theory appeared to be increasingly incorrect, and statistically valid studies showed that the market for green products had not grown at all, and that in fact it was static. Similarly, studies in the early 1990s indicated that as much as 20% of the outbound tourism market in the world could be categorized as ecotourism while, by 2002, a study of the US market showed that ecotourism was actually only 5% of the market and had remained static in the 1990s.

Statistically reliable studies on the market for certified sustainable tourism have not been undertaken. Anecdotal information indicates that businesses may be able to more effectively position their businesses in the marketplace if they follow sustainable practices, and that certification may help to validate these practices in the marketplace – but that this process will take between 8 and 15 years.

Multiplicity of brands has left certified tourism products without market traction and certification cannot effectively help to brand tourism enterprises. Efforts to create marketing consortiums of certified product have not created strong Internet presences, and the lack of marketing experience and funding for certification consortiums appears to be making these efforts unsuccessful.

The chapter explored whether certification is a viable tool for providing information for wholesalers. This is particularly pertinent in Europe, where legislation will require wholesalers to purchase tourism products that meet sustainability standards. However, evidence already exists from previous initiatives that wholesalers in Europe have not found certification labels useful in marketing to their customers due to absent consumer interest or understanding of the numerous certification labels presently on the market. The question remains whether wholesalers from Europe will rely on certification programmes to provide the supplier information they need to meet European legislative standards. The authors find that most wholesalers have a record of using their own inspections programmes at present, and it is unlikely that they will rely on certifiers not affiliated with their businesses for the information they require. Finally, alternative approaches to marketing sustainable tourism were explored in this chapter, based on marketing theories, and it was found that a more subjective, experience-oriented approach to marketing sustainable tourism is more likely to succeed than an objective, standards-oriented approach.

Further research will be needed to prove or disprove the arguments put forward in this chapter. While the authors do not contest that certification of tourism has a role in reinforcing the quality and sustainability standards management applies in tourism development, this chapter concludes that the case for certification increasing market access to businesses around the world is so weak that it cannot be used by NGOs, governments and donors as an argument for funding support of certification projects.

Acknowledgement

The authors would like to acknowledge the contribution of Dr Harold Goodwin from Greenwich University in drafting this chapter.

References

ABTA (2000) *ABTA Visitor Survey.* Association of British Travel Agents, London.

Ackerstein, D. and Lemon, K. (1999) Greening the brand: environmental marketing strategies and the American consumer. In: Charter, M. and Polonsky, M.J. (eds) *Greener Marketing: A Global Perspective on Greening Marketing Practice.* Greenleaf, Sheffield, UK, pp. 233–254.

Bien, A. (2005) *Marketing Strategy for Sustainable and Ecotourism Certification, EcoCurrents First Quarter 2005.* The International Ecotourism Society, Washington, DC.

Cambridge Reports/Research International (1992) *Green Consumerism: Commitment Remains Strong Despite Economic Pessimism.* Cambridge Reports, London.

Cortese, A. (2003) Socially conscious consumers? To marketers, they're LOHAS. *New York Times* 21 July.

ECEAT (2005) Tourlink: towards a sustainable tourism supply chain. Available at: http://www.greentravelmarket.info/default.asp?site=background&menu=st_press&main=/portal/st_press.htm

Ecotrans and FUR (2003) German tourists expect environmental quality – Reiseanalyse 2002. Ecotrans, Saarbruken, Germany.

Epler Wood, M. (2004) *The Green Market Gap, Epler Wood Reports.* EplerWood International, Burlington, Vermont. Taken from results of International Market Study for Awa/Huaorani Territories, Ecuador, Proyecto Caiman, USAID, Quito, Ecuador. Available at: http://www.eplerwood .com/reports.php

Epler Wood, M., Wight, P. and Corvetto, J. (2005) *A Review of Markets, Business, Finance and Technical Assistance Models for Ecolodges in Developing Countries.* IFC, World Bank, Washington, DC. Available at: http://www.ifc.org/ifcext/enviro.nsf/AttachmentsByTitle/p_donor2004/$FILE/SBAP_2004.pdf

ETC (2002) *Visitors' Attitudes to Sustainable Tourism.* English Tourism Council, London.

Fairweather, J., Maslin, C. and Simmons, D. (2005) Environmental values and response to ecolabels among international visitors to New Zealand. *Journal of Sustainable Tourism* 13(1), 82–98.

Font, X. (2001) Conclusions: a strategic analysis of tourism ecolabels. In: Font, X. and Buckley, R. (eds) *Tourism Ecolabelling: Certification and Promotion of Sustainable Management.* CAB International, Wallingford, UK, pp. 259–270.

Font, X. (2005) Sustainability standards in the global economy. In: Theobald, W. (ed.) *Global Tourism.* Butterworth-Heinemann, Oxford, UK, pp. 213–229.

Font, X., Tapper, R. and Kornilaki, M. (2004) Green purchasers: sustainable supply chain management in tourism. In: *Tourism: State of the Art II Conference.* Glasgow, UK.

GG21 (2004) Green Globe 21 – Newsletter No. 21, December 2004. Available at: http://www.greengolbe21.com/Documents/Newsletters/December2004.htm#8

GG21 (2005) Green Globe 21 – Newsletter No. 23, February 2005. Available at: http://www.greenglobe21.com/Documents/Newsletters/February2005.htm

Goodwin, H. and Francis, J. (2003) Ethical and responsible tourism: consumer trends in the UK. *Journal of Vacation Marketing* 9(3), 271–284.

Hartman, H. and Hartman Group (2003) *Reflections on a Cultural Brand.* The Hartman Group, Bellevue, Washington, DC.

Inter-American Development Bank (IDB) and Multilateral Investment Fund (MIF) (2003) *Donors Memorandum International Accreditation System and Consolidation of National Systems for Certification to Facilitate SME Competitiveness and Market Access*, TC-03-03-03-4-RG. IDB and MIF, Washington, DC.

King, J. (2002) Destination marketing organisations – connecting the experience rather than promoting the place. *Journal of Vacation Marketing* 8(2), 105–108.

Lübbert, C. (2001) Tourism ecolabels market research in Germany. In: Font, X. and Buckley, R. (eds) *Tourism Ecolabelling: Certification and Promotion of Sustainable Management.* CAB International, Wallingford, UK, pp. 71–86.

Newton, T., Quiros, N., Crimmins, A., Blodgett, A., Kapur, K., Lin, H., Luo, T., Rossbach, K. and Dunivan, D. (2004) *Assessing the Certification of Sustainable*

Tourism Program in Costa Rica. School for Field Studies, Center for Sustainable Development Studies, Alejuela, Costa Rica.

Planeta.com (2003) Ecotourism Marketing and Certification Forum. Available at: http://www.planeta.com/ecotravel/tour/marketingcert.html

Plog, S. (2004) *Leisure Marketing.* Pearson Education, Upper Saddle River, New Jersey.

Ray, P. and Anderson, S.R. (2000) *The Cultural Creatives*. Three River Press, New York.

Tearfund (2002) *Worlds Apart.* Tearfund, London.

TOI (2002) *Tourism Ecolabel Schemes: a Supply Chain Management Tool for Tour Operators*. Tour Operators Initiative for Sustainable Tourism Development, Paris.

TOI (2004) *Supply Chain Engagement for Tour Operators: Three Steps toward Sustainability.* Tour Operators Initiative for Sustainable Tourism Development, Paris.

Tourism Concern (2001) *Responsible Tourism Survey.* Tourism Concern, London.

UNEP (2005) *Marketing Sustainable Tourism Products.* United Nations Environment Programme, Paris. Available at: http://www.uneptie.org/pc/tourism/private_sector/Marketing%20sustainable%20tourism%20htm.htm

USGA (2004) Good news for the bottom line and environmentally sensitive golf course development. Available at: http://www.usga.org/turf/green_section_ record/2004/nov_dec/good_news.html

Weeden, C. (2002) Ethical tourism: an opportunity for competitive advantage. *Journal of Vacation Marketing* 8(2), 141–153.

WTO (2001) *The British Ecotourism Market.* World Tourism Organization, Madrid, Spain.

WTO (2002) *The US Ecotourism Market.* World Tourism Organization, Madrid, Spain.

11 Consumer Demand for Quality in Ecotourism

ZOË CHAFE

Worldwatch Institute, Washington, DC, USA

Chapter Profile

An analysis of market studies and traveller surveys indicates that consumer demand for ecotourism appears to be strong and continues to grow. Tourists report strong interest in conserving the environment at tourism destinations, participating in educational and cultural exchange and contributing to host communities, either economically or voluntarily. Using consumer profiles from market studies, and examining the larger 'responsible' purchasing sector, one sees the potential for ecotourism to reach a broader audience. Ecotourism certification programmes are proliferating and generating interest from tourists – when they understand the concept. Travel agents and written travel resources are the most logical choice to further educate tourists about ecotourism products and services, as they continue to serve as a direct liaison to individual consumers. By harnessing latent consumer demand for ecotourism, building on the successes of the responsible purchasing trend and reaching out to travel information sources, ecotourism has the potential to reap the benefits of broadening public interest.

Introduction

Ecotourism has, since its inception in the mid-1980s, been advocated as a means of conserving sensitive ecosystems and generating income for local communities (Honey, 2002). The World Bank, like most other multilateral lending agencies, has embraced ecotourism as a means of development, and the United Nations recognized 2002 as the International Year of Ecotourism. The International Ecotourism Society (TIES) defines ecotourism as 'responsible travel to natural areas that conserves the environment and improves the well-being of local people' (TIES, 2004). The concept, however, is little more than words on paper unless committed businesses offer genuine products that adhere to the principles of ecotourism, and consumers (travellers) are willing to purchase those products, often at a higher price than other mainstream tourism options. As ecotourism becomes a familiar concept, by this name or others related (sustainable tourism, geotourism, responsible tourism), it is important to understand who the ecotourists are, what products they are seeking to purchase and what concepts they are interested in supporting when they travel.

This chapter analyses the current consumer demand that exists for ecotourism, sustainable tourism and/or responsible tourism. It uses surveys and polls carried out and analysed by academics, industry groups, non-governmental organizations (NGOs) and businesses to present evidence that tourists are interested in purchasing ecotourism products. By analysing consumer profiles, developed through market studies, the chapter explores specific niche markets with which the ideals embodied in ecotourism (cultural and environmental awareness and respect, environmental conservation, empowerment for local people) seem to resonate – yielding potentially untapped ecotourism consumers. It then examines the rapid rise in the overall 'responsible' purchasing sector, on the notion that consumers interested in other types of responsible purchasing might also be interested in ecotourism.

Certification for ecotourism serves two purposes: it can inform consumers about the quality of a tourism product or service, and it can also increase the value of the certified product. The latter part of the chapter examines consumers' perceptions of certification, and their willingness to pay for such quality assurance.

Finally, the chapter proposes that travel resources, playing a unique role as a source of information for the pre-departure tourist, are well suited to educate tourists about certified tourism products/services and ecotourism opportunities. Ecotourism, as a global phenomenon, has reached its adolescence. By studying consumer demand for ecotourism, one ascertains that there is broad support among a limited, but growing, number of tourists. There is still great potential for growth in the ecotourism and certified ecotourism products market, though this growth hinges on well-targeted marketing campaigns.

Survey and Poll Results on Demand for Ecotourism

Given the complexities of the ecotourism concept, researchers have found collecting data on ecotourism travellers quite difficult, and quantitative data on the subject have, until recently, been fairly scarce. Over the past decade, however, a number of universities and industry groups have sought to quantify the scope of both domestic and international ecotourism markets by interviewing tourists about their interests, values and spending habits. The survey questions focus on the three 'legs' of ecotourism – environmental, social and economic responsibility – as well as the quality of tourism products and services, knowledge of certification programmes, motivations for travelling and special interests.

Not all surveys are created equal: the surveys outlined in this chapter vary by sample size, respondent type, location and method. These are all important attributes to consider, as the survey method alone has the potential to greatly influence, even sway or bias, the results. Leggett *et al.* (2003) noted that results in a willingness-to-pay survey were 23% higher when administered through face-to-face interview, rather than using a self-administered (control) format.

Despite the inherent biases and faults in the variety of polls presented, it is possible to identify general trends by tracking the results of similar questions across various populations. Most of the surveys presented here are not statistically compatible. However, the results do begin to paint a picture of the ecotourism market that exists, and one that could exist. The diversity of populations interviewed begins to create an international perspective, though one notable caveat is that the information available is restricted almost exclusively to travellers from the industrialized world, which is composed of countries with high UN Human Development Index scores.

Several trends emerge from the assemblage of surveys examined. Taken as a whole, key aspects of the growth in consumer demand for various facets of ecotourism are: (i) a growing awareness of alternatives to mass tourism; (ii) concern about environmental degradation; (iii) interest in exploring new cultures; and (iv) self-reported willingness to pay for responsible travel products. The sections that follow outline the evidence and limitations that further define these trends.

Tourists seek quality vacations

Taking a vacation requires (often significant) investments of time and money, so it is natural that tourists want to ensure the best possible return in terms of quality for their investments while on vacation. It is not surprising, therefore, that price and quality remain among the top priorities cited by those choosing a vacation. After determining whether a tourism product or service has a fair price and is of sufficient quality, the purchaser might consider the environmental and social characteristics of the product. In a survey of 2032 UK adults, Tearfund (2000) found that 'the three main criteria are weather, cost and good facilities. But [UK] tourists do show concern about ethical policies and environmental considerations.' Building on Maslow's well-known hierarchy of needs, which shows that humans need to satisfy the most basic physiological and emotional needs before they can seek creativity and address morality, ecotourists must first be assured that they are purchasing a product of high quality before they consider whether it is environmentally or socially responsible (see Fig. 11.1).

Demand for environmental conservation

Over the past few decades, stunning information has become available detailing the degree to which the world's environment has been irreparably changed.

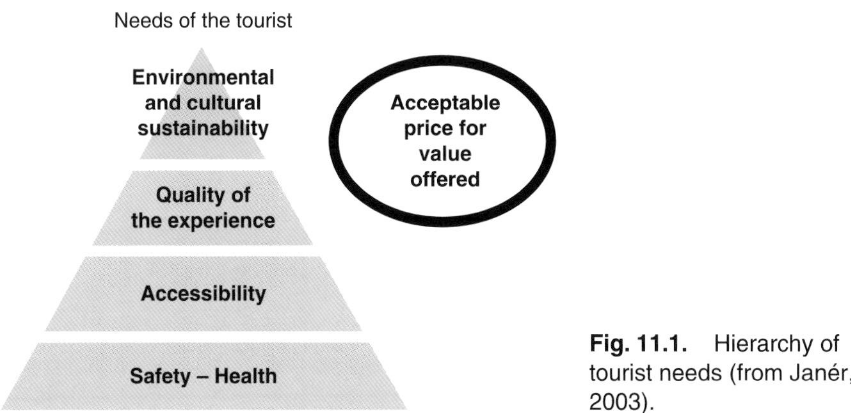

Fig. 11.1. Hierarchy of tourist needs (from Janér, 2003).

Conservation International, for example, has pinpointed 34 biodiversity hot spots – those areas rich in species diversity and threatened by human activity – which contain half of the world's plant species and 42% of the terrestrial vertebrates on only 2.3% of the world's land surface (Conservation International, 2005). Public concern for the protection of natural areas is shown in a variety of tourist surveys (see Table 11.1). Approximately 50–75% of tourists expressed a strong interest in visiting natural areas, conserving the environment at their destinations and patronizing accommodation that adheres to environmental standards.

In a survey of market characteristic studies, EplerWood International (2003) found that ecotourists across the world are interested in admiring and viewing natural scenery (70–85%), wildlife viewing (40–70%), hiking and walking (20–60%), guided interpretive tours (50–60%), visiting parks and protected areas, and learning about nature or culture (70+%), though the high percentages found in the responses should be expected as all activities are inherent to the definition of ecotourism. At least 85% of the tourists that visit Costa Rica consider national parks and rainforests the most important places to visit in the country (Rivera, 2002), and 70% of British adults surveyed agreed that short visits to local wildlife conservation projects would make their vacation more enjoyable (Responsibletravel.com, 2004).

The surveys referenced above also reveal tourists' displeasure at the decreasing environmental quality at popular destinations, such as beaches and national parks, highlighting the synergies between expectations of quality in tourism and the values contained within the concept of ecotourism. The gap between moral motivations for conserving environmental resources and having the quality of environmental resources impact a vacation is shrinking as tourists are faced with clear examples of environmental degradation. Tourtellot noted in 2002, for example, that more than half of US tourists surveyed (54%) notice that there are fewer unspoiled destinations than there used to be. No longer an idealistic expectation, environmental conservation has become a necessity to protect the quality of tourism destinations, and tourists increasingly recognize this. However, it remains unclear exactly how

Table 11.1. Results of selected consumer surveys.

Survey	Year	Countries	Survey population	Key findings
Travel Industry Association of America and National Geographic Traveler	2002	USA	8000 US adults 18+ (percentages reflect answers of those that have travelled more than 50 miles)	• 71% say it is important their visits to a destination not damage its environment • 53% agree their travel experience is better when learning about the destination's customs, geography and culture • 61% agree their travel experience is better when destination preserves natural, historical and cultural sites
Tearfund	2000	UK	2302 UK adults 15+ (percentages reflect answers from those that have travelled overseas)	• 46% want information on local customs, appropriate dress and behaviour • 54% think tour operators and guides should provide such information, while 52% think travel agents should • 55% would pay more for responsible tourism, and 5% was the average amount they would pay extra
	2001	UK	100 UK-based tour operators	• Nearly 50% of respondents (32 of 65 operators) have a responsible tourism policy • 30% of respondents said clients were asking more about social, economic and environmental issues in tourism
Responsibletravel.com	2004	UK	1002 UK adults	• 88% say tour operators should have a responsibility to benefit local people and preserve the environment • 89% say their holiday would be more enjoyable if they learned some of the local language, met local people • 89% say their holiday would be more enjoyable if their hotel had adequate waste and sewage treatment facilities

International Hotels Environment Initiative	2002	UK, USA, Australia	300 travellers at airports	• 87% of UK travellers surveyed (63% Australia, 60% US) expect hotels to guarantee good wages and working conditions • 0% of UK travellers surveyed (26% Australia, 14% US) actually asked if hotels have an environmental policy
ECOTRANS	2002	Germany	7872 German adults 14+	• 50% want to vacation in areas where the environment is intact or unspoiled • 42% consider environmentally friendly accommodation the most important environmental factor for future trips
Foster	2001	Australia	115 tourists at Visitor Info Centres around Victoria, Australia	• 39% expect accredited tour operators to be more expensive, while 54% expect them to be about the same • 71% would use an accredited operator in the future, after learning what accreditation meant

environmental degradation influences travel choices. In some cases, there may be a rush to see relatively unspoilt destinations, especially if it seems likely that quota systems will be introduced to mitigate problems stemming from heavy visitation.

Seeking environmental quality

As mass tourism destinations become increasingly overused and degraded, some ecotourists are consciously seeking destinations with intact environments. There is a clear relationship between the types of activities in which ecotourists engage (birdwatching, hiking and horseback riding, for example) and the need to preserve the environment in which the activities are physically taking place.

A 2002 survey of 7872 adult Germans found that the interviewees placed special importance on environmental quality: 65% of those surveyed (extrapolated to 39 million in the general German population) want clean beaches and water, and 42% (25 million) 'think that it is particularly important to find environmentally-friendly accommodation' (Ecotrans, 2002). In Britain, the figure is even higher: nearly all British tourists surveyed (83%) indicated that dirty beaches and a polluted sea 'mattered a great deal' in choosing or recommending travel destinations (Goodwin, 2001). And an overwhelming 89% of the 1000 British adults surveyed on behalf of Responsibletravel.com in 2004 agreed that their vacations would be more enjoyable if their hotel had adequate waste and sewage treatment facilities.

Additionally, a survey of American tourists found that 61% thought travel experiences are better when the destination is a well-preserved natural, historical or cultural site (TIA and NGT, 2002). Nearly 91 million US travellers (59%) support controlling access to and/or more careful regulation of national parks and public lands in order to preserve and protect the environment (TIA and NGT, 2002), showing strong support for conservation-oriented land retention. The survey does not distinguish between domestic and international travel.

Avoiding damage to the destination's environment

As tourists become increasingly cognizant of the damage that mass tourism can cause to heavily travelled destinations, a subset are looking for ways that they can help to stop the trend. Keeping in mind that the vast majority of the survey results discussed here pertain to the general population, it appears that some tourists accustomed to visiting mainstream tourism destinations are seeking out responsible travel alternatives.

Both British and American travellers unequivocally hope to tread lightly on the land while vacationing. In Britain, 87% of tourists interviewed in 2002 stated that it was either very or fairly important that their vacations not damage the environment; this was up from 85% in 2000 (Goodwin, 2001; Goodwin and Francis, 2003). Another study from 2003 found that, in the USA, more than three-quarters of travellers 'feel it is important their visits not damage the environment' (TIA and NGT, 2003). Additionally, 66% of British travellers said that they had placed importance on the fact that their last trip 'had been specifically designed to cause as little damage as possible to the environment' (Tearfund, 2000). In 2004, 67% of British adults surveyed agreed that they did not like the way mass tourism damages the environment at resorts (Responsibletravel.com, 2004), showing that they are aware of the damage already occurring.

Tourists are interested in taking trips that do not degrade the environment. However, in order to fulfil that interest, the tourists must have access to tourism products that are indeed environmentally sensitive and ecologically innovative. When seeking out such products, many tourists look directly to their accommodation for leadership. More than two-thirds of US and Australian travellers and 90% of British tourists consider active protection of the environment, including support of local communities, to be part of a hotel's responsibility (IHEI, 2002). A 2004 survey showed that 88% of British adults think tour operators should have a responsibility to preserve the local environment and operate in a way that benefits local people (Responsibletravel.com, 2004).

Environmental practices can be a defining characteristic in tourist retention. In a 1997 survey, 18% of British tourists said that a hotel's lack of concern for the environment would prevent them from returning to the same place again (MORI, 1997). Unfortunately, this survey stops short of asking whether tourists have actually ever complained to hotels when they encounter a lack of concern for the environment, but the results send a clear message to accommodation that, without environmental awareness, hotels risk losing return visits from a significant portion of their clientele.

Seeking businesses with an environmental attitude

Travel operators that engage in true ecotourism understand and embrace the environmental realm of sustainability. Many ecotourism travellers now do their best to seek out such tour operators, to the exclusion of mainstream operators.

According to survey results from the Travel Industry Association of America and National Geographic Traveler, approximately one in three US travellers is influenced by a travel company's efforts to preserve the environment, history or culture of the destinations the company visits (TIA and NGT, 2002). A similar 2003 study of 3300 American travellers found that 35% of respondents 'select travel companies that strive to preserve and protect the environment'. When extrapolated, these results represent approximately 54 million American travellers. Furthermore, 11% of the 3300 American survey respondents say that, of all factors they consider, environmental performance is a top priority for them when choosing which travel companies to patronize (TIA and NGT, 2003). This trend shows that a niche segment of tourists are undeniably concerned with a company's environmental attitude and record. Unfortunately, many well-intentioned travellers are sidetracked by 'greenwashing' – false promises from below-par operators that fail to truly operate according to the principles of ecotourism. However, with increasing tourist interest, environmental performance looks poised to become an increasingly important aspect of business practice in the ecotourism industry.

Demand for social sensitivity and cultural experience

Whether or not tourists go on vacation with the explicit goal of being immersed in local culture, the majority report that they are interested in learning about aspects of local culture and heritage, often by attending an art performance or trying new foods at the destination. Tourism has provided such intercultural opportunities since its origination, and cultural education remains a colourful drawing point for tourists of all persuasions.

Many tourists actively seek out opportunities for cultural experiences while on vacation. For example, more than half (52%) of the American travellers surveyed in one study said they seek destinations with a wide variety of cultural and arts events/attractions (TIA and NGT, 2003). A series of surveys found that more than three in four British tourists acknowledged that their trip should include visits to experience local culture and foods. This number increased between 2000 to 2002 (77% to 81%) (Goodwin and Francis, 2003). A separate survey found that 86% of the British adults responding to the questions want to eat local produce and discover local recipes while on vacation (Responsibletravel.com, 2004). From Thailand to Tuscany, specialized cooking courses have blossomed in the past decade, with many catering principally to foreign tourists.

Beyond pure 'consumptive' interest in the cultural aspects of tourism, several recent studies show that travellers tend to be concerned about respecting local cultures. A survey by Switzerland Travel Writers found, for example, that an overwhelming 95% of Swiss tourists consider respect for local culture to be highly important when choosing a holiday (FTTSA, n.d.). And more than half (62%) of the US travellers surveyed in 2003 said that it is important that they learn about other cultures when they travel, a key step beyond the entertainment enticement of cooking classes or dance performances (TIA and NGT, 2003).

Finally, travellers have an active interest in receiving information on local culture, including the local language. Some 42% of British tourists look for the quality of local social, economic and political information available when booking trips; and 37% identified opportunities to interact with local people as an important factor in evaluating their vacation (Goodwin and Francis, 2003). A 2004 study indicated that 89% of the British adults responding to the poll want to learn some of the local language when they travel, and they are interested in meeting local people (Responsibletravel.com, 2004). A separate study found that 75% of British and Australian travellers and 33% of US tourists favour seeing local people on their hotel beach (IHEI, 2002), another place where tourists might be able to practise local languages.

Demand for local economic benefit

Ecotourism has the potential to benefit a local economy in several ways. Tour operators and accommodation often provide skills training and jobs, sometimes in areas marked by high unemployment. Local entrepreneurs may produce food or crafts to sell through tour operators and accommodation. Taxi drivers, porters and bicycle repairmen could find that tourism increases their business. In one way or another, many members of a destination community will be economically affected by tourism. For every person directly employed by the tourism industry, other family members may benefit from the financial flow to that family, and indeed to the community in general.

The multiple impacts of tourism dollars on a specific community constitute a phenomenon sometimes known as the local multiplier effect. This refers to the unusually significant impact that tourism may have on the economic system of a destination community. For every dollar that a tourist pays to a local business for a tourism-related product or service, a portion of that sum will in turn be spent in the community by the recipient. For example, if a birdwatcher purchases a tour from an ecotour guide, there is a good chance that the guide will turn around and spend a portion of their earnings purchasing food or other goods in the local area. The grocer from whom the guide buys their goods will then, in turn, spend a portion of their keep in the same local community. In this way, the community benefits from more than just the transaction between the tourist and the guide. The earnings from the tourists reverberate throughout several local transactions, potentially reinvigorating the economy.

There are, of course, obstacles to successfully fostering this multiplier effect, and both tourists and governments are becoming aware of the potentially serious barriers that can exist. True ecotourism focuses, in part, on ensuring genuine returns to the local community. Many ecotourism operators focus on employing local residents and purchasing locally produced supplies in order to keep money circulating within the destination community. In some cases, however, much of the tourists' money does not stay within the economy of the host community. Rather, a significant portion of the money spent on a trip can be diverted to international vendors or to businesses in distant places in the destination country. In either of these cases, the overall economic benefit to the destination community can be severely compromised.

Financial leakage can occur throughout the supply chain: on airfare to the destination, on booking fees or commissions, or simply on hotels that are owned by or employ international staff. Tourists might also purchase international goods, such as imported liquor, paying mostly for transportation fees or international taxes, and leaving little profit to the local seller. In other cases, it may be out of the tourists' hands; for example, the accommodation might be unable to source local goods without compromising quality standards, because of an undependable supply (UNEP, 2001). Whatever the reason, economic leakage from host communities is a common and, unfortunately, a pervasive occurrence. To harness the potential advantages of the multiplier effect, both tour operators and tourists have important roles to play.

More and more tourists are aware that the purchasing choices they make while on vacation can have a profound effect on those hosting their visit. The majority of US (57%), Australian (62%) and British (74%) travellers favour hotels that employ local staff. An even higher proportion from each country surveyed expects that the hotels they patronize 'guarantee good wages and working conditions', according to results from airport surveys of 300 travellers completed in 2002 (IHEI, 2002). Nearly half (49%) of the Americans questioned in 2003 prefer trips with small-scale accommodation run by local people (TIA and NGT, 2003). The obvious challenge is that the traveller must somehow ascertain, often before arriving at the destination, which tour operators and accommodation are truly locally owned and provide good working conditions.

Looking beyond preventing the negatives, such as averting financial leakages and retaining tourism dollars within a community, some innovative travel companies have focused on positive economic efforts by voluntarily giving back in some way to the local community. This growing trend towards travellers' philanthropy highlights the positive contributions many companies choose to make to the communities that allow them to operate (Center on Ecotourism and Sustainable Development, 2004). This approach appears to be very popular with tourists, so much so that travellers' philanthropy projects are an attribute almost expected in some circles.

Travellers' philanthropy involves giving time, talent or treasure to benefit a community to which tourists travel or in which a tour business operates. Travellers' philanthropy projects are often creative and should always be designed with the unique needs of a host community in mind. They should also be sustainable beyond the tenure of the company sponsoring the project.

Some companies see their travellers' philanthropy projects as charitable offshoots of their main tourism endeavours. These companies might ask tourists if they are interested in matching corporate contributions to a community development fund. A second grouping of businesses regard the projects as integral to the tourism experience, and these companies might organize tours that spotlight positive contributions they have made to a destination community. For example, CC Africa, a safari business headquartered in South Africa offers a tour at its Phinda Game Reserve that showcases nearby nursery schools and medical clinics funded by traveller and corporate donations to the company-initiated Africa Foundation (CC Africa, n.d.). A third grouping of tour businesses considers travellers' philanthropy an integral part of good business practice. Giving back to those the company works with tends to breed high employee morale, positive reception in the community and happier guests. Companies such as the long-standing US-based tour operator Lindblad Expeditions rarely trumpet their financial contributions, preferring to quietly notify guests of the initiatives they have undertaken. These companies often find that simply informing guests of their community-based efforts inspires a cascade of unsolicited donations.

Some tourists consider more than just the potential economic benefits their visit might have on vacation destinations. In some cases, tourists wish to seek out companies that give back to the communities in which they operate. Approximately half of Australian (62%), British (57%) and US (49%) travellers surveyed say it is very important that hotels support local businesses and invest in local schools and hospitals (Goodwin and Francis, 2003).

In an informative corollary, small-sized British tour companies, surveyed in 2000, estimated that approximately 70% of their trips' costs remained in the local economies of their destinations. Medium-sized companies put the figure at 35%, while larger tour companies were unable to create an estimate (Goodwin and Francis, 2003).

Demand for information and active learning

Education and information-sharing are an integral part of ecotourism, whether they come from informal conversations or through formal channels such as operator-provided materials or guided tours. As in the section earlier in this chapter on prioritizing cultural sensitivity, the surveys noted below show that travellers express a strong interest in learning from the trips they take, both before they depart and during their vacation.

Most surveys that ask travellers about their interest in learning during their trips show strong support for an educational component, and a subset wish this to start before they depart. A 2003 study found that more than half (53%) of US tourists surveyed agree that they have a better travel experience when they learn as much as possible about their destination's 'customs, geography, and culture' (TIA and NGT, 2003). Some 37% of British tourists echoed that they try to learn about local culture before they travel (Meyer, 2003). This idea was reinforced by yet another survey, in which over half (52%) of British respondents indicated that they are interested in finding out more about local social and environmental issues before booking a trip (Goodwin, 2001). And, in a question that links cultural respect with education and learning, a 2004 study found that 88% of British adults want to be given advice on local cultures and customs (Responsibletravel.com, 2004).

The strong support for including educational components in a travel experience holds true for interest in information about the ethical dilemmas associated with tourism, as well as for environmental aspects of travelling. Nearly two in three British tourists surveyed (63%) want information on the ethical issues associated with their vacation (Tearfund, 2000) and more than three in four (78%) British package vacation travellers reported that the inclusion of social and environmental information in tour operators' brochures is important to them. Over half (52%) of British respondents indicated they are interested in finding out more about local social and environmental issues before booking a trip (Goodwin, 2001).

In Australia, the opportunity to 'learn about the environment' was the motivation most frequently cited by those choosing to patronize ecotourism operations (Enhance Management, 2000). An overwhelming majority (82%)

of Dutch tourists surveyed believe that integrating environmental information into all travel brochures is a good idea (FEMATOUR, 2000). With such support for information about destinations and about tourism in general, one would expect each tour operator to devote some time and money into developing introductory fact sheets or presentations about the social, environmental and economic issues associated with their trips.

However, many outside a top tier of ecotourism companies, such as Micato Safaris, Intrepid Travel and Lapa Rios, routinely fail to provide such information. Seeking to fill this specific information gap, The International Ecotourism Society, a global non-profit industry and traveller group, recently published a brochure entitled *Your Travel Choice Makes a Difference* (The International Ecotourism Society, 2006). It focuses on tips for being a responsible tourist, and lists responsible travel resources pertinent both to those planning a trip and those travelling (see Fig. 11.2).

The Ecotourism Market Segment

The surveys reviewed above have indicated that many tourists are seeking out a specific type of tourism experience, one that, whether they are aware of it or not, follows the principles of ecotourism. These tourists are aware of social issues, engaged in environmental sensitivity and interested in the economic impact of their travels. Though they appear as little more than numbers on paper once translated into survey results, the people behind the percentages are real travellers. And many market analysts have been trying to identify just who these people are, and how much they are willing to spend on ecotourism.

There have been many attempts to analyse populations interested in responsible products, including ecotourism. Table 11.2 begins to pick apart just a few of the market segment studies related to ecotourism that have been popularized. One of the first responsible purchaser studies in recent years came in the form of a book entitled *The Cultural Creatives: How 50 Million People are Changing the World* (Ray and Anderson, 2000). The analysis in this volume set the stage for interest in a burgeoning marketing niche or sector now referred to under the umbrella 'lifestyles of health and sustainability', or LOHAS, segment.

More recently, National Geographic Traveler commissioned a report by the Travel Industry Association of America to address the concept of geotourism, tourism that sustains or enhances the geographical characteristics of the place being visited: its environment, culture, aesthetics, heritage and the well-being of its residents. While not focusing on the principles of ecotourism specifically, the results of this massive survey have relevance and applicability to ecotourists.

Table 11.2 illustrates the ecotourism market segment relative to other types of mainstream tourism and responsible tourism. Mainstream tourism remains the dominant choice among all tourists, in part because of the lack of alternative options. However, even within mainstream tourism, there

Making informed choices before and during your trip is the single most important thing you can do to become a responsible traveller.

Planning your Trip

With a little planning, you can improve the quality of your trip, while making a real difference to the people and places you visit.

1. Search the web: Look for websites specializing in responsible travel, ecotourism, or sustainable tourism.

2. Consult guidebooks: Choose guidebooks with information on your destination's environmental, social and political issues, and read before booking. Guidebooks vary in quality, even within a series, but *Lonely Planet*, *Rough Guides*, and *Moon* are among the best.

3. Make contact: Call or email tour operators that have firsthand knowledge of the place you are considering visiting. Check the websites of all accommodations.

Fig. 11.2. *Your Travel Choice Makes a Difference* brochure.

Look for green certification

4. Ask questions: Let tour operators/hotels know that you are a responsible consumer. Before you book, ask about their social and environmental policies. For instance: What is your environmental policy? What percentage of your employees are local citizens? Do you support any projects to benefit the local community?

5. Choose wisely: Are the businesses you're considering certified? Do they have eco-label ratings, or have they won eco-awards?

What is Certification?

Have you heard of the AAA or 5-star rating systems? These long-standing labels judge hotel quality and services. Over the last decade, many 'green' certification programs have been created. These use independent auditors to rate the environmental and social impacts of hotels (or other tourism businesses). They help travellers to make responsible choices. A growing number of companies have earned eco-labels. We encourage you to patronize those that have.

Fig. 11.2. (Continued).

Table 11.2. Classifying responsible market segments in the USA (from Ray and Anderson, 2000; TIA and NGT, 2003; LOHAS, 2005).

Publication/study	Market segment	Size of population/market
The Cultural Creatives: How 50 Million People are Changing the World	Cultural creatives: ecotourists, volunteer travellers, interested in experiential vacations. They are careful consumers, and prefer print or radio to television	Estimated at 50 million US adults in 2000. Average income is US$52,000 per year
Geotourism: The New Trend in Travel, commissioned by National Geographic Traveler, conducted by Travel Industry Association of America	Geo-savvies, urban sophisticates, good citizens: share a belief in preserving and protecting destinations	A combined total of 55.1 million Americans, with an average income of about US$70,000 per year
Lifestyles of health and sustainability	LOHAS: interested in ecotourism as part of an 'ecological lifestyle', valuing health, the environment, social justice, personal development and sustainable living	Estimated at US$226.8 billion in May 2005 – 63 million consumers, or 30% of the adult US population

are pockets that focus on volunteer vacations or education-oriented study trips. Subgroups, such as adventure tourism and nature tourism, occupy additional niches in the travel industry. At the intersection of nature tourism and responsible tourism is ecotourism. Though ecotourism garners only a small fraction of the overall tourism industry, Fig. 11.3 shows that it holds much in common with other sections of the industry as well.

Growth in responsible consumption

A long-standing question has been whether there exists a latent but potentially much larger ecotourism market waiting to be developed through enhanced marketing, better product development and outreach to amenable consumers. One way of beginning to address this question is to measure the number of people that express interest in attributes pertaining to ecotourism, even if they do not yet fully understand the principles and complexities of the definition of ecotourism. Examining the market trends for other responsible or ethical products, such as fair trade and organic goods, may shed light on the potential for forward growth in the ecotourism market.

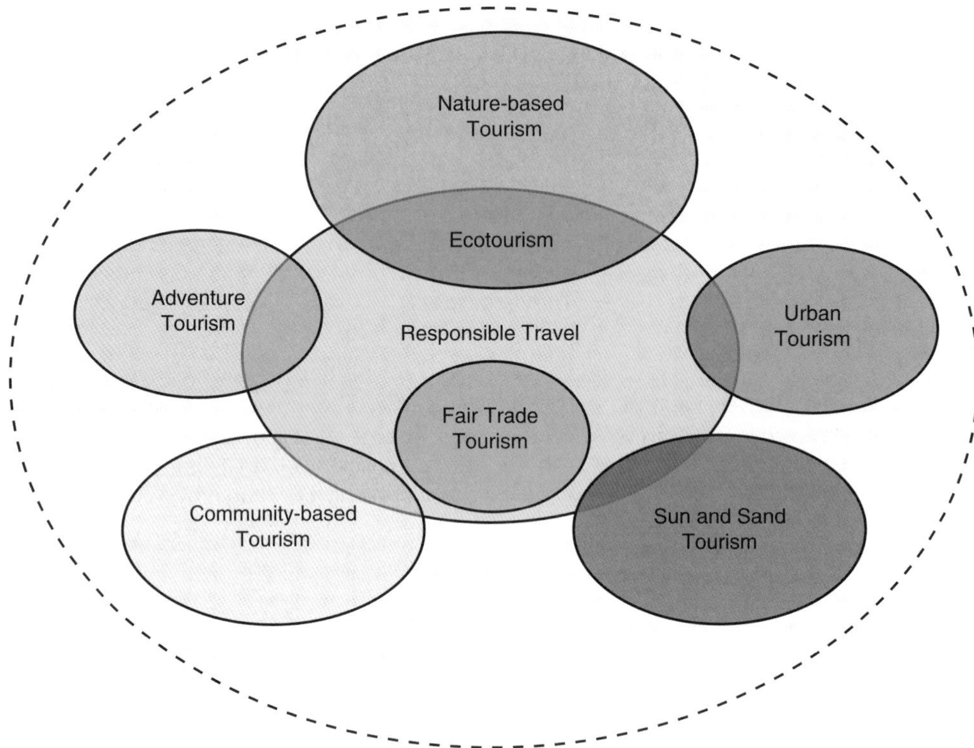

Fig. 11.3. Locating ecotourism.

Fair trade products, by definition, provide living wages and safe working conditions for farmers and other labourers around the world. Several trademarks and labels spotlight products that have been certified to meet standards in those areas. (The term fair trade refers to a broad spectrum of products that purport to meet the characteristics listed above, while various trademarks, such as the Fairtrade mark or Transfair USA, certify that the creation of certain products does indeed meet specific fair trade attributes.)

Support for fair trade products, which has continued to grow since the term's initial introduction in 1994, illustrates consumers' willingness to choose, and pay a premium for, the products of companies that guarantee good working conditions and fair wages for their producers (Tearfund, 2000; MORI, 2003). Fair trade coffee sales grew by 90% in the USA during 2003 (Moskin, 2004), while Fairtrade-branded food sales in the UK more than doubled in the 3 years before 2003 (MORI, 2003). And during 2004 sales of UK Fairtrade-branded products hit £140 million for the year, a 51% rise over 2003 (Fairtrade Foundation, 2005a).

There appear to be two major factors behind the increases in sales of Fairtrade-branded products in both the USA and the UK: first, a significant diversification of the product line; and secondly, quick increases in the recognition of the trademark (as well as the concept). The number of internationally certified Fairtrade products exploded from 150 in 2003 to 834 in 2005, a fivefold increase in just 2 years (Fairtrade Foundation, 2005b). A recent MORI survey (Fairtrade Foundation, 2005a), commissioned by the Fairtrade Foundation in the UK, found that 50% of the UK adults surveyed recognized the Fairtrade mark, up from 25% in 2003. The combination of these two factors has spawned a dramatic rise in spending on fair trade products in the UK.

Beyond fair trade products, the marketing research firm RoperASW has surveyed Americans to assess overall willingness to integrate environmental issues into consumer behaviour. The firm estimates that 16% of adult Americans are 'green' consumers and that an additional 33% of the population can be persuaded to base spending choices on environmental values (Cortese, 2003).

Meanwhile, estimates of the 'lifestyles of health and sustainability' (LOHAS) market segment point to a well-defined category of consumers that is based on shared values. The LOHAS market was estimated at US$226.8 billion in May 2005, according to Natural Business Communications (in the USA). This includes an estimated 63 million consumers, or 30% of the adult US population, who value health, the environment, social justice, personal development and sustainable living (LOHAS, 2005).

Broader calculations show that the 'ethical consumption market' in the USA increased 15% between 1999 and 2000, and that, for markets in which there exists an ethical alternative, ethical consumer purchases increased 18.2% between 1999 and 2000 surveys. Ethical products are chosen for positive reasons (such as being 'cruelty-free'), passed over for negative reasons (grown in inhumane conditions) or assessed by the producing company's overall ethical record. The ethical purchasing sector appears to be growing, though it remained below 2% of the total market share in the UK in 2001, the latest year for which data were available (1.68% in 2001) (Co-operative Bank, 2002). Many of the principles used to select ethical products might also be applied to ecotourism, yielding significant overlap between the two sectors. The British non-profit Tearfund foresaw growth in this regard, stating that 'ethical tourism will rightly be a big issue in the new millennium' (Tearfund, 2000).

The growth in ethical consumption is mirrored in the development of environmentally and socially responsible products aimed at all aspects of life, including the investment industry. Consumers now have the power to screen companies according to their specific standards, bypassing those involved with weapons production, for example, and choosing instead to support those with clean environmental records. A variety of investment firms specialize in this type of investing, helping to channel interested consumers' money to laudable companies. In the UK ethical banking and investment increased at a rate of about 20% per year between 1999 and 2001, showing a promising outlook for the ethical purchasing sector (Co-operative Bank, 2002). In 2003, investments using socially responsible criteria topped US$2.63 trillion worldwide, with US$2.16 trillion of this total within the USA. Western Europe's socially responsible investment reached US$413 billion in 2003, and is growing rapidly (Assadourian, 2005). The market segment interested in ethical, or socially responsible, investment is just one more for which possible overlap with ecotourism should be considered.

The latent market for ecotourism

Market increases in a variety of converging, though still distinct, market segments draw attention to the fact that more and more people are choosing to spend their money in accordance with their values. As responsible choices for consumption and investment become available, interest in the products continues to grow (though it often takes some time for a particular market to begin rapidly increasing). Concurrently, high percentages of tourists who may not think of themselves as ecotourists as such, indicate that they feel strongly about environmental and social responsibility issues. When it comes to ecotourism, then, where are the millions of consumers represented in these studies and statistics?

Measured in a variety of ways, a section of the general population will predictably express interest in the pillars of ecotourism: social, environmental and economic sustainability, and nature-based tourism combined with a focus on local ownership. However, tourism operators routinely report that marketing a trip around the concept of ecotourism does not necessarily increase occupancy, nor does it often affect value.

In a study of 'reputable' US-based ecotourism operators, EplerWood International (2003) found that, although the operators classified 42% of their clients as very concerned with ecological and social issues, the operators perceived that only 8% showed a specific interest in these issues when booking their trip. These observations seem to point to a mismatch: perhaps the tourists are interested in ecological and social issues, but do not want to spend time thinking about them when choosing a vacation. Alternatively, maybe the tourists are not actively expressing their interest in certain issues to tour operators while planning a trip. Another possibility is that the tour operators are not picking up tourists' interests that the tourists believe they are adequately communicating prior to a trip.

In a study by the International Hotels Environment Initiative (IHEI), now known as the International Tourism Partnership, reports from travellers themselves indicate that, though the tourists do often have significant interest in environmental or social issues, they are not taking the initiative to actively communicate that interest to tour operators or accommodation (IHEI, 2002). The study found that, despite the majority of those surveyed expressing interest in hotels with a responsible environmental policy, only 14% of US travellers, and 26% of Australians, actually ask hotels if they have an environmental policy. Not a single British traveller spoke to the hotel about their policies (IHEI, 2002).

The apparent discrepancy between tourists' values or interests and the lack of effective communication between tourists and tour operators presents both challenges and hope for an emerging ecotourism market. Clearly, a number of tourists report that they do care about the aspects of travel embodied in ecotourism (IHEI, 2002; TIA and NGT, 2002, 2003; Responsibletravel.com, 2004). However, it is important to note that several studies question whether the number of people reporting to care about environmental or social issues is higher among some types of surveys, as there exists a social pressure to appear concerned with such issues.

Researchers, as well as tour operators, remain perplexed on the issue of miscommunication between principled travellers and those serving them. Regarding the lack of expected ecotourism business, factors of convenience and marketing may weigh heavily against ecotourism: it is often simply easier to patronize all-inclusive mainstream tourism resorts, book package tours and sail on enormous cruises – so much simpler, in fact, that these factors could continue to trump the moral values that would otherwise compel a significant segment of the travelling population to seek out ecotours.

Another complex, but vitally important, question is whether tourists are truly interested in actively pursuing social and environmental issues when they are on vacation. While many people are interested in social and environmental issues, only a select few plan a vacation solely to learn or to find out how environmentally sustainable their trip could be. 'People's motives for travel are not environmental, but what they would like to do on holiday can be', says Noel Josephides, of tour operator Sunvil Holidays (McGrath, 2004). Josephides illustrates an important distinction between motives for travel and actions while travelling. Although a tourist might not book a vacation because of environmental concerns, that vacation can become an opportunity to learn about the concerns along the way, or to patronize businesses that have similar underlying values. This distinction has profound implications for the way that ecotourism is marketed and the type of information that is provided for potential tourists both before and during their trip.

To reach the latent market, that is, those travellers that attest to having interest in environmental and social issues but are not yet familiar with ecotourism, one must think about the types of decisions travellers in this latent market are making, when they are making travel decisions, what information they are using to make the decisions, and how best to provide new information during that process. Couching environmental and social issues in terms of the quality of a tourism product may provide a new market opening. Creative marketing ideas, which play to tourists' interest in purchasing an enjoyable vacation while the tourists are engaged in the buying process, may prove effective in introducing tourists to responsible tourism options. For example, when advertising a visit to travellers' philanthropy projects, marketing the experiential aspect of the tour might play to tourists' interests in a quality vacation, with engagement in the travellers' philanthropy aspects coming after the experience.

Research on the LOHAS market in the USA indicates that 60% of consumers are influenced by friends and family they trust when making decisions about healthy or environmentally friendly products and services. Reliance on family and friends' advice ranks higher than looking at company web sites (48%), product packaging (47%) and information from the government (40%)

(Natural Marketing Institute, 2004). When speaking with friends and family, a prospective traveller may be less hesitant to verbalize interests in patronizing environmentally and socially responsible tourism businesses, providing an opportunity for those in the know to steer them towards responsible operators. However, if prospective travellers are among the first in their families or their areas to seek out ecotourism possibilities, they may find themselves at a loss for dependable advice.

Justin Francis, co-founder of the online responsible travel site Responsibletravel.com, agrees that ecotourism and, more broadly, responsible tourism need to be marketed differently from how they have been in the past. 'People aren't ever going to go into a travel agent and ask for a responsible holiday,' says Francis, 'but what they are increasingly asking for is a local guide or to eat in a local restaurant, which is more sustainable' (McGrath, 2004). Rather than taking a pre-planned trip that is centred completely around ecotourism, it seems as though tourists are piecing together the responsible portions themselves. They may take a fairly mainstream trip, but seek to be responsible where they have a choice.

The issue, then, is how to best prepare prospective travellers to make the best decisions possible, and to consider all the ways in which their travel could impact the places that they visit. The International Ecotourism Society's *Travel Choice* brochure (see Fig. 11.2) is one example of an increasingly popular trend towards 'do-it-yourself' responsible tourism lists provided by ecotourism and responsible tourism proponents. Other interesting references of this sort are provided by the web site responsibletravel.com, and by Rainforest Alliance's sustainable tourism programme (rainforestalliance.com/programs/tourism/travelers/index.html). There are also several substantial books that provide more in-depth guidelines (DFID and Rough Guides, 2004; Patullo and Minelli, 2006). These publications serve the dual purpose of familiarizing travellers with the ideas behind ecotourism, and then giving travellers the information they need to take actions on their own, whether they are travelling with a responsible tourism provider or not.

This tactic has the potential to be particularly effective, given the ever-increasing number of travellers that plan their vacations over the Internet. Without the guidance of a travel agent, they will still be able to reference material such as the *Travel Choice* brochure when considering destinations and accommodation, transport or activities.

Another important way of communicating with consumers is through certification, or ecolabelling, for tourism. Certification is a process by which goods or services (in this case, tourism services and accommodation) are inspected and declared to have met a certain public standard. A variety of ecotourism and responsible tourism certification programmes, including Blue Flag, Certification for Sustainable Tourism, Fair Trade in Tourism South Africa, Green Globe, and Nature's Best, exist already, and more appear all the time. The main difficulty, for the subject of consumer demand, is that consumers are often daunted by the variability between different labels, the variety in standards and enforcement, and the lack of advertisement to communicate the meaning of most labels. The following section considers whether certification is working for consumers and, if not, whether it could be improved as a means of communicating information about ecotourism travel choices.

Certification as an indicator of quality

Ecotourism certification, by indicating the fact that select accommodation or operators have met standards, provides a measure of quality for tourists interested in choosing between a variety of similar companies. The type of quality measured by certification programmes varies widely, but reliable marks should include basic quality assessments, as well as environmental and social ratings. For example, the Fair Trade in Tourism South Africa trademark assures would-be customers that lodges provide fair wages and safe working conditions. The Blue Flag seal, on the other hand, speaks to high water quality and the types of services available at beaches. The programmes also vary in the level of quality that the logos or trademarks themselves represent. Some programmes are much more stringent in their examinations and renewal inspections than others. Despite these differences, and despite the unfortunate possibility of bogus greenwashing ecotourism certification (labels that are meaningless, but intended to lure in consumers) appearing, ecotourism certification does provide consumers with a potentially powerful amount of information.

Research from Mintel shows that consumers are indeed keen to find quality in both the types of basic facilities and the types of activities available (Mintel International Group, 2003). A survey of 2000 UK adults in both 2001 and 2003 showed that the top factor in whether tourists rate a vacation enjoyable is 'high standard of accommodation and facilities'. More than half of those surveyed (55%) agreed with that statement in 2003. Sightseeing, whether historical, cultural or wildlife-based, ranks third, with 45% in 2003. Experiencing a different culture comes next, popular with 32% in 2003. (Each statistic mentioned here showed an increase of 2–3% over 2001.) Additionally, a select group of tourists do state that ethical practices are integral to a successful trip. In 2001, some 20% of UK tourists surveyed mentioned that 'knowing that I have booked with a company that has good ethical practices' makes a good trip (though this number fell to 18% in 2003) (Mintel International Group, 2003).

To demonstrate just how important it is to ensure basic quality in ecotourism, one need only look at the negative side of the statistics. In an amalgamated study of all types of tourism, the standard of accommodation was the biggest overall source of travellers' complaints against the UK's biggest travel suppliers in 2004, according to the Co-op Travel Trading Group, with some 24% of complaints pertaining to accommodation in 2004 (down from 35% in 2003) (Davies, 2005). If tour operators are going to successfully reach out to other sections of the population, this statistic serves as a reminder that basic services must be perfected before environmental and social aspects gain the attention of a discerning tourist. The fact that many ecotourism certification programmes do not include basic quality assurance criteria only serves to reinforce this problem.

Role of certification in consumer decisions

Tourists may encounter ecotourism certification at a variety of points, either in their travel planning process or while on a trip. A tourist may already have some familiarity with either the concept of certification or the concept of ecotourism, but perhaps has not yet encountered the intersection of the two. In other cases, the consumer may be new to both concepts. It is important that initial information either about a specific label or about certification or ecotourism in general be applicable for a range of audiences.

A study conducted in Victoria, Australia, indicated that most tourists (61.3%) were initially unfamiliar with the concept of tourism certification (or accreditation, as the concept is termed in Australia) (Foster, 2001). After learning about certification, many cited the fact that the operator would be 'trustworthy' and have 'improved standards' as reasons that they would use a certified operator in the future. The change in tourists' attitudes recorded by this survey indicates that simply spreading knowledge of the concept of certification might increase consumer demand for certified products. After being given information about the process, tourists associated the process of certification with positive characteristics of tour operators (Foster, 2001).

Another Australian study reported similarly positive findings after surveying travellers and educating them about the existence and purpose of an ecolabel (Enhance Management, 2000). The 2000 survey for Tourism Queensland found that, after receiving a brief description of the NEAP ecolabel (now known as EcoCertification) and its purpose, the majority of those surveyed said that they would be either 'a lot more likely' or 'a little more likely' to select certified businesses and products. Additionally, most of the travellers reported that they would pay at least 5% more to use certified businesses (Enhance Management, 2000). The results of this survey indicate that increased marketing and education about certification programmes could significantly raise tourist support for such initiatives.

In some cases, certification programmes are not yet present at a destination, but consumers posed with the idea of a certification label are enthusiastic about the concept of certification, and many say they would indeed make use of such a programme. In a survey of German tourists, the overwhelming majority (71.1%) of domestic travellers and more than half of the German tourists travelling outside Germany (59.5%) agreed that an environmental label for tourism would be useful (Hildebrand, 2000). About half of all German tourists surveyed (52.8% travelling within Germany and 46% travelling outside Germany) agreed that they would use an ecolabel, if available, in the choice of a vacation (Hildebrand, 2000).

A small segment of Germans surveyed by the organization ECOTRANS in 2002 reported that they placed high importance on the development of a uniform measure of environmental quality at the regional level. In the travel survey of nearly 8000 Germans, 14.2% (8.5 million) said that 'easy access to information on all tourism products in Europe with certified environmental quality (ecolabels)' was 'of peculiar importance' to them (Ecotrans, 2002).

To complement the promising theoretical support for ecotourism certification reported in the surveys discussed above, there are several reports that address the effectiveness of existing certification programmes. A poll of tourists to the Baltic Island of Hiiumaa, part of the Western Estonian Archipelago Biosphere Reserve, found that 50% of the island's visitors were aware of the local Green Label certification scheme, and that some 70% of these had chosen accommodation with the label (UNESCO, 2002). This is an inspiring result, documenting the correlation between high awareness of an ecotourism label and consumer use of the standard to choose certified products.

A study of Danish tourists staying in certified hotels raises another important point related to tourism certification: that tourists already familiar with ecotourism labels may be willing to pay more for certified products. A survey of nearly 500 Danish tourists staying at least 1 night in Green Key-certified hotels found that 69% were willing to pay extra for hotels with ecolabelling. More than one-third (34%) of the tourists expressed willingness to pay US$0.25–5.00 more to stay in a certified hotel, with 2% willing to pay up to US$25 more to stay in a certified hotel (Green Globe 21, 2002).

Certification: the tour operators' perspective

With tourists' interest in ecotourism and certification growing, tour operators are not ignoring these trends. Recognizing that ecotourism could expand their customer base and that certification represents a potential price increase, many tour operators are exploring either or both of these two options. To gauge current interest levels, Green Globe sent a survey to 115 Australian and international businesses and organizations that either supply the travel and tourism industry or have made a public commitment to environmental and social sustainability (Green Globe 21, 2004). Nearly all respondents (89%) said that issues of sustainability and corporate social responsibility were extremely important to their organizations, while 84% of respondents said that minimizing their organization's environmental impacts, or assisting their clients to do so, was extremely important. In terms of actual implementation, about half of the organizations (48%) had already participated in an environmental benchmarking or certification scheme, or stated that they planned to participate. Even more organizations (68%) participated in charitable giving to environmentally or socially responsible projects, mirroring increasing interest in travellers' philanthropy and similar social responsibility initiatives (Green Globe 21, 2004).

Large travel companies are beginning to highlight the linkages between sustainable tourism, including ecotourism, and the quality of the destinations and products they offer. Before being closed for tactical business reasons in 2004, Virgin Travelstore, a flight consolidator, announced it would donate funds to sustainable tourism efforts for each of the 3000 agents the company was to visit during a promotional tour of the UK. The donations were to go to the Travel Foundation, which was launched in 2003. Travelstore director Carol Smallman acknowledged, 'Sustainable tourism is crucial to our industry, and the people we all work with across the globe' (Travelmole.com, 2004).

Beyond donations to side projects, many tour operators are integrating principles of ecotourism and responsible travel into their everyday operations, recognizing that these principles are fundamentally important to their activities. In a 2001 study of British tour operators, half of the respondents (49%) said they had developed some form of a responsible tourism policy. An additional 26% said they were planning to produce such a policy in the future. Though these policies can take many forms and include a variety of different directives, the 2001 study found that most responsible tourism policies were composed of written principles that guided the operators' activities, while other policies consisted of suggestions for how tourists should behave (Tearfund, 2001). These policies are an important step towards transforming diverse tour operators' attitudes and activities, despite being more difficult for tourists to understand and evaluate than certification marks.

With an expanding number of certification schemes, it is increasingly difficult to estimate the overall proportion of tourism businesses applying for and earning ecotourism certification marks. One survey, by certification organization Green Globe, found that just under half (48%) of the Australian and international organizations queried in 2004 had participated in, or planned to participate in, an 'environmental benchmarking or certification scheme', while 84% of the organizations state that 'minimizing their . . . impacts on the environment and assisting their clients to do the same' are extremely important (Green Globe 21, 2004). While not representative of the global situation, this survey does indicate that a significant number of organizations are considering the benefits of ecotourism certification, and that an even higher number recognize the benefits that environmental sensitivity could provide both for their business and for the customers they serve.

Why certify?

When seeking to understand the perceived benefits that spur tourism businesses to participate in ecotourism certification schemes, the best sources of information are the businesses that have undergone the process of applying for such schemes. When large-, medium- and small-sized British tour operators were surveyed, most operators agreed that tourists use responsible tourism practices 'nearly every time' to choose which tour operator to support (Goodwin and Francis, 2003), indicating that consumer interest in responsible tourism is encouraging the businesses to pursue the sometimes arduous process of becoming certified. However, another report found that only 30% of British companies surveyed said that their customers were asking more about the social, environmental and economic issues associated with tourism (Tearfund, 2001).

At the same time, however, a 'significant' number of specialist tour operators stated that clients were more interested in these issues after they returned from a trip, having personally experienced the situations and seen the potentially negative effects of tourism (Tearfund, 2001), indicating that travellers themselves can become educated about certification and associated responsible travel issues while on a trip. These tourists are potentially valuable because they can leverage messages about certification and responsible travel by communicating them to friends and family upon their return. This conclusion is supported by additional findings from the same survey, in which more than 20 of the 65 British companies surveyed said their responsible tourism policy is designed to educate tourists. Approximately 25 respondents agreed that the responsible tourism policy is an integral part of the underlying principles upon which their company operates.

Paying more for certification

With increasing interest in ecotourism certification exhibited by consumers, more travel operators are poised to begin testing certification as a viable business option. For most operators, the process of certification is a positive way to reflect upon existing business policies and/or to develop better practices. It also provides a time to reflect on the goals and strategies of the business, integrating responsible travel principles where appropriate. Beyond internal strategies, businesses are beginning to closely study findings showing that consumers are willing to pay more for travel products that have been ecotourism-certified.

Findings from around the world present a rough portrait of travellers' self-reported spending priorities. In 2003, Mintel found that 17% of UK adults surveyed would pay more to stay in an environmentally friendly hotel (Mintel International Group, 2003). Another study, conducted in Victoria, Australia, indicated that more than half (55.3%) of those surveyed would expect to pay more when using an accredited/certifed operator, citing the potential for better service and recognizing that the accreditation would cost the business money (Foster, 2001).

Some surveys ask tourists about business practices related to ecotourism certification, if not about certification directly. The support voiced for these responsible practices indicates potential support for certification, provided the tourists become aware of ecotourism certification and its relationship to the issues they currently support. In the UK, one in five British tourists surveyed (21%) would pay more for an international trip if their money supported a local charity (Goodwin, 2001; Tearfund, 2001), and half (46%) of British adults surveyed want information on ways that they can support the local economy and local people at their destinations (Tearfund, 2000).

Given that a section of the population is interested in supporting ecotourism and responsible travel, the next question is just how much more tourists would be willing to spend for responsible or ecotourism-certified travel products. In a survey of British tourists, respondents were asked whether they would be willing to pay more for their vacations if the vacation included responsible tourism aspects (Tearfund, 2000). The conclusion from this survey was that 'tourists are not always simply looking for the lowest price: they are willing to pay for principle' (Tearfund, 2000).

Education enhances demand

One of the most important aspects of ecotourism certification revolves around the potential to engage tourists in a conversation over what constitutes responsible travel and how tourism businesses should be evaluated on the principles inherent to ecotourism. Some tourists are anxious to engage in such a conversation. Other tourists are more focused on enjoying a vacation, knowing that their travels are not harming the environment or exacerbating existing social and economic problems in destination communities. For this reason, education around certification is of vital importance and must be well planned.

The best time for tourists to become aware of ecotourism certification and responsible tourism principles is before travel begins. Prospective travellers often turn to trusted friends and family members for travel advice, as previously discussed. Many rely on Internet web sites to learn about destinations and book travel, and others turn to travel agents for information and travel advice.

Travel web sites and travel agents have the potential to create a significant impact on tourist education if they familiarize themselves with ecotourism certification and responsible travel options. Equipped with such knowledge, they will be better sources of information for curious travellers. Additionally, by recommending certified products, travel agents will be able to ensure a high-quality experience for their customers.

Travel web sites, books and newspaper columns are all prime sources by which a wider population of potential tourists could be reached. These written forums provide the perfect opportunity to explore issues related to ecotourism, explain certification and demystify the myriad certification labels that tourists are likely to encounter. The inclusion of pertinent certification labels and standards in descriptions of destinations would improve public recognition of the certification labels, while also adding information and value to the analysis presented.

Without better education, tourists may learn about the importance of ecotourism and responsible tourism principles the hard way. 'It is down to the education of people to show them what tourism does to a destination,' says Roy Dey-Graff of Gullivers Travel Associates, a travel agency (McGrath, 2004). That education can come either in the form of proactive information sharing or through increasingly negative experiences at overrun tourism destinations, where environmental degradation and social issues related to the tourism industry make a good vacation increasingly difficult to find.

Some travel agents, such as Solimar Marketing in Washington, DC, have taken the ecotourism market very seriously, centring their expertise around ecotourism and marketing their services as niche ecotourism planning. The online travel consolidator Expedia recently announced a partnership through which it will create a special portal dedicated to travel to World Heritage Sites (World Heritage Alliance, 2006). However, such positive examples are few and far between.

Given the relatively small percentage of all travellers that will actively seek out ecotourism experiences, many travel agencies are reluctant to put the time and effort into receiving training about what they perceive to be a niche market. With the expansion of ecotourism principles to other parts of the mainstream tourism industry, however, it will become increasingly important that travel agents are able to cater to questions about accommodation quality and social, environmental or economic equity concerns with equal expertise.

Conclusion

Ecotourism is at a crossroads: after developing a healthy base of support over the past 20 years, the industry is moving increasingly towards certification and standard setting. This chapter has reviewed the need for and implications of setting standards for quality and responsible tourism. Ecotourism has a very significant role to play in the global economy, though it is difficult to estimate just how much potential for growth there is within the industry. The local multiplier effect predicts that tourism revenues that remain within a host community can continue to benefit the community long after the tourist leaves.

By reviewing a variety of surveys and studies that examine consumers' views about tourism preferences and responsible tourism issues, it appears clear that a sizeable portion of the population reports interest in supporting more responsible tourism and, in some cases, ecotourism. However, tourists are concerned, foremost, with the quality and value of their vacation. After basic quality standards are met, environmental, social and economic considerations may come into play.

Tourists are interested in the quality of the environment they visit, shying away from areas that are visibly polluted or degraded. They also state that do not want to cause environmental damage on their vacations, a sentiment that may spur them to learn more about environmental issues. A section of these travellers are willing to seek out companies that actively avoid environmental damage along the way.

Tourists are also interested in exploring other cultures in a respectful way. Many want to learn local languages, eat foreign foods and mingle with those living in the places they visit. They are interested in patronizing businesses that pay their employees fair wages, and they would sometimes pay more to ensure that the business gives back to the community that supports its presence. Recognizing the importance of putting tourism revenues straight into host communities, tourists are increasingly seeking out opportunities to spend money with businesses that will retain the money in the local community.

Many tourists are inquisitive about the places they are visiting, as well as the impacts of their travels. Education about responsible travel and ecotourism certification is extremely important, but must be done in a way that makes the information available to a diverse population of consumers. Some tourists come with familiarity about aspects of certification or ecotourism; others will embark on trips with no prior knowledge of the concepts. By learning about certification programmes, however, tourists can begin to make travel decisions that are truly in line with their values. Fortunately, tourists are overwhelmingly receptive to information about their travels, and express interest in learning about culture, language and environmental issues, with certification falling in line with these subjects.

Though it is difficult to pinpoint exactly who currently chooses ecotourism trips, an analysis of market segments can provide an estimate of the size of the potentially untapped ecotourism market. Using surveys that quantify the market segments whose preferences and values overlap with the principles and values inherent to ecotourism, it is possible to infer how many tourists might be interested in ecotourism if provided with information about such travel opportunities.

The responsible tourism market is riding on the tail of successful growth in related markets, such as ethical investment and fair trade products. Many of the consumers currently spending money in those markets may well be interested in ecotourism travel, though it is difficult to say how active they would be in seeking out responsible trips.

A common complaint from tour operators is that they often hear that consumers are interested in environmental, social and economic issues, but their travellers rarely voice such preferences to them directly, before or during a trip. There is a mismatch between the behaviour operators observe and the values that travellers reportedly prioritize.

Ecotourism certification can help travellers make decisions about the types of tour operators and accommodation they patronize, either before or during their trip, and select consumers report that they often support certified businesses when they are aware of the certification mark.

Successful certification programmes will ensure high-quality tourism while also guaranteeing that a particular company meets stringent standards for socially, environmentally and economically responsible travel. Unfortunately, many existing ecotourism schemes have eschewed basic tourism quality components.

The lack of existing consumer awareness about certification presents a serious challenge, one that is only exacerbated by the differences between the myriad ecotourism certification programmes that currently exist. Surveys show that consumers do often think highly of certification programmes, once they are aware of them. This fact gives hope that, with proper marketing, the proportion of travellers using such labels could increase dramatically (Enhance Management, 2000; Foster, 2001).

Tour operators see ecotourism certification as a way to improve business practices, and to differentiate their product. They may also engage in ecotourism certification to improve the efficiency of their operations or learn more about sustainable practices, two things that could boost their returns. Though tour operators hope that certification will eventually draw in consumers who may also pay a higher price for a certified product, this is infrequently the primary reason for going through the certification process. Some tourism businesses recognize that responsible tourism principles lead to better products, and that it is advantageous to integrate these principles into everyday business practices. Many are giving back to the communities in which they operate through travellers' philanthropy projects or other social investments.

Education about ecotourism certification and responsible travel principles is critical, both to reducing the negative impacts associated with tourism and to expanding the number of tourists interested in ecotourism. Travel agents and print travel resources are valuable means of spreading information about responsible travel prior to a traveller initiating a trip. During a trip, tour operators can guide tourists in being respectful travellers, while weaving ecotourism messages into their everyday activities.

Further research should focus on creating a global profile of ecotourism patterns and tracking money spent on responsible travel over time. A major weakness in resources available for this study comes from the fact that the majority of tourist surveys are focused on just a few industrialized countries (the USA, the UK, Australia, Germany, Denmark) and it is difficult and potentially irresponsible to suggest that the results obtained through such surveys could be applied universally.

Much remains to be learned about how individual travellers decide where to spend their money and how they implement their values while travelling. Exit surveys of tourist spending habits, as well as their behavioural patterns, would guide future recommendations on how best to steer tourists towards more responsible purchasing and spending choices. This is a challenge because tourists on vacation often do not want to be disturbed by questioning or surveys.

Despite these shortcomings, the results compiled in this study indicate considerable potential for the spread of both ecotourism and associated certification programmes. With travellers increasingly choosing to use their money in line with their values, something that tour operators have encouraged through the development of responsible tourism products over the last 20 years, ecotourism is set to expand as a travel market over the coming years.

References

Assadourian, E. (2005) Socially responsible investing spreads. In: *Vital Signs* 2005. Worldwatch Institute, Norton, Washington, DC, p. 99.

CC Africa (n.d.) Phinda Private Game Reserve. Available at: www.ccafrica.com

Center on Ecotourism and Sustainable Development (2004) Travelers' Philanthropy: Helping Communities Build Economic Assets and Sustain Environmental and Cultural Resources in an Era of Rapid Globalization. Available at: www.travelersphilanthropy.org

Conservation International (2005) Biodiversity Hotspots. Available at: www.biodiversityhotspots.org

Co-operative Bank (2002) *Ethical Purchasing Index 2002*. Co-operative Bank, Manchester, UK.

Cortese, A. (2003) Socially conscious consumers? To marketers, they're LOHAS. *New York Times*, 21 July.

Davies, P. (2005) Accommodation biggest gripe amongst holidaymakers. Travelmole.com, 18 March.

Department for International Development (DFID) and Rough Guides (2004) *Rough Guide to a Better World.* Rough Guides, London.

Ecotrans (2002) Holiday 2002: German Tourists Expect Environmental Quality! Press release, 27 March, Saarbrücken, Germany.

Enhance Management (2000) *NEAP Consumer Survey: August 2000.* Prepared for Tourism Queensland, Brisbane, Australia.

EplerWood International (2003) *A Review of International Markets, Business, Finance and Technical Assistance Models for Ecolodges in Developing Countries.* International Finance Corporation/GEF Small and Medium Enterprises Program, Burlington, Vermont, p. 26.

Fairtrade Foundation (2005a) Awareness of Fairtrade Mark Rockets to 50%. Press release, May, London.

Fairtrade Foundation (2005b) Fairtrade shows massive public response to man-made 'economic tsunamis'. Press release, 28 February, London.

FEMATOUR (2000) Feasibility and market study for European eco-label for tourist accommodation. Conducted by Consultancy and Research for Environmental Management (CREM), The Netherlands; and CH2M-HILL, Spain (subcontractor), Amsterdam. Available at: europa.eu.int/ecolabel

Foster, D. (2001) The customer's perception of tourism accreditation. Presented at 5th National and 8th International Research Conference on Quality and Innovation Management, Melbourne, 12–14 February 2001.

FTTSA (n.d.) The Power of Socially Conscious Tourists. Available at: www.fairtourismsa.org.za/fairtrade/

Goodwin, H. (2001) Responsible tourism and the market. Unpublished. Available at: www.haroldgoodwin.info

Goodwin, H. and Francis, J. (2003) Ethical and responsible tourism: consumer trends in the UK. *Journal of Vacation Marketing* 9(3), 271–284.

Green Globe 21 (2002) *Green Globe 21 Newsletter*, No. 27, September. Green Globe 21, Canberra, Australia.

Green Globe 21 (2004) *Green Globe 21 Update*, No. 14, May. Green Globe 21, Canberra, Australia.

Hildebrand, C. (2000) Probleme, und Tendezen bei der Entwicklung eines einheitlichen Unweltgutezeichens fur das Hotel, und Gaststattendewerbe, Fachhochshule Munchen, Studiengang Tourismus. May. With Herbert Hamele, Ecotrans, unpublished. [In FEMATOUR (2000).]

Honey, M. (ed.) (2002) *Ecotourism and Certification: Setting Standards in Practice.* Island Press, Washington, DC.

International Hotels Environment Initiative (IHEI) (2002) Consumer Attitudes Towards the Role of Hotels in International Environmental Sustainability. Press release of report commissioned by Small Luxury Hotels of the World, Surrey, UK, 23 July. Available at: www.hotel-online.com/Neo/News/PR2002_3rd/Jul02_IHEI.html

Janér, A.E. (2003) Hierarchy of tourism needs (apud Maslow), from presentation on sustainable tourism. Available at: www.ecobrasil.org.br or www.pcts.org.br

Leggett, C., Kleckner, N., Boyle, K., Duffield, J. and Mitchell, R. (2003) Social desirability bias in contingent valuation surveys administered through in-person interviews. *Land Economics* 79(4), 561–575.

LOHAS (2005) *LOHAS Journal Online.* Available at: www.lohasjournal.com (17 May)

McGrath, G. (2004) Is consumer demand the only hope for sustainable tourism? Travelmole.com, 13 May.

Market and Opinion Research International (MORI) (1997) *Tourism, the Environment, and Consumers.* MORI, London.

Market and Opinion Research International (MORI) (2003) *Fair Trade Recognition.* MORI, London. Available at: www.fairtrade.org.uk/pr100503.htm

Meyer, D. (2003) *The UK Outbound Tour Operating Industry and Implications for Pro-Poor Tourism.* Pro-Poor Tourism Working Paper No. 17, London.

Mintel International Group (2003) *Eco and Ethical Tourism – UK.* Mintel International Group, London.

Moskin, J. (2004) Helping Third World one banana at a time. *New York Times*, 5 May.

Natural Marketing Institute (2004) *Understanding the LOHAS Consumer.* Natural Marketing Institute, Harleysville, Pennsylvania.

Pattullo, P. and Minelli, O. (2006) *Ethical Travel Guide.* Tourism Concern, Earthscan, London.

Ray, P. and Anderson, S. (2000) *The Cultural Creatives: How 50 Million People are Changing the World.* Harmony Press, New York.

Responsibletravel.com (2004) *Summary of Responsible Travel 'Had Enough?' Survey Results.* With Taylor Nelson Sofres. Responsibletravel.com, Brighton, UK.

Rivera, J. (2002) Assessing a voluntary environmental initiative in the developing world: the Costa Rican Certification for Sustainable Tourism. *Policy Studies* 35. [Referencing INCAE, *Tourism in Costa Rica: A Competitive Challenge,* Costa Rica, 2000].

Tearfund (2000) *Tourism – an Ethical Issue: Market Research Report.* Tearfund, London.

Tearfund (2001) *Tourism – Putting Ethics into Practice.* Tearfund, London.

The International Ecotourism Society (TIES) (2004) *A Simple User's Guide to Certification for Sustainable Tourism and Ecotourism.* The International Ecotourism Society, Washington, DC.

The International Ecotourism Society (TIES) (2006) *Your Travel Choice Makes A Difference.* Brochure. TIES, Washington, DC.

Tourtellot, J. (2002) The hidden clout of travelers. *National Geographic Traveler*, May/June.

Travel Industry Association of America (TIA) and National Geographic Traveler (NGT) (2002) *Geotourism Study: Phase I – Executive Summary.* TIA and NGT, Washington, DC.

Travel Industry Association of America (TIA) and National Geographic Traveler (NGT) (2003) *Geotourism: The New Trend in Travel. Overview of American Travelers.* TIA and NGT, Washington, DC.

Travelmole.com (2004) Virgin Travelstore gets eco-friendly. Travelmole.com, 28 April.

UNEP (2001) Economic Impacts of Tourism. Available at: www.uneptie.org/pc/tourism/sust-tourism/economic.htm

UNESCO (2002) Towards more responsible tourism. In: Hadley, M. (compiler) *Biosphere Reserves: Special Places for People and Nature.* UNESCO Publishing, Paris.

World Heritage Alliance (2006) Expedia, Inc. and UN Foundation introduce World Heritage Alliance at WTTC. Press release, 5 April. Washington, DC.

12 Quality in Ecotourism: the Community Perspective

Abigail Rome

Tierra Vista Consulting, Silver Spring, Maryland, USA

> We would like to have more visitors so that we can have more for our families. At the same time, the entire region will benefit . . . I want the world to know that there are proud indigenous communities working to protect what God created. We like all that is natural; it is beautiful . . . There are many countries where people are [finally] recognizing their identity, and there are people [such as tourists] who want to help us with this. The tourist that comes here wants to learn and understand us, not only to have a vacation. This makes us very happy.
>
> (Lucas Angel Chavez, Kekoldi Indigenous Reserve, Hone Creek, Costa Rica)

Chapter Profile

Community perspectives on quality in ecotourism are best determined by consulting people working in community-based tourism (CBT) because they have created tourism businesses with specific objectives that reflect their values, needs and standards. This chapter presents the voices of CBT members to identify the characteristics of tourism that most connote excellence to communities. Ten characteristics are identified. Five are associated with stated tourism objectives to provide a variety of personal and community-level benefits; three are additional side benefits; and two relate to the quality and number of tourists. As many of the principles of CBT are the same as those of ecotourism, the voices and values expressed by CBT members can also serve as indicators of quality for communities engaged in ecotourism.

Introduction

The majority of the published literature on communities and ecotourism falls into two categories: reviews of sociocultural impacts of tourism on indigenous peoples and/or local communities (e.g. Brandon, 1996; Epler Wood, 1998; Wearing, 2001) and recommendations on how to ensure that communities participate actively and maintain control over tourism activities and impacts occurring on their lands (e.g. Drumm, 1998; Sproule and Suhandi, 1998; Häusler and Strasdas, 2003). While all these studies provide useful information, especially for planning and implementing sustainable tourism programmes with communities, they miss an important feature. They are written by conservation and development professionals, tourism planners, consultants and academics, and therefore express the perspective of outsiders, not that of community members themselves.

The best way to accurately identify the community perspective on quality in ecotourism is to consult the community; however, defining community presents some challenges. A 'community' may simply be a group of people living in close proximity, or it may be a social unit that shares common interests, work, philosophies and identities. This chapter adopts the definition of 'community' offered by Potts and Harrill (1998): 'a limited number of people in a somewhat restricted social space or network held together by shared understandings and a sense of obligation'.

However, in some cases, communities in tourist destinations around the world do not share common values pertinent to the tourism activities being carried out around them, while some communities have consciously decided to engage in tourism. In these cases they share common interests and objectives, and collaborate in the planning, management, revenue generation and monitoring of tourism. They are practitioners of what is called community-based tourism (CBT), also described as a form of tourism in which a significant number of local people have substantial control over and involvement in tourism development and management. Most of the benefits remain within the local economy, and even those community members who are not directly involved in tourism enterprises gain benefit as well (Häusler and Strasdas, 2003).

This chapter examines the tourism perspectives of community members who have chosen to engage either in community-based tourism or in ecotourism partnerships. In both cases, community members are active participants. In partnership arrangements, communities join forces with a private tourism company and/or a non-governmental organization (NGO) to take advantage of the skills, knowledge and capital of each partner in developing a tourism business. Satisfying the needs and concerns of the community are among the primary objectives of such arrangements.

The lessons learned from community members who live and work in CBT projects are valuable for determining what communities are looking for when engaging in any type of tourism. Specifically, they can shed light on what communities perceive as quality or excellence in ecotourism. In fact, many of the principles of CBT are similar to those of ecotourism – e.g. community control and empowerment, natural and cultural sustainability, economic sustainability and cross-cultural learning and sharing (TIES, 2005). It should be made clear, however, that CBT and ecotourism are not one and the same. For example, CBT need not always be conservation-oriented. Its focus is on maintaining and sharing culture and lifestyles, while generating income for individuals and supporting community development. At the same time, while ecotourism always seeks to benefit communities, many ecotourism businesses are not controlled or managed by local peoples.

Community members working in CBT and ecotourism partnerships have identified goals and objectives, and in doing so have defined what quality in tourism represents for them. While this includes ensuring community-wide benefits, it does not guarantee community-wide consensus. That is, there may be some residents who are not actively engaged in tourism and who may have differing opinions on the value and impacts of tourism. While their voices are equally important, they are not the main focus of this study. The challenges that they, as well as CBT practitioners themselves, face are real, but, because they fall outside the task of defining quality in ecotourism and community-based tourism, they will only be addressed peripherally.

Methodology

The research for this chapter is based on two main data sets. The first data set is a series of conversations between the author and members of the Asociación Costarricense de Turismo Rural Comunitario (ACTUAR). With support from the United Nations Development Programme (UNDP) Small Grants Programme, ACTUAR promotes the environmental, social, cultural and economic sustainability of community-based rural tourism initiatives through assistance with marketing, capacity building and resource management. The purpose of the conversations was to give community members an opportunity to talk about how they are being affected by and benefiting from tourism. This research is part of a project that will give a voice to the 'travelled upon', that is, people living in tourism destinations, by disseminating their stories via a monthly e-newsletter and a web site (www.lifeamongvisitors.org). Community members were interviewed with open-ended questions about the benefits and changes they have experienced as a result of engaging in CBT. While they were not queried directly about what they consider to be quality in tourism, their objectives and expectations became evident through the interviews.

The second data set is a summary of lessons learned from the Trueque Amazónico, a year-long research exchange between representatives of three indigenous ecotourism partnerships in the Amazon regions of Bolivia, Ecuador and Peru to discuss their experiences with ecotourism. While the author participated in one of the workshops, the source used for this chapter is a report by Amanda Stronza, project manager, entitled 'Trueque Amazónico: lessons learned in community-based ecotourism' (Stronza, 2004). Additional conclusions regarding community perspectives come from the author's personal conversations with members of CBT operations around the world, as well as relevant literature.

Prior to a discussion of the results, several caveats must be mentioned. First, this chapter contains generalizations about communities. The author is fully cognizant that each community is different and there is significant diversity within communities. Nevertheless, a framework is offered that attempts to address the perspectives of the majority of people living near and working in CBT initiatives. The author hopes that readers will approach what follows with a generous mind and an acceptance for apparently sweeping insights. Ten characteristics of quality in tourism are presented as viewed by the generic 'community'. Each characteristic is described in detail, and examples are provided, mostly from Latin America. To simulate direct consultation with community members, many of the examples will be direct quotes from CBT practitioners. Unless otherwise identified, quotes come from interviews conducted in early 2005 with the author.

Quality in Community-based Tourism

The perspective of any group of stakeholders regarding quality or excellence reflects the values of that group. Therefore, the characteristics that local communities regard as measures of tourism quality mirror the values, concerns and needs of the community. They are the benefits and positive aspects realized through their experiences with tourism. Ten characteristics of quality in CBT have been identified and have been grouped into three categories.

The major reasons that communities engage in tourism or rural community-based tourism operations are to fulfil certain objectives that bring benefits to themselves and to their communities. They want to:

1. Generate income for individuals and their families.
2. Maintain cultures, traditions and lifestyles.
3. Improve and develop their communities.
4. Conserve and protect their environment.
5. Ensure equitable benefits and democratic processes.

While not always initially identified as objectives, community members who are fully engaged in tourism often realize other additional benefits. These include:

6. Education and training.
7. Personal growth.
8. Increased opportunity for individuals and the community.

At the same time, certain characteristics of tourist relationships can determine whether tourism is successful and beneficial. Community members often discover that quality in tourism also depends on the quality and number of tourists. They value and experience superior tourism when there is a(n):

9. Mutual respect between visitors and hosts.
10. Ideal number of tourists.

While these characteristics of tourism quality have been identified and classified by the author, the community's perspective will be offered through the voice of local residents. At times, the personal statements may elucidate more than one valued characteristic of tourism. This is because community members' objectives are closely intertwined. For example, an indigenous person who conserves their culture is simultaneously protecting environmental resources as integral parts of their community's tradition and heritage; or, after receiving training, community members mature in their grasp of technical, informational and administrative skills, as well as in more personal ways.

Objectives in Developing Tourism Programmes

Income generation

Primarily, community members look to tourism as a way of gaining an income. Local people may be directly employed in a lodge, as a manager or administrator or as a guide or they may benefit indirectly by providing food, handicrafts, transport and other products or services for visitors. In addition to being paid for their work, community members may enhance their personal revenue by generating business profits. Some communities have established distribution systems that provide all members with income whether or not they are directly involved in the tourism operation. This ensures wider community support for tourism, while allowing community members to continue to engage in a diversity of income-generating activities.

The economic benefits of tourism are extremely important for communities because rural destinations, where most ecotourism and some community-based tourism occurs, generally offer few employment alternatives. Even when the income generated through tourism is from part-time work, as is the case in many of the small, community-based operations, the income helps families meet basic economic needs. Rosa Emilia Cruz of Hone Creek, Costa Rica, clearly states her group's objectives in developing a rural tourism programme:

> We wanted tourism because we needed to make more money. We have kids in school and some of the women are single and have no other sources of income. We wanted to be able to have an income while protecting our health and the environment . . . When groups come and it's my turn to cook for them, I make some money. Other days, other women in the group cook and get paid. We need this income. This is our purpose for working.

This is supported by the experience of Lucas Angel Chaves of the Kekoldi Indigenous Reserve in Costa Rica, who states:

> Tourism has also been beneficial for me and for the community and for other communities, too. We're not working directly with tourism but the majority of the population works in handicrafts and they bring them here [to sell]. This has opened the doors to many families, not only from our community but from many others. We've seen that when you know how to do good work, tourism brings money for families. Most of the artisans are single indigenous women who need to be both mother and father. This work really helps them resolve economic problems, for instance enabling them to help their children with school expenses.

Maintaining traditional cultures and lifestyles

Some places that become tourism destinations do so because of the unique attractions, whether they are natural, cultural and/or social, that they offer to visitors. Congruently, communities living in tourism destinations are often highly aware and protective of their natural wealth, cultural heritage and social structure. This is especially true in cases where indigenous cultures and communities have continued to maintain their identities and way of life in a rapidly changing and modernizing world. They value their history, current lifestyles and environment, and look to tourism as a way to preserve these aspects of their identity. Their involvement in tourism means that they are able to remain in their community and make a living, rather than moving to the city for a job. They can maintain family stability, traditional lifestyles and local resources while keeping cultural knowledge alive.

While some communities develop tourism programmes to generate personal income and conserve cultures and destinations, others use it to support complementary existing activities, which also have income-generating potential. In the case of Rosa Emelia Cruz's community, she and other village women initially formed the El Yue Association of Family Producers to raise organic bananas, vegetables and herbs, as a way to supply healthy food to their families and neighbours. After a few years, in order to secure land and supplement the revenue they were receiving by selling their produce, they decided to develop a small tourism facility. They built two cabins and a dining room/kitchen and now invite visitors to stay with them, learn about their farm and enjoy other nearby attractions.

The situation at Lucas Angel Chaves's community is similar, where he and other Bribri-Cabecar Indians of south-eastern Costa Rica started breeding iguanas for cultural and conservation reasons in the mid-1990s. Shortly afterwards they developed a visitor programme to support their work. As spokesman for the Kekoldi Wak Kak Koneke (caretakers of the forest) organization, he explains how ecotourism has allowed them to maintain an important and traditional indigenous resource:

> We use the money [from visitor fees] to maintain the site and care for the iguana. We say that every person who comes and pays the entrance is another member, another supporter of the project. Each visitor gives so that others may come and see the iguanas too. If it wasn't this way, it would be impossible, because we always need resources and materials to be able to work. We have no interest in making a profit. We do this for love, because we love the species. The iguana is very important for us. We use the skins for handicrafts and also for medicinal purposes. In the past, the fat of the iguana was used to resolve bronchial problems. This is part of our history, our culture that we've maintained from [long ago]. This project encompasses something really important in the history of our indigenous people. We fight [to conserve our history] and we work with the help of the visitors who help finance the project.

Establishing a tourism programme to maintain traditional cultures and lifestyles can provide benefits as well as challenges. Members of the indigenous

Amazonian communities of San José de Uchupiamonas in Bolivia, Infierno in Peru and Kapawi in Ecuador, all participants in the Trueque Amazónico, discussed how ecotourism has influenced the management of cultural resources. For example, they mentioned that tourism has favoured the re-evaluation of culture and the feeling of pride in being 'native' and has prompted a new interest in 'cultural rescue'. Tourism has also brought increased exposure to Western culture. In cases where some of those outside characteristics are assumed by the population, it does not necessarily mean that people are no longer 'native'. For example, what people are wearing, driving, cooking or lighting their homes with does not necessarily define their status as indigenous. They mentioned that it is vital to respect culture and local desires when determining whether and how to present and represent culture to tourists and essential to establish and uphold codes of conduct for showing culture and community to tourists (Stronza, 2004).

These findings demonstrate that tourism has stimulated a re-evaluation by community members of cultural and traditional resources and how they should be presented. Communities want to ensure that these resources are maintained as authentically as possible, and are not presented as a 'show' simply to entertain visitors.

Non-indigenous communities are also concerned about the impacts of tourism, especially on their lifestyles. ASACODE is an association of small landholders in San Miguel de Sixaola, Costa Rica, working to preserve declining natural resources. Members run a lodge and educational programmes to present local culture, agricultural techniques and natural history. When José Luis Zuñiga, a key ASACODE organizer, was asked how many tourists they would like to see each year, he replied:

> We don't want a Monteverde [cloud forest community and reserve with high volumes of tourists] here. We want to continue to be farmers, but we want a better quality of life. In Monteverde and the beaches, you don't see people working. You just see them sitting around waiting for tourists to come. Here no. We're working. I don't live from tourism. It's an alternative.

These villagers are adamant in their desire to ensure that tourism does not disrupt their current lifestyles and activities. They want to continue working the land and living much as they are accustomed. However, the very act of engaging in a new form of employment such as tourism requires making changes and is likely to cause some conflicts between traditional and tourism-based lifestyles. A community working in tourism finds itself carrying out new and different daily activities, learning new skills and information, engaging in relationships with a variety of people from afar, gaining new values and experiencing changes in both the natural environment and the community itself.

However, these changes are not always positive. Members of the Trueque Amazónico discussed negative changes in community life as a result of working in ecotourism. These changes included the time and distance spent by ecotourism workers away from their families, and a rise in jealousy and suspicion towards those who work in the ecolodge. They also mentioned some loss of community spirit, specifically with regard to communal work. There is now more interest in individual gain through paid employment, and not in voluntary work for the community. Some people have become dependent on profits from tourism and have abandoned other subsistence and income-earning activities. A variety of community issues normally addressed at community meetings are not heard because ecotourism occupies most of the agenda (Stronza, 2004).

Likewise, a study of the impacts of ethnic tourism on gender roles in two communities, one matriarchal and one patriarchal, in Yunnan Province, China, found that in both communities mothers have less time for their families. In addition, the women of the matriarchal village expressed concern over the preservation of their traditions, saying that tourism brought crime, cultural misrepresentation and, most importantly, amorous temptations to women and girls (Morais *et al.*, 2005).

To avoid conflicts communities have implemented a variety of measures to mitigate the change inherent in becoming or developing a tourism destination. Many communities have constructed their lodges away from their village to separate tourists from villagers. Others have engaged in zoning their village or forest so that tourists and tourism activities are limited to certain areas or times of the day or year. Tourists use trails specifically designed for them, as opposed to those used by locals, sacred sites have restricted or closed access to visitors, and visits to see where locals live and work may be available only at scheduled times. Communities, such as those participating in the Trueque Amazónico, have established codes of conduct so that visitors avoid disrupting local lifestyles or natural resources. They say, 'The goal is to protect tourism from the community, and also the community from tourism' (Stronza, 2004).

Community development

While acknowledging that communities involved in tourism want to maintain traditional lifestyles, they also want to raise their standard of living. They embrace certain aspects of development, such as enhanced health care, access to water and electricity, increased communication with the outside world and more diverse and higher-quality educational opportunities. Tourism can improve the well-being of the larger community in a range of ways. For instance, community members running Chalalan Lodge in southern Bolivia mentioned a variety of associated community development benefits in their village of San José de Uchupiamonas. They include:

- Improving opportunities for education, local transportation and access.
- Providing more and better resources for health care.
- Developing professional relationships with government institutions in Bolivia.
- Slowing outmigration from San José and consolidating the community.
- Self-determination of the community, both in practice (legally) and in perception.

- Contributing to overall improvement of quality of life.
- Providing an additional market for various community-produced goods and services, including agricultural products and handicrafts.
- Improving public services in the community, including telephone, potable water, bathrooms with plumbing and a medical clinic (Stronza, 2004).

Infrastructure developed or brought in for tourism can also benefit communities. Transportation services to bring tourists to lodges are often available to local residents on boats that ply the rivers in the Amazon or on small tourist planes. Solar panels or other energy sources supplying ecotourism operations may also be available to local residents; likewise, radio or cellphone communications introduced to facilitate tourism can be used by all in cases of emergency.

Travellers' philanthropy also provides additional support for health or educational facilities and services. Donations come either from tourists or from businesses that devote a percentage of their profits to community projects and funds. For instance, the Jean Michel Cousteau Resort near Savusavu, Fiji, contributes to the Savusavu Community Foundation, a charitable organization providing health care, education, transportation and cultural support for local peoples (G. Taylor, Savusavu, Fiji, personal communication, 2005). Likewise, Myths and Mountains, a tour operator based in Nevada, USA, offering cultural and environmental tours in South-east Asia and South America, has established a non-profit organization called READ (Rural Education and Development). READ provides educational scholarships, builds and stocks community libraries and encourages self-sustaining initiatives that build literacy in Nepal (A. Neubauer, Washington, DC, personal communication, 2004).

While the examples above illustrate how privately owned companies contribute to community development, community-based lodges often develop similar programmes. For example, Chalalan Lodge in the Bolivian Amazon is owned and managed by the village of San José de Uchupiamonas. They created a business model where 50% of the profits go to shareholders (74 families, representing most of the community) and 50% go to a community organization (which includes families who did not invest in the lodge) to be used for education, health, sports, establishing land tenure and other matters (Stronza, 2004). Likewise, visitation at the Kapawi Lodge in the Ecuadorean Amazon supports FINAE, the Ecuadorean Achuar Federation, and the 58 surrounding Achuar communities through monthly rent payments and a US$10/tourist fee. This revenue is used for education, health, micro-enterprise development and maintenance of a community airstrip, as well as administration of FINAE (Stronza, 2004).

Although these initiatives can assist in improving community well-being, most of these communities realize that a tourism business alone is not enough to support an entire community. Not everyone can or wants to be directly involved in tourism, and the industry is highly sensitive to outside influences that might negatively influence profits. Therefore, communities that are savvy to tourism's risks recommend establishing complementary activities or projects, such as fish farming, agroforestry and handicrafts production, ensuring that as many community members as possible have ongoing revenue streams (Stronza, 2004). The education and training available to communities for tourism development can also help local people establish other businesses.

Yet, while community development is generally considered beneficial, especially in rural or developing country destinations, not all tourism impacts are positive for communities working to maintain their lifestyles, cultures and environment. For example, in parts of Africa, women traditionally gather and socialize at water sources. When development influenced by tourism and other factors brings potable water into villagers' homes or yards, women no longer congregate as readily. As a result, social interactions and cultural traditions are affected. Another example of where community development may lead to breakdown of tradition is in health care. When Western or modern medicine is more easily available, communities may gradually cease to use traditional medicines and lose their knowledge of plant-based remedies.

Conservation and protection of environmental resources

Communities as well as conservationists often develop ecotourism programmes specifically as a way to protect their natural environment, which is faced with threats such as logging, mining, oil drilling and hunting. Ecotourism can be used to deter proponents of these environmentally destructive activities by offering a more environmentally friendly income generation alternative. This was the case of the Cofan Indians in the Ecuadorean Amazon, who resisted threats of oil companies and established a community-based ecotourism lodge in the village of Zabalo (Tidwell, 1996).

In Hojancha, in Costa Rica's Nicoya Peninsula, the community faced a different challenge, where the river that fed the town was drying up because of forest clearing upstream. Del Fin Mendez Cruz talks of the history of the Monte Alto Reserve:

> By 1992, only about 5% of the primary forest was left. That is when we started to get worried, especially when we saw how the river was drying up. I said that the only way we could protect the forest was to buy the land [where the river starts]. When in private hands, it's very difficult to protect natural forest because the farmer needs to cut trees in order to produce crops. [We knew that if you recuperate] the forest, you can recuperate the fauna and the water.

In this case the community banded together and raised money to buy land, but then found they needed additional money to ensure its conservation. With the help of governmental and non-governmental organizations, the community successfully gained a grant, enabling them to construct an ecolodge and environmental education centre. Now these facilities and their programmes fund the land and water conservation work of the Monte Alto

Foundation, provide jobs for community members, and raise environmental awareness of Costa Rican and foreign visitors. Del Fin is proud of the community initiative:

> Hojancha is the [community conservation] leader in Guanacaste [Province]. The water situation is much better now. In 1992, there were a lot of problems. There wasn't any water. The river was dry – like a desert. It was a disaster. It passes right through the Hojancha and is very important [for the community]. Now, the river is fine. It's completely changed.
>
> I think it's important to fulfil a goal. My goal was that there would be forest here again. We were lucky to have this project, and now we know that the forest will last for ever. We're leaving this for the next generation. They'll know the animals, even the ones that had disappeared. There are 160 species of birds here. People have realized that this project is going to last. I've always thought that when you live in a community, you benefit from what's there, but you also need to give back to it.

In the small village of Gandoca, on the north coast of Costa Rica next to the border with Panama, a group of homeowners work together to provide lodging for volunteers who come each year to patrol the beaches and protect sea turtles during the nesting season. When Carmen López Umaña was asked what benefits tourism brings, she focused on visitor contributions to conservation while acknowledging that the benefits are community-wide:

> The community benefits because the volunteers come and patrol the turtles and their eggs when they're laying them. We don't have enough people here to go and patrol the beach every night. And if we did [the patrolling], how would we make a living? No one is going to pay us to do it. The volunteers come and pay us to stay in the cabins and help us care for the turtles.

These examples are in contrast to others in which there may be conflict between conservation of natural areas and the desire to maintain traditional uses and lifestyles. While ecotourism promotes limiting the harvest of non-renewable resources such as hunting, fishing, logging and mining, local residents may be opposed to regulation of resource use. In fact, indigenous people in Alaska, the Amazon and elsewhere view hunting and/or fishing as important activities that must be maintained to conserve their culture and lifestyles. However, when there is excessive fishing or hunting and/or these activities occur close to the ecolodge, these may conflict with ecotourism principles and practices.

To return to a less controversial aspect of natural resource management, ecotourism can generate political and economic support for conservation and environmental protection. By providing new local and national revenue streams, ecotourist dollars can help governments see the value in conserving natural areas, stimulating them to establish parks and protected areas. At the same time, ecotourists often serve as advocates for conservation of the places they visit (as well as their own homelands and waters). After visiting and enjoying natural areas, they may lobby for their protection and donate money to local conservation and management programmes.

Equitable benefits and democratic processes

Another objective of communities that involve themselves in tourism is ensuring that the benefits and opportunities are distributed equitably and democratically among community members. They do not want tourism to negatively influence the social framework of the village; such destabilization may be the result of income inequalities in cases where community members who work directly in tourism receive higher or steadier salaries than those who do not.

Xiomara Sosa Lopez of Gandoca, a village on the Atlantic coast of Costa Rica, discussed how she and other local home-stay providers ensure that disadvantaged members of the community share the tourism wealth:

> [Having volunteers here from March to July] has now become a custom. I like it when there are visitors here. In fact, everyone in the community likes it for the money. Many people raise chickens, pigs, plantains, cassava and we buy their products for the visitors. I also hire someone from the community to help me cook and clean. I always hire someone local so that the community benefits. We're not selfish – we like to share the money in the community, especially with people who have few resources. Another important thing is that we have an open policy that says anyone from the community can work in tourism, not just those of us who are already doing it.

While the residents of Gandoca embrace equal opportunities for the entire community to work in tourism, such impartiality is not always possible. An individual's ability to engage in community-based tourism may depend on their resources, education level, skills, gender and overall community values, and members who do not qualify may be denied employment. For instance, in communities such as Gandoca where home stays are provided, participants must have a large enough house to offer lodging to visitors; or, in some indigenous communities, women are prohibited from working outside the home. People who do have the skills to work as guides, cooks, managers or administrators in or around lodges may also be left out. In these cases, communities engaged in CBT must find other ways to provide tourism benefits for those who desire them.

At the Trueque Amazónico, the communities engaged in long discussions on how to make decisions about distributing economic benefits. They demonstrated a strong concern for the process to be democratic, embracing Chalalan's model in Bolivia. In their village of San José de Uchupiamonas, profits are divided equally among shareholders and the Organización Territorial de Base (OTB), the community organization that provides support for community needs such as education, health, sports and land legalization. While both shareholders and OTB beneficiaries are members of the community and are owners of the land that the lodge occupies, shareholders also work in and/or provide capital for the ecotourism project. This system ensures that everyone in the community benefits, while those who contribute time and energy benefit even more. One community member explains:

> To participate, you have to have been born in the community and have a home there as well. We cannot turn away some families. There are families who have

> entered the community, and they are now San Josésanos. Now what we have to do is measure the participation because in one way or another, a shareholder has to contribute. What we know is that we cannot marginalize people. At the end of last year, we had Christmas gifts, and we requested that they go to everyone. Everyone has a right, because [they have] a share of territory and live in the community.
>
> (Stronza, 2004)

The other two participating communities, Infierno in Peru and Kapawi in Ecuador, make decisions about income distribution at community assemblies to which all residents are invited. However, they voice concerns about how to ensure that democracy and equity are addressed, as explained by a stakeholder from Chalalan: 'Just being a member of the community, one has contributed nothing. The benefits should be earned. People should fight for their benefits. Being a community member is a requirement, but the contribution and interest are important' (Stronza, 2004). The response from an Infierno representative confirms this sentiment: 'It doesn't make sense for community members to receive benefits simply for being community members. In Infierno, we are doing that but have to analyse the situation better' (Stronza, 2004).

Additional Benefits that Communities Receive from CBT Tourism

Education and training

One of the less tangible, non-economic benefits from tourism development that community members experience is access to education and training. Capacity building, as these opportunities are often called, is an important component of development projects and programmes, and is available to those directly involved in tourism development as well as to other community members. In Costa Rica, the UNDP Small Grants Programme provides support for construction of community-based tourism operations as well as training in a range of areas, including hotel management, hospitality, accounting, financial management, organization and self-esteem. In other Latin American countries, the Inter-American Development Bank has funded tourism development programmes that include training as a major component. The skills and knowledge provided serve the community as a whole because they are useful in developing a wide range of small businesses.

As a result of these programmes, participants learn new ways of making a living. For instance, in Costa Rica they are learning how to form partnerships and gain support from other individuals and organizations and they are changing how they view the concept of work. Gerardo 'Beto' Mora of El Copal Ecolodge talks about the communities of El Humo and Pejibaye near Cartago:

> [People] are thinking of work in new and different ways than what we're used to. There are people who think it's very easy [to work in tourism], but . . . There

> is nothing easy in this life. Those who don't work can't live. So you have to think about finding people and organizations who can support you and be partners. They can give a hand when you're in a difficult situation. If someone helps you out, you can find a way to make it work. That's something new for us, because as former farmers we've been used to working on our own.

Liliana Martinez Gonzalez from the Isla de Chira in the Gulf of Nicoya, Costa Rica, realizes the value of the business, administration, organization and personal growth training she received from the UNDP. It allowed her and several other women to succeed in building a successful lodge, in spite of the doubts and strong criticism from their husbands and neighbours. She points out that once the tourism operation was up and running, other, once-sceptical members of the village requested training for themselves to help them develop their own small businesses and conserve their natural resources. As she explains:

> Little groups of women came to us to ask us for help. They were afraid, but we said [to ourselves] we have to get them some training like we had. Since we were a well-formed group, now known by the institutions, we went to them and said that there is a group of women who want to get trained. Now we have 20 or 40 women from different villages who gather at our place to get training, and gradually they begin to gain strength.

Likewise, once residents of small villages in the cloud forests outside Quito, Ecuador, were trained and had worked at the nearby, NGO-owned Maquipucuna Reserve and Ecolodge, they gained the skills needed to develop their own community-based lodges. Now, community-based operations such as Santa Lucia and Yunguillas share tourists and volunteers, who visit all three lodges, as well as tourism attractions and activities, with Maquipucuna (F. Molina, Santa Lucia, personal communication, 2004). This coordinated approach results in a broader, more diverse market, increased employment and more revenue for all of the nearby ecotourism providers and villages.

Many tourism lodges offer opportunities for national or international volunteers to stay in the lodge and work either on the property itself or in the community. The services provided vary from place to place but may include:

- Providing classes or workshops in foreign languages, environmental education, organic gardening, handicrafts development, computer skills, etc.
- Conducting applied research including ecological, agroforestry, silvopastoral systems, ethnobotany, archaeology, folklore, health, etc.
- Providing assistance with community building projects such as school or hospital construction or disaster relief.
- Offering health services such as vaccinations, dental check-ups or first aid.

Communities are generally appreciative of the contributions, many of which they would not receive without the presence of tourism accommodation in the area.

However, training opportunities made available to some community members and not others can be a cause for conflict. More highly educated or more experienced people may have access to better jobs and/or receive higher wages and tips, creating economic disparities between villagers. In communities that are not traditionally hierarchical, such as the San in South Africa, the advancement of more educated individuals may negatively influence cultural and societal relationships (Moses *et al.*, 2002). Communities that encourage sharing of knowledge and skills between interested members can reduce this potential source of friction.

Personal growth

After becoming involved in tourism, receiving training and gaining experience working in tourism, community members often find they have grown in unexpected ways. Many report becoming more outgoing and comfortable talking with strangers and foreigners. They lose their shyness and gain confidence in themselves and what they have to offer. Patricia Chavez of El Copal near Cartago, Costa Rica, discusses the new-found joy she has in meeting people from other countries:

> Now we want to get to know those who come. At first, we're a bit timid to meet new people. At first we don't understand each other [because of language differences], but we use sign language and soon we get excited, and we start to understand each other. It's fun.

After receiving training in self-esteem, organizational development and other topics relevant to developing community-based rural tourism, Rosa Emilia Cruz from El Yue said:

> Our self-esteem has improved, thanks to the workshops we've received and activities we've done. The majority of the women here used to feel like they had to do whatever their husbands said. They were afraid to be independent, but now that has changed.

The women on the Isla de Chira learned valuable lessons about themselves and also made profound changes in their community when they succeeded in building a lodge and boat and running a rural tourism programme. Speaking about the small group of committed women involved in the project, Liliana Martinez Gonzalez said:

> We soon began to realize that we were women and that we had many rights, especially the right to work freely, not pressured by others. We had rights to do what we needed to do for our lives. When we realized all these rights, it felt like a huge liberation. It was a liberation that allowed us to proceed more quickly, not weighted down any more with guilt or doubts that maybe the men were right [when they told us we were crazy], and that we were doing bad things.

Not only did the women involved gain new insights about themselves and their neighbours, but so did other members of the community. Liliana goes on to say:

> [After a while] the community began to see the change in the four women who were left in the project. When we attended meetings of church committees,

> school or health committees, we were taken into account. When they saw that these women were becoming more powerful, that they were a force in the community, the men began to have hope in these women. They saw that the women had worked and succeeded in something. They had put their minds to it and accomplished their goal.
>
> One day 32 men, all fishermen, came here while we were working. They stood in a line and said, 'We didn't know what class of women we had on this island. You are very brave women. You are women who have given the entire island hope. In you and your project we have seen faith. We have seen the faith that you had, and look what you accomplished.'

While these changes in individuals and communities appear to be positive, there are places where new perspectives brought about by tourism can cause problems and/or bring about unforeseen cultural change. For example, in communities that maintain specific gender-based roles, the empowerment of women and their engagement in new activities may impair their ability to maintain traditional practices and uphold traditional values. In addition, as demonstrated in Isla de Chira, conflicts between men and women about gender roles and responsibilities can foment familial and community discord.

Returning to more positive examples of communities gaining new perspectives, many who have engaged in tourism now think differently about their natural surroundings. In Isla de Chira, the success of the women's lodge affected how the villagers view conservation and environmental protection, as Liliana explains:

> This [project] was an entryway into changing the situation on the island. The people began to remove their blinkers, to see what was possible to accomplish with hard work, faith and hope. They realized that indeed we can continue living on this island. We can conserve and protect the forest. Before they thought that they needed to cut trees because they had to cook with wood. But when they saw that we women could cook without wood and even build a whole lodge without cutting trees, they were impressed. They had witnessed the great lengths that these women had gone to haul wood from the mainland, so that they didn't have to cut one tree on the island. It was a very direct message and important lesson for them.

Local people who have been trained as guides gain pride in themselves and their community. While many of them were already well versed in local ecology, birds and plants, as well as community history and culture, they often did not know the value of this knowledge. Only after visitors express amazement and appreciation for a guide's extensive understanding of animal behaviour or medicinal plants do rural villagers realize the value of their knowledge. The result is often a strong boost of self-esteem.

Community members in Costa Rica find that they have new and increased appreciation for what they always took for granted in their own backyards. They had grown up with the forest around them and did not realize its value until it started to disappear. Now that people from around the world travel long distances to see their forest, local people are beginning to realize that they do indeed have something special to share and to protect. Patricia Chavez explains:

> Before, we never knew the importance of the forest or tourism. We'd say what's the forest for? Now that we have tourists we see them get excited about the natural beauty we have here. We're thrilled to see that we have something to offer to foreigners and even to Ticos [Costa Ricans]. Now we meet more people and learn from them, and they [also learn] from us.

Her husband, Gerardo 'Beto' Mora, adds:

> I think that thanks to this [ecotourism] project we, at least in my case, have learned to value nature and the animals. I don't like hunters in the forest. And, our life is getting better. We're leaving something for the future, for our kids so they'll learn to value nature, too. I feel content. I feel I've changed how I am. I have committed myself to the environment. If I can increase the size of the forest and protect the watershed and find a way to protect the springs, we'll all benefit.

Increased opportunities for individuals and the community

Community members see tourism as a way to increase opportunities for themselves, their children and the community as a whole. Education, training and the skills they gain through their involvement in tourism open doors for them to work in new jobs and other fields. The relationships they develop with tourists, the tourism industry and other organizations provide them with opportunities to be involved in a variety of initiatives that have impacts beyond the community. The new perspectives they gain through involvement with travellers affect the way their families and other community members view their place in society and the world, as described by Liliana of Isla de Chira:

> The kids have new hopes now. They want to study. When visitors come speaking other languages, the kids want to be able to speak with them. They are interested in bettering themselves. Before, they used to think that you go to elementary school and when you finish, you fish. That's all there was to do. Now they want to improve the community, to make improvements in the trails, roads and boats.

Guido Mamani, general manager for the Chalalan Ecolodge and resident of San José de Uchupiamonas in southern Bolivia, describes significant changes in his village since they became successful in their ecotourism venture:

> Years ago, people abandoned San José, but now they are returning because they have pride in the success of Chalalan. They see opportunity here. As many of us have received training to work in our tourism business, everyone sees the value of education. The community now expects a good education for all its youngsters. This helps us develop a variety of sustainable community-related businesses which improve our living standards. Before, San José was a place of suffering; now it is a place of opportunities.

New opportunities resulting from their work in tourism have also arisen for the community of Infierno at Posada Amazonas in southern Peru. They reported their ability to communicate directly with donors, NGOs and other sources of potential support for development in Infierno. New gender relations have developed, in particular, an acknowledgement of the abilities and opportunities for women to assume non-traditional roles, as well as greater participation of women, especially in the production of handicrafts (Stronza, 2004).

Encounters with tourists may result in new opportunities for local people. For example, Julieta Mena, a Quitirrisi indigenous artesan from Canton Mora outside San José, Costa Rica, had the opportunity to travel to the USA and give basket-weaving classes. Her trip was sponsored by a group of women who had come to Costa Rica as tourists, met Julieta and were impressed with her handiwork, energy and enthusiasm. She reports some of her impressions:

> In Minnesota, I saw that the people were very polite and the city was so clean, really clean, unlike Costa Rica. One day we were walking and I saw a woman who saw some litter on the ground and picked it up. I thought, how nice, if only people in Costa Rica did that. The other thing that really impressed me was I saw women doing hard work – driving trucks and cleaning the streets. Here in Costa Rica those are men's jobs. But women there were doing men's work. Before I thought that women can't really work, that we could only do housework. But now I realize that women can work hard too. Like men. They have the same rights.
>
> For me, it was a really nice experience. Sometimes, I would think life is so difficult. I didn't realize that I could excel at something, that I can be independent and go other places and have other opportunities. I have to thank them because they gave us this opportunity to know another country.

Characteristics of Tourist Relationships

Mutual respect between visitors and hosts

Usually the lives, lifestyles, cultures and native environments of communities engaged in tourism are different from those of the tourists who visit them. As a result, it can be easy for either group to make value judgements based on what they see and experience. This can lead to uncomfortable situations and/or conflict between individuals or within the community. Mature or experienced community members recognize the importance of developing mutual respect between individuals, no matter what their level of education, cultural or historical background, skin colour, religion or other characteristic.

José Luis Zuñiga of San Miguel de Sixaola, Costa Rica, articulates the need for mutual respect:

> When [visitors] come here, they experience a cultural change. We need to respect the differences between us. Once [visitors] respect us and we respect them, then we begin to share. For example, in the morning we get up early and

> ask [the guests] who wants to learn how to cook. It makes us laugh because they don't know how to cook. But I put myself in their place. If I were to go to the US, I wouldn't know how to do their things. If you put me in front of a computer, I don't know how to use it. I'm like a baby, not knowing what to do. I learn to respect them. Respect is everything.

Rural villagers also appreciate the opportunity to meet and converse with people from around the world, to share stories and experiences and to learn. As they get to know people with different lifestyles and habits, they gain respect for people from other places and cultures. They are no longer afraid or critical of the differences. Gerardo 'Beto' Mora of El Copal describes how ecotourism and new relationships and communications with foreigners have affected him:

> Life isn't easier with tourism. It's different. It's not only about working in the field. It's learning to live together. The most important experiences I've had have been with young volunteers. They're Canadian and Australian. I've never worked with people who don't speak Spanish. We've learned how to exchange ideas about how they live. And we tell them how we live differently. I've learned what they discover when they come to a forest like this. For example, the Canadians are not used to seeing a natural forest.

In describing what he likes about tourists, a resident of Infierno in the Peruvian Amazon illustrates the value of respect between visitor and host:

> I think tourists are good people, not only because they provide us with money, but also because they allow us to learn about their culture. The most important part is the social. The tourists are open, and talk honestly, from their hearts. We can learn from them.
>
> (Stronza, 2004)

Ideal numbers of tourists

While rural communities want tourism to help them maintain traditional lifestyles and cultures and protect their natural environments, they do not want to be overwhelmed by too many visitors with alternative interests and concerns. Nor do they want to spend all of their time serving guests as they have their own families and livelihoods to maintain. At the same time, they want sufficient numbers of visitors to make it worthwhile for them to be engaged in tourism. Many villagers have taken risks, spending time, money and energy to develop their lodges and programmes, and want their investments to pay off. Therefore, they try to ensure that numbers of tourists are sufficient to provide revenue and satisfy community needs, but not so high as to disrupt their lives and communities.

Xiomara Sosa Lopez of Gandoca expresses the need for a balanced approach:

> We want even more benefit from tourism, but we don't want massive tourism like in Puertoviejo. We want to work in rural community-based tourism. We don't want to be millionaires from this. We want a good life, but not an exaggerated one.

Rodolfo Goodman of Guias Mant in Manzanillo, Costa Rica, agrees, explaining that the tourism experience is better for the community as well as the visitor when groups are small:

> We need more money, but we don't want big groups. We want tourists who come and stay in small cabins or rent a room. We want them to work with local people. We enjoy them more and they like it better, too.

While still in the early stages of their rural community tourism project, Liliana of Isla de Chira knows that her group needs more income, but sees the need to control numbers and types of tourists:

> We'd like more people, and people who stay for several days. If there are more visitors, then there is more work for more people here. But we want to be careful of the type of people who come here. We want responsible people who appreciate the quiet, safe life we have here. We have children and we want them to always be safe.

In the early stages of community-based tourism development, and often even in later stages, one of the biggest challenges that communities face is marketing. Often, because of their remote location, lack of knowledge about the outside world and marketing practices and lack of resources, they are unable to promote their tourism programmes. As a result, they often have insufficient numbers of tourists and are unable to fulfil their objectives. One solution to this problem is to establish partnerships with NGOs, the tourism industry, international organizations and/or governmental tourism promotion programmes for marketing support.

Conclusion

This chapter has examined how communities perceive quality in tourism by examining what rural residents of some communities say and feel about their experiences of community-based tourism. Ten characteristics were identified by local communities that they regard as measures of tourism quality. These characteristics reflect their community values, concerns and needs. Their characteristics were systematized into a framework, but derived from listening to local voices – reflecting the standard principles of ecotourism. The five objectives that communities stated for actively engaging in community-based tourism – generating income, maintaining cultures, traditions and lifestyles, improving their communities, protecting their environment, and ensuring equitable benefits and democratic processes – mirror the principles of ecotourism outlined in a variety of definitions (Blamey, 2001). The additional benefits encountered – capacity building, personal growth and increased opportunity – as well as expressed preferences for numbers and quality of tourist–host relationships, shed further light on community values.

The relevance of these findings for ecotourism developers and managers is paramount. Given that ecotourism practitioners want a win–win–win solution, in which economic, environmental and sociocultural sustainability criteria are met, they must ensure that quality in ecotourism extends to communities. This means they need to work towards ascertaining that the communities they work with experience the benefits and expectations for quality that have been expressed.

However, conflicts exist between ecotourism and community-based tourism, similar to those already described. This is because expectations for quality in ecotourism as expressed by other stakeholders (and outlined in this volume) are not always the same as those of the community. While tourists and tour operators have certain standards of quality for products and services, these are often different from those of host communities. As communities adapt and modify their lifestyles, practices and environments to meet the expectations of tourists and tourism proponents, authenticity is lost. At the same time, ecotourism cannot be successful without such compromises. The challenge for both ecotourism and community-based tourism will be to balance traditional community values and perceptions of quality in tourism with those of the tourists and the tourism industry.

References

Blamey, R.K. (2001) Principles of ecotourism. In: Weaver, D.B. (ed.) *The Encyclopedia of Ecotourism.* CAB International, Wallingford, UK, pp. 5–22.

Brandon, K. (1996) *Ecotourism and Conservation: A Review of Key Issues.* Environment Department Paper no. 33, World Bank, Washington, DC.

Drumm, A. (1998) New Approaches to community-based ecotourism management. In: Lindberg, K., Epler Wood, M. and Engeldrum, D. (eds) *Ecotourism: A Guide for Planners and Managers,* Vol. 2. Ecotourism Society, North Bennington, Vermont, pp. 197–214.

Epler Wood, M. (1998) *Meeting the Global Challenge of Community Participation in Ecotourism: Case Studies and Lessons from Ecuador.* Nature Conservancy, Arlington, Virginia.

Häusler, N. and Strasdas, W. (2003) *Training Manual for Community-based Tourism.* InWEnt – Capacity Building International, Bonn, Germany.

Morais, D.B., Yarnal, C., Dong, E. and Dowler, L. (2005) The impact of ethnic tourism on gender roles: a comparison between the Bai and the Mosou of Yunnan Province, PRC. *Asia Pacific Journal of Tourism Research* 10(4), 361–367.

Moses, K., Thoma, O. and Thoma, A. (2002) Will tourism destroy San cultures? *Cultural Survival Quarterly* 26(2), 39–41.

Potts, T.D. and Harrill, R. (1998) Enhancing communities for sustainability: a travel ecology approach. *Tourism Analysis* 3, 133–142.

Sproule, K.W. and Suhandi, A.S. (1998) Guidelines for community-based ecotourism programs: lessons from Indonesia. In: Lindberg, K., Epler Wood, M. and Engeldrum, D. (eds) *Ecotourism: A Guide for Planners and Managers,* Vol. 2. Ecotourism Society, North Bennington, Vermont, pp. 215–235.

Stronza, A. (2004) Trueque Amazónico: lessons learned in community-based ecotourism. Unpublished manuscript, Critical Ecosystems Partnership Fund.

The International Ecotourism Society (TIES) (2005) *Community-based Tourism Course.* George Washington University, Washington, DC.

Tidwell, M. (1996) *Amazon Stranger: A Rainforest Chief Battles Big Oil.* Lyons and Burford, New York.

Wearing, S. (2001) Exploring socio-cultural impacts on local communities. In: Weaver, D.B. (ed.) *The Encyclopedia of Ecotourism.* CAB International, Wallingford, UK, pp. 395–410.

13 The Prospects and Dilemmas of Indigenous Tourism Standards and Certifications

Luis A. Vivanco

Department of Anthropology, University of Vermont, USA

Chapter Profile

The rise of tourism standards and certification programmes presents new opportunities for indigenous communities to redress histories of exploitation and marginalization by the tourism industry. Yet indigenous voices have been notably absent in the development of standards and certification programmes. The purpose of this chapter is to discuss why this lack of engagement might be the case, to evaluate current indigenous involvement in and attitudes toward tourism certification programmes and to consider some of the major opportunities and dilemmas standardization and certification initiatives represent for indigenous peoples. These themes were discussed in a recent indigenous-centred conference called 'Rethinking Indigenous Tourism Certification', which is also discussed in this chapter. Certification advocates and indigenous communities alike have much to gain by first constructing a space in which the parties can dialogue over certification's potential applications and consequences for indigenous communities. If indigenous involvement is deemed desirable, it will be necessary to create flexible and customized frameworks and programmes where diverse and localized concerns, if not also standards and concepts of quality, are foundational elements.

Introduction

> This ecotourism is an interesting issue; it requires a constant faith in neoliberalism. But to believe in catechisms after 500 years is to forget the damage that they've done to the earth, it's like forgetting the war they've made on us.
>
> (Latin American indigenous leader, in García, 2002)

Since its conception, ecotourism has been promoted as a means for indigenous peoples to generate economic growth while protecting fragile natural resources and endangered lifestyles. Many indigenous communities around the world, faced with weak prospects for non-extractive economic development and the corrosive pressures of assimilation, have found that ecotourism offers new opportunities for income and the chance to communicate distinctive cultural perspectives on the natural world. Yet the relationship between ecotourism and indigenous peoples has been fraught with profound difficulties and dilemmas, not least because many indigenous communities enter global tourism markets in the most disadvantaged positions, the result of decades of political and economic marginalization, weak or no control over their territories because of encroachments and expropriation, few resources to invest in infrastructure, limited training in tourism and little access to marketing. These factors are often compounded by the fact that tourism was imposed by non-indigenous agents or states (McLaren, 1999; Tourism Concern, 2002).

Furthermore, as expressed in the quotation that opens this chapter, ecotourism has been perceived by some indigenous peoples as inseparable from other modernizing 'catechisms' whose intellectual and practical origins lie elsewhere, distant from indigenous societies. This particular observation, as well as others that were similarly blunt, was made during the International Forum on Indigenous Tourism, which took place during March 2002 in Oaxaca, Mexico (García, 2002). Meant to coincide with, but independent of, the 2002 UN International Year of Ecotourism, the forum gathered almost 200 indigenous representatives and leaders from 19 countries to analyse and deliberate on the opportunities and dilemmas of ecotourism in their particular communities.[1] In their concluding document, the Oaxaca Declaration, participants affirmed:

> Indigenous Peoples are not objects of tourism development. We are active subjects with the rights and responsibilities to our territories and the processes of tourism planning, implementation, and evaluation that happen in them. This means we are responsible for defending Indigenous lands and communities from development schemes imposed by governments, development agencies, private corporations, NGOs, and specialists.
>
> (Oaxaca Declaration, 2002)

Central to this assertion is that, whatever concrete economic opportunities might be generated by ecotourism development schemes, as long as such development is conceived as formulaic or not under some level of control by community members or authorities, indigenous political rights and cultural values can be compromised. From this point of view, ecotourism is not simply or just an economic and conservation 'opportunity', as it is so often represented by ecotourism specialists and promoters, but a potential 'threat' to indigenous political and livelihood priorities. It is clear that indigenous involvement in ecotourism (as operators, guides, host communities, etc.) requires more significant discussion and analysis of its potential cultural, natural and political consequences than currently tends to occur.

Enter recent international efforts to develop standards for ecotourism and sustainable tourism certification, led by international environmental and development institutions, academics, multilateral lending banks, certain governments and tourism industry leaders (Buckley, 2001; Font and Buckley, 2001; Font, 2002; Honey, 2002). The discussions taking place around best practices, quality control and certification have referred to local community enterprises, including indigenous tourism, as beneficiaries of technical assistance and access to certified ecotourism and sustainable tourism markets, and confirmed the desirability of indigenous participation in programme design and implementation (Honey and Rome, 2001: 59; ITRI, 2003; Rainforest Alliance, 2003a). Yet indigenous voices and perspectives have been notably mute, if not largely absent, in such discussions, and, while there is some indigenous involvement in certain tourism certification programmes, on the whole there has been remarkably little engagement of such issues in indigenous communities and networks involved in, or wanting to become involved in, ecotourism.

The purpose of this chapter is to discuss why this lack of engagement might be the case, to evaluate current indigenous involvement in and attitudes toward tourism and ecotourism certification programmes and to consider some of the major positive opportunities and dilemmas certification initiatives represent for indigenous peoples. It should be said that indigenous communities around the world already participate in commodity certification programmes, especially organic and fair trade coffee, timber, cacao and textiles, and display a range of attitudes towards certification, from enthusiasm to hostility (World Rainforest Movement, 2004). But, as I shall discuss here, certifying tourism is distinct from certifying other products and goods, and carries its own particular social and political implications. Indigenous communities and networks are just barely beginning to deliberate on the issues raised by certification and accreditation regimes. These issues range from foundational concerns, such as the fact that standards and programmes are being developed and implemented largely without indigenous involvement, to questions over what communities have to gain by certifying tourism and whose standards will count. Reflecting some concerns expressed in academic discussions about the 'audit society' (Power, 1997; Strathern, 2000), some indigenous activists have also expressed preoccupation that standardization and certification are used to guarantee compliance with technical requirements but do not necessarily guarantee either genuine outcomes for indigenous peoples or ethical behaviour.

This chapter looks at some of the challenges facing the international ecotourism movement to ensure the legitimacy and relevance of standardization and certification for indigenous communities and tourism enterprises. It also reports on a recent important initiative that has sought to open debate and deliberation on whether certification can support appropriate tourism outcomes for indigenous people, which is an online forum during 2004, entitled 'Rethinking Indigenous Tourism Certification', that was hosted by the US-based indigenous peoples' tourism organization, Indigenous Tourism Rights International (ITRI, 2004). The lesson of both of these themes is that a successful framework for working with indigenous communities and organizations must be based on approaching them not simply as recipients of ready-made certification programmes defined by metropolitan tourism consultants and experts, because this will merely serve to further marginalize indigenous peoples from the important decision-making processes that affect their lives. Instead, certification advocates and indigenous communities alike have much to gain by first constructing a space in which the parties can dialogue over certification's potential applications and dilemmas for indigenous communities, and then, if indigenous involvement is deemed desirable, creating flexible and customized frameworks and programmes where diverse and localized concerns, if not also standards and concepts of quality, are foundational elements. If this does not occur, there is a possibility that certain indigenous communities will reject certification as a recent innovation, if not catechism, of neoliberal globalization.

From Indigenous Peoples in Tourism to 'Indigenous Tourism'

Any adequate understanding of the opportunities and dilemmas facing indigenous involvement in ecotourism certification must first deal with the complex status of ecotourism within indigenous communities (Sofield, 1993; Zeppel, 1998; Weaver, 2001; Duffy, 2002). It could be argued that indigenous experiences of tourism and ecotourism are as diverse as the 300 million people who occupy the category 'indigenous'. The term is the product of colonial reductionism: it is a singular identity imposed on diverse peoples who do not fit Western criteria of cultural progress. Such a definition has been related to a legacy of discrimination, forced assimilation through resettlement and education, and outright genocide and ethnocide (Bodley, 1998). Reflecting the unequal power dynamics that have defined them, most contemporary definitions emphasize the particular relationship indigenous peoples have with nation states and capitalism: they are typically original inhabitants of a territory, often small-scale societies, who have been marginalized in the construction of dominant national identities, state bureaucracies and capitalistic markets (Bodley, 1998; Niezen, 2003). In recent decades, the people who themselves inhabit the category have adapted, re-imagined and collectively transformed what it means to be indigenous in more positive terms. Indeed, one of the most important forces to emerge on the international political scene has been an indigenous peoples' movement, typically mobilizing around principles of self-determination as expressed in the International Labour Organization's (ILO) Convention 169 and the United Nations Draft Declaration on the Rights of Indigenous Peoples (Niezen, 2003). At the heart of such political expressions have been assertions of certain shared legal rights and cultural experiences, but also the irreducible cultural particularities of specific indigenous groups (Niezen, 2003).

These assertions are increasingly being made in the context of tourism and ecotourism, and are responses to the ways in which the tourism industry has used and abused indigenous communities and lands. Tourism in indigenous communities has historically been based on the considerable curiosity of non-indigenes in their lifestyles, landscapes, spiritualities and artistic expressions (Swain, 1989; Butler and Hinch, 1996). Such 'niche market potential' – that indigenous communities and their traditions represent fertile grounds to attract tourists – feeds the widespread idea among tourism operators, development agencies and indigenous communities themselves that tourism represents an important opportunity for economic development and poverty alleviation. But, because of the severe obstacles facing them, including weak abilities to communicate what they know or need to know about tourism, indigenous peoples have typically not been able to control the terms of the interaction with tourists, much less the global tourism industry (Johnston, 2000). Consequently, tourism has often created conflict and resentment, especially once its negative social and ecological impacts become known. These include, among others, displacement for hotel and infrastructure construction, desecration of burial and other sacred sites, disruption of religious ceremonies, introduction of diseases, labour exploitation (even forced labour), pressure to turn cultural traditions into commodities, being overrun by outsiders who do not respect local values, treating indigenous peoples as zoo specimens, plundering of cultural artefacts and wildlife, prevention of communities from pursuing traditional subsistence patterns based on hunting and fishing, and sexual exploitation (Sofield, 1993; Butler and Hinch, 1996; Zeppel, 1998; McLaren, 1999; Mowforth and Munt, 2003). In such instances, tourism is less a tool for indigenous development than a mechanism for even further domination and marginalization, and basic concerns about the connection between tourism and the degradation of human rights are justified.

Ecotourism, as envisioned by organizations like the International Ecotourism Society (TIES), Rainforest Alliance, United Nations Environment Programme (UNEP), Conservation International and others, seeks an alternative form of tourism development, based in or at least supporting community processes, and with practices of environmental sustainability and habitat protection at the forefront. Under the right conditions of scale and community participation, ecotourism can become a means of generating nature appreciation among hosts and guests, valuing cultural heritage and utilizing natural resources to generate income (Honey, 1999; Epler Wood, 2002). And yet indigenous peoples and their representatives have also expressed justifiable scepticism about ecotourism development on their homelands. Examples of communities being expelled and cut off from the natural resources upon which they rely, in the names of nature protection and ecotourism development, have moved one Maasai activist to observe, 'The designation of ecotourism sites tends to disentitle the poor by depriving them of their traditional use of land and natural resources' (Kamauro, 1996: 62; Duffy, 2002; Tourism Concern, 2002). Such incidents may not be 'genuine ecotourism' according to definitions promoted by leading international environmental and tourism organizations, but, for a local community that has been denied access to natural resources by government natural resources planners or tourism operators invoking the language of 'ecotourism', such a distinction is largely academic.

Compounding such issues, there is often an undeniable gap between local values and needs and the short-term profit-driven equations of ecotourism developers. One especially profound conundrum is expressed in the words of Roy Taylor of the North American Indigenous Peoples Biodiversity Project: 'the way that conservation is practiced in the West is viewed as conservation-for-development and that is not necessarily consistent with our traditional view of guardianship and protection. We wouldn't even use the word conservation' (cited in McLaren, 1999: 26). Indeed, the pressure to turn lands and cultural traditions into commodities for tourism consumption is one of the most important dilemmas a community has to face (Hinch, 1998). Furthermore, there is often little understanding of indigenous decision-making processes by external agents. As Johnston (2000: 90) observes:

> Business owners not only become impatient with indigenous decision-making processes, but also ultimately retain an image of themselves as community benefactors. Consequently, corporate good will rarely translate into adequate information sharing. This puts indigenous peoples at an extreme disadvantage in negotiations, and can quickly lead to problems, e.g. premature decisions by community authorities in favour of tourism, incomplete accounting of the possible opportunity costs of tourism, or foreclosure of the potential to establish more beneficial management regimes for tourism.

One area of necessary vigilance is joint ventures, like ecolodges and other co-management schemes, which sometimes provide for ownership transfer and have been largely presented as win–win scenarios. They are seen as one solution to the problem of tourism's leakage, or the fact that the vast amount of money spent by tourists tends not to stay in communities (Third World Network, 2001). But without adequate information sharing between external tourism companies and indigenous communities, many communities have little knowledge of the workings of global tourism markets, often do not feel as if they are co-owners of the venture and can end up merely providing inexpensive labour for hotels (Johnston, 2000: 90).

Another significant area of concern is intellectual property and traditional resource rights. Ecotourism development in remote areas often accompanies and can even become a vehicle for the illegal collection of plants, animals, insects, minerals, cultural artefacts and, most importantly, knowledge, especially when there is weak land tenure, ineffective regulation governing access or no protective mechanisms against bioprospecting and biopiracy (Zeppel, 1998; García, 2002; Vivanco, 2002b). Additionally, indigenous symbols, imagery and art are commonly used in the promotion of ecotourism products, although indigenous peoples are often not consulted, much less compensated, for the use of their imagery or the photographs of them that appear in marketing and postcards (Brown, 2003). Another key 'cultural' component of ecotourism is often no more than insulting and simplistic staged performances that play up stereotypes of exotic indigenous otherness and noble savagery (Johnston, 2000).

In fact, indigenous leaders and activists have reiterated again and again that prior informed consent and clear jurisdiction are essential components of sustainable tourism and community livelihood, and the most successful examples of indigenous control over tourism visitation and development have been based on these conditions, as well as clarity of land rights, the application of customary laws and relatively tight control over visitor movements through codes of conduct and constant vigilance (Zeppel, 1998; Johnston, 2000). Indeed, a distinction is often made between the marketing-driven 'greenwash' examples of ecotourism – which often reflect the worst exploitative and destructive tendencies of the tourism industry (Honey, 1999) – and a cautious optimism towards forms of hosting visitors designed and implemented in terms of local needs, values and capacities. Santa María de Yavesía, a small Zapotec village in the Sierra Juarez of Oaxaca in Mexico, is but one example among many that demonstrates the broader lessons shared by many indigenous communities pursuing ecotourism in such ways (Vivanco, 2002b). The community decided early on that it would resist creating 'attractions' simply to bring tourists. Instead, they have approached ecotourism holistically, viewing their involvement in tourism as an opportunity to share with visitors their culture's long history of sustainable involvement with the landscape, and as support for their ongoing efforts to define their political and cultural autonomy within the Mexican nation.

This project, which invites visitors to walk through community-owned forested land guided by locals, is integrated into the community's other productive uses of the forest, including a spring-water bottling plant and the collection of non-timber forest products. Instead of becoming a 'monocrop', tourism provides an important avenue of economic diversification for the community without displacing other productive activities. Decisions regarding tourism activities and the distribution of their modest economic benefits are made by communal authorities and in community assembly, and work on the project (such as guiding and trail work) is organized through traditional means, such as *tequio*, a responsibility to voluntarily participate in community affairs such as the maintenance of infrastructure. Visitors cannot simply show up in the village unannounced, but must coordinate with village authorities prior to their arrival. Community members also feel very strongly, as reiterated by many other indigenous groups, that they have the right and responsibility to protect certain sacred spaces, activities, rituals and knowledge from tourists, so visitor movements and the information they receive are carefully monitored and controlled by vigilant guides and community authorities.

Perhaps this example and others like it reflect ideals of 'genuine ecotourism', although residents of Yavesía have expressed ambivalence, if not outright scepticism, about the term. On the one hand, it is a convenient and widely recognized marketing tool that can attract visitors and even funding for capacity building and infrastructure. But, on the other, ecotourism is often seen as yet another modernization fad promoted by national and international interests seeking to develop indigenous peoples and their lands, if not also a label under which tourism's abusive elements have continued. Importantly, indigenous peoples are beginning to act in coordinated ways to share experiences about and define tourism on their own terms, in international meetings like the 2002 International Forum on Indigenous Tourism and in organizations and networks like the US-based Indigenous Tourism Rights International, Federación Plurinacional de Turismo Comunitario del Ecuador

(Plurinational Federation of Community Tourism of Ecuador), Red de Turismo Indígena de Mexico (Indigenous Tourism Network of Mexico) and Aboriginal Tourism Australia, among others. They are consciously moving from being objects to subjects of tourism development, from 'indigenous peoples in tourism' to what some are calling 'indigenous tourism'.

For tourism scholars (e.g. Swain, 1989: 87; Sofield, 1993; Butler and Hinch, 1996; Zeppel, 1998), 'indigenous tourism' tends to be characterized as culturally based tourism development under local control. Butler and Hinch (1996: 9), for example, define it as 'tourism activity in which indigenous people are involved either through control and/or by having their culture serve as the essence of the attraction'. But, in the international indigenous peoples' movement and an increasing number of communities, where leaders and activists are reluctant to impose prescriptive definitions and development schemes on the many societies that they come from and represent, 'indigenous tourism' encompasses inherent diversity. It is not a marketing of indigenous cultures as tourism products, much less a singular or normative development strategy. It emphasizes that tourism is an arena of cultural and political struggle and revitalization. Within this framework, certain factors are paramount, including the fact that tourism must respect and be accommodated to local traditions; there must be substantial community or local control over the social and natural resources involved in tourism; tourism must be integrated into other productive activities so that the community does not become dependent on tourism markets; tourism exists on a small (family or community) scale; decisions about tourism management are made in customary fashion (traditional authorities, community assembly, etc.); and there is resistance to reducing tourism to an economic activity alone, seeing it instead as part of a wider strategy of reinforcing or revitalizing political and cultural autonomy through inter-cultural encounters.[2] Because they often emphasize the articulation of indigenous political and cultural goals through tourism, such developments have important consequences for the applicability of ecotourism certification in indigenous communities.

Certifying Indigenous Tourism

In a global commercial environment, certifications provide a common set of accepted practices and standards, providing a guarantee that these standards are being met. Certifications give an appearance of legitimacy, which is becoming increasingly important as other sources of legitimacy, such as community and the state, decline in importance (Power, 1997).

Certification standards, assessment and compliance auditing also often appear obscure, mundane and neutral, since they are largely based on technical criteria. But, as the definition of who and what is auditable and certifiable widens, it is becoming clear that these are not merely mundane or obscure procedures. This is because standards and auditing often embody and reflect certain powerful social norms and processes. This is the gist of arguments about the 'audit society', that is, that we are witness to a rapidly globalizing condition in which social activities are increasingly being redefined and regulated in terms of audits and market certifications, and the logic of neoliberalism – privatization, efficiency, profitability, universal standards of quality, etc. – is more deeply embedded as the central mode of organizing society (Power, 1997; Strathern, 2000). Indigenous peoples are understandably concerned about what the implications of this might be for their own activities, especially since they have had little participation in the international discussions taking place around the design and implementation of certification schemes, especially in tourism.

Certification and quality assurance regimes are currently being developed and implemented to counter the abuse of the term ecotourism (Honey, 2002). Indigenous perspectives – whatever their attitudes towards the term – tend to support the assertion that ecotourism's legitimacy is in question, and that, in theory at least, certification may provide one way to redefine the legitimacy of the activity. For instance, one indigenous Ecuadorean leader has observed:

> This term has been used by the private sector, alleging coordination with our communities that brings us benefits. At the same time, in our country the term ecotourism has been totally manipulated so that everyone started thinking solely in terms of the economic benefits that would come if you just mentioned that your product is ecotouristic, without even complying with the criteria denominated as such.
>
> (ITRI, 2004; my translation)

For those indigenous communities and businesses following principles of responsible ecotourism, certification can provide a potentially useful tool that helps create a framework under which conscientious consumers can patronize the businesses that most closely follow ecotourism ideals, and indigenous communities and businesses can better understand the environmental and sociocultural impacts of tourism activities. It can also be, as one native Hawaiian tourism representative has observed, 'a socio-political attempt to preserve the integrity and dignity of the destination by insisting that tourism practitioners abide by standards of behaviour and authenticity that does [sic] not diminish the integrity of the people or the place' (ITRI, 2004).[3]

Visitor codes of conduct and management plans, which have become increasingly common means for indigenous communities and businesses to standardize and assert control over tourism development and tourist activities, do not necessarily present the same opportunities as certification. For example, provided the certification scheme is well organized and funded for marketing, being certified can create advertising opportunities, which is a perennial problem for many indigenous enterprises that do not have the resources to gain access to international, even national, channels of tourism information and marketing. Even the Internet, which has become a key tool for marketing across the industry, is not a facile solution for this problem, because remote communities may not have electricity and telephones, much less easy access to the Internet. Although indigenous tourism infrastructure tends to be small-scale, and therefore may not use large amounts of non-renewable energy or produce large amounts of effluents (making certain process-oriented best practices typical in many certification programmes less applicable than in mainstream tourism), audits and certification can also potentially bring access to certain kinds of useful technical knowledge for infrastructure development and management, not to mention training and skills to improve the 'quality of service' expected by consumers. If the certification programme addresses fair trade issues, such as justice, fairness and transparency in the distribution of tourism's benefits at the community level, it could offer an appealing way to enter into the global tourism economy on favourable terms. Finally, if adequate funding were available (which is currently lacking), an indigenous-specific certification programme could support the particularistic vision and values of indigenous tourism and communities, while strengthening the collaborative organizing efforts of national and international indigenous peoples' networks and political movements.

There are relatively few examples of formal indigenous involvement in existing tourism and ecotourism certification programmes. Where it has happened, there are various modes of indigenous participation, including involvement as stakeholders in the creation of certification criteria and as clients of mainstream ecotourism certification programmes. While some of these programmes may provide for indigenous involvement, they do not prioritize specifically indigenous values or concerns. For example, Guatemala's Green Deal Certification programme for Tourism Quality was created by Alianza Verde in 1999 for tourism businesses operating in the Maya Biosphere Reserve (Alianza Verde, 2004). This programme does not prioritize indigenous participation, although Maya Itzá (a specific Maya group) was consulted as stakeholders in the creation of certification criteria, along with representatives of conservation groups, the private business sector, government and community enterprises. The Maya-run Bio-Itzá ecotourism project is the only certified indigenous enterprise, and, according to the executive director of Alianza Verde, it scored higher than the other businesses in its initial audit for certification (Saúl Blanco, personal communication, 2004). Also in this category is the Swedish Ecotourism Association's Nature's Best ecotourism labelling programme, which has been offering certification for ecotourism products since 2002 (Nature's Best, 2002). Some nomadic Sami reindeer herders have gained certification for their tourism products, and programme criteria require that ecotourism offerings respect rights of public access and receive permission to operate on non-public lands, ensuring that ecotourism operations on Samic lands or migration corridors respect concerns of informed consent and land rights. Yet another example is the Australian Nature and Ecotourism Accreditation Program (NEAP, now known as EcoCertification Program). According to Chester and Crabtree (2002: 171), 'Although the focus of ecotourism in Australia is primarily on the natural values of an area, many of these sites also have significant cultural value, particularly indigenous cultural value.' As a result, NEAP criteria require 'minimal impact on and presentation of [indigenous] culture, including involving indigenous communities in the delivery of the ecotourism product' (Chester and

Crabtree, 2002: 171). Tourism businesses must consult with traditional custodians and, where appropriate, restrict access to areas of spiritual significance. A final example in this category is Fair Trade Tourism South Africa, which launched its Fair Trade in Tourism trademark in 2002 (FTTSA, 2004). Principles with relevance to indigenous peoples include fair distribution of income; the right of all participants in a tourism activity to participate in decisions that concern them; cultural respect, including fair and safe labour conditions, gender equality and tolerance of sociocultural norms; safety and security for host and visitor; transparency of ownership and sharing of profits; and, finally, sustainability through economic viability and resource use. Their goal is to encourage and help publicize fair and responsible business practice in mainstream tourism, while also creating opportunities for smaller-scale businesses to gain access to markets (see Chapter 14 in this volume).

It is noteworthy that these examples, while relevant in various ways to indigenous communities and businesses because of their commitments to cultural respect and protection, if not also to involving indigenous actors as stakeholders, are not certifying 'indigenous tourism' per se. That is, they do not privilege or target specifically indigenous concerns or businesses, and the programmatic balance leans more towards environmental and business best practices for mainstream ecotourism or sustainable tourism operations and products. As a result, most certified businesses or products under these programmes are not indigenous or even community-based.

In cases where organizations have developed indigenous culture-specific certification programmes, there are more explicit treatments of cultural protection, traditional authority and authenticity issues. One example is in Hawai'i, where the Native Hawaiian Hospitality Association (NaHHA) has been working towards the creation of greater opportunities for native Hawaiians in tourism, as well as the preservation and perpetuation of Hawaiian values, customs, language and artefacts through tourism. NaHHA, which is a membership organization (and does not purport to speak for all native Hawaiians), has a certification programme for training native Hawaiian tour guides for their Waikiki Historic Trail tours, as well as a programme that trains certified trainers for Na Mea Ho'okipa (Hospitality) workshops for the hospitality industry (ITRI, 2004). In the future, there are plans to develop a certification programme for hotels, retailers and others in which operational standards are based on Hawaiian values and practices of hospitality. Another example is Aboriginal Tourism Australia's (ATA) 'Respecting Our Culture' (ROC) label, launched during 2003, which endorses both Aboriginal and non-Aboriginal tourism businesses that follow certain cultural protocols, environmental management regimes and business practices in the context of tourism in Aboriginal communities and lands (see ROC, 2004). As in Hawai'i, indigenous imagery and culture have long been used by the Australian tourism industry, with little of tourism's benefits flowing back to Aboriginal communities. Created on the basis of consultations carried out in communities, with elders and traditional custodians of the land, as well as with industry and government representatives, ROC requires that businesses demonstrate written endorsement from traditional authorities and custodians of the land, and emphasizes cultural and artistic authenticity and property rights. It also provides workshops and technical assistance for Aboriginal peoples and communities to help them understand the workings of the tourism industry and product development. Although the demand for Aboriginal tourism experiences in Australia has been increasing, it is still small-scale and ATA does not expect the programme to grow very large (ITRI, 2004).

In spite of such concrete examples, the application of certification regimes in indigenous tourism has not materialized on any large scale, and, in fact, knowledge of the principles upon which certification is based, not to mention the workings of actual programmes, is still extremely scarce, especially in the global South. This was demonstrated in the bilingual (English and Spanish) online forum 'Rethinking Indigenous Tourism Certification', which was organized and hosted for 1 month during 2004 by Indigenous Tourism Rights International (hereafter referred to as Tourism Rights). Tourism Rights organized this forum precisely because members of its network of indigenous communities and tourism businesses, many of them based in Latin American countries, where ecotourism and sustainable tourism are becoming increasingly important civil society issues, had expressed a clear need for information and discussion on the theme.[4] The initiative was designed to provide a space for indigenous peoples to learn about and discuss the merits, details and dilemmas of certification, including some of the opportunities and case studies discussed above. Recognizing the urgent need to begin an international discussion of indigenous involvement in tourism certification but lacking funds for a meeting, Tourism Rights decided to hold the forum online with volunteer moderators, instead of organizing a more desirable face-to-face forum. Organizers knew full well the severe limitations of this technology, especially that members of disadvantaged and marginal communities would not have access to the Internet, much less for a month. But 189 people signed up as participants, representing 34 countries, and they were mainly members of community-level tourism projects and representatives of community and indigenous tourism networks. A dozen or so non-indigenous certification experts and programme representatives were invited for limited participation.[5] Because it is one of the only efforts of its kind, that is, an indigenous-centred discussion on tourism certification, it is worthwhile to present some of the major concerns and perspectives expressed during this forum, as they indicate some of the difficulties and dilemmas of implementing tourism certification schemes oriented towards indigenous communities.[6]

It rapidly became clear in the online discussions that, even though Tourism Rights scheduled more advanced discussions on the theme, such as close analysis of actual certification programmes (including the examples discussed above), tourism marketing strategies and the development of indigenous alternatives to certification, participants were more preoccupied with basic issues. These included finding out who was promoting certification and why, learning about how these actors had (or had not) collaborated with indigenous peoples in these processes and discussing both the potentials and pitfalls of certification from the perspectives of their particular communities. Justifying submission of such basic questions, one Mexican participant wrote:

> Pardon the many questions, but in truth it is because we have been objects for so long, and we have been objects of study and information extraction to justify the work of other people who, at the end of the road, all they do is justify their own work because it is fashionable, and then they leave without saying goodbye.
>
> (ITRI, 2004; my translation)

Viewed from this perspective, tourism certification can be judged as double-edged, in that, whilst offering certain kinds of opportunities for tourism businesses, it also represents new kinds of risks for indigenous communities.

For the organizers and participants of the online forum, accountability, legitimacy and responsibility are universal human problems, and yet every culture approaches and resolves these problems on its own terms. The notion of certification and audits carried out by an external party, practices whose origins lie in First World financial markets and institutions, where independent verification defines the legitimacy of certification, does not rest easy in or automatically translate to some cultural contexts. For instance, in many indigenous societies, legitimacy may be demonstrated by lineage, differentiated access to specialized knowledge, fulfilment of obligatory communal responsibilities, and so on, and responsibility and accountability are guaranteed through specific cultural institutions, ceremonies, spiritualities and social practices. Legitimacy in many indigenous settings thus often comes from the communities and their specific sources of authority (Bissett *et al.*, 1998; ROC, 2004). This contrasts markedly with formal certification programmes that have, in part, arisen in a historical period of declining community and state legitimacy because of economic globalization (Strathern, 2000). Given the colonial histories of dispossession and domination, not to mention rocky relationships with international environmental and development institutions, it is not surprising that many indigenous peoples feel reluctance to letting external actors define the legitimacy of their activities.

It is also important to point out that, in its contemporary Western meaning, audit is as much an idea and a willingness to be audited as it is a technical practice (Power, 1997). It implies a voluntary commitment to participate in an activity whose effect is to narrow the diversity of productive practices, as practices come in line with industry-accepted standards. For indigenous communities already participating in certification and fair trade programmes (for timber management, coffee, textiles, etc.), participation in these markets is oriented towards a particular outcome, the commodity itself. As a number of communities have discovered, there are good reasons to adopt certain universal production and quality standards, such as gaining access to higher market prices and technical assistance, or because there is already a tradition of organic production that fits well into certification programmes.

But, as some of the Tourism Rights forum participants observed, participation in certification programmes also involves key trade-offs. For instance, being certified can require high costs and substantial training to join a programme and maintain certification. Problems of equity and access are compounded by the fact that certification often involves burdensome bureaucratic procedures and paperwork, and few programmes provide suitable institutional support, training or technical assistance. Even worse, there is little concrete evidence of tangible economic benefits for producers. Because indigenous tourism businesses tend to be micro-scale (family-based or community-level) and cut off from easy access to funding, there is little likelihood that they can afford infrastructure or best practices based on specialized technologies or complex management systems, especially in circumstances where basic struggles like access to electricity, clean water, education, land rights, cultural recognition, and so on are paramount. Indeed, some participants in the online forum affirmed that concerns like certification and quality assurance are irrelevant unless a community's basic needs are met. Employing a wide definition of 'basic needs', one South American participant wrote, 'Whatever the case, to begin the process of CERTIFICATION we believe that there first needs to be organizational strengthening, which will raise self-esteem, strengthen cultural identity, value the environment, all of which will bring benefits and sustainable community development' (ITRI, 2004, my translation, capitals in original).

Furthermore, forum participants asserted that tourism is a distinctive kind of productive activity, quite unlike a coffee bean or textile. That is because tourism is a service industry based on a specific set of social relationships between hosts and visitors and between hosts and hosts, and the outcome of tourism is those specific relationships, not a thing or commodity. The very reason tourists tend to go to indigenous communities is to participate in these distinctive social relationships, and there is a certain level of irony in proposing standardization on a broad scale for an activity that is defined by its non-prescriptive diversity. Indeed, as one South American participant observed, in the context of indigenous tourism the quality of the service is based on the quality of the experience, which is itself based on the very specific qualities of the social relationships that are constructed within particular indigenous communities (ITRI, 2004). Certifying that tourism activities meet certain external standards of accountability, efficiency, best practice or quality lets outside auditors and institutions define the appropriateness of the activities, processes and relationships constructed around tourism. Summing up his community's concerns about certification, another South American representative asserted, 'One of the reasons we do not agree with existing certification is that all the tools it uses have been developed in the majority of cases by external consultants who do not know the reality of the communities' (ITRI, 2004, my translation).

A major reason for this concern is that external standards can compete with or displace culturally and gender-specific concepts and practices of accountability, how to host guests, how to manage relationships with the natural world, and so on. That is why one participant from Mexico insisted that indigenous communities must recognize that certification is, at base, an ethical issue. As he said:

> Tourism is a service based on social relations. Social relations that are, or should be, product of historical and cultural questions, and not solely technical and specialized questions like certification. For example, trust in our communities is product of a culture and very specific form of education and communication . . . and the question here is who has the right to question our trust, even worse, questioning our trust is questioning our history, our culture, in sum, our way of being, and this I do not believe we should permit, because processes of certification are mining our culture, our way of being. Therefore I repeat, I believe that at bottom the issue of certification has ethical aspects.
>
> (ITRI, 2004, my translation)

According to this perspective, participating in an externally defined certification programme amounts to letting outside auditors define whether or not an indigenous community's claims are trustworthy. This represents a basic challenge to local and culturally specific ways of establishing and communicating trustworthiness and ethical compromise, which themselves could represent an important part of the tourism experience. Furthermore, in emphasizing the ethical nature of certification, there is an implicit critique of process-oriented auditing practices, based on the fact that audits do not necessarily certify ethical behaviour and outcomes, but compliance with technical requirements (such as is the case with ISO 14001 and Green Globe standards). Indeed, some academic analysts of auditing have made a similar point: that, as long as there is a tendency to abstract auditing processes from the actual outcomes of organization, 'one can be very good, in a quality assurance sense, of doing morally questionable things' (Power, 1997: 84).[7]

A number of participants in the online forum also expressed their preoccupation that certification can represent a challenge to community structures and solidarity. One of these is greater long-term dependency on specialized international markets. One Mexican participant expressed concern about:

> Producers and communities [being] more dependent on a 'certified' market, and they remain subjects of and hooked into a demanding market, and they have to 'satisfy the demands of this market', and this has nothing to do with the autonomy of the indigenous communities, or with a local development linked to the culture and tradition of indigenous communities.
>
> (ITRI, 2004, my translation)

Certification can carry consequences for community solidarity, as this same individual observed about his region's experiences with coffee and timber certification:

> Producers [who participate in coffee and timber certification programmes] live and form part of a community and an indigenous people, which in the end is what is at risk, because these producers become 'privileged entities', existing above the community that covers them, and this generates internal problems within the community . . . Certification creates producers of first and second

> class, those that become privileged sons of the system, the others become a shame; the first become receptacles of economic and institutional support, the second become an object of dispute by NGOs and official institutions, trying to get them to leave their 'natural' state and so they can sit at the table with the privileged sons, those certified by the modern world. That is to say, [it is] modern inclusion and exclusion.
>
> (ITRI, 2004, my translation)

He concluded that, while certification programmes may celebrate how consumers are helping ensure the sustainable use of the natural world, there has been little public discussion about the social sustainability of the sacrifices communities make in participating in certification programmes, especially when those programmes and their criteria are not defined by indigenous peoples themselves.

Another key area of concern for forum participants was over the relationship between indigenous peoples and the international actors and organizations pushing for ecotourism and sustainable tourism standards and certification, including the Rainforest Alliance, TIES, UNEP and the World Tourism Organization (WTO). There was a widespread feeling among forum participants that international environmental, tourism and development organizations based in the North are pressing the discussion on certification ahead, in some cases with funding from multilateral lending agencies, but without meaningful indigenous participation. Participants were especially concerned about a 2003 US$3 million grant the Inter-American Development Bank's Multilateral Investment Fund provided for the Rainforest Alliance, with the purpose of furthering the work of the Sustainable Tourism Certification Network of the Americas and ensuring that small and medium-sized businesses have the necessary preparations for and access to certification programmes (Rainforest Alliance, 2003b). This immediately raises concerns about how these organizations have used the name of indigenous peoples to gain funding, and how their activities will directly impact or benefit indigenous communities.

Representatives of TIES and Rainforest Alliance were invited to participate for a week during the early part of the forum to discuss these concerns, because these two organizations have solicited and received such funding, and because they have expressed the importance of indigenous 'stakeholder involvement' in developing sustainable tourism and ecotourism certification frameworks. Representatives explained that they are not promoting any particular certification programmes at this point. Rather, they are working together with other international organizations (primarily the UNEP, the WTO and the Sustainable Tourism Certification Council) to determine the proper sociocultural, environmental and economic standards for certification, and to develop ways to ensure the participation of a wide cross-section of businesses in certification programmes (ITRI, 2004). Forum participants expressed preoccupation over the generalized lack of indigenous knowledge about, not to mention direct participation in, these discussions and processes.[8] They also reaffirmed that the legitimacy and relevance of any programmatic and information-sharing activities with potential impacts on their communities and territories must be based on respecting indigenous rights to land, culture and resources. They also depend on previous consultation and well-informed participation in the planning, implementation and evaluation of tourism certification programmes, as confirmed by ILO Convention 169 and the United Nations Draft Declaration on the Rights of Indigenous Peoples. Participants expressed their preoccupation that the funder for these initiatives, the Inter-American Development Bank, does not yet have, although is in the process of defining, an indigenous peoples policy to ensure that programmes they fund respect such rights. The reason for concern here is that, without a stated indigenous peoples policy, neither the funders nor the funded agencies are accountable to the rights of indigenous peoples.

The participation of representatives from the Rainforest Alliance and TIES was valuable in clarifying that their goal is not to promote any one single certification programme, but to establish baseline standards upon which an international accreditation body will eventually operate. This immediately raises a keen political question, one that was raised at various moments during the Tourism Rights forum, which is 'Who certifies the certifiers?' On the one hand, this is about whose voices and issues are currently being heard – and, more crucially, not heard – in the design and implementation of certification programmes and the international development of baseline standards. But, on the other hand, this question rather misses the point, especially if 'the certifiers' (those who define the baseline standards) represent a wide range of interests and perspectives through a collaborative and inclusive process of multiple stakeholders, as representatives of the Rainforest Alliance and TIES emphasized. There is another issue here, however, and that is that the outcome of auditing and certification is to create a sense of reassurance about the product or service one is purchasing, and any number of certifying bodies and schemes can emerge to fulfil this function (Strathern, 2000). In this sense, the question is not who certifies the certifiers, but how those who disagree with certifiers will create competing certification programmes and accreditation criteria.[9] This proliferation is a common dilemma for all market-based certifications, for, as one analyst has observed, certifications are like dandelions: once there is one, they seem to spring up everywhere, and the question of whether or not they are weeds or flowers is determined by the beholder (Tourigny, 1990). If so, the very real problem here is how to not overwhelm and confuse consumers with so many certified labels, which dilute the distinctiveness or appeal of any one particular certification scheme and can undermine a sense of reassurance about all of them.

Conclusion

It is quite likely that, in spite of this recognized problem with the proliferation of certification programmes, there will be an increase in efforts to develop programmes applicable to indigenous communities and tourism enterprises, in more diverse contexts and possibly on an even larger scale than currently exists. Certain factors are likely to be of general importance in these efforts, factors that go beyond the more obvious ones that are applicable to both indigenous and other rural peoples, such as the fact that certification cannot be too expensive or require serious investments in infrastructure if it is going to be relevant or accessible.

First, certification programmes must be flexible and particularistic enough for them not to compete with or undermine priorities deemed locally relevant within indigenous communities, whatever they may be, ranging from political and cultural self-determination to land rights to struggles over how indigenous culture is portrayed through tourism imagery. Tourism certification risks irrelevance if it merely creates a new dependence on external auditors and specialized international markets, and does not address how it can serve concerns of autonomy, local concepts of ethical practice and the strengthening of indigenous jurisdiction. Mechanisms for the protection of cultural and intellectual property, including evidence of codes of conduct and monitoring, are essential aspects of this.

Secondly, certification programmes must ensure that they do not turn control over the planning and implementation of tourism projects to itinerant outsiders (consultants, auditors, cosmopolitan resource managers, etc.). This is especially important because it means turning control over to the very actors who have not prioritized, or have even excluded, indigenous participation in the creation of certification programmes and standards in the first place. It is worth re-emphasizing that, in many indigenous contexts, legitimacy still extends from the community, and a legitimate process of defining certification must be based on the informed consent and participation of communities and their authorities. This is no panacea, since disputes over land rights and resources within communities or with external agents (like governments) tend to undermine consensual processes. Nevertheless, there is an argument to be made that auditing and certification should be defined and carried out through indigenous-centred or controlled technical collaboration.

Thirdly, there should be special attention to collaborative and joint ventures, ensuring practices of transparency and negotiated fair distribution of profits. Finally, tourism certification must not displace and undermine local and culturally specific concepts and practices of accountability, best practice, natural resource management, hosting of guests, etc., but in fact must address and incorporate them, as is the case with Aboriginal Tourism Australia's Respecting Our Culture programme. This can become the grounds upon which indigenous peoples can communicate their distinctive cultural vision, social practices and ethical relationships with tourists. But it also represents one of the broadest challenges to the industry and certification advocates who assume that their criteria of quality and best practice are the necessary ones upon which to base certification.

The Tourism Rights online forum demonstrated that, among indigenous communities and networks involved in ecotourism, there is currently a wide variety of attitudes towards certification programmes and regimes, both as a conceptual innovation in tourism practice and as concrete programmes. Attitudes ranged from scepticism to cautious interest and conditional support, and even include a proposal for an indigenous-led 'counter-certification' that 'breaks all the rules of the international organizations . . . that is more social-cultural, that opens doors to all criteria and actors, that doesn't exclude anybody' (ITRI, 2004). The fact that there is no predetermined or singular indigenous position on ecotourism certification and quality assurance reflects the plurality of the peoples who occupy the label, the ways they have integrated tourism into their community development and nature conservation efforts and their previous experiences with certification. But there is also a widespread lack of knowledge about ecotourism certification and quality assurance issues in indigenous communities and networks, especially in the global South, and certification advocates have an important task ahead of them in finding ways to communicate with indigenous peoples and their representatives if they are to advance certification to the levels of inclusivity they claim to want. This will require a concerted openness on the part of the ecotourism industry, certification advocates and indigenous peoples themselves to open new spaces for dialogue, as well as a willingness to construct a flexible framework for certification that is both relevant and legitimate for indigenous interests and values.

At the heart of this imperative are certain key factors. One of these factors is that tourists tend to visit indigenous peoples and their territories because they seek an inter-cultural encounter, where local values and standards help shape the relationship between hosts and visitors. A second factor is that indigenous peoples are increasingly viewing tourism as a site of cultural and political revitalization, struggle and reaffirmation, but on the condition that they retain rights of informed consent, if not also some level of negotiated, if not a priori, control over tourism development. A third factor is the necessity for and often-confirmed right of indigenous representatives to participate in the international discussions around creating a framework for effective ecotourism certification. Finally, following closely from the previous statement, is a purely economic factor: the leaders of the certification movement will have to be willing to financially invest in indigenous participation and attendance in international discussions on certification. In all four cases, the prospects of certification in indigenous tourism and ecotourism in indigenous communities rely on rethinking the framework that informs certification so that it does not operate solely in terms of universal, Western standards of best practice and quality. If it does, then certification risks being written off as a new 'catechism' defined largely by metropolitan activists, scholars and organizations. And, with no real opportunity for indigenous peoples to exercise their collective rights of refusal or participation, concepts such as best practices, quality assurance and certification will at best be irrelevant and at worst serve to perpetuate indigenous marginalization in important civil society discussions. Even worse, the international ecotourism movement would miss an important opportunity for an inter-cultural dialogue of its own about how to make ecotourism practices more accountable to its rhetoric.

Acknowledgements

I am grateful to Rosemary Black and Alice Crabtree, who have been patient, thorough and thoughtful editors. I am also grateful to the anonymous reviewers for their close readings and advice. The research on which this chapter is based would not have been possible without the support and openness of Indigenous Tourism Rights International and its Advisory Council members who were involved in the online forum 'Rethinking Indigenous Tourism Certification', especially Deborah McLaren, Carol Kalafatic, Cresencio Resendiz-Hernandez, Chuck DeBurlo, Milo Sybrant and Norbert Hohl. This research was undertaken while on a Fulbright research and teaching fellowship in Costa Rica, and I am grateful to the Costa Rica office of the Rainforest Alliance, especially Ronald Sanabria, Damaris Chavez and Alejandrina Acuña, and Amos Bien of the International Ecotourism Society for their support of my research on sustainable tourism certification.

Notes

[1] This forum was held independently of the IYE because of the concern among the organizers and participants that the UN and its co-planners appeared to be more concerned about celebrating ecotourism's role in promoting the UN's Agenda 21, rather than a critical review of community-level experiences of ecotourism, and to protest at a general lack of indigenous participation in the planning of the year's activities. See Pleumarom (2001); Vivanco (2002a).

[2] In recent years, these values have been expressed in various international meetings, such as the International Forum on Indigenous Tourism and its Oaxaca Declaration (2002), the Statement on the Process of the Regional Meeting on Community-based Ecotourism in Southeast Asia held in Chiang Mai, Thailand (Regional Meeting on Community-based Ecotourism, 2002) and the San José Declaration on Rural Community Tourism (Redturs, 2003).

[3] Although this can be controversial because, as this same individual noted, 'it tends to be seen as an imposed regulatory program designed to create a gatekeeper system that limits free enterprise' (ITRI, 2004).

[4] Although held in English and Spanish, Tourism Rights volunteers were also translating the discussion into Hindi, Nepali and Swahili. Translation was also facilitated by Babblefish software, a translation program.

[5] Forum organizers insisted on a format of limited involvement of non-indigenous participants to ensure that certification advocates and analysts could present their points of view, but to provide a space for an autonomous discussion to emerge on tourism certification. Non-indigenous 'guests' included the Rainforest Alliance, the International Ecotourism Society, Nature's Best (Sweden) and several non-affiliated consultants.

[6] The anonymous perspectives presented here were chosen on the basis of several criteria. One is simply to give a broad perspective on the diversity of voices expressed, balancing positive, negative and ambivalent perspectives on certification. Another is on the basis of how much discussion was provoked around the submission and its themes. A final criterion is the fact that the perspective was shared or echoed by others.

[7] This perspective ignores the fact that many ecotourism certification programmes, including the examples of programmes discussed earlier in this chapter, are a judicious mix of process- and outcome-oriented criteria.
[8] Indigenous Tourism Rights International has been invited as a 'stakeholder' in the Sustainable Tourism Certification Network of the Americas, which is being coordinated by the Rainforest Alliance.
[9] This situation is the case in sustainable timber certification, where there are two major competing certification bodies with distinct standards: the Forest Stewardship Council and the Sustainable Forestry Initiative. The former is based on a collaborative–activist model, that is, the initiative is an effort to introduce sustainable practices largely by activists from outside the industry, while the latter is an industry-self-regulation model (operated by the American Forestry and Paper Association) (C. Danks, personal communication, 2004).

References

Alianza Verde (2004) Programa de Certificación de Calidad Turística Green Deal. Available at: http://www.alianzaverde.org/pagina2.htm (accessed on 15 November 2004).

Bissett, C., Perry, L. and Zeppel, H. (1998) Land and spirit: Aboriginal tourism in New South Wales. In: McArthur, S. and Weir, B. (eds) *Australia's Ecotourism Industry: A Snapshot in 1998*. Ecotourism Association of Australia, Brisbane, pp. 6–8.

Bodley, J. (1998) *Victims of Progress,* 4th edn. McGraw-Hill Humanities/Social Sciences/Languages, New York.

Brown, M. (2003) *Who Owns Native Culture?* Harvard University Press, Cambridge, Massachusetts, 315 pp.

Buckley, R. (2001) Tourism ecolabels. *Annals of Tourism Research* 29(1), 183–208.

Butler, R.W. and Hinch, T. (1996) Indigenous tourism: a common ground for discussion. In: Butler, R.W. and Hinch, T. (eds) *Tourism and Indigenous Peoples*. International Thomson Business Press, London, pp. 3–19.

Chester, G. and Crabtree, A. (2002) Australia: the Nature and Ecotourism Accreditation Program. In: Honey, M. (ed.) *Ecotourism and Certification: Setting Standards in Practice*. Island Press, Washington, DC, pp. 161–185.

Duffy, R. (2002) Ecotourism and indigenous communities. In: Duffy, R. (ed.) *A Trip Too Far: Ecotourism, Politics, and Exploitation*. Earthscan Publications, London, pp. 98–126.

Epler Wood, M.E. (2002) *Ecotourism: Principles, Practices and Policies for Sustainability*. United Nations Environment Programme Division of Technology, Industry and Economics, Paris, 62 pp.

Font, X. (2002) Environmental certification in tourism and hospitality: progress, process, and prospects. *Tourism Management* 23(3), 197–205.

Font, X. and Buckley, R.C. (eds) (2001) *Tourism Ecolabelling: Certification and Promotion of Sustainable Management*. CAB International, Wallingford, UK, 359 pp.

FTTSA (Fair Trade Tourism South Africa) (2004) Fair Trade in Tourism trademark. Available at: http://www.fairtourismsa.org.za/index.html (accessed on 15 November 2004).

García, J.J. (2002) *Voces del Foro Internacional Indígena de Turismo*. Ojo de Agua Comunicación, Oaxaca, Mexico. 22-minute video production.

Hinch, T. (1998) Ecotourists and indigenous hosts: diverging views on their relationship with nature. *Current Issues in Tourism* 1(1), 120–124.

Honey, M. (1999) *Ecotourism and Sustainable Development: Who Owns Paradise?* Island Press, Washington, DC, 405 pp.

Honey, M. (ed.) (2002) *Ecotourism and Certification: Setting Standards in Practice.* Island Press, Washington, DC, 407 pp.

Honey, M. and Rome, A. (2001) *Protecting Paradise: Certification Programs for Sustainable Tourism and Ecotourism.* Institute for Policy Studies, Washington, DC.

ITRI (Indigenous Tourism Rights International) (2003) Indigenous Tourism Partnerships Tourism Standards and Certifications. Available at: www.tourismrights.org (accessed on 15 November 2004).

ITRI (Indigenous Tourism Rights International) (2004) Rethinking Indigenous Tourism Certification. Online conference, 31 May–2 July 2004. Available at: http://www.tourismrights.org (accessed on 2 July 2004).

Johnston, A. (2000) Indigenous peoples and ecotourism: bringing indigenous knowledge and rights into the sustainability equation. *Tourism Recreation Research* 25(2), 89–96.

Kamauro, O. (1996) Ecotourism: suicide or development? In: *Voices from Africa #6: Sustainable Development.* UN Non-Governmental Liaison Service, New York. Available at: www.unsystem.org/ngls/documents/publications.en/voices.africa/number 6/vface.12.htm (accessed on 1 March 2007).

McLaren, D. (1999) The history of indigenous peoples and tourism. *Cultural Survival Quarterly* 23(2), 25–30.

Mowforth, M. and Munt, I. (2003) *Tourism and Sustainability: Development and New Tourism in the Third World*, 2nd edn. Routledge, London, 334 pp.

Nature's Best (2002) Nature's Best, A Quality Labelling System for Swedish Ecotourism (Criteria Document). Available at: http://www.naturesbest.nu/en/grunddokument.asp

Niezen, R. (2003) *The Origins of Indigenism: Human Rights and the Politics of Identity.* University of California Press, Berkeley, California, 272 pp.

Oaxaca Declaration (2002) Declaration of the International Forum on Indigenous Tourism, Oaxaca, Mexico, 18–20 March 2002. Available from Indigenous Tourism Rights International, info@tourismrights.org

Pleumarom, A. (2001) Do We Need an International Year of Ecotourism? Available at: http://www.twnside.org.sg/title/iye1.htm (accessed on 18 April 2002).

Power, M. (1997) *The Audit Society: Rituals of Verification.* Oxford University Press, Oxford, 200 pp.

Rainforest Alliance (2003a) *Sustainable Tourism Stewardship Council: Raising the Standards and Benefits of Sustainable Tourism and Ecotourism Certification. Final Report, March 2003.* Rainforest Alliance, New York.

Rainforest Alliance (2003b) Ecotravel friendly options to expand significantly in Latin America. Press release. 18 November 2003, The Rainforest Alliance, New York.

Redturs (2003) San José Declaration on Rural Community Tourism. Available at: http://www.redturs.org/inicioen/inicio/index.php?option=com_content&task=view&id=2&Itemid=1 (accessed on 1 March 2007).

Regional Meeting on Community-Based Ecotourism (2002) Statement on the Process of the Regional Meeting on Community-based Ecotourism in Southeast Asia held in Chiang Mai, Thailand, 3–7 March 2002. Available at: http://209.85.165.104/search?q=cache:fWv_0RtmUDoJ:turismo-sostenible.rds.hn/document/IYE_Indigenous_Perspective.pdf+Clearinghouse+for+rethinking+ecotourism+chang+mai&hl=en&ct=clnk&cd=4&gl=us&client=safari (accessed on 1 March 2007).

ROC (Respecting Our Culture) (2004) Respecting Our Culture. Available at: http://www.rocprogram.com/ (accessed on 15 November 2004).

Sofield, T.H. (1993) Indigenous tourism development. *Annals of Tourism Research* 20, 729–750.

Strathern, M. (2000) Introduction: new accountabilities. In: Strathern, M. (ed.) *Audit Cultures.* Routledge, London, pp. 1–18.

Swain, M. (1989) Gender roles in indigenous tourism: Kuna *Mola*, Kuna Yala, and cultural survival. In: Smith, V. (ed.) *Hosts and Guests: The Anthropology of Tourism,* 2nd edn. University of Pennsylvania Press, Philadelphia, Pennsylvania, pp. 83–104.

Third World Network (2001) NGO Statement to Government Delegates at the UN. Available at: http://www.twnside.org.sg/title/eco4.htm (accessed on 21 September 2001).

Tourigny, A. (1990) Certification: what, why, and how. In: *Proceedings of the American Society of Association Executives, 8th Annual Management Conference, 1990*, pp. 206–212.

Tourism Concern (2002) *Ecotourism Evictions.* In Focus 42, Tourism Concern, London.

Vivanco, L. (2002a) The International Year of Ecotourism in an Age of Uncertainty. *Clearinghouse for Reviewing Ecotourism*, Vol. 23, available from the Tourism and Investigation Monitoring Team: tim-team@access.inet.co.th

Vivanco, L. (2002b) Ancestral homes: indigenous peoples are pushing for tourism alternatives that respect community, culture, and the land. *Alternatives Journal* 24(8), 27–28.

Weaver, D. (2001) Indigenous territories. In: Weaver, D. (ed.) *Ecotourism.* John Wiley and Sons, Milton, pp. 256–261.

World Rainforest Movement (2004) Malaysia: Indigenous communities reject timber certification. Available at: http://www.wrm.org.uy/bulletin/80/Malaysia.html (accessed on 24 November 2004).

Zeppel, H. (1998) Land and culture: sustainable tourism and indigenous peoples. In: Hall, C.M. and Lew, A.A. (eds) *Sustainable Tourism: A Geographical Perspective.* Longman, New York, pp. 60–74.

14 Assuring Community Benefit in South Africa through 'Fair Trade in Tourism' Certification

JENNIFER SEIF[1] AND ANNA SPENCELEY[2]

[1]*Fair Trade in Tourism South Africa, South Africa;* [2]*International Centre for Responsible Tourism, South Africa*

Chapter Profile

South Africa provides particularly fertile ground for applying the concept of 'fair trade' to tourism. This chapter discusses the work of Fair Trade in Tourism South Africa (FTTSA), a non-profit initiative that has developed a primarily social certification programme based on fair trade principles and practices. The programme recognizes and supports tourism establishments in South Africa that operate fairly and contribute to the country's socio-economic transformation objectives. The chapter draws in part on research into the perceived benefits and likely impacts of FTTSA certification. By way of conclusion, the authors consider how FTTSA could inform tourism certification programmes in other destinations.

Introduction: Defining Fair Trade in Tourism

In the past decade, the concept of 'fair trade in tourism' has emerged as a powerful critique of mass tourism and other forms of global travel that impact negatively on destinations and their inhabitants. This critique was led mainly by European advocacy organizations, including Tourism Concern in the United Kingdom (UK) and Arbeitskreis Tourismus and Entwicklung (akte) in Switzerland (Kalisch, 2001; akte, 2003).

Fair trade in tourism or 'FTT' is rooted in the global fair trade movement, which started in Europe in the 1960s to address imbalances in international trade in agricultural commodities like coffee, tea and fruit. This is achieved through trading partnerships and, from 1988,[1] the labelling of goods exported by developing countries, usually for consumption in high-income countries located in the 'North'. Fair trade is based on the premise that socially informed consumers will pay a premium price in exchange for a reliable guarantee that certain social, labour and environmental standards have been met during the production process (Kocken, 2003). Premiums are then passed on to producers, who are required to invest the money in social development projects that benefit workers and communities.

Although fair trade started out as something of a fringe movement, fairly traded products are becoming mainstreamed. In 2003, the retail value of fairly traded products in the UK was estimated at £92 million, up nearly 50% from the previous year (DFID, 2004: 72). In 2004 this increased by a further 50% to reach £140 million (Bretman, 2005). According to the UK Fairtrade Foundation, a total of 700 certified food and catering products are currently on offer to British consumers, up dramatically from 140 in 2003, and can be purchased in workplaces and a range of major supermarkets (DFID, 2004).

FTT interrogates the extent to which the concept and practice of fair trade (including trading partnerships, consumer awareness raising and labelling or certification) can inform tourism development both internationally and within destinations (Evans and Cleverdon, 2000; Kalisch, 2001; Pluss, 2003). On the one hand, tourism is similar to other global export industries to the extent that it is characterized by North/South imbalances and exploitative practices and is subject to international trade negotiations, most notably the General Agreement on Trade in Services. On the other hand, however, tourism is not a commodity industry: trade in services is very different from trade in agricultural goods, and the tourism supply chain is highly complex. For these latter reasons, neither the global Fairtrade Labelling Organization (FLO) nor any of its 19 affiliated national initiatives have yet attempted to regulate tourism (R. Roth, Stellenbosch, personal communication, 2005), although FLO is widening its scope to embrace new types of agricultural products like wine and fruit juice as well as non-agricultural commodities like clothing and sports balls (FLO, 2005).

The international network on FTT facilitated by Tourism Concern during 1999–2002 was a first attempt to address this gap. The networking process helped to foster some degree of consensus internationally regarding FTT principles and criteria, as indicated in Table 14.1. The network also defined FTT as 'a key aspect of sustainable tourism [that] aims to maximize the benefits from tourism for local destination stakeholders' (Kalisch, 2001: 11). The deliberate linking of FTT to sustainability in tourism is intended to illuminate the power relations that characterize the global industry, often to the detriment of local destination stakeholders. Sustainability in tourism has since the 1980s (when the concept of 'sustainable development' first became part of the world development agenda[2]) been associated rather narrowly with environmental and natural resource management. Hence the rise of 'ecotourism' as a development and marketing tool and the proliferation of 'ecolabelling' schemes around the world. Although ecotourism development has begun to take into account the socio-economic concerns of local people (TIES, 2004), it still fails to address the underlying structural relations that constrain local economic, social and human development. FTT speaks to this issue by focusing explicitly on the distribution of power within the industry and the power relations that underpin exploitative industry practices. These inequalities are evident in environmental degradation as well as poor labour standards, high outward

Table 14.1. Principles and criteria for fair trade in tourism (FTT) (from Kalisch, 2001: 12; akte, 2003; Seif, 2003).

FTT principles defined by Swiss 'Fair Trade on Holiday' campaign	FTT criteria defined by the International FTT Network	FTT criteria defined by Fair Trade in Tourism South Africa (FTTSA)
A fair exchange with my hosts matters a lot to me.	Fair trade partnerships between tourism and hospitality investors and local communities.	Fair wages and working conditions.
My holiday should benefit the local population to the best extent possible.	Fair share of benefits for local stakeholders.	Fair operations and purchasing.
I make sure that I pay fair prices.	Fair trade between tourists and local people.	Fair distribution of benefits.
I appreciate the beauty of nature and respect the attractive landscape as the place where my hosts live and earn their livelihoods.	Fair and sustainable use of natural resources.	Respect for human rights, culture and environment.
I take time for my holidays.	Fair wages and working conditions.	Ethical business practice.

'leakages' of revenue, unequal access to resources and at times inequitable practices within distribution channels (Kalisch, 2001; Harris, 2003).

Perhaps it is not surprising that the ongoing process to define and promote FTT has been keenly informed by 'Southern' perspectives and experiences of international development, drawn from countries like India, Brazil, The Gambia, Uganda, Namibia and South Africa – countries all strongly affected by unequal terms of trade in tourism and other sectors. In these and other developing countries, where conditions of poverty, inequality and exclusion are prevalent and are strongly tied to external as well as internal power relations, there is a marked push to develop FTT practically. This includes tackling such issues as how to define and measure 'community benefit' and how to structure conditions of supply and distribution (e.g. Tourism Watch and Equations, 2004). Destination-based methodologies complement the approach to FTT (and fair trade more generally) conventionally taken within tourist-generating countries like Switzerland (refer to Table 14.1), where the logical emphasis is on advocacy and consumer awareness raising, as well as the roles and responsibilities of independent travellers and outbound tour operators (akte, 2003).

To date, only one country represented in the International FTT Network – South Africa – has piloted a 'labelling' system: the Fair Trade in Tourism South Africa (FTTSA) certification trademark. This is an important milestone in the ongoing process to define and implement FTT, given that labelling or certification is so central to the fair trade movement. FTTSA has developed a set of predominantly social standards against which tourism products in South Africa can be assessed, and ultimately certified, for fair trade practices. Before examining FTTSA in detail, it is useful to describe the context of tourism development in South Africa.

Tourism in Post-apartheid South Africa

Tourism is South Africa's 'new gold'. The industry has over the past decade grown faster than the economy as a whole, and currently contributes roughly 10% of gross domestic product (GDP) and directly employs more than half a million people (DEAT *et al.*, 2004: 6–7). In 2004, South Africa recorded 6.67 million international arrivals, up 3.67% from 1994. About a third of these are classified as overseas arrivals, primarily from Europe and North America, with the remainder being African intra-regional arrivals. The total value of international arrivals in 2004 was about US$840 million (SAT, 2005).

Tourism is widely seen as a sector especially well suited to poverty reduction, based on a number of factors, including: the labour-intensive nature of the industry; its dependence on natural and cultural assets (which are assets that poor people often have access to); the diversity of the industry, which facilitates wide participation, including the participation of women; and the necessary proximity of the customer to the producer, which creates opportunities for formal and informal linkages (e.g. souvenir selling) (Ashley *et al.*, 2000; WTO, 2002).

South Africa's national tourism White Paper (Government of South Africa, 1996) draws on these insights to provide the policy framework for national tourism development. The White Paper uses the language of 'responsible tourism development' to highlight the enormous potential of the tourism industry to create jobs, alleviate poverty, stimulate black economic empowerment (BEE)[3] and promote the development of small, medium and micro-enterprises (SMMEs). It also draws attention to South Africa's rich natural and cultural diversity, and the potential of tourism to generate income and livelihoods and to alleviate poverty for rural as well as urban communities.

The need to unlock this potential is huge. Poverty, unemployment and inequality are on the rise in South Africa, with strong spatial, gender and racial biases (Bond, 2000; Turner and Meer, 2001). The South African government calculates the national unemployment rate at 26.5% (Statistics South Africa, 2005), although some believe that real unemployment in South Africa is as high as 40% (e.g. Streak and van der Westhuizen, 2004). In 2002, 21.9 million or nearly half (48.5%)[4] the population were living below the national poverty line of R354 per month (about US$2 per day)[5] (UNDP – South Africa, 2003: 41). Growing inequality is further evidenced in the country's high Gini coefficient,[6] which rose from 0.596 in 1995 to 0.635 in 2001 (UNDP – South Africa, 2003: 43). In 2002, the poorest half of all South Africans earned 9.7% of national income, while the richest 20% of the population took a massive 65% of all income (Jacobs *et al.*, 2005).

Against this backdrop of growing poverty, inequality and exclusion, a range of public- and private-sector initiatives has been created to unlock the potential for tourism growth and development. The most recent such initiative takes the form of an industry-specific BEE Charter and Scorecard, designed to measure and monitor the extent to which black people[7] (and especially black women) are included within the tourism industry (DEAT, 2005). The tourism BEE Scorecard sets measurable targets for industry regarding ownership and control of economic assets, human resource development, affirmative action and preferential procurement. The application of the Scorecard is voluntary; however, favourable BEE credentials will increasingly become a necessity for firms seeking to do business with government and with other businesses seeking to meet their own sector-specific BEE targets.

The current focus on BEE and in particular the focus on black ownership of business assets threatens to overshadow or crowd out other developmental priorities. Research commissioned by the Tourism Business Council of South Africa shows that private- and public-sector pursuit of narrowly defined BEE objectives can and often does conflict with other priorities like developing local business, supporting good labour practice and encouraging environmental sustainability (Sykes, 2004: 10). This research raises a number of timely questions concerning the trade-offs companies make when pursuing specific policies. While the current emphasis on BEE is understandable, given the legacies of apartheid, BEE growth may ultimately occur at the expense of other development objectives, with potentially negative implications for alleviating poverty, inequality and unemployment. Particularly in tourism, there is also a risk that the growing focus on BEE will obscure broader debates about sustainability, labour standards, corporate citizenship and the like. This is particularly worrying in an industry such as tourism, which is characterized globally as well as in South Africa by poor wages and working conditions, reliance on casual labour, high resource inputs per customer and relatively low levels of corporate social responsibility (Kalisch, 2002; Beddoe, 2004).

The FTTSA Certification Scheme

FTTSA was established in mid-2001 following a 2-year pilot project, which entailed extensive stakeholder consultation to test the relevance and meaning of the FTT concept for South African tourism. These stages were facilitated by the South African country office of the IUCN (World Conservation Union), based on its understanding that inequitable tourism development has negative implications for the conservation of biodiversity and natural resources (IUCN – South Africa, 2005). FTTSA separated from IUCN at the end of 2004 and now operates as an independent non-profit company registered in South Africa. This move was meant to enable the long-term sustainability of FTTSA as well as the independence of the FTTSA certification mark (Seif, 2005).

The FTTSA certification programme measures business performance in relation to social, labour, economic and, to a lesser degree, environmental standards, based on an intensive assessment process. The programme took approximately 2 years to develop, including the development of assessment tools and procedures, the training of independent consultants, defining costs and benefits and designing a monitoring and evaluation plan. A key feature of FTTSA is its dual-facing nature, which enables it to speak to universal principles and standards of fairness and justice, on the one hand, and to destination-specific concerns and development imperatives, on the other. By way of illustration, the FTTSA certification framework accounts for globally accepted core labour standards like the prohibition of child labour and freedom of association, while also focusing on affirmative employment and training, preferential procurement, land restitution and other practices that are key to redressing the legacies of colonialism and apartheid. Critically, FTTSA is also able to assess wages, prices and other economic indicators in relation to the South African context (Seif, 2003).

FTTSA certification is voluntary and available to tourism products such as accommodation and activity-based operations. To qualify for FTTSA certification, a tourism product must complete a three-phased assessment process, outlined in Fig. 14.1. In short, this process measures the extent to which applicants operate fairly, through analysis of internal conditions (e.g. wages and working conditions, workplace culture and policies, job mobility and training, distribution of revenue, waste and water management) as well as external relationships and linkages (e.g. procurement, recruitment and employment, community social investment, conservation activities). The whole process is based on learning and feedback. Unsuccessful applicants are provided with detailed feedback and are encouraged to reapply following a waiting period. Successfully certified establishments must meet certain improvement targets to retain their certification annually (Seif and Gordon, 2003).

The costs of FTTSA certification to the tourism product are twofold. The first is the on-site assessment cost, which includes the assessor's fee and 40% of the assessor's travel costs. The majority of FTTSA applicants are able to qualify for a subsidy of up to 50% by registering with the national Tourism Enterprise Programme (TEP), a national fund to promote small business development in tourism. The real cost to an applicant for a typical 3-day assessment is thus about US$500. This cost is payable every 2 years to facilitate the biennial reassessment of all FTTSA-certified enterprises. In addition to the assessment costs, qualifying businesses pay an annual user fee, which is determined according to a sliding scale based on the size of the business and its published rates. The minimum annual fee is US$75, which would be payable by a micro-enterprise, while the highest fees collected to date are around US$4000 per annum. The sliding scale of annual fees, as well as the subsidies provided by TEP, ensures that the costs of FTTSA certification do not pose a barrier for small businesses or community-based enterprises, which is a notable weakness of many certification schemes globally.

Step 1	Step 2	Step 3
Self-Assessment	**Assessment**	**Adjudication**
Applicant completes questionnaire, which is reviewed by an independent panel, comprised of FTTSA National Co-ordinator and two external experts.	Specially trained consultant ('independent assessor') conducts on-site evaluation, to verify and supplement self-assessment data. Assessment lasts 1 to 3 days depending on size and complexity of business. FTTSA has trained 11 local consultants, who are contracted in as required.	Assessor's report is panel-reviewed. Successful applicants reassessed annually (paper audit alternates with on-site assessment every 12 months). Unsuccessful applicants must wait 6 months to reapply. All applicants provided with written feedback.
No cost to applicant	Applicant pays consultant fee (about US$250 per day at current rate of exchange[a]) and 40% of transport costs. Many applicants can qualify for up to 50% subsidy via the national Tourism Enterprise Programme (TEP), which supports small and medium-size enterprise (SME) development.	Certified establishments pay annual user fee, calculated on a sliding scale linked to rates and capacity. FTTSA retains the right to adjust fees annually.

[a]The South African currency (rand) has appreciated considerably in recent months, which tends to distort the US$ amounts presented in this chapter. Here a good benchmark is professional consulting fees in South Africa, which typically range from R2500 to R4500 per day, compared with the FTTSA assessor fee: R1500 per day from 1 August 2005 to 31 July 2006.

Fig. 14.1. The Fair Trade in Tourism South Africa certification process (from Seif and Gordon, 2003).

The FTTSA certification trademark is compatible with a number of other certification and quality assurance schemes on offer in South Africa. The strongest synergy is with the voluntary national star grading system, managed by the Tourism Grading Council. Star grading assesses the quality of different types of tourist establishments (e.g. hotels, guest houses, conference centres, campsites, home stays), but does not currently cover social or environmental criteria. With regard to environmental certification, there has been limited uptake in South Africa of international environmental management system (EMS) standards like ISO 14001 and Green Globe. A local equivalent, the Heritage Ecotourism Rating Programme, has attracted about 40 members, mostly hotels in South Africa, Swaziland, Lesotho and Botswana (Spenceley, 2005). In contrast to FTTSA, Heritage is a for-profit business based on the International Hotels Environment Initiative, and incorporating primarily process-based criteria (Koch *et al.*, 2002).

One of FTTSA's potential competitors is Proudly South African (PSA), a type of import substitution initiative endorsed by government and organized labour. PSA membership is based on self-reporting and self-monitoring of four basic criteria: (i) local content; (ii) fair labour practice; (iii) quality; and (iv) environment (PSA, 2001). However, 'self-certification' raises a number of questions concerning credibility and reliability. Interestingly, the national responsible tourism guidelines (DEAT, 2002), which were launched during the run-up to the Johannesburg World Summit on Sustainable Development, also propose a system of self-monitoring and self-regulation by 'responsible' businesses and industry associations. It is as yet unclear what proportion of the tourism private sector actually has the capacity and even the will to self-monitor and self-regulate. Bigger players, like Conservation Corporation Africa, which has developed an internal appraisal system to audit environmental and, to some extent, social performance within its nature-based accommodation establishments (Spenceley and Seif, 2003), are hardly typical of the industry as a whole. The lack of accepted criteria and monitoring procedures, coupled with confusing messages about 'responsibility' from within the industry itself, could dilute the message of responsible tourism in South Africa.

FTTSA strengths and weaknesses

A major strength of FTTSA is that it occupies a specific and clearly defined niche within the broader umbrella of responsible tourism. FTTSA focuses primarily on the socio-economic dimensions and impacts of tourism, which are extremely salient in post-apartheid South Africa. Gender equality, employee benefit and the protection of children and other vulnerable groups, as well as community support and empowerment, are priority areas for FTTSA. More especially, FTTSA's rights-based approach to development provides a basis for interrogating the extent to which increased tourism arrivals and other customary indicators of national tourism 'success' actually benefit poor people, including the rural poor, for whom the tourism economy often has strong potential to contribute to sustainable livelihoods (Spenceley, 2003a). Finally, as a market-oriented intervention based on knowledge and empowerment, FTTSA provides a useful and much needed counterpoint to the many supply-side initiatives that characterize tourism development in South Africa today (Seif, 2001, 2003).

An additional strength of the FTTSA programme is thus the rigour and independence of the assessment process. Research commissioned by IUCN – South Africa indicates that tourism industry stakeholders consistently point to the credibility, professionalism and integrity of the FTTSA trademark (Steyn and Newton, 2004: 9–10; Tholin, 2004a). In contrast to the 'self-certification' utilized by other ethical and responsible tourism initiatives, the FTTSA mark (like fair trade labels more generally) provides consumers, product owners and the industry in general with assurances that certified products comply with globally and locally recognized standards of fairness and sustainability (Harris, 2003: 40). In addition to assuring the market, assessment-based certification conveys valuable learning opportunities to product owners, as discussed in greater detail in the next section below.

The intensive nature of the FTTSA assessment process may also be seen as a weakness – depending on the extent to which the numbers of products certified are seen to be a key indicator of success. Since October 2003, FTTSA has certified a total of 29 products, ranging from large mainstream establishments to community-owned and operated ones. Figure 14.2 shows the current geographical spread of FTTSA-certified products across South Africa. FTTSA-certified products are clustered rather logically around the country's major tourism areas and icons: (i) Cape Town and the Western Cape; (ii) the Garden Route; and (iii) the Kruger National Park. In addition to the numbers of products certified, key indicators for FTTSA are thus the types and geographical distribution of products certified, in relation to FTTSA's goal of mainstreaming FTT principles and creating space and opportunity for community-based and other emerging tourism enterprises (Seif, 2005).

FTTSA's unhurried rate of product acquisition can be attributed to a number of factors, including lack of industry awareness about FTT and certification more generally; the absence of clearly defined criteria during the start-up phase; lack of time, capacity, documentation and/or confidence amongst potential applicants; competition from other initiatives like star grading and industry associations; and lack of capacity and resources within FTTSA itself. Significantly, the costs of certification to product owners do not appear to be a limiting factor (Steyn and Newton, 2004; Tholin, 2004a; Benesh, 2005).

On the one hand, the slow rate of product acquisition has constrained the institutionalization of FTTSA within the industry and the uptake of certified products by international tour operators, for example, operators in the UK that are seeking to render their operations more responsible in relation to various codes of conduct and other industry voluntary initiatives (Mvula, 2005). On the other hand, however, the 'low road' to product acquisition does to some extent reinforce the 'prestige' status of FTTSA certification. The incremental approach has also enabled FTTSA to optimize its own knowledge and learning along the way (Steyn and Newton, 2004). When benchmarked against the

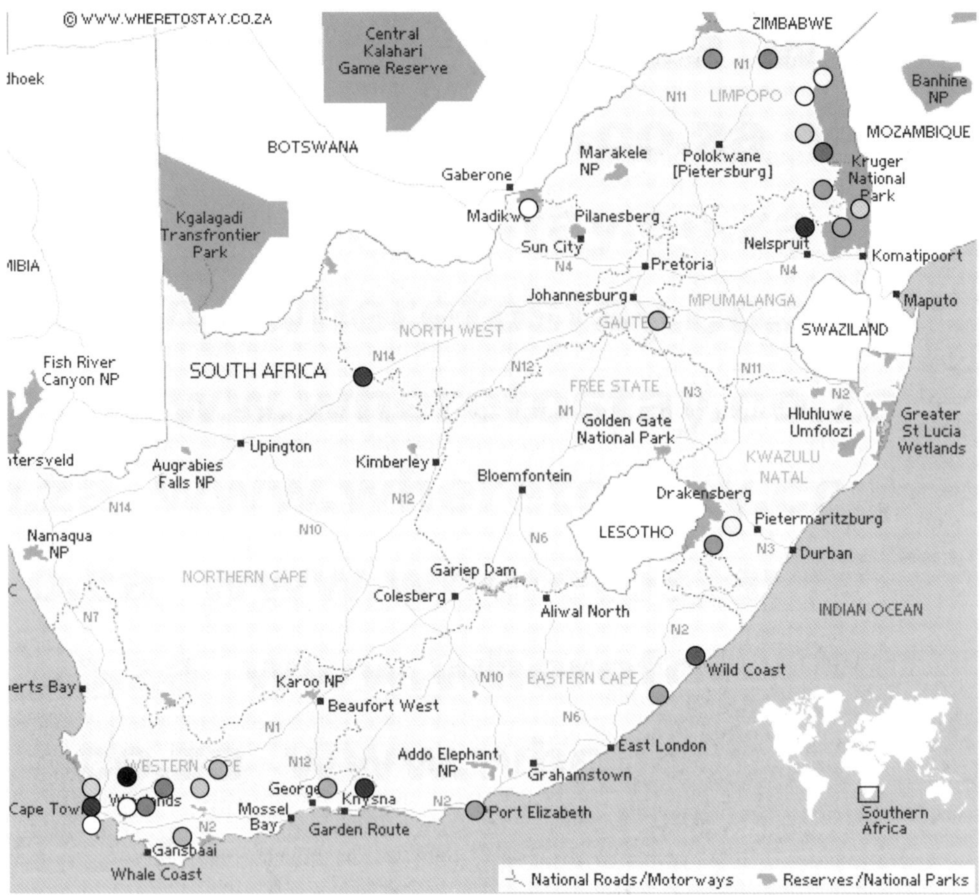

Fig. 14.2. Geographical distribution of Fair Trade in Tourism South Africa products (May 2007).

quantitative performance of other destination-specific certification schemes, FTTSA is about average. One such national scheme, the Certification for Sustainable Tourism (CST) in Costa Rica, has certified about 55 hotels since 1998.[8] Unlike FTTSA, CST is financed directly by its national government.

Ultimately, the success of FTTSA hinges on its ability to build a diverse portfolio of certified products within the next 2 to 3 years. This means that FTTSA must accelerate the rate of product acquisition, while simultaneously retaining its existing clients. The FTTSA portfolio should show good geographical distribution and a balance between different product types as well as between 'mainstream' and 'emerging' products, including good-quality community-based tourism enterprises (CBTEs). At the same time, FTTSA should continue to build brand awareness, especially in South Africa. A larger and more diverse portfolio of products as well as higher brand recognition within the industry will in turn provide a platform for linking FTTSA-certified products to travel channels and consumer markets. Box 14.1 describes the results of an industry awareness survey conducted by FTTSA in May 2004 and again in May 2005.

Benefits and impacts of FTTSA certification

During FTTSA's planning phase, it was assumed that tourism products would be attracted to the certification programme primarily for marketing and promotional purposes. This notion of market benefit was premised on indications of positive demand internationally for 'ethical' and 'responsible' travel. Research into this field suggests a growing aspiration by European and North American consumers for travel that respects the integrity of destinations, host populations and the environment (see Table 14.2). Unfortunately, there has to date been no research into South African consumer demand for responsible tourism, nor has this topic been treated anywhere else on the African continent.

Box 14.1. FTTSA brand awareness (from Tholin, 2004b; and De Lijser, 2005).

In April 2004 and 2005, FTTSA conducted a survey to assess brand awareness amongst the South African tourism industry. The survey was distributed as an electronic mailshot just before the annual Tourism Indaba trade fair, which takes place every May. The target group was the listed Indaba exhibitors from South Africa. There were 192 responses in 2004 and 125 responses in 2005, representing response rates of 16% and 11.7%, respectively.

The research shows that FTTSA brand recognition is growing. In 2004, 26% of respondents recognized a visual representation of the FTTSA trademark (left). This figure increased to 49% in 2005.

In both years, of the respondents who knew the trademark, about 70% indicated they knew what the trademark stands for. Many respondents also wrote down a brief explanation, which in most cases was accurate. Keywords used to describe the mark were: integrity, professionalism, quality, transparency, equality and credibility.

In 2004, 40% of total respondents had heard previously about FTTSA as an organization. This figure rose to 52% in 2005. Interestingly, some respondents visually recognized the trademark but had not heard of FTTSA. Most of these people belonged to the group that could not explain what the trademark stands for.

Table 14.2. Summary of findings on consumer attitudes to environment and sustainable tourism (from Spenceley, 2003b).

Issue	Proportion of sample	Source and sample size[a]
Importance of environmentally sensitive policies and practices		
More likely to book hotels with a good environmental attitude	87% British 60% Australians 54% Americans	IHEI study, cited in Anon. (2002) ($n = 300$ travellers at airports in the UK, Australia and the USA)
Important that their holiday does not damage the environment	71%	Stueve *et al.* (2002) ($n = 4300$ adults in the USA)
Important that the holiday should not damage the environment	2000 – 85% 2002 – 87%	MORI study for ABTA, cited by Goodwin and Francis (2003) ($n = 963$ British public in 2000; $n = 713$ in 2002)
At least fairly important to use a company that accounts for environmental issues when arranging holidays and business trips	1995 – 52% 1997 – 61%	Martin and Stubbs (1999) (British public)
Importance of socially responsible policies and practices		
More likely to book holiday using company with a written code guaranteeing good working conditions, protection of the environment and support of local charities in the tourist destination	1999 – 45% 2001 – 52%	Tearfund (2001, 2002) (1999: nationally and regionally representative sample of $n = 2032$ adults in the UK; 2001 $n = 927$)
Knowing that they had booked with a company with good ethical practice made their holiday enjoyable	24%	Mintel (2001) ($n = 2028$; UK holidaymakers = 1636, July 2001)
Important that holidays benefit people in the destination (e.g. through jobs and business opportunities)	2000 – 71% 2002 – 76%	MORI study for ABTA, cited by Goodwin and Francis (2003) ($n = 963$ British public in 2000; $n = 713$ in 2002)
Respect towards the ways of living and the traditions of the local host population is the most important criterion when booking a holiday	95%	Forschungsinstitut für Freizeit und Tourismus (FIF), Müller and Landes (2000) (German tourists)

[a]The sample size is indicated where known.

Interestingly, stakeholder surveys conducted by FTTSA as well as by independent consultants have shown that, in practice, market benefit is not so strongly associated with FTTSA certification, either in terms of what FTTSA's clients expect (Tholin, 2004a; Benesh, 2005), or in terms of where key industry stakeholders, including government bodies and industry private associations, believe the longer-term impacts of FTTSA are likely to lie (Steyn and Newton, 2004). Rather, the main benefits to the private sector appear to revolve around knowledge and empowerment through information sharing, networking and benchmarking. FTTSA's clients consistently point to the value of the feedback received through the FTTSA assessment process, and of the opportunities for peer exchange that are created through affiliation to FTTSA (Steyn and Newton, 2004; Tholin, 2004a; Benesh, 2005).

The immediate effects of this 'information dividend' are most commonly focused around improved human resource management, although FTTSA's clients also report improved understanding and performance with regard to other operational issues, including risk management, natural resource management, social investment and the management of HIV and AIDS in the workplace. More widely, FTTSA is seen to be creating space and opportunity in the industry for entrepreneurs and employees to take risk and initiative, for example by insisting on 'fair trade' procurement and workplace empowerment (Steyn and Newton, 2004: 10).

This compelling evidence of developmental benefits and future impacts does not discount the significance of FTTSA branding and associated market linkages, especially for smaller clients. Small businesses like those featured later in this chapter have reported immediate market advantage deriving from new linkages with international tour operators, as well as improved uptake by domestic travellers as a direct result of media coverage facilitated by FTTSA. The market benefits of certification are likely to become stronger over time as the FTTSA brand develops and as the market for responsible travel matures, internationally as well as domestically. FTTSA itself is realistic about the market at this stage, but believes that demand for fair travel will grow over the long term, and that in the meantime certification will enable FTTSA-certified establishments to access the niche market, no matter how small it is (Steyn and Newton, 2004: 9).

Market benefit is of especial value to CBTEs and other new entrants to South African tourism, as they tend to lack market knowledge and other resources and are generally constrained in their capacity to access and penetrate markets (Seif, 2001). For such enterprises, a link with one specialist operator or a specific niche market, however small, can provide the basis for immediate as well as longer-term viability (see Box 14.2). The likely positive impact of FTTSA on demand for community tourism is validated by a recent Pro-Poor Tourism (PPT) survey of UK independent tour operators active in South Africa. Tour operators interviewed concurred that consumer take-up of community tourism will likely improve with expanded use of the FTTSA logo (Jackson *et al.*, 2004: 3). FTTSA is thus helping to create a more enabling environment for more equitable tourism in South Africa (Steyn and Newton, 2004). This will ultimately be measured in terms of new attitudes and

Box 14.2. Sample of local industry opinion on what it means to be certified with an FTTSA trademark (from Tholin, 2004b).

'It affords a guarantee to potential tourists that the product they are using is genuinely concerned about its place in society and its effect on the people and the environment it is part of.' – Hog Hollow Country Lodge

'It means that you practise the correct way of operating your business that is fair to all involved and in accordance to the principles set by the Fair Trade in Tourism organization.' – Cape Town Tourism representative

'Fair working conditions, no exploitation of locals/culture/staff.' – *African Frontiers*

'Although many companies might employ Fair Trade practices, certification is a viable and credible recognition. The establishment should be proud to broadcast that it is a practitioner of Fair Trade, which has a positive contribution to the development of our community and our country.' – Bill Harrop's 'Original' Balloon Safaris

behaviours by industry as well as by consumers towards community tourism and the whole notion of 'community benefit' (discussed in greater detail below), which will hopefully help to unlock the industry's potential to contribute meaningfully to poverty alleviation and sustainable livelihoods as envisaged by the 1996 tourism White Paper (Steyn and Newton, 2004; Seif, 2005).

Complementary Models of Community Benefit

The concept of 'community-based tourism' (CBT) features prominently in South African tourism development. Strasdas (2002) describes CBT as tourism where a significant number of local people have substantial control over and involvement in the management and development of tourism activities, and where the majority of benefits remain within the local economy. He further specifies that local involvement may range from scenarios where an entire community is involved in a tourism venture to joint ventures between a community or some of its members and private-sector partners. There are also subsets of CBT, for instance community-based ecotourism (CBET), which Kiss (2003) argues goes beyond simply employing local people or contributing to community projects. For her, CBET entails the direct and active involvement of communities, ranging from consultation to partial or total community ownership.

Both definitions are based on an intuitive description of such key terms as 'local' and 'community', which is fairly common in the academic and technical literature on CBT. A more rights-based approach is taken by FTTSA, which defines CBT as tourism activity that is 'based on communally owned resources (e.g. land, indigenous knowledge), where the people that collectively own these resources ("the community") have legal ownership of the enterprise, either wholly or in part' (Seif and Gordon, 2003). For FTTSA, ownership is the defining feature of a CBTE because it conveys certain rights and responsibilities to stakeholders, for instance with regard to governance and the distribution of benefits. The benefits of ownership should translate into social infrastructure or other forms of social investment financed through tourism receipts or, ultimately, dividends from shareholdings. This type of CBT development is usually achieved with inputs by governments, NGOs and donor agencies, who provide capital, training and institutional support. During the mid-1990s in South Africa, there was a tendency to develop 'pure' CBT – owned and operated by communities for the benefit of communities. While this was understandable given apartheid's legacies of abuse and dispossession, the failure of many such projects has over the past decade engendered new models of CBT based on partnership between communities and the private sector, with the public sector playing a necessary role where state assets are involved (Lund, 2004).

As this suggests, ownership and control are not the only modalities of 'community benefit'. For the majority of tourism development stakeholders in South Africa, this is a concept that encompasses a range of transactions and activities. More specifically, community benefit can be measured in terms of jobs, income, contracts, skills, knowledge and other resources conveyed to communities and to individual entrepreneurs within communities through tourism. This way of conceptualizing community benefit is typically associated with PPT (Pro-Poor Tourism), which advocates that the private sector can contribute effectively to poverty alleviation through improved procurement, employment and social investment practices (Ashley *et al.*, 2000, 2005; Mahony and van Zyl, 2001; Spenceley and Seif, 2003).

Needless to say, these two ways of understanding or defining community benefit are not mutually exclusive. To qualify for FTTSA certification, a tourism enterprise must create 'community benefit' in various forms, although FTTSA maintains that privately owned enterprises should not be held to exactly the same expectations and requirements as CBTEs, and vice versa. Significantly, FTTSA's approach to community benefit differs from that taken by commodity-based fair trade organizations, which dictate that premiums paid by consumers must be invested in social and community infrastructure projects (i.e. to benefit communities). In tourism, at least in South Africa, this primary objective of fair trade is expected to be part of the business model. This is an extremely important point of departure, for two reasons. First, it eliminates the need for FTTSA to involve itself in pricing, which is one of the most contentious aspects of the FLO (Fairtrade Labelling Organization) system (R. Allen, Stellenbosch, personal communication, 2005). Secondly, it renders community social investment initiatives inherently more sustainable, because they are financed either through business revenue, guest donations or a combination of both.

The remaining sections of this chapter will focus on two distinct and yet complementary models of creating community benefit through tourism, which illustrate different ways of achieving community benefit: one urban and privately owned; the other rural and wholly owned and managed by a community trust. Both cases achieved FTTSA certification in early 2004. While it is premature to specify the impacts of FTTSA certification, it will be useful to consider the added value of certification in each context, based on available data.

Calabash Tours

Calabash Tours, established in 1997 in Port Elizabeth (see Fig. 14.2 above), defines itself as a 'commercial venture with a strong social agenda' (African Insight, 2005). Calabash used to operate a small, seven-room guest lodge; however, this component of the business was sold in early 2005 to enable owners and staff to focus on its core business: popular 'township tours', which tell the history of the city and of apartheid more generally, while providing mostly foreign tourists with opportunities to interact with township residents. Calabash is a service provider to a number of large inbound tour companies, and can accommodate groups of all sizes as well as independent travellers.

Calabash is co-owned by a married white couple who have three employees: all young black men who were previously unemployed. All but one of the staff hail from Port Elizabeth's surrounding black townships. The wages paid by Calabash are more than double industry norms,[9] and the company is in the midst of a restructuring process that will provide staff with an opportunity to obtain equity in the business (P. Miedema, Port Elizabeth, personal communication, 2005). Calabash also employs guides on a full-time basis, challenging the industry norm of paying only for services rendered or employing only during the tourist season (mid-October to mid-May).

Calabash creates benefits for urban communities around Port Elizabeth in a number of ways. First, the company pays a fair price for services rendered by township suppliers, including catering (e.g. drinks, meals) and entertainment, and visitors also have opportunities to purchase arts and crafts directly from township producers. Secondly, Calabash Tours works closely with the Calabash Trust, which was established in 2001 in response to spontaneous donations by guests. A good example of travellers' philanthropy (CESD, 2004), the Trust has to date collected approximately US$100,000. It has also accrued sizeable contributions of clothing, books, furniture and building materials, in support of education, nutrition and health projects based in urban communities regularly visited by Calabash tours. Thirdly, Calabash provides a social dividend for township residents, in the form of respectful and economically beneficial interactions with tourists. This is in contrast to much of the township tourism on offer throughout South Africa today, which is characterized, still, by voyeurism and outward leakage (Scheyvens, 2002; Hornby *et al.*, 2003).

Calabash was certified by FTTSA in February 2004. The total financial cost to Calabash was roughly US$900, including US$500 towards the assessment[10] and an annual user fee in the amount of US$400. In return, Calabash receives a combination of development support and market benefit, as indicated by the following communication from Calabash co-owner Paul Miedema:

> We claim to be a responsible tourism practitioner. By applying for the trademark we can be put to the test to whether in fact this is the case. Even the process of applying has made us realize we have overlooked one or two aspects. We see FTTSA as credible in terms of awarding the trademark. We often feel frustrated that we are unable to find partners who share our vision. By becoming part of FTTSA we can link with other tourism organizations and share experiences and best practices. Most of all, we believe we need to be evaluated to ensure that the claims we make of having developed a sustainable approach to township tourism are in fact shared by our peers.
>
> (P. Miedema, Port Elizabeth, personal communication, 2003)

Preliminary research demonstrates that expectations about networking, benchmarking and self-improvement are already being realized and are likely to be maintained over the longer term (Tholin, 2004a; Benesh, 2005). This research also suggests that the costs of certification (which can be considerable, especially for smaller and more marginal businesses) are offset by the benefits, and that the process is widely seen by applicants as good value for money (Tholin, 2004a) and as an effective organizational developmental tool (Steyn and Newton, 2004). Exposure in the media, which FTTSA's non-profit status helps to facilitate, is helping to raise Calabash's profile in the industry and is drawing increased attention to the Calabash Trust. These aspects of FTTSA certification are already bearing fruit: in November 2004, Calabash was named as a joint overall winner in the first annual Responsible Tourism Award competition at the World Travel Market in London. In accepting the award, Miedema cited the FTTSA assessment and certification process as a key reason for their edge in the competition (FTTSA, 2004a). As Calabash continues to grow its business, increased tourism revenues will convey knock-on benefits to township residents.

Masakala Traditional Guesthouse

Masakala Traditional Guesthouse is situated in a peri-urban settlement adjacent to the town of Matatiele in the southern Drakensberg Mountains (see Fig. 14.2). The Mehloding ('green pastures') Community Tourism Trust (MCTT), founded in 2002 and representing more than 25 villages in the area, owns the guest house and a nearby adventure trail, which is still under development. Masakala is managed by a village-based community tourism organization, which is represented on the MCTT board. According to the Trust Deed, profit from tourism activities is paid into the Trust and subsequently distributed to specific social infrastructure projects (e.g. roads, schools), although to date no funds have yet been disbursed due to a lack of operating profit.

Masakala opened for business in 2002, and offers guests comfortable accommodation plus home-cooked meals based on local recipes and local produce, some of which is grown organically (see Fig. 14.3). Masakala provides full-time employment and on-the-job training for three local residents, whose remuneration is aligned to national minimum wage legislation, including two women who are being trained in guest-house management. Additional ad hoc employment is generated for resident tour guides, who facilitate guided walking tours to view rock art, bird viewing, horse riding and cultural entertainment. Guests also have opportunities to visit community development projects and to purchase locally produced crafts. On average 40% of guest-house revenue is retained in the village through a combination of guest-house purchases for goods and services, wages and commissions, as well as community levies (FTTSA, 2004b).

The infrastructure for the trail and guest house was built using money from the national government's Poverty Relief Fund (a financial instrument

(top left) Masakala Traditional Guesthouse is comprised of two rondavels; (top right) local rock art guide; (right) view from Masakala.

Fig. 14.3. Masakala Traditional Guesthouse.

designed to create short-term employment for poor people through labour-intensive public works projects). The MCTT is also supported by local and provincial government, local NGOs and a range of donors, including the New Zealand government, which has provided technical assistance over a 4-year period. MCTT stakeholders were involved in the FTTSA pilot project (1999–2000), which endowed the local tourism development process with a strong appreciation of FTT principles and an aspiration for FTTSA certification, which Masakala achieved in May 2005. The total cost of certification to Masakala was US$360, including US$333 towards the assessment fee[11] and a nominal US$27 annual user fee.

Though not involved in the everyday management of the business, FTTSA adds value to Masakala through the facilitation of market and business linkages. More concretely, FTTSA certification provides tangible relief to Masakala (and to other new entrants to the industry) in the form of web site presence, media and trade exposure, shared knowledge and expertise and opportunities to network and exchange information with peers. The FTTSA certification trademark also conveys credibility, which helps to position enterprises like Masakala in an increasingly crowded and competitive industry that is in many ways sceptical about CBT. Moreover, Masakala staff and stakeholders are empowered by the knowledge that their guest house operates in a fair and sustainable manner that complies with industry and general requirements. Indeed, Masakala provides the industry and moreover the whole of South Africa with evidence that, no matter how small or rural or disadvantaged or 'community-based', a tourism venture can and should be run professionally, equitably and sustainably.

Conclusion

A number of lessons about certification and development can be drawn from the experiences of FTTSA to date. In the first instance, FTTSA demonstrates the importance of context and timing: the initiative emerged at the right time and place, and is evolving in a socio-economic and political context that is conducive not only to social and economic justice, but to change and innovation. The notion that tourism should be fairer is strongly aligned to ongoing national efforts to build diversity and transform the industry in South Africa. FTTSA also demonstrates the importance of positioning to ensure synergy, not duplication, with other efforts to transform and grow South African tourism. FTTSA offers industry a proactive and transparent certification model that conveys benefits to qualifying establishments, while also helping to mainstream FTT principles and practices. That the South African tourism industry has performed relatively well over FTTSA's inception phase is an additional, if unplanned, success factor (WTTC, 2002, 2004; SAT, 2005).

Secondly, certain features of the FTTSA system have contributed to its initial achievements. These features include: strong vision; a developmental approach focusing on knowledge and empowerment; a clear and transparent schedule of costs and benefits; buy-in by key stakeholders, including mainstream product owners; a focus on internal business conditions as well as the external environment; transparent measuring and reporting of business performance; clear and consistent communication; strong external and internal communications; and a focus on monitoring and evaluation of results and impacts (Steyn and Newton, 2004). Despite these strengths, FTTSA has struggled with product acquisition, which is likely to remain its primary challenge over the next 3 to 5 years, based on the experience of comparable programmes globally. Assessment and certification costs must also be continually managed in ways that do not create barriers to small and emerging product owners.

Thirdly, FTTSA consciously certifies all types of tourist establishments – mainstream and emerging, rural and urban, large and small – as a means of integrating community-based and other structurally disadvantaged enterprises into the wider industry. FTTSA helps to level the playing field for CBTEs and other emerging enterprises to achieve the same status and trademark as more established, mainstream operators. Thus, Masakala Traditional Guesthouse shares a certification mark and industry position not only with Calabash but also with industry leaders like Sabi Sabi Private Game Reserve, Singita and Spier. A common commitment to fairness and community benefit transcends the commercial and psychological boundaries between established businesses and emerging ones, which is critical to the long-term success of CBT not only in South Africa but globally.

Fourthly, FTTSA's dual approach to certification as both a developmental process and a marketing tool sets FTTSA apart from other schemes on offer in South Africa, and possibly from other ecotourism certification schemes globally. The FTTSA approach is based on direct and indirect support to FTTSA-certified establishments around such themes as branding, joint marketing, networking, benchmarking and information sharing. As FTTSA grows, this basket of benefits will undoubtedly evolve, in relation to the needs of trademark users but also in parallel to growing brand recognition and growing demand for fair and responsible travel options within consumer and trade markets.

This observation points to a fifth and final critical success factor for FTTSA and for other certification systems in destinations, namely its ability to speak simultaneously to global and local concerns and imperatives. One of the most important features of FTTSA is its capacity to grasp and act upon the dynamics of its external environment, while remaining true to its vision and principles. In many ways, FTTSA is piloting the concept of social certification globally. As stakeholders in other destinations seek to incorporate or replicate aspects of the FTTSA model, it will be necessary to invest sufficient time and resources to developing standards and systems appropriate and relevant to the needs and development imperatives of local destination stakeholders, as well as tourists and tour operators. The example of FTTSA and the possible expansion of socio-economic certification thus make a compelling case for global exchange and collaboration that go beyond conventional North–South discussions of 'standards' to embrace South–South collaboration to define and address the problems and developmental challenges that certification and other tourism development strategies are ultimately meant to address.

Acknowledgements

The authors would like to thank Mesfn Debrezion, Busani Tshabangu and Camilla Ottosson for their assistance in compiling this chapter.

Notes

[1] In 1988 the world's first fair trade label (Max Havelaar) was established in The Netherlands (Kocken, 2003: 3).
[2] The classic definition of 'sustainable development' was presented in a 1987 report entitled *Our Common Future* and subsequently known as the Brundtland Report: 'sustainable development is development that meets the needs of the present without compromising the ability of future generations to meet their own needs'. (http://www.srds.ndirect.co.uk/sustaina.htm)
[3] Black economic empowerment is defined by the South African government as:

> an integrated and coherent socio-economic process that directly contributes to the economic transformation of South Africa and brings about significant increases in the numbers of black people that manage, own and control the country's economy, as well as significant decreases in income inequalities.
>
> (DTI, 2003: 12)

[4] Unemployment figures are based on Adelzadeh (2003) Measurement of poverty and deprivation in South Africa. Background submission for the UNDP South Africa Human Development Report.
[5] The poverty line is calculated according to the Statistics South Africa Income and Expenditure Survey (1995), http://wwwstatssa.gov.za
[6] A measure of inequality where 0 represents perfect equality and 1 perfect inequality.
[7] South African legislation defines 'black' to include all people of colour: Africans, Indians or Asians and coloureds (people of mixed race).
[8] Certification for Sustainable Tourism (CST). http://www.turismo-sostenible.co.cr/EN/home.shtml (accessed on 20 October 2005).
[9] In this instance national minimum wage guidelines for unskilled workers in domestic and agricultural work do not apply. The South African government has specified a minimum wage of about US$120 per month for domestic workers in urban areas like Port Elizabeth; however, there is no analogous position within Calabash.
[10] Calabash qualified for a 50% subsidy on its assessment cost, paid by the Tourism Enterprise Programme (TEP). Most FTTSA assessments are conducted by a pair of assessors, to promote co-learning, as was the case with regard to Calabash. FTTSA carries the costs associated with the second consultant. As with all assessments, Calabash provided accommodation for the assessors, and FTTSA covered the costs of travel.
[11] Masakala also qualified for a 50% subsidy from TEP. Two consultants also conducted this assessment.

References

Adelzadeh, A. (2003) *South Africa Human Development Report 2003*. UNDP, Oxford University Press Southern Africa, Cape Town.

African Insight (2005) *Partners/Preferred Suppliers*. Available at: http://www.africaninsight.co.za/preferred.htm (retrieved 15 August 2005).

Anon. (2002) British holidaymakers most likely to favour hotels with responsible environmental policies. *Caterer and Hotelkeeper*, 1 August, 6.

Arbeitskreis Tourismus and Entwicklung (akte) (2003) Postcard campaign 'Fair Trade on Holiday'. In: *Documentation-Kit of the akte-Campaign on Fair Trade in Tourism*. akte, Basle.

Ashley, C., Boyd, C. and Goodwin, H. (2000) *Pro-poor Tourism: Putting Poverty at the Heart of the Tourism Agenda*. National Resource Perspectives No. 51. Overseas Development Initiative, London.

Ashley, C., Poultney, C., Haysom, G., McNab, D. and Harris, A. (2005) *How to. . . .? Tips and Tools for South African Tourism Companies on Local Procurement, Products and Partnerships*. ODI and Business Linkages in Tourism, Johannesburg (series of five booklets).

Beddoe, C. (2004) *Labour Standards, Social Responsibility and Tourism*. Tourism Concern, London.

Benesh, M. (2005) *Second Annual FTTSA Client Satisfaction Survey*. FTTSA, Pretoria, 26 pp.

Bond, P. (2000) *Elite Transition: from Apartheid to Neoliberalism in South Africa*. Pluto Press, London, 318 pp.

Bretman, I. (2005) Fairtrade fruit from South Africa – UK market trends. Presentation to Fairtrade South Africa annual stakeholders meeting, 13–14 May 2005, Stellenbosch. Available at: http://www.fairtrade.org.za/FTSAConference/Documents/FTF%20UK%20Presentation.ppt (retrieved 15 June 2005).

Center on Ecotourism and Sustainable Development (CESD) (2004) *Travellers' Philanthropy: Helping Communities Build Economic Assets and Sustain Environmental and Cultural Resources in an Era of Rapid Globalization*. CESD, Washington, DC, and Stanford, California.

De Lijser, I. (2005) *FTTSA Brand Awareness Survey*. Unpublished FTTSA report, Pretoria.

Department for International Development (DFID) (2004) *The Rough Guide to a Better World*. DFID, London.

Department of Environmental Affairs and Tourism (DEAT) (2002) *Guidelines for Responsible Tourism Development*. Department of Environmental Affairs and Tourism, Pretoria.

Department of Environmental Affairs and Tourism (DEAT) (2005) *Tourism BEE Charter and Scorecard*. Department of Environmental Affairs and Tourism, Pretoria.

Department of Environmental Affairs and Tourism (DEAT), South African Tourism (SAT) and Department of Trade and Industry (DTI) (2004) *The Global Tourism Competitiveness Project: A Report on the Global Competitiveness of the South African Tourism Sector*. DEAT, Pretoria.

Department of Trade and Industry (DTI) (2003) *South Africa's Economic Transformation: A Strategy for Broad-based Black Economic Empowerment*. Department of Trade and Industry, Pretoria.

Evans, G. and Cleverdon, R. (2000) Fair trade in tourism – community development or marketing tool? In: Richards, G. and Hall, D. (eds) *Tourism and Sustainable Community Development*. Routledge, London, pp. 137–153.

Fair Trade in Tourism South Africa (FTTSA) (2004a) *FTTSA-certified Calabash Lodge and Tours Wins International Responsible Tourism Award*. Media release issued 10 November 2005. Available at: http://fairtourismsa.org.za/news/messages/10112004.html

Fair Trade in Tourism South Africa (FTTSA) (2004b) *Case Study No. 2 – Masakala Traditional Guesthouse.* Available at: http://fairtourismsa.org.za/news/messages/10112004.html

Fairtrade Labelling Organization (FLO) (2005) *Products.* Available at: http://www.fairtrade.net/sites/products/products_02.html (retrieved 15 October 2005).

Goodwin, H. and Francis, J. (2003) Ethical and responsible tourism: consumer trends in the UK. *Journal of Vacation Marketing* 9(3), 271–284.

Government of South Africa (1996) *White Paper on the Development and Promotion of Tourism in South Africa.* Department of Environmental Affairs and Tourism, Pretoria.

Harris, H. (2003) Fair trade in tourism: theory and praxis. MSc thesis, Canterbury Christ Church College, Canterbury.

Hornby, K., Knuckle, A., Makarem, D. and Shugert, M. (2003) Soweto: growth engine or explosion? An exploration of the economic rationale and social consequences of tourism to the Soweto District of Johannesburg, South Africa. Unpublished paper, Kellogg School of Management, Northwestern University, Chicago, Illinois.

IUCN – South Africa (2005) *2004 Annual Progress Report.* IUCN – South Africa, Pretoria.

Jackson, N., Haysom, G. and Nyathi, Z. (2004) *A Step in the Right Direction? UK Tour Operator's Opinions on Pro-Poor, Transformation and Responsible Tourism in South Africa.* Pro-Poor Tourism, London.

Jacobs, A., Meintjies, C. and Mouton, A. (2005) *Quantification of Poverty in South Africa.* Development Bank of Southern Africa, Johannesburg.

Kalisch, A. (2001) *Tourism as Fair Trade: NGO Perspectives.* Tourism Concern, London.

Kalisch, A. (2002) *Corporate Futures: Social Responsibility in the Tourism Industry.* Tourism Concern, London.

Kiss, A. (2003) Is community-based ecotourism a good use of biodiversity conservation funds? *Trends in Ecology and Evolution* 19(5), 232–237.

Koch, E., Massyn, P.J. and Spenceley, A. (2002) Getting started: the experiences of South Africa and Kenya. In: Honey, M. (ed.) *Ecotourism and Certification: Setting Standards in Practice.* Island Press, Washington, DC, pp. 237–263.

Kocken, M. (2003) *Fifty Years of Fair Trade – A Brief History of the Fair Trade Movement.* Unpublished report.

Lund, S. (2004) The proposed tourism PPPs toolkit. Presentation to Tourism PPP consultative workshop, 1–2 December, Kopanong Conference Centre, Benoni, Gauteng.

Mahony, K. and van Zyl, J. (2001) *Practical Strategies for Pro-Poor Tourism. Case Studies of Makuleke and Manyeleti Tourism Initiatives: South Africa.* Pro-Poor Tourism Working Paper No. 2, ICRT/IIED/ODI, London.

Martin, A. and Stubbs, R. (1999) *Future Development in Tourism.* Market and Opinion Research International (MORI), London.

Mintel International Group Ltd (2001) *Ethical Tourism.* Mintel International Group Ltd (provided by MarketResearch.com), electronic document (pdf format).

Müller, H.R. and Landes, A. (2000) *Tourismus und Umweltverhalten.* Befragung zum Reiseverhalten, Forschungsinstitut für Freizeit und Tourismus (FIF), Hans Imholz-Stiftung. Switzerland Travel Writers and Tourism Journalists Club (STW), Zurich.

Mvula, C. (2005) *Fair Trade in Tourism – Overcoming the Barriers to Supplier Certification.* Expression of Interest submitted to the UK Travel Foundation.

Pluss, C. (2003) Fair trade – Also in tourism! *Trialog* 79, 38–43.

Proudly South African (PSA) (2001) *About Proudly South African.* Proudly South African. Available at: http://www.proudlysa.co.za/about/index.html (retrieved 8 July 2004).

Saunders, G. (2005) Deciphering the tourism puzzle. Presentation by Grant Thornton, Johannesburg, 21 June 2005.

Scheyvens, R. (2002) *Tourism for Development: Empowering Communities.* Prentice Hall, Harlow, UK.

Seif, J. (2001) *Facilitating market access for South Africa's disadvantaged communities and population groups through 'Fair Trade in Tourism'.* Unpublished paper delivered to the International Conference on 'Tourism as a Catalyst for Community-Based Development', University of Pretoria.

Seif, J. (2003) Fair trade in tourism – the example of South Africa. *Trialog* 79, 44–50.

Seif, J. (2005) *Establishing Fair Trade in South African Tourism.* Final Report to DFID Business Linkages Challenge Fund, FTTSA, Pretoria, 49 pp.

Seif, J. and Gordon, K. (2003) *Trademark Users' Guide – Fair Trade in Tourism South Africa*, 2nd edn. IUCN, Pretoria.

South African Tourism (SAT) (2005) *Annual Tourism Report for 2004.* South African Tourism, Chislehurston, Johannesburg.

Spenceley, A. (2003a) *Tourism, Local Livelihoods and the Private Sector in South Africa: Case Studies on the Growing role of the Private Sector in Natural Resources Management.* Sustainable Livelihoods in South Africa Research Paper 8, Institute of Development Studies, Brighton, UK.

Spenceley, A. (2003b) Managing sustainable nature-based tourism in Southern Africa: a practical assessment tool. Doctoral thesis, University of Greenwich, UK.

Spenceley, A. (2005) *Tourism Certification Initiatives in Africa.* The International Ecotourism Society (TIES), Washington, DC.

Spenceley, A. and Seif, J. (2003) *Strategies, Impacts and Costs of Pro-Poor Tourism in South Africa.* Pro-Poor Tourism Working Paper No. 10, ICRT/IIED/ODI, London.

Statistics South Africa (2005) Key economic indicators. Available at: http://www.statssa.gov.za/keyindicators/keyindicators.asp (retrieved 15 October 2005).

Steyn, L. and Newton, D. (2004) *Draft IUCN Impact Assessment Report.* IUCN, Pretoria.

Strasdas, W. (2002) *The Ecotourism Training Manual for Protected Area Managers.* German Foundation for International Development (DSE), Zschortau, Germany.

Streak, J. and van der Westhuizen, C. (2004) *Fitting the Pieces Together – a Composite View of Government's Strategy to Assist the Unemployed in South Africa, 1994–2004.* Idasa, Pretoria. Available at: http://www.sarpn.org.za/documents/d0000962/index.php (retrieved on 15 October 2005).

Stueve, A.M., Cook, S.D. and Drew, D. (2002) *The Geotourism Study: Excerpts from the Phase 1, Executive Summary.* National Geographic Traveler and the Travel Industry Association of America, Washington, DC.

Sykes, P. (2004) *SMME Potential in Tourism Supply Chains: Six Case Studies.* Tourism Business Council of South Africa and W.K. Kellogg Foundation, Pretoria (unpublished).

Tearfund (2001) *Guide to Tourism: Don't Forget your Ethics!* Tearfund, London.

Tearfund (2002) *Worlds Apart: A Call to Responsible Global Tourism.* Tearfund, London.

The International Ecotourism Society (TIES) (2004) What is ecotourism? Available at: http://www.ecotourism.org/index2.php?what-is-ecotourism (retrieved 25 July 2005).

Tholin, J. (2004a) *FTTSA Client Satisfaction Survey.* IUCN – South Africa, Pretoria.

Tholin, J. (2004b) *FTTSA Annual Brand Awareness Survey.* IUCN – South Africa, Pretoria.

Tourism Watch and Equations (2004) *Towards Democratising Tourism. Understanding Development Through Tourism: A Critique and Strategising Alternatives.* A summary of interventions of International Tourism NGOs in the World Social Forum 2004, Mumbai, India.

Turner, S. and Meer, S. (2001) *Conservation by the People in South Africa: Findings from TRANSFORM Monitoring and Evaluation, 1999.* PLASS Research Report No. 7, Programme for Land and Agrarian Studies (PLAAS), University of the Western Cape, Cape Town.

United Nations Development Programme (UNDP) – South Africa (2003) *South Africa Human Development Report 2003. The Challenge of Sustainable Development in South Africa: Unlocking People's Creativity.* Oxford University Press (for UNDP – South Africa), New York.

World Tourism Organization (WTO) (2002) *Tourism and Poverty Alleviation.* WTO, Madrid.

World Travel and Tourism Council (WTTC) (2002) *South Africa: The Impact of Travel and Tourism on Jobs and the Economy.* WTTC, London.

World Travel and Tourism Council (WTTC) (2004) *South Africa: Travel and Tourism Forging Ahead.* The 2004 Travel and Tourism Economic Research, WTTC, London.

15 Certification in Protected Areas: a Western Australian Case Study

Colin Ingram

Department of Environment and Conservation, Perth, Australia

Chapter Profile

This chapter uses the case study of Western Australia (WA) to examine from the perspective of a protected area manager the issues surrounding the development of tourism certification programmes in Australia and their relationship with protected area management. In the past 10 years since tourism certification programmes were introduced in WA, many of the expected benefits have not been realized due to the costs and time incurred by tourism operators, inconsistent and generally low uptake by tourism operators and parochial attitudes towards certification programmes among state government agencies. To increase the uptake among operators the issues of cost and time, auditing and incentives need to be addressed. Possible reasons for this slow uptake and the implications for park agencies are discussed in this chapter. The chapter also examines some of the developmental, historical and geopolitical issues that have contributed to both the successes and the shortcomings in the development of tourism certification programmes in Australian protected areas.

Introduction

Tourism is the world's largest industry (Tisdell and Roy, 1998), with global visitation exceeding 760 million for 2004 (WTO, 2005), representing a growth rate of 10% over the last 20 years. This growth is occurring at the same time as there is mounting evidence of serious global environmental problems to which tourism contributes, such as climate change, species loss, habitat destruction, water availability and pollution. Despite awareness of these trends some observers believe that the tourism industry has been slow to respond to environmental issues, show leadership or take firm action to contribute to changing, managing or even acknowledging their impacts (Worboys and De Lacy, 2003). According to Worboys and De Lacy (2003), no industry, including the tourism industry, is insulated from such global and local environmental problems. This is particularly relevant to tourism enterprises that operate in high-quality natural and cultural environments such as protected areas. Tourism certification is one example of leadership and action taken by the tourism industry to address these concerns.

In Australia, both government and non-governmental organizations have taken a lead in supporting or developing tourism certification programmes that attempt to address the need for better environmental practices in the tourism industry. National park agencies, which are predominantly involved in the protection and management of important natural environments, have a particular interest in the development of such programmes.

The first broadly based industry-led tourism certification programmes in Australia have been in place for almost 10 years and yet widespread adoption of these programmes still remains low. Possible reasons for this slow uptake and the implications for park agencies are discussed in this chapter. The chapter also examines some of the developmental, historical and geopolitical issues that have contributed to both the successes and shortcomings in the development of tourism certification programmes in Australian protected areas.

This chapter uses the state of Western Australia as a case study to explore issues relating to the development of various tourism certification programmes in Australia from the perspective of a protected area manager. This state has been chosen because of the significant role played by a number of organizations in either developing or facilitating tourism certification, including the Western Australian government tourism agency (Western Australian Tourism Commission), the peak tourism industry body (Tourism Council of Western Australia) and the protected area agency (Department of Conservation and Land Management – CALM).

Protected Areas

Protected area[1] creation and designation constitutes the primary strategy of most countries to protect biodiversity[2] and outstanding landscapes (Wells *et al.*, 1992; Pouliquen-Young, 1997; Eagles *et al.*, 2002). In addition to their biodiversity values, protected areas often contain areas of outstanding natural beauty, wildlife or natural heritage (DITR, 2003) and their existence provides important opportunities for people to experience nature and recreate in natural environments (Worboys *et al.*, 2001; Eagles *et al.*, 2002).

The Australian protected area system of national parks, marine parks, forests and other reserves includes over 77 million ha of land and water and attracts over 80 million visits per annum (Steffen, 2004; TTF, 2004). These areas make up approximately 10% of Australia's continental land mass, and represent 85 bioregions (DEH, 2000). These bioregions define unique biogeographical regions and highlight the diversity of life and ecological systems that exists in Australia. Managing Australia's protected area network is largely a state government responsibility and operated by separate state-based conservation agencies, such as the Western Australian Department of Conservation and Land Management. All these agencies operate under separate Acts of Parliament. Generally speaking, these statutes provide powers to create and manage national parks and other reserves (including state forests in some states), for a range of values including the conservation of plants, animals, ecosystems and outstanding landscapes and in some cases cultural sites and values (both indigenous and non-indigenous) throughout the state. These statutes also provide opportunities for people to recreate and enjoy national parks and reserves to the extent to which those natural and cultural values are not impaired.

The statutory objectives of state park agencies are similar throughout Australia and generally relate to the conservation and protection of flora and fauna, the management of land and water for conservation and biodiversity, and the promotion and facilitation of public recreation, which includes tourism.

In Western Australia protected areas are managed under the *Conservation and Land Management Act* (1984), CALM. The CALM Act defines the purpose of national parks and conservation parks as:

> To fulfil so much of the demand for recreation by members of the public as is consistent with the proper maintenance and restoration of the natural environment, the protection of indigenous flora and fauna and the preservation of any feature of archaeological, historic or scientific interest.
>
> (CALM Act 1984 #465)

Tourism and Protected Areas

Tourism can provide an economic justification for the establishment of protected areas (Worboys *et al.*, 2005) and provide incentives for existing protected areas through improved support and financial returns. In Australia, many of the globally recognized tourism icons are located within protected areas (Figgis, 1999), including Uluru Kata-Tjuta, the Great Barrier Reef and Kakadu. Tourism in and adjacent to protected areas provides significant economic benefits for both regional areas and the Australian economy (TTF, 2004). For instance, a recent estimate of the value of Australia's tourism, with much of this based on natural, wildlife or cultural icons was A$70 billion (Steffen, 2004). Direct tourism expenditure of A$100 million has been reported from the Wet Tropics World Heritage area of northern Queensland alone (Lindberg and Denstadli, 2003), and in Western Australia the Cape Range National Park and Ningaloo Marine Park are reportedly worth A$127 million per annum (Carlsen and Wood, 2004).

During the late 1980s and 1990s, protected areas in Australia (and in other developed countries such as New Zealand and Canada) faced shrinking budgets and greater areas of land to manage, as well as experiencing increased visitation (Eagles, 1994). Many protected area agencies faced a dilemma, with increasing costs from managing the impacts of growing visitor numbers and increased demands on services and access, at the same time as decreasing government funding. Not surprisingly, in light of tourism's dependence upon protected areas as tourism drawcards and increasingly harsh economic rationalization, park managers began to look to the opportunities offered by tourism. The managers found the potential for funding shortfalls could be replaced or ameliorated by innovative links and partnerships with the tourism industry, through either cash contributions or in-kind support (for conservation efforts, reduced management resources, etc.) as an attractive and obvious solution. However, the relationship between protected areas and tourism is dependent on the tourism industry recognizing the importance of protecting the full range of values that are afforded by protected areas. The recognition by operators that the maintenance of the natural and cultural values of the parks they visit is integral to their business is critical to this relationship.

Tourism and park agencies have a somewhat ambiguous relationship. Initially tourism was regarded as simply a commercialization of recreation activities that have traditionally been regarded as a legitimate purpose of national parks. It is in the legal context of providing for recreation that tourism is able to operate and exist in the protected area system. Park agency responsibilities often include the provision of facilities and services that are fundamental to recreation, and yet also support tourism. Despite this situation, most park agencies do not see themselves as part of the tourism industry – their basic obligation and prime reason for existing are to ensure the protection and conservation of the natural and cultural heritage. However, it is undeniable that education and interpretation are important to help ignite a conservation ethic and encourage appropriate behaviour, and therefore they do have a role in protected area management. This fact has been embraced by many park agencies, with their own interpreters and educators often playing a crucial part in providing information and even supporting interpretive activities and guided tours. For example, the New South Wales National Parks and Wildlife Service developed and delivered successful Seasonal Ranger Programs in the 1970s and 1980s, involving guided tours and activity programmes, which served as a model for other agencies. These ranger-led programmes identified and established a growing demand for nature-related tourism services. However, limitations on government resources, the need for continuity of delivery, the growth of vehicle-based touring and the advent of the Federal Government National Competition Policy[3] (competitive neutrality) meant that private operators increasingly took over the role of providing guided and interpretive activities.

A general assessment of the involvement of Australian park agencies with tourism in the late 1980s and early 1990s can be summarized as follows:

- Most agencies were still coming to terms with how to manage tourism.
- Most agencies did not differentiate the management of tourism from recreation.
- Most agencies had not developed strong administrative structures or systems for managing tourism.
- Most agencies did not regulate tourism.
- Policy and strategy for tourism management were immature or absent.

- Most agencies were still struggling with the ethics of raising revenue from tourism.
- Most agencies did not employ staff with tourism management competencies.

In the 1990s, as the ecotourism and nature-based tourism industries rapidly emerged in Australia, park agencies were forced to develop more effective administrative structures to deal with visitor and tourist management. The growing numbers of tourists to Australia and increasing interest in and participation in ecotourism and nature-based activities were causing increasing concerns about negative environmental impacts at icon sites (e.g. Uluru Kata-Tjuta) and an increasing realization that tourism was a growth industry. Some state protected area agencies embraced the growing tourism industry as an opportunity; others paid little attention to it, hoping it would go away, while others perceived it as a threat to conservation. In Western Australia CALM saw tourism as an essential partner in achieving the conservation objectives of the agency (Sharp, 1992; Shea and Sharp, 1993; CALM, 1994).

Growth of the Nature-based and Ecotourism Industry in Australia

Between 1970 and 1990 world tourism grew by 260% (Wearing and Neil, 1999), mainly associated with the continued growth of the consumer society and characteristic of the dominant world view whereby, in the post-war era, social and economic development prevailed at the expense of nature. More recently, ecotourism (defined as nature-based tourism that involves education and interpretation of the natural environment and is managed to be ecologically sustainable (DoT, 1994)) has developed as an alternative form of tourism in response to the growing concerns in the 1980s over the impacts of mass tourism on the environment. Ecotourism is thought to be the fastest-growing component of the world's fastest-growing industry (Page and Dowling, 2002). This growth is largely fuelled by a new breed of travellers who are well educated and who value nature for its own sake (Worboys *et al.*, 2001).

The exceptional growth of nature-based tourism between 1994 and 2004 is best demonstrated by the growth of licensed tourism operators in protected areas in Western Australia and the growth in visitors to Western Australian national parks, forests and reserves (see Fig. 15.1 and Fig. 15.2, respectively).

In the early 1990s an infant ecotourism industry began to emerge in Australia with considerable encouragement and institutional support from the Federal Government, which saw value in helping to develop a quality ecotourism industry. The introduction to the *National Ecotourism Strategy* (NES) makes this clear, with the then Minister for Tourism, Michael Lee, stating: 'Ecotourism provides an opportunity for Australia to take advantage of

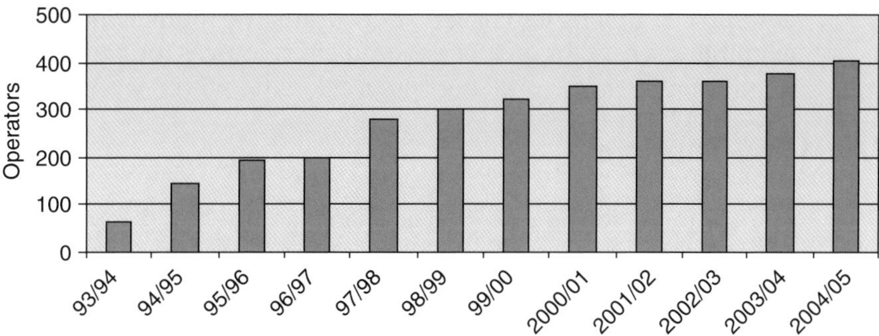

Fig. 15.1. Licensed tour operators, Western Australia, 1994–2005 (from CALM, 1993/94–2004/05).

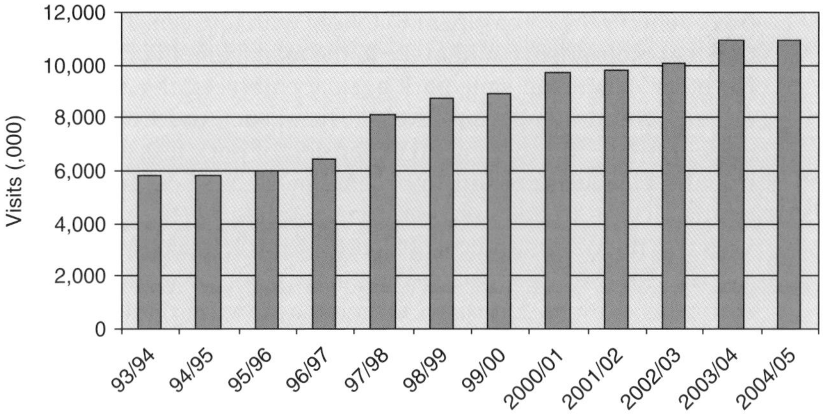

Fig. 15.2. National park visitation, Western Australia, 1994–2005 (from CALM, 1993/94–2004/05).

its unique natural environment by targeting the growing domestic and international market for environmental tourism experiences' (DoT, 1994). Governments around the world tend to embrace tourism because of its significant potential economic and social contribution. Australia is no exception, and promoting and developing nature-based and ecotourism has the added advantage of providing significant economic returns for rural and regional Australia (Australian Government, 2003). It is estimated that 70% of total domestic visitor nights and 58% of the domestic tourism dollar is spent in regional locations, with Australians spending A$51 billion on travel within Australia in 2002 (Barry and Robins, 2001; Australian Government, 2003).

In Western Australia, CALM also embraced the growing numbers of nature-based and ecotourists because of the potential they offered 'to assist conservation of biota and landscapes as well as contribute to the State's economy' (Shea, 1997). Ecotourism was seen as an opportunity for CALM to develop champions for conservation within the tourism industry and assist in building a case for greater government resources for parks.

CALM and Tourism

The response to the growing eco- and nature-based tourism in Western Australia was atypical of other park agencies around Australia. This can be partly attributed to the commercial experience that the former Forest Department brought to CALM as the dominant influence in the new agency when it formed in 1985. The introduction by the State Treasury in 1994 of net appropriation (retention of revenue) provided departments with the incentive and flexibility to maximize revenue-generating opportunities, to recover full costs, to rationalize 'free' or cost-inefficient services and to initiate new activities. The use of royalties to fund forest management provided an obvious precedent for the Department to follow with tourism. The financial contribution that ecotourism could make to the management of parks was appealing. No other Australian state park agency embraced the opportunity provided by ecotourism more than CALM. The agency did this by expanding lease opportunities, introducing an expansion of park fees and encouraging staff to build partnerships and to become more business-focused and entrepreneurial. These trends are best demonstrated by the redevelopment of the Valley of the Giants and construction of the Tree Top Walk (Box 15.1).

CALM also began to broaden 'user pays' programmes, including park entry fees, with an unofficial target of achieving A$10 million in park revenue within 10 years. In the period between 1993/94 and 2003/04, CALM increased park revenue by almost 500% (see Fig. 15.3). This was achieved by opening up new tourism opportunities in the Kimberley Ranges and Shark Bay, building the Valley of the Giants Tree Top Walk, remodelling Yanchep National Park as a cultural centre for Aboriginal education, increased merchandising and expanding the park entry fee and camping fee system. Between 1990 and 1998 CALM increased the number of parks applying a park entry fee from five to 24 parks (CALM, 1995).

However, these economic successes were matched by a tourism industry that seemed intent on rapidly expanding to take advantage of the wave of interest in nature-based tourism before it evaporated, with only a limited consideration of their own environmental impacts. It appeared that the label 'ecotourism' was being exploited by an increasing number of tourism operators keen to capitalize on the perceived marketing opportunity ecotourism provided, without necessarily delivering a genuine ecotourism product. Nature tourism was perceived by operators as an easy industry to enter, with very low barriers, and the term 'eco' was often applied to any tourism product vaguely related to nature. Thus the credibility of the industry was low, and the number of true ecotourism operators appeared to be small. At the same time, nature tourism was increasingly being criticized as unsustainable and the credibility of CALM's accommodation of nature-based tourism was being questioned. However, the release of the National Ecotourism Strategy

Box 15.1. Redevelopment of the Valley of the Giants and construction of the Tree Top Walk.

Tourism growth in the 1980s saw rapidly increasing visitation to the south-west forests of Western Australia. In 1989 the number of people visiting the Valley of the Giants had grown to 100,000 and was causing increasing environmental impacts. Soil compaction caused by vehicles and pedestrians and the decline in ground humus contributed to the collapse of the popular Giant Tingle tree in 1990.

The management plan for the area recommended a major redevelopment at the Valley of the Giants to minimize the environmental impact and preserve the grove of veteran Tingle forest, which was the central tourist attraction. Today's Valley of the Giants forest experience includes an architecturally designed Tree Top Walkway, an adjoining visitor centre and a series of ground-level interpretive boardwalks and hardened paths.

The redevelopment has changed the visitor flows at the site and greatly reduced the environmental impacts. Large coach groups, which had previously caused environmental impacts as they were led through the Valley of the Giants at ground level, now use the elevated Tree Top Walk to experience the attraction. Individuals and smaller groups can still walk through the Tingle forest at ground level, as soil compaction has been reduced due to the provision of boardwalks and paths.

Visitor impact within the Tingle forest has been reduced and this major tourist attraction has been developed, offering an educational experience for all ages and abilities, while accommodating increased visitor numbers. Since visitors now schedule a stop in the district instead of passing through, significant economic benefits have been generated for the surrounding communities of Denmark and Walpole.

The redevelopment of the Valley of the Giants area during the 1990s is an excellent example of how tourism development can bring about positive conservation and economic outcomes through minimizing impacts, increasing environmental awareness and raising revenue to support conservation management.

(DoT, 1994) and later the Western Australian Nature-based Tourism Strategy (WATC and CALM, 1997) provided some support and justification for CALM's bold approach of expanding recreation and tourism programmes in Western Australian protected areas.

In contrast to some of the other Australian states, Western Australia's relatively undeveloped national parks and state forest allowed park planners to construct a more strategic approach to the overall development of recreation and tourism, attempting to maximize the opportunities that were arising through the growth in eco- and nature-based tourism. CALM's Recreation and Tourism Strategy (CALM, 1996) highlighted this approach by stating the objectives of protected areas as 'generating wealth through commercial recreation and tourism ventures' and that 'CALM will pursue innovative ways of attracting resources by involving community and industry in managing and protecting the public estate.'

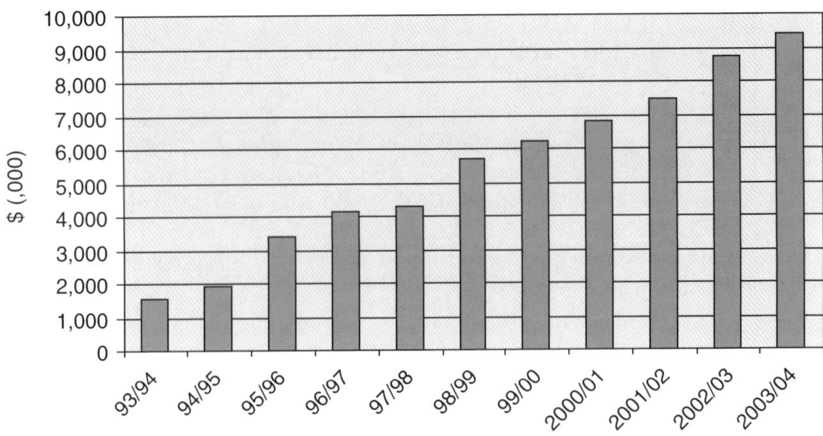

Fig. 15.3. National park revenue – CALM, Western Australia, 1994–2004 (from CALM, 1993/94–2003/04).

However, the strategy also highlighted that 'recreation and tourism opportunities should be evaluated to determine their compatibility with CALM's conservation objectives' (CALM, 1996), suggesting that, despite the desire for tourism revenue, CALM's primary consideration was the protection of biodiversity and conservation values. This meant that CALM needed to manage and regulate undesirable activities and encourage more sustainable tourism, using traditional tools such as licensing and permits as well as more innovative approaches like partnerships with the tourism industry to reward operators that demonstrated best practices through certification programmes.

Protected area licensing

Traditionally, Australian state park agencies tend to use regulatory systems to control operator behaviour (DITR, 2003). The reasons are both historical and political and relate to the cultural environment in which the first national parks were created. In Australia compliance with formal and informal protected area enforcement has generally been high and has been supported by judicial systems; hence park agencies have tended to persist with the use of a regulatory and enforcement culture. Park agencies believe their role in regulating tourism operations is a key part of the agency's management tools for protecting park values, and that resources need to be applied to licensing. The regulatory approach relies on ensuring compliance with licence conditions and imposing fines and/or withdrawing licences in the event of regular breaches of those conditions.

Tour operator licensing in Australian protected areas differs considerably from state to state. In Western Australia there are Commercial Activity Regulations, which control and license the activities of vehicle- and boat-based tourism operators. CALM, through its licensing system, emphasizes the protection of environmental standards to ensure that tourism activities are sustainable and public safety is achieved. CALM's *Tour Operator Handbook* (CALM, 1999, 2004d) sets out stringent environmental and safety conditions for operators conducting tours on land and waters under its control. However, more recently, agencies have realized that the singular application of a regulatory approach (licensing and law enforcement) may not be the most effective means of achieving protection of natural assets and may in fact limit successful management by alienating the stakeholder group that could help provide additional support and resources.

Certification

Certification provides a means by which the tourism industry can demonstrate that it can deliver services at recognized standards and in an environmentally and socially acceptable manner. Ecotourism certification programmes provide criteria that ensure that the negative impacts of tourism are minimized and positive effects (such as returns to conservation) are maximized. As such, certification has the potential to provide park agencies with a means of identifying genuine sustainable ecotourism operators with practices that lead to fewer negative environmental or ecological impacts and use natural resources more efficiently, which benefits areas of high conservation significance. Industry-based certification programmes, especially with regard to ecotourism-specific programmes, have an important part to play in raising the standards of tourism.

Protected areas and the introduction of tourism certification

The Western Australian Tourism Commission (WATC) and CALM saw certification as an opportunity to improve operator standards. CALM also viewed it as an opportunity to share some of the responsibility for managing the resource. Involving the industry in the management of its own standards and taking responsibility for its own impacts was something that appealed to the agency, and they realized that more effective management of protected areas was possible if a bilateral approach involving a strong and effective partnership between the tourism industry and government was developed. The nature-based tourism industry would also gain from actively engaging and involving park agencies in the development of eco- and nature-based certification because the agencies control access to national parks and the majority of wilderness areas. This concept was given impetus in Western Australia with the preparation of the Nature-based Tourism Strategy (WATC and CALM, 1997) and the signing of a Memorandum of Understanding (MOU) between CALM and WATC (CALM and WATC, 1997). Both documents recognize the benefits of strong relationships between tourism and conservation of the natural environment and provide a framework and direction for both agencies to work more closely together.

The MOU emphasizes joint implementation of the Nature-based Tourism Strategy, which includes a commitment to 'encourage the adoption of tour operator certification programs and identify minimum levels of standards of services and products'.

During the initial phases of tourism certification development, many state park agencies were supportive and keen to provide input, but with certification being an industry-based activity that was self-regulated and subject to market forces, rather than government regulation. It was felt that 'certification systems should not be administered by governments but established and operated by industry' (Foster, 2000). In the case of Western Australia, however, CALM and other state agencies were prepared to play a supporting or facilitating role in certification development but felt that, if it was to be successfully adopted by the tourism industry, it required ownership by the industry.

In general, Australian park agencies became involved in certification for several reasons:

- Accountability (building community and political support): Park agencies need to be able to justify both internally and externally that tourism activity in protected areas operates in a sustainable manner. In Western Australia park management plans now have key performance indicators that require the agency to be accountable to the provisions of the plan.
- Expediency: The growth of eco- and nature-based tourism has meant that Australian state tourism organizations (STOs)[4] have been required to work more closely with park agencies to deliver the economic benefits of tourism growth. State government policy has driven park agencies to cooperate in delivering tourism outcomes, including the use of certification programmes.
- Leverage: Certification provides protected area managers with the ability to offer commercial tour operators the opportunity to improve their practices in return for benefits offered through licensing concessions, such as lowered fees and longer licence terms.
- Sharing responsibility for management: To date, protected area managers' main tourism management tools have been regulations. This approach is labour-intensive and combative and undermines successful partnership approaches. Certification was viewed as a tool that allows for collaboration with the industry and also moves some of the responsibility for tourism industry impacts and behaviours to individual operators. This is consistent with the principle of stewardship, where operators recognize what is good for the protected area is good for them, as it is their product. Certification has the capacity to foster cooperation between the protected area manager and operators towards a common goal of conserving the values of the protected status that tourists want to experience.
- Credibility: Certification provides governments with a mechanism for marketing credible tourism products to international wholesalers. Certifying its tourism products can enhance Australia's reputation as a safe, clean, friendly and reliable tourism destination. Many of Australia's

natural icons are the flagships for major domestic and international marketing campaigns and, while tour operators only transport a small percentage of total park visitors, their behaviour and standards can influence Australia's credibility as a tourism destination.

Linking industry certification and park licensing

In recent years, two park agencies (Victoria and Western Australia) have linked certification to greater licence security by offering the incentive of longer licence terms in return for certification uptake (i.e. better environmental practices). Normally all general licences were renewed on an annual basis. Traditionally, tour operators have expressed concern with the lack of long-term security in accessing protected areas, so linking industry certification to extended tenure and licensing is a tangible way of rewarding tourism enterprises.

In Western Australia there were two major industry-led tourism certification programmes available:

1. A tourism business certification programme, known as the National Tourism Accreditation Program (NTAP), developed in Western Australia by the Tourism Council of Australia, Western Australia (TCAWA) in 1996. This programme was originally known as the Quality Assurance Certification Program.
2. A nature-focused sustainable tourism/ecotourism certification programme, EcoCertification, a national industry-association-led programme launched in 1996 as the National Ecotourism Accreditation Program (NEAP); it was revised in 2001 and reviewed, revised and relaunched as the EcoCertification Program in 2003 (EAA, 1996; EA, 2003b).

EcoCertification and NTAP have some essential differences. First, EcoCertification is nature product-based, whereas NTAP accredits the entire business operation and focuses on business processes. Secondly, NTAP has a whole-of-industry focus whereas EcoCertification deals with the niche market of nature-based and ecotourism. Neither programme originally addressed all the components of the principles of sustainability (environmental, social, economic). None the less, both forms of certification have the same overriding goal, to improve business practices and through that enhance customer satisfaction. Currently, CALM rewards tour operators meeting either of these programmes with extended-term licences.

CALM and licensing incentives

CALM considered certification as a method of assessing whether an operator was demonstrating industry best practice in both business standards and environmental practices. This was important in areas and activities of environmental sensitivity; where the fragility or the capacity of the site or the nature of wildlife interaction is limited, the numbers of licences issued is limited and made available through a publicly advertised competitive process. This ensures that these areas or wildlife interactions can be managed sustainably. Restricted-entry licences also have the effect of bestowing a commercial advantage on licence holders by artificially limiting competition.

The mandatory requirements for restricted-entry licensees conducting commercial tourism activities in protected areas were introduced in 2002, with the requirement for tourism operators to hold both EcoCertification and NTAP certification. This applied to about 40 licensed operations across the state. In 2004 this requirement was altered to require only one of the recognized certifications because NTAP was developing its own environmental module as part of its programme and EcoCertification included a generic business module as part of its certification.

CALM's licence condition for restricted-entry operators requires:

> The Operator must achieve and maintain either the National Tourism Certification Program with the Advanced Environmental Management Module (NTAP) administered by Tourism Council Western Australia or EcoCertification from the Ecotourism Association of Australia or an equivalent environmental certification program.

The remaining 350 tourism operators (general-class licensees) have had the opportunity since 2002 to obtain 3–5-year licences after achieving certification from one or more of the tourism certification programmes. However, the uptake of incentives has been weak, but is steadily increasing. The number of NTAP-accredited operators in Western Australian protected areas in 2004/05 was 136 (CALM, 2005b). While this represents around a third of all operators operating in the state's protected area system, certification is a mandatory licence condition for 41 of these operators. Table 15.1 provides a summary of tourism certification levels in Western Australia's protected areas since 2003. At 30 June 2005 only 36 general-class operators eligible to take out longer-term licences had chosen to take advantage of the privilege (CALM, 2005b), suggesting that either security of licence is not a concern to operators or the costs associated with certification outweigh other benefits, including the incentives offered by CALM. The reasons for this low uptake are explored in the following sections by examining the two major tourism-led certification programmes' development, their ideology and their political operating landscape.

Business Certification Programmes

Business certification encompasses a number of different voluntary industry standards that were created to provide a tool for developing better business practices and customer service (TCWA, 2003). Business certification standards include a benchmark of industry requirements and tools to help plan, develop, improve and document good business practices and procedures (TABV, 2005). These programmes often have requirements such as having relevant licences and insurances, preparation and implementation of a

Table 15.1. Summary of tourism certification levels in Western Australia's protected areas (from CALM, 2003, 2004a, 2005a).

	No. of CALM licences with certification at 30 June 2003	% of all operators	No. of CALM licences with certification at 30 June 2004	% of all operators	No. of CALM licences with certification at 30 June 2005	% of all operators
NTAP	94	26%	115	30%	136	33%
EcoCertification	12	3%	36	10%	32	8%

business plan, customer service policies and procedures, risk management planning and procedures, staff training and development and booking and financial procedures, as well as environmental policies and practices. The commonly promoted benefits include improved business operations, greater industry and consumer recognition through marketing and advertising, marketing and advertising discounts, access to government marketing channels, and extended park agency licence periods. Business certification is granted to the operating entity.

Better Business Tourism Certification Program

The purpose of the first tourism business certification programme developed in Victoria by the Victorian Tourism Operators Association (VTOA) in 1991 was principally to ensure that operators, especially those in the higher-risk adventure tourism market, had adequate public liability insurance. This was largely driven by concerns from protected area managers upon whose land many of these operators conducted their tours. This scheme (now called the Better Business Tourism Certification Program (BBTAP)) attracted membership from other states because tourism operators wanted access to cheaper insurance premiums. Unfortunately, the insurance advantages, which were a major selling point of the programme, suffered the same fate of most insurance during recent public liability problems. BBTAP has suffered like many certification programmes from a lack of consumer awareness. It has concentrated its resources on promoting programmes to businesses, but has not had the resources to mount advertising campaigns to inform the consumers of the benefits of using a certified business. It is apparent that certified operators have not reaped the marketing benefits that were promised by VTOA.

National Tourism Certification Program (NTAP)

As the government agency responsible for tourism development in Western Australia, the Western Australia Tourism Commission (WATC) recognized that certification could also be a powerful form of marketing if operators could meet consumer demands for high standards of service. Quality assurance was critical to raising standards to an acceptable level. WATC, like other government agencies, believed that the tourism industry needed to have ownership of the development and administration of certification and sponsored the development of the first generation of the Tourism Council of Australia, Western Australia's (TCAWA) business certification programmes.

This programme was based principally on the International Organization for Standardization (ISO) 9000 family (updated to ISO 9001 in 2001), which define requirements for Quality Management Systems (ISO, 2005), including customer's quality requirements and applicable regulatory requirements, whilst aiming to enhance customer satisfaction and maintaining continual improvement in performance. This was released in 1996 as the Quality Assurance Accreditation Program (QAAP) specifically for tourism in Western Australia.

However, the QAAP was considered too cumbersome and rigid (mainly because ISO 9000 was structured and designed to suit industries other than tourism) and the programme was reviewed and revamped into the National Tourism Accreditation Program (NTAP). Interest from other state and territory tourism organizations and peak tourism industry bodies led the WATC and the TCWA to offer the programme under licence to State Tourism Councils in South Australia, Tasmania, the Northern Territory and the Australian Capital Territory.

Business-based certification programmes are designed primarily to ensure reliable and consistent business management practices that improve both safety and service to customers. The Tourism Council of Western Australia (TCWA) assumed that business certification would have little relevance to protected area managers, and their interests were given little consideration. Yet protected area managers actually have much to gain from the introduction of better tourism business practices.

A national approach was considered necessary to ensure that consistency was achieved and scarce resources were not squandered through the creation of duplicated programmes. While comprehensive national certification coverage was not achieved through either NTAP or the BBTAP business certification, it did gain strongholds in all states and territories in Australia except for New South Wales (NSW) and Queensland. It is clear that the overall effectiveness of tourism certification uptake depended on two things: first, ensuring the integrity of certification programmes to retain or regain the confidence and support of industry; and, secondly, gaining national coverage of generic (business systems) certification, which meant gaining the support of both NSW and Queensland. The lack of endorsement of NTAP by both of these states removed any hope of reaching the critical mass necessary to further drive national uptake of certification. Queensland concentrated on promoting NEAP (now known as EcoCertficiation) and the state agency, Tourism Queensland, provided significant resources to support this approach. It is unclear why NSW did not endorse NTAP or BBTAP. At various stages, both Queensland and NSW argued that existing laws and regulations already covered the requirements of BBTAP and NTAP, and these programmes were regarded as superfluous.

TCA's determination to establish a national certification framework and business certification system led to the creation of the Australian Tourism Accreditation Authority (ATAA) in 1998 (Foster, 2000). ATAA was a self-formed 'Authority' created by the states and territories with the rights to use NTAP (WA, ACT, SA, Tasmania and NT) and Victoria. The body had no government authority or endorsement, although its objective was to establish certification at the national level and ensure that all tourism certification programmes included comparable generic criteria. Victoria retained BBTAP and conformed to the new ATAA criteria. Certification programmes delivering the ATAA criteria were deemed to have met the Australian Tourism Certification Standard. The standard included compliance with generic business components, including adherence to industry sector standards and codes of conduct, risk management procedures and training, corporate strategic business and marketing plans, human resource management policy and procedures, customer service procedures, ethical and environmental policies and procedures and general maintenance schedules and procedures. Sector-specific components (e.g. caravan parks, wine cellar door) would be added to this mix.

By mid-2003 over 2500 tourism businesses throughout Australia had met the Australian Tourism Certification Standard (TCWA, 2003). The Bureau of Tourism Research (BTR) estimates suggest that there are about 290,000 tourism-connected businesses[5] and 60,000 tourism characteristic businesses[6] in Australia (BTR, 2003). In 2003 the number of certified businesses represented only 4% of all recognized tourism businesses nationally.

EcoCertification Program (formerly known as the Nature and Ecotourism Accreditation Program – NEAP)

In 1993 the relatively newly formed Ecotourism Association of Australia (EAA) held its inaugural conference, with a focus on defining ecotourism standards and expressing strong support for the development of an ecotourism certification programme. Events were overtaken by the Commonwealth Department of Tourism releasing the National Ecotourism Strategy (DoT, 1994), which highlighted a need for national leadership in the development of an ecologically sustainable tourism industry and 'the need for an integrated approach to the planning, development and future management of ecotourism'. The strategy recognized that the development and implementation of an industry-led national system of certification was a priority. Some of the reasons stated for the need for a national ecotourism certification programme were to:

- Differentiate and designate bona fide ecotourism operators.
- Minimize impacts and improve the ecological sustainability of tourism in Australia.
- Enhance the reputation of Australian ecotourism in both domestic and international markets.

- Allow natural resource managers to better monitor ecotourism operators and better protect natural and cultural values.
- Supply consumers with information upon which they can make more accurate comparisons on different enterprises and activities.

Consultation to obtain the views of key stakeholders about the creation of a national ecotourism certification scheme involved a major survey and a series of workshops in all states and territories (Manidis Roberts Consultants, 1994b). A steering group of the Australian Tourism Industry Association (ATIA – shortly rebranded as Tourism Council Australia – TCA), the Ecotourism Association of Australia (EAA), the Australian Conservation Foundation (ACF) and the Commonwealth Department of Tourism (DoT) oversaw the process. Despite this level of consultation, initial steps were hampered by perceptions within park agencies of being a Federal Government-driven initiative, with clear influences from the Report of the Ecologically Sustainable Development Working Group (1991), the National Tourism Strategy of 1992 and the National Strategy for Ecologically Sustainable Development, 1992.

Protected area managers were obviously involved as major stakeholders because they controlled many of the sites for ecotourism and had the potential to support the certification process. A national reference group was established, with park agencies providing two representatives at director level in the group. Ministerial briefing notes prepared by senior CALM staff that attended the Perth Consultative Workshop indicate that there appeared to be limited understanding of what a certification scheme was intended to accomplish, and that the consultation process:

> was unlikely to result in a meaningful certification scheme that has broad industry support. It is more likely that a meaningful certification scheme could only be achieved through greater participation and ownership by the industry itself and better consultation with stakeholders to identify key issues.
>
> (CALM, 1995)

The final report and proposed National Ecotourism Certification Scheme (Manidis Roberts Consultants, 1994a) was rejected by a range of key industry stakeholders. The EAA, VTOA and TCA provided feedback that the programme and administrative structures were too complex, involved significant multilayering and would necessitate an expensive new bureaucracy. Funding the programme administration and implementation would be expensive, and unless significantly subsidized would lead to minimal industry participation (Charters, 2000; Chester and Crabtree, 2002).

During 1995 EAA lobbied the Federal Government Department of Tourism to continue with the idea of ecotourism certification and the Federal Government agreed to support development of a revised programme. However, grant funding was tied to being administered by the peak mainstream tourism body (TCA), and the programme was to be developed by a partnership between EAA and the Australian Tour Operator Network (ATON) (the national body created by VTOA to bring together tour operators). At that time, ATON (through VTOA) was the only industry body that had a successful track record of developing and running a certification programme (the BBTAP). The National Ecotourism Accreditation Program (NEAP I) was released in 1996, with an administrative structure jointly shared by EAA and ATON. There were limited provisions that encouraged operators to take up both the ecotourism and the ATON business certification programmes at a reduced rate, but this was not marketed to any great extent. The partnership between EAA and ATON remained in place until 2000, when EAA gained sole ownership of the programme. VTOA and ATON withdrew from direct involvement in delivering certification programmes at this time, with the BBTAP going to the Victorian Tourism Accreditation Board (VTAB).

The NEAP certification was developed to provide industry, protected area managers, local communities and ecotourists with an assurance that certified products were backed by a commitment to best practice ecological sustainability, natural area management and provision of quality ecotourism experiences (EAA, 1996). The programme certifies product in three major sectors – accommodation, tours and attractions – and originally provided two levels of certification, 'Ecotourism' and 'Advanced Ecotourism'. Certification criteria originally fell into four main areas: provision of interpretation, environmental sustainability, contributions to conservation and working with and providing returns for local communities. It included requirements such as staff knowledge, interpretation, safety and emergency planning, management of waste, noise and litter, water and energy conservation and impact management. NEAP I was revised, rebranded and expanded to include an additional nature tourism level for the second generation of the programme in 2000, the Nature and Ecotourism Accreditation Program or NEAP II (EAA, 2000). The programme has since been updated and again rebranded as the EcoCertification Program (popularly known as NEAP III). (See Chapter 22 for a more detailed discussion on NEAP.)

Certification: Meeting the Needs of Western Australia and CALM

Western Australia's major marketing focus has been based largely on the natural attributes and environmental drawcards of the state. The Western Australian Tourism Commission has prepared, marketed and released a series of programmes aimed at engaging tourists in environmental projects by contributing physically and financially to ecotourism facility developments and research projects – known as 'Be Touched by Nature – Environmental Tourism Packages', as well as a campaign called 'Holidays of an Entirely Different Nature' (WATC, 2001). The ethos of these campaigns was to showcase Western Australia as a unique nature-based tourism destination and to facilitate the funding of conservation projects throughout the state. For a state that is heavily marketing the natural environment and experiences in protected areas, it is necessary to work towards improving standards specifically for nature-based tourism operators.

CALM, whilst interested in ensuring that high environmental standards were integrated into tourism enterprises operating in protected areas under their jurisdiction, also faced additional pressures. The change in government funding policies relating to cost recovery placed increased demands on protected areas to raise revenue through 'user pays' systems, and increasing costs brought financial pressures. All protected area managers have a duty of care under a common law claim in negligence (McDonald, 2003). In Western Australia there is a statutory obligation under the Occupiers Liability Act, 1985, to ensure the safety of all visitors entering protected areas. In the 9-year period since 1997, CALM's public liability premiums rose 121% at a total cost of $A3.9 million – largely attributed to increasing litigation (John Ireland, personal communication, July 2005, based on data from the government insurer – RiskCover). Therefore park agencies were seeking ways to minimize insurance costs by shifting or sharing the risk. Certified operators also enhance the park agency's financial security, as better accounting systems ensure that licence and per person entrance fees are paid.

The requirements for high-quality natural tourist experiences, environmental management, good financial systems and appropriate business planning – including risk management and staff training – are all elements found in either one or the other of the two main tourism certification programmes discussed. As programmes have evolved and key issues such as environmental sustainability, safety, risk management and insurance have gained greater importance, park agencies look to certification and the industry to ensure that these areas are properly addressed. However, it is critical that certification programmes are credible and this relies on accurate assessment and auditing of certification standards.

In the case of NTAP, audits are conducted internally and cannot be considered independent. The lack of independent third-party auditing appears to be due to financial costs and the lack of willingness to pay for certification by tourism enterprises.

Until recently, NEAP/EcoCertification relied on self-assessment, with referee checks and a small percentage of on-site audits. Criticism about self-assessment was rife, with concerns expressed by some operators and park agencies who felt that some certified product was not meeting the standards. Ecotourism Australia has recently established a more independent audit programme for its EcoCertification product, with the aim of having all certified operators audited at least once during their 3-year certification period. Although this represents an improvement to the initial auditing schedule, such a time frame is probably insufficient to ensure effective compliance.

Certification must be credible to gain the support of park agencies and state tourism organizations (STOs). To date, EcoCertification has failed to gain the support of protected area managers (with the exception of pilot audits for NEAP financed by Tourism Queensland) and STOs to assist in financing the new auditing programme. It is also evident that neither NTAP's nor EcoCertification's current fee schedule raises sufficient funds for appropriate independent third-party auditing to be self-financed. The viability of certification programmes and their ability to be self-sufficient and fund relevant auditing procedures are in part dependent upon achieving a critical mass of certified operators, particularly in remote areas. The emergence of an environmental module as part of NTAP may make it impossible for EcoCertification to achieve this critical mass in Western Australia and other states supporting the NTAP model.

Certification programmes: duplication or competition?

Maintaining and conserving natural and cultural values is an essential prerequisite to providing nature-based tourism experiences, suggesting a synergistic advantage for EcoCertification and park agencies to work together. However, the role that tourism and tourism certification can play in conservation and park management is the subject of considerable ongoing debate. The Tourism and Protected Areas Forum (TAPAF), a loose association of senior managers from Commonwealth, state and territory government agencies responsible for tourism (STOs) in Australian protected areas, which includes both park agencies and state tourism organizations, was formed to share information and develop consistent approaches to the management of tourism in protected areas. TAPAF has debated the value of certification as a management tool, and the value of specific programmes has come under scrutiny. EcoCertification's emphasis on environmental sustainability is appealing to park agencies, but mainstream business tourism certification schemes also meet some of an agency's needs.

CALM considers that neither programme meets its needs entirely, and contends that the programmes do not duplicate one another but complement each other: hence the requirement for both programmes. The basis of this argument is the triple-bottom-line approach to sustainability, a concept being strongly pushed by the Western Australian state government through a State Sustainability Strategy (Government of Western Australia, 2003). While the environmental and social elements of the triple bottom line were self-evident as being integral to the operations of protected area managers, CALM argued that economic sustainability also applied to the management of protected areas and not just the operator. Park agencies, like other economic entities, rely on financial resources to manage their estate; therefore the commercial activity they were licensing needed to be economically sustainable from a monitoring and management point of view. As many of the licensed operators paid the user-pays fees on a credit-approved system, and these funds are auditable and used primarily for the purpose of funding the monitoring and management of tourism operations, then CALM would expect the operator's business practice to be robust and of acceptable practice. Issues such as customer service and safety were also a concern of CALM, and the NTAP best addressed these needs.

NEAP/EcoCertification has now been in the market for almost 10 years. If the number of certified operators is used as a performance measure, the programme has failed to deliver for protected areas. In 2003/04 Ecotourism Australia recorded 146 businesses holding EcoCertification nationally (EA, 2003a). This had grown to 188 by 30 June 2005 (EA, 2005a). There were 34

Table 15.2. Number of NEAP/EcoCertified businesses in Australia and Western Australia (from EAA, 1998, 2001; EA, 2005a, b).

	1998/99 (NEAP I)	2001 (NEAP II)	2005 (EcoCertification)
No. of certified businesses nationally	45	78	240
No. of certified businesses in WA	2	6	34
No. of certified businesses operating in WA protected areas	1	5	32
No. of certified businesses in Queensland	21	43	82

Western Australia businesses with EcoCertification in 2005 (EA, 2005a), 32 of which operated in protected areas (CALM, 2005b). CALM's mandatory certification requirements for restricted entry licences have largely been responsible for this growth. These numbers represent a very small percentage of the estimated 3000 nature and ecotourism businesses (EA, 2005a) operating Australia-wide, and represent only about 8% of all licensed operators in WA protected areas (see Tables 15.1 and 15.2).

This lack of NEAP/EcoCertification take up in WA can be attributed to four perceived problems with the programme:

1. Narrow focus on ecotourism.
2. Level of marketing support provided by STOs.
3. Relevance of NEAP/EcoCertification.
4. Competition with NTAP.

Narrow focus of NEAP/EcoCertification

One of the main barriers in the initial roll-out of NEAP was its narrow ecotourism focus. The philosophy and definition of ecotourism formed the scope for the certification programme. This meant that many nature-based operators, who were happy to pursue environmental initiatives but did not wish to pursue other elements of ecotourism (interpretation, returns to conservation and community) or did not want to market themselves as ecotourism products, were excluded. NEAP was perceived as an exclusive programme concerned more with protecting the image of ecotourism than using certification as a tool to improve standards of all enterprises operating in the natural environment. Pressure from some park agencies and within the EAA (McArthur, 1998) highlighted the need for NEAP to be more encompassing and include all operators operating in natural areas, and this was combined with the realization by the programme managers that the programme needed to expand to be self-financing (A. Crabtree, personal communication, 2002). In 2000, after much consultation and debate, the revised NEAP II provided a broader three-tier approach incorporating an entry-level certification category for nature-based operators and two levels of ecotourism certification.

Despite broadening NEAP in 2000, there appeared to be a culture within the EAA and among the NEAP Assessment Panel that resented the inclusion of nature-based operators into the NEAP system. There appeared to be some philosophical differences within the EAA as to the propriety of certifying operators that were not attuned to the concept of ecotourism and even less to understanding or practising it. The expanded programme did introduce a different breed of operator to the programme – with many operators inducted into the concept of performance improvement and quality assurance for the first time. Many operators appeared to struggle with certification and the certification process and did not reach the final stages. While the certification of exemplary operators is desirable, CALM considered it essential that all tourism enterprises operating in protected areas apply sustainable practices. From the perspective of ecological sustainability, it is of mutual interest to programme managers, operators and park agencies alike that certification programmes are as inclusive as possible. Certification programmes need to aim at recognizing existing best practice products/operators and engaging and developing those that are not to the point where they can achieve some level of certification. Without these dual aims, certification will not meet its objectives of a truly sustainable industry.

State tourism organization support for NEAP

The EAA (later renamed Ecotourism Australia – EA) has strong links with Queensland, with its office having always been based in that state and a large proportion of its executive members being based there. Tourism Queensland (TQ) has, over the years, played a significant role in funding and supporting the development and implementation of the NEAP programme – a fact that NEAP has always acknowledged (Chester and Crabtree, 2002). This close relationship is highlighted by TQ staff holding senior positions on the EAA Executive Board, and often providing significant grant, marketing, workshop or lobbying support. Specific activities included NEAP marketing and promotional materials and a NEAP-oriented visiting journalists programme (Charters, 2000), as well as grant funding for on-site audits and audit protocols and a state-wide protected area agency consultation/lobby tour by two NEAP members during the development of NEAP II. Tourism Queensland also conducts a number of more general support programmes to encourage ecotourism and sustainable tourism development, with quality publications, industry education, marketing support to certified operators and consumer-understanding programmes. It is therefore not surprising that Queensland has attracted the highest number of businesses with NEAP-certified products and consequently NEAP has been perceived as a Queensland-based and -driven programme.

The extent of marketing NEAP/EcoCertification by STOs outside Queensland has been very limited. Some STOs only recognized programmes that met the Australian Tourism Accreditation Authority (ATAA) standard, something that NEAP could not obtain until the criteria had been considerably changed to include more generic business components. This did not occur until NEAP III (EcoCertification) was released in 2004. NEAP did establish some marketing arrangements with the Australian Tourism Commission, but this had little relevance to many of the small regional operators in WA who were the basis of the state's nature-based industry. The lack of strong STO support outside Queensland therefore reinforced the perception that NEAP was not a truly national programme.

Relevance of NEAP

Western Australia and some of the other more isolated states and territories (SA, NT) had not evolved a large or mature tourism industry at the time NEAP was first released. In the case of WA, most visitors were from within the state, and the majority of the tourism operators were small-scale. They seldom used the travel industry sales distribution network and were not exposed to the more sophisticated approach required to service the needs of international travellers. This contrasted to Queensland, which had a higher number of international visitors and a more commercially oriented ecotourism industry, with several large players involved in icon areas such as the Great Barrier Reef and Fraser Island (e.g. Quicksilver Connections, Kingfisher Bay Resort and Village) and later on Sky Rail in the Wet Tropics World Heritage Area. Accordingly, NEAP was most relevant to tourism destinations like Queensland, which, due to strong tourism growth, had already experienced some negative impacts of tourism, and had a more established and arguably more sophisticated tourism industry.

Competition with NTAP

The lack of significant uptake of NEAP/EcoCertification in Western Australia can also be partially attributed to the problems associated with what was perceived as a competing programme, the NTAP. Whilst the NTAP criteria did not overlap, the reality is that voluntary certification programmes compete for resources. CALM certainly received feedback from operators that did not see a benefit of having to apply to two separate tourism certification programmes, and resented both the time and costs involved in doing so. Research by Shadbolt (2003) indicates that certification programmes impose significant costs on operators and guides (seeking individual professional certification), not only in application and annual fees but in hidden costs such as time, training, research and preparation for the certification application process. The relative cost of certification appears to be much higher for smaller businesses than for large businesses that have greater resources.

This element of competition between the two certification programmes was exacerbated by the position of the WATC. WATC owns the NTAP and licenses the TCWA to operate it in Western Australia. The WATC's failure to support ecotourism certification, while at the same time heavily marketing Western Australia's natural environment, was driven by a conflict of interest that highlighted the obvious inconsistency between its marketing campaigns and its lack of support for NEAP.

Recent developments

Duplication between NTAP and EcoCertification

The development of NEAP III in 2002 introduced a business component to the programme to enable EcoCertification to meet the national ATAA Standard and hence become eligible for various incentives offered to ATAA-endorsed programmes. This meant that tour operators in WA only needed to comply with the EcoCertification Standard to become eligible for the 5-year licences. NTAP decided, in the interest of its programme, to offer an environmental sustainability module similar to that of NEAP, so that tourism enterprises were also eligible for the extended tenure with NTAP certification.

Development of a national accreditation body

The Federal Government-provided funding for TCA in 1999 to support a national certification framework (the ATAA) had not achieved widespread support. The White Paper on tourism (Australian Government, 2003) highlighted the need to establish a genuine industry-led, national, voluntary, tourism certification system within an established and more comprehensive national framework. A National Tourism Certification Working Group was established in 2003, with A$2 million in funding. Australian park agencies were included as key stakeholders, with the Department of Industry, Tourism and Resources (DITR) recognizing that tourism certification programmes have not adequately met the needs of protected area managers.

Under the direction of the Working Group and the DITR, a draft national framework was developed, which included the dissolution of the ATTA and the creation of the Tourism Accreditation Australia Limited (TAAL). TAAL is an incorporated association with board membership reflecting the sectorial and geographical interests of the Australian tourism industry. As a consequence of the role played by protected area managers in the National Certification Forum in 2003, DITR produced, in cooperation with state and territory park agencies, a draft Standard for Commercial Tour Operator Certification in Protected Areas, which details the essential requirements to be included in any tourism certification programme operating in protected areas. The new national tourism certification approval body (TAAL) was to have ensured that these guidelines were addressed when approving applications for certification programmes that operate in protected areas.

In 2004, on the eve of implementing a business plan that would have established a truly national framework and ensured that tourism certification programmes could operate more viably, the Federal Government withdrew funding for the implementation of the plan. The reasons are unclear; however, it is clear that the government turnaround was unexpected, the industry has been left floundering and Australia is no closer to achieving a truly national tourism certification system.

In mid-2005 the Federal Minister for Tourism announced that the A$2 million allocated in the tourism White Paper for tourism accreditation would be reallocated to Decipher Technologies Pty Ltd (a business arm of the Sustainable Tourism Cooperative Research Centre) to develop a tourism business and accreditation portal. The proposed web site is meant to 'assist industry to develop and market tourism accreditation and relevant products' (Bailey, 2005). As a consequence of this change in policy by the Federal Government, the draft Standard for Commercial Tour Operator Certification in Protected Areas has not been adopted.

CALM Benchmarking

In recent moves CALM's national park management plans now include key performance indicators to measure management effectiveness. This places greater pressure on protected area managers to manage the performance of commercial tour operators. CALM has developed benchmark indicators to assist in assessing applications for the reallocation of restricted licences to operate semi-permanent safari camps in the World Heritage-listed Purnululu National Park (CALM, 2004c). Licence holders will be independently audited every 12 months against their proposals and the benchmarks, with the view of moving the operations from the benchmark standards towards best practice. The lack of a credible auditing process for either of the voluntary certification programmes (EcoCertification or NTAP) has meant that, while CALM will continue to encourage operators to seek certification, it does not consider that the programmes are able to fulfil the necessary auditing and reporting requirements against the park's management plan and focus on the level of detail required to deal with these types of specific proposals in sensitive areas.

CALM's own auditing process will place a greater financial and operational burden on the operator than either certification programme because of the more complex nature of the requirements of the operational conditions, but is considered as necessary because the current certification programmes do not provide this level of monitoring. It is desirable that in the future certification programmes can achieve credible on-site audits at a level to satisfy this need, and hence the economies of scale will reduce cost to operators.

Discussion

The previous discussion has raised some concerns, challenges and benefits of certification programmes for protected area managers and agencies. In general, Australian park agencies seek a range of benefits from certification programmes:

- Tangible benefits in the form of improved environmental performance and/or a contribution to park management programmes.
- An effective tool in managing the balance between protection and use.
- Regular and effective auditing.

- Tangible benefits delivered to operators.
- Equitable support by STOs to all accredited certification programmes.
- Cost-effective certification products for operators.
- Consultation and negotiation with certification programme managers over the content and standards of certification programmes.
- Greater emphasis on risk management and safety.
- Reduced confusion among consumers.
- Transfer of administering the annual verification of compliance certificates (insurance, other licences, etc.) to certification programme managers.
- The progressive raising of the minimum standard at each level of certification.
- Improved standards for the advanced level of certification.

Park agencies also seek to use certification programmes to improve the sustainability of tourism operations in protected areas, improve visitor safety and raise the level of visitor satisfaction. Specifically they can use the programmes as a:

- Credible and effective incentive for licensing benefits such as longer-term licences and licence fee discounts.
- Prerequisite for restricted-access areas/opportunities.
- Means of progressively increasing the standards necessary for licensed access to limited-entry areas and opportunities (e.g. preferential access to special areas).
- Means of achieving performance reporting on the level of environmental performance (environmental sustainability) and levels of visitor satisfaction with commercial tourism operations.
- General demonstration that the tourism industry is responding effectively to environmental management and visitor safety issues.

It is also anticipated that in the future protected area managers will consider ways of integrating businesses that service the free independent traveller (FIT) market into certification processes. The FIT is an important segment of the tourism market and, while not well serviced by traditional tour operators, is serviced by the general travel sector (wholesalers, retailers and inbound operators often prepare itineraries for FITs). NEAP/EcoCertification or NTAP does not currently cover these sectors, and certification programme providers will need to consider how they might approach this sector of the industry and encourage certification. The need to bring FITs into the equation is highlighted by recent research by Roy Morgan's Holiday Tracking survey 2001/02 (TTF, 2004), which indicates that only 1% of people visiting a national park form part of a commercial tour group. In Western Australia's protected areas this figure is significantly higher – between 15 and 18% (CALM, 2004b). None the less, this is still a small proportion of total visitors to be focusing on with so much effort. It is apparent that this fact has not been lost on park agencies, which have taken a much broader management perspective. As certification is likely to impact on only a small proportion of park visitors, park agencies have not enthusiastically embraced certification. Park agencies have been realistic and never viewed certification as a panacea for managing all the impacts of tourism, but have recognized it is one of a suite of possible tools that can assist in providing effective management of tourism within protected areas. The more commonly used tools for visitor management, such as planning, zoning, transportation management, pricing, regulation and enforcement, good design and infrastructure, and information and education (Eagles *et al.*, 2002), will not become redundant. While the benefits of certification may only have a marginal impact on conserving the values of protected areas at this stage, park agencies have become involved in certification because it appears to have other positive effects than raw numbers suggest because:

- Tour operators have a commercial incentive to cut environmental corners.
- Tour operators can set a good or bad example that independent tourists may replicate.
- Commercial operators are expected to be more accountable.
- Certification can reduce park agency administration and monitoring.

Unfortunately, this back-seat approach of park agencies, combined with the failure of certification programme managers to better engage park agencies and develop an effective partnership, has certainly limited the potential success of mutual certification benefits and the take-up of voluntary programmes in protected areas. The fact that park agencies control access to many of the iconic nature-based tourism destinations in Australia and the vast majority of nature-based operators conduct their business at least partially in protected areas demonstrates that park agency support and involvement is crucial to the success of certification programmes.

Conclusions

Australia's protected areas are predominantly located in regional locations, and tourism is now a well-established industry within these areas. Properly managed, tourism can provide economic benefits both within and adjacent to national parks (Wearing and Neil, 1999). Increasingly, the economic and social impact of tourism in regional areas, based predominantly in protected areas, has administrative and political implications for park agencies. While it is now recognized that tourism can be used to help pay for conservation, if the balance of power shifts towards tourism and away from conservation, park values risk being irreversibly compromised. Figgis (1999) describes ecotourism as creating a double-edged sword:

> on the one hand a powerful economic argument for the creation and proper management of protected areas for their value as tourism products and on the other hand it devalues their purpose as biodiversity reserves because it creates a tendency for protected areas to be regarded first and foremost as an economic resource.

This dilemma creates pressure for tourism interests to prevail over conservation and in turn to create significant tension within park agencies, which have a dual role of providing for both tourism and conservation. For these agencies, the challenge is in achieving an acceptable balance between conservation and social and economic interests. Driml and Common (1995) suggest that an 'optimal economic solution that coincides with conservation objectives for a particular protected area is arrived at when constraints that maintain a defined standard of environmental quality are incorporated in this balance'. While this will not always provide acceptable outcomes for tourism stakeholders, the process of certification can assist operators and park agencies in defining the environmental standard and balancing economic realities.

In the 10 years since tourism certification programmes were first introduced to WA, many of the original objectives and expected benefits of certification have not been achieved or fully realized. Operator uptake has been limited, the industry has been confused about the need for generic versus sectorial certification, tourism operators have been burdened with costs, bureaucracy and paperwork, and cooperation between competing programmes has been limited. This has resulted in a catch-22 situation, where economies of scale and the necessary critical mass of certified product have not resulted, and regular and credible audits in remote areas are consequently expensive and consumer recognition remains low.

It is evident that in Australia parochialism has played a significant role in preventing uptake of different certification programmes and has significantly shaped the evolution of a number of different programmes, reflected in a fragmented certification landscape. States that have pioneered particular certification programmes have protected and promoted their own programme, often at the expense of the national interest. NEAP/EcoCertification, BBTAP and NTAP have all suffered similar problems. TQ's support for NEAP and WATC's support for NTAP and the unwillingness or inability of the two key tourism states (NSW and Queensland) to embrace a national approach to tourism certification seem to have hindered, and perhaps even discredited, the concept of certification in Australia. Certainly they seem to have stifled the development of a national programme and have added to the confusion among consumers and tourism enterprises. In WA, the perception that NEAP was entirely Queensland-focused, did not understand the WA market, was unwilling to have local representatives servicing the industry and were competing with the WA certification programme hindered uptake in the state. Unfortunately NTAP did not serve the major focus of protected areas, conservation. The desirability of having a single hybrid programme that incorporates elements of the two programmes is clear. Such a programme would allow operators to complete one application (and reduce administration costs) and meet park agencies' needs with a strong environmental focus but also credible business viability, appropriate risk management strategies and good financial skills. Indeed, CALM initiated negotiations between NTAP and NEAP to allow the programmes to form a partnership to achieve the objective of one programme. In principle, agreement was achieved, but EA unexpectedly added generic business components to the EcoCertification Program and NTAP responded by developing an environmental sustainability module, and these actions shelved the opportunity to work together.

A strong and effective national tourism certification body provides the best opportunity to improve the viability and promotion of all certification programmes by creating the necessary critical mass to make certification an essential business activity, and will assist better links and collaboration with the different certification programmes. The Federal Government's decision to abandon support for TAAL has also hindered the short-term chances of creating a national framework.

The recent move by DITR and TAPAF to develop standards based on the principles of triple-bottom-line sustainability is a direction that park agencies should support. While the status quo with regard to EcoCertification and NTAP in WA is unlikely to be resolved and strong, effective and collaborative arrangements are unlikely to eventuate, it is both parties that must share the responsibility. On a more positive note, both programmes have succeeded in improving the tourism industry's appreciation for the need for tourism certification. The initial narrow focus of NEAP has been addressed, although the lack of comprehensive national marketing, promotion and delivery programmes through the engagement of state partners has not yet occurred. NTAP has been more successful in gaining national presence, particularly in Tasmania, South Australia and Western Australia (but is yet to gain a foothold in those states with the greatest share of the tourism market, NSW and Queensland).

To meet the growing expectations of the community, including protected area managers, through government policy and to achieve recognition that it is worthy of a higher level of self-regulation, the tourism industry needs to accept the need for credible measures to demonstrate that a relaxation in the regulatory approach is warranted. All stakeholders will benefit if this can be achieved. The cost in time and resources invested by tourism operators is limiting the tourism industry's ability to adapt and grow within a fast-moving market that requires a level of flexibility. Auditing is the linchpin of any credible certification programme. Robust and regular independent auditing of programmes is the most desirable situation. Annual reviews and reporting on operations are preferable to allow park agencies to meet their reporting responsibilities and also provide regular feedback to operators. A higher participation level of certified operators will increase the viability of any auditing process.

However, it is unlikely that the incentives provided by park agencies alone will significantly impact on certification uptake. Broader industry-wide packages of coordinated and tangible incentives, such as cost savings and improved business turnover for certified operators, need to be developed. Such incentives might include 'certification-only access' to marketing programmes run by STOs, and financial incentives such as discounted marketing and membership fees for state tourism industry bodies, discounts on park agency licence fees and reduced insurance premiums.

To date, tour operators do not appear to be convinced that there are significant benefits to be gained from certification. From a park agency's perspective, there is a lack of adequate mutual benefits. This appears to be a result of poor engagement between park agencies and certification programme managers. Despite these shortcomings, certification has been a useful educational tool and has the potential for improved understanding and appreciation for the need for more sustainable tourism practices across the entire industry, from consumers to protected area mangers and operators alike.

Acknowledgements

The author would like to thank Rod Quartermaine and Alice Crabtree for their comments and assistance in writing this chapter.

Notes

[1] A Protected Area is defined by the World Conservation Union (International Union for Conservation of Nature or IUCN) as an area of land and/or sea especially dedicated to the protection and maintenance of biological diversity and of natural and associated cultural resources and managed through legal and effective means (IUCN, 1994).

[2] Biodiversity is the variety of all life forms – the different plants, animals, fungi and microorganisms, the genes they contain, and the ecosystems of which they form part. Biological diversity is considered at three levels: genetic, species and ecological (CALM, 2004e).

[3] National Competition Policy is an agreement between all Australian governments to promote enhanced competition within Australia. Competitive neutrality principles aim to remove unfair advantages government business activities have over private-sector rivals as a result of public ownership. These advantages may include exemption from taxes, lower costs of finance and exemption from regulation affecting private-sector activity (NCC, 2005).

[4] A state tourism organization (STO) is the government body responsible for the marketing and development of tourism at the state and territory level.

[5] Tourism connected businesses are those businesses other than those defined as tourism characteristic for which a tourism product is directly identifiable and where products are consumed by visitors in volumes that are significant for the visitor and/or producer (e.g. food and beverage, manufacturing, petrol stations, retailing) (Cooper and Hall, 2005).

[6] Tourism characteristic businesses are defined as a business that would either cease to exist in their present form or would be significantly affected if tourism were to cease (e.g. accommodation, travel agents, tour operators) (Cooper and Hall, 2005).

References

Australian Government (2003) *Tourism White Paper: A Medium to Long Term Strategy for Tourism.* Department of Communications, Information Technology and the Arts, Commonwealth of Australia, Canberra.

Bailey, F. (2005) Decipher to Develop National Tourism Accreditation Portal. Department of Tourism, Industry and Resources. Available at: http://minister.industry.gov.au/index (18 July 2005).

Barry, T. and Robins, P. (2001) Tourism trends and opportunities: what do they mean for regional Australia? Based on a paper presented at *Outlook 2001, ABARE's National Outlook Conference.* Bureau of Tourism Research, Canberra.

BTR (2003) *Tourism Businesses in Australia.* Occasional Paper No. 34, Bureau of Tourism Research, Canberra.

CALM (1993/94–2004/05) *Annual Reports.* Department of Conservation and Land Management, Perth, Australia.

CALM (1994) *Policy 18 – Recreation, Tourism and Visitor Services.* Department of Conservation and Land Management, Perth, Australia.

CALM (1995) *National Ecotourism Accreditation Scheme*, Vol. 1, 1995–2004, CALM File 036931F0808, Department of Conservation and Land Management, Perth, Australia.

CALM (1996) *People in CALM Places – Recreation and Tourism Strategy.* Department of Conservation and Land Management, Perth, Australia.

CALM (1999) *Tour Operator Handbook: Official Manual of Licence Conditions for Tour Operators Entering CALM Managed Lands.* Department of Conservation and Land Management, Perth, Australia.

CALM (2003) *Annual Report 2002/2003.* Department of Conservation and Land Management, Perth, Australia.

CALM (2004a) *Annual Report 2003/2004.* Department of Conservation and Land Management, Perth, Australia.

CALM (2004b) *RATIS: Recreation and Tourism Information System.* Department of Conservation and Land Management, Perth, Australia.

CALM (2004c) *Semi-permanent Accommodation in Purnululu National Park: Expressions of Interest and Request for Proposals – Guidelines for Submissions.* Department of Conservation and Land Management, Perth, Australia.

CALM (2004d) *Tour Operator Handbook: Terrestrial.* Department of Conservation and Land Management, Perth, Australia.

CALM (2004e) *Towards a Biodiversity Conservation Strategy for Western Australia: Discussion Paper.* Department of Conservation and Land Management, Government of Western Australia, Perth, Australia.

CALM (2005a) *Annual Report 2004/2005.* Department of Conservation and Land Management, Perth, Australia.

CALM (2005b) *RATIS: Recreation and Tourism Information System.* Department of Conservation and Land Management, Perth, Australia.

CALM and WATC (1997) *Memorandum of Understanding between the Western Australian Tourism Commission and the Department of Conservation and Land Management.* Department of Conservation and Land Management and Western Australian Tourism Commission, Government of Western Australia, Perth, Australia.

Carlsen, J. and Wood, D.S. (2004) *Assessment of the Economic Value of Recreation and Tourism in Western Australia's National Parks, Marine Parks and Forests.* Sustainable Tourism Cooperative Research Centre (STCRC), Brisbane, Australia.

Charters, A.I. (2000) Nature and Ecotourism Accreditation Program. In: Charters, A.I.E. and Law, K.E. (eds) *Best Practice Ecotourism in Queensland.* Tourism Queensland, Brisbane, Australia, pp. 33–55.

Chester, G. and Crabtree, A. (2002) Ecotourism and certification: setting standards in practice. In: Honey, M. (ed.) *Australia: the Nature and Ecotourism Accreditation Program.* Island Press, Washington, DC, pp. 161–186.

Cooper, C. and Hall, C.M. (2005) *Oceania: A Tourism Handbook.* Channel View Publications, Clevedon, UK.

DEH (2000) *Interim Biogeographic Regionalisation for Australia.* Department of Environment and Heritage, Canberra.

DITR (2003) *Pursuing Common Goals – Opportunities for Tourism and Conservation.* Department of Industry, Tourism and Resources, Canberra.

DoT (1994) *National Ecotourism Strategy*. Commonwealth Department of Tourism, Commonwealth of Australia, Canberra.

Driml, S. and Common, M. (1995) Economic and financial benefits in major protected areas. *Australian Journal of Environmental Management* 2(1), 19–29.

EA (2003a) *Directory of Certified Ecotourism Operators, 2003/04*. Ecotourism Australia, Brisbane.

EA (2003b) *EcoCertification*, 3rd edn. Ecotourism Australia, Brisbane.

EA (2005a) *Australian Ecotourism Directory, 2005/06*. Ecotourism Australia, Brisbane.

EA (2005b) EcoTourism Product Search, Ecotourism Australia. Available at: http://www.ectourism.org.au (accessed 1 August 2005).

EAA (1996) *National Ecotourism Accreditation Program*. Ecotourism Association of Australia, Brisbane.

EAA (1998) *Australian Ecotourism Guide 1998/99*. Ecotourism Association of Australia, Brisbane.

EAA (2000) *NEAP: Nature and Ecotourism Certification Program*. Ecotourism Association of Australia, Brisbane.

EAA (2001) *Australian Ecotourism Guide 2001*. Ecotourism Association of Australia, Brisbane.

Eagles, P.F.J. (1994) Ecotourism and parks: do or die. In: *Changing Parks, A Conference on the History, Future and Cultural Context of Parks and Heritage Landscapes. Peterborough, Ontario*. University of Waterloo, Ontario, Canada.

Eagles, P.F.J., McCool, S.F. and Haynes, C.D. (2002) *Sustainable Tourism in Protected Areas: Guidelines for Planning and Management*. IUCN – the World Conservation Union, Gland, Switzerland.

Figgis, P.J.F. (1999) *Australia's National Parks and Protected Areas: Future Directions*. Australian Committee for IUCN Inc. (World Conservation Union), Eagle Press, Adelaide.

Foster, D. (2000) *The Customer's Perception of Tourism Accreditation*. Centre for Management Quality Research, RMIT University, Melbourne.

Government of Western Australia (2003) *Hope for the Future: the Western Australian State Sustainability Strategy*. State Government of Western Australia, Perth.

ISO (2005) ISO 9000 and ISO 14000 – in brief. International Standards Organization. Available at: http://www.iso.org/iso/en/iso9000-14000/understand/inbrief.html (16 August 2005).

IUCN (1994) *Guidelines for Protected Area Management Categories*. Commission on National Parks and Protected Areas, Gland, Switzerland.

Lindberg, K. and Denstadli, J. (2003) *The Impacts of National Park Visitation on Rural Economies and Government Revenue in Queensland*. Sustainable Tourism Cooperative Research Centre, Goldcoast, Australia.

McArthur, S. (1998) *Embracing the Future of Ecotourism: Sustainable Tourism and EAA in the New Millennium*. Unpublished report.

McDonald, J. (2003) Financial liability of park managers to visitor injuries. In: Buckley, R., Pickering, C. and Weaver, D.B. (eds) *Nature-based Tourism, Environment and Land Management*. CAB International, Wallingford, UK, pp. 35–50.

Manidis Roberts Consultants (1994a) *Formulating a National Ecotourism Accreditation Scheme*. Information leaflet.

Manidis Roberts Consultants (1994b) *An Investigation into a National Ecotourism Accreditation Scheme*. Commonwealth Department of Tourism, Canberra.

NCC (2005) National Competition Program Agreements, National Competition Council. Available at: www.ncc.gov.au (accessed 27 July 2005).

Page, S.L. and Dowling, R.K. (2002) *Ecotourism*. Pearson Education, Harlow, UK.

Pouliquen-Young, O. (1997) Evolution of the system of protected areas in Western Australia. *Environmental Conservation* 24, 168–181.

Shadbolt, R. (2003) Ecotourism certification as a tool for raising guiding standards – options for Rottnest Island. Unpublished.

Sharp, J.R. (1992) *Ecotourists: Saving or Sinking Noah's Ark, Ecotourism Business in the Pacific: Promoting a Sustainable Experience*. Department of Conservation and Land Management, Perth, Australia.

Shea, S.R. (1997) Integrated Approach to Conservation, Public Land and Wildlife Management and Commercial Forestry – Case Study Western Australia. Presented to the *New Zealand Forest Research Institute's 50th Jubilee Celebration Day, Rotorua, New Zealand*. Department of Conservation and Land Management, Perth, Australia.

Shea, S.R. and Sharp, J.R. (1993) Western Australia's Natural Advantage – Capitalising on the Nature Based Tourism Potential of the North, in Management. A paper presented to the *Northern Australia Development Council's Over the Horizon Conference. Exmouth, Western Australia*. Department of Conservation and Land Management, Perth, Australia.

Steffen, C. (2004) Parks and tourism perspectives: an industry perspective. In: Buckley, R. (ed.) *Tourism in Parks: Australian Initiatives*. International Centre for Ecotourism Research, Griffith University, Goldcoast, Queensland, Australia, pp. 55–78.

TABV (2005) Tourism Accreditation: Frequently Asked Questions for Businesses, Tourism Accreditation Board of Victoria Inc. Available at: http://www.tourismaccreditationvic.com.au (16 July 2005).

TCWA (2003) *National Tourism Accreditation Program, Strategic Plan 2004–2008*. Tourism Council of Western Australia, Perth, Australia.

Tisdell, C.A. and Roy, K.C. (eds) (1998) *Tourism and Development: Economic, Social, Political and Environmental Issues*. Nova Science Publishers Inc., Commack, New York.

TTF (2004) *A Natural Partnership: Making National Parks a Tourism Priority: Executive Summary*. Tourism and Transport Forum Australia Ltd (TTF), Sydney.

WATC (2001) *Western Australian Environmental Tourism Packages*. Western Australian Tourism Commission, Perth.

WATC and CALM (1997) *Nature-based Tourism Strategy for Western Australia*. Department of Conservation and Land Management, Western Australian Tourism Commission, Perth, Australia.

Wearing, S. and Neil, J. (1999) *Ecotourism: Impacts, Potentials and Possibilities*. Butterworth Heinemann, Oxford.

Wells, M., Brandon, K. and Hannah, L.J. (1992) *People and Parks: Linking Protected Area Management with Local Communities*. International Bank for Reconstruction and Development, Washington, DC.

Worboys, G. and De Lacy, T. (2003) Tourism and the environment: it's time! In: *11th National Ecotourism Australia Conference. National Wine Centre, Adelaide, South Australia*. Sustainable Tourism Cooperative Research Centre, Goldcoast, Australia.

Worboys, G., Lockwood, M. and De Lacy, T. (2001) *Protected Area Management: Principles and Practice*. Oxford University Press, Melbourne, Australia.

Worboys, G., Lockwood, M. and De Lacy, T. (2005) *Protected Area Management: Principles and Practice*, 2nd edn. Oxford University Press, Melbourne, Australia.

WTO (2005) World Tourism Barometer, World Tourism Organisation. Available at: www.world-tourism.org (accessed 4 May 2005).

16 Certification of Protected Areas: the Case of PAN Parks in Europe

XAVIER FONT[1] AND SUE CLARK[2]

[1]Leeds Metropolitan University, Leeds, UK; [2]Glion Institute of Higher Education, Switzerland

Chapter Profile

This chapter reflects on the ability of PAN (Protected Area Network) Parks to deliver the expected benefits of certification to both national parks and stakeholder tourism businesses in Europe. The anticipated benefits included an improvement of the product through better management and an increased volume of business from certification branding and marketing. There is some evidence of increased performance in the field but little evidence of additional trade. This is unfortunate as the expected increase in business was a key pull factor for applicants. PAN Parks promotes and certifies stakeholder partnerships for continuous improvement towards sustainability. The challenges arise from certifying not one firm but a partnership, which makes it harder to locate responsibilities and identify budgets and mandates. The costs of implementing the certification programme are high because of different languages, cultures and geographical constraints, and PAN Parks is presently only reaching the low-hanging fruit. A period of consolidation and capacity building needs to occur so that economies of scale reduce the costs of getting new parks to meet the standards and that appropriate marketing benefits are provided for certified parks.

Introduction

Little research has been undertaken on the benefits that certification brings to the PAN Parks applicant. This chapter reviews the perception of national park managers and local partner tourism firms that are either certified or are candidates of PAN Parks (see Fig. 16.1), the certification programme for European protected areas initiated in 1997 by the World Wide Fund for Nature (or, in the USA, World Wildlife Fund – WWF) and the Dutch Leisure Company Molecaten. The Protected Area Network (PAN) of Parks has four aims: first, to create an European network of wilderness protected areas; secondly, to improve nature protection by sustainable tourism development; thirdly,

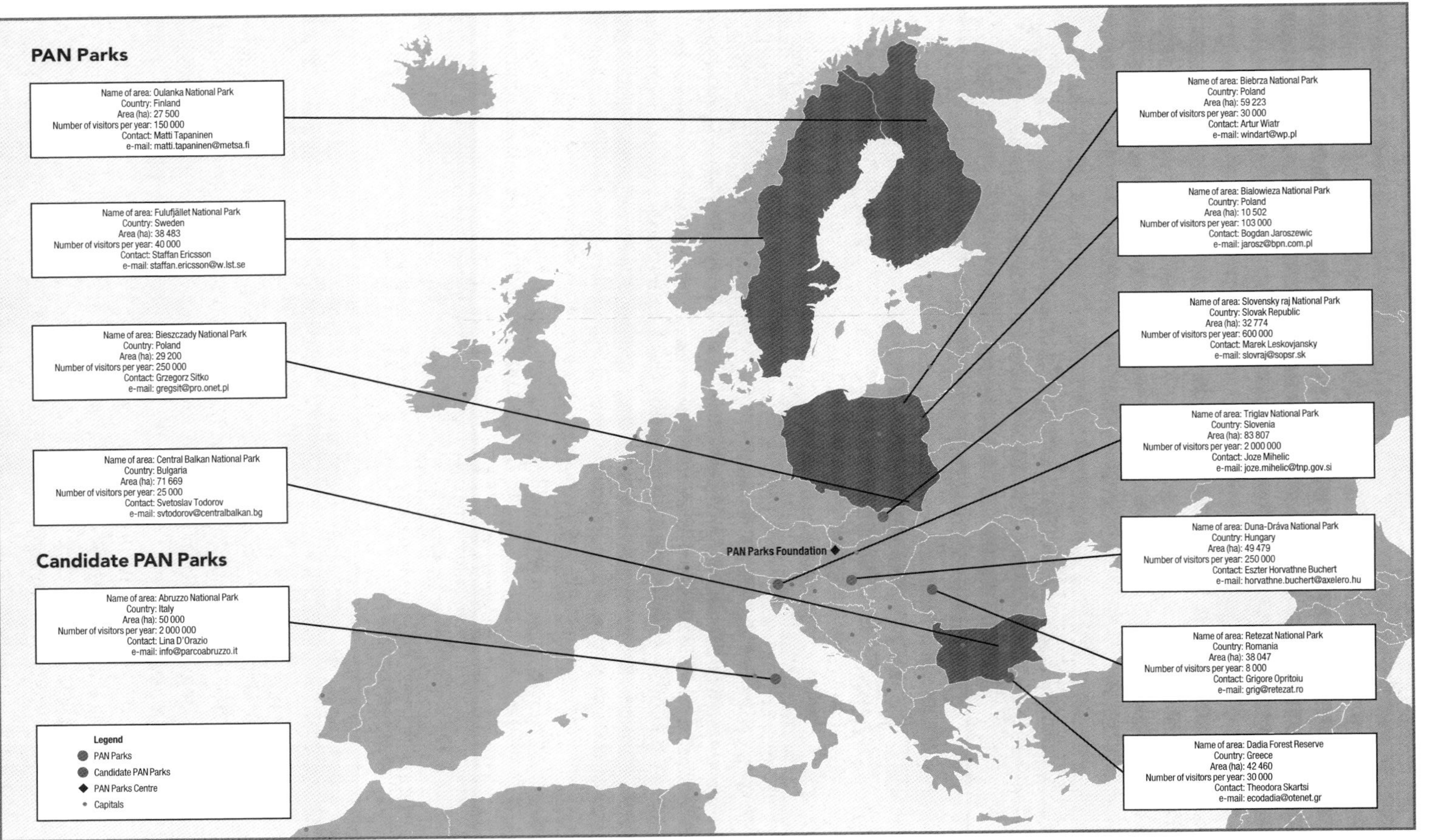

Fig. 16.1. Certified and candidate PAN Parks.

to provide a reliable trademark that guarantees nature protection and is recognized by all Europeans; and, finally, to involve local businesses in the development of a sustainable tourism strategy that forms part of the verification process itself. As such, this new trademark is awarded to parks with outstanding nature and high-quality tourism facilities that are balanced with wilderness protection, and to the tourism business partners who contribute to make this happen. The PAN Parks trademark aims to communicate to tourists that their visit contributes to the protection of the natural area. In this manner, tourism provides a unique chance to raise people's awareness of their environment and to communicate conservation messages.

WWF developed the PAN Parks programme as a sustainable development tool to promote conservation by emphasizing the benefits of sustainable production and consumption through a partnership approach. The key element of this partnership is assigning intrinsic economic value to nature preservation long-term, rather than consumption of resources within protected areas. Among the management tools applied by parks and their business partners to meet nature management and quality requirements are those based on protection of ecosystem dynamics, as well as systems to meet key performance indicators on visitor management, tourism strategy and contribution of business partners (Font and Brasser, 2002). Critical to the vision of PAN Parks is the belief that local communities immediately adjacent to the parks should benefit economically in a way that is sustainable and in keeping with the natural values of the area. The initiative aims to put economic value into European nature, as a means of affording greater protection. By so doing, it aims to create a form of tourism that is not a threat but an opportunity. Partnerships with nature conservation organizations, travel agencies, the business community and other interest groups on a local, national and international level are set up to try and ensure the effectiveness of the process PAN Parks envisions for itself.

This vision is a brand bringing together parks with natural heritage and model management practices that enables visitors to enjoy wilderness, in the form of ancient forests and wild mountain ranges, peatlands and unspoiled rivers. PAN Parks documentation (Kun, 1999) cites specific benefits that are conveyed to applicants who are interested in starting the process of verification. The concept provides a nature conservation-based response to the growing market for nature-oriented tourism. The brand uses the bylines 'people, respect, nature' and 'preserve, support and enjoy Europe's wilderness' to convey a message linking people and economic benefit directly with the preservation of nature and the wilderness concept. The unique selling proposition is that the parks are the natural treasures of Europe where visitors are welcome and their visit can help protect the area. The programme aims to bring four benefits:

1. Independent verification aiming at improving the quality of management and the wilderness experience for visitors in European protected areas.
2. Strong marketing of the concept and certified parks in cooperation with tourism businesses, especially tour operators.
3. Developing a common communications approach towards people interested in green tourism.

4. Creating partnerships with local communities and local/small-scale businesses in order to implement a sustainable tourism development strategy on a regional scale.

PAN Parks aims to be the 'flag carrier' for key sites of European nature and wilderness areas, the guardian of Europe's iconic natural heritage sites. The network is proposed to expand throughout Europe and to include protected areas reflecting the natural diversity of the whole region. Within this vision are inherent problems relating to the reality of protected area status in much of Europe. Many protected areas are not managed effectively for biodiversity, with logging, mining and hunting continuing to be pursued as everyday activities. WWF believes in the need for a greater number of effectively managed protected areas linked by corridors, protected by buffer zones and designed to maximize resilience to threats. When WWF surveyed some 3000 protected areas in 39 European countries, only 134 (fewer than 1% of Europe's total protected areas) met the conservation organization's criteria for well-managed parks that could allow them to eventually meet the requirements needed to achieve the PAN Parks trademark (Kun, 2002).

For a park to pre-qualify as a potential PAN Park it requires 20,000 ha of protected land, with at least 10,000 ha of protected core zone – the minimum deemed necessary to provide a wilderness experience by restoring and/or maintaining natural processes in ecosystems, a tall order for much of Europe. This essentially means that only the most peripheral and/or economically depressed regions in Europe will qualify, with most of these located in Central and Eastern Europe and Scandinavian countries. The report by Kun (2002) identifies protected areas in relatively good condition and with good potential for achieving the PAN Parks trademark in Scandinavia, Russia, Central Europe and the east Mediterranean. However, the findings also show that most protected areas in Western Europe, on the Atlantic coast and in the west Mediterranean are in a relatively bad condition. Lack of protection in supposedly protected ecosystems and natural processes in eight Baltic and Adriatic coast regions is alarming (Kun, 2002).

Problems already exist in relation to appropriate tourism development within those areas designated as having high potential to become certified by PAN Parks. For example, most Central and Eastern European countries have existing tourist destinations, usually catering to regional and domestic visitors. Bulgaria has a rapidly developing coastal tourism product, which is attracting an increasing number of international mass tourists, drawn by the low cost. Inland, the Central Balkan National Park attracts mostly Bulgarians travelling from Sofia, though there are some examples of specialist small-scale tour operators focusing on the park and its activities. Poland's national parks already receive quite high levels of visitation, mostly from domestic tourists or those from bordering countries. Otherwise the country is not particularly renowned for its tourism product apart from historic cities such as Krakow.

Despite the different nature of their tourism products and levels of development, these countries face similar challenges in developing international tourism. First, they must develop the infrastructure necessary for quick access beyond the gateway points to diversify tourism products and spread economic benefits geographically. In Bulgaria, for example, the problem of poor roads is compounded by poor signposting, which is mostly in Cyrillic script, posing another barrier to the international tourist. In most countries, international tourism concentrates on the capital cities (TTI, 1999), while in the Adriatic and parts of the Mediterranean it is locked in coastal resorts (Hall, 2003). Secondly, in Bieszcady and the Central Balkans, there have been problems with poor-quality accommodation. However, in the course of research for this chapter, it was found that many local businesses are trying hard to create high-quality accommodation and attractions. The problem is compounded by difficulties in both communication and levels of service quality. This relates to the third point that staff training, particularly at supervisory and management levels, is critical to meet international standards of service delivery without destroying the integrity of local culture. Fourthly, most countries have inadequate facilities for hiking and adventure activities, particularly for independent tourists but also for groups (Nowaczek and Fennell, 2002; Hall, 2003). These needs express themselves in a shortage of marked trails, poor interpretation, a lack of proper guiding and inadequate equipment for many of the activities that are offered.

Scandinavian countries also have the natural characteristics that make them suitable for establishing PAN Parks, but share only some of the challenges of their Central and Eastern European counterparts in so far as their most suitable sites are on the periphery of Europe (see Brown and Hall, 2000, for a review of the challenges and opportunities of tourism in peripheral areas). The latitude, high prices and healthy economies mean that the majority of tourism will be domestic, relying on unique selling propositions to attract international niche tourist markets (Andersson and Huse, 1998). Oulanka National Park in Finland, for example, is relatively well promoted to both domestic and overseas markets and receives significant numbers of Dutch tourists, drawn by winter tourism, 'Lapland' and the tranquillity of the area.

Methodology

This chapter reviews the ability of the PAN Parks certification programme to deliver benefits to applicants, and considers the challenges confronting this organization in doing so, including expectations and perceived benefits under the headings of improved management and marketing. The challenges and costs relating to the management of the expectations created and the actual achievement of these benefits are then discussed, with an emphasis on meeting the criteria and the verification requirements. In a series of interviews, relevant stakeholders in PAN Parks were asked to comment on their views of the potential benefits of PAN Parks, and these were compared with the aims of the PAN Parks Foundation and the literature. Open-ended face-to-face interviews were held with stakeholders involved in each of the currently verified PAN Parks. These stakeholders included national park staff at all levels, local business people, community representatives and in some cases local and regional government officials. The interview questions were informed by the outcomes of the consultation undertaken during the International Year of Ecotourism for the World Ecotourism Summit regional preparatory meetings, which highlighted a range of benefits and costs, summarized in Table 16.1 (Sallows and Font, 2004).

Between April and October 2004, interviews were carried out in four certified national parks: Central Balkans (Bulgaria), Fulufjället (Sweden), Oulanka (Finland) and Bieszcady (Poland), as well as candidate parks Monte Sibillini and Abruzzo (Italy) and Duna Drava (Hungary). It should be noted that the

Table 16.1. Park managers' perceived benefits and costs of certification as a sustainability tool: International Year of Ecotourism results (adapted from Sallows and Font, 2004).

Benefits	Challenges and costs
Management • Source of criteria for sustainability and quality (manuals, advice) • Environmental and social improvement • Improved efficiency • Developing product goodwill through marketing of certification • Improved sustainability – social, environmental and economic *Marketing* • Method does differentiate quality of service/product • Expected that it will increase competitiveness in the marketplace • Expected increased access to government incentives/benefits (marketing, grants) • Access to better markets of tourism • The development of consumer-friendly products *Credibility* • Consumers benefit by having a sustainable product offering • It represents the development of a new tourism market segment • Fosters a good reputation for a business • Effective for branding tourism products • Promotes a higher-value clientele	• Not an effective tool to generate demand, market is not present • When known, the market perceives that certification increases prices • No regulatory systems or legislation to support implementation • Challenge of implementing monitoring system • There are no accepted ecotourism criteria • Inequitable access to certification • Certification could legitimize larger companies and disenfranchise local communities and small firms • Expensive tool • Low feasibility of implementation in developing countries • Perception it could become part of political favours and corruption • Cost of developing reliable, effective baseline data • The benefits derived from current certification programmes come at too high a cost • Lengthy development and application in terms of training, process, systems, facilities, promotion and capacity building • Enormous financial costs in terms of technology and technical expertise • The need for capacity building • The establishment of an auditing framework • Limitations to the size of the ventures, reducing the amount of revenue from certification • Time required for implementation

parks are in countries with widely different cultures and levels of economic and tourist development. However, what was most notable was that many of the issues pertinent to local communities were in fact very similar whether, for example, in Finland or Bulgaria. What these communities have in common is more than what divides them, for the purpose of providing quality ecotourism: that is, being remote rural areas with relatively high unemployment and low incomes was found to be a more significant factor than the relative wealth of their respective countries. Although all areas are relatively poor in terms of comparison with national and European standards, the problems of 'real rural poverty' are much higher in Bulgaria and Poland than in Sweden and Finland, both of which have well-structured social benefit systems. And yet the interviewees repeatedly mentioned a number of common problems for their poor-quality product, such as rural economic deprivation, ageing populations as young people leave to explore urban opportunities, relatively low levels of business experience, lack of contact with foreigners and poor language skills. These reasons may have been mentioned because parks that have applied to PAN Parks for verification are primarily located in areas within Europe that are less well known and are seeking to increase their profile with tourists or as a mechanism to lobby for the maintenance of protected areas by governments. In general, the most popular European parks have not applied for PAN Parks status because they either do not possess the necessary criteria or, as in the case of Mercantour (France), they became nervous about the potential influx of tourists if they became a PAN Park, or because they perceive PAN Parks to have insufficient benefits for the effort required.

Benefits of PAN Parks

The benefits mentioned by the interviewees coincide closely with the aims set out by PAN Parks and those identified in the literature (Font and Buckley, 2001; Honey, 2002; WTO, 2002; Sallows and Font, 2004). Two categories of benefits were mentioned: management benefits, which will help improve the sustainability and quality of the tourism product; and marketing benefits, usually in the form of additional business from increased exposure to international markets. This categorization may seem artificial at first; however, it allows comparison in future research against other policy tools that might contribute only either to product development or to marketing. The four key management benefits mentioned were increased quality of tourism product, conservation benefits, stakeholder collaboration and training, while the dominant marketing benefits are branding, tourist demand and political and public support for conservation.

Management of PAN Parks

PAN Parks applicants expect that this programme will improve the quality of the tourism product, both in the parks and in the adjacent communities, as pride of place is maintained or restored. Partners focus on the management of the visitor experience within the context of expectations derived from a branded product. However, currently there are no data available to confirm that visitor satisfaction has increased as a result of service improvements derived from being certified, and, as the first PAN Parks were only verified in 2002, such data will not be available for some time.

Nevertheless, PAN Parks can claim to have supported increased protection of nature. Two of the first certified parks, Fulufjället and Central Balkans, became national parks at the same time as they were certified by PAN Parks. Certification has created a particular dynamic within the local communities adjacent to the parks: that is, people living around both new parks perceive that they have lost economic benefits through the loss of traditional activities such as hunting and forestry. Yet PAN Parks is at pains to compensate for such losses to the local communities involved through the introduction of new activities, such as tourism, by placing an intrinsic economic benefit and value on conservation.

PAN Parks has become an important vehicle for stakeholder relationships, addressing many institutional constraints in the development of tourism, and the expectations of many interviewees is that certification can become a tool to increase efficiency of business communications. PAN Parks cooperates with national parks, local communities and businesses, international organizations and business partners for the benefit of both nature conservation and the local economy. 'The establishment of partnerships helps the sustainable development of visitor services, promotes the area's tourist potential, and helps provide employment for local people', said Zbigniew Niewiadomski, Deputy Director of Bieszcady National Park (personal communication, September 2003).

Applying for PAN Parks certification has meant that the park and local firms have had to develop joint plans and programmes of action in a way that had not happened previously. These partnerships increase the planning and the development of local opportunities that can create a platform for sound ecotourism product development (WTO, 2003). In Fulufjället, Oulanka and Central Balkans, local PAN Park groups are operating and, at the time of writing this chapter, it is hoped that they will be established in Bieszcady and Retezat also. The format of the local goup varies between countries and reflects local law and situations, as a key part of their activitiy is to develop a sustainable tourism development strategy that is acceptable to partners and appropriate to the region.

The challenge is to use certification as an enabling process, and yet this approach conflicts with the trend in Eastern Europe to move away from regulating growth, as this is reminiscent of old communist ways, and many are suspicious of further intervention. Self-regulation is likely to bring its own share of complexities, starting with the challenge of educating both the public and private sector on its meaning, benefits and implementation. In Eastern European countries there is a lack of coordination between public-sector agencies, as well as no tradition of entrepreneurial public–private-sector partnerships (Nowaczek and Fennell, 2002). It is unrealistic to expect the creation of stakeholder partnerships in the short term, as experienced in donor-funded projects that required local partnerships in Romania and Bulgaria (Roberts and Simpson, 1999). The experience of the Pirin Tourism Forum is similar to that of the local PAN Parks groups (the networks set up around parks to manage the process of writing and implementing a sustainable tourism development strategy) in developing local capacity and supporting and ensuring quality tourism products. This forum has faced considerable inter-municipality competition for breaking away from joint strategies (Roberts and Simpson, 1999). In this context it is understandable that the most challenging of the PAN Parks criteria have been those that require public–private-sector partnership. The PAN Parks verification team had to accept a two-stage certification process, first focusing on environmental criteria, and leaving as second stage the social/tourism management-related criteria that require partnerships.

Bieszcady's local PAN Parks coordinator, Gregory Sitko (personal communication, 8 October 2004), explained that intially they thought PAN Parks would be like surgery that would solve their problems and start bringing tourists in immediately. Since then, they realize that what it has done is give them the understanding and capacity to take control, and from here to take decisions that they follow through.

There are expectations from the parks and local communities of certification being a vehicle for training. Glion Institute of Higher Education (Switzerland) carried out a training needs assessment during 2004 to prioritize the needs of both park staff and local businesses. The results of this exercise reveal a striking commonality of needs, indicating that foreign languages, marketing, interpretation of nature and visitor management are of primary importance to all parks. Parks have also struggled with the preparation and application of sustainable tourism development strategies. The training will be delivered by PAN Parks' own network meetings, focusing on the identification of training needs. It is hoped that external funding will allow futher specific training at the local level.

PAN Parks is aiming for a change from consumptive to non-consumptive use of these protected areas. This means reducing, and in the core zones forbidding, activities such as hunting, fishing and grazing, as well as motorized transport such as snowmobiles. The loss of these activities is perceived as a serious disadvantage by many people and there are real difficulties for some domestic markets to appreciate the concept of ecotourism and to behave accordingly in protected areas (Nowaczek and Fennell, 2002). In Oulanka in Finland, there have been problems with semi-domestic reindeer entering the park and, in both Oulanka and Fulufjället, the traditional 'rights of everyman' for free access to all public lands have created issues concerning the zoning of highly fragile areas. In addition, around the Central Balkan Park, many traditional local accommodation providers claim to have suffered a significant decrease in visitors since hunting was prohibited. These restrictions on activities are accepted by the local stakeholders because there is an expectation that these activities will be replaced by lower-impacting tourism. The financial benefits arising from efficiency-based cost cuts, for example in hotels through water–waste–energy management, are not available to national parks and will not offset the costs of participating in a certification programme. PAN Parks is therefore expected to be a vehicle to realizing expectations of an economic turnaround and creating economic benefits that can substitute for any loss of traditional activities and can help retain younger people in rural communities. The implications of these points are reviewed below in the marketing section.

Marketing of PAN Parks

Over two-thirds of the benefits stated by the interviewees related to marketing, in terms of both expectations and concerns about the inability to deliver: in particular, issues related to PAN Parks providing the potential for being part of an internationally known and recognized quality brand. Business stakeholders viewed marketing as essentially connected with promotion, rather than product development, which is more a management benefit, while park authorities usually had difficulties in coming to terms with marketing in relation to their own activities.

PAN Parks sees its trademark as a new opportunity for green tourism development, which will attract tourists who want to enjoy true wilderness, in the knowledge that their visit does little harm to the environment. The organization expects that it will also open economic opportunities to local businesses who are invited to become PAN Parks partners. PAN Parks aims to improve the management of protected areas, using sustainable tourism as a tool. PAN Parks partners can use PAN Parks international communications and marketing channels to gain support in effectively combining sustainable tourism development and nature protection. The current certified PAN Parks, however, are not the most spectacular nature sites in Europe, though they are some of the most valuable and endangered. However, the two things are not the same and the tourist does not get the 'wow factor' from these parks. Their remoteness is partly the reason why they are less developed, and yet it does not necessarily add value to the tourist experience. The concept of PAN Parks is quite difficult for consumers to understand, and much more needs to be done to clarify the nature of the brand and what it stands for before the public can become supporters of PAN Parks. A similar example, if not a original concept but an effective promotional tool, is the World Heritage brand. These sites as designated by UNESCO and have a high level of brand recognition, and yet concerns have been expressed that this brand has become overstretched and its credibility could start to wane. PAN Parks has to be aware of the same phenomenon in the long term. That said, World Heritage Site (WHS) designation was not devised with marketing in mind, and yet it was found that WHS branding has a significant impact on international tourism visitation, as tour operators advertise the fact that their trips include WH sites, and park managers use this status in lobbying stakeholders (Buckley, 2004).

As the PAN Parks brand is not only applied to the parks themselves but also to participating tourism businesses, it is critical to see brand marketing as important beyond the promotion of managing nature and wilderness alone. Instead, in order for the local communities to optimize their benefits, they must understand that local hospitality and other offerings to tourists must also be of a high standard. During the annual PAN Parks conference in the Central Balkans (October 2004), several local entrepreneurs said this was usually equated to 'international-style hotels and restaurants'. This might be seen to contradict the ethos of ecotourism and locally sustainable tourism, which favour local distinctiveness and uniqueness as part of the tourism product. What is needed is high-quality, small-scale accommodation (some large enough for specialist tour operators with small groups), excellent local guiding and quality activities for tourists, for example hiking and canoeing, local retailing and local food. Where possible, PAN Parks should strive to highlight and promote local culture, food and retailing to optimize economic benefits and match tourists' expectations. If the PAN Parks brand is to be taken seriously by tourists, local products must be high-quality.

The designation of a quality brand to a national park, to a tour operator or to a local business partner may raise the expectations of the tourists. Currently, one of the key issues that PAN Parks faces is that these expectations of high quality may not be met. From the conservationist's point of view, there is no doubt that the quality of the natural environment is the key concern. However, tourists want quality in terms of scenery and/or flora and fauna. PAN Parks must be aware of the competition it faces, especially in Northern Europe; for example, reaching Oulanka (Finland) takes as long and can cost as much as reaching some of the African game parks or some US national parks.

From a marketing perspective, the challenge is in creating a message that raises appropriate expectations that can be met satisfactorily. At the moment, this message is lacking or at best confusing. More research should be done (and is planned) on what the PAN Parks brand means to people, particularly in relation to wilderness. Wilderness as a concept is difficult to define and in fact is rather hard to translate in some European languages. Main entrances to at least two of the parks, Oulanka and Fulufjället, are often crowded and sometimes littered, thereby negating the feeling of the wilderness experience. Certified PAN Parks have actually only existed since 2002 and therefore perhaps it is not surprising that their visibility has been limited. To assist marketing, PAN Parks has given each of the parks a small grant to create a visibility package for the brand. In Fulufjället a map was created, in Oulanka a tourist trail, and in Bieszcady each entrance ticket to the park has the PAN Parks logo on it.

Marketing benefits need to be understood more broadly than attracting additional visitors; namely in the context of wider public and political support for protected areas through changing attitudes and stimulating their economic value. These benefits are the main interest of the park authorities. PAN Parks has managed to attract support from non-governmental organizations (NGOs) and officials in each of the countries where it has certified a park. For example, WWF recognized the three first PAN Parks in Sweden, Finland and Poland as model parks for nature tourism and effective park management on 17 September 2002, with an international launch of the new trademark for tourism and nature protection. The following year, Central Balkan National Park was opened as a national park and received its certificate from the Prime Minister of Bulgaria. The Bulgarian government used this event to promote themselves as ready to join the European Union and were obviously proud of joining a new venture like PAN Parks. However, it remains to be seen if the high level of political support evident at the opening fanfare of all these parks will translate into long-term support for management and conservation issues. On a more positive note, in 2005 WWF International reported to PAN Parks that the Swedish Ministry of Environment had indicated a requirement that in future all Swedish national parks should strive to achieve the standards set by PAN Parks.

Certification's Ability to Meet Expectations

While both certified and applicant PAN Parks report a range of benefits, there is an equally long list of challenges and costs that parks face both to behave in a more sustainable way and to prove this to PAN Parks for verification purposes. Many of these were raised in the context of improved management and marketing of the certified parks in previous sections. This section will discuss the feasibility of providing benefits through working towards the set of criteria, and the ability of the verification procedures to ensure standards.

There are few attempts to certify tourist destinations as a whole, with the Green Globe destination standard and the European Federation of Parks (EUROPARC) Charter for Sustainable Tourism being the exceptions. This is because of the complexity of setting meaningful and measurable indicators, coupled with the challenges of setting implementable plans for action that identify responsibilities. The most challenging part of the PAN Parks requirement is the need for a sustainable tourism development strategy based on public–private dialogue and partnership. The benefits of such partnerships in managing national parks are well established in a variety of contexts (Eagles *et al.*, 2002; Tourism Council Australia, 2003), and stakeholder collaboration is key to the certification of destinations through programmes such as Green Globe. Fulufjället's PAN Parks coordinator Janet Jander said the main benefit of PAN Parks certification was to use this opportunity to look beyond their geographical boundaries and to acknowledge they have a role to play in the livelihoods of neighbouring communities. She said this should have been done earlier, but the opportunity had not arisen until PAN Parks was presented as a vehicle (personal communication, 8 October 2004). What makes PAN Parks different is the way in which partnerships are embedded in the criteria. Each park is required to have its own local group responsible for local verification, coordination of activites and management of the park and its partners. In recognition of local cultural differences, the local groups have been given freedom to adopt a format that best suits their specific requirements. This contributes to ecotourism quality because one of the principal characteristics of ecotourism is the involvement and agreement of the local community in setting the agenda for its own tourism development.

Three aspects of the verification process undertaken by PAN Parks ensure that local communites are empowered to prescribe the kind of tourism development that is most relevant and appropriate to them. The first aspect is the Sustainable Tourism Development Strategy. PAN Parks has developed a manual that provides guidelines for the preparation of such a strategy. However, each park is free to develop a strategy that is relevant to local conditions and the existing level of tourism development.

Secondly, each of the local PAN Parks groups can define its own area to include those communities and attractions it deems appropriate. In the case of Fulufjället, where the local population closest to the park is about 300 people, it was considered essential to draw in communities like Sarna from slightly further afield and outside the park's buffer zone.

Thirdly, the local PAN Parks group themselves are trained for and become responsible for verifying and certifying their own local membership. In this way, an internal quality mechanism is set up, which has the potential to regulate the integrity of local tourism development and commitment to locally sustainable ecotourism. The existing groups in Fulufjället and Oulanka have adopted a fairly informal forum structure without taking a legal identity. Groups are still in the process of formation in the Central Balkans, Bieszcady and Retezeat, but are expected to have a more formal legal status. However, there are challenges in running partnerships with limited mandates and no funding. How local PAN Parks groups will be funded and who will participate are repeated points of discussion at annual conferences and networking events. It is hoped the local groups will be representative of a range of tourism stakeholders and will seek and achieve consensus. The objective of PAN Parks is not only to provide for an exchange of ideas but also to promote the implementation of local projects and initiatives. To address this issue the PAN Parks Foundation established a Small Grants Fund supporting candidate PAN Parks in building the potential to contribute to the Foundation's goals, which are effective management of protected areas and sustainable tourism development. It is intended to give financial help to protected areas for the implementation of PAN Parks principles and criteria. Currently, the Small Grants Fund only accepts applications from PAN Parks and candidate PAN Parks; consequently, the cost–benefit of providing such grants has not been evaluated to date, but it is certainly instrumental in setting partnerships in motion.

The consequences of community partnerships are that PAN Parks is setting standards for larger sites, with more than one management or operating unit, and yet a key challenge comes from setting and ensuring standards for sites such as national parks where the land is owned and managed, or at least used, by more than one management unit. For those principles and criteria where the national park authority has sole responsibility and control over the management of the verification process and has managed to find evidence of compliance, the park authority has been fairly sure about the information. The greatest challenges relate to the management of collaboration and partnerships, particularly where responsibilities for improvements are shared and where sources of impacts cannot be identified or managed. This is most obvious in implementing the Sustainable Tourism Development Strategies. As protected areas tend to be geographically the responsibility of more than one municipality, strategies for the park that include neighbouring communities need to be the result of collaboration across different municipalities and individual businesses, with separate budgets and no structures to enforce implementation of decisions taken.

There are also specific challenges in setting standards, particularly social standards, because these can be ambiguous and because the assessment methodologies are not consistent (Font and Harris, 2004). These issues are also evident in PAN Parks, where social standards relate mainly to collaboration and partnerships. Partnerships provide access for joint decision making, and PAN Parks provides a framework for this to take place. The question here is, how are the processes required by PAN Parks affected by inherent power relationships between the players? Can PAN Parks legitimize inequitable power, or does it empower in an equitable way? The measures of participation in PAN Parks are rather crude, in relation to the conceptualization of measures of partnership developed by Roberts and Simpson (1999), after Jamal and Getz (1995). The challenge is also that these basic measures of participation do not encapsulate the true meaning of partnerships, and the PAN Parks process could be legitimizing them. Additional challenges arise as a result of the expectation that each local PAN Parks group will decide its own standards for local business partners that are locally relevant. PAN Parks is training these groups in establishing procedures to set their own standards. It considers that there are benefits in incorporating bottom-up standards. The benefits are engaging local people in the debate of what sustainability means in their hometowns, as well as ensuring that the standards set are relevant. Some interviewees were concerned about the transparency and credibility of the certification system, especially when verification of local business partners is undertaken by others from the local community, and the associated conflicts of interest.

Some of the interviewees mentioned the challenges and costs of PAN Parks working across geographical, linguistic and cultural barriers: the linguistic challenges (for example, all the work is produced in English, including standards and manuals, despite the fact that it is not the first language of any of the people implementing the work in the field) but also challenges arising from misunderstandings due to linguistic and cultural barriers. There are also challenges arising from the translation needs for verification purposes, as the verifiers need a local expert to translate some documents as well as explain local conditions and this means that certain indicators may not be interpreted correctly. Geographical diversity increases the operating costs of verification because ecology and wildlife management needs are different between the north and south of Europe, and verifiers need to be aware of traditions and good practices for each location. This means that the documents setting the standards are rather generic, leaving the specific site implementation down to interpretation by individual park authorities and the verifying team. The consequence is that parks sometimes struggle to understand what is expected from them, and there are many possible interpretations of the minimum threshold needed to verify that an indicator has been fulfilled.

Several interviewees expressed concern over the cost of upgrading facilities. For some of the criteria, both parks and tourism businesses will have to make investments to upgrade their tourism facilities to show that negative impacts are being reduced. So far, the work done has been to record previous work, and to set systems in place to manage processes, with no evidence available from the park authorities or the tourism businesses about actual investments to improve the sustainability of their facilities. Monitoring of how business partners are certified in the near future will provide more evidence to elaborate on this point. In order to match the expectations of PAN Parks' partners with the reality of meeting the sustainability processes and standards, in the light of the many challenges mentioned, significant amounts of money and time will need to be invested. The expense of an application for PAN Parks certification does not cover the cost of operating the certification programme. As a result, applicants to many certification programmes complain about the high cost of certification (see also Table 16.1) and in many cases certification programmes have had to set membership and verification fees to cover only variable costs, without making a contribution to the fixed costs of running the programme (Toth, 2002; Font, 2005). As application and verification costs do not cover the cost of operating the programme, the funding members, WWF Netherlands and the Molecaten Groep, are still subsidizing the fixed costs of running the programme, and PAN Parks has difficulty in raising finances from elsewhere. As has been stated elsewhere in this chapter, both of these organizations envisage that their contributions will decline in the short term and finances will need to come from elsewhere for PAN Parks to become self-sufficient. This raises issues for the organization that are perhaps beyond the scope of this chapter but nevertheless present a significant challenge for the realization of the benefits for nature and the local community that PAN Parks proposes.

The consequences of these challenges are that PAN Parks, like many other certification programmes, is collecting mainly the most accessible parks. The parks that have been certified to date generally already have good conservation and visitor management systems, and the main emphasis of their work is to improve their contribution to sustainable tourism in the region. The same issue was identified repeatedly in presentations from six certification programmes on the benefits gained from certification at the World Travel Market in 2004. The Central Balkans (Bulgaria) and Retezeat (Romania) have benefited from USAID funds to put the structures in place to manage their parks, and in the first case to develop a national strategy for ecotourism. Also national parks and state-owned properties that have a strong centralized management function at state level are more likely to have internal management structures that require regular reviews and reporting mechanisms, while smaller sites will not be in a position to generate these data from their current information systems operations. This raises questions on the ability to transfer practice to other programmes and the expectation on these pioneer pilot sites to transfer the lessons learned to others.

Conclusion

The PAN Parks certification programme is a sustainable development tool being used to promote conservation by emphasizing the benefits of sustainable production and consumption through a partnership approach. It is being used to support a number of European parks in maintaining Europe's remaining wilderness and benefiting the local communities in their hinterland areas. The programme is not operated on a cost-efficient basis and for this reason can only currently survive by supporting a small number of parks. The network of parks is expanding, but at a slower pace than the funding members, WWF and Molecaten, had expected because of the need for parks to receive support from the programme. For the PAN Parks brand to be part of the public consciousness, there needs to be a crticial mass of parks participating. Unfortunately the existing certified PAN Parks are not sites that are widely known by Europeans as key natural areas. Europeans are not generally aware of national parks outside their own country, and it is doubtful if many Western Europeans are aware of the high natural values of parks existing in countries like Poland and Bulgaria.

Systems to make PAN Parks more financially self-sustaining have been put in place in terms of external sponsorship. Certainly, PAN Parks cannot become self-sustaining unless all stakeholders, including the tourists and local and international businesses, are committed to the programme. Currently, in overall terms, it is impossible to state whether or not the PAN Parks certification programme has achieved any of the expected benefits. In terms of the parks, local businesses and the tourists, the benefits for all are mostly long-term and those challenges cited in this chapter will require considerable investment of both time and money. Park authorities as well as the PAN Parks Foundation hope this process will encourage wider public and political support for protected areas through changing attitudes and stimulating their economic value. Communities near PAN parks expect increased visitor numbers and employment opportunities. In contrast, to many park staff the concept of attracting more visitors to natural areas is something of an anathema; in fact, many would willingly prefer to limit rather than encourage visitation. Learning about sustainable tourism development strategies and stakeholder collaboration requires a significant sea change in attitudes and culture. Overall, PAN Parks is providing a useful tool to mobilize park authorities to consider their responsibility towards neighbouring communities and open their doors to collaborative arrangements with the tourism sector, but not without the danger of over-promising and under-delivering.

References

Andersson, T. and Huse, M. (1998) Scandinavia: challenging nature. In: Williams, A.M. and Shaw, G. (eds) *Tourism and Economic Development: European Experiences.* Wiley, Chichester, UK, pp. 325–344.

Brown, F. and Hall, D. (2000) *Tourism in Peripheral Areas.* Channel View, Clevedon, UK.

Buckley, R. (2004) The effects of World Heritage listing on tourism to Australian national parks. *Journal of Sustainable Tourism* 12(1), 70–84.

Eagles, P., McCool, S.F. and Haynes, C.D. (2002) *Sustainable Tourism in Protected Areas: Guidelines for Planning and Management.* IUCN – the World Conservation Union, Gland, Switzerland, and Cambridge, UK.

Font, X. (2005) Sustainability standards in the global economy. In: Theobald, W. (ed.) *Global Tourism.* Butterworth-Heinemann, Oxford, UK, pp. 213–229.

Font, X. and Brasser, A. (2002) PAN Parks: WWF's sustainable tourism certification programme in Europe's national parks. In: Harris, R., Griffin, T. and Williams, P. (eds) *Sustainable Tourism: a Global Perspective.* Butterworth-Heinemann, Oxford, UK, pp. 103–118.

Font, X. and Buckley, R. (eds) (2001) *Tourism Ecolabelling: Certification and Promotion of Sustainable Management.* CAB International, Wallingford, UK.

Font, X. and Harris, C. (2004) Rethinking standards: from green to sustainable. *Annals of Tourism Research* 31(4), 986–1007.

Hall, D. (2003) Rejuvenation, diversification and imagery: sustainability conflicts for tourism policy in the eastern Adriatic. *Journal of Sustainable Tourism* 11(2/3), 280–294.

Honey, M. (2002) *Ecotourism and Certification: Setting Standards in Practice.* Island Press, Washington, DC.

Jamal, T.B. and Getz, D. (1995) Collaboration theory and community tourism planning. *Annals of Tourism Research* 22(1), 186–204.

Kun, Z. (1999) *PAN Parks Principles and Criteria.* PAN Parks, Gyor, Hungary.

Kun, Z. (2002) *Potential PAN Parks in Europe – a Quick Scan of Protected Areas against Selected PAN Parks Indicators.* PAN Parks, Gyor, Hungary.

Nowaczek, A. and Fennell, D. (2002) Ecotourism in post-communist Poland: an examination of tourists, sustainability and institutions. *Tourism Geographies* 4, 372–395.

Roberts, L. and Simpson, F. (1999) Developing partnership approaches to tourism in Central and Eastern Europe. *Journal of Sustainable Tourism* 17(3/4), 314–330.

Sallows, M. and Font, X. (2004) Ecotourism certification criteria and procedures: implications for ecotourism planning and environmental management. In: Diamantis, D. (ed.) *Ecotourism: Management and Assessment.* Thomson, London, pp. 89–109.

Toth, R. (2002) Exploring the concepts underlying certification. In: Honey, M. (ed.) *Ecotourism and Certification: Setting Standards in Practice.* Island Press, Washington, DC, pp. 73–102.

Tourism Council Australia (2003) *Pursuing Common Goals: Opportunities for Tourism and Conservation.* Department for Industry, Tourism and Resources, Commonwealth of Australia, Canberra, Australia.

TTI (1999) *Tourism in Central and Eastern Europe.* Travel and Tourism Intelligence, London, UK.

WTO (2002) *Voluntary Initiatives for Sustainable Tourism.* World Tourism Organization, Madrid, Spain.

WTO (2003) *Co-operation and Partnerships in Tourism: a Global Perspective.* World Tourism Organization, Madrid, Spain.

17 Professional Certification: a Mechanism to Enhance Ecotour Guide Performance

ROSEMARY BLACK

Charles Sturt University, Albury, NSW, Australia

Chapter Profile

The pivotal role of the tour guide in the tourism industry has been recognized and the recent increase in nature-based and ecotourism has highlighted the vital role the guide plays in these sectors. Evidence suggests that some ecotour guides may not be adequately performing all their roles. To assist in improving guide performance and raising guiding standards, a number of quality assurance mechanisms can be used, including professional certification, the focus of this chapter. In Australia, two professional certification programmes for ecotour and nature guides have been developed and implemented over the past 15 years: the first was Savannah Guides and more recently the EcoGuide Australia Certification Program.

Introduction

This chapter examines ecotour guides and the application of professional certification as one mechanism to enhance tour guide performance, and then looks at two Australian professional certification programmes that have been developed for ecotour and nature-based guides. The first part of the chapter looks at some empirical studies of ecotour guides, the key roles of the guide in ecotourism and a range of quality assurance mechanisms for achieving high ecotour guide standards. The second part of the chapter focuses on two professional certification programmes for nature and ecotour guides that have been developed in Australia, Savannah Guides and the EcoGuide Australia Certification Program (EGACP). These two programmes were selected because they have been developed specifically for nature and ecotour guides, they represent two of the most developed and well-established programmes and they are also the most well documented.

The ecotour guide has been described as the 'heart and soul of the ecotourism industry' (Epler Wood, 1998), a position supported by others

(Weiler and Ham, 2001; Page and Dowling, 2002). The ecotour guide can play a vital role in protecting the natural and cultural environment by performing a number of roles such as interpreter of the environment, motivator of environmentally responsible behaviour and conservation values and specialist information giver (Weiler and Davis, 1993).

The term 'ecotourism guide' was probably first mentioned by Manidis Roberts Consultants in their investigation of ecotourism accreditation for the Australian government (Manidis Roberts Consultants, 1994). This term was then shortened to 'ecotour guide' in 'A National Ecotourism Education Strategy' (Social Change Media, 1995) and has been adopted for this chapter (Weiler and Crabtree, 1998). An ecotour guide is defined by Black (2002) as a:

> nature-based guide who is working for an ecotour operator and is therefore expected to guide in a manner consistent with the principles of ecotourism. This includes interpretation of the natural and cultural environment, using minimal impact practices, and ensuring sustainability of the natural and cultural environment.

In contrast, a nature-based guide is 'a person who guides tours which are primarily oriented toward providing an experience that is dependent upon the natural (but may include cultural) environment' (Black, 2002).

As the term implies, 'ecotour guides' may be employed in the ecotourism industry, whether it is the public or private sector. It is a relatively new term and has been derived from the term 'ecotourism'. Although the term 'ecotour guide' is not widely used in the industry, the advent of the EGACP in Australia, a professional certification programme for nature and ecotour guides, is likely to increase its exposure and usage.

Ecotour Guiding – Some Empirical Studies Based on Specific Tours and Geographical Areas

With the increasing interest in ecotourism and nature-based tourism during the 1990s, a number of studies have been undertaken that focus on nature and ecotour guides either on specific tours or within certain geographical areas.

A study undertaken by Weiler *et al.* (1992) involved analysing secondary data and collecting primary data from a sample of nature tour operators. Based on the findings of this study, they adapted Cohen's model of the principal components of the tour guide's role to explain the role of the nature guide in providing and achieving environmentally responsible tourism. This involved adding a third dimension, resource management, to Cohen's model (see Table 17.1). Their study is based on content analysis of the Australian Tourism Industry Association *Code of Environmental Practice* (Australian Tourism Industry Association, 1990) and advertising brochures from nature-based tour operators, as well as university and non-profit tour operators, and was supplemented with data from a mail survey of tour operators. The inclusion of resource management in the model requires the tour guide to

Table 17.1. Roles played by the tour guide/leader in nature-based tourism (from Weiler *et al.*, 1992).

	Outer-directed (resourced from outside the group)	Inner-directed (resourced from inside the group)
Tour management (focus on group)	'Organizer'	'Entertainer'
Experience management (focus on individual)	'Group leader'	'Teacher'
Resource management (focus on environment)	'Motivator'	'Environmental interpreter'

focus on the environment, and involves two roles. The first is the motivator, which involves influencing the tourists' behaviour and impacts on the site, and the second is that of environmental interpreter, which involves increasing the tourist's appreciation and understanding of the environment to facilitate responsible tourist behaviour in the long term.

The tour management, experience management and resource management dimensions are useful additions to the literature to help explain the roles of the guide in the nature-based tourism industry. Weiler *et al.*'s (1992) study fills an important gap in the literature, reflecting the current growth and focus on ecotourism and nature-based tourism and the role of the guide in these experiences. Weiler *et al.* (1992) suggest that further research should examine the relative importance of the six roles and the implications for tour promotion, tour guide recruitment and training.

As Weiler and Ham (2001) noted, there has been almost no published research that tests and applies the theoretical frameworks developed by Holloway (1981), Cohen (1985) and Weiler *et al.* (1992), with the exception of Haig (1997). Haig explores the role of the guide in the ecotourism experience and in the developing concern among tourists for the environment. His study investigates the tourists' perception of the guides' importance and the skills needed in an ecotourism experience. He surveyed ecotourists from two commercially operated eco-travel organizations, one resort-based and the other tour-based. He found that ecotourists as a group rated the role of organizer as the most important role for a guide, followed by interpreter, teacher and motivator for environmentally responsible behaviour. The least important role was entertainer. The two groups of ecotourists differed in their rating of roles, with the resort-based group placing greater importance on the roles of entertainer (and possibility social facilitator) and interpreter. These two roles fit with Cohen's argument that the social component of the guide's role is more likely to be important in facilities that offer group activities. The roles of entertainer and interpreter relate to the 'inner-directed' sphere of Weiler *et al.*'s (1992) nature-based tour guide model. In contrast, Haig's tour-based group placed importance on Cohen's instrumental leadership roles, such as access to non-public areas, physical orientation of the experience and responsibility for the safety and comfort of the group. These roles are associated with Cohen's original guide and are more group-focused. Haig (1997) finds that the group that considered the guide to be 'extremely important' rated the guide's role in order of importance from organizer to motivator (of environmentally responsible behaviour) and interpreter. This supports Weiler *et al.*'s (1992) proposition that the motivator and interpreter roles of a guide are important in achieving the goals of environmentally responsible tourism.

The Key Roles of the Guide in Ecotourism

To date, much of the literature has strongly focused on identifying and analysing the various roles of the guide in mass tourism and many studies acknowledge the multifaceted nature of guiding (Holloway, 1981; Cohen, 1985; Weiler *et al.*, 1992; Pond, 1993).

The roles that a guide plays in tourism depend on a number of factors, including the setting and purpose of the tour, the motivations and experience of the tourists, the characteristics and motivations of the guides themselves and the expectations of the tour operators. However, there are times when the roles may be in conflict (Holloway, 1981; Cohen, 1985) and roles may often be performed simultaneously (Pond, 1993). In a small survey of guides, tour operators and visitors, Pond (1993) found that, while the respondent groups placed different emphasis on the roles of a guide, all agreed that one of the features of professional guides is their ability to perform a wide range of duties and functions simultaneously. The roles of the guide have been identified in a number of key empirical studies based on guides working in both the mass tourism and nature-based/ecotourism environments. However, particular focus will be given to the key roles of the ecotour guide.

As previously outlined in Chapter 1, indicators suggest that ecotourism and nature-based tourism are increasing (Derrett, 2001; Hawkins and Lamoureux, 2001). As more people visit natural areas as part of an ecotourism or nature experience, the demand for travel professionals such as ecotour guides also increases. Hawkins and Lamoureux (2001) suggest that over the last few years there has indeed been an increase in the number of tourism professionals such as travel agents, tour operators and tour guides that specialize in the ecotourism and/or nature tourism markets.

A number of studies focusing on tour guiding have identified a range of roles that the guide can play in tourism (Holloway, 1981; Cohen, 1985; Pond, 1993), such as leader, information giver, interpreter, organizer and mediator. More recent studies indicate that the guide has more specialist roles to play in ecotourism and nature-based tourism (Weiler and Davis, 1993; Haig, 1997; Black, 1999; Weiler and Ham, 2001), requiring skills in interpretation, motivating visitors to modify their behaviour to minimize impacts on the resource and instilling conservation values, and providing associated underpinning knowledge/expertise.

A number of studies have investigated and acknowledged the role of the guide in ecotourism and nature-based tourism (Weiler *et al.*, 1992; Roggenbuck and Williams, 1993; Black, 1999; Weiler and Ham, 2001). Weiler *et al.* (1992: 233) note that 'Tour leaders as role models for visitors must exhibit environmentally responsible behaviour, must hold environmentally responsible attitudes, and most importantly, must have the skills and abilities to promote these attitudes in visitors.' They argue that only guides who have appropriate skills, knowledge and attitudes should be allowed to take on the important role of ecotour guides. They consider that this can be guaranteed through mechanisms such as training or professional certification of individual tour guides.

A guide in the ecotourism industry needs to be aware of the environmental and sociocultural impacts caused by ecotourism. This awareness may enable the guide to assist in the management of protected areas by promoting minimal impact behaviour and assisting in enforcing national park regulations. High-quality guides may also encourage conservation action among both tourists and the local community. However, long-term follow-up with tourists and trained guides is needed to identify whether this is occurring and what the mechanisms might be to strengthen it (Black *et al.*, 2001).

Black and Weiler (2005) reviewed a number of studies that focused on the roles of general and ecotour guides and that aimed to identify guide roles that have been highlighted in the literature, and, in particular, focused on the roles of the ecotour guide. Their analysis identified ten main roles, including leader, interpreter, social catalyst, cultural broker and tour manager. Six of the studies identify the role of information giver, while all of the studies reviewed identify the role of interpreter, suggesting that this is a role that is widely acknowledged as a key role of a guide, irrespective of the tour setting. Few of the studies that focus on the guide in mass tourism identify the role of motivator of environmentally responsible behaviour and conservation values (see Schmidt, 1979; Holloway, 1981; Cohen, 1985; Pond, 1993). However, a number of more recent studies focusing on nature-based and ecotourism tours and ecotour guides identify this role (Weiler and Davis, 1993; Haig, 1997). Interestingly, given the remote location of many ecotours none of the studies identified the role of risk manager or provider of safety and first-aid, and yet in Australia first-aid certification is a national standard and is a widely accepted and utilized form of quality assurance and professional certification.

As well as illustrating the more generic roles of a general guide, such as leader and tour manager, Black and Weiler's (2005) analysis shows that the ecotour guide also performs a number of roles more specifically related to ecotourism, such as specialist information giver, interpreter and motivator of environmentally responsible behaviour and conservation values. However, their review of the literature found that guides are underperforming in some areas.

Mechanisms for Achieving High Ecotour Guide Standards

To ensure that guides can competently fulfil all these demanding roles, many see a need for the development and enforcement of guiding standards (Weiler and Davis, 1993; Weiler and Ham, 2001; Black and Weiler, 2005). Improved guiding standards can potentially be achieved through a number of different mechanisms, including support from professional associations, codes of conduct, awards for excellence, formal training programmes, licensing and professional certification (Black, 2002). Professional certification is distinct from ecotourism certification that is generally applied to programmes or products or services. Professional certification is a term that is used consistently across many professions to describe 'the formal recognition of professional or technical competence' (Lysaght and Altschuld, 2000). It is generally a voluntary process, depending on the profession and level of responsibility and legal requirements. Professional certification of tour guides is found in Australia (for example, the EcoGuide Australia Certification Program and Savannah Guides), in some developing countries and in North America, with the exception of a few major US cities (Pond, 1993). The definition used in this chapter refers to an individual's ability to perform professional duties (Altschuld, 1999). Professional certification indicates that the individual has attained a certain level of competence (e.g. knowledge and skill) in the field, usually determined through an examination or series of assessments. To be certified, the individual's level of skill and proficiency must be ascertained.

In a recent paper, Black and Weiler (2005) examined a range of quality assurance and regulatory mechanisms that have the potential to enhance the performance of tour guides with respect to the key roles they are expected to perform. A range of mechanisms can be used to improve guide performance, including the implementation of codes of conduct, professional associations, awards of excellence, training, professional certification and licensing. Black and Weiler (2005) assessed each of these mechanisms in relation to its usefulness in delivering outcomes that may help guides perform their various roles, together with an overview of the advantages and disadvantages of implementing that mechanism. The six mechanisms reviewed were:

- Codes of conduct.
- Professional associations.
- Awards of excellence.
- Training.
- Professional certification.
- Licensing.

Each of the mechanisms is discussed in relation to its characteristics and outcomes and its advantages and disadvantages. Specifically, they looked at whether the mechanism is compulsory or voluntary for guides helps achieve or raise guiding standards, rewards excellence, raises awareness among guides and improves guiding credibility in the industry. As Black and

Weiler (2005) note, 'Many of these initiatives are used by other sectors of the tourism industry to improve professionalism, standards, training and an enhanced tourist experience (Manidis Roberts Consultants, 1994; Issaverdis, 1998; Honey and Rome, 2001; Harris and Jago, 2001).' They concluded that there is a need to develop, implement and monitor the effectiveness of a range of quality assurance and regulatory mechanisms to assist guides in fulfilling the full range of roles required of a guide, and to enhance their performance. In particular, they proposed that a multi-mechanism approach has the greatest potential to raise guiding standards and enhance performance across all roles, but requires significant financial and human resources. However, they suggest that the development of a professional association whose core business is to support guides in performing their various roles could be the most cost-effective short-term strategy, with a longer-term goal of developing an integrated strategy that incorporates training, certification and/or licensing and an award-of-excellence programme.

In Australia, in response to the fragmented, uncoordinated and unregulated nature of the tour guiding industry, Guiding Organizations Australia (GOA) (see www.goa.org.au) was formed in 2003 as a not-for-profit organization to bring some consistency and unity to the eight tour guide and related associations across Australia, and attempt to find some common ground for a national tour guide certification framework. To date GOA has been developing its own corporate processes and networks, and has not commenced certification, although it is anticipated that the framework will link to the National Tourism Training Package (see www.ntis.gov.au).

Earlier chapters in this volume have mentioned other quality contol mechanisms to assist in raising tour guiding standards and professionalism. Peter Mason's chapter (Chapter 4) covered codes of conduct and briefly mentioned the role of codes of conduct for guides, and Chapter 3 by Stuart Toplis on awards of excellence mentioned the value of awards for individual professionals like guides.

The focus of this chapter is professional certification, using the case studies Savannah Guides and the Australian EcoGuide Certification Program, as one quality assurance mechanism that has the potential to improve or raise guiding standards and hence ecotourism quality.

Savannah Guides

Earlier in the chapter we have seen that guides have an important role to play in the ecotourism and nature tourism experience – such as providing specialist information, interpreting sites and encouraging and motivating environmentally responsible behaviour and conservation values. High guiding standards can assist in serving this wide range of interests and can benefit the visitor, the operator and the environment.

As outlined in Chapter 2, the recent growth, particularly in Australia, of quality assurance measures, including certification and professional certification in the tourism industry, was discussed. The growth of certification and professional certification is attributed to the tourism industry's recognition that consumers' expectations are higher, and that consumers have a heightened awareness of service quality, improved safety and sustainable environmental issues (Toplis, 2000). A number of quality assurance mechanisms are available to raise guide standards and performance. One of these mechanisms is professional certification, which can be used to improve professionalism, standards, training and quality in their service sector. Savannah Guides and the EGACP are examples of professional certification programmes aimed specifically at ecotour and nature guides.

Savannah Guides Ltd was really the first effective programme to certify tour guides in Australia and link to the national competency standards. Established in 1988, Savannah Guides is a regionally and ecosystem-based professional certification programme established to certify guides and operators based in the tropical savannahs of northern Australia. The Gulf Local Authorities Development Association established Savannah Guides as a non-profit company. Its original purpose was to provide access for tourists into natural environments on private, leased or public land, and in a way that would ensure the protection of the region's assets. The mission of Savannah Guides is:

> To be an economically sound, community-based, professional body, maintaining high standards of:
>
> - Interpretation and public education.
> - Training and leadership.
> - Natural and cultural resource management.
>
> Through the promotion of ecologically sustainable tourism principles, Savannah Guides will enhance regional lifestyles and encourages the protection and conservation of the natural and cultural resources of the Tropical Savannahs of Northern Australia.
>
> (Savannah Guides, 2000: 1)

Initially, members came from local communities within the Queensland Gulf Savannah but the network has since expanded to include the tropical savannahs of northern Australia. Members are drawn from the tropical savannahs of northern Australia, a region including Queensland, Northern Territory and Western Australia. Savannah Guides is currently managed by a six-member board of management and employs a part-time coordinator.

The process of becoming a member of Savannah Guides involves satisfying a number of criteria, including:

- A commitment to the mission of Savannah Guides.
- Formal accreditations, licences and qualifications.
- Participation in Savannah Guide Schools.
- Assessment of guiding or management skills by peers.
- Acceptance of the nomination by the Board of Directors (Savannah Guides, 2004).

Guides are carefully selected for the programme to ensure that individuals have good communication skills, a reasonable knowledge of technical matters and a strong commitment to Savannah Guides' philosophy. The natural ability of individual guides has been a critical factor, with much of the learning process involving experienced guides acting as mentors and instilling an ethos of self-learning, self-improvement and a strong desire to elevate the profession of guides.

Savannah Guides have a number of membership categories. Enterprise membership is where existing tour operators are linked to the Savannah Guides network and their tour operations are endorsed as of a high standard. The benefits to these members are staff development, site management, corporate imagery, visitor referral, tour packaging, buying networks and industry networking.

Members may progress from entry-level to master-level enterprise, which allows for a higher participation level in marketing activities, and a generally higher level of involvement in the organization. Enterprise membership levels are: Savannah Guide Site (e.g. a nature-based tourist attraction), Savannah Guide Operator (e.g. a safari company), Savannah Guide Station and Savannah Guide Master Operator. Individual membership levels are; Site Interpreter (guide at stationary enterprises), Roving Interpreter (guide with mobile operators), Savannah Guide (senior guide/supervisor at enterprise) and Special Member (non-guiding senior representative of enterprise).

Currently there are two Savannah Guide Stations, three Savannah Guide Master Operators, seven Savannah Guide Sites and five Savannah Guide Operators (Savannah Guides, 2004). All of those involved in the programme must demonstrate a commitment to conservation values, meet strict standards of operation and abide by professional codes of conduct. Knowledge and professionalism are fundamental to Savannah Guides' operating philosophy. To gain certification all guides must attend two Savannah Guide training schools. This ensures an extended training and induction period at the enterprise and in terms of Savannah Guides (Savannah Guides, 2004). The content of the programme reflects its regional basis. Peer-group assessment underpins the training methodology. At least two training schools are conducted each year, at varying locations across the savannahs, and they feature experts in related fields, including Aboriginal culture, ecology, land management and tourism. All Savannah Guides must demonstrate a commitment to conservation values, meet strict standards of operation and abide by the professional code of conduct.

Guides are required to attend one Savannah Guides School every 2 years to maintain and improve their knowledge and skills. Peer-group assessment is the primary form of assessment and this process is benchmarked against the Tourism Training Package. In addition, optional formal assessments of units from the Tourism Training Package allow guides to work towards formal qualifications. These assessments occur during the training schools. A number of Savannah Guides members have completed the national Certificate IV in Assessment and Workplace Training course, thus providing guides the opportunity to access formal tour guiding qualifications. Ongoing contact with other guides and enterprises provides training environments at Savannah Guides Schools, familiarization tours, locum employment and social visits. The interaction at the Schools with the enterprise-level membership also facilitates communication and cooperation between guides, especially in areas such as resource and information sharing.

Savannah Guides has been recognized nationally and internationally with several tourism awards, including the prestigious Best Tourism Organization (World) in the British Airways Tourism for Tomorrow Awards (Savannah Guides, 2000). Further information on Savannah Guides can be found at their web site (www.savannah-guides.com.au).

The EcoGuide Australia Certification Program

In contrast to Savannah Guides, which is a regionally based certification programme, the EcoGuide Australia Certification Program is a national ecotour guide certification programme that has recently been developed and implemented. The EGACP represents one initiative that has been developed to assist in raising the standard of ecotour guiding in Australia. The following sections outline the background to the initiation of the project to develop the EGACP, the basic components of the programme development process and the programme's current status.

Background to the development of the EcoGuide Australia Certification Program

It was the *National Ecotourism Strategy* (Commonwealth of Australia, 1994) that first raised the issue and possibility of a certification system for guides employed in the ecotourism industry. The report indicated that certification of guides would 'encourage the delivery of high-quality, sustainable tourism products and the provision of accurate interpretive services' and 'to allow natural resource managers to monitor ecotourism operators and guides working within their region' (Commonwealth of Australia, 1994: 39). In particular, the report highlighted the need for skilled and knowledgeable guides in the ecotourism industry: 'Well-trained operators and guides who can deliver accurate information and informative materials and presentations. Tour leaders and operators should have a good knowledge of ecology, cultural issues, conservation and minimal impact practices and be skilful in interpretation' (Commonwealth of Australia, 1994: 41).

The concept of an ecotour guide certification programme was later followed up in a report by Manidis Roberts Consultants (1994), which examined the concept of a broader national ecotourism accreditation scheme. The findings of the Manidis Roberts report suggest that, from early on in the discussions on ecotourism accreditation, there has been a recognition that the guide contributes to a high-quality ecotourism experience. The report states that: 'A national ecotourism guide training and certification system should be prepared and introduced in parallel with the proposed National Ecotourism Accreditation Scheme' (Manidis Roberts Consultants, 1994: 31).

Broadly, the report recommends that the proposed scheme requires 'qualified ecotourism guides' and recommends that recognized ecotourism guide training programmes be established in parallel with the further development and implementation of the proposed certification scheme. The report further suggests that the proposed National Ecotourism Accreditation Scheme and ecotourism guide certification system should build on existing areas of expertise and develop specific competencies for ecotourism guiding. The recommendations, together with more detailed information provided in the report, give some initial guidance to the development and implementation of an ecotourism guide certification scheme.

The 'National Ecotourism Education Strategy' (Social Change Media, 1995) also endorsed the concept of ecotour guide certification. The report indicated that any national ecotour guide certification scheme should be developed in tandem with the proposed ecotourism accreditation scheme, to ensure that operators are 'qualified to meet specific ecotourism competencies' (Social Change Media, 1995: 70). The report stated that much of the groundwork for the development of a national ecotourism training programme already existed, and that any ecotour guide certification system should build on existing national competency standards. A specific recommendation of the report was that 'the development of an ecotourism accreditation scheme should look closely at the work done by Inbound Tour Operators Association (ITOA) to see if their system is suitable for modification, to produce an ecotourism specific stream' (Social Change Media, 1995: 70).

In line with the recommendations of the Manindis Roberts report, it was decided to pursue the concept of a national ecotourism accreditation programme, which would certify ecotourism products in the accommodation, tours and attractions sectors. Although the concept of ecotourism guide certification was not officially pursued at that time, the seed had been planted. In 1996 the National Ecotourism Accreditation Program, known as NEAP, was launched and was jointly administered by EA (Ecotourism Australia) (then the Ecotourism Association of Australia) and the Australian Tourism Operators Network (ATON) (Ecotourism Association of Australia, 2000). The programme, now called the EcoCertification Program, is currently administered solely by EA.

At the same time, research was being conducted in the area of ecotour guiding, mainly by Alice Crabtree and Betty Weiler. In 1994 they were involved in producing the *National Ecotourism Education Strategy* (Social Change Media, 1995). This was the first of several projects that included a focus on ecotour guides. Following extensive industry and community consultation, the report found that the guides who were surveyed thought that guide training was important and that further training opportunities were needed. However, the study also noted that the demands on tour guides and the lack of adequate rewards were issues that needed to be addressed at the same time as training issues. The report recommended the revision of existing national tour guide competency standards, more specific ecotourism-related competency standards be developed, and that a speciality ecotour guide category be added to the tour guide competencies. Due to a change in the Federal Government, the 'National Ecotourism Education Strategy' was never formally released, so many of its recommendations have never been implemented.

Following the recommendations of the Manidis Roberts report and the *National Ecotourism Education Strategy* (Social Change Media, 1995), Tourism Training Australia, the national tourism training organization, began developing specific national competency standards for ecotour guiding, interpretation and ecotourism operations. These ecotour guide competencies acknowledged the specialized roles of the guides working in the nature-based and ecotourism industries.

As part of the 'National Ecotourism Education Strategy' (Social Change Media, 1995), a *Directory of Ecotourism Education in Australia* (Commonwealth of Australia, 1996) was also produced. This directory listed all the training courses and curricula relating to ecotourism education, including ecotour and nature-based guiding, and highlighted the lack of training in non-urban areas, and the over-abundance of degree-level and full-time courses of study.

The 'National Ecotourism Education Strategy' and the *Directory of Ecotourism Education* provided the lead into another project, called 'Developing Competent Ecotour Guides'. The project was funded by the Australian National Training Authority (Research Advisory Council) (ANTARAC) and subsequently managed by the NCVER (Weiler and Crabtree, 1998). This research study aimed to assess the performance of nature-based/ecotour guides on the job. The research involved using a number of data collection methods to assess guides' performance on the job, using a set of criteria that had been developed from previous research and the literature. These criteria assessed the guides' competencies in five specific areas: group management, leadership, communication/interpretation, minimal impact and cultural awareness.

The outcomes of this study (Weiler and Crabtree, 1998) represent an important milestone towards the development of a national ecotour guide certification programme. First, a set of potential instruments for on-the-job assessment of selected components of guide competencies had been developed and piloted, and, second, a national nature/ecotour guide database had been established for EA as a communication and recruitment tool for guides. A key finding of the report (Weiler and Crabtree, 1998) was that, although guides performed well on most of the performance criteria dealing with site knowledge, tour management and interpersonal communication skills, they performed poorly on indicators relating to interpretation methods and conservation themes. Based on these and other findings, the researchers suggested that ecotour guides might not be fulfilling their potential to deliver a quality visitor experience and impart strong conservation messages.

All of the research and industry developments described previously laid the foundations for the initiation and development of a national ecotour guide certification programme in Australia. A number of papers (Black and Weiler,

2002, 2005) emanating from Black's doctoral thesis have already described aspects of the EGACP. The thesis critically analysed the development of the EGACP, and based on the study findings and lessons learnt presented a general model for tour guide certification. This model has the potential for application and use for other countries and sites and would be particularly useful for planners and managers of existing and future tour guide certification programmes. A more detailed account of the background to and description of the development of this certification programme, using the analogy of the human life cycle, was subsequently completed by Black and Weiler (2002). Their chronological review of the EGACP reflects the successes and challenges of developing ecotour guide certification. They take the development process of the EGACP through the stages of birth, growth and maturation. Initially the idea for a tour guide certification programme was discussed over a 7-year period from 1991 to 1997. From 1997 to 2001 the EGACP was conceived, born and matured into a fully fledged programme, having been launched in November 2000.

The funding application to the Australian Federal Government to develop the EGACP argued the pivotal role of the guide in tourist satisfaction and in protecting Australia's natural and cultural heritage. The main benefits identified in the proposal were raising the standards of ecotour guides, improving the working conditions and benefits for guides, increasing the professionalism of ecotour guides, assisting employers in recruitment, identifying training gaps and providing ecotour guides with a national portable qualification and professional recognition.

The proposal involved the development of a National Ecotour Guide Certification Program, later called the EcoGuide Australia Certification Program, including a pilot period and an implementation strategy. As part of the project, it was proposed that a guide workbook and preliminary assessor's manual would be produced. The proposal recommended that a steering committee of industry representatives be established to ensure that effective cooperation and coordination occurred between the relevant agencies and organizations.

The project to develop the EGACP began in May 1998. The anticipated outcomes of the project were to have a professionally produced certification programme, a web page and an implementation strategy. The performance indicators were:

- Portable qualifications that are recognized by employers in all states and territories involved in the process.
- Protected area managers, NGO and commercial tour operations conducting joint training and exploring assessment programmes.
- Cost-effective and easy availability of industry-based assessors available in all states/territories.
- Links between ecotourism operators, mainstream tourism and specialist industry sectors, natural resource managers and NGO groups involved in tourism/guiding.
- A national database of ecotour guide assessors and certified guides.

The programme was developed and managed by a project manager (Alice Crabtree), who worked collaboratively with a project team and an industry steering committee. This committee aimed to represent a range of industry stakeholders from tourism, ecotourism, guiding, heritage interpretation, tourism training and protected area management agencies and statewide representation. In addition, a national telephone survey of nature-based tour operators, ecotour/nature guides and protected area managers was undertaken (Black, 2002). The aim of the survey was to assess ecotour/nature guides', nature-based operators' and protected area managers' views towards the proposed EGACP and tour guide certification, their willingness to pay for such certification, the benefits and services they deemed essential in return for certification fees and their awareness of the EGACP.

When the EGACP was launched in November 2000, the programme consisted of an EcoGuide Workbook, which has since been revised, available as a hard-copy book and as a web-based document on EA's web site (www.ecotourism.org.au); a preliminary EcoGuide assessor's manual, which has since been finalized; a fledgling network of EcoGuide assessors; a marketing brochure; a business plan; and a programme logo.

The EcoGuide Australia Certification Program: in detail

The EGACP is a professional certification programme that awards an industry 'qualification' that recognizes guides that achieve certain competencies and specified industry standards. The programme is voluntary and designed to recognize and reward best practice nature and ecotour guiding. All types of guides are encouraged to become certified, including interpretive rangers, commercial guides and volunteers. In contrast to training programmes, the EGACP aims to assess guide's skills, knowledge, attitudes and actions. The programme is designed to be equally relevant and accessible to guides who have gained their skills and experience (competence) through life experience and on-the-job training and to those who have gained competencies through formal training.

To make the programme more relevant and appealing to guides, it incorporates a pathway for certified guides if they wish to gain formal, nationally recognized qualifications. This process involves the certified guide approaching a registered training organization (such as a technical and further education institution) that offers tour guide training to be recognized for the competencies they have been awarded through the EGACP. Although this option was built into the development of the programme, the administrative arrangements have not been established to allow guides to easily gain these formal qualifications.

In terms of assessment, the programme aims to be as user-friendly as possible and provides flexibility, a range of assessment options and progressive assessment, so that guides can proceed through the programme at their own pace. An assessor mentors each applicant through the programme. The programme developers sought to ensure that assessors were of high calibre and to this end they must have workplace assessor qualifications and experience as a tour guide and supervisor.

A significant achievement of the programme developers was the linkage between the EGACP and the EcoCertification Program (then called the Nature and Ecotourism Accreditation Program), which certifies nature and ecotourism products. The two programmes work in tandem to provide standards for nature and ecotourism that ensure quality and continual improvement in the Australian industry. The latter programme emphasizes the importance of having guides and other key staff in contact with customers who are able to provide accurate information, having been adequately trained in ecotourism and interpretive techniques. To achieve advanced certification or bonus points, Lead or Head Guides that operate in protected areas must be formally qualified as nature/ecotour guides or can demonstrate competence in the criteria used for nature/ecoguide certification programmes such as the EcoGuide Australia Program, IATG/ITOA Guide Qualification Program or Savannah Guides.

According to Crabtree and Black (2000), the EGACP is designed to provide a range of benefits for a variety of nature and ecotourism stakeholders (see Box 17.1).

To enter the programme, guides need to prove their eligibility, which is that they have at least 12 months' relevant work experience as a tour guide or they have a recognized and approved formal guiding or ecotourism qualification and a minimum of 3 months' work experience as a tour guide. Once guides have proved their eligibility, they may apply for certification. The certification assessment process involves three stages:

Stage 1 – application by candidate.
Stage 2 – assessment preparation.
Stage 3 – assessment.
Stage 4 – assessment report, EcoGuide Panel review and certification.

Part of the certification process involves the guides signing a code of ethics (see Box 17.2). In signing the code, guides are declaring their intent to provide high-quality nature and ecotourism experiences in a safe, culturally sensitive and environmentally sustainable manner (Crabtree and Black, 2000).

The certification criteria for assessing guides is based on the basic skills, knowledge, attitudes and actions nature and ecotour guides are expected to demonstrate in their work. Specifically, the criteria are based on work experience as a guide and a commitment to the code of ethics, combined with a specified set of industry standards. These industry standards are the national competencies from the Australian Tourism Training Package previously referred to. Competencies are the skills and knowledge an individual needs to perform their job to the required industry standard. The competencies were selected after extensive consultation with the steering committee and other relevant industry organizations and include 13 competencies. There are nine core competencies that are generic tour guiding competencies, such as occupational health and safety, tourism industry knowledge, working

Box 17.1. Benefits of the EcoGuide Australia Certification Program (from Crabtree and Black, 2000).

Benefits to nature and ecotour guides

- A recognized industry qualification
- Baseline benchmark to determine the degree to which their services meet the standards of best practice nature and/or ecotour guiding
- An opportunity to promote guiding services as genuine nature/ecotourism
- A defined competitive edge rewarded through factors such as better job opportunities
- Access to relevant, appropriate and reduced-cost training materials and networking opportunities
- Pathway to nationally recognized and portable formal qualifications within the Australian qualification framework (Certificate III Tourism (Guiding), also beginning of the pathway for Certificate VI in Tourism (Guiding) and Certificate VI in Tourism (Natural and Cultural Heritage))

Benefits to nature and ecotourism operators

- A simple method of recognizing and recruiting quality guides
- A standard or benchmark within which guide performance can be continually improved to a standard recognized as best practice
- An opportunity to promote guided products as best practice nature and/or ecotour guiding, giving greater product appeal and a marketing advantage
- Improved guiding practices that lead to fewer negative environmental and cultural impacts and increased client satisfaction

Benefits to nature and ecotourism consumers

- An assurance of guides that are committed to providing quality nature or ecotourism experiences in a safe, culturally sensitive and environmentally sustainable manner

Benefits to protected area managers

- Improved guiding practices that lead to fewer negative environmental impacts
- Guides who role-model and ensure good environmental and culturally appropriate behaviour
- Guides committed to a partnership in providing a front line of defence in environmentally sensitive or fragile areas
- Ability to identify operators who employ staff with appropriate training and qualifications for reviewing permit applications in sensitive areas
- A framework of standards applicable to interpretive rangers

Benefits to the environment

- Guides providing relevant and appropriate interpretation that inspires clients and workplace employees and encourages minimal impact actions and a conservation ethic. This is reinforced by the guide practising and modelling behaviour in support of minimal impact principles

Box 17.2. EcoGuide Australia Certification Program code of ethics (from Crabtree and Black, 2000).

The certified nature or ecotour guide:

- Adopts best practice standards in relation to safety, interpretation, customer service, product promotion and their own leadership and presentation.
- Is committed to implementing minimal impact principles and practices.
- Endeavours to maximize the positive and minimize the negative economic, social, cultural and experiential impacts of the tours they conduct.
- Is committed to eco-efficient resource use.
- Respects and, where appropriate, seeks to build good relationships with local people, colleagues, customers and any other visitors to an area.
- Is committed to ongoing professional development.

with colleagues and in a socially diverse workplace, working as a guide and preparing and presenting tour commentaries. In addition, there are four further ecotourism-specific competencies, such as planning and developing interpretive activities, minimal impact practices, basic knowledge and protocols with respect to indigenous people and culture, and appropriate content and specialist interpretive content.

2000 to the present

It has been 4 years since the launch of the programme and during that time it has experienced highs and lows. Between 2000 and 2002, there was considerable exposure of the programme through the EcoGuide Australia marketing brochure, a regular guiding insert in the quarterly Ecotourism Australia newsletter and the establishment of the National EcoGuide Award for Excellence. The programme is currently managed and administered by EA, with assistance and input from an EcoGuide Australia Committee, comprising members of the EA board, a network of independent assessors and a programme manager with EA. Since early 2003, the Committee has achieved some significant successes, including holding an EcoGuide assessors workshop to provide input into the EcoGuide assessor's manual and EA policy, finalization of the EcoGuide assessor's manual, revision of the EcoGuide Workbook to ensure consistency with the assessor's manual, new logos and cloth badges and a business plan for the programme. Despite all these initiatives, the programme has not been as successful as anticipated, with limited uptake of the programme by guides. In 2003 the Committee set a target of 100 new EcoGuide assessments and during that year guide assessments were held in South Australia, Fraser Island and other regional locations around Australia.

In 2000 there were about 50 guides certified under the programme and there are currently 57 certified guides, demonstrating the low uptake of the programme by guides. Although there is no accurate figure on the number of ecotour/nature guides in Australia, there were 250 ecotour/nature guides listed on the EAA Nature and Ecotour Guide database in 1999, which suggests that there are potentially many more ecotour/nature guides that could become certified. There may be a number of reasons for this poor uptake, including insufficient promotion of the programme to the ecotourism industry and guides in particular, lack of perceived benefits for the guides and the industry and lack of recertfication of certified guides.

Challenges and the future

The experience of the EGACP has many lessons for other organizations planning to develop and introduce a certification programme for tour guides. First, Ecotourism Australia has limited staff and financial resources to support the programme and this may have influenced the manner in which it was promoted and supported administratively. In addition to gaining funding to develop a programme, it is imperative that funding be secured for its implementation, as programmes are particularly vulnerable in the early stages of implementation, when there is likely to be little or no income. Funding is necessary to cover the initial gap and for the ongoing operation of the programme. The financial viability of a programme may be strengthened through sponsorship, subsidization or developing some form of industry-wide scheme that has a 'core' component common across all programmes and a number of criteria specific to particular areas (Black, 2002).

Secondly, when the programme was launched in 2000, there were a number of programme components that were not fully functional and in place. These were the EcoGuide Assessor's Manual, which has subsequently been finalized, and a fledgling network of qualified assessors. Sufficient time and resources must be allocated during the development phase to ensure that all programme components are fully functional once the programme is launched. The lack of qualified assessors and a draft assessors' manual probably meant that fewer guide assessments were carried out and there were insufficient assessors promoting the programme.

Thirdly, a vital component of any new programme is its promotion and selling the benefits of the programme to potential guides and tour operators. These groups must be convinced of the programme's benefits, and in particular its tangible benefits. The programme marketing brochure highlighted the benefits of the programme to a range of stakeholders, including guides, operators, visitors and training providers. For guides the stated advantage of certification was to gain an industry qualification and a pathway to nationally recognized formal qualifications, which would provide a defined competitive advantage. Although this opportunity still exists, EA has not established a formal link with a registered training organization or facilitated a pathway for guides to acquire formal qualifications.

It would appear that few of the promised benefits have materialized and it is likely that some guides have failed to recertify because their expectations of the programme have not been met. This is a major issue, given that guides surveyed in the national survey (Black, 2002) who had previously been certified under the now disbanded ITOA Australian Guide Qualification Program were disillusioned and had received no tangible benefits under that programme. It is essential that, if the programme is sold on the basis of providing benefits, then these must be forthcoming: otherwise, guides will not recertify and the credibility of the programme and the sponsor organization is affected.

Further information on the EcoGuide Australia Certification Program may be found at: http://www.ecotourism.org.au

Conclusion

The pivotal role of the tour guide in the tourism industry has been recognized and the recent increase in nature-based and ecotourism has highlighted the vital role the guide plays in these sectors. To assist in improving guide performance and raising guide standards, a number of mechanisms can be implemented, including professional certification. Australia is a world leader in ecotourism policy and programmes, and this chapter has highlighted two Australian professional certification programmes that aim to improve tour guide performance and ensure high professional standards in ecotour and nature guiding. It has presented the role of the tour guide in ecotourism and the history of tour guide certification in Australia and described some of the recent industry initiatives in Australian ecotour guiding, in particular the development of Savannah Guides and the EGACP. It has summarized the industry and research developments that laid the foundations for, and led to, the development of the EGACP and highlighted some of the challenges of implementing such a programme.

References

Altschuld, J.W. (1999) The certification of evaluators: highlights from a report submitted to the Board of Directors of the American Evaluation Association. *American Journal of Evaluation* 20(3), 481–493.

Australian Tourism Industry Association (1990) *Code of Environmental Practice for Australian Tourism Industry.* Australian Tourism Industry Association, Sydney, NSW.

Black, R.S. (1999) Ecotour guides: performing a vital role in the ecotourism experience. In: Liaw, J. and Majungki, J. (eds) *Proceedings of the World Ecotourism Conference: The Right Approach.* Kota Kinabalu, Sabah, 17–23 October 1999.

Black, R.S. (2002) Towards a model for tour guide certification: an analysis of the Australian EcoGuide Program. Doctoral thesis, Department of Management, Monash University, Melbourne, Victoria, Australia.

Black, R.S. and Weiler, B. (2002) Tour guide certification in the Australian ecotourism industry: conception to adulthood. In: *CAUTHE Conference Proceedings,* part 2. CAUTHE, Fremantle, Western Australia.

Black, R.S. and Weiler, B. (2005) Quality assurance and regulatory mechanisms in the tour guiding industry: a systematic review. *Journal of Tourism Studies* 16(1), 24–37.

Black, R.S., Ham, S.H. and Weiler, B. (2001) Ecotour guide training in less developed countries: some preliminary research findings. *Journal of Sustainable Tourism* 9, 1–10.

Cohen, E. (1985) The tourist guide: the origins, structure and dynamics of a role. *Annals of Tourism Research* 12, 5–29.

Commonwealth of Australia (1994) *National Ecotourism Strategy.* Australian Government Printing Service, Canberra, ACT.

Commonwealth of Autralia (1996) *Directory of Ecotourism Education in Australia.* Commonwealth Department of Tourism, Canberra, ACT.

Crabtree, A. and Black, R.S. (2000) *EcoGuide Program Guide Workbook.* Ecotourism Association of Australia, Brisbane, Queensland.

Derrett, R. (2001) Special interest tourism: starting with the individual. In: Douglas, N., Douglas, N. and Derrett, R. (eds) *Special Interest Tourism.* John Wiley & Sons Australia, Milton, Queensland, pp. 1–24.

Ecotourism Association of Australia (2000) *The EcoGuide Program.* Ecotourism Association of Australia, Brisbane, Queensland.

Epler Wood, M. (1998) New directions in the ecotourism industry. In: Lindberg, K., Epler Wood, M. and Engeldrum, D. (eds) *Ecotourism: A Guide for Planners and Managers.* Ecotourism Society, North Bennington, Vermont, pp. 45–62.

Haig, I. (1997) Viewing nature: can a guide make a difference? Masters of Arts thesis in Outdoor Education, Department of Outdoor Education, Griffith University, Brisbane, Queensland.

Harris, R. and Jago, L. (2001) Professional accreditation in the Australian tourism industry: an uncertain future. *Tourism Management* 22, 383–390.

Hawkins, D.E. and Lamoureux, K. (2001) Global growth and magnitude of ecotourism. In: Weaver, D. (ed.) *The Encyclopedia of Ecotourism.* CAB International, Wallingford, UK, pp. 63–72.

Holloway, J.C. (1981) The guided tour: a sociological approach. *Annals of Tourism Research* 8(3), 377–401.

Honey, M. and Rome, A. (2001) *Protecting Paradise: Certification Programs for Sustainable Tourism and Ecotourism.* Institute of Policy Studies, New York.

Issaverdis, J.P. (1998) Tourism industry accreditation – a comparative critique of developments in Australia. Master of Business in Tourism Development, Victoria University, Melbourne, Victoria.

Lysaght, R.M. and Altschuld, J.W. (2000) Beyond initial certification: the assessment and maintenance of competency in professions. *Evaluation and Program Planning* 23, 95–104.

Manidis Roberts Consultants (1994) *An Investigation into a National Ecotourism Accreditation Scheme.* Commonwealth Department of Tourism, Canberra, ACT.

Page, S.P. and Dowling, R.K. (2002) *Ecotourism.* Pearson Education, Harlow, UK.

Pond, K.L. (1993) *The Professional Guide.* Van Nostrand Reinhold, New York.

Roggenbuck, J. and Williams, D.R. (1993) Commercial tour guides' effectiveness as nature educators. In: Cushman, G. and Veal, T. (eds) *Leisure and Tourism: Social and Environmental Change. World Leisure and Recreation Association Congress.* Centre for Leisure Studies, UTS, Sydney, Australia, pp. 651–655.

Savannah Guides (2000) *Savannah Guides: Protectors of the Outback* (brochure). Savannah Guides, Cairns, Queensland.

Savannah Guides (2004) Savannah Guides homepage. Available at: http://www.savannah-guides.com.au (accessed on 14 July).

Schmidt, C.J. (1979) The guided tour. *Urban Life* 7(4), 441–467.

Social Change Media (1995) A national ecotourism education strategy. Unpublished report, Newcastle, NSW.

Toplis, S. (2000) Evaluating the effectiveness of the Australian Tourism Awards in promoting ecological sustainability in the Australian Tourism industry: A Victorian perspective. Doctoral thesis. Department of Hospitality, Tourism and Leisure, RMIT University, Melbourne, Australia.

Weiler, B. and Crabtree, A. (1998) *Developing Competent Ecotour Guides.* National Centre for Vocational Education Research, Adelaide.

Weiler, B. and Davis, D. (1993) An exploratory investigation into the roles of the nature-based tour leader. *Tourism Management*, April, 91–98.

Weiler, B. and Ham, S.H. (2001) Tour guides and interpretation. In: Weaver, D. (ed.) *Encyclopedia of Ecotourism.* CAB International, Wallingford, UK, pp. 549–563.

Weiler, B., Johnson, T. and Davis, D. (1992) Roles of the tour leader in environmentally responsible tourism. In: Weiler, B. (ed.) *Ecotourism Incorporating the Global Classroom.* University of Queensland, Brisbane, Queensland, pp. 228–233.

18 Putting the Ecotour Guide Back into Context: Using Systems Thinking to Develop Quality Guides

Jon Kohl

Interpretive Planner and Trainer, Fermata, Inc., Costa Rica

Chapter Profile

Ecotourism strives to improve the environmental, cultural and social conditions of a place. Thus those who work as ecotour guides, ultimately, should serve that goal. Advocates of ecotour quality, however, often focus on measuring only a guide's personal qualities rather than on the guide's achievement of ecotourism's goal. With the increasing complexity of conservation issues, an enlarged definition of guide quality that includes conservation success can only be possible if ecotourism managers use systems thinking. This allows them to understand the multiple interactions between a guide and his/her complex context. By understanding the context and the guide's role in it and building in long-term learning mechanisms, ecotourism is more likely to reduce persistent policy resistance and better serve conservation and community.

Introduction

There are moments in society when one-time encounters serve their purpose: catch and release, love 'em and leave 'em and sudden-death kung fu matches. But training ecotour guides – training them and setting them free – can no longer remain one of them. To be an ecotour guide requires more than mastering natural and cultural history, practising environmental interpretation, navigating confusing trails, speaking multiple tongues or basking in the applause of fervid park visitors. To be an ecotour guide is to carry the flying colours of ecotourism, promoting conservation of natural and cultural heritage through tourism.[1] Thus any definition of ecotour[2] guide quality, any certification, any measure thereof, must incorporate consideration of conservation success. That society's penchant for reductionist thinking has cut ecotour guide training from its complex context must end if ecotour guides are to truly effect natural and cultural resource conservation.

 Quality Assurance and Certification in Ecotourism (eds R. Black and A. Crabtree)

Reductionist Thinking Cuts Training from Its Context

For tens of thousands of years, folk societies lived in a holistic world, consisting of all nature's cycles, ecological interactions and connections among different planes of existence. But then a curious thing happened on a dark November night in 1619. Through a series of dreams, René Descartes envisioned a flurry of symbols such as thunderclaps, books, an evil spirit and a delicious melon, from which he perceived that the universe is both rational and united through cause and effect. And over the next 30 years Descartes would introduce reductionism, 'the study of the world as an assemblage of physical parts that can be broken apart and analyzed separately' (Wilson, 1998: 31).

And so Western society began breaking things down in order to understand their complexity. First scientists became increasingly specialized, moving from general naturalists to adopting titles from arduously named sub-field specializations. Universities splintered into departments, companies created autonomous operating units.

Reductionist thinking branched off linear thinking, seeing the world as a one-way chain of cause and effect. Event A causes Event B, which causes Event C. OPEC reduces oil production, which increases prices, which annoys car owners, who buy hybrid cars. Such thinking ignores feedbacks between different variables, important delays, historical trends and, most of all, the relationships that influence behaviour resulting in these events.

We teach our children to be reductionist, even though evidence suggests that naturally they start out thinking intuitively in wholes (Senge, 1990). We use highly fragmented curricula that do not connect students with the world, with culture, with each other or even with themselves (Woodhouse, 1996).

Conventional teaching practice reflects fragmentary, linear thinking as well. Information flows one way from expert teacher to student or nature guide. The establishment knows what is best for every student, even if their needs and contexts vary. Unfortunately, over time, the idea of recombining the fragments together again to learn about complex wholes got lost. What make things complex and dynamic are the relationships and feedbacks between parts. If one studies separately me and my brother, one cannot speak to our relationship. As physicist, David Bohm, says, it is like trying to reassemble the fragments of a broken mirror to see a perfect reflection (Senge, 1990).

There should be little surprise, then, that, if society and the education system in particular chop up the world with a reductionist cleaver, then vocational training, such as ecotour guide training, does as well. Do any of these characteristics sound familiar?

- One curriculum fits all guides.
- One-shot training is expected to improve guiding capacity.
- Training courses are mostly theoretical, with little or no authentic practice or simulation.
- Courses are short, say, a couple of weeks or fewer.
- Experts design training programmes.

- Little, if any, feedback from students to teachers exists that either: (i) improves the way the course is taught or (ii) promotes mutual learning between instructors and students.
- Training programmes have implicit structural incentives to turn out graduates, with degrees or certification.
- Courses take place both 'out of site' and 'out of sight' of the guide's local context.

In the following section, we use the case study of one international conservation organization that transformed its guide training programme from a reductionist to a more holistic approach.

Rare's Nature Guide Training Program Began Reductionist

In 1994 an enterprising conservation organization, RARE Center for Tropical Conservation (referred to as Rare), teamed up with a private non-profit service teaching organization, WorldTeach, to create a novel brand of guide training in Costa Rica.

Because Rare focuses on grass-roots conservation, long-term partnering and local capacity building, it tries to develop programmes in terms of local needs rather than what its staff likes to do. So it conducted a survey that revealed great demand among both non-profit and for-profit ecotourism practitioners for bilingual nature guides. Rare then elicited the help of WorldTeach, an organization that trains volunteer teachers and deploys them around the world for up to a year to teach English to local people. Together they created a course for rural adults with little formal education that teaches basic skills necessary to work as local nature guides. Those included English, natural history and some guiding skills. The course aimed principally to provide local natural resource users (typically hunters and gatherers, considered poachers by the surrounding protected areas) with a sustainable lifestyle and income through ecotourism.

The programme was especially innovative because Rare trained WorldTeach volunteers about natural history and some guiding skills before the student guides arrived and integrated that knowledge into an immersive English-learning environment. Instructors transferred several pedagogical strategies used for English as a second language to natural history and guiding instruction, such as English for a Specific Purpose and the communicative approach. The innovation and its early success in teaching English to rural people in Costa Rica launched the programme in coming years to become Rare's well-known Nature Guide Training Program (NGTP) in Latin America.

Despite its success (that is, the popularity of the programme among donors and parks, the number of guides trained and the number of countries in which the programme worked) and since its inception, NGTP regarded its graduates as the final product, independent of any other ecotourism development effort. It did not try to integrate guides into larger conservation or business programmes, and it created a top-down curriculum executed by instructors (see Fig. 18.1). The programme was born reductionist, and it would take years to escape it. But the transition it is promoting between reductionist and holistic designs makes it an apt example for this chapter.

The Rise of Systems Thinking

Society grows more complex in a thousand ways. Technological advance requires more sophisticated systems for research, delivery and control. Globalization increasingly links finance, transportation, communication, security and cultures across the world. Population growth forces people to live closely together, requiring new lifestyle norms and accommodation. The number of societal relationships climbs exponentially, imbuing systems with their structure and behaviour.

Logically, conservation problems grow increasingly complex as well. A common conservation scenario involves scores to hundreds of variables: immigration rate, population growth, resource exploitation, law enforcement, economic situation, forest cover, ecosystem health, attitude towards nature, social stability, activity of conservation organizations. Together these variables result in system behaviours such as: repeating business cycles; exponential population growth, overshoot and collapse; rich get richer, poor get poorer; accelerating deforestation rate; and others.

Fig. 18.1. The original Nature Guide Training Program trained guides out of context, a strategy that would eventually change. Here Jorge interprets the mangroves in Honduras. (Photo by author.)

Reductionist thinking has not handled complex situations well. So, in the past couple of decades, there has been an upsurge in all things holistic. Social movements emphasizing integration and holism include environmentalism, human/animal rights, gender equity, Eastern religions in the West, recovering Native American traditions, green politics, steady-state economics, holistic medicine, green architecture, organic diets and vegetarianism, sustainable development, holistic education, total quality management, adaptive management, ecosystem management and systems thinking.

In this chapter we observe how systems thinking can improve ecotour guide quality. In mounting this argument, I draw especially from Peter Senge's book, *The Fifth Discipline: The Art and Practice of the Learning Organization* (1990), which unites systems thinking and organizational learning.

Systems thinking perceives a world of wholes rather than of parts. It emphasizes interrelationships and processes rather than linear cause and effect and snapshots in time. Systems thinking aims to find high leverage points in a system where the greatest and most enduring change can come with the least effort, in order to avoid policy resistance that often puts the brakes on interventions. Policy resistance occurs when other actors in a system, with their own goals, respond to an intervention in a way that neutralizes or worsens the effects sought by the original policy (Sterman, 2000). For example:

- Building wider nature trails in order to ease visitor congestion attracts more visitors due to greater accessibility, thus increasing congestion again.
- Conservationists train local poachers as ecotour guides. Yet the reduction in poachers creates a void that attracts more poachers because the demand for bush meat remains high.
- A coastal village promotes ecotourism to improve community welfare. Tourism booms. Outsiders build hotels, restaurants, shops, nightclubs, roads and street lights. The town grows, becomes crowded, garbage piles up, the water isn't safe for swimming, and eventually tourism dries up. Now the community has many expensive problems with which to deal and little income.
- Ecotour guides are trained and hired to bring more money into a park. Their training raises expectations of park managers, who then neglect proper business planning and the guides cost more money than they can bring in. Later the guides are laid off due to lack of funds.
- Guides on staff are sent to a guide training course to improve the quality of their performance. When they return, managers expect to see an immediate jump in customer satisfaction. When they do not, they decide that further investment in the guides is a waste of money. The guides are eventually fired as ineffectual.

The above discussion should suffice in relating the notion that a linear, reductionist perspective often leads people to misunderstand system behaviour, resulting in persistent policy resistance.

In the following sections, we shall begin viewing guides as wholes (not just entertainers, a business input or an empty vessel into which ecotour knowledge is poured) within larger wholes. We shall see that, due to complexity, there are no right answers and whatever solutions we devise must continually improve over time; but this can only happen with continuous learning, both by guides and by ecotourism managers.

What Should We Measure to Determine Ecotour Guide Quality?

Traditional ecotour guide quality indicators measure a legitimate but reductionist part of the story. Most indicators focus on guides themselves, such as their knowledge, skills, understanding of the park, and, of course, customer satisfaction at the end of their programmes.

While these measures rate the guide's personal performance, none rates the guide's contribution to larger ecotouristic or business objectives.[3,4] By applying a systemic view of the context, the whole, rather than just a part (such as the guide's personal capacities), ecotour guide quality ultimately depends on the guide's contribution to the larger objectives for which the guide has been recruited and trained to serve.

Since ecotourism can aim to conserve a particular place, whether a 100-metre nature loop trail or 1000 islands in Indonesia, it necessarily works in a complex system involving hundreds of interrelated variables and an overall system behaviour. As tempting as it might be, we cannot simply extract out education or conservation or standard-of-living variables from the morass of activity in which we labour and leave the rest for others to contemplate.

Certainly this enlarged purview will rankle with reductionist thinkers, who grew accustomed to measuring only how well guides can relate stories, the rapport they create with visitors and the conservation messages they share. While ecotourism managers must continue measuring these fine aspects of performance, their consideration will be absorbed into a larger picture of ecotour guide purpose and results.

While visitors on a guided hike may experience a sublime and spiritually transformative connection to a place, there may be little evidence that their participation in the programme has measurably contributed to conservation. If this is the case, the ecotour guide cannot ultimately consider him- or herself a success. Besides facilitating a positive visitor experience, then, the second function of a quality ecotour guide is to channel visitors' actions in order to meet these higher programmatic objectives of ecotourism, such as returns to conservation, local empowerment, fairer distribution of wealth and turning a profit.

What kinds of actions might guides promote among their self-actualized visitors? The following examples of actions make no reference to context or objective, so their applicability to any particular scenario remains general.

Conservation-related actions

- Become a member of a park friends group.
- Give a monetary donation to a conservation project (see Ham and Weiler, 2003).
- Donate computer equipment, binoculars, radios, books, camera equipment, etc.
- Donate services like translation, financial analysis, artwork or web design.
- Donate quality trip photographs of the protected area.
- Procure volunteers to work with the park.
- Make contacts for park management with university research programmes, donor agencies, Rotary Clubs and student exchanges.
- Set up pen pals with local schools in other countries.
- Join clean-up projects.
- Perform habitat restoration (plant trees, build bird boxes), adopt a creek.
- Write letters to politicians, newspapers and those involved in tourism.
- Report illegal actions seen on site.
- Protect wildlife from pets and other domestic animals.

Business-related actions

- Encourage other potential customers to purchase the same product.
- Make additional purchases such as souvenirs or add-on components, or patronize local businesses (restaurants, ecolodges, other operators).
- Become a member or supporter of tour operator conservation activities.
- Write positive reviews about the ecotourism product in periodicals.
- Fill out evaluation forms for the trip.

Definition of Quality Ecotour Guiding

We have established that an ecotour guide works for a particular location, which is characterized by complexity, and must help meet the specific objectives of ecotourism programmes designed to improve conservation of that site, as well as meeting business objectives. Thus, we can define quality and what should be measured as the following:

> A quality ecotour guide exhibits not only high proficiency in personal guiding skills (communication, group management, customer service skills, etc.) but also meets specific ecotourism programme objectives in the manner predetermined for guides by the programme design.

This description implicitly includes all traditional measures of guide quality (i.e. customer satisfaction, guide knowledge, guiding skills, etc.: see Weiler and Ham, 2001), as well as the guide's tools for reaching the programme objectives. I include the term 'predetermined' because, as often happens and has happened with Rare's NGTP, without specific objectives, anything positive counts as success. For example, although it was not specified as an objective, if a guide gets promoted to park administrator, NGTP claims success, as it did in Honduras. In another case, the guide moved on to become an expert kayaker and NOLS-certified trainer. This impressive achievement by a Mexican guide graduate was never an objective of the programme. Other guides create their own mini-guide training programmes, teach English, get hired by prestigious international tour operators, become environmental officers, and exhibit a wide range of other outcomes. Because they are not planned outcomes, most of them do not help meet the programme's objectives or even aid the target site's conservation. I do not discourage any organization from taking credit for such achievements, but they cannot stand alone in place of planned programme results.

Similarly some programmes (such as NGTP in past years) practise what is derisively called 'bean counting'. In more sterile language, these programmes confuse outputs with outcomes.[5] This is especially characteristic of institutions, like university programmes, designed to generate guides. Their banner of success rests on the number of guides trained or certified. This output indicator only represents the productivity of the programme (not even the quality) and tells us nothing about the guide's capacity to promote conservation or business at particular sites.

Now we have identified the travails of reductionist thinking and defined ecotour guide quality, we can discuss how to develop this quality for business and conservation objectives.

Design the Overall Ecotourism Programme for Business and Conservation

An important way to increase the quality of the guide in order to make meaningful contributions to the conservation objectives of ecotourism is for the programme itself to be designed in such a fashion as to permit significant conservation achievements. Thus, good project design based on the contextual situation in which ecotourism takes place, as well as an approach that promotes continuous learning, is essential to the success of ecotour programmes and their supporting guides.

The following section outlines guidance in designing and managing projects, using an adaptive project management framework based on the work by the Conservation Measures Partnership's (CMP) 'Open standards for the practice of conservation' (2004a). If indeed the quality of guiding depends on the guide's ability to help projects meet their objectives, then the effectiveness of project design is a crucial element in ensuring that quality. In other words, it is not just a function of how to train the guide, but the project context in which that guide works that determines quality.

Adaptive project management is based on a systems approach. Its basic process behaves as a single cycle (Fig. 18.2). That is, a manager designs a project and through monitoring receives feedback, used to improve the design,

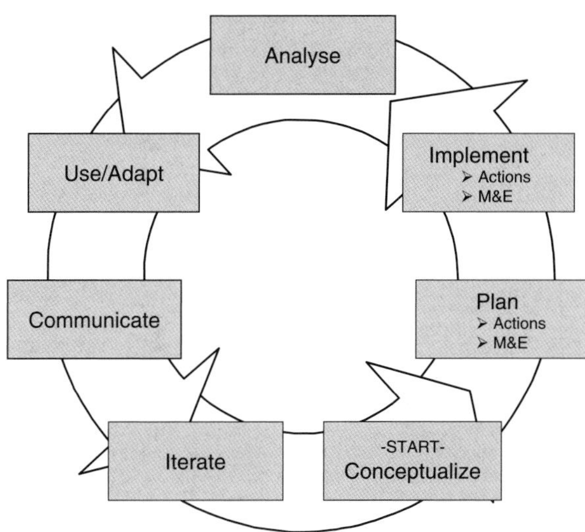

Fig. 18.2. Generalized project management cycle.

which receives further feedback and ideally enjoys continual improvement over the project's lifetime.

Elements throughout the project design cycle contain practices that improve its effectiveness and quality. This array of elements originates with the work of CMP, a consortium of international conservation organizations founded in 2003 'that seeks better ways to design, manage, and measure the impacts of their conservation actions' (CMP, 2004b). By conforming to an accepted standard, a conservation organization will have an industry-wide benchmark by which it can audit projects to the degree to which it is meeting its conservation objectives, and not just distributing press releases with that conclusion. While CMP is interested in conservation in particular, the standard of effective project design applies to all kinds of development projects.

The following summarized steps come from CMP's 'Open standards for the practice of conservation' (CMP, 2004a).

Conceptualize

A surprising number of projects lose their way very early in their journey. They never fully define their problem or understand the dynamic that drives it. Without such an understanding, it is nearly impossible to identify high leverage points and avoid policy resistance. Under these conditions, a programme can employ the world's best tour guides with little hope of achieving meaningful conservation. For this reason, quality in ecotourism must encompass the broad systemic context of a conservation problem (hereinafter called 'a threat') and intervention; without the conservation aspect, only traditional guide quality measures remain.

A programme must be clear about which threat it addresses and model that threat appropriately. While the conservationist must analyse threats to protected resources, on the business side of ecotourism, the practitioner must also investigate the potential market, including demand, customer profiles, political stability, competitive advantage, market saturation, market receptiveness, etc. Many business tools measure these as well.

During conceptualization, the practitioner not only describes the dynamics of the threat in the particular site, but also – specifically – how ecotourism, alone or in concert with other interventions, aims to mitigate or eliminate it. The construction of the model necessarily requires the modeller to clarify assumptions about the relationships between variables (see Box 18.1 on guiding assumptions).

The most common and perhaps simplest strategy for ecotourism is the generation of resources to support particular conservation activities. The following example outlines a real scenario, though the ecotourism response is mostly fictional. Rare guide graduates currently participate in the situation described.

Forest fire prevention in Tikal National Park, Guatemala

Tikal National Park (see Fig. 18.3) prepares fire brigades to fight its seasonal forest fires, but the resources needed for suppression are limited, especially in years of above-average dryness. Rare has suggested that ecotourism generate resources to support forest fire prevention. While the project needs money most of all, it can also benefit from donated tools and expert advising. The park then sets objectives of how much it would like to raise through ecotourism. It might say that, with US$10,000 in donations this year, 50 shovels and off-season advising from a fire ecologist, it could meet its expected needs.

Rare has trained guides, some of whom together have formed a cooperative ecotour operator, Conservation Tours Tikal, which sells interpretive products, as well as supplying additional locally provided services such as transportation, food and housing. The cooperative has designated 5% of net annual profits to park conservation efforts, which, if projections prove true, would yield about US$5000 to the fire prevention programme. The guides committed themselves to raising an additional US$5000 through solicited donations from visitors. Thus, the guides integrate the theme of fire into their interpretive tours and after each programme the guides solicit from visitors monetary and in-kind donations and they also ask for a contact with a volunteer fire ecologist.

To understand the role of ecotourism in contributing to the resolution of the problem or mitigation of the threat, it is necessary to model the problem. Models are by definition a simplified view of reality, focusing on aspects important to answering a particular question. The process, no matter what kind of model we create, involves identifying and surfacing assumptions about which variables are important in the dynamic of a problem and their relationships to other variables.

There are a variety of methodologies for modelling, but most involve diagramming at some point. Even sophisticated computer modellers start

Box 18.1. Seeing 20/20: 20 good and 20 not-so-good ecotour guide assumptions.

Convention observes that things seem clearer in 20/20 retrospection. Given that reductionist thinkers react to events, retrospect will always reveal unforeseen surprises in system behaviour. Systems thinkers, on the other hand, try to be generative rather than reactive by identifying structures to be changed in advance of the events, to which linear thinkers react. The following list of assumptions may help guide trainers generate better learning and conservation-promoting structures.

Not-so-good Assumptions

1. Give a guide some English and some natural history and away they go.
2. Short-term training will provoke enough interest and understanding for the guide to take over from there.
3. Non-profit and government agencies who train guides don't need to know a lot about the tourism industry or business in general to make effective ecotour guides.
4. Tourism companies do not need to know a lot about conservation to train effective ecotour guides.
5. Local people are the threat to biodiversity and therefore if we turn them into nature guides they: (a) won't cause more damage and (b) will teach their community not to do damage.
6. A well-trained guide can be effective in an environment unfamiliar with the training and its theories.
7. Good guides usually contribute to conservation. The fault is not in the contribution but our ability to detect and measure it.
8. Where there are good guides, tourists will follow.
9. Local guides are always better than urban or non-local guides.
10. Experts in tourism and guiding know better than local guides what should be taught in an ecotour training course.
11. If tourists say they are happy, then the guide must be a success.
12. If we teach guides the theory, they will be able to apply it in the field themselves.
13. Practice tours in the context of a course are sufficient for guides to later build, execute and improve actual tours in their parks.
14. Follow-up and monitoring are nice additions when there is money to implement them.
15. Creating a few local jobs for nature guides will win over the hearts and minds of the community towards the benefit of conservation of their protected area.
16. Generating income from a few local guides will have a significant economic multiplier effect for community economic development.
17. By teaching people to be local guides, they can also double as effective environmental educators.
18. Encouraging foreign visitors to perform conservation actions, anywhere, is an indicator of ecotour guide success.
19. Employing ecotour guides increases the park's ability to monitor its conservation targets.
20. Ecotour guide training success can be measured by the number of guides trained and the number of courses given.

Box 18.1. (Continued).

Good Assumptions

1. Actual learning doesn't take place during a formal course.
2. A guide without a context is a wheel without a car.
3. For a guide to be an effective agent of ecotourism, he/she needs a lot of well-informed supervision and planning.
4. One-off short courses often waste time and money as well as raising guides' expectations unnecessarily.
5. It is more important that programme managers be systems thinkers than the guides themselves.
6. The ecotourism programme, not the guide, has conservation goals. Thus the programme, not the guide, usually decides how the guide will achieve the goals.
7. Guides do not link directly to conservation without being involved in a larger conservation strategy.
8. Like most professions, it requires years of training and practice to become a professional-level ecotour guide, though this level is not necessary for all strategies.
9. Guides learn best when they perceive that their training meets their needs.
10. Since a guide is responsible for conservation benefits as much as any other person working in the ecotourism project, if conservation does not result, the guide and the rest of the team are responsible. It is reductionist to say that the guide is an unqualified success even though the overall project fails.
11. Private-sector guides need a wider range of skills than park guides employed by management agencies.
12. Developing, maintaining and improving a body of guides require more structured learning than occasional in-service training.
13. A guide facilitates positive visitor experiences and channels specific visitor actions towards specific conservation objectives.
14. Many local guides on a site do not necessarily result in many benefits for the site. The relationship between the number of guides and benefits depends on the structure of the system.
15. Interpretation, environmental education and even ecotourism are means to greater ends. If the project does not clearly define how these tools contribute to the ends and does not have objectives to define those outcomes, then the programme will not succeed.
16. Understanding that a guide is in a context increases the chances that the guide will positively change that context.
17. Personal visions may be consistent with the shared vision, but are never the same and never static.
18. Measuring only a guide's personal qualities says little about that guide's potential to contribute to conservation.
19. Anything positive that a guide does should not be mistaken for actions that contribute to the programme's objectives.
20. Policy resistance is the reward that goes to those who try to solve whole problems by inspecting only the problems' parts.

Fig. 18.3. Tikal monuments sit amidst the forests of the park (photo by Marisol Mayorga).

with a sketch. Figure 18.4 presents a modified causal loop diagram used in the systems dynamics field (Sterman, 2000).

The diagram answers the question 'How does ecotourism contribute to the reduction of forest fires in Tikal National Park?' Before explaining the

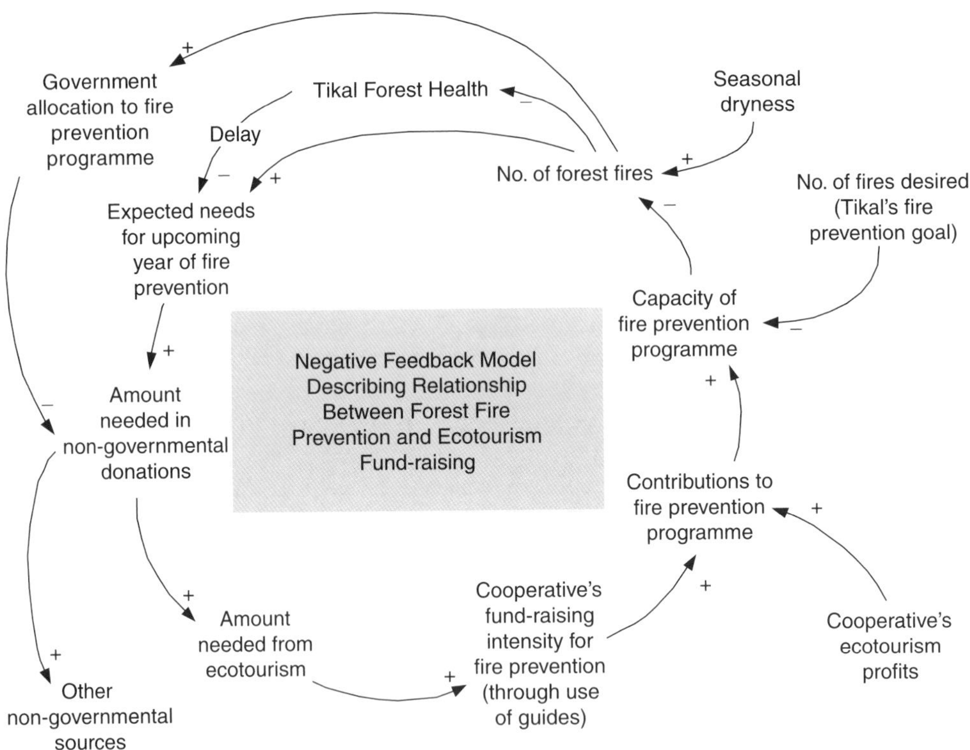

Fig. 18.4. Negative feedback model describing the relationship between forest fire prevention and ecotourism fund-raising.

content of the model, it is necessary to understand how to read it. First note that the model is circular. Since feedbacks are the building blocks of systems,[6] we can see that every variable is eventually affected by variables it affects. Thus, cause and effect happen in a circle or cycle, not in straight lines with no feedbacks.

System behaviour often involves time delays. Delays in response are responsible for so much of system behaviour that systems thinkers include exceptional time delays in the diagrams, like the one seen between Tikal forest health and expected needs for an upcoming year of fire prevention. This delay indicates the long time scientists need to collect enough data and report conclusively on forest health, much longer than the political response to the number of forest fires the previous season.

The number of forest fires immediately affects the government's willingness to combat forest fires, affects overall forest health and is feedback to managers on how much they need to adjust their fire suppression effort for the following year. When they compare their needs to budget allocations, they know how much money they need from other sources. They direct their own ecotourism or that of the cooperative to increase contributions, which increases the capacity (and hopefully effectiveness) of the programme, which then affects the number of forest fires.

Overall, the model represents a negative feedback loop since, as the number of forest fires increase, that triggers a series of relationships that produces more money for forest fire prevention, thus correcting an imbalance in forest fires. The goal (number of forest fires desired) indicates where managers think that balance should be.

Plan

Strategic plan

After having analysed the context, the business environment and the threat, we need to begin designing the programme, in which ecotour guides will exercise their art. All plans must start with governing ideas – vision, mission, goals, objectives and possibly core values. While these ideas may have directed analysis in the previous step, it is during the planning phase that planners cast them concretely, clearly and rendered into operation. This is true for both conservation and business aspects. Based on governing ideas, the plan develops the most efficient and equitable strategies to accomplish its objectives.

Action plan

The action plan follows the strategic plan. The action plan details which actions the programme will execute and how their successful implementation should result in the fulfilment of objectives. Managers choose activities, considering high leverage points in the system. These points promote efficiency (with time and money) and minimize policy resistance.

In our Tikal example, some activities necessary for the cooperative to make contributions include the following:

1. Identify the needs of the fire prevention programme.
2. Design product interpretation to include a fire theme.
3. Train guides to link programme needs and potential donors.
4. Ensure that a financial mechanism exists to register donations and that they are channelled to the programme.
5. Set up a rewards system to encourage guides to solicit and achieve visitor donations.

Monitoring and evaluation plan

In order for learning to take place, a programme must intentionally build in feedbacks so that managers know how well their interventions are achieving planned results. If the feedback is relevant, timely and noticed, then the programme should be able to adapt and grow in its effectiveness.

As with other aspects of good project design, indicators tie directly into the activities, objectives and model used to design the programme.

Some indicators that may be useful in measuring the success of ecotour guides include:

1. Natural history knowledge.
2. Quality of interpretive skills.
3. Customer satisfaction.
4. Trail damage or trash recovered along guide's route.
5. Guide's financial contribution as percentage of guiding target to conservation.
6. Success of fire prevention unit to which ecotourism's contributions are being applied.
7. Target number of forest fires.

Note that it can be difficult to calculate how much responsibility guides themselves share in an overall conservation programme. Certainly a percentage of programme success can be calculated based on the proportion of funding contributed by guides. Rare's Public Use Planning Program calculates visitor contributions to larger conservation projects this way. But, if an overall project is not yielding conservation benefits, it would be wrong to call the guides' work successful in terms of conservation, even though they may be successful financially. The guide is, after all, part of the team.

Budget

Once project designers have completed the action and monitoring and evaluation (M & E) plans, we should be able to budget how much it will cost to run the plan. Again a budget should be tied to strategic and action plans. It is always a part of a business plan (National Parks Conservation Association, 2004).

Implement plans

Now that the project has been designed, it must be implemented.

Analyse

As the M & E plan generates data during implementation, programme managers need to analyse them. Hopefully results will indicate how managers can modify their programme for improvement. Improvement will take place throughout the entire process from situational analysis, through all forms of planning, implementation, even to the conception of the basic problem itself. Unfortunately, this is a step often underestimated by project managers, leaving them with significant amounts of data but no one or no way to analyse it. It is, therefore, important to plan for analysis as early as possible in the project management cycle.

Use and adapt

Of course, collecting and analysing data are of no value if those results are not turned into learning and improving the capacity of the programme to produce the desired results.

Communicate

Every project needs to communicate to various programme stakeholders, whether donors, clients, collaborators, academics, policy makers or news media. In our example, some audiences include Tikal park staff, UNESCO (principal donor), other sites where similar results are taking place, news media, area tourism associations and professional community.

Iterate

This step indicates that updates and improvements in the project will then pass through the project management cycle. Since we are dealing with complex scenarios where there is no right answer, the best we can hope for is continual improvement throughout the project life cycle (Senge, 1990).

Rare's Nature Guide Training Program Becomes Systemic

In 2001, Rare entered into a 4-year agreement with the United Nations to pilot-test linkages between ecotourism and biodiversity conservation at six World Heritage Sites. Consequently the organization took a couple of important steps in trying to make its programme implementation more systemic. First, Rare formed Rare Enterprises, a division that develops local ecotourism enterprises and includes a local ecotourism planner training programme, trail building programme, regional marketing and business development and NGTP, and increasingly aims to integrate these programmes.

As part of this 4-year project, Rare teamed up with Foundations of Success (FOS), a non-profit network of individuals and institutions that seeks to improve the practice of conservation and to develop tools and a means of managing adaptively. With FOS's help, Rare developed a site assessment methodology that attempts to look at a full range of contextual considerations before designing any particular intervention, including guide training (Rare, 2005).

FOS helped Rare develop monitoring plans and a solid conceptual understanding of programme interventions, and set up mechanisms for learning. NGTP had to pass through all these steps to understand the connection between nature guides and conservation. Figure 18.5 shows the diagram used to explain the linkages. While linear, it makes numerous explicit assumptions that connect nature guides to biodiversity conservation.

Another important step was to begin a long process of integrating its different ecotourism tools (NGTP, promoters, trail development and others)

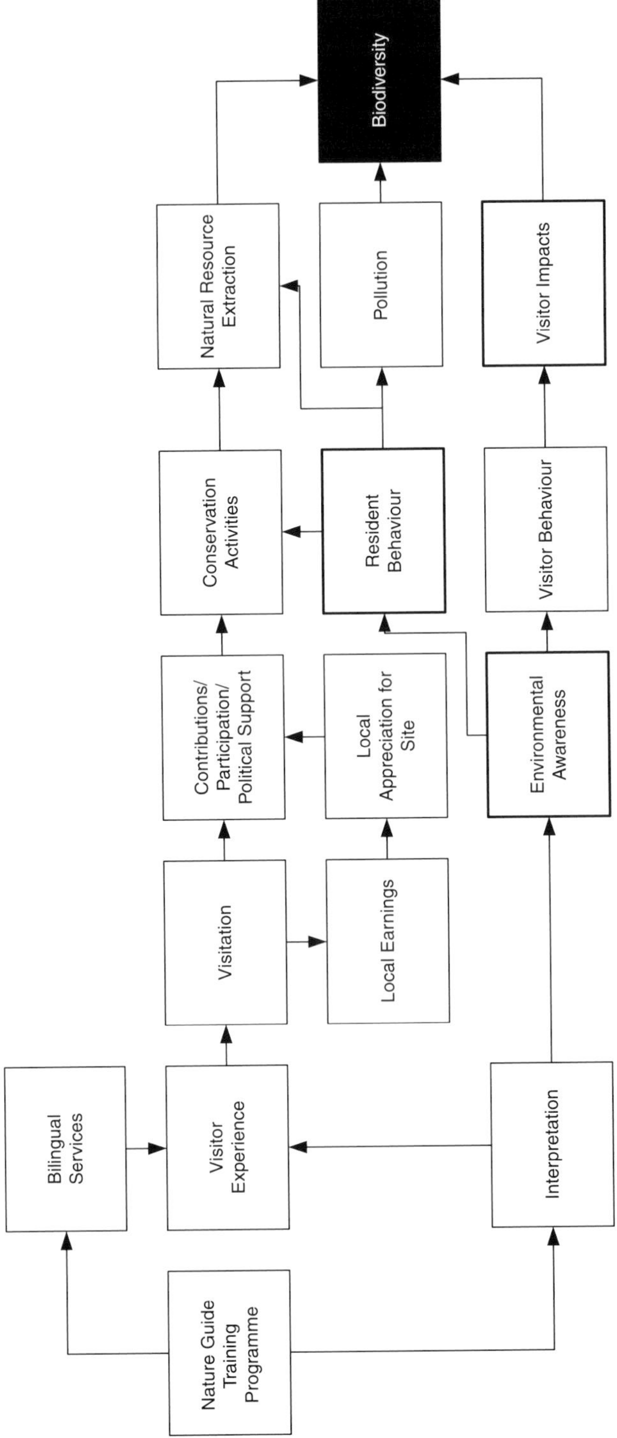

Fig. 18.5. Rare model linking nature guide training with biodiversity conservation.

and link them to market demand – thus beginning to adopt a more systemic approach. Previously Rare would run a guide training programme, then promote a training programme, and then try to integrate sites into regional markets; yet, in the last couple of years, Rare has shifted its focus to analysing a site in terms of ecotourism demand and supply, conservation threats and objectives, stakeholders and other aspects in a more holistic site assessment. Then with stakeholders it defines ecotourism objectives and connections to conservation. Thereafter, it also defines how different ecotourism tools can be combined to produce desired results.

Rare no longer trains nature guides without first having undertaken some business planning and deciding what inputs are necessary for ecotourism development and in what order. Rare no longer views its guides as final products, but rather as smaller wholes in a larger ecotourism whole. By adopting a more systemic approach to a site's needs and dynamics in terms of conservation and ecotourism, it tries to break down the artificial and reductionist barriers between guide development, business planning, conservation planning and community development. It is a long road, but their approach has already left other guide training programmes behind in linear history (Fig. 18.6).

Training is Part of a Larger Learning Process

Extracting training from its context like a splinter from a toe would reduce the training's applicability to a site's complexity and the likelihood that the

Fig. 18.6. Quality of interpretive guides must be measured not only for the individual guide's performance but for the success of the programme in which he or she practises (photo by Matt Humke).

guide will have the means to continue learning in years ahead. Thus, one-off, isolated training programmes cannot usually meet the spirit of the enlarged definition of ecotour guide quality or the definition of learning, which is to increase the capacity to produce results that we really want in life. In this section, I offer some key systemic ways in which the training can promote a greater integration of guide and system.

Shared vision binds guide to context and purpose

The first rule of learning is that people learn best when they feel their needs are being met. Thus a clear fit between their personal vision and the vision of their organization and their training programme motivates learning. Senge (1990) explains that a shared vision brings people together, but cannot be created with just one session. People and organizations accommodate each other's vision in an ongoing and evolving dance. Every potential guide has a vision of benefits that guiding will bring. The closer their vision fits the vision of the training programme and the ecotourism in which they will work, the more relevant they see the training and the faster they will learn. But resources are limited and teachers will not always be around to help. For learning to continue after the main training finishes, a guide needs to learn to learn. In order to pursue the necessary inputs to a guide's learning, they must have a vision of what they are trying to build. Without a blueprint, the guide cannot easily know which materials to acquire to build their house.

NGTP has suffered the problem of training guides to work in conservation, but not helping them sufficiently to understand their role in it. If they are to solicit donations, they need to better understand the needs of fire prevention and how to link those needs to potential donors. They need to be able to recognize a successful fire prevention programme if they are to explain with enthusiasm and clarity what the solicitation is for and why it is important.

Curriculum teaches guides to understand complex contexts

Aside from defining the knowledge and skills that a guide should have about the generic craft and vision of guiding, the curriculum should also include material to help the guide understand their conservation issues, the context and how they will relate to it. Generic curricula do not bridge the needs of the guide to fully understand their role in the context itself. NGTP has been very effective at this point. For every training site in which Rare has worked, the guide training staff write a customized *Guide's Guide*. This volume, written in the guides' native language and one of five volumes comprising the guide training assessment manual (Rare, 2001), presents general information on biology and conservation but also provides extensive research on each site to make as much of the material as relevant as possible to the guide's reality. Staff usually add a chapter or more to the book interpreting issues of that particular site. For example, in the south-east Mexico manual, Rare included a chapter on the Natural History Institute and its role in Chiapas's conservation history. NGTP managers also scour the generic curriculum for every opportunity to modify it to the needs of the particular student body and make it relevant to the guides' work.

The role of the training team in facilitating guides' adaptation to the ecotourism programme

Trainers know the material of their course. They were trained to impart lessons to prospective guides. With this linear approach, however, trainers are unlikely to understand the context, the ecotourism programme, the conservation strategy or even how to help guides develop a personal vision.

Thus, a training programme can integrate a guide and their studies much more to the context by preparing the training staff for this task. First, staff need to understand the context and importance of a guide's vision in motivating and directing a guide's learning. Then they need training themselves to participate in the continuous adaptation and elicitation of personal visions.

Aside from vision, the team should be trained in group learning. Senge (1990) discusses how for any invention to become an innovation that can be replicated reliably, at scale and at a reasonable cost requires the synergistic interplay of core technologies. For example, between the time the Wright brothers demonstrated that flight was possible and McDonnell Douglas introduced its commercially successful DC-3 in 1935, 30 years passed. It was not until the DC-3 integrated five critical components that commercial flight became possible. Those components comprised the variable-pitch propeller, retractable landing gear, lightweight moulded body, radial air-cooled engine and wing flaps.

We still do not know all the core components for ecotour guide training. How it is done will emerge from a continual process of learning and improvement. Thus, the training team cannot just impart expert knowledge, but needs to learn together to develop that knowledge and try to develop core technologies. Senge (1990) proposes five disciplines necessary for team members to learn together: systems thinking,[7] mental models, building share vision, personal mastery and team learning. While NGTP trains its staff to work together as a team, it does not focus on explicit team learning, perhaps the most important aspect of team function.

Training structure provides interaction and learning with context

There are several ways to modify a typical one-off training course structure to promote greater interaction with context and improved longer-term learning. As Senge (1990) points out, mastery of a discipline occurs as the novice learns the rules of action, experiments with them and then after a while is able to implement those rules from the subconscious under stress and ambiguity – 'people will have adapted the rules into their own particular model, speaking in their own voice' (p. 377). Consider average times for different kinds of apprenticeships, from 2 years for a drywall finisher to 5 years as an electrician. To become an experienced ecotour guide will take a period measured in years as well.

For most of NGTP's existence, guides participated in a course of 70–80 days' duration. During the course, each guide performs up to ten guided tours in English, starting at 10 minutes and working up to the final 45-minute tour. Then WorldTeach volunteers accompany guides for a month in their own communities. Thereafter Rare staff would make occasional visits.

Rare has deemed this insufficient time for learning and too much uninterrupted course time (C. Mayoral, NGTP manager, Arlington, Virgina, personal communication, 2004). NGTP is now adopting a format similar to the Rare Ecotourism Promoters Course (capacity-building programme that prepares local people to facilitate the creation or development of local ecotourism ventures) and the Public Use Planning courses – which is to break up coursework into three segments separated by a period of at least 2 months when practitioners do real-life work at their site (Rare, 2004), where their mistakes have consequences. Throughout this period, Rare staff remain only a call away and often visit at strategic moments to help guides through tough periods. When guides return, the simulations during workshops are much richer and the guides boast real-life experience to share with each other. While still not as authentic as a tradesperson's apprenticeship, the course does mix a great deal of authentic, real-time experience into its training.

Then, after the formal coursework finishes, neither promoters nor public use coordinators actually graduate until they have produced a major product. For example the coordinators must finish the entire first round of planning and have their strategic park plan approved by authorities. Rare is phasing out the bestowing of certificates for simply passing a course. It focuses now on making sure people can do the work in their given context. Promoters, coordinators and soon guides will no longer be extracted from their context and trained independently of it. The days of one-off training courses are numbered.

Preparing the Context to Receive and Support Guides

One hallmark of traditional, reductionist training is its isolation from the reality in which guides will work. Curriculum designers work far away, training sites are often far away, and trainers do not know the context or the people there. Yet, for ecotour guide training to develop the highest-quality guides, who can contribute to conservation and business, the programme needs to integrate into the local context in a way similar to schools involving parents.

If parents understand what their children are learning, they can support and supplement that learning. If parents understand how children are learning, they are more likely to accept and approve the techniques (e.g. field trips). Likewise the guides' own environment needs to be receptive and understanding of the new ways they bring home.

NGTP has for the past several years placed increasing emphasis on working with guide supervisors. It had one experiment in Honduras where it actually designed a supervisor training programme where supervisors came during the course to work with their guides. A problem that often haunts training is that a newly trained employee returns to an environment that has not changed. US Peace Corps volunteers often complain that after their 2 years away in a foreign country they change remarkably in maturity and outlook and yet when they return home little has changed. No one understands their new perspective or experience and sometimes counterculture shock[8] sets in. The effect is worse in a work environment where supervisors may not allow the modifications necessary for the guide to practise new approaches. For example:

- Supervisors do not help guides create or approve interpretive themes because they do not understand their value.
- Senior management allocates money for follow-up training but only for information-intensive courses that do not reinforce new guiding skills.
- The guide sees the connection between ecotourism and conservation but is not responsible for setting up the infrastructure to make that connection achievable.
- Guides want to solicit donations but no financial mechanism exists to account for donations or the park may not be able to accept donations.
- Staff do not have any concept of guide quality so the guide has no support to develop their nascent lessons. There may be institutional incentives (such as saving money) that actively promote poor quality.

If these types of situations arise, the danger of the reductionist assumption becomes apparent that simply training the guide and releasing them back into their small pond will be sufficient for continued growth. To address these situations NGTP currently uses at least three strategies to develop an environment that supports guides.

Visioning with supervisors

As mentioned above, NGTP is always looking for new cost-effective ways of involving supervisors. One strategy is to ensure that future supervisors participate in visioning workshops at the outset of any new site where Rare Enterprises will work. In addition to the general visioning workshop, different interventions, such as NGTP and Public Use Planning, have their own specific workshops to prepare potential supervisors. Public Use Planning even develops a social contract to which supervisors must agree. It has the objective of ensuring that supervisors realize, if not share, the vision of the training and they agree to carry out tasks to support the public use coordinator.

Prearranged jobs

NGTP had discovered on previous occasions that, when parks pay to train guides, they often could not guarantee them work. In these situations, rates of guides abandoning guiding often proved high within the first year. Now Rare Enterprises tries not to train anyone unless they either are already on staff or have a specific opportunity to exercise their new motivation in a manner such that Rare can continue to work with them.

Support network

I prefer not to use the word 'follow up' as it implies a nice but non-essential addition to the 'real' training. The period many people call 'follow up' is actually the most crucial time for learning because guides are for the first time practising, erring and learning in a real-life situation. NGTP and other Rare programmes strive to develop formal support networks both through staff and through other graduates. In the past this was not emphasized; the assumption was that if guides wanted to support each other they would. In Honduras, for example, guides formed an association, elected officers and did some fund-raising before the course ended. Rare did not support that association in its formative days and it slid slowly into oblivion.

Now NGTP plans to maintain contact with all graduates and perhaps support more formal associations among them. Also, contact and access to Rare staff may be extended further into the future. Currently the Public Use Program envisions at least a 3-year programme, while NGTP only fund-raises for a 1-year intervention, after which no formal structure exists to support guides. Another programme, called Rare Pride, which is a conservation education programme with graduates around the world, actively takes advantage of virtual networks, chat rooms and other forms of Internet-based communication to keep its graduates together and learning.

The Path Ahead

NGTP and guide training in general are in a time of transition as proposals for more holistic approaches appear in many different fields. Based on the experiences of Rare and its programme, recommendations follow for all guide training programmes that seek long-term benefits from their efforts:

1. Train team members in several or all of the five disciplines of a learning organization as described in Senge's (1990) *Fifth Discipline*.
2. Training staff, not just programme managers, should have more experience in the site to help guides adapt to their context.
3. Trainers should see themselves as facilitators of vision and be involved in the visioning process, rather than just a one-shot vision workshop.
4. Programmes should establish infrastructure to offer technical assistance to guides over the years, not just for 1 year. Rare, in one instance, has considered establishing a central guide training school, spinning it off to another organization or facilitating a guide-run international organization.

5. Programmes should try to identify core technologies of guide training. While there is no Holy Grail of guide formation, the notion of synergy between core components could reframe the pursuit to improve the methodology in such a way as to accelerate learning.
6. Make holistic learning a central tenet throughout the training process, not just in the monitoring and evaluation.

This discussion has now come full circle, bringing us back to the original question and intent of this chapter and book. What do we measure to ensure ecotour guide quality? Are certification and licensing the right mechanisms?

Certainly there is great need for measuring the traditional and highly specific aspects of guiding. In fact, NGTP uses a tool called the Tour Guide Checklist, with over 70 specific items organized along 20 Characteristics of a Good Guide. In this sense, certification covers part of the guide's fare. It does not indicate if the guide is really prepared to contribute in a manner specific to a particular site's conservation. Also it does not indicate if the project has been designed specifically to ensure that the guide can contribute in a specific manner to conservation.

Many guide training and certifying programmes focus on outputs rather than outcomes. That is, they grade themselves on the number of people certified or graduated. NGTP did this once, but now one of the overarching themes leading NGTP to the future is that training the most technically skilled guides in the world does not ensure or even indicate if any real conservation is taking place (C. Mayoral, NGTP manager, Arlington, Virginia, personal communication, 2004). If no real conservation is taking place, it is not ecotourism and the guides as well as the programme are not ultimately successful.

In order to implement this expanded definition of assuring quality in ecotour guide training, programme managers must look beyond their curricula, training materials and personal performance indicators to assure quality; they must also assure that the guide is trained within a context, one that is both receptive to new approaches and one that has specific built-in mechanisms that define how the guide contributes to the ecotourism programme's objectives. That is quality through a systems perspective.

At the rate at which biodiversity, local cultures, languages and diversity in general are being lost on our planet, nothing short of a significant outcome-based measure for ecotour quality will do. Quality is not only in the eye of the beholder, but in the jungles, coral reefs, deserts, indigenous communities and other last refuges of diversity in decline.

Notes

[1] In this chapter, all references to conservation refer not only to natural resources but also to cultural resources, both past and present. Thus community development that aims to maintain the health and character of local communities I assume for convenience to be subsumed under this term.

[2] The International Ecotourism Society defines ecotourism as 'responsible travel to natural areas that conserves the environment and improves the well-being of local people' (http://www.ecotourism.org/index2.php?what-is-ecotourism).
[3] Although project planners distinguish between goals and objectives, I shall not discuss these differences in this chapter. For more information on this topic, see Margoluis and Salafsky (1998).
[4] By this definition, freelance guides (such as those that graduate from university programmes) are not ecotour guides until they work within an ecotourism programme or business.
[5] Outcomes are the ultimate results for which the programme strives. Outputs are intermediary products that move a programme closer to its outcomes.
[6] A feedback is the effect a result has on the variables that caused that result. For example, if I slam a door on my finger (the result), my body sends a screaming signal of pain from the contact, causing me to withdraw my hand (one of the variables that produced the result). This is negative feedback that works to correct an imbalance (damage to my body). A positive feedback works to accelerate the effect. For example, if I make money on the stock market, I get a signal that makes me happy and encourages me to invest again in the stock market. If I continue to do well, then I might get addicted.
[7] Senge calls systems thinking the 'fifth discipline', after which he named his book. Without systems thinking, he argues, teams can never have a realistic idea of the kinds of leverage points needed to reach their visions.
[8] That is, a volunteer has to readapt to his or her own culture. He or she is often acutely aware of perceived deficiencies in his or her own culture and few can understand or empathize. Without proper social support, the person may suffer depression.

Organizational Links

Rare, www.rareconservation.org
WorldTeach, www.worldteach.org
Society for Organization Learning, www.solonline.org (founded by Senge)
Foundations of Success, www.fosonline.org
Conservation Measures Partnership, www.conservationmeasures.org

References

Conservation Measures Partnership (2004a). Open standards for the practice of conservation.

Conservation Measures Partnership (2004b) Available at: www.conservationmeasures.org.

Ham, S.H. and Weiler, B. (2003) Toward a theory of quality in cruise-based nature guiding. *Journal of Interpretation Research* 7(2), 29–49.

Margoluis, R. and Salafsky, N. (1998) *Measures of Success: Designing, Managing, and Monitoring Conservation and Development Projects*. Island Press, Washington, DC, 363 pp.

National Parks Conservation Association (2004) The Business Plan Process Meets National Parks. Available at: www.npca.org/across_the_nation/americansfor nationalparks/learn_more/park_data/business_plan.asp (accessed in June).

Rare (2001) *Interpreting for Conservation: A Manual for Training Local Nature Guides*, 5 vols. RARE, Arlington, Virginia.

Rare (2004) *Park Planning for Life: Manual for Public Use Coordinators*. RARE, Arlington, Virginia.

Rare (2006) *Site Assessment Manual*. RARE, Arlington, Virginia.

Senge, P.M. (1990) *The Fifth Discipline: The Art and Practice of the Learning Organization*. Doubleday Currency, New York, 424 pp.

Sterman, J.D. (2000) *Business Dynamics: Systems Thinking and Modeling for a Complex World*. McGraw-Hill, New York, 982 pp.

Weiler, B. and Ham, S.H. (2001) Tour guides and interpretation. In: Weaver, D. (ed.) *Encyclopedia of Ecotourism*. CAB International, Wallingford, UK, pp. 549–563.

Wilson, E.O. (1998) *Consilience: The Unity of Knowledge*. Vintage Books, New York, 368 pp.

Woodhouse, M.B. (1996) *Paradigm Wars: Worldviews for a New Age*. Frog, Berkeley, California, 632 pp.

19 Towards Developing Tour Guides as Interpreters of Cultural Heritage: the Case of Cusco, Peru

GEMMA MCGRATH

University of the Arts, London College of Communication, London, UK

Chapter Profile

Over the last 10 years heritage tourism has become an increasingly popular activity for visitors and has been actively promoted by governments. The debate on sustainability within the discipline of tourism studies during the late 1980s coincided with the growth of ecotourism as a tourism activity (Cooper *et al.*, 1993; McGrath, 1994). In the UK, this debate then shifted to encompass cultural heritage and its management during the late 1990s. This chapter looks at the role tour guides play in developing more sustainable tourism at archaeological sites in Peru (McGrath, 2005).

Introduction

The chapter is structured in three parts. The first outlines why Cusco's archaeology requires skilful interpretation and sensitive visitor management, but it also highlights how a lack of quality assurance and a lack of integration of key stakeholders have created operational issues in the region.

The second part of the chapter focuses on interpretation as a strategic planning tool in order to overcome some of the key issues facing less developed world regions promoting heritage tourism. The final section recommends the redesign of tour guide training to encourage quality assurance in both curriculum design and service delivery. The need to develop training that enables guides to be interpreters of their heritage is discussed in the context of the need for tourism and interpretation to work for conservation. The design of appropriate training is recommended for delivery to the local indigenous people living near the sites who currently cannot participate in the industry. Developing a vision that allows tour guide training to support the diffusion of the conservation message emerged as a key opportunity from the study. The fine-tuning of curriculum is required to facilitate inspirational tour guiding, whether for heritage or ecotourism development.

Country Overview

Peru is the third largest country in South America and, as shown in Fig. 19.1, is bordered by five different countries and lies to the west of the continent on the Pacific Ocean.

Peru contains a wealth of natural attractions, abundant wildlife and vibrantly diverse cultures in its people, adding a 'human' dimension to its heritage. Approximately half the population is native Indian, while a third is made up of the Spanish–Indian mix, the *mestizo*, 12% are white and only 5% are black. The majority of the population, 71%, live in the urban areas, with only 29% found in the rural areas. The official language is Spanish, but the highlanders, who call themselves *campesinos*, which means country people, speak both the indigenous languages of Quechua and Aymara widely. The majority of the *campesinos* have native languages as their mother tongue, though most, depending on their level of education, can also speak and write Spanish.

In 2000, the average rate of poverty in urban areas was recorded at 36.9%, while the average rural poverty rate was nearly double, at 70% (Peruvian National Institute for Statistics and Information, 2001). There are marked socio-economic contrasts between the different ethnic groups that comprise the 27 million individuals who make up Peru's population (World Development Indicators, 2004). Modern-day ethnic power relations in Peruvian society have not changed much since the arrival of the conquistadores, despite the development of democracy. The current President of Peru, Alejandro Toledo, however, was sworn in as Peru's first democratically elected president of Quechua ethnicity in 2001. He identified tourism as a development option for Peru in his inaugural speech and posed for his photographs at Machu Picchu.

Tourism in Peru

Peru has remained one of the most popular countries to visit in the South American continent over the last 30 years. This popularity is due to the spectacular landscapes across three distinct and contrasting environments: immense desert coastline, vast tracts of tropical rainforest and the Andes, the second greatest mountain chain in the world after the Himalayas. These lend themselves to the development of three main types of tourism product: cultural, adventure and ecotourism. According to PromPeru (2002, 2003) the overwhelming majority of visitors come to Peru because of its archaeological wealth, although they may also undertake some elements of other types of activity during their stay. Many of its cultural attractions, such as its archaeological sites, are set

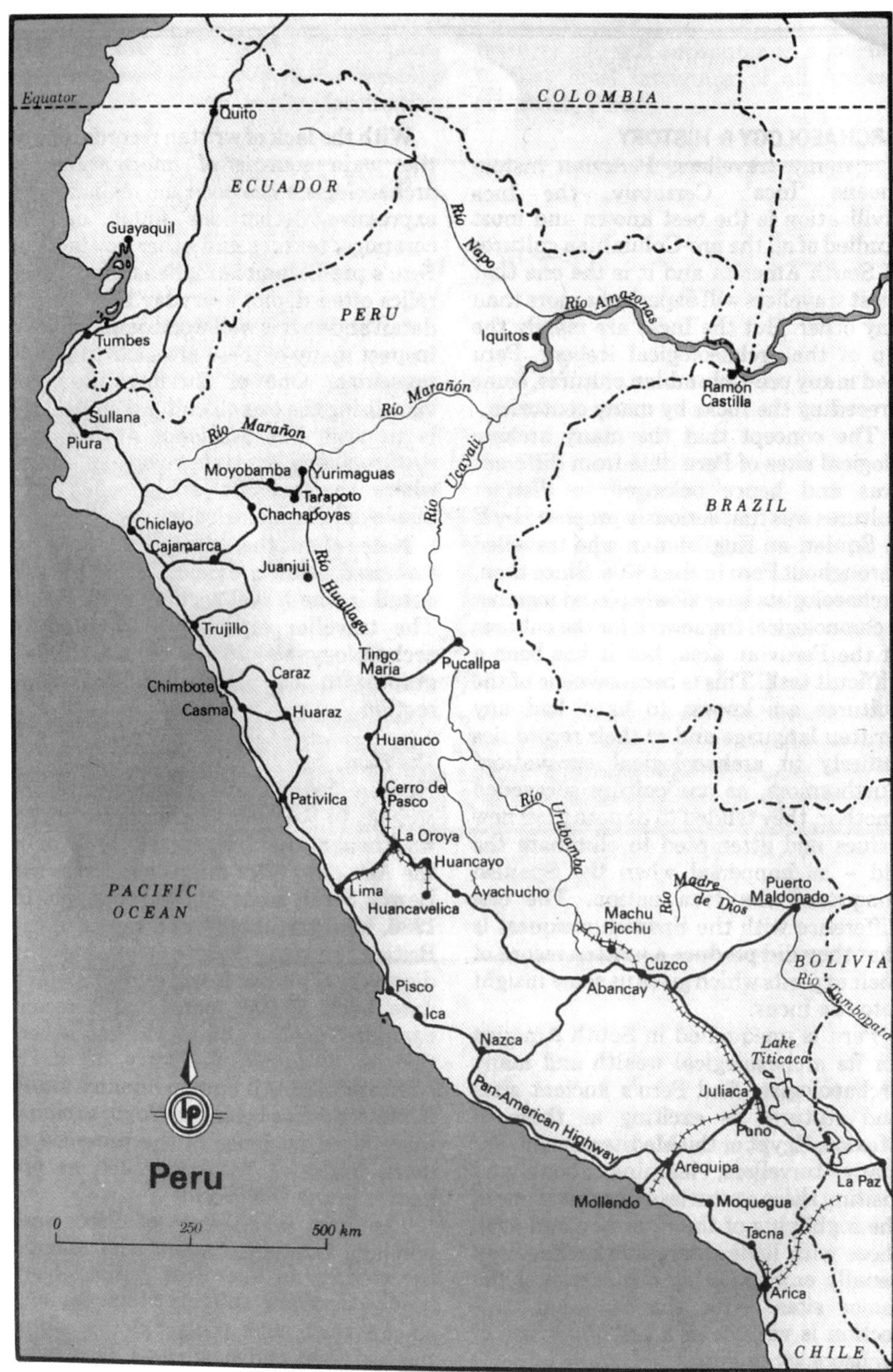

Fig. 19.1. Map of Peru, showing its location within South America (from Rachowiecki, 1987, reproduced with kind permission from Lonely Planet).

amidst stunning natural surroundings and so visitors often engage in different types of tourism simultaneously.

Due to economic and political turmoil, Peruvian tourism experienced two significant troughs in the early 1980s and 1990s. In 1992, there were 216,534 international visitors to Peru, but, by 1994, a sharp increase to 386,120 was recorded and largely attributed to the improved economic conditions brought about by the capture of Guzman, the head of the Maoist terrorist group, the Shining Path. Able to market itself as a safe destination, Peru has seen this trend continue, with the year 1998 logging a record 833,807 international visitors, responsible for generating US$631 million income (Pacific Consultants International, 1999). In 2000, the 1 million target was achieved, 2 years ahead of its forecast. Tourism accounts for nearly 11% of Peru's GDP, but the current volume of visitors is now resulting in problems with over-congestion (Ladkin and Bertramini, 2002). These arrivals have put pressure on the carrying capacity of the destination, but this is as much to do with a lack of planning for the tourism that is aggressively promoted overseas, as it is linked to the current approach to heritage management that is dominant in the respective bodies responsible for tourism and archaeology (McGrath, 2005).

The problem of over-congestion is compounded by the fact that tourism is not evenly distributed in Peru, with at least 80% of all visitors going to Cusco, on account of it being the gateway to Machu Picchu and the wealth of Inca archaeology in the region. As Rachowiecki (1987: 9) states: 'For many travellers, Peruvian history means, "Inca" . . . But the Incas are merely the tip of the archaeological iceberg. Peru had many pre-Columbian cultures preceding the Incas by many centuries.' The use of icons from a variety of Peru's pre-Columbian cultures could alleviate some of this congestion. If the Institute of National Culture (INC) – under whose jurisdiction are the nation's archaeological sites – and the Ministry of Tourism (MINCETUR) promoted other parts of the country, it could allow for tourism-related income to be better distributed.

Tourism in Cusco and the Cusco Region

Cusco is located in the south-eastern highlands of the country and lies at 3326 m above sea level. The city of Cusco lies within the Department of Cusco, which holds some of the finest scenery of the Andean region. The city of Cusco was the capital of the Inca Empire as well as the most important place of pilgrimage in South America in modern times. The INC has identified no fewer than 3600 known archaeological sites in the Cusco region (Jenkins, 2000). Cusco is considered a key tourism destination in the most popular tourist circuit of Lima–Arequipa–Puno–Cusco–Lima.

As case-study sites for the research, the author focused on two archaeological sites, Raqchi and Ollantaytambo, as shown in Fig. 19.2 (McGrath, 2005). Ollantaytambo site is considered one of the most significant monuments in Peru, while Raqchi is much less well known. As with many of the

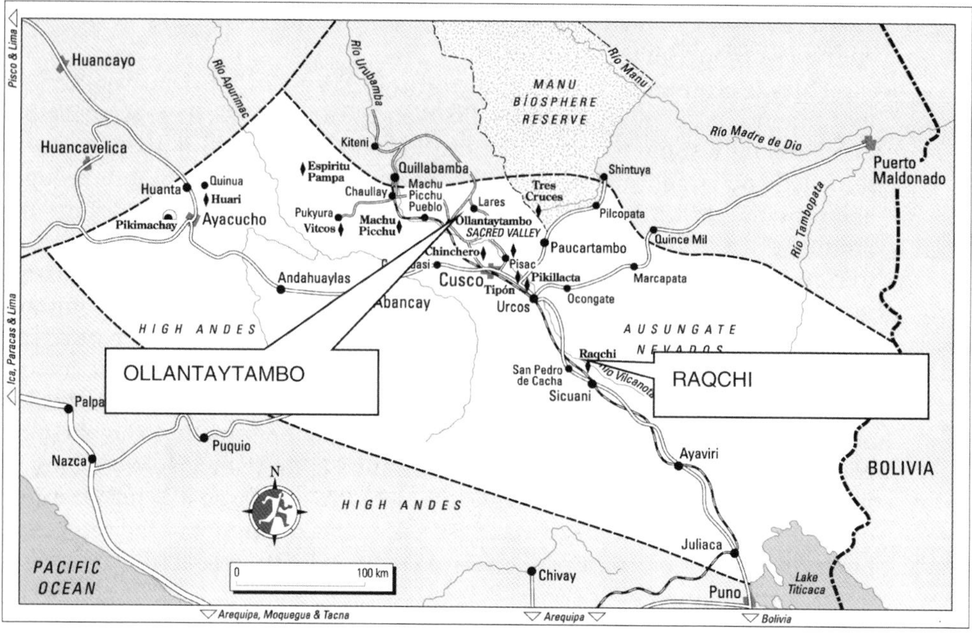

Fig. 19.2. Cusco region and location of Raqchi and Ollantaytambo (adapted from Jenkins, 2000, and reproduced with kind permission).

smaller Inca sites, it has recently found itself placed on the tourist circuit by a tourism industry developing new itineraries to add to its portfolio.

Incaismo is a special case of the wider literary, intellectual and political movement known in Peru (and in other Latin American countries, notably in Mexico) as *indigenismo*. In Peru, the roots of *indigenismo* go back to the 19th century, when it got turned into a protest ideology, capturing the imagination of left-wing intellectuals.

Monuments, museums, architecture and archaeology in Cusco are to a great extent highly visual representations of *Incaismo*. It also contains evidence of pre-Inca and post-Inca cultures, with some architecture being purely from the colonial era. There are examples of *mestizo* monuments, where Spanish construction has been undertaken upon Inca foundations. However, as Van den Berghe and Flores Ochoa (2000) explain: 'Practically every tourist gets exposed to Inca matters, and the vast majority would not have come but for them'. The phenomena of *Incaismo* and international tourism especially, though unrelated in origin (Van den Berghe and Flores Ochoa, 2000), have become inextricably connected; they now 'feed into one another to create a dynamic new reality'.

Incaismo became the perfect template for the country's nationalist myth formation, and tourism has revived *Incaismo* by consolidating a national identity, which has become an exportable commodity. This has allowed Cusco to come full circle to the time when it was the capital of Peru and the

Incas named it the 'navel of the world', which is currently used as a slogan in its tourism promotion.

Myth and Mystery and the Need for Quality Interpretation

Linked to *Incaismo*, indeed wrapped up in it, is the important element of myth involved in the packaging of tourism products. If *Incaismo* is part of Peru's mythical allure, Machu Picchu's mystique further placed Cusco on the tourist map (Van den Berghe and Flores Ochoa, 2000). The romanticism of its discovery in 1911 as the 'Lost City of the Incas' has given way to extensive and varying accounts of this find (Hemming, 1970). The 'Sacred Valley of the Incas', where Ollantaytambo site and town are located, has been imbued with myth and legend about its construction and the history of how it was toppled by the Spanish. According to Rachowiecki (1987), 'Cusco is a city steeped in history, tradition and legend. Indeed it is often difficult to distinguish where fact ends and myth begins.'

Tourists have a complex relationship with myth and the mysteries alluded to by legend. On the one hand, they are attracted by myth, while, on the other hand, it can also create frustration for the visitor. The myth is the 'pull' factor for stimulating demand, but a 'push' factor can occur if the visitor does not feel the guide is able to 'demystify' the sites. The 'push factor' here is alienation – a distancing and a disconnection that can occur in the absence of an interpretation process. The myth and magic of Peru's past require skilful interpretation if visitors are to get the most satisfaction from their experience. The unravelling of fact from fiction and what cannot be known from the archaeological record is required by the tour guide if an understanding is to be gained of the visited sites.

Interpretation and Tour Guides in Peru

Interpretation is not currently used strategically in Peru, in other words, it is not used to orient or manipulate the visitors to move around sites in a particular route, nor is it used as a visitor management tool as yet (Hall and McArthur, 1996). This was highlighted as a major weakness in the Master Tourism Plan for Peru (Pacific Consultants International, 1999). The supply of interpretation in Peru is under the jurisdiction of the INC, although most of it is limited to non-verbal media in the form of information panels at some sites. While the very size and architecture of the archaeological sites may keep the visitor engaged and interested, the use of interpretation could also facilitate improved site and visitor management and the development and diffusion of the take-home conservation message.

In the light of growing visitor arrivals, the creation of an interpretation strategy for the country is imperative in order to safeguard the fabric of its built heritage. According to Sayers (1989: 166), the lack of interpretation supply is a classic symptom of unplanned tourism development: 'Tourism goes its own way, conservation struggles on and interpretation is best left to local guides, albeit sometimes excellent, and touts.'

The current approach, however, reveals a traditional approach to heritage management, unlike the approach recommended by ICOMOS (1999: 1), which expounds the value of 'reasonable access' to the site. The sole use of tour guides as the interpretation supply in Cusco exacerbates the characteristic of variability implicit in service delivery. Misguiding information can lead to misunderstandings between guide and tourist, which are the exact opposite of interpretation's intended outcome. At the wider destination level in Cusco, gaps in communication exist between the different stakeholders implicated in developing tourism. There is scope for the service provided by guides to be improved and developed to more consistent, high-quality levels. The development of professional interpreter guides at archaeological sites has the potential to allow for other wider-destination benefits to flow from it (Moscardo, 1996; Uzzell and Ballentyne, 1998; McGrath, 2005). At present, there are few quality assurance measures and several constraints to the development of professional tour guiding (for either natural or cultural contexts), as the sections that follow outline.

Types of Guides in Peru

The title *guía* is used quite loosely in the region and it can refer to the three types of tour guide that exist in Peru. In the second part of this chapter, the development of guides types around the world is discussed in more detail. In Peru, *guía* can be used to refer to a university graduate who is a specialist in Inca history, which, using Cohen's (1985) classification, would be a 'mentor-type' guide. The title *guía* is also used to refer to an adventure guide, who may or may not have formal training, but who knows the area and can offer visitors safety, guidance and companionship, when undertaking activities such as trekking or white-water rafting. This type would come under Cohen's 'pathfinder' classification. According to the stakeholders from the tourism and archaeology communities who were interviewed for the research (McGrath, 2005), many of the pathfinder guides do not receive formal training but gain employment in the industry for their knowledge of the area and expertise in a physical activity such as trekking. However, despite this, both these types of guide are considered to be official and enjoy a central position within the industry. The third type of guide in Peru is the *guía local* (local guide), and this title is usually given to those who have had no formal training. The majority of these guides come from the native Indian population living near archaeological sites in the rural areas. These guides are usually bilingual Spanish and Quechua speakers and often assist the visiting official guides, who are predominantly from the urban-dwelling mestizo population.

In Peru, the title 'official guide', therefore, can denote two things. The first is that the guide has undergone formal training and the other indicates that these guides, unlike the 'local guide', lie inside the tourism system and therefore carry the stamp of approval from the organizations involved in tourism development. While many guides in Peru work to high professional standards, there is no discrete national body that organizes entry to the profession, although all guides need to be registered with the regional tourism boards in order to work within the industry. However, apart from gaining a degree or a diploma in a relevant subject, in order to qualify for the profession, at present, there is no additional specialist course in Peru. The predominant type of guide available for cultural sightseeing in Peru is the 'mentor-type' guide, whose emphasis is the transfer of knowledge, rather than the interpretation of it for the visitors. Therefore, the notion of a professional tour guide, such as the Blue Badge guide in the UK, does not currently exist and, due to their training and the nature of the country's heritage management, the types of guide currently working in Peru constrain the extent that interpretation is able to function to its full potential.

Types of Training for Guides in Peru

There are two training routes to becoming a tour guide in Peru. The first is to undertake a degree in a related subject area at a university, and then majoring in either tourism or guiding within the course. The second route is to undertake a diploma at a college of higher education (*instituto*) in either tourism or tour guiding. Despite these different routes, for the end-user, the visitor, there is no visible way of recognizing that a tour guide is qualified as there is no badge with a readily identifiable icon for guides to wear in order to show that they belong to an official body representing the profession.

According to the guides themselves, however, there are noticeable differences between the guides who have come to tour guiding via the two different routes. An element of hierarchy and some rivalry exists between the college-trained guides and the university-trained ones. The college guides claimed that the university-trained guides have too much of an academic slant to their training and this does not allow for them to develop their presentation skills, while the university-trained guides suggested the courses delivered by the colleges lack rigour and overemphasized communication skills in the field by way of compensation. The courses via either route usually last between 3 and 4 years.

A review of the routes available for entry into the profession of guiding in Peru emerges as a legitimate need. The need for guides who are capable of interpreting places is especially magnified in the context of developing heritage tourism at archaeological sites. However, while this may be a valid recommendation, it is important that the relevant stakeholders identify this as a need within the destination (Senior, 1993; Tosun, 2000).

Tour Guide Quality and Visitor Satisfaction

Many archaeological sites are located in the rural areas and, as such, access is difficult. This means that even independent visitors may opt for day trips sold by agencies, which include guided tours. Therefore, most visitors are likely to experience at least one Peruvian guide during their holiday. Coupled with the fact that tour guides are the mainstay of interpretive supply in Peru, this puts them in a central position within the tourism system, in so far as they come into contact with the majority of tourists in the country. Guides are often seen to occupy a privileged position by other residents of the destination because of their contact with a tourist, which gives guides a perceived closeness to the West, to which other residents may not have access.

This central position and the visitor satisfaction implications have not gone unnoticed by the government. Tour guide behaviour and service delivery quality, in this light, emerge as key to destination image and improved public relations overseas. The quality of tour guides' services has been assessed by the promotional body for tourism, PromPeru (2002, 2003), and was found to be average. In addition, while the findings from the study by this author revealed that members of both the archaeology and tourism worlds agreed that the tour guide is an essential part of the industry, there was also consensus amongst the respondents that too much variability existed between guides and such patchy performance was a problem for visitor satisfaction and potentially for Peru's image. The respondents identified two key issues concerning the variability. The first was the accuracy of commentary–knowledge and the problems of lack of foreign language competence. Other areas highlighted as issues, regarding the guides in general, were fabrication and exaggeration, particularly where 'pathfinder' and 'local' guides were concerned. The majority of tour guides who have either a diploma or a degree in tour guiding work as 'mentor-type' guides in Peru.

By the same token, however, the guides interviewed for the study stated that among their frustrations were not having open access to updated archaeological records and the lack of evaluation of their work. This lack of performance monitoring and professional development also needs to be addressed as part of the redesign of any tour guide curricula in Peru.

Parker and Potter (1997), writing from their perspective as archaeologists and from their experiences with the project 'Archaeology and the Public in Annapolis, USA', express how guides can provide visitors with the increased understanding and enjoyment on sites. They distinguish run-of-the-mill guiding scripts with the true dialogue possible for guides to have with their visitor audiences, though this does depend on the culture and ethos of the archaeology's management. They state (Peter and Potter, 1997: 38) that 'Most historical interpreters and tour guides are asked to present third- or fourth-hand information. Quite honestly, I don't envy people who have to interpret this way.' Although the guides in this case were actually archaeologists, such an approach would be relevant in Cusco as most guides are initially graduates in related disciplines. Potter and Parker (1997: 42) explain this training approach:

> interpreters were not trying to be clones of the tour's authors, they were freer than many interpreters to respond to a question by saying 'I don't know', and seek answers from artefact bags, excavation notes or other crew members – right in front of inquiring visitors.

Such an approach aims to turn the usual service encounter inside out in that behind-the-scenes work is actively shown centre stage. While such an approach may be simpler to implement in a developed context than a developing one, elements of it could be modified to suit the operating environment in Peru.

The findings from the case-study sites of Ollantaytambo (McGrath, 2005) revealed high satisfaction with the guide (the majority were 'mentor types') and little variance across the sample, which highlights, despite the limitations of the current training system, the guide's potential to be an interpreter of heritage. A correlation was also found between those who had a guide and those tourists who experienced higher overall satisfaction at the site.

Despite the positive findings of the study, the author identified the need to protect Peruvian tour guides from some of the more challenging aspects of postmodern Western audiences, as an additional reason for redesigning tour guide training. The author's experience of tour leading in Peru prior to undertaking this study enabled observations of tourists becoming angry with guides, especially over the veracity of facts, as well as guides having to cope with obviously bored tourists, who did not hide the fact! While visitors on a tour bus or in the tour party may be a 'captive' audience, this does not mean that they will be 'captivated' by the guide's commentary. The quality of the guide's presentation of his or her knowledge is what allows visitors to gain deeper access to the visited world. Moreover, it is in the presentation of the knowledge that there lies the opportunity for guides to deliver the all-important conservation message to the audience.

The Development of Sustainable Tourism at Heritage Sites

The traditional approach to managing heritage, be it cultural or natural, is based on the premise that the resource, built or natural, is the main focus, often to the exclusion of the local community and any visitors (Miller, 1982; Hall and McArthur, 1996). This approach tends to prevail, though not exclusively, in developing countries, but when a site becomes a visitor attraction, even with low levels of visitation, such management can be problematic.

The notion of stakeholders beyond the organization officially responsible for a site, or the development of interpretation, is rare in this type of approach. Once a site becomes a visitor attraction, such management, however, often reveals itself to be unsuitable, unlike an integrated approach, which, as its name suggests, is concerned with bringing together all the stakeholders implicated in the development of tourism. Moreover, its practice is often an indicator of an integrated approach to tourism development at a wider, destination level. In this way, an integrated approach to developing heritage tourism will seek to develop quality assurance indicators, such as consistent and high service quality, satisfied visitors, improved destination image and improved site sustainability. The often-tense relationship between tourism and archaeology is really the manifestation of the tug of war between the approaches over how to manage resources.

Moreover, within the discipline of archaeology, different management approaches are also found in different world regions, much in the way that is also true for tourism development. New archaeology (Shanks and Tilley, 1992), which developed during the late 1970s in the USA, has a similar philosophy to an integrated approach to heritage management in that its aims are to widen access to the remains of the past and to focus on all the stakeholders involved in a site's development (Hall and McArthur, 1996). This approach is still not common in some parts of the world, largely because of varying development levels (Rotow, 1959).

As Hall and McArthur (1996: 4) express it, an integrated approach to heritage management:

> therefore requires an approach which integrates the human dimensions of heritage with the traditional resource-oriented concerns for heritage managers, planners and interpreters to meet the wide range of demands placed upon them from organisations, visitors and the community at large.

Moving from the traditional approach characterized by separation and towards an integrated management approach to heritage is not to throw the baby out with the bath water. Indeed, the resource-oriented concerns still need to be present in any management endeavour: planning, budgeting, resource allocation, site maintenance and health and safety in and around the site. However, added to these basics of management is the need to develop a 'market orientation' (Westlake and Cooper, 1991) in order to achieve the dual aims of protecting the heritage and allowing the heritage to reach the wider audience interested in understanding it.

In short, this will involve the development of a human resource training programme, the supply of appropriate, quality interpretation for each particular site and a suitable marketing strategy. In more developed areas, particularly with regard to the development of heritage tourism at archaeological sites, the participation of local stakeholders has become an indicator of sustainability. The inclusion of local people living on or near a site in a developing area of the world can allow tourism to support long-term conservation goals (Hall and McArthur, 1996; Jameson, 1997). Such inclusion can involve the education of local people in the real value of the site over the long term as a tourist attraction and, at a basic level, garnering their support as custodians can mean a reduction of site looting. However, this inclusion needs to consider allowing local people to in turn be supported by the site, in the form perhaps of having the right to undertake tours for visitors or sell handmade souvenirs in the area.

Interpretation as a Mediator and Strategic Management Tool

One key difference between the traditional and the integrated approach is the way interpretation is used. The traditional approach tends to use interpretation at a one-dimensional level, offering basic information to the visitor about an attraction, while an integrated approach usually aims to harness the strategic elements of interpretation, which range from physical orientation to visitor and site management to marketing (Westlake and Cooper, 1991; Hall and McArthur, 1996; Nuryanti, 1996; Helmy and Cooper, 2002). When used in this way, interpretation can come to fulfil its original goal of assisting conservation aims, which, as Pond (1993: 71) points out, is one of interpretation's key aims: 'Interpretation has a noble origin. Its creators believed that there were certain places so magnificent or significant as to oblige one generation to preserve them for the enjoyment of those to follow.'

In many developing-world areas, the mainstay of interpretation offered is in the form of tour guides, and, in these areas, heritage is usually managed with a traditional approach. While the use of guides for interpretation can have many benefits, poor guiding has several drawbacks. The use of humans as interpreters can present problems with the visitor experience, if they are not trained to a good standard. One problem lies in the subjectivity of what such a standard is to each world region, which is reflected in the variety of training courses available. If developed well, however, there are well-documented advantages (Pond, 1992) to using tour guides as an interpretation tool though, for some commentators, the disadvantages of poorly trained or non-performing guides can have serious effects on visitor experience and visitor satisfaction. Risk (1994) discusses this in the context of guides in museums and galleries, and Keck (2001) does so in the context of the guide on tour.

Figure 19.3 shows how interpretation can play a mediation role between a site and its visitors, and particularly between the bodies responsible for the discrete stakeholders. The outer border around individual boxes in this diagram represents the destination at the wider level.

Therefore, taking as a premise that interpretation can operate as a mediator in the often-tense relationship between archaeology and tourism bodies, this section explores how developing the tour guide role can help both strengthen stakeholder participation and develop quality assurance measures surrounding tour guide quality. The 1999 International Cultural Tourism Charter drafted in Mexico (ICOMOS, 1999: 1) refers to the paramount importance of interpretation in generating 'intellectual and/or emotive access to heritage and cultural development'. Where tour guides provide the mainstay of interpretation, it is these types of access, emotional and intellectual, that need to be considered by the planners and designers of interpretation. Due to the fact that so much of the world has been mapped and explored, visitors can access information about destinations and attractions with relative ease. Visitors who hire a tour guide may not only be in search of facts about the visited site, but may be searching for the type of access they

Fig. 19.3. Interpretation for conservation: a mediator in the tourism–archaeology relationship.

cannot provide for themselves. Increasingly, as the world continues to be opened to tourism and information becomes more accessible, tour guides will need to help visitors to 'get under the skin' of the visited area rather than just providing physical access. Providing 'emotional' as well as 'intellectual' access is important if guides are to develop into interpreters of places and remain a relevant part of the tourism industry of the 21st century. This is particularly important in areas such as Peru, where the introduction of technology-based interpretation (in the form of audio-guides commissioned by the INC for commentary on its sites) has begun to be proposed by entrepreneurs as solutions to some of the issues of working with human interpreters (Pond, 1993; McGrath, 2005). Such a shift would cause a major negative economic impact on Peru, as tour guiding provides a significant employment opportunity. This highlights the urgency of improving the quality of the current tour guiding in Peru.

Of equal importance is the use of interpretation as a strategic tool in the management of a site. Strategic use of interpretation allows visitor demand to be managed as well as facilitating orientation and flow at the site or attraction. In a modern context, interpretation is an indicator of sustainable development. Effective use of interpretation involves the destination (the supply-side) being in control of the visitors (the demand-side) and manipulating them to the destination's needs. This approach is known as a market orientation and allows destinations to use tourism to thrive and develop (Westlake and Cooper, 1991). Appropriate use of interpretation allows a destination or an attraction to take control of its resource management, which in turn allows those who have come to the place to enjoy an improved visitor experience. This in turn satisfies them as customers and creates good word of mouth and may result in repeat visits.

The Evolution of the Role of the Tour Guide

The tour guide is perhaps one of the oldest forms of interpretation (Pond, 1993). The two types of guide that have developed over time, the 'pathfinder' and the 'mentor' types, stem from different origins (Cohen, 1982, 1985). Currently, the pathfinder-type guides are more commonly found working in a natural context, at either incipient or geographically peripheral destinations (in relation to the tourism-generating regions), and their strength is leading groups through difficult physical terrain. The mentor-type guides, however, are more commonly found in a cultural context, at either more mature or more central destinations (in relation to the tourism-generating regions), while their strength is leading groups through difficult intellectual terrain.

The pathfinder guide is usually found leading visitors in ecotourism sites such as on safaris or on fishing or trekking expeditions, where they are hired for their knowledge of the area's geography. This is the case in Peru, though in other countries the pathfinder-type guide has a wider role. The mentor tour guide abounds in cultural destinations located in the less developed countries of the world, though not exclusively so. Rather like the privileged position held by schoolteachers in the West until the 1950s (Cohen *et al.*, 2002), the mentor tour guide's key asset is their knowledge base and, as Dahles (2002: 786) expresses it, 'the transfer of information takes on an almost academic nature'. The information selected, however, is not always due to personal preferences of versions of history, but instead to versions they have been asked to put forward by whoever is their employer, normally either the state, a private company or themselves (Cohen, 1985). Dahles (2002: 786) states: 'Information is considered to be a vital element in the mentor's task . . . An extensive body of knowledge is required to establish the professional status of the mentor.'

Another type of guide has emerged in the developed countries, the professional tour guide. The key difference between this third generation of guide and its predecessors is that the professional guide has usually undertaken specialist training provided by an official tour guide body. In the UK, to cite one example, the Blue Badge training course for guiding offers entry to the profession via a rigorous process that emphasizes the importance of both knowledge and presentation skills. Figure 19.4 shows the tour guide's evolution over time. The mentor guide type, in particular, has evolved into the professional guide in countries where such training provision exists.

With regard to the differences between the pathfinder and mentor guide, it is important that the correct guide be used for the correct destination (Poynter, 1993) and yet this is not always a simple objective to achieve for the tourism industry. Figure 19.5 shows the optimal operational contexts for the different types of guide. In the current tourism industry, in both developed and developing areas, the mentor type of guide has come to occupy a more central position than the pathfinder type because of the growing importance qualifications have gained in the labour market over the last 30 years. This is not, however, to say that tour guides who offer site-specific commentary in ecotourism destinations such as national parks, nature trails and mountain treks, rather than just showing visitors the way, do not also occupy a central role. In these instances, the guides are acting as a hybrid of the original pathfinder and mentor guide and taking the shape of a professional interpreter guide. This type

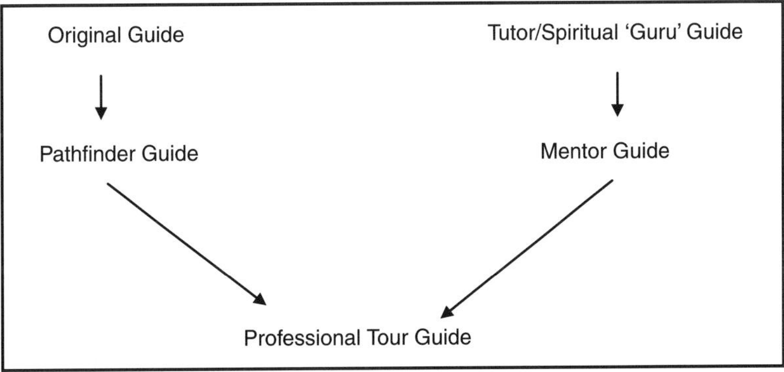

Fig. 19.4. Ancestry and evolution of guide types (adapted from Cohen, 1985).

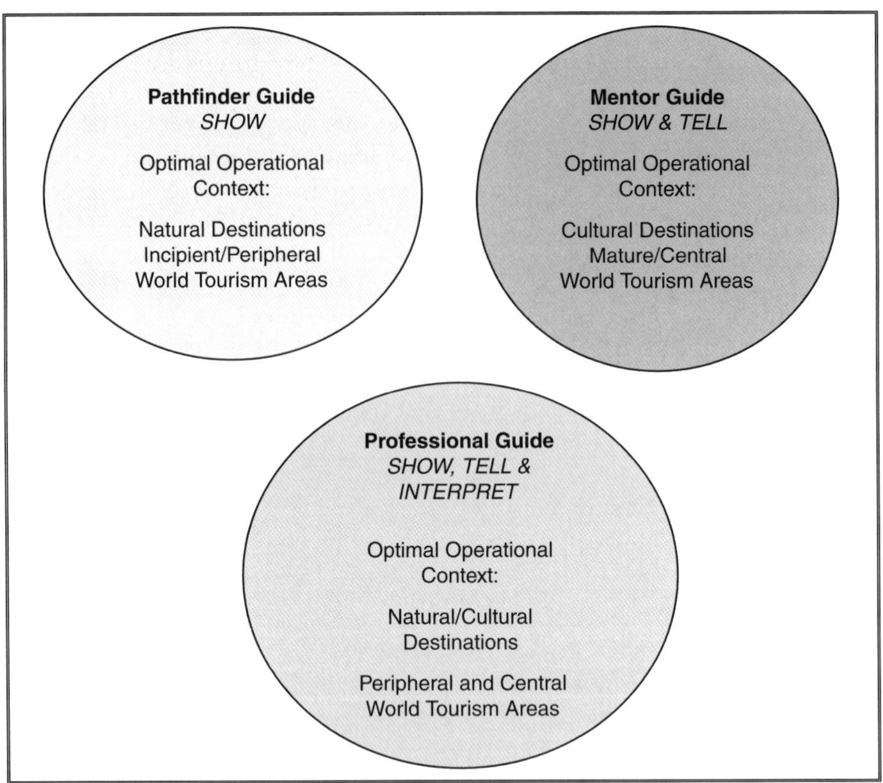

Fig. 19.5. The range of key tour guide types and their optimal operational contexts.

of guide is lacking in Peru as there is a need for guides who can both lead through difficult physical terrain (such as the Inca Trail to Machu Picchu) and offer site commentary on both the natural heritage and the cultural heritage.

Currently in Peru, there is a clear distinction between the type of guide who accompanies visitors on the trail (the pathfinders) and the ones who arrive by train at Machu Picchu with visitors (the mentors) to explain the significance of the archaeological complex. For the visitor who is interested in the natural aspects of the trail but also the cultural aspects of the site, this creates a lack of choice. The pathfinders working the Inca Trail do not generally have tour guide training, but are employed for their physical fitness and their knowledge of the area. The mentor guides are generally older than the pathfinders and some have incorporated elements of the natural environment into their commentaries, but the development of training that would allow the pathfinders to interpret the landscape they lead in would increase the quality of the visitor experience and empower these guides in their role and within the tourism system. Such training may also consider the importance of providing first-aid training for all pathfinder guides, including the handling of oxygen cylinders in the case of visitors suffering from mountain sickness.

Difficulties can be encountered when guides are employed out of their optimal operating context (Poynter, 1993). When guides are not properly trained to undertake the activities set for them or when guides are trained but placed in charge of a type of tour for which they do not possess appropriate training or experience, it is likely to cause problems at some stage on the tour. The author has observed situations where guides, imparting what the visitors considered incorrect information about the site, anger visitors. In Peru, these situations have arisen when a pathfinder guide has accompanied a group on the Inca Trail and then has been expected by the agency to also guide the same group around the archaeological complex of Machu Picchu. Some of these guides confided in the author (McGrath, 2005) that they do not feel confident in this task due to lack of training and their site knowledge is usually gleaned piecemeal from overhearing other guides on site, notably the mentor guides.

The Professional Tour Guide

The key difference the professional tour guides can make is that they interpret the destination as a whole: its people, its archaeology and its landscape. Rather than translating and imparting facts from previously published sources, the professional tour guide is able to make skilful use of these facts in order to pursue a key objective, to create sense of place for the visitor. As Dahles (2002: 786) explains:

> Guides are becoming interpreters . . . Pivotal to the interpreter's role is the art of storytelling . . . there is a shift away from the didactic legislator who instructed tourists to look, what to look for, and when to look, towards an encouragement to look with interest at an enormous diversity of artefacts, cultures, and systems of meaning.

In short, because visitors can access information about sites for themselves, they are usually, and legitimately, expecting to get something extra from the guide that they feel unable to supply for themselves. Since postmodern tourists have developed confidence in the art of travel, they may not feel the need for a tour guide in the way they may have previously. The professional guide flourishes in developed world areas where the audience is likely to be postmodern. Figure 19.6 sets out the differences of focus of the three main types of guides.

Whether the visited place be a rainforest or an ancient ruin, one of the key advantages to developing professional tour guides within a quality-assured system of training is that inspirational guiding has a higher probability of existing. In turn, high-quality guiding can encourage sensitivity towards conservation issues in visitors and therefore allow the original aims of interpretation (Tilden, 1977) to remain present within the tourism industry as it is known today. An interpreter tour guide can engage an audience and may possibly effect changes, however slight, in attitude towards the heritage visited. Therefore, with the appropriate input, tour

(Original Guide)	(Tutor Guide)	(Interpreter Guide)
Pathfinder Guide	**Mentor Tour Guide**	**Professional Tour Guide**
Intimate Geographical Knowledge of Visited Place(s)	Intimate Subject Knowledge of Visited Place(s)	Combines Elements of Mentor and Pathfinder Guide's Subject
Focus on External World	Focus on Internal World	Focus on Navigation between External and Internal World
SHOW	**TELL**	**PROVIDE FRAMEWORK FOR MEANING**

Fig. 19.6. Development of guide by type of knowledge and focus: original, tutor and interpreter guide.

guides can be developed as an integral output within an overall conservation strategy.

While the pathfinder shows and the mentor tells, the professional guide provides a framework for meaning to emerge for the visitors. The professional tour guide's focus is both inner- and outer-directed and as such can encourage visitors to use any prior knowledge they have about the site to make new connections and reveal relationships between subject areas (Tilden, 1977). Such a framework can allow for the visit to be interactive rather than a one-way discourse from guide to visitor and thereby create a more meaningful visit.

The more confident a guide can be as a curiosity stimulator, rather than sole knowledge imparter, the more likely it is that a tour will succeed. In this way, to a large extent, the success of a guide depends upon how their positional power is used (Hales, 1993). In turn, this depends on the nature of guide training received, the extent to which they are made aware of this issue and how much licence guides are given to entertain pluralistic interpretations of sites. This is, however, largely contingent on the nature of the wider operating environment of the destination.

The Position of Tour Guides within Developing and Developed Countries

There are important differences in the position and place the tour guide occupies within the developed and developing areas of the world. Pond (1993: i) refers to guides as 'the orphans of the industry' but, while little, if any, attention has been given to the subject of tour guides in academia until recent years, the position of guides in developing-world areas, in society and in the industry generally remains central. Meanwhile, in developed areas, the guide's position has shifted to a more peripheral place, due to two key external environment factors, namely the introduction of technology-based interpretation and the development of postmodernism, which Smart (1993: 12) defines as: 'Post-modernity is a way of living with doubts, uncertainties and anxieties which seem increasingly to be a corollary of modernity, the inescapable price to be paid for the gains . . . associated with modernity.'

There is still considerable contention as to definitions of postmodernism, though there seems to be agreement about the timing of the beginning of the movement. If modernism extended from the 1950s until the early 1970s, postmodernism took over from then, and this has had implications for the development of interpretation, as it also has for tourism. During the 1980s and early 1990s, the development of high-tech interpretation became popular, particularly in the UK, and critics of this movement (Hewison, 1987; Baker, 1988; Fowler, 1989) suggested that this was because newly introduced admission fees to previously free-entry museums and galleries had to be justified. The shift from human-based interpretation, however, has also been understood as a cost-cutting exercise in the long term. In addition to the influence of postmodernism, over the last 30 years, the evolution of the tourist as a mature, more independent consumer has also been a factor in the repositioning of the guide in the more developed countries.

The dimensions of the tour guide's role have been analysed by Cohen (1982, 1985), who found that there are two main realms in which they operate: the inner-directed and the outer-directed sphere. Within these spheres are the discrete skill and knowledge competencies involved in guiding; these range from foreign language skills to site-specific commentary, destination information (cultural and natural), interpretation skills, sensitivity to group dynamics and administrative and organizational skills. In some countries, guiding has become developed to a professional level while, in others, entry qualifications have not as yet been outlined. In some countries, specific bodies have been long established to set standards and validate training for the profession, notably in the UK, the USA, Australia and Canada. In the main, these are found in the more developed areas of the world, but not exclusively, as recent developments in Belize (Juneau Consulting, 2001) and Bolivia demonstrate. According to the European Federation of Tourist Guides Associations (www.touristguides.europe.org), each member country's guide training course is embedded in the nation's educational framework, though the EFTGA highlights the importance of standardizing key areas of proficiency, which it refers to as 'knowledge' and 'the art of guiding'. Under the category of 'knowledge' it states:

> Each and every country will share a number of common subjects. The depth with which these are studied will vary from country to country. In some history will be more important than geography, and vice versa. In some, ancient archaeology will prevail; in others, industrial archaeology. In all . . . guides need to know the cultural context of their heritage.

In its definition of the art of guiding it refers directly to the original principles set down by Tilden (1977): 'This is a common skill . . . It is the skill of allowing the visitor to look and see and to understand. It is a skill which, if well performed, is invisible. If it is missing, it is all too visible.' It also adds interesting comments on the importance of the quality of foreign language skills: 'It is essential that these languages be easily listened to by nationals over a full day. Oral language skills are of great importance.'

This is relevant to how training curricula for the guiding role across different countries (especially between the developed and developing regions) differ in their emphasis and balance of skills and knowledge competencies. According to the Institute of Tourist Guiding, a standard-setting body based in London, which sets the Blue Badge Guide exams, most of their curriculum design work around the world involves refocusing on the importance of presentation skills in order to convey destination knowledge.

The power resources that the human interpreters hold over a group are especially problematic within the context of a postmodern society. It is 'knowledge' power (Hales, 1993) that the guide is expected to hold and this, along with other competencies, is what the visitor is traditionally paying for by employing a guide. This knowledge ranges from basic visitor orientation to information about the culture and heritage of the people who built the archaeological sites, in the case of Cusco, the Incas.

Cohen and Cohen (2002) point out how the era of postmodernism has seen the rise of questioning long-held traditions and the acceptance of authority, and how the status of knowledge has undergone radical change. He quotes Martusewicz (1992: 131–32), following Lyotard, (1984): 'our assumptions about what constitutes everyday knowledge as well as academic knowledge, indeed the very possibility of knowing, have been placed deeply in question.'

In the developing regions of the world, freer of the impacts of technology-based interpretation and postmodernism, the guide still holds a respected role within both the tourism industry and society at large. In developing countries, the tour guide could still be considered the 'king of interpretation', not least because the profession remains male-dominated, but also because guides are often the only type of interpretation available. This is also because tour guides have the power and prestige that comes from being in a position to associate with tourists and, by extension, have greater perceived access to the Western world and information about its workings.

Implications for the Tour Guide–Visitor Encounter

The differences in the place and position of tour guides in more and less developed world regions have important implications for the quality of the visitor–guide encounters. In these encounters, two different worlds are, in effect, meeting or colliding, depending on the type of management operating within the wider environment. It is exposure to the postmodernism of Western tourists that has impacted their outlook and hence their expectations and subsequent visitor experience of a destination. It is unlikely that tour guides from developing regions will be familiar with fragmented, pluralistic narratives, though the extent of this would depend on which world regions are involved. This has implications for international heritage tourism in general, and specifically for the balance of emphasis between skills and knowledge components in guide training. These implications are linked to service quality, visitor satisfaction with the experience, destination image and overall site sustainability.

In terms of the knowledge component, it is likely that tour guides operating within a developing region would tend to offer singular and perhaps definitive interpretations of a heritage site to visitors, with an emphasis on imparting facts and figures about a place, rather than bringing a place to life by interpreting the place's possible meanings. Of equal importance to destination knowledge is the skills element of the role, though in developing areas this may be given less importance as a competency (K. Prince, London, personal communication, 2004). The UK Institute of Tourist Guiding reports that their experience of consultancy with countries such as Latvia, Malta, Cyprus, Fiji, Papua New Guinea and the Caribbean nations, as well as Mongolia, is on rebalancing the curricula for guides by emphasizing the paramount importance of developing presentation skills, as well as knowledge (K. Prince, London, personal communication, 2004).

In this light, what emerges is that there is scope for the tour guide (in the context of developing regions) and the visitor to be communicating at cross purposes. This issue raises key questions about developing tour guide training. In the context of different operating environments, how can the quality of a tour guide's performance be controlled without imposing a Western postmodern slant on it? One answer lies in training emphasizing the equal importance of presentation skills and site-specific knowledge. This issue is also linked to standardization of certain aspects of this universal tourism service, with an international audience in mind, while preventing local colour getting squeezed out. Ultimately, the redesign of training must be appropriate for a country's individual needs and, in order for it to be successfully implemented, it is advisable for such initiatives to emerge from within.

Tour Guides as Interpreters of and Bridges to the Visited World

The various sub-roles within the tour guide's role (ambassador, mediator, 'culture-broker' and interpreter) have been well-documented (Schmidt, 1979; Cohen, 1982, 1985; Pond, 1993; Ap and Wong, 2001). In the context of heritage tourism at archaeological sites in particular, it is this author's view that the role of the guide as an interpreter is crucial for successful visitor experiences. The guide as interpreter is even more important when tour guides are working with prehistoric sites, which may be even more spatially bare and temporally remote from the present time and from the visitors' world. Echoing the principles set out by one of the forefathers of interpretation (Tilden, 1977), Cohen (1985) expresses the importance of the tour guides revealing the meaning of a destination as a whole, rather than piecemeal. He states that the tour guide is responsible for 'the translation of the strangeness of a foreign culture into a cultural-idiom familiar to the visitor'.

In order to successfully develop as an 'interpreter', a guide needs to be encouraged to think of themselves as a 'bridge' between the visitors' world and the visited world. McDonnell (2001: 1) uses the metaphor of the bridge to discuss how the tour guide is facilitating 'cultural transference' between a site and a tour party. Figure 19.7 shows how a tour guide is an interpreter of a destination, not a mere translator of it, when they provide passage from one side of the bridge (the visitors' world) to the other side (the visited world). As such, the guide can not only protect visitors from the frustration and boredom of a meaningless experience, but also hopefully inspire interest in the issues at stake at the site, and possibly plant the seed of a change in attitude towards conservation, which may continue to grow long after the holiday has concluded.

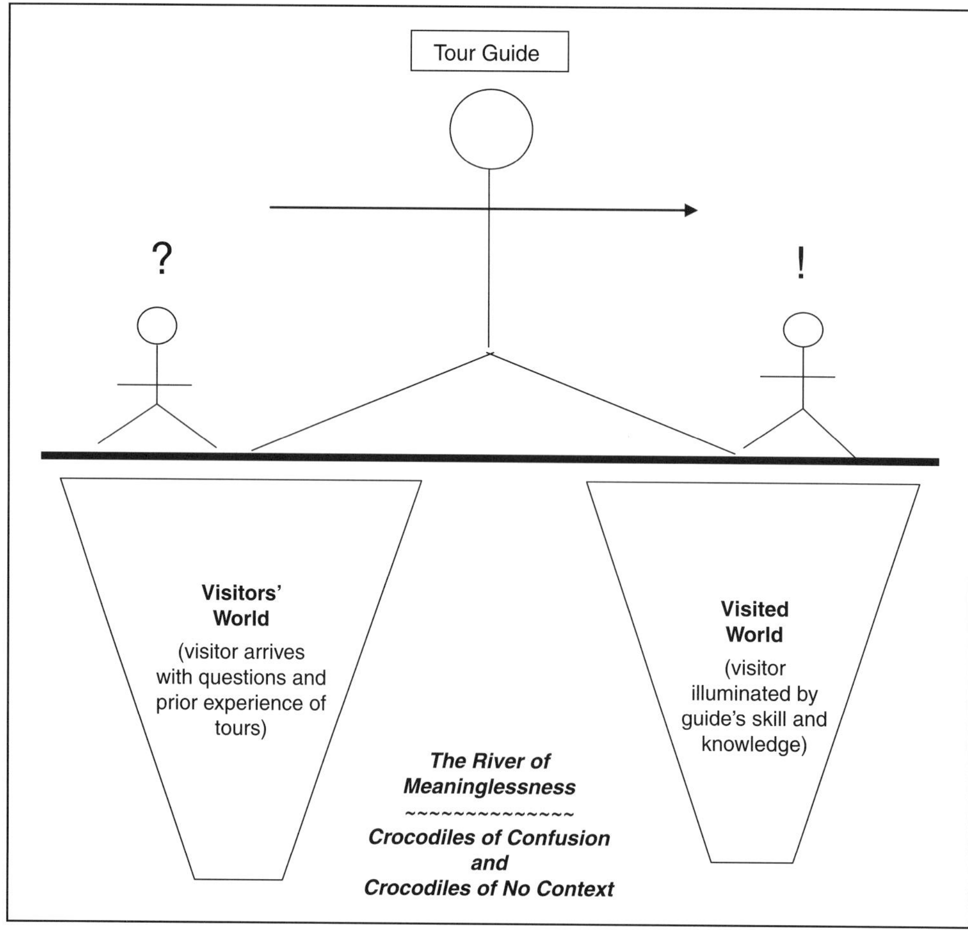

Fig. 19.7. The tour guide as bridge: one foot in the visitors' world and the other in the visited world, protecting the tour party from falling into the river of meaninglessness.

If the quality of the bridge the tour guide provides in their guiding is sturdy and not of the ropy variety, then it is possible for visitors to avoid floundering in the 'river of meaninglessness' and encountering either a 'crocodile of confusion' or a 'crocodile of no context'. Both these are dangerous as they pose a threat to the visitor experience and they short circuit some of the communication between visitor and site that comes via the guide, which is one of the 'discourses' that Adler (1989) talks of in relation to sightseeing.

Moscardo (1996, 1999) focuses her work on the importance of interpretation fostering mindfulness in visitors. The use of an interpretation programme, whatever the mix of techniques, she suggests, needs to allow visitors to move from a dizzy pre-visit state to a receptive state of mind in order to ensure that visitor attention is focused during the visit for lasting post-visit effects. One of the cardinal sins of tour guiding is the use of information with no attempt to interpret the attraction for the visitors. Mackesy (1994: 50) summarizes this in his vivid description: 'Guided tours are things that bring back the worst childhood memories: studying the patterns on the backs of coats while an inaudible blue rinse drones on about regency panelling.' It is difficult to be receptive as a visitor if you have been alienated, bored or frustrated by the interpretation at a site. Moscardo (1999) echoes this by maintaining that interpretation per se will not turn mindless visitors into mindful ones; what is needed is for interpretation to deliver context. If visitors are unable to evaluate and make sense of the guide's message, the interpretation is unlikely to provide a gateway to anything but alienation and dissatisfaction. Moscardo (1996, 1999) emphasizes the importance of facilitating 'mindfulness' in visitors, because it allows for the all-important conservation message, whether working with the built or natural heritage, to get through.

The development of an affective component in interpretation, as well as a cognitive one, can help ensure that the conservation message be taken away more effectively by the visitors (Hall and McArthur, 1996; Uzzell and Ballantyne, 1998; Weiler and Ham, 2002). In the context of developing heritage tourism or ecotourism, such an approach to interpretation can allow tourism to work for conservation, instead of against it. This links with the other important benefit of developing a strong 'interpreter' element in the tour guide role. In order to be an interpreter, it is necessary to have a foot in the visitors' world and the visited world and to be a 'bridge' between these two worlds. The greater the sociocultural and economic differences between these, the more salient a need this becomes, and this is important for developing regions supplying tourism experiences.

The interpreter guide also has the potential to (and is in a position to) act as a bridge between the tourism and archaeology stakeholders, which, in the context of traditional heritage management, tend to keep themselves at a distance from one another, which creates greater opportunity for misunderstanding, tension and conflict and less chance of finding common ground. Figure 19.8, however, shows how the tour guide can be a living link between these communities and could work on behalf of their shared objectives. In Fig. 19.8 the tour guide is also acting as a bridge and a go-between for the archaeology and tourism bodies at a destination. In this scenario, the guide's

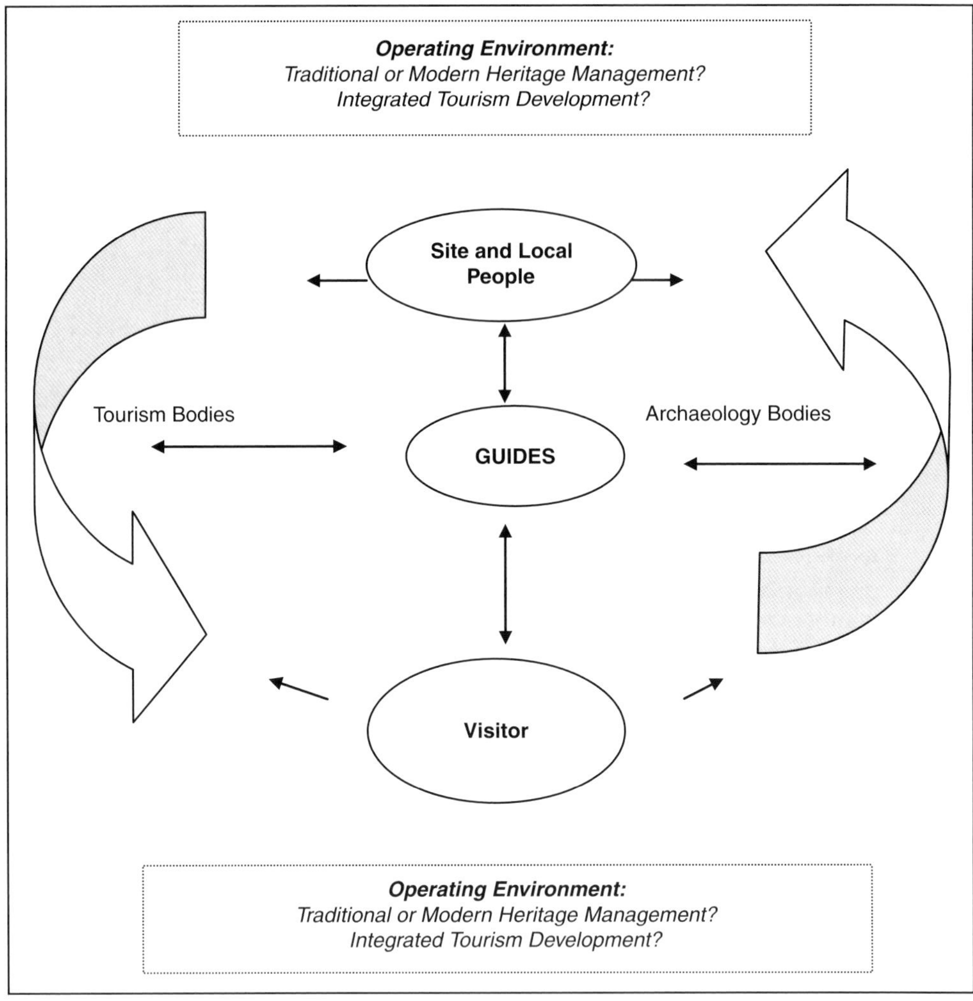

Fig. 19.8. The tour guide's potential as bridge between the stakeholders of an archaeological site.

role at archaeological sites can facilitate understanding and communication between the stakeholders because it touches upon the discrete worlds that overlap in the provision of heritage tourism.

In a sense, the tour guide must be a portal into another world culture, as well as an alchemist who can turn the base metal of facts into the gold of narrative and transportation to another time and place, and this is particularly true of guiding in the subject of the ancient past. As such, the tourists' gaze can be fascinated rather than frustrated (Urry, 1990), as they will have been granted real access to the places they have travelled to not only see, but feel and get a sense of, which links directly to the original motivation of 'cultural tourists' (Adler, 1989; Boniface, 1993; EC, 1993). This will require a high level of presentation skill on the part of the guide, but will have several benefits, not only to the visitor, but also to all the stakeholders involved in heritage tourism at archaeological sites. These issues are especially pertinent to the case-study region of Cusco, Peru.

Redesign of Training for the Development of Professional Tour Guides

In the case of Peru, the training available emphasizes either the knowledge or the skills component of the role. It is clear that both components need to be developed in the training and that integrating elements from both may make an important improvement. In order to simplify the process of redesign, but also to implement an element of professionalism, it is proposed that a postgraduate conversion course be designed to last one academic year. In this way, the undergraduate degrees or diplomas undertaken will therefore not also require revalidation. Such a proposal could also work for other areas experiencing similar issues to those in Peru.

In the light of the problems raised and discussed in this chapter, it is proposed that students choose between two key specialist routes within the course, focusing more either on nature (for the pathfinder type of guide) or on culture (for the mentor type of guide). However, whichever specialist route is chosen, both would expose the student to the drawbacks of just imparting information to visitors and the advantages of interpreting an attraction. Subjects such as first aid, health and safety and botany are recommended to be included in both courses, as they are relevant to both ecotourism and cultural tourism activities. Currently, guides on the Inca Trail do not always carry oxygen cylinders and, where they do, are not always instructed on how to use them. The emphasis of the course is recommended to deepen specialist knowledge, but also to highlight the importance of interpretation skills so that a destination as a whole can begin to be accessed emotionally, as well as cognitively, by the visitor. In this way, the quality of such training may allow for tour guides, as is the case in Belize (Juneau Consultancy, 2001), to be developed as a unique selling point for Peru as a whole. This is especially important for countries where the mainstay of interpretation is the tour guide.

Despite the importance of developing an appropriate training course for guides, research on the issue of training evaluation has revealed little systematic analysis (Roggenbuck and Williams, 1991; Black *et al.*, 2001). Any review of training will be implemented more successfully if the need is identified from within a country and especially if done so by key stakeholders (Reed, 1997, 2000; Bramwell and Sharman, 1999). Tour guides, particularly in developing regions, have considerable contact with visitors, and their position, as ambassadors, as mediators and as 'culture brokers', is significant. In Indonesia (Dahles, 2002), this has not been lost on the government, and tour guides are employed very much as the country's public relations spokespersons, carefully presenting and concealing what is and is not considered suitable for tourists consumption. The redesign of training, in terms of the selection of material, could well be viewed as a political issue. In order to overcome this, the focus of the training can be kept to refining presentation skills rather than the content. While destination knowledge may be a political issue, the style and structure with which it is delivered need not necessarily be so.

It is important that moving towards the development of professional tour guides does not come to mean the imposition of Western training models. As stakeholders in the development of tourism services, the domestic tourism market, which is a growth market in Peru (PromPeru, 2003), also needs to be considered in the redesign of tour guide training. A major part of integrated heritage tourism is the inclusion of all the stakeholders involved in its development. In developing regions such as Cusco, some elements of the ethnic power relations at play between the official and local guides can begin to be addressed by extending training opportunities to local people.

Building Bridges – Access to Appropriate Training for Local Guides

In need of creation, rather than of review, is the concept of the development of appropriate training for local people who want to work as local guides. At present in Cusco, as in other world regions, local guides have a marginal role in tourism, often being employed by the official guides at a site entrance to give their version of the history of the place to their tour party. The local guide may speak in their native tongue and the official guide will translate into either Spanish or the appropriate foreign language for their party. The official guide will either pay the local guide directly or encourage the party to tip them for their input. The main difference between the commentary of the two guides is, as their title suggests, that the 'official guide' is likely to offer visitors what may be considered to be an 'official' version of events linked to the archaeological record, to which they will have had access while training. The local guide, on the other hand, with no access to training or archival documentation (and often with only experience of primary schooling), is likely to offer a commentary that focuses more on local legend and myth surrounding the site passed down to them in the oral tradition. In the case of Peru, the difference in the type of commentary a local guide and a mentor guide may deliver to a group has caused concern at the MINCETUR and at the INC. Despite this concern, however, few of those interviewed demonstrated an interest in the idea of extending training opportunities to the local guides, citing levels of education, language and cultural barriers as reasons (McGrath, 2004).

However, if learning is about opportunities for transformational change (Blanton, 1981; Kolb, 1984) and if tourism is to work for conservation in Peru, then an appropriate curriculum design is also required for local guides. Empowering local communities as custodians of the national heritage allows a virtuous circle of protection for it to ensue (McEwan *et al.*, 1993; Hall and

McArthur, 1996). Bridges need to be built in order to allow rural communities ways in to participate in tourism (see Fig. 19.9).

The design of a training programme for local guides would need to be underpinned with a review of other subjects, such as world geography, regional geography and introductions to the subject disciplines of archaeology and Inca culture and heritage. It would need to prepare the local guides to be able to understand where, as guides, they fit into in the overall tourism system in order to afford a level of protection to cope with the demands of the role (Riley, 1995; Black *et al.*, 2001). This training could come in the form of workshops to give the phenomenon of the tourism experience some context for those who are working in this system (as guides, souvenir sellers or suppliers of accommodation), but who themselves have yet to be tourists (Blanton, 1981).

Towards Developing Tour Guide Training that Facilitates Conservation

The benefit of training that emphasizes the importance of the 'interpreter' element of the tour guide role is that it could result in guides having the ability to move visitors through the stages of the cycle shown in Fig. 19.10. The tour guide has the potential to be a catalyst for the conservation movement, in either a natural or cultural context, though, ultimately, the fulfilment of this potential is contingent on the quality of guide training, which is also dependent on the operating environment, as was discussed in the previous section of this chapter.

It is recommended that the stakeholders, such as archaeologists, professional interpreters, botanists and tourism specialists, implicated in the development of heritage tourism in Peru be invited to propose inputs to the curricula for training professional tour guides. The input of these groups may have a positive impact on the outputs of the tour guide performance and it may also facilitate the much-needed starting point for dialogue between the stakeholders. Clarifying what the guide's role means to each of the discrete groups would be an advantage in the move towards using interpretation for conservation. The key here is for the all-important conservation message to be integrated into the tour guide's role – which is in the interests

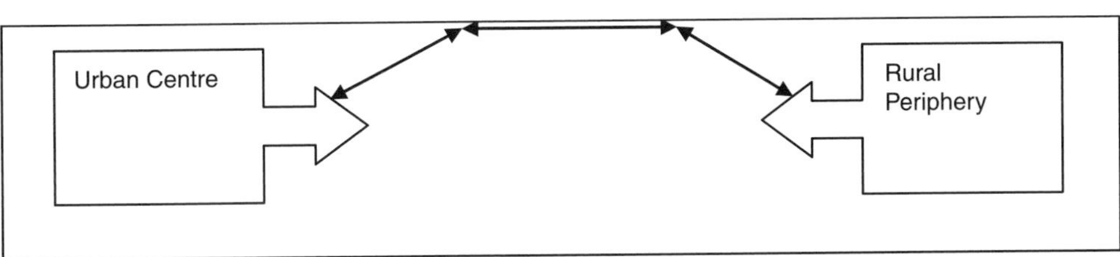

Fig. 19.9. Building bridges for access to training between urban centres and the rural peripheries.

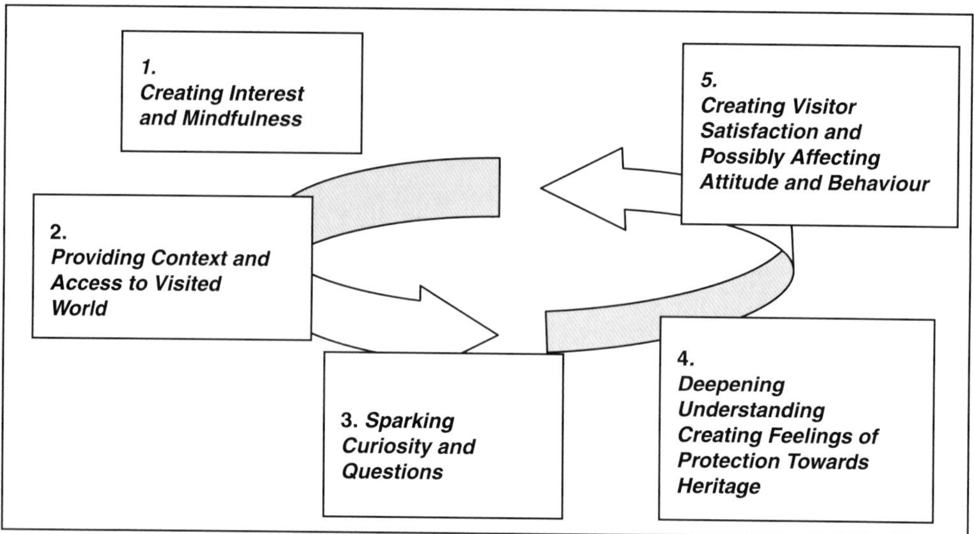

Fig. 19.10. Virtuous circle: guiding for conservation builds in five stages, from creating interest to creating visitor satisfaction and possibly affecting attitude and behaviour.

of both the tourism industry (economic sustainability) and the archaeology community (the sites' sustainability). Table 19.1 shows the salient roles of the guide from the point of view of both the tourism and the archaeology bodies, and those that could be common salient points within an integrated heritage tourism context, when 'interpretation' is the linchpin between the stakeholders. The seventh principle of the ICOMOS-ENAME Charter (2004) is relevant here:

> The training of qualified professionals in the sub-fields of heritage interpretation, such as conservation, content creation, management, technology, guiding, and education, is a crucial objective. Standard curricula should be formulated. In addition, basic academic preservation programmes should include a component of Interpretation in their courses of study.

The central column of Table 19.1 shows that, within the context of integrated heritage management, the tour guide has many sub-roles that are salient to the worlds of both tourism and archaeology. As such, the development of professional interpreter guides may be able to bridge the distances that currently exist between the INC and MINCETUR in Peru. Such a development may allow for greater inter-organizational collaboration to begin within the region of Cusco and within Peru.

Conclusions

This chapter has outlined the importance of developing inspirational tour guiding as part of sustainable visitor management, particularly in the

Table 19.1. The sub-roles of the tour guide and those which are of more salient concern to tourism and archaeology, respectively, and those of mutual interest in the context of integrated heritage tourism development (adapted from Black and Weiler, 2004).

Salient tour guide sub-roles for the tourism industry	Salient tour guide sub-roles in integrated heritage tourism development context	Salient tour guide sub-roles for archaeology
Interpreter/educator	Information giver	Interpreter/educator
Public relations/company representative	Leader	Motivator of conservation values
Information-giver	Motivator of conservation values	Navigator/protector/broker/mediator
Tour and group manager/organizer	Social role/catalyst	
Leader	Cultural broker/mediator	
Social role/catalyst	Navigator/protector/broker/mediator Facilitator of access to non-public areas Interpreter/educator	

context of heritage sites. The use of interpretation as a mediator between a site's stakeholders and as a strategic management tool was also discussed as an important part of integrated tourism planning. Focusing on the case study of Cusco in Peru, it is recommended that, for tour guiding to flourish, a review of training needs to be undertaken in order to increase tourism's capacity to work for conservation in the region. Improving the quality of the official tour guides means that they could develop as 'interpreters' of sites for visitors and locals and as 'bridges' between the stakeholders of archaeological sites. Including local guides into the system by allowing them access to training will also increase site sustainability.

Such recommendations involve long-term development, which is contingent on cultural and structural changes within the key tourism and archaeology groups. It is advisable that a shift from the traditional approach to heritage management gives way to the development of an integrated approach in order for the changes at the operational level to be implemented. For Peru, and world regions experiencing similar issues in heritage or ecotourism development, a move towards joint thinking in this area is recommended. In the short term, however, the issues raised by tour guides in Peru may indeed be the catalyst necessary for change to ensue.

References

Adler, J. (1989) Origins of sightseeing. *Annals of Tourism Research* 16, 7–29.

Ap, J. and Wong, K.K.F. (2001) Case study on tour guiding: professionalism, issues and problems. *Tourism Management* 22, 551–563.

Baker, F. (1988) Archaeology and the heritage industry. *Archaeological Review from Cambridge* 7(2), 141–144.

Black, R., Ham, S. and Weiler, B. (2001) Ecotour guide training in less developed countries: some preliminary research findings. *Journal of Sustainable Tourism* 9(2), 147–156.

Black, R. and Weiler, B. (2005) Quality assurance and regulatory mechanisms in the tour guiding industry: a systematic review. *Journal of Tourism Studies* 16(1), 24–37.

Blanton, D. (1981) Tourism training in developing countries: the social and cultural dimension. *Annals of Tourism Research* 8(1), 116–133.

Boniface, P. (1993) *Managing Quality Cultural Tourism*. Routledge, London.

Bramwell, B. and Sharman, A. (1999) Collaboration in local tourism policy-making. *Annals of Tourism Research* 26(2), 392–415.

Cohen, E. (1982) Jungle guides in northern Thailand: the dynamics of a marginal occupational role. *Sociological Review* 30(2), 234–266.

Cohen, E. (1985) The tourist guide: the origins, structure and dynamics of a role. *Annals of Tourism Research* 12, 5–29.

Cohen, E., Ifergan, M. and Cohen, E. (2002) A new paradigm in guiding: the *Madrich* as a role model. *Annals of Tourism Research* 29(4), 919–932.

Cooper, C., Fletcher, J., Gilbert, D. and Wanhill, S. (1993) *Tourism: Principles and Practice*. Pitman Publishing, London.

Dahles, H. (2002) The politics of tour guiding: image management in Indonesia. *Annals of Tourism Research* 29(3), 783–800.

European Commission (EC) (1993) *Cultural Tourism in Europe*. European Commission, Brussels, Belgium.

Fowler, P. (1989) Heritage: a post-modern perspective. In: Uzzell, D. (ed.) *Heritage Interpretation*. Belhaven Press, London, pp. 57–63.

Hales, C. (1993) *Managing through Organisation*. Routledge, London.

Hall, M. and MacArthur, S. (1996) *Heritage Management in Australia and New Zealand*, 2nd edn. Oxford University Press, Melbourne, Australia.

Helmy, E. and Cooper, C. (2002) An assessment of sustainable tourism planning for the archaeological heritage: the case of Egypt. *Journal of Sustainable Tourism* 10(6), 514–534.

Hemming, J. (1970) *The Conquest of the Incas*. Macmillan, London.

Hewison, R. (1987) *The Heritage Industry: Britain in a Climate of Decline*. Methuen Press, London.

ICOMOS (1999) International Cultural Tourism Charter Managing Tourism at Places of Heritage Significance, 8th draft. For adoption by ICOMOS at the 12th General Assembly, Mexico, October.

ICOMOS-ENAME Charter (2004) Charter for the Interpretation of Heritage and Culture. Available at: http://www.enamecharter.org/downloads.html

Jameson, J. (ed.) (1997) *Presenting Archaeology to the Public: Digging for Truths*. Altamira Press, California.

Jenkins, D. (2000) *The Rough Guide to Peru*. Penguin, London.

Juneau Consulting (2001) *Belize Guiding Case Study*. Prepared by Egret Communication/ARA Consulting, part of Juneau Tourism Management Planning Process.

Keck, R. (2001) Far horizons: managing problems on a package tour. *International Travel News*, February, 1–5.

Kolb, D. (1984) *Experiential Learning*. Prentice Hall, Upper Saddle River, New Jersey.

Ladkin, A. and Bertramini, A. (2002) Collaborative tourism planning: a case study of Cusco, Peru. *Current Issues in Tourism* 5(2), 71–93.

Lyotard, J. (1984) *The Post-Modern Condition: A Report on Knowledge*. University of Minneapolis, Minneapolis, Minnesota.

Mackesy, S. (1994) Courtly behaviour. *Independent*.

Martusewicz, R. (1992) Mapping the terrain of the post-modern subject. In: Pinar, W. and Reynolds, W. (eds) *Understanding Curriculum as Phenomenological and Deconstructed Text*. Teachers College Press, New York.

Mathieson, A. and Wall, G. (1982) *Tourism: Economic, Physical and Social Impacts*. Longman, Harlow.

McDonnell, I. (2001) *The Role of the Tour Guide in Transferring Cultural Understanding*. Working paper. University of Technology, Sydney, Australia.

McEwan, C., Hudson, C. and Silva, M. (1993) Archaeology and community: a village museum in Ecuador. *Museum International* 45(2), 42–45.

McGrath, G.M. (1994) Destination resource management: integrating ecotourism in Costa Rica. MSc thesis, University of Surrey, Guildford, UK.

McGrath, G.M. (2004) Including the outsiders: the contribution of guides to integrated heritage tourism management in Cusco, Southern Peru. *Current Issues in Tourism* 7(4,5), 426–432.

McGrath, G.M. (2005) Tour guides as interpreters at archaeological sites: heritage tourism in Cusco, Peru. PhD dissertation, University of Surrey, Guildford, UK.

Miller, K.R. (1982) The natural protected areas of the world. In: McNeely, J., Jefferey, A. and Miller, K. (eds) *Proceedings of the 3rd World Congress on National Parks and Protected Areas, 11–12 October, Bali, Indonesia*. UNDP, USA, pp. 20–23.

Moscardo, G. (1996) Mindful visitors: heritage and tourism. *Annals of Tourism Research* 23(4), 376–397.

Moscardo, G. (1999) *Making Visitors Mindful: Principles for Creating Sustainable Visitor Experiences through Effective Communication*. Advances in Tourism Application Series, Sagamore Publishing, Illinois.

Nuryanti, W. (1996) Heritage and post-modern tourism. *Annals of Tourism Research* 23(2), 249–260.

Pacific Consultants International (1999) *Peru Master Plan. Revised Strategic Institutional Plan of the Ministry of Foreign Trade and Tourism (MINCETUR) (2004–2006)*. Pacific Consultants International, Lima, Peru.

Parker, B. and Potter, J.R. (1997) The archaeological site as an interpretative environment. In: Jameson, J. (ed.) *Presenting Archaeology to the Public*. AltaMira Press, Lanham, Maryland.

Pond, K.L. (1992) *The Professional Guide: Dynamics of Tour Guiding*. John Wiley and Sons, New York.

Poynter, J.M. (1993) *Tour Design, Marketing and Management*. Regents/Prentice Hall, Upper Saddle River, New Jersey.

PromPeru (2002) *Visitor Satisfaction Survey*. Mincetur, Lima, Peru.

PromPeru (2003) *Visitor Satisfaction Survey*. Mincetur, Lima, Peru.

Rachowiecki, R. (1987) *Peru: a Travel Survival Kit*. Lonely Planet, South Yarra, Victoria, Australia.

Reed, M. (1997) Power relationships and community-based tourism planning. *Annals of Tourism Research* 32(3), 566–591.

Reed, M. (2000) Collaborative tourism planning as adaptive experiments in emergent tourism settings. In: Bramwell, B. and Lane, B. (eds) *Tourism Collaboration and Partnerships: Politics, Practice and Sustainability*. Channel View Publications, Clevedon, UK, pp. 247–271.

Riley, M. (1995) Interpersonal communication: the contribution of dyadic analysis to the understanding of tourism behaviour. *Progress in Tourism and Hospitality Research* 1, 115–124.

Risk, P. (1994) People-based interpretation. In: Harrison, R. (ed.) *Manual of Heritage Management*. Butterworth-Heinemann, Oxford, UK.

Roggenbuck, J.W. and Williams, D.R. (1991) *Commercial Tour Guides' Effectiveness as Nature Educators*. Congress of the World Leisure and Recreation Association, University of Technology, Sydney, Australia.

Rotow, W.W. (1959) *The Stages of Economic Growth*. Cambridge University Press, Cambridge.

Sayers, D. (1989) Interpretation: a key to tourism and conservation expansion in developing countries. In: Uzell, D. (ed.) *Heritage Interpretation*, Vol. 2: *The Visitor Experience*. Belhaven Press, London, pp. 165–169.

Schmidt, C.J. (1979) The guided tour. *Urban Life* 7(4), 441–467.

Senior, B. (1993) *Organisational Change*. Pearson Education, Essex, UK.

Shanks, M. and Tilley, C. (1992) *Reconstructing Archaeology: Theory and Practice*. Routledge, London.

Smart, B. (1993) *Postmodernity*. Routledge, London.

Tilden, F. (1977) *Interpreting Our Heritage*, 3rd edn. North Carolina Press, Chapel Hill, North Carolina.

Tosun, C. (2000) Limits to community participation in the tourism development process in developing countries. *Tourism Management* 21, 613–633.

Urry, J. (1990) *The Tourist Gaze*. Sage, London.

Uzzell, D. and Ballantayne, R. (1998) *Contemporary Issues in Heritage and Environmental Interpretation*. Stationery Office, London.

Van den Burghe, P. and Flores Ochoa, J. (2000) Tourism and nativistic ideology in Cusco, Peru. *Annals of Tourism Research* 27(1), 7–26.

Weiler, B. and Ham, S. (2002) Tour guide training: a model for sustainable capacity building in developing countries. *Journal of Sustainable Tourism* 10(1), 52–69.

Westlake, J.N. and Cooper, C. (1991) Planning for tourism at local level: maintaining the balance. Paper delivered at the Conference 'Tourism and the Environment', Lesbos, Greece, October 1992.

Web sites

Blue Badge Guides, http://www.blue-badge.guides.co.uk
City and Borough of Juneau, Alaska, http://www.juneau.org/tourism2/cbjtourism/belize.pdf
ICOMOS, http://www.icomos.org/tourism/charter.html
Institute of Tourist Guides (ITG), http://www.itg.co.uk
Peruvian National Insitute for Statistics and Information (INEI), http://www.inei.gob.pe
PromPeru, http://www.peru.org.pe
World Development Indicators, http://www.publications.worldbank.org
World Development Indicators (2004), http://web.worldbank.org

20 Ecotourism Certification in New Zealand: Operator and Industry Perspectives

TARA ROWE AND JAMES HIGHAM

University of Otago, New Zealand

Chapter Profile

This chapter examines New Zealand ecotourism operator perceptions of environmental certification programmes. It reports on an empirical study that reveals that ecotourism business operators hold clear views on the merits of environmental certification, and the relative merits of other environmental management initiatives such as self-regulation through voluntary codes of conduct. The study confirms that membership of environmental certification programmes is most likely if businesses have been in existence for more than 10 years and if they account for five employees or more. However, at present, a minority of New Zealand ecotourism businesses fit this description. As such, most ecotourism business operators continue to view investment in environmental certification as a potentially ineffective use of limited human and/or financial resources. It is concluded that investigating and overcoming barriers to the environmental certification of ecotourism businesses in New Zealand remain a priority for the sector.

Introduction

Environmental sustainability and the use of natural resources are serious issues facing the tourism industry, given increasing concerns for human-induced environmental change (Harper, 2001). The tourism industry in New Zealand and elsewhere depends upon the sustained quality of natural environments, and yet there is much debate as to how the tourism–environment relationship may be best managed (Bass *et al.*, 2001; Buckley, 2002; Giro, 2002). For many years, management of the environment and natural resources in tourist areas has been based upon government legislation (INSULA, 2003). However, environmental deterioration caused by tourism development and tourist activities continues to be a growing concern (Forsyth, 1997). This does not necessarily suggest that government legislation is insufficient, but legislation alone has often proved inadequate or ineffective (INSULA, 2003). There is an additional need for flexible, efficient and effective schemes to support the management of tourism in natural areas.

In New Zealand, the natural environment has long been a central part of the tourism product. Areas designated for conservation and rural landscapes provide a substantial resource base for recreation and tourism (Hall and Kearsley, 2001). New Zealand has long traded on its reputation as a 'clean and green' destination. Since 1999, Tourism New Zealand (TNZ) (a government-funded board charged with the international marketing of New Zealand as a tourism destination) has, through its global marketing campaign '100% Pure New Zealand', branded New Zealand as an ecotourism destination. However, there has been considerable debate on what should be done regarding environmental management, and by whom (Dewar, 1999; Buhrs, 2000; Memon and Perkins, 2000). While trying to attract visitors to New Zealand to experience the natural environment, little effort has been invested in management practices to protect the environment (Simpson, 2003).

Buckley (2002) believes, perhaps somewhat pessimistically, that few commercial tourism operators have genuine concern for environmental deterioration in protected areas unless it affects their immediate commercial viability. Furthermore, Simpson (2003: 271) declares that in New Zealand 'it often appears that the tourism industry, including some ecotourism operators, continue to regard environmentalism as a necessary evil, something that is promotionally useful but operationally restrictive'. Since 1984, environmental reforms in New Zealand have been comprehensive, and yet there remains a common view that there has been a lack of progress in addressing environmental issues, both at the general level (e.g. recycling, the use of public transport) (Memon and Perkins, 2000) and at a level specific to tourism (e.g. impact mitigation, energy efficiency) (Kearsley and Higham, 1997).

Within this context, the development of effective management tools for the ecotourism industry remains an urgent priority. For example, Higham and Carr (2003: 29) assert that, with the development and maturation of the New Zealand ecotourism industry, it has become critical that certification of operators takes place. This chapter examines the awareness and perceptions of New Zealand ecotourism operators of environmental certification schemes. Specifically it examines whether ecotourism operators in New Zealand see any value in environmental certification schemes and what, if any, barriers to entry they perceive.

Development of Ecotourism in New Zealand

New Zealand's tourism industry is heavily reliant upon natural resources (Van Aalst and Daly, 2002; Higham and Carr, 2003). New Zealand currently receives approximately 2 million international visitors per annum (Tourism New Zealand, 2003). Most visitors consider New Zealand to be an ecotourism destination (Simpson, 2003). However, despite the growing importance of ecotourism in New Zealand, several critical issues are yet to be adequately addressed. Higham and Carr (2003) note that defining ecotourism remains a significant challenge in New Zealand and that this is possibly a barrier to effective product development and visitor management. Gaps in the legislative framework for managing ecotourism (e.g. relating to the rapid development of marine ecotourism) remain. Progress towards establishing quality standards and the adoption of environmental certification schemes has been both belated and slow.

An increasingly complete profile of ecotourism businesses in New Zealand has emerged in a generally piecemeal fashion over the last two decades (Warren and Taylor, 1994). New Zealand ecotourism operations are generally small in size and owner-operated. A high proportion of ecotourism operators are inexperienced business people and have chosen to enter the industry for lifestyle reasons (Warren and Taylor, 1994). Many ecotourism operations, particularly in the marine tourism context, are recently established (Dickey, 2003; Orams, 2003) and are often formed to generate secondary family income (e.g. diversified from farming or fisheries). The number of visitors to these businesses varies greatly, ranging anywhere from two to four visitors per week to over 100,000 per year (Higham *et al.*, 2001). Many are undercapitalized and the success rates for these small businesses are low (similar to small businesses in other sectors of the New Zealand economy), especially during the first 3–5 years (Warren and Taylor, 1994).

Key Ecotourism Industry Stakeholders in New Zealand

Nationally there are several government agencies that have important roles to play relating to the tourism industry. Tourism New Zealand (TNZ), the Tourism Industry Association of New Zealand (TIANZ), the Ministry of Tourism and the Department of Conservation (DoC) are key players in the New Zealand tourism industry (Simpson, 2003). TNZ, for example, which is responsible for the international marketing of New Zealand, has embraced ecotourism as part of its international marketing campaign (Orams, 2003). The role of Tourism New Zealand, however, is not in the area of ecotourism management practices; their role focuses strictly on the promotion and marketing of New Zealand to overseas markets. Notably, there has recently been a shift in TNZ focus away from an emphasis on increasing visitor numbers towards promoting longer visitor stay and higher visitor expenditure (TIANZ, 2002b), which can be considered a positive step towards more sustainable management of visitor impacts.

The Ministry of Tourism provides policy advice for the Minister for Tourism (Ministry of Tourism, 2004b). The Ministry also works with other government departments on key tourism policy issues (e.g. use of the environment, resources), and provides access to government-funded tourism research and statistics. The Ministry produced in collaboration with TIANZ the Tourism 2010 National Tourism Strategy (Ministry of Tourism, 2004b), which was developed in close consultation with the industry and the academic community. The strategy seeks to direct the continuing development of the tourism sector and maximize the potential that the tourism industry offers over the coming years, whilst ensuring environmental sustainability (TSG, 2001). Although it does not represent a form of regulation, the document does offer many suggestions and recommendations towards managing tourism and the natural environment sustainably.

The Tourism Industry Association of New Zealand (TIANZ) is a membership-based organization that represents the interests of over 3500 New Zealand tourism businesses. TIANZ was a driving force behind the creation of the New Zealand Tourism 2010 Strategy. A key area for TIANZ is industry development, which includes sourcing and providing programmes for the industry that can contribute to improvements in business and performance results (TIANZ, 2002b). TIANZ has recognized ecotourism and nature tourism as unique sectors of the tourism industry (TIANZ, 2002b), and has developed quality standards specific to the sector. These quality standards are delivered through the Qualmark certification programme.

The Department of Conservation (DoC) is charged with managing in accordance with the Conservation Act 1987 New Zealand's extensive conservation estate. DoC manages commercial use of public lands (national parks and reserves) by way of granting and administering concessions, or permits, allowing a level of commercial tourism activity to take place in selected areas. A concern for some stakeholders is the process by which these concessions are granted (Warren and Taylor, 1994; Warren *et al.*, 2003). The Department grants concessions for operators on a case-by-case basis, under different conditions, with different requirements for monitoring. This has resulted in frustrations for operators due to inconsistencies in conditions and charges (Warren *et al.*, 2003). Pressure exists for the Department to adhere to requirements of the Conservation Act 1987 while generating income through issuing and administering commercial concessions.

The Resource Management Act (RMA) 1992 is the primary legislation in New Zealand that is aimed at sustainable development. In addition to providing a consent process for proposed developments, it requires that the effects of proposed activities are considered, and impact mitigation measures put in place where necessary (Memon and Perkins, 2000). The RMA 1992 is administered by local/regional government to whom development consent applications are submitted for approval. Development proposals (e.g. energy generation schemes such as hydroelectric developments) are considered by central government if deemed to be of national significance. The RMA 1992 seeks to encourage developers to become involved in setting environmental plans and impact measures. While Dewar (1999) states that there is little guidance on tourism and the RMA from central government and that businesses and industry have been compromised by the time frames involved in processing consent applications, Local Government New Zealand has recently published a *Good Practice Guide to Tourism and the RMA* (August 2004). This document was produced in recognition of local government's major role in sustainable tourism planning and development. It directly relates to the implementation of some ten of the 43 suggested recommendations of the 2010 New Zealand Tourism Strategy (Beca Carter Hollings & Ferner Ltd and Tourism Resource Consultants Ltd, 2004).

The Search for Sustainable Ecotourism in New Zealand

The New Zealand tourism industry is challenged by the quest for sustainable tourism development. While many operators seem uncertain of where to begin, there have been various efforts aimed at sustainable tourism development in New Zealand. In 2000 TIANZ facilitated the national introduction of Green Globe (GG) (see Chapter 6) into the New Zealand tourism industry, through the development of an environmental plan (EP) (explained in detail in the following section). Subsequently the development of quality tourism standards (QTS) took place in 2003, which TIANZ claims provides a client-focused, cost-effective, quality standard for providers of tourism products (TIANZ, 2004). These standards cover a number of fields, including the eco/nature tourism sector (TIANZ, 2004), and are administered, marketed and accredited through Qualmark. Qualmark is a government/private-sector partnership that licenses tourism businesses to use the Qualmark logo. The Qualmark system is designed to assess the components that contribute to the delivery of high-quality visitor experiences. Its core activities have traditionally been in the accommodation sector (star grading system); however, the QTS programme allows the scheme to be expanded to cover more tourism industry sectors. Participation in the Qualmark certification programme is voluntary and based on payment of an annual licence fee. The annual licensing fee for Qualmark is variable, as it is influenced by the number of employees a business has, and can also be influenced by the size of the business (e.g. operating from more than one location). The joining fee for Qualmark is NZ$175.00, and the annual licensing fee begins at NZ$595.00 (Qualmark, 2005).

There are currently over 1250 New Zealand tourism businesses that have registered with Qualmark (Ministry of Tourism, 2004a); however, by the end of 2005, Qualmark hopes to have 1550 tourism businesses accredited (Qualmark, 2004). While Qualmark does not focus entirely on the environmental aspects of quality standards (as GG does), the programme has six 'quality areas for assessment' for their endorsement system of non-accommodation businesses (Qualmark, 2005). These comprise: (i) customer service; (ii) facilities and equipment; (iii) you and your staff; (iv) environmental and cultural impacts; (v) general safety and welfare; and (vi) overall business operations. There are additional 'bolt-on' criteria that businesses will be assessed against, specific to their operation (e.g. adventure tourism, ecotourism, horse trekking, etc.). Until recently, Qualmark was the only quality-standard certification programme in existence in New Zealand (TIANZ, 2002a); however, Green Globe has recently launched its International Ecotourism Certification programme (Green Globe 21, 2004). These standards were based on Ecotourism Australia's EcoCertification Program, formerly known as the Nature and Ecotourism Accreditation Program (see Chapter 22).

Three geographical areas in New Zealand have taken a regional approach in supporting initiatives to incorporate sustainability standards into their tourism industry. Green Globe has been adopted by the South Island community of Kaikoura, the third community in the world to undertake the benchmarking process, and the first in New Zealand. In the North Island, Rotorua developed a sustainability charter in 1998, bringing together leading industry and community stakeholders to develop a 'grass-roots' approach. The philosophy in this case is that some improvement in environmental performance is better than no improvement at all (Tourism Rotorua, 2004). The initiative has been recognized as an effective way to raise awareness in small and medium enterprises, and is considered complementary to more formal schemes such as GG (Titchener, 2004). A sustainability charter for tourism businesses has also been developed in the North Island region of Northland. The Northland Sustainable Tourism Project aims to assist Northland tourism businesses to work together to protect and enhance their social, cultural, economic and natural environments. The charter's principles were created uniquely for the Northland region and its operators in a process that was guided by the industry and its key stakeholders. The Ministry of Tourism has committed resources for full implementation in the Northland region (Woolams, 2005). Businesses will be supported to make progress towards sustainability, and may be able to use their achievements as a springboard onto existing certification schemes available in New Zealand (Woolams, 2005).

Another environmental initiative in New Zealand is the use of visitor codes of best practice (see Chapter 4). These voluntary schemes may be adopted by tourism operators to manage environmental impacts and provide an approach to self-regulation. In New Zealand, codes of best practice are widely used in the industry. One example is the Sea Kayak Operators Association of New Zealand (SKOANZ) Code of Practice. This code was developed and widely adopted in 1997. It sets out minimum standards and accepted industry practices for all members of SKOANZ (SKOANZ, 2003). It comprises four separate components: safety (primary focus), legislation, the environment and customer service.

Ecotourism Operator Perspectives on Environmental Certification Schemes

Recent research has examined New Zealand tourism operator perspectives on environmental certification schemes (ECS) (Cheyne and Barnett, 2001). Their study was driven by the adoption of GG by the TIANZ, which included a negotiated free entry for New Zealand businesses entering the first stage of the GG programme – developing an environmental plan (EP). This strategic partnership did not include costs for businesses progressing to stage two (commitment to certification), or stage three (independent certification) (TIANZ, 2001). In early 2001 TIANZ distributed general information about GG and developing an EP to its members. The EP is a one-page statement outlining a business's commitment towards environmental improvement (TIANZ, 2001). The EP uses ten key performance areas, which were aligned to those identified by GG, in which companies should seek continual environmental improvement. A sample of 238 completed questionnaires was generated by Cheyne and Barnett (2001), representing operators from various sectors of the tourism industry (the majority of respondents were from the hospitality, adventure and outdoor activities sectors). Results indicated that most operators generally agreed that belonging to an environmental certification scheme would provide benefits for their business, but that barriers to entry included lack of the awareness, knowledge and time required to complete application processes (Cheyne and Barnett, 2001). This study extended to various sectors of the tourism industry and did not isolate the responses of ecotourism business operators.

In response to the need for sector-specific insights, a quantitative research project was developed in 2003 to specifically explore commercial ecotourism operator perspectives on environmental certifications schemes in New Zealand (Rowe, 2004). The research sought to quantify the extent to which New Zealand ecotourism operators currently use environmental certification schemes, and assess their awareness and perceived value on different aspects of environmental certification. The term 'environmental certification scheme' was defined according to Honey and Rome (2001: 17) as any 'voluntary procedure that assesses, monitors and gives written assurance that a business, product, service or management system conforms to specific requirements. A marketable logo or seal is awarded to those that meet or exceed baseline standards.'

The research was conducted using a questionnaire that addressed in three separate parts the profile of New Zealand ecotourism businesses, operator perspectives on environmental certification and perceptions of Green Globe. The majority of questions were closed-ended, employing five-point Likert scales to assess degrees of operator agreement or disagreement with specific statements. Several variables used in the survey were retained from Cheyne and Barnett (2001) to allow comparison of responses.

The research utilized an existing database of New Zealand ecotourism operators (Higham *et al.*, 2001), which identified that in 1999 there were 230 ecotourism businesses in New Zealand. The database was updated in August 2003. In line with the criteria developed in creating the original database, an operation needed only to declare themselves to be 'ecotourism' in order to be included in the 2003 ecotourism database. Additionally, operators who declared that they offered an ecotourism experience, used the term 'eco' in the title of their operation or described the product or service offered as ecotourism were included in the database. Thus, operators were not evaluated or screened prior to inclusion on the database but rather included on the basis of self-declaration. A total of 51 new ecotourism operations appeared in the updated database, which, when combined with operator attrition ($n = 55$), resulted in a slightly reduced total of 226 New Zealand ecotourism operators in 2003. This exercise confirmed the dynamic nature of commercial ecotourism business operations in New Zealand. Eighty per cent of operators from the 1999 database were still in operation (perhaps indicating a maturing of the sector, given the earlier findings of Warren and Taylor, 1994), and 17 businesses had changed the name of their operation during the interim period.

All operators that appeared in the 2003 ecotourism database were invited to complete an online survey. An email was sent as the initial communication with operators, providing a hypertext link to the online survey. All operators were offered the choice of completing the online survey or receiving a postal survey. The questionnaire was password-protected; the password was provided only for those invited to complete the survey (Litvin and Kar, 2001). Respondent confidentiality was provided as all responses to the survey were directly downloaded into an SPPS data file upon completion and electronic submission of the online questionnaire. The survey generated a total response rate of 36%. Seventy-four responses were received from the online survey, and seven from completed postal surveys. The valid response rate was 29% due to partial incompletion rendering some survey returns insufficient to be included in the analysis. Data analysis was performed using frequency and descriptive techniques, as well as bivariate analysis via cross-tabulations. Chi-square tests of significance were applied to all cross-tabulation analyses and in some such cases data recoding was performed to reduce degrees of freedom.

Profiling New Zealand Ecotourism Operators

The design of the survey sought initially to profile New Zealand ecotourism operators in such terms as number of employees, years/months of operation, number of visitors per year and location of business. Additionally the operator profile included types of resources used by the operators and membership of environmental certification schemes (Table 20.1).

Ecotourism operators were widespread and their activities took place in areas that could be described as natural and rural as well as in urban areas in many parts of New Zealand. The distribution of responding operators was consistent between the North Island (48.5%) and the South Island (50%). Sixty-five per cent of respondents indicated that they held a Department of Conservation (DoC) concession. Of the 66 operators in total, there was a much higher proportion of concession holders in the South Island (31:2) than the North Island (12:20). Twenty-four per cent of respondents indicated that they were current members of an environmental certification scheme, one-quarter had considered becoming certified, and 43% had never considered joining a certification scheme. Operators who were certified indicated that the application was completed by the owner (20%), manager (9%), a student (2%) or other staff (2%) (the remainder provided no response to this question).

Analysis showed that small operators, defined as those with five employees or fewer, were less likely to be members of an environmental certification scheme ($\chi^2 = 16.015$, df $= 5$, $P \leq 0.007$). Operators with more than

Table 20.1. New Zealand ecotourism operator profile ($n = 66$).

Characteristic		Response (%)
Number of full-time employees	1–2	51
	3–5	24
	6–10	18
	21+	7
Operate throughout the year	Yes	73
	No	27
Age of operation	≥4 years	20
	5–9 years	29
	10+ years	51
Predominant type of customer	Domestic	30
	International	64
	Equal mix	6
Total number of visitors per year (no.)	Minimum	12
	Maximum	300,000
Location of ecotourism activity	North Island	48.5
	South Island	50
	No response	1.5
Top five natural resources used	Scenery	86
	Wildlife	80
	Streams/rivers	59
	Land use	51
	Rainforest/forest	45
DoC concession holder	Yes	65
	No	35
Member of an ECS	Yes	24
	No	71
	No response	5
Member of Green Globe	Yes	23
Member of Qualmark	Yes	1
Operate in accordance with code of best practice	Yes	88
	No	9
	No response	3

six employees were most likely to be a member of an environmental certification scheme. Another significant factor for operator membership status was the longevity of the business. Eighty-one per cent of environmental certification scheme members had been in operation for more than 10 years, whereas businesses that had been operating less than 4 years represented only 6.3% of members ($\chi^2 = 8.006$, df = 2, $P \leq 0.018$). Ninety-four per cent of operators who were members of an ECS indicated that they had a predominantly international visitor base ($\chi^2 = 8.519$, df = 3, $P \leq 0.036$). Almost all members of environmental certification schemes were also DoC concession holders (94%) ($\chi^2 = 7.757$, df = 1, $P \leq 0.005$). Marine mammal tour operators were found to be those most likely to be members of an environmental certification scheme ($\chi^2 = 11.176$, df = 1, $P \leq 0.001$). This is due in large part to the fact that most of these businesses need to comply with the Marine Mammal Protection Act (MMPA, 1978) and the Marine Mammal Protection Regulations (MMPR, 1992) in order to be permitted to operate.

Responding operators viewed membership fees (60%) and the perceived time involved in completing the required paperwork (64%) as barriers to joining an environmental certification scheme (Table 20.2). Non-members of environmental certification schemes were most likely to consider membership fees a barrier to joining (70%), while 44% of current environmental certification scheme members disagreed that fees were a barrier ($\chi^2 = 6.937$, df = 2, $P \leq 0.031$). It was evident that operators who are not members of an environmental certification scheme perceive that entry into such schemes is associated with high costs. Operators were largely undecided whether they would be willing to absorb the membership costs of an environmental certification scheme (44%); however, a significant proportion (51%) of operators who were members of environmental certification schemes agreed that they would be willing to absorb the cost of membership ($\chi^2 = 10.678$, df = 2, $P \leq 0.005$). Thirty-nine per cent felt that the consumer should absorb the financial costs associated with environmental certification schemes. The actual costs of environmental certification vary between schemes (e.g. Green

Table 20.2. New Zealand ecotourism operator perceptions on joining an environmental certification scheme (%), $n = 66$.

Variable	1	2	3	4	5	M	Std dev.
Membership fees a barrier to joining	20	40	26	12	2	2.35	0.98
Time developing an environmental plan a barrier to joining	11	35	20	29	5	2.80	1.11
Time completing required paperwork a barrier to joining	14	50	15	18	3	2.47	1.04
Lack knowledge to complete an EP	5	9	27	41	18	3.59	1.03
Willing to absorb extra cost of being a member	3	18	44	29	6	3.17	0.90
Expect cost of being a member to be absorbed by the consumer	5	39	33	18	5	2.79	0.95
Benefits of being environmentally certified outweigh the barriers to joining	5	18	49	23	5	3.05	0.88

1 = strongly agree, 2 = agree, 3 = undecided, 4 = disagree, 5 = strongly disagree.

Globe, Qualmark, The Natural Step, ISO 14000 and Enviro Mark). Most schemes have a sliding fee structure which may be significant in terms of this result. The Green Globe fee structure is: (i) affiliates: companies $100, communities $1000; (ii) benchmarking:[1] companies $200–$1000, communities $3000–$5000; and (iii) certification:[2] companies $200–$1000, communities $3000–$5000 (Koeman *et al.*, 2002).

Although 46% of operators identified time to be a barrier to completing an environmental plan (EP), most (60%) felt they had the knowledge required to complete an EP. Seventy per cent of the operators who felt they had the knowledge to complete an EP also held DoC concessions ($\chi^2 = 11.039$, df = 2, $P \leq 0.004$), indicating that prior energy has been invested in developing an environmental plan for the actual establishment (i.e. permitting) of the businesses in question. A significant number of operators (93%) who operated in accordance with a code of conduct stated that they perceived the time involved in completing the required paperwork to be a barrier to joining an environmental certification scheme ($\chi^2 = 12.290$, df = 4, $P \leq 0.015$).

Responding operators provided various insights into perceptions of environmental certification schemes (Table 20.3). The majority of New Zealand ecotourism operators agreed with the statements that environmental certification schemes could improve relationships with the local community (57%) and help with public relations (56%) and that customer demand for environmentally certified business is increasing (74%). However, despite this, many operators were undecided whether environmental certification schemes would actually increase the credibility of their ecotourism operation. Forty-one per cent of operators remained undecided on the marketing benefits of environmental certification schemes and many operators (49%) were undecided whether the benefits of being environmentally certified would outweigh the costs. Similar results were found around perceptions that media publications (travel guides, brochures) were more effective means of market communication than being a member of an environmental certification scheme. An analysis of the status of operators as affiliated, benchmarked or certified might have added value to this analysis but this level of detail was not achieved in the design of the operator survey. It is recommended that future research in this field should extend to ascertaining the status of operators who claim to be members of environmental certification schemes.

A significant number of operators considered endorsements by media and travel guides to be more powerful marketing than environmental certification (67%) and also agreed that most ecotourists were largely unaware of environmental certification schemes ($\chi^2 = 25.777$, df = 4, $P \leq 0.001$). While many operators agreed that demand for environmental certification is increasing (74%), 23% of respondents were undecided about this (Table 20.3).

In contrast, it was found that 88% of businesses were operating in accordance with a code of best practice (only 9% indicated that they were not) (see Table 20.1). New Zealand ecotourism operators who had been in business for more than 10 years were more likely to follow a code of conduct, compared

Table 20.3. New Zealand ecotourism operator perceptions of environmental certification schemes (%), *n* = 66.

Variable	1	2	3	4	5	M	Std dev.
Increase profitability	3	8	51	38	–	3.24	0.725
Increase customer satisfaction	2	18	48	24	8	3.18	0.875
Increase employee satisfaction	3	21	42	30	3	3.09	0.872
Improve relationships with the local community	3	54	29	11	3	2.56	0.844
Help with public relations	14	42	29	11	4	2.50	1.011
Increase a business's credibility as an ecotourism provider	11	26	48	12	3	2.71	0.924
Marketing advantage over competitors	3	27	41	23	6	3.02	0.936
Customer demand for environmentally certified businesses is increasing	23	51	23	3	–	2.06	0.762
Endorsements by media, publications and travel guides are more powerful marketing than most ECS	8	20	38	27	7	3.08	1.042
Most ecotourists are aware of ECS	–	3	33	41	23	3.83	0.815

1 = strongly agree, 2 = agree, 3 = undecided, 4 = disagree, 5 = strongly disagree.

with those who had been in business for 5–9 years and 4 years and under ($\chi^2 = 11.817$, df = 4, $P \leq 0.019$). Also significant was the number of operators (64%) who followed a code of best practice and perceived most ecotourists to be unaware of environmental certification schemes ($\chi^2 = 10.397$, df = 4, $P \leq 0.034$). In terms of value, most operators perceived there to be some value in joining environmental certification schemes (57%), although over a quarter (26%) saw no value in environmental certification whatsoever. Forty-eight per cent of operators considered certification as a means of supporting/validating the '100% Pure New Zealand' campaign, although a similar proportion (42%) did not consider this to be the case. Those who felt that certification does not validate the '100% Pure New Zealand' campaign were also more likely to see cost ($\chi^2 = 18.361$, df = 6, $P \leq 0.005$) and time completing an EP ($\chi^2 = 21.634$, df = 6, $P \leq 0.001$) as barriers, and were less likely to consider certification to improve relationships with the local community ($\chi^2 = 14.397$, df = 6, $P \leq 0.026$), help with public relations ($\chi^2 = 25.061$, df = 6, $P \leq 0.001$), enhance credibility ($\chi^2 = 16.831$, df = 6, $P \leq 0.010$) and provide a marketing advantage ($\chi^2 = 13.570$, df = 6, $P \leq 0.035$).

Green Globe

Many of the sampled ecotourism operators in New Zealand were undecided about their perceptions of the Green Globe (GG) certification scheme (Table 20.4). Most operators were undecided on their perception of belonging to GG; however, compared with the previous section, a significant number of respondents (85%) agreed that both certification schemes in general, as well as GG specifically, help with public relations ($\chi^2 = 27.046$, df = 4, $P \leq 0.001$). A strong relationship existed between operators who were members of GG ($n = 15$) and the perceptions that GG increases employee satisfaction ($\chi^2 = 15.422$, df = 4, $P \leq 0.004$) and improves relationships with the community ($\chi^2 = 12.682$, df = 4, $P \leq 0.013$). Operators who were members of GG agreed that membership of this scheme increases profitability ($\chi^2 = 15.129$, df = 4, $P \leq 0.004$). For operators with a predominantly domestic market base, only 10% agreed that GG could give a marketing advantage over competitors ($\chi^2 = 13.272$, df = 6, $P \leq 0.039$).

Many operators perceived barriers to joining GG (Table 20.5). These barriers include cost (62%), time involved in developing an EP (54%) and time involved in the paperwork (59%). A significant proportion of operators who were not members of an environmental certification scheme (60%) agreed that the costs of belonging to GG would be a barrier to joining ($\chi^2 = 8.225$, df = 2, $P \leq 0.016$). Significant relationships were identified between those operators who held DoC concessions and their perceptions of barriers to joining GG. More operators who held DoC concessions agreed that the cost was a barrier (76%) than those who did not (24%) ($\chi^2 = 9.555$, df = 2, $P \leq 0.008$). Seventy-two per cent of operators holding DoC concessions agreed

Table 20.4. New Zealand ecotourism operator perceptions of Green Globe membership (%), $n = 66$.

Variable	1	2	3	4	5	M	Std dev.
Increase profitability	–	11	48	35	6	3.36	0.75
Increase customer satisfaction	–	15	48	27	9	3.30	0.84
Increase employee satisfaction	2	21	42	30	5	3.15	0.86
Improve relationships with community	–	24	50	21	5	3.06	0.80
Help with public relations	–	40	38	20	2	2.82	0.80
Give a marketing advantage over competitors	2	30	47	18	3	2.91	0.81

1 = strongly agree, 2 = agree, 3 = undecided, 4 = disagree, 5 = strongly disagree.

Table 20.5. New Zealand ecotourism operator perceptions of joining GG (%), *n* = 66.

Variable	1	2	3	4	5	M	Std dev.
The cost of belonging to GG is a barrier	26	36	29	7	2	2.23	0.97
The time in developing an EP is a barrier	15	39	21	21	3	2.58	1.08
The time in completing required paperwork for GG is a barrier	24	35	24	15	2	2.35	1.06
I lack the knowledge required to develop an EP	2	9	27	47	15	3.65	0.90

1 = strongly agree, 2 = agree, 3 = undecided, 4 = disagree, 5 = strongly disagree.

that the time involved in completing the paperwork is a barrier to joining GG ($\chi^2 = 9.463$, df = 2, $P \leq 0.009$). Clearly concern exists regarding multiple environmental quality and certification programmes and the costs of compliance and/or membership of differing schemes.

Discussion: Ecotourism Operator Responses to Environmental Certification

Approximately 18,000 small to medium-size tourism businesses exist in New Zealand, of which 13,500 (82%) employ fewer than five people (Department of Labour Te Tari Mahi, 2004) and only ten are substantial enough to merit stock exchange listing (TIANZ, 2002b; Simpson, 2003). The findings of this research highlight that the New Zealand ecotourism sector is not different from other tourism businesses in size; 75% of respondents have fewer than five employees. Many tourism businesses in New Zealand confront significant seasonality challenges and are scarcely viable in the off season (Department of Labour Te Tari Mahi, 2004). Given that most ecotourism businesses operate at a micro-management level, it is not surprising that one-quarter do not operate throughout the year. The longevity of ecotourism businesses appears to be increasing; half of the survey respondents (51%) had been in operation for more than 10 years. This differs from Higham and Carr's (2002) research, which reported at that time that most New Zealand ecotourism operators were less than 10 years old, indicating an increasingly established and maturing ecotourism sector. This research found ecotourism in New Zealand to be dynamic in nature, with a number of businesses entering and exiting the sector between 1999 and 2003. The total number of New Zealand ecotourism operators has not radically changed in the past 4 years.

In 2001, Cheyne and Barnett's tourism industry-wide study of certification schemes indicated that 9% of tourism operators had taken up membership of environmental certification schemes. The 2003 study indicated that 25% of ecotourism operators were members of environmental certification schemes. It also emerged that small-scale ecotourism operations (five employees or fewer) were less likely to be certified. Given that 75% of ecotourism operators fit this description, the probability of New Zealand ecotourism operators becoming certified will remain low until entry barriers of relevance to small businesses are adequately addressed. The age of the operation also influenced the likelihood of membership of a certification scheme. The businesses that have been in operation for more than 10 years represent 81% of certification scheme members; very few members (6.3%) have been operating less than 4 years. Eighty per cent of ecotourism operators have now been operating for more than 5 years, which might augur well for expanding membership of environmental certification schemes.

TIANZ (2002b) reports that 60% of New Zealand tourism is generated by domestic visitors; however, New Zealand ecotourism operators identified that 64% of their customers were from international origins. It is evident that commercial ecotourism businesses in New Zealand cater particularly for international visitors. This suggests that New Zealand ecotourism operators could benefit from adherence to an international certification scheme (e.g. Green Globe), as opposed to a less internationally recognized domestic quality standard such as Qualmark. Generally the promotion of tourism environmental certification is primarily addressed to consumers or tourists as a target group (Spittler and Haak, 2001). Labels can improve the image and/or sales of a company (Gallastegui, 2002) but only where consumers are able to recognize credible certification brands. This emphasizes the importance of understanding operator perceptions of the effectiveness of different environmental certification schemes.

The perception widely held by New Zealand ecotourism operators that most ecotourists are generally unaware of environmental certification schemes is supported by Synergy (2000), although more recent research into market demand for the certification of tourism operators is now available (see Font and Epler Wood, Chapter 10 and Chafe, Chapter 11, this volume). None the less, operators generally agreed that customer demand for environmentally certified businesses is increasing (74%). New Zealand ecotourism operators, however, indicated that demand for environmentally certified businesses in New Zealand is not strong. Further marketing of environmental certification schemes could potentially influence tourist and operator awareness. While operators agreed that levels of customer demand are increasing, 38% were undecided whether endorsements by media and travel publications are more powerful marketing tools than environmental certification. Thus there appears to be a necessity for the industry to contemplate approaches that will increase levels of awareness of environmental certification schemes on the part of ecotourism operators as well as tourists.

Certification at any level involves a time commitment by the staff of a business, and meeting the costs of operating environmentally sustainable businesses perhaps explains why larger-scale operations are more likely to commit to certification programmes (Sasidharan and Font, 2001; Font, 2004). New Zealand operators were critical of the fee structure of most programmes, highlighting the perception of high costs and fees as a barrier to considering, let alone pursuing, membership. Toth (2002) disagrees, suggesting the idea that cost is a barrier is simply a myth, and some programmes could provide ample benefits to repay the fees. Myth or no myth, sliding fee scales are now a common incentive, with larger companies paying higher fees than smaller companies. Recent research suggests that sustainable tourism certification criteria can lead to short-term returns on investment through 'eco-efficiencies', reported to be up to 30% savings (e.g. energy and water savings) (Sanabria *et al.*, 2003). Regardless of these views, scepticism within the New Zealand industry towards the relative merits, costs and savings of the programmes is indeed a barrier (Cheyne and Barnett, 2001). Synergy (2000) and various other reports (e.g. Sanabria *et al.*, 2003) state that many smaller businesses are excluded from certification programmes because of the complexity of the business planning required to adopt a certification scheme. It is conceivable that the complexities of certification applications (and the possible cost of hiring an outside consultant) are viewed as an important part of the certification process, and one that will incur considerable cost.

Operators were predominantly aware of several perceived benefits of environmental certification, including that it could improve relationships with local communities (58%) and assist with public relations (56%). A substantial number of operators considered environmental certification to play several valuable roles, including supporting the country's clean and green image and enhancing their ecotourism business's credibility. None the less, many New Zealand ecotourism operators were not willing to absorb the cost of certification, nor did they believe that they had the time to complete the requirements of certification.

At present, operating in accordance with a code of best practice remains the preferred option in terms of demonstrating a commitment to the environment. Just as businesses that have been operating for more than 10 years are more likely to be certified, so too are they likely to be adhering to a code of best practice. Adherence to a code of best practice could be interpreted as a means to demonstrate a commitment to responsible business practice. However, this is particularly the case if businesses are also committed to other formal environmental initiatives (including schemes such as Green Globe, Qualmark, The Natural Step, ISO 14000 and Enviro Mark), due to weak quality controls associated with voluntary codes (Weaver, 2001). None the less, following a code of best practice can perhaps be viewed as an evolutionary step towards becoming a member of an environmental certification scheme as businesses become more established over time.

Those operators who were members of GG ($n = 15$) served predominantly international visitor markets. GG is a globally recognized certification programme and operators clearly understand the value of offering a logo or programme that is both recognized and meaningful to their customers.

Interestingly, the one respondent who was certified only with Qualmark reported a predominantly domestic market. Operators who were members of GG felt that the programme increased employee satisfaction (53%), improved relationships with the community (53%) and increased profitability (73%). These findings suggest that operators have responded positively to the GG programme in those cases where GG, and the benefits that it may offer, fits the profile of the business in question, particularly as it relates to visitor markets.

Conclusions

Ecotourism in the New Zealand context has been commercially developed relatively belatedly and may be considered a maturing industry sector. While the total number of commercial ecotourism operators has plateaued in recent years, there remains a steady turnover of businesses as some new players enter the ecotourism sector replacing those that fail. The ecotourism sector is particularly reliant on the perception that New Zealand is a '100% Pure' destination, as promoted by Tourism New Zealand. This is a perception that is actually somewhat removed from the reality (Higham *et al.*, 2001). The environmental performance of many ecotourism operators, and the communities within which they are located, indicate much potential for further improvement (Higham *et al.*, 2001). The relatively low levels of response to environmental certification that are evident in this chapter are perhaps another indicator of this fact. The profile of ecotourism businesses in New Zealand helps to explain this situation. Many are small-scale, highly seasonal, undercapitalized and, in some instances, barely viable. This is a situation with many parallels in the international context (Blamey, 2001).

That said, some operators have emerged as industry leaders. Examples of leaders in this research include those operators who adhere to a code of best practice, have a DoC concession and are members of an ECS (23% of the study sample). Some of these operators have been recognized nationally and internationally through industry awards. However, at present, there remains little urgency and no requirement to adhere to environmental certification standards, and this is perhaps a consequence of programmes providing a lack of demonstrated tangible benefits (e.g. marketing benefits, preferential access or filtering of concessions, government support of improved image) for their members. Although many New Zealand ecotourism operators agreed that customer demand for certified businesses is increasing, they did not agree that demand in New Zealand was strong. Additionally, while a significant number of operators in the ecotourism sector are operating at a micro-management level and do not operate throughout the year, investing in certification was often viewed as an ineffective use of limited financial and/or human resources. Barriers to environmental certification were clearly articulated by operators, particularly those running small-scale businesses. Instead, the adoption or development of codes of best practice is widespread, and it is possible that this is an evolutionary step towards formal environmental certification. In order to make practical the more widespread environmental certification of ecotourism operators, it may be necessary for TIANZ and the Ministry of Tourism to seek to address perceived barriers to the certification of ecotourism businesses as they currently exist.

Notes

[1] Regional and national fee levels may vary from this global fee; does not include cost of on-site audit.

[2] Does not include fee for required certification assessment by accredited certification firm.

References

Bass, S., Font, X. and Danielson, L. (2001) *Standards and Certification: A Leap Forward or a Step Back for Sustainable Development?* International Institute for Environment and Development, London.

Beca Carter Hollings & Ferner Ltd and Tourism Resource Consultants Ltd (2004) *Tourism and the RMA Good Practice Guide.* Local Government New Zealand.

Blamey, R.K. (2001) Principles of ecotourism. In: Weaver, D.B. (ed.) *Encyclopedia of Ecotourism.* CAB International, Wallingford, UK, pp. 5–22.

Buckley, R. (2001) Major issues in tourism ecolabelling. In: Font, X. and Buckley, R. (eds) *Tourism Ecolabelling: Certification and Promotion of Sustainable Management.* CAB International, Wallingford, UK, pp. 271–348.

Buckley, R. (2002) Tourism ecolabels. *Annals of Tourism Research* 29(1), 103–108.

Buhrs, T. (2000) The environment and the role of the state. In: Memon, P. and Perkins, H. (eds) *Environmental Planning and Management in New Zealand.* Dunmore Press, Palmerston North, pp. 27–35.

Cheyne, J. and Barnett, S. (2001) Environmental certification schemes: a New Zealand case study of operator perceptions. In: Joppe, M. (ed.) *Optimising Your Destination: Finding a Balance, Travel Tourism Research Association Conference, Niagara Falls, Ontario, 14–16 October 2001*, pp. 23–29.

Department of Labour Te Tari Mahi (2004) Tourism Skills Shortage Report, Industry Profile: Tourism, Skills Action Plan. Available at: www.dol.govt.nz (accessed 10 September 2004).

Dewar, K. (1999) Sustainable management – enacting the RMA. In: Monin, N., Monin, J. and Walker, R. (eds) *Narratives of Business and Society: Differing New Zealand Voices.* Longman, Auckland, pp. 265–277.

Dickey, A. (2003) Ecotourism in New Zealand: a spatio-temporal analysis. Unpublished dissertation, University of Otago, New Zealand.

Font, X. (2004) Sustainability standards in the global economy. In: Theobald, W. (ed.) *Global Tourism.* Butterworth-Heinemann, Oxford, pp. 213–229.

Forsyth, T. (1997) Environmental responsibility and business regulation: the case of sustainable tourism. *Geographical Journal* 163(3), 270–281.

Gallastegui, I.G. (2002) The use of ecolabels: a review of the literature. *European Environment* 12, 316–331.

Giro, F. (2002) World Ecotourism Summit final report: Theme B: Regulation of ecotourism: institutional responsibilities and frameworks. In: *World Ecotourism Summit 2002, Quebec, May.*

Green Globe 21 (2004) International Ecotourism Standard. Available at: www.greenglobe21.com (accessed 29 April 2005).

Hall, C.M. and Kearsley, G. (2001) *Tourism in New Zealand: An Introduction.* Oxford University Press, South Melbourne.

Harper, C.L. (2001) *Environment and Society: Human Perspectives on Environmental Issues.* Prentice Hall, Upper Saddle River, New Jersey.

Higham, J. and Carr, A. (2002) Ecotourism visitor experiences in Aotearoa/New Zealand: challenging the environmental values of visitors in pursuit of pro-environmental behaviour. *Journal of Sustainable Tourism* 10(4), 277–308.

Higham, J. and Carr, A. (2003) Scope and scale of ecotourism in New Zealand. In: Fennell, D.A. and Dowling, R.K. (eds) *Ecotourism Policy and Planning.* CAB International, Wallingford, UK, pp. 235–255.

Higham, J., Carr, A. and Gale, S. (2001) *Ecotourism in New Zealand: Profiling Visitors to New Zealand Ecotourism Operations.* Research Paper Number Ten, Department of Tourism, University of Otago, Dunedin.

Honey, M. and Rome, A. (2001) *Protecting Paradise: Certification Programs for Sustainable Tourism and Ecotourism*. Institute for Policy Studies, Washington, DC.

International Scientific Council for Island Development (INSULA) (2003) *Tools for Managing Sustainable Tourism.* Available at: www.insula.org (accessed 1 November 2003).

Kearsley, G.W. and Higham, J.E.S. (1997) *Management of the Environmental Effects Associated with the Tourism Sector. Review of Literature on Environmental Effects.* Report to the Ministry for the Environment submitted to the Parliamentary Commissioner for the Environment Te Kaitiaki Taiao a Te Whare Paremata, Wellington, New Zealand.

Koeman, A., Worboys, G., Lacy, I.D., Scott, A. and Lipman, G. (2002) Green Globe: a global environmental certification program for travel and tourism. In: Honey, M. (ed.) *Ecotourism and Certification: Setting Standards in Practice.* Island Press, Washington, DC, pp. 299–324.

Litvin, S.W. and Kar, G.H. (2001) E-surveying for tourism research: legitimate tool or a researcher's fantasty? *Journal of Travel Research* 39, 308–314.

Memon, P.A. and Perkins, H.C. (2000) Environmental planning and management: the broad context. In: Memon, P.A. and Perkins, H.C. (ed.) *Environmental Planning and Management in New Zealand.* Dunmore Press, Palmerston North.

Ministry of Tourism (2004a) On Track to 2010, Issue One, August, 1–6. Available at: www.tourism.govt.nz (accessed 6 September 2004).

Ministry of Tourism (2004b) Homepage. Available at: www.tourism.govt.nz (accessed 10 September 2004).

Orams, M. (2003) Marine ecotourism in New Zealand: an overview of the industry and its management. In: Garrod, B. and Wilson, J.C. (eds) *Marine Ecotourism: Issues and Experiences.* Channel View Publications, Clevedon, UK, pp. 233–248.

Qualmark (2004) 1200 Quality Tourism Businesses to Choose From, Media Release, 25 May.

Qualmark (2005) *Joining Qualmark: Tourism Businesses.* Available at: www.qualmark.co.nz (accessed 10 April 2005).

Rowe, T. (2004) New Zealand ecotourism operators' perception of environmental certification schemes. Unpublished Master of Tourism thesis, University of Otago, New Zealand.

Sanabria, R., Skinner, E., Font, X., Maccarrone-Eaglen, A., Sallows, M. and Frederiksen, M. (2003) *Sustainable Tourism Stewardship Council (STSC). Raising the Standards and Benefits of Sustainable Tourism and Ecotourism Certification.* Rainforest Alliance, New York.

Sasidharan, V. and Font, X. (2001) Pitfalls of ecolabelling. In: Font, X. and Buckely, R.C. (eds) *Tourism Ecolabelling: Certification and Promotion of Sustainable Management.* CAB International, Wallingford, UK, pp. 105–120.

Sea Kayak Operators Association of New Zealand (SKOANZ) (2003) Code of Practice. Available at: www.seakayak.org.nz (accessed 15 December 2003).

Simpson, K. (2003) Ecotourism policy and practice in New Zealand's national estate. In: Fennell, D.A. and Dowling, R.K. (eds) *Ecotourism Policy and Planning.* CAB International, Wallingford, UK, pp. 255–273.

Spittler, R. and Haak, U. (2001) Quality analysis of tourism ecolabels. In: Font, X. and Buckley, R. (eds) *Tourism Ecolabelling: Certification and Promotion of Sustainable Management.* CAB International, Wallingford, UK, pp. 213–245.

Synergy (2000) *Tourism Certification: An Analysis of Green Globe 21 and Other Tourism Certification Programmes.* World Wildlife Fund, Godalming, UK.

Titchener, G. (2004) Pathways to sustainability: community charters and collective intelligence. In: *National Extension Tourism Conference (NET), People Places and Partnerships: Keys to Success, Kissimmee, Florida, 27–30 September 2004.*

Toth, R. (2002) Exploring the concepts underlying certification. In: Honey, M. (ed.) *Ecotourism and Certification: Setting Standards in Practice.* Island Press, Washington, DC, pp. 73–102.

Tourism Industry Association of New Zealand (TIANZ) (2001) *The Nature of Good Business, EP Guidelines.* Available at: www.tianz.org.nz (accessed 2 October 2003).

Tourism Industry Association of New Zealand (TIANZ) (2002a) *Quality Tourism Standard: Nature Tourism,* Version 1.0, October. Available at: www.tianz.org.nz (accessed 10 August 2003).

Tourism Industry Association of New Zealand (TIANZ) (2002b) *Tourism Industry Briefing to the Incoming Government.* Available at: www.tianz.org.nz (accessed 28 September 2003).

Tourism Industry Association of New Zealand (TIANZ) (2004) *Quality Tourism Standards.* Available at: www.tianz.org.nz (accessed 12 December 2004).

Tourism New Zealand (TNZ) (2003) *International Visitor Arrivals.* Available at: www.tourisminfo.govt.co.nz (accessed 6 August 2003).

Tourism Rotorua (2004) *Rotorua Sustainable Tourism Charter.* Available at: www.rotoruanz.com (accessed 7 September 2004).

Tourism Strategy Group (TSG) (2001) *New Zealand Tourism Strategy 2010.* Ministry of Tourism, Wellington, New Zealand.

Van Aalst, I. and Daly, C. (2002) *International Visitor Satisfaction with their New Zealand Experience: The EcoNature Tourism Product Market: A Summary of Studies 1990–2001.* PS Services, Wellington, New Zealand.

Warren, J., Blaschke, P., Taylor, N. and Gough, J. (2003) Recognising, planning for and managing limits to tourism development in natural areas. Paper presented at: *Taking Tourism to the Limits: An International Interdisciplinary Conference in the Waikato, The Waikato University, Hamilton NZ, December.*

Warren, J.A.N. and Taylor, C.N. (1994) *Developing Ecotourism in New Zealand.* The New Zealand Institute for Social Research and Development Ltd, Christchurch.

Weaver, D. (2001) *Ecotourism.* John Wiley & Sons Australia, Milton.

Woolams, R. (2005) *Northland Sustainable Tourism Charter Project Inc.* Sustainability Assessor, Enterprise Northland, Whangarei.

21 Towards an Internationally Recognized Ecolodge Certification

HITESH MEHTA

Edward D. Stone Jr and Associates, Florida, USA

Chapter Profile

The growing marketing hype and misuse of the term 'eco' appear to subvert whatever integrity the term and the concept behind ecolodges once had. Marketers, travel magazine writers, aid agencies, conservation organizations and even ecotourism associations indiscriminately label any accommodation located in a natural setting as an 'ecolodge'. This results in market confusion, and a mismatch between ecotourists who have chosen an ecolodge in the belief that there would be appropriate returns to the local community and conservation – and what is actually delivered. In some cases using the term ecolodge is more about jumping on the bandwagon in the expectation of greater market appeal than it is about a commitment to conserving the environment and local cultures.

To reduce the dilution of the ecolodge concept, this chapter argues for an internationally recognized ecolodge standard to help eliminate the widespread greenwashing in the tourism industry. After defining the concept of ecolodge and introducing the components/principles that differentiate ecolodges from traditional hotels, this chapter reviews four certification programmes from around the globe that incorporate ecolodge criteria and analyses them against the proposed components/principles.

The chapter aims to lay the foundations for creating an international certification for ecolodges as one option, incorporating some key principles and best components from the four existing certification programmes addressing ecolodges that were reviewed and analysed.

Introduction

In the last 15 years, ecolodges have developed and appear to be flourishing around the world, from Fiji to Ecuador. To date, there are over 20 ecolodges, with community-owned ecolodges being the current trend. In developing ecolodges, innovative developers and designers are synthesizing traditional and high-tech concepts for land and site planning, architectural design and construction, and creating plans that incorporate local community involvement while showing an increasing sensitivity to existing ecosystems and still bringing about genuine economic gains. By blending the wisdom of the past with current knowledge and technology, ecolodges are being built that fulfil a number of aims and benefits. For visitors, they are being built to provide a healthy and comfortable place to enjoy nature, with buildings that blend into the surroundings, conserve material resources in their construction, save energy and water resources in their operation and, most importantly, involve the local population through the design, construction and operational stages (Gardner, 2001). Outstanding examples of ecolodges include Kapawi Ecolodge in the Ecuadoran Amazon, Chumbe Ecolodge in Zanzibar and Il Ngwesi Ecolodge in northern Kenya.

The benefits of ecolodges are numerous and can include the empowerment of local communities, preservation and conservation of surrounding flora and fauna and education of visitors and staff. Several recent ecotourism projects are demonstrating that involving indigenous peoples in the planning process can help towards the sustainability of both the natural and cultural resources – for example, Wen Hei Ecolodge in Yunnan, China, and Adrere Amellal Ecolodge in Siwa Oasis, Egypt. In contrast to most conventional planning processes, the planning of ecolodges incorporates community empowerment techniques, where planners are employed to ensure that all additions to the built environment and infrastructure are at a scale that is appropriate and within the limits of acceptable change. Some of the techniques include planning workshops whereby indigenous stakeholders are encouraged to help draw up the physical plans for ecolodges. This type of participatory design is most successful when it is incorporated into the lives of indigenous communities through economic development resulting in some kind of monetary generation (Mehta, 2001).

Despite the benefits of ecolodges, the ecolodge industry is currently at a crossroads. In the last decade, ecolodges can be shown to have generated revenue for local economies worldwide (such as Sukau Rainforest Ecolodge in Malaysia, Lapa Rios in Costa Rica, etc.), provided new incentives for governments (for example, Australia and Brazil) and local communities (Masai in Kenya and San in Botswana) to preserve protected areas and species, and heightened overall local awareness of the importance of conservation. Unfortunately, ecolodges, like all tourism accommodation, also have negative impacts. For example, inappropriate development of lodges in sensitive environments can also create significant pressures on and threats to the natural and cultural resources (e.g. pollution, over-consumption of scarce resources, etc.) that sustain it (Mehta, 1997). Some examples include the lodges along the Mara River in Kenya and in the Amazon rainforest of Brazil. However, from these often-costly lessons, we are learning that the benefits of ecolodges can only be sustained through well-planned and carefully implemented projects that place the long-term well-being of the natural and cultural resources as a high priority. In addition to the negative impacts of ecolodges, there are other challenges to creating authentic ecolodges, and this is combined with 'greenwashing' and general confusion amongst tourists as well as consultants (architects, landscape architects, engineers, etc.).

One of the challenges is that design firms, consultants, academics, web sites (www.ecoclub.com, 2003) and construction companies with little or no experience in ecolodge design, construction and operation are increasingly positioning themselves as green 'experts' (www.ecoclub.com, 2003). Some ecolodges are not being planned or built properly, are underfunded and the staff poorly trained. Operators and owners need to be advised by an internationally accepted certification body that what they are selling are not ecolodges. They are causing more harm than good by misinforming their consumers about the product. They are what can be referred to as the 'fish and chicken vegetarians' of the tourism industry (Mehta, 2000).

The second challenge is the lack of government regulations. The majority of government agencies around the world do not have specific regulations or minimum standards for ecolodge design and development (Sweeting *et al.*, 2000). It has therefore fallen on a few developers, landscape architects and architects to develop their own design and construction criteria and codes of ethics that guarantee minimal environmental and social impact, as well as having a harmonious and sustainable interaction between the physical structure and the surrounding environment. Some examples include Jean Michel Casteau's Recife Resorts, which developed their own design and construction guidelines, and EDSA, the landscape architecture and planning firm that has its own site selection criteria. However, currently none of these criteria or ethics are available to the general public.

The third challenge is the lack of international standards for ecolodges. The development of true ecolodges requires a strong commitment to both nature and culture, a thorough understanding of technology and, above all, shrewd marketing strategies. Within the field of ecotourism, there is perhaps no more important and potentially achievable goal than setting internationally viable sustainability standards for ecolodges. The importance of developing such ecolodge standards has been recognized by the International Ecotourism Society (TIES) and they have held two international Ecolodge Forums and Field Seminars in 1994 and 1995 in the US Virgin Islands and in Costa Rica, respectively. As a follow-up of the 1994 forum, TIES published the first book in the industry dedicated to ecolodges: *The Ecolodge Sourcebook for Planners and Developers*.

The continued demand for ecolodges in the late 1990s (Epler Wood *et al.*, 2004) prompted the writing of guidelines to allow for the creation of authentic ecolodges. TIES began this process by publishing *The International Ecolodge Guidelines* in 2002 (Mehta *et al.*, 2002). The aim was to provide a framework for the design, development and operations of ecolodges to ensure the social and ecological integrity of their given environments, and thereby allow for sustained benefits from ecotourism without damaging or destroying the natural resources on which they depend. These guidelines have helped developers, practitioners and local communities to gain a better understanding of how to achieve the benefits of an ecolodge, and have also helped conservation and tourism agencies to set up criteria to determine whether a lodge is an ecolodge or not.

The logical progression is from ecolodge guidelines to ecolodge certification. Guidelines are mainly used by developers, non-governmental organizations and consultants, and their use has helped develop sensitive accommodation; however, their use has not been able to stem the greenwashing. Given this situation, this chapter argues that there is a need for international ecolodge certification as a means of delivering authentic ecolodges. While the benefits and challenges of certification have been debated amongst ecotourism experts elsewhere (see Chapters 2, 6 and 22 in this volume), this chapter aims to provide the foundations for a certification system for ecolodges but does not attempt to provide details of such a system.

The objective of this chapter is to address the transition from ecolodge guidelines to certification and assist in developing a more transparent and consistent ecolodge market, with standardized components and principles.

Ecolodge Definitions

This section of the chapter addresses the term 'ecolodge' and attempts to clarify the definition. In order to create an internationally recognized certification system, it is crucial that the particularities and requirements of ecolodges be widely understood by all concerned. Since the term ecolodge emerged in the early 1990s several definitions have been put forward by various ecotourism organizations and 'experts' using different criteria systems that evaluate accommodation facilities.

The term ecolodge was first coined in 1994 during the first TIES Ecolodge Forum in Maho Bay and defined as 'an industry label used to identify a nature-dependent tourist lodge that meets the philosophy and principles of ecotourism' (Russel *et al.*, 1995). However, some felt that this was too broad and lacked specificity as it incorporated the term 'ecotourism', which has also commonly been misinterpreted and misunderstood.

In 1997, Hector Ceballos-Lascurain refined the definition, stating that:

> The most important thing about an ecolodge is that the ecolodge is not the most important thing. It is the quality of the surrounding environment that counts most: the nearby natural and cultural attractions – and the way ecotourism circuits are set up, operated and marketed, and the way in which local populations are actively involved in the process.
>
> (Ceballos-Lascuráin, 1997)

However, again the term ecotourism is used and it does not emphasize what is considered by some as one of the most crucial aspects of an ecolodge – planning, design and construction.

During the 1990s the definition of ecolodges evolved and, although in the mid-1990s there was very little mention of the cultural component in ecolodges (Russel *et al.*, 1995), it is now one of the key principles (Mehta *et al.*, 2002), so much so that Maho Bay Camp, the first 'ecolodge', would fail to meet today's criteria of what constitutes an ecolodge because the social component is practically non-existent and the benefits to local communities are minimal.

In 1999 Mehta (1999), following a review of existing certification programmes that incorporate ecolodge criteria and his own personal experience in planning and building ecolodges, identified ten key principles that constitute an ecolodge. The principles were:

1. Helps in the conservation of the surrounding flora and fauna.
2. Has a minimal impact on the natural surroundings during construction.
3. Fits into its specific physical and cultural contexts through careful attention to form, landscaping and colour, as well as the use of vernacular architecture.
4. Uses alternative, sustainable means of water acquisition and reduces water consumption.
5. Provides for careful handling and disposal of solid waste and sewage.
6. Meets its energy needs through passive design and renewable energy sources.
7. Uses traditional building technology and materials wherever possible and combines these with their modern counterparts for greater sustainability.
8. Endeavours to work together with the local community.
9. Offers interpretive programmes to educate both its employees and tourists about the surrounding natural and cultural environments.
10. Contributes to sustainable local development through education programmes and research.

Not all ecolodges will meet all the principles, as individual circumstances or location may make different principles irrelevant. For example, if an accommodation facility is located near a freshwater river or in a rainforest, it would not be necessary to spend money to have water-harvesting technologies. Likewise, in some areas, there may be no local materials available and therefore it would be prudent to import environmentally friendly foreign materials. With this in mind, this author developed a criteria system in 2002 for determining whether an ecolodge is truly an ecolodge (Mehta *et al.*, 2002). For an accommodation facility to be called an ecolodge, it had to satisfy five of the above-mentioned criteria, three of which embodied the three main principles of ecotourism, namely protection of nature, benefits to local people and offering of interpretive programmes. With this criteria system, there was flexibility depending on the individual circumstances of the ecolodge.

Utlizing the existing ecolodge definitions (Mehta *et al.*, 2002), the following definition is proposed:

> An ecolodge is a five- to 75-room, low-impact, nature-based, financially sustainable accommodation facility that helps protect sensitive neighbouring areas; involves and benefits local communities; offers tourists an interpretive and interactive participatory experience; provides a spiritual communion with nature and culture; and is planned, designed, constructed and operated in an environmentally and socially sensitive manner.

The Development and Operation of Ecolodges

Before analysing current certification programmes that incorporate ecolodge criteria, it is important to understand the key stages that are important in the development and operation of an authentic ecolodge.

Site selection, analysis, planning and design

The success of an ecolodge can centre on the initial site evaluation and selection. Careful evaluation, in some instances, may reveal that the site is not appropriate for development at all. Some of the criteria that should be used for evaluations are: access; location; existing infrastructure; slope; views; cultural resources; adjoining protected areas; availability of environmentally friendly materials; and market demand.

Once the site has been selected, the next development process is research and analysis. The majority of site analysis techniques that are being practised today are objective, and so tend to be rather unidimensional. A subjective approach is needed in order to create a plan that is in total harmony with the existing landscape. A sense of place and the feeling of sacredness are missing from most existing tourism lodges. Ecolodge sites need to provide the ecotourist with a spiritual communion with nature and the feeling of being 'at one with nature'. In the context of the ecosystem theory, holism is based on the concept that non-living components and living components function together as a whole according to well-defined biological laws.

Once a thorough site analysis has been conducted, sustainable site planning and design can lead to a closer harmony between an ecolodge and its setting and will help to lessen environmental impacts. Integral to ecolodge site planning and design is consideration of land use, human circulation, existing structures (if any), facilities and utilities in the natural and human environment. Information and data on the project and site are best laid out clearly in accurate scale plans, showing location, layout, general size and shape and orientation of the different elements of the project.

Biophysical impacts

The basic measures of the sustainability of an ecolodge are how it impacts on the environment, both negatively and positively. These impacts begin with the construction phase and continue with day-to-day operations. The goal from an economic, social and moral standpoint is to plan, construct and operate an ecolodge development so that negative impacts are reduced and positive impacts are increased, so that the ecolodge is sustainable. Ecolodges are selling biological and cultural diversity. So, if the ecolodge is designed, built and operated in a way that degrades the biophysical assets, its credibility, and that of the 'ecologically sustainable hospitality industry', is damaged; the ecolodge loses its selling point and any community support – and may ultimately fail.

Since ecolodges are to be used mainly by nature tourists, who are concerned with conservation, ecolodges should provide practical examples of harmonious interaction with nature. They should not only strive to minimize negative impacts but also provide alternative, more sustainable ways of living.

Ecolodges should play a proactive role in the conservation of biodiversity. A trend that began in Costa Rica but is spreading to other parts of the globe is the increasing participation of ecolodges in the preservation and conservation of the surrounding flora and fauna. Lodge owners now realize that, without animal species such as the quetzal and the elephant, there will be no ecotourists. There can be no greater irony than an ecolodge owner working in partnership with the local communities to earn a good reputation when the same lodge despoils its environment through inappropriate technologies, insensitive location and unsuitable design.

Eco-architectural design and environmental management systems

A fresh view of lodge architectural design is necessary if the hospitality industry is to be extended successfully into sensitive areas: eco-architectural design should be based on a blend of traditional technology and materials, along with modern concepts and appropriate technology. The considered inclusion of local people and the proper conservation of natural and cultural resources are crucial determining factors, particularly as many typical ecolodges are sited in or around protected areas and, in most cases, are neighbours to indigenous people.

Significant technological trends over the past decade have had a major influence on the character, pattern and architectural form of ecolodges. In a few cases, the design of the lodge has been driven by the technology. Probably the most notable technological trend is the new paradigm of 'designing for deconstruction' (DFD). Also, the concept of life cycle analysis of building materials has shifted from a 'cradle to grave' to a 'cradle to cradle' philosophy, which professes that all buildings have a certain lifespan, so it is important to plan ahead and determine the life cycle of materials used in the ecolodge. Designers should ask the question, 'How can the material be recycled or reused after the ecolodge is demolished?' Life cycle analysis raises the fundamental question of what the life of the building should be, which is an aspect rarely given much systematic consideration by most architects.

Some of the main environmental management systems principles that need to be considered for ecolodges include water conservation and harvesting, energy conservation and use of alternative energy, waste water and sewage treatment and solid waste management. Many of these issues are incorporated into most existing ecotourism certification programmes, and this section will explain some of the main principles.

In the case of water conservation and harvesting, rain and snow harvesting as well as water conservation technologies, such as low-flow shower heads and grey-water irrigation, can be used. Alternative energy sources and energy conservation technologies can be applied, such as solar, wind and geothermal power and the use of low-wattage light fittings and energy-saving kitchen equipment. In the case of waste management, which is a crucial principle especially for ecolodges because of their remote locations, strategies such as sorting of solid waste (plastics, glass, paper, etc.), composting of kitchen waste, use of dry decomposting toilets and constructed wetlands to treat sewage are some of the techniques utilized by designers.

Socio-economic and cultural impact

The need for integration and participation of neighbouring communities, both in tourism projects and in the conservation of natural resources, has been greatly emphasized over the past 10 years. In theory, an ecolodge project should create jobs and promote sustainable development of the area and community involved, from the environmental, cultural and economic point of view. In practice, this has proved to be challenging.

Without doubt, the most innovative current international trend in ecolodge development is the process that empowers indigenous populations. Active participation of people from the early planning and design phases, through consultation and construction and finally financial equity and operations, is crucial to the success of an authentic ecolodge. 'Ecotourism must bring about integrated development of the area where the ecolodge development is taking place' (S. Selengut, New York, personal communication, 1999). Several projects in Ecuador, Kenya and Canada built within the past decade have demonstrated that working hand in hand with the local people can result in a win–win situation (Mehta, 2001). More recently, ecolodge development in Kenya has demonstrated that it is possible to have community-owned ecolodges that are financially successful. Currently, the East African countries of Rwanda and Uganda are in the process of developing community-owned and joint-venture ecolodges.

Legal and financial factors

An aspect of ecolodges that until recently has not been given priority is the business aspect of ecolodges. It was not until TIES published *The Business of Ecolodges* (Sanders and Halpenny, 2000) that financial sustainability was considered. This worldwide survey showed that over half of the lodges were running at a loss (Sanders and Halpenny, 2000). There were a number of reasons for this situation. First, most of the properties were 'mom and pop'-operated and, while the owners were committed to the concept of ecotourism, they lacked adequate business experience and knowledge and for many it was a lifestyle decision. Secondly, many of the ecolodges were new businesses and not making a profit, and, thirdly, others had no budgets for marketing and were not attracting customers.

The sustainability of an ecolodge depends not only on its compatibility with the natural environment but also on its financial profitability and legal soundness. No venture will survive if it cannot generate an income that sufficiently covers all of its expenses. Failure to create an appropriate legal and financial foundation will put a venture at risk should government authorities, creditors or plaintiffs challenge it.

Ecolodge operation and management

Ecolodge owners and operators are in a unique position to demonstrate the significance and viability of ecolodge practices and concepts through their daily operations. By providing a role model, the owner/operator can ensure that the fundamentals of ecotourism are on show to inspire and educate local communities and officials, and garner accolades and support from guests. If the ecolodge can successfully convey a commitment to ecotourism through its operations, staff and daily activities, it will benefit from valuable word-of-mouth marketing.

An important aspect of ecolodge operations, which is often ignored, is the quality of food and beverages served in the restaurant. Food is a key aspect of any guest's experience and therefore careful attention needs to be given to preparation, taste and delivery.

Marketing and promotion

Compared with conventional tourist accommodation, marketing an ecolodge demands an ethical and honest presentation of the product and a greater degree of responsibility in the use and management of resources. Ecolodges draw from a definite and growing market, and yet it continues to be a niche market within the global accommodation context. In addition to this market, there is a large market of potential travelers who have a budding interest in nature-based tourism and adventure tourism, who can potentially be converted into true ecotourists. This segment of the market is a more conventional travel audience, one that requires a more sophisticated level of promotion, in terms of both content and quality.

Education: training and interpretation

As identified earlier in this chapter, one of the key principles of ecolodges is the provision of education and interpretation. Education is one of the cornerstones of all ecolodge operations and one of the three main identifying characteristics separating an ecolodge from traditional lodging. However, there is a need to educate and train ecolodge owners and potential investors to understand the importance of interpretation in ecolodge facilities. The surrounding communities, an integral part of all ecolodge development, should also be taught the significance of investments in ecolodge development, the need to conserve faunal and floral species, the intricacies of sustainability and the community impacts of ecolodge operations.

Ecolodges should provide opportunities to experience nature and culture in ways that lead to a greater understanding, appreciation and enjoyment for guests. The primary importance of interpretation for ecolodges is the potential it has to differentiate ecolodges from mainstream tourism lodges and hotels. At the heart of any ecolodge should lie a creatively organized and delivered interpretation package that enriches guest experiences and knowledge and thus increases client satisfaction.

Monitoring and evaluation

The basic concept of monitoring is to measure various parameters over time, and to identify and predict change or impact (both positive and negative). Monitoring should be a fundamental part of all in-house ecolodge operations, because it helps the operators understand the impacts the ecolodge is having on both the natural and the social surroundings. The final application of monitoring is to use it to make more informed decisions, such as to proactively change operation practices before negative impacts reach a critical level.

A Review of Existing Ecotourism Certification Programmes that Incorporate Ecolodge Criteria

In this section, the previously mentioned stages and principles of ecolodges have been used to compare and evaluate four existing ecotourism certification programmes that incorporate ecolodge criteria:

- EcoCertification (NEAP edition III) – Australia.
- Green Globe – International Ecotourism Standard (IES).
- CST (Certificate of Sustainable Tourism) – Costa Rica.
- Eco-Rating Scheme – Kenya.

While there are many other certification programmes around the world, such as Green Leaf (Thai Hotel Certification Program), ECOTEL and ISO 14001, the above four were selected because they had a number of criteria specifically relating to ecolodges. Table 21.1 compares the various components and principles relating to ecolodges covered by each programme and those not covered. In the following section, the four certification programmes are introduced and analysed in relation to their respective criteria relating to ecolodges.

CST (Certificate of Sustainable Tourism) – Costa Rica

The CST programme was developed by the Sustainability Programs Department of the Costa Rica Tourist Board and the Costa Rica National Accreditation Commission and is managed by the Costa Rica Tourist Institute (ICT).

Table. 21.1. Summary of ecotourism certification programmes incorporating ecolodge criteria.

	CST	Eco-Rating scheme	EcoCertification (NEAP edition III)	Green Globe IES
Site selection and planning	×	×	✓	✓
Eco-architecture design techniques	×	×	×	×
Community participation in planning	×	×	×	×
Minimal impacts during construction	×	×	✓	✓
Traditional building technology and materials	✓	×	✓	✓
Form of architecture fits into physical and/or cultural context	×	×	✓	✓
Air, noise and visual pollution	✓	✓	✓	✓
Conservation of surrounding flora and fauna	✓	✓	✓	✓
Water conservation	✓	✓	✓	✓
Energy conservation	✓	✓	✓	✓
Solid waste disposal	✓	✓	✓	✓
Sewage treatment	✓	✓	✓	✓
Offer interpretive programmes and training	✓	✓	✓	✓
Contribute to local development	✓	✓	✓	✓
Financial sustainability and legal compliance	✓	✓	✓	✓
Marketing and promotions	×	×	✓	✓
Food and beverages	✓	×	×	×

The CST programme focuses on hotels and not lodges. It seeks to categorize and certify each tourism company according to the degree to which its operations comply with a model of sustainability. To this effect, four fundamental aspects are evaluated:

1. Physical–biological environment.
2. Hotel facilities (internal environmental practices).

3. Customers.
4. Socio-economic environment.

The CST programme provides a system of sustainability levels, on a scale of 0 to 5, with each number indicating the relative position of the lodge or hotel in terms of sustainability. This scheme provides a way to classify the lodges and hotels in terms of 'levels' in a system similar to the commercial categorization of hotels using a stars system.

The CST programme is centred on accommodation facilities and on the built product, e.g. visitor centres and museums. There are no criteria related to the planning and construction process, two aspects that are vital to the site and surroundings and may create tension with local communities even before the ecolodge is built. The use of environmentally friendly materials during the design stage is not included and waste water is mentioned but no specific questions address sewage treatment. However, the programme gives adequate attention to private reserves, and hotels can gain points by having their own private reserve, but they can be certified with little commitment to conservation, which should be mandatory for any ecolodge (Blake, 2001).

As can be seen from Table 21.1, the CST programme does not consider the following components and principles of ecolodges:

- Site selection and planning.
- Eco-design techniques.
- Aesthetics – visual aspects.
- Inclusion of locals in the planning process.
- Sustainable construction.
- Use of environmentally friendly materials.
- Marketing.

Eco-Rating scheme

The Eco-Rating scheme is a voluntary certification initiative developed by the Ecotourism Society of Kenya on behalf of the Kenyan tourism industry. It aims to identify and reward best practices in environmental, economic and social arenas within the industry. The scheme has three levels of certification, namely bronze, silver and gold, and presently focuses on accommodation facilities, including hotels, lodges, camps and *bandas* (rondavels). The scheme is in its infancy stage and no lodge to date has received silver or gold rating (J. Kepher-Gona, executive officer, ESOK, personal communication, 2004). The scheme has been operational for several years and there are over 21 lodges and hotels that have been given bronze status.

The scheme drew in part from the CST certification programme but addresses some issues specific to Kenya's tourism industry, such as the sale of environmentally friendly wood curios.

The principal goal of the Eco-Rating scheme is to encourage businesses to conserve the natural resource base upon which tourism is dependent.

Its focus is on tourism businesses interested in and committed to embracing 'best practices' in their operations. It aims at providing these businesses with an opportunity to review and improve their operations towards 'best practice', leading to overall improvement in environmental performance. Under this scheme, 'best practice' includes among other things:

- Protecting, conserving and investing in the environment.
- Minimizing and reducing wastes.
- Preventing pollution.
- Support of local communities and economies.
- Responsible use of resources such as land, water, energy, etc.
- Education of tourists.

The Eco-Rating scheme evaluates five criteria:

1. Environmental.
2. Economic.
3. Social.
4. Policy and management systems.
5. Communications.

Similarly to the CST programme, the Eco-Rating scheme evaluates hotel/lodge operations only and there are no criteria for planning, design and construction. The strength of the Eco-Rating scheme is without doubt the benefits to local communities. Of all the four certification programmes reviewed, the Eco-Rating scheme had the most detailed criteria regarding support for local communities and economies. The scheme encourages the development of community-owned ecolodges more than any other certification programme.

As can be seen from Table 21.1, the Eco-Rating scheme does not consider the following components and principles of ecolodges:

1. Site selection and planning.
2. Eco-design techniques.
3. Aesthetics – visual aspects.
4. Inclusion of locals in the planning process.
5. Sustainable construction.
6. Use of environmentally friendly materials.
7. Marketing.
8. Food and beverages.

EcoCertification (NEAP edition III) – Australia

The EcoCertification programme is an initiative of Ecotourism Australia (EA), the largest national ecotourism association in the world. Originally launched in January 1996 as the National Ecotourism Accreditation Program (NEAP I), the EcoCertification programme certifies products, not companies, and has been developed to specifically address the need to identify genuine ecotourism and nature tourism operators in Australia (see Chapter 22 in this volume).

The criteria have been designed to evaluate nature tourism and ecotourism accommodation and tour and attraction products, which can achieve certification at one of the following three levels: Nature Tourism, Ecotourism or Advanced Ecotourism, which incorporates a more stringent set of assessment criteria. Advanced Ecotourism can also be obtained through innovative best practices that exceed the main EcoCertification programme standards. An important part of the programme is the inclusion of regular reviewing and upgrading of the criteria.

After assessing over 400 ecotourism products under the NEAP editions I and II criteria, as well as additional consultation, industry comment and application in the field (www.ecotourism.org.au, 2004), the assessment criteria were revised and in November 2003 the EcoCertification (NEAP edition III) programme was launched. NEAP III has numerous upgrades on and refinements to its predecessor, NEAP II.

Additionally, EcoCertification (NEAP edition III) now includes coverage of the three objective elements of sustainability: environmental, economic and social. This triple-bottom-line approach has been achieved by expanding NEAP principles from eight to ten. EcoCertification (NEAP edition III) is based on a self-assessment model and was reviewed in November 2006. Initially, no on-site verification is required because of the remote locations of the products and the impracticality and lack of affordability of inspecting the products (S. Pahl, CEO Ecotourism Australia, personal communication, 2004).

Comparisons with other programmes found that EcoCertification (NEAP edition III) is the most advanced ecotourism accommodation certification programme in the world. The award criteria system is not only detailed and extensive but demanding as well. It is strong on the interpretation and training aspect and also clearly distinguishes between new and old products.

However, even after expanding the principles, EcoCertification (NEAP edition III) still does not cover all the components and principles necessary for an ecolodge. Compared with other certification programmes, in particular the Eco-Rating scheme, the local communities section is weak, especially regarding encouragement of community-owned and operated ecotourism products.

As seen in Table 21.1, EcoCertification (NEAP edition III) does not consider the following components and principles of ecolodges:

1. Eco-design techniques.
2. Inclusion of locals in the planning process.
3. Food and beverages.

Green Globe International Ecotourism Standard

Green Globe is an Affiliation, Benchmarking and Certification programme for sustainable tourism. It has four different certification standards (see Chapter 6 in this volume). The Green Globe International Ecotourism

Standard was reviewed as it has the most detailed criteria system (compared with the other Green Globe standards) for both new and existing accommodation facilities. Also, it is geared towards international certification, which is not the case with the other three programmes (CST, Eco-Rating and EcoCertification are national programmes) reviewed in this chapter. However, mention should be made of the Green Globe Design and Construct Standard, which is one of the most innovative certification programmes regarding tourism accommodation facilities, with a focus entirely on the pre-operations (i.e. design and construction phase) stages of a project.

The Green Globe International Ecotourism Standard is a licensed product of Ecotourism Australia and the Cooperative Research Centre (CRC) for Sustainable Tourism (based in Australia) and has been developed by Green Globe for its exclusive use internationally. The Green Globe International Ecotourism Standard is based principally on the NEAP II programme combined with elements of the Green Globe Benchmarking performance system.

Before its introduction, Green Globe International Ecotourism Standard was piloted with a number of ecotourism operations from several countries and products. It should be noted, though, that no accommodation facility has yet been certified under the Green Globe International Ecotourism Standard. The reason is that it is a new programme and demanding. Most products in developing countries would not be able to obtain certification due to the stringent evaluation criteria, which have been borrowed from the Australian certification programme (C. Parsons, Global Manager, Green Globe, personal communication, 2004).

The principal objective of the Green Globe International Ecotourism Standard is to facilitate environmentally sustainable ecotourism (www.greenglobe21.com, 2004). This Standard is expected to provide a basis for assessing a baseline environmental management performance standard for ecotourism products and recognizing best practice ecotourism. The Green Globe International Ecotourism Standard provides operators with a framework to benchmark their operations/ecotourism products in terms of environmental and social performance, to achieve certification and to continually improve their performance.

However, the Green Globe programme as it is operated today is confusing. As a new accommodation facility, you can either apply under the 'Accommodation' category in the Green Globe Company Standard or as a 'product' under the International Ecotourism Standard or as a 'hotel', 'resort' or 'park accommodation' under the Design and Construct Standards. Green Globe is aware of this confusion and the complicated application process is currently being simplified (C. Parsons, Global Manager, Green Globe, personal communication, 2004).

Since the Green Globe International Ecotourism Standard was prepared with input from some of the same authors as NEAP edition II, the programmes have similarities. Due attention has been given to interpretation, training aspects and natural and environmental management systems, and the programme clearly distinguishes between new and old products.

The review of the Green Globe International Ecotourism Standard reveals that the section on building materials is weak and there is no mention of traditional construction techniques and, similarly to EcoCertification (NEAP edition III), the local communities section needs to be strengthened. Green Globe International Ecotourism Standard is geared mainly towards more developed countries, and the main disadvantage is that the criteria are too stringent for most countries in the developing world. On-the-ground logistical situations are extremely different from those in Australia, especially in places in sub-Saharan Africa and South America.

As noted in Table 21.1, the Green Globe International Ecotourism Standard fails to consider the following components and principles of ecolodges:

1. Eco-design techniques.
2. Inclusion of local communities in the planning process.
3. Use of environmentally friendly building techniques.
4. Food and beverages.
5. Financial sustainability.

The Way Forward

The review of the four internationally recognized certification programmes above indicates that none of them consider all the various components and principles that are needed to plan and construct a genuine ecolodge. Certified ecolodges in these programmes might not achieve the level of quality in terms of delivering the genuine win–win–win of ecotourism. What this means is that an accommodation facility can be certified by any one of the above reviewed programmes and yet not be a genuine ecolodge as per the definition stated earlier in this chapter.

One option, therefore, is the creation of an internationally recognized ecolodge certification programme that is accessible to all owners, operators and communities. To avoid greenwashing, an authentic programme specific to ecolodges needs to be prepared that considers the following issues:

- Site selection and planning.
- Eco-architecture design techniques.
- Community participation in planning.
- Minimal impacts during construction.
- Traditional building technology and materials.
- Form of architecture fits into physical and/or cultural context.
- Air, noise and visual pollution.
- Conservation of surrounding flora and fauna.
- Water conservation.
- Energy conservation.
- Solid waste disposal.
- Sewage treatment.
- Offer interpretive programmes and training.

- Contribute to local development.
- Financial sustainability and legal compliance.
- Marketing and promotions.
- Food and beverages.

All of the programmes reviewed certified a wide variety of accommodation types and in so doing compromised on some of the important principles that constitute genuine ecolodges. One of the benefits of certifying ecolodges separately from nature lodges and traditional hotels is that they will be held to a much higher standard than regular businesses, which may put them at an economic disadvantage. While this may be true, ecolodges must meet high standards in order not to endanger the environment on which they depend (Blake, 2001). Also, it must be emphasized that, with the future niche tourism market trends, ecolodges may well have a stronger economic advantage over nature lodges and traditional hotels. The other reason for creating an internationally recognized ecolodge certification system is to eliminate 'greenwashing'. In addition to following the principles and components already discussed, an internationally recognized ecolodge certification programme will need to:

- Carry out aggressive marketing and education of tourists about the programme. This is to reduce the lack of consumer awareness and demand. Even though marketing to consumers is expensive, there are many ways to create awareness with a small budget: the Internet, international conferences, newspaper articles and on-site brochures produced by the respective ecolodges. One of the biggest weaknesses in the above-mentioned certification programmes is that most consumers are only aware of the programmes and their positive impacts after they have reached their destinations.
- Brand and promote a credible and effective programme to consumers through a centralized umbrella accreditation body. Even though this is a challenging task, a centralized body like the World Tourism Organization (WTO) or the Sustainable Tourism Stewardship Council (STSC) would give credibility to this new programme and help clarify the confusion regarding the various certification programmes and logos. Consumer awareness is key to the success of this programme, as currently consumers find it hard to distinguish between the different sustainability programmes and ecotourism. Having the ecolodge certification programme administered by a centralized body will help to identify ecolodges as a specific product.
- Improve communication regarding the components and principles of ecolodges and their merits to lodge businesses. One of the documents that needs to be prepared is a report on best practice ecolodges, which would include all the practices, including planning and design, construction, and the significant savings from the use of environmentally friendly technologies.
- Recognize the potential of local communities in the pre-construction phase and include local skills in the construction phase. The

involvement of local communities in the planning and design phases of the project should be a mandatory criterion.

- Have detailed questionnaires for each component (see Table 21.1). Questionnaires similar to those used by international sustainable tourism awards, such as World Legacy Awards and Tourism For Tomorrow, could be utilized. The ecolodge questionnaires would be generic and not be specific to individual countries.
- Have a weighting scale that is objective. This weighting scale would have to be developed by an independent international ecolodge expert group, and assessment would need to be done by certified assessors with a sound knowledge of all the components and principles of ecolodges.
- Reward owners who keep on improving. If the rating system is based on 'leaves', for example, then any upgrades undertaken by the owners should be rewarded with an extra leaf. For example, if an ecolodge owner has two 'leaves' and they have improved on one of the components mentioned earlier, then they should be rewarded with a three-'leaf' designation.
- Award certification logos only to those ecolodges that have achieved the minimum performance standards, rather than for commitment to improvement. This is to avoid the misuse of the logos. Some of the existing programmes award logos to those hotels that have not met the minimum criteria and this leads to misinformation to the guests.
- Motivate owners to improve by creating exchange programmes between certified ecolodges and by helping them market their products if they achieve a higher rating.
- Enforce on-site evaluations by trained and knowledgeable professionals. This is crucial to the authenticity of ecolodge certification. The evaluations would have to be done by environmental management specialists who are well trained in both conservation and social issues.
- Have an application process that is accessible and equitable. This is challenging because of the different types of ecolodges. The whole system needs to be set up so that any ecolodge should be able to apply for certification even if it does not have enough money.
- Improve integration of the economic, environmental, social and spiritual aspects of ecolodges.

As stated earlier, it is not the aim of this chapter to provide details for any proposed certification programme for ecolodges; however, consideration needs to be given to issues such as how we can have standards that are equally applicable to developing countries and developed countries. The standards would need to be performance standards and not prescriptive standards, similar to the *International Ecolodge Guidelines* book, which is being used successfully in many different parts of the world.

An international ecolodge certification programme would take several years to develop and establish and would have to be a low-budget programme for it to be a financially viable certification programme that is dedicated to ecolodges only. However, in order to embrace the rest of the tourism sectors, marketing would be required to non-ecotourists and this will help to effect genuine change.

The ecolodge industry is increasingly confronted with arguments about its authenticity regarding environmental protection and community development and is facing serious and difficult choices about its future. If we are to move forward, lodge owners, operators, consultants, ecolodge marketing web sites and the media will be required to become better educated about the key components and principles that constitute ecolodges.

One way forward is the creation of an international certification programme focusing specifically on ecolodges. Such a programme would provide a set of criteria to ensure genuine ecolodges. This type of programme would assist in identifying genuine ecolodges and establish a set of criteria to enable ecolodge owners to evaluate their accommodation for further improvement.

References

Blake, B. (2001) *A New Key to Costa Rica*. Ulysses Press, Berkely, California.

Ceballos-Lascurain, H. (1997) *Concept Paper on Ecolodge Development in Coastal and Desert Zones of Egypt*. Winrock International, Cairo, Egypt.

Epler Wood, M., Wight, P. and Corvetto, J. (2004) *A Review of International Markets, Business, Finance and Technical Assistance Models for Ecolodges in Developing Countries*. International Finance Corporation (IFC)/GEF Small and Medium Enterprise Program, Washington, DC.

Gardner, J. (2001) Accomodations. In: Weaver, D. (ed.) *The Encyclopedia of Ecotourism*. CAB International, Wallingford, UK, pp. 525–534.

Mehta, H. (1997) Designing and developing ecotourism hotels. Research paper presented at the Ecotourism at a Crossroads Conference and Field Seminar. The Kenya Wildlife Society, Nairobi, Kenya.

Mehta, H. (1999) International trends in ecolodges. Research paper presented at the 1999 World Ecotourism Conference and Field Seminar. The International Ecotourism Society, Kota Kinabalu, Malaysia.

Mehta, H. (2000) The evolution of ecotourism in Florida. Research paper presented at the Florida Center for Environmental Studies Third Annual Conference on Ecotourism on Public and Private Lands in Florida, Palm Beach Gardens, Florida.

Mehta, H. (2001) *Community Empowerment through Participatory Design*. Green Hotelier 1/2001, International Hotels Environment Initiative, London.

Mehta, H., Baez, A. and O'Loughlin, P. (eds) (2002) *The International Ecolodge Guidelines*. The International Ecotourism Society, Burlington, Vermont.

Russel, D., Bottrill, C. and Meredith, G. (1995) International ecolodge survey. In: Hawkins, D.E., Epler Wood, M. and Bittman, S. (eds) *The Ecolodge Sourcebook for Planners and Developers*. The International Ecotourism Society, Burlington, Vermont, p. 15.

Sanders, E. and Halpenny, E. (2000) *The Business of Ecolodges*. The International Ecotourism Society, Burlington, Vermont.

Sweeting, J., Bruner, A. and Rosenfeld, A. (2000) *The Greenhouse Effect – An Integrated Approach to Sustainable Tourism and Resort Development*. Conservation International, Washington, DC.

WWF-UK (2000) *Tourism Certification: An Analysis of Green Globe 21 and Other Tourism Certification Programmes.* Worldwide Fund for Nature, London.

Web sites

Retrieved 1 August 2004: Beatrice Blake, Comparing the ICT's Certification of Sustainable Tourism and the New Key to Costa Rica's Sustainable Tourism Rating, August 2001, www.planeta.com/planeta/01/0104costa.html

Retrieved 5 August 2004: Eco Certification Program Application Document, http://www.ecotourism.org.au/eco_certification.asp

Retrieved 6 August 2004: http://ecoclub.com/experts.html

Retrieved 2 September 2004: Planeta web site, http://groups.yahoo.com/group/ecotourism_certification/

Retrieved 10 October 2004: http://ecoclub.com/philosophy.html

Retrieved 10 October 2004: http://www.greenglobe21.com/AboutEcotourism.aspx

Retrieved 16 October 2004: CST web site, http://www.turismosostenible.co.cr/EN/directorio/hotel_busq_habs.phtml?busqueda=habs&ch=2

Developing an international standard for 'green' tourism, a report by OECD-UK, 2003. Retrieved 16 October 2004: http://webdomino1.oecd.org/comnet/ech/tradeandenv.nsf/viewHtml/index/$FILE/green.pdf

22 The Australian EcoCertification Program (NEAP): Blazing a Trail for Ecotourism Certification, but Keeping on Track?

RIK THWAITES

School of Environmental Sciences, Charles Sturt University, Albury, Australia

Chapter Profile

The Australian EcoCertification programme (originally known as the National Ecotourism Accreditation Program or NEAP) blazed a trail in developing the world's first ecotourism-specific certification programme in 1996, and has been heralded as an example of a successful ecotourism certification programme. The programme has been credited with improving standards and professionalism in the Australian ecotourism industry, providing encouragement and tangible rewards for operators who demonstrated sustainable environmental and sociocultural practices and used as a blueprint for the development of other ecocertification programmes, including Green Globe's International Ecotourism Standard.

The EcoCertification programme was developed primarily as a tool to identify genuine and quality ecotourism product. The criteria were developed from the principal components of most ecotourism definitions – nature-focused product that was environmentally sustainable, included interpretation, provided returns for both local communities and environments and was culturally sensitive. This chapter provides an insight into the development of the programme and identifies key changes introduced as a result of experience, the inbuilt demand for continuous improvement, internal politics and external pressure and forces. The realities of establishing and operating an ecotourism certification programme and the evolution of the programme through to the third version are followed in order to learn from the successes and triumphs as well as the setbacks.

Chapter Context

Regarded as the world's first national certification programme for ecotourism (Charters, 2000), the National Ecotourism Accreditation Program (NEAP) was launched in Australia in 1996. A second, updated version was launched in 2000 under the slightly altered title of the Nature and Ecotourism Accreditation Program, known as NEAP II, and a third version of the programme was launched in 2003, relabelled as EcoCertification. This chapter seeks to build on the discussion of the progress of NEAP presented in Chester and Crabtree (2002) by reflecting further on the experience of the ongoing development and management of this programme through versions II and III (EcoCertification). A fourth generation of the programme was released in July 2006 with the launch of the online application form. This new version is not discussed in this chapter, but contains only minor changes from the previous EcoCertification programme, with some clarifications and updated criteria reflecting new standards, technologies and expectations.

The author teaches ecotourism at Charles Sturt University and has been involved in a number of certification projects with tourism operators, including presenting workshops to operators, arranging for students to assist operators through the certification process and, from 2000 to 2003, being a member of the NEAP assessment panel dealing with applications, operators and referees. Since the introduction of EcoCertification, the author has had no direct involvement in the development or implementation of the programme. While operator connections have been maintained, specific information regarding EcoCertification has been gained from published sources and from interviews with Ecotourism Australia (EA) staff responsible for managing the programme.

Introduction: Context of Ecotourism Certification in Australia

Tourism is a major contributor to the Australian economy. In 2001/02 tourism generated over AU$17 billion in export earnings, or 11.2% of total export revenue and, with AU$51 billion of domestic tourism expenditure, directly contributed 4.5% of the nation's GDP (Commonwealth of Australia, 2003). The tourism industry directly employs around 550,000 people, or 6% of national employment, and indirectly employs a further 397,000 (2001/02 figures).

Matters of environmental degradation, conservation and sustainable development have seen active public debate and action in Australia in recent decades. The publication of the *National Strategy for Ecologically Sustainable Development* (Commonwealth of Australia, 1992) included a chapter on tourism. Two years later, the *National Ecotourism Strategy* (Commonwealth of Australia, 1994) provided a set of guidelines for achieving well-managed ecotourism, and proposed the establishment of high-quality industry standards and a national ecotourism certification system, thus providing a firm conceptual grounding for later activities within the ecotourism arena in Australia. While the national policy environment has moved on, particularly with the development of the *Tourism White Paper* (Commonwealth of Australia, 2003), which provided no focus on ecotourism in the discussion of regional tourism and tourism sustainability in protected areas, Fennell (2003: 109) was of the view that the *National Ecotourism Strategy* (Commonwealth of Australia,

1994) has been 'instrumental in demonstrating to the rest of the world the advanced state of ecotourism in Australia'.

In the late 1980s and early 1990s, there was considerable debate in Australia, and other parts of the world, over the need for 'accreditation' in the tourism industry (Commonwealth of Australia, 1995). This led to the establishment of a Guide Accreditation Scheme by the Inbound Tour Organization of Australia (ITOA) in 1992, followed by the Victorian Tour Operators Association (VTOA) Accreditation Program in 1993, which became a condition for operators to receive a licence to operate on public lands in Victoria (Commonwealth of Australia, 1995). This programme was closely followed by other state and sector-based operator 'accreditation' programmes. (Since this time, use of the term 'accreditation' has changed in line with internationally accepted use, and the term 'certification' has been adopted by EA to describe the procedure whereby an independent body provides assurance that tourism products, services or systems conform to specified requirements. The term 'accreditation' is still used for this procedure in some quarters in Australia, but in this chapter will only be used where it is part of a title or programme name.)

Early meetings of the Ecotourism Association of Australia (EAA) in 1992 and 1993, renamed Ecotourism Australia (EA) in 2003, recognized the importance of protecting the use of the term 'ecotourism' and rewarding sound ecological practice (Chester and Crabtree, 2002). The push towards creating an ecotourism certification programme reflected the need to create a way of distinguishing quality ecotourism product that would deliver sustainability and benefit to operators, customers and the environment, from more dubious operators. It was considered that there were too many operations misusing the ecotourism term, seeking marketing advantage without attempting to deliver genuine ecotourism product.

So, with a world-leading *National Ecotourism Strategy*, the establishment of a national ecotourism body and development of state policies on nature tourism and ecotourism, and a climate favouring certification, the scene was set with exceptional institutional 'hardware' for the development of ecotourism certification in Australia.

NEAP

In 1994, the Australian Federal Government Department of Tourism hired consultants to investigate the creation of a national ecotourism certification system that would facilitate the application of agreed industry standards by ecotourism operators. The outcome proposed was a large and cumbersome national administrative bureaucracy, but little was provided in the way of practical certification criteria (Charters, 2000; Chester and Crabtree, 2002).

With funding from the Commonwealth Government and together with the Tourism Council of Australia and VTOA, the EAA set out to develop a certification scheme. The government funding provided support only for development of the scheme. The project partners had limited funds for subsidizing promotion and ongoing management, so the scheme had to rapidly become self-funding. Recognizing that the ecotourism industry in Australia consisted largely of small-scale operators, certification would need to be offered at a relatively low cost (Charters, 2000). This in turn meant that the programme would have to be 'lean and mean', with low operating costs (Chester and Crabtree, 2002). Around 50 tour operators provided an industry perspective on the practicality of the programme by reviewing draft criteria, administrative structures and fees. Launched into the market in 1996, the first version of the National Ecotourism Accreditation Program (NEAP) was designed with a heavy reliance on volunteers for its management, that is, it was not developed on a fully commercial costing basis, but required the substantial input of time and other support from individuals and organizations. It is worth noting that two of the nine characteristics identified by Charters (2000) for the programme to be successful related to the economics of the programme: 'affordability' – that the programme be within the financial reach of all operators – and 'self-funding' – that the programme generate sufficient funds to survive independently in the long term.

A number of descriptions have been written of the development of NEAP, including Charters (2000) and Chester and Crabtree (2002), both drawn on above. It is not the intention of this chapter to repeat all the information contained in these previous works, although it is important to begin by outlining the structure of the programme. This chapter will focus on changes to the programme, including the most recent version, EcoCertification, and reflect on the experience of implementing the programme.

Programme Structure

An important consideration in the development of NEAP was the matter of what should be certified, the business or the product. It was decided that the certification should be provided for individual products, not the operating entities. It was believed that, as many operators have diverse businesses and a range of products, some of which may follow ecotourism principles while others may not, that such operations would be excluded from certification if the focus were on the operation as a whole (Chester and Crabtree, 2002). Thus distinct products of a larger operation can be certified independently of the rest of the operation, to ensure a rigorous application of ecotourism principles (Honey and Rome, 2001).

Three different types of products (or sectors of the ecotourism industry) are identified in the programme: accommodation where infrastructure and services are supplied to house visitors overnight in nature; tours where guides lead an excursion that combines activities such as walking, driving or riding with viewing and interacting with nature; and attractions that combine a natural area focus with fixed infrastructure designed to help people explore and learn (Ecotourism Australia, 2003).

NEAP was designed to encourage continuous improvement among operators, and the programme has been completely updated twice (in 2000 and 2004) to reflect improved industry standards and performance.

The original version of NEAP provided certification at two different levels, Ecotourism and Advanced Ecotourism. The lower level would provide for a minimum set of requirements that a tourism product must meet to be certified as ecotourism, while the upper level would reward a higher level of achievement (Chester and Crabtree, 2002), thus providing incentive for operators to seek improvement and rewarding those operators who adopt best practices.

As a basis for certification, the programme defined ecotourism as 'ecologically sustainable tourism with a primary focus on experiencing natural areas that fosters environmental and cultural understanding, appreciation and conservation' (EAA, 2000: 4). Following from this definition, eight fundamental principles of ecotourism were identified, under which detailed criteria could be set to assess operator practice: natural area focus, interpretation, environmental sustainability, contribution to conservation, working with local communities, the cultural component, customer satisfaction and responsible marketing. To qualify for ecotourism certification, products needed to meet 'minimum requirements' set out as 'core' criteria under each of these eight principles. Advanced Ecotourism certification was assessed on the basis of calculation of points for the achievement of 'bonus criteria' and 'innovative best practices', practices identified by the operator that go beyond the identified requirements of the criteria.

An expanded and updated version of NEAP released in 2000 (NEAP II) incorporated a third level of certification under the new category of nature tourism. This opened up the programme to a wider range of operations and products based in natural areas but not meeting the strict definition of ecotourism, and by doing so recognized that all tourism in natural areas should be sustainable and encouraged a wider set of operators to consider the sustainability of their practices. The system of core and bonus criteria was retained, though the criteria were updated and in many cases made more stringent, particularly in relation to the 'bonus' criteria for Advanced Ecotourism certification. 'Nature tourism' was separately defined, requiring a product to meet core criteria in only four principles, those relating to natural area focus, environmental sustainability, customer satisfaction and responsible marketing. Certified nature tourism was thus considered to be a subcomponent of ecotourism, having to meet the same core criteria of some principles, such as environmental sustainability, but excluding criteria under other principles that are considered fundamental for ecotourism certification, such as interpretation (Table 22.1).

Nature tourism is defined in the programme as 'tourism with a primary focus on experiencing natural areas that ensures environmentally sustainable use of natural resources' (EAA, 2000: 4).

EcoCertification

The experience of developing and managing the programme allowed NEAP and EAA to contribute internationally to discussions regarding ecotourism

Table 22.1. NEAP II certification principles and eligibility for different levels of certification (from EAA, 2000).

Principles The nature tourism or ecotourism product:	Nature tourism	Ecotourism	Advanced Ecotourism
Focuses on directly and personally experiencing nature	✓	✓	✓
Provides opportunities to experience nature in ways that lead to greater understanding, appreciation and enjoyment (provision of interpretation)	Optional	Mandatory but not necessarily core to experience	Core element of experience
Represents best practice for environmentally sustainable tourism	✓	✓	✓
Positively contributes to the conservation of natural areas		✓	✓
Provides constructive ongoing contributions to local communities		✓	✓
Is sensitive to and involves different cultures, especially indigenous cultures		✓	✓
Consistently meets customer expectations	✓	✓	✓
Is marketed accurately and leads to realistic expectations	✓	✓	✓

and sustainable tourism certification. NEAP representatives participated in the international certification conference held in 2000 in New York. This conference resulted in the Mohonk Agreement, which offers a set of principles and elements considered necessary as part of any 'sound' ecotourism certification programme (Honey, 2002). In 2002, Green Globe and EAA jointly launched the International Ecotourism Standard. This was developed by NEAP and EAA, based largely on NEAP II, but also drawing on the requirements of the Mohonk Agreement and the existing Green Globe approach to certification. This exercise contributed greatly to consideration of where to take NEAP in its third version.

The most recent version of NEAP was launched in December 2003 (along with a rebranding of the EAA and change of name to Ecotourism Australia – EA). Recognizing the need for globally consistent use of terminology following Mohonk, reference to 'accreditation' was dropped, and the new programme was called 'EcoCertification'. While many parts of the NEAP II document were redrafted to reflect new understandings and requirements, EcoCertification also represented something of a departure in that its scope was expanded to include two further principles not considered under earlier NEAP versions: business management and operational planning, and business ethics. As a result, EcoCertification now presents a comprehensive 'triple-bottom-line' approach covering the three elements: economic, social and environmental sustainability (EA, 2003).

The major driving factor behind these additions to the programme was the desire to meet the requirements of the 'Australian Tourism Accreditation Standard'. With the proliferation of certification schemes there was a move in the late 1990s to establish a national tourism accreditation scheme (that is, 'certifying the certifiers', in the language of Mohonk) comprising a national framework and standard for certification schemes (TAA, 2005 and Chapter 15 in this volume). With the creation of a single national system and its recognition by different levels of government and government agencies, endorsement under this national system would be imperative for any certification scheme to remain credible and relevant to operators.

The Australian Tourism Accreditation Standard is largely focused on elements of business planning and management, components that were not adequately dealt with under NEAP II. The desire to be recognized under the national standard thus provided a strong incentive for EcoCertification to expand the principles covered, and to apply the new set of principles across all three categories of certification (Table 22.2). EcoCertification achieved national accreditation status in April 2004.

Programme Assessment and Administration

The assessment of tourism products throughout all versions of NEAP and EcoCertification has been based around self-assessment by an operator of the nominated product(s) against relevant criteria and completion of the application document. This document is submitted with product brochures/web

Table 22.2. EcoCertification programme principles applied for eligibility under different categories (from EA, 2003).

Triple bottom line	Principles	Nature tourism	Ecotourism and Advanced ecotourism
Economic sustainability	Business management and operational planning	✓	✓
	Business ethics	✓	✓
	Responsible marketing	✓	✓
	Customer satisfaction	✓	✓
Environmental sustainability	Natural area focus	✓	✓
	Environmental sustainability	✓	✓
	Interpretation and education	n/a	✓
	Contribution to conservation	n/a	✓
Social sustainability	Working with local communities	n/a	✓
	Cultural respect and sensitivity	n/a	✓

site details and nomination of two referees. An assessor is responsible for checking all the documentation and ensuring that all relevant criteria have been met, determining the bonus and innovative best practice points and contacting referees. Once awarded, certification is valid for 3 years, with the operator paying an initial application fee and an annual fee.

With the evolution and growth of NEAP, administration and assessment arrangements have undergone a number of changes. The programme has always had a management committee to oversee its development and administration. Initially, this incorporated representatives from EAA, VTOA and an independent chair and was responsible for management, promotion and ongoing development of the programme. Programme administration was provided from the EAA office. At this stage, assessment of applications was undertaken in-house by the EAA administrative officer on a fee-for-service basis, with help from members of the NEAP committee. As the number of applications increased, a team of independent assessors was established, who made recommendations to the NEAP committee for the final decision.

In 2001, EAA took over sole ownership of NEAP, and management was changed to reflect this change. Independent assessment and audit groups were established, with a single independent chair sitting on a NEAP Management Group, made up otherwise of EAA committee members and an Executive Officer (Fig. 22.1). The Assessment and Audit Groups were established to be independent of the EAA, thus separating the tasks of programme management from assessing and auditing products and avoiding perceptions of conflict of interest in the awarding of certification (Chester and Crabtree, 2002). The Assessment Group included up to five assessors, subcontracted to assess applications and advise the Executive Officer of assessment decisions, develop assessment protocols, provide feedback for operators and pass information on to the Audit Group. The Audit Group was established to develop audit protocols and implement audits, with the authority to revoke or suspend certification. The NEAP Management Group retained the higher-level functions of strategic planning and policy setting, managing the business and ongoing review and development of the programme (EAA, 2001).

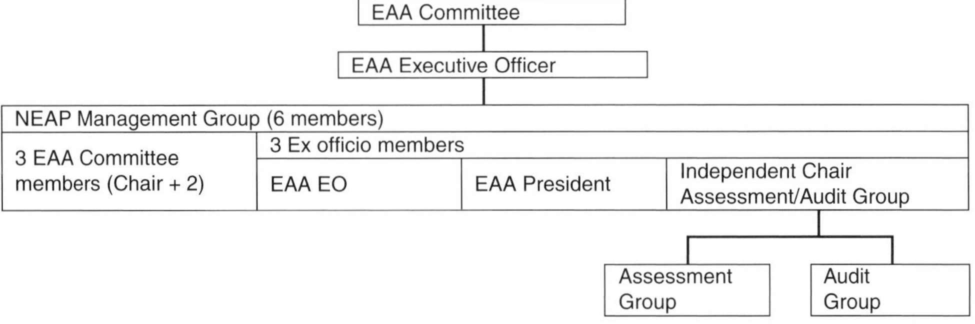

Fig. 22.1. NEAP corporate structure (from EAA, 2001).

Programme Credibility

Given an initial self-assessment process, credibility of NEAP has depended on verification by assessors of information provided, as well as review via auditing. The review of brochures and web sites and contacting referees have proved to be a powerful means of verification of information provided in application documents and identifying areas where further information is required or where further work or modification by the operator is needed.

Additional verification comes from the audit process, including both paper and on-site audits. Achieving a programme of on-site audits to ensure credibility of the programme has proved to be the real challenge. While the intention was that these be random physical audits, made with a 60-day notice to the operator, these were rarely carried out through the early years of NEAP. The critical point to consider here is that the programme was established to be self-funding and affordable to small operators. The first priority of the programme was to get a functioning and affordable certification scheme on the market, able to gradually build its membership. However, on-site auditing is an expensive and demanding process and, at least early on, was beyond the budget and the limited organizational capacity of the programme.

Pressure for change intensified, with the Mohonk Agreement in 2000 identifying that scheme integrity requires audits by suitably trained and independent auditors (Honey, 2002). Consultants were engaged to develop a NEAP audit protocol, and a programme of on-site audits to test the protocols was rolled out from December 2001 to April 2002 (Chester and Crabtree, 2002). A grant from Tourism Queensland enabled audits to be undertaken across a variety of operations in different states, and included both on-site and desk audits to identify cost-effective audit methodologies.

Assessment under EcoCertification

The launch of EcoCertification in 2003 saw changes to the assessment and audit process that represent the latest step in the evolution from a 'lean and mean', volunteer-driven programme into a more professional, funded programme seeking the highest standards. The administrative structure established in 2001 was simplified, with the abolition of the independent NEAP Assessor Group and removal of a position on the programme Management Committee for an Independent Chair of the Assessment and Audit Groups. Trained assessors now work individually on a subcontract basis, with the responsibility of reviewing documentation and contacting referees, and make their recommendations directly to the CEO of EA.

This change has resulted in some clear efficiency benefits. Under the previous arrangement, assessments regularly took 6 weeks or more, with assessors having to balance the demands of the assessment process, including contacting referees and chasing missing information, and their other (full-time) jobs, and final decisions having to wait for a monthly teleconference. Under EcoCertification, a smaller number of professional assessors (two) work independently of each other, responsible to the CEO of EA. With an improved system of chasing missing information and no monthly meetings, turnaround time is now about 2 weeks for correctly completed applications, making the programme more attractive in the marketplace.

While this new system saves considerable time and expense, the replacement of a panel to make decisions by individual assessors making recommendations to the CEO of EA reduces the distance between the assessment decision and the administration, and also removes much of the protection afforded to the assessors and the EA from potential accusations of conflict of interest or from inappropriate pressure to make particular decisions. This is not to suggest that any impropriety has occurred under the new system or that the system is any less rigorous, only to suggest that perhaps the inbuilt protection from abuse has been reduced.

Perhaps a greater enhancement to the rigour of the programme, and thus its credibility, has been the commitment to on-site auditing by independent, third-party auditors. With the launch of EcoCertification, Ecotourism Australia was committed to seek a 100% audit of all EcoCertified product/operators over the 3-year term of the programme. The proposal was not for upfront on-site assessment (perhaps the ideal situation but extremely expensive), but provides for single visits to be made to a region to audit all local operations, recognizing the large size of Australia and the expense of travelling to isolated destinations.

In May 2004 expressions of interest were called for from professional auditors, with the intention of establishing a national pool of independent third-party auditors. Fees proposed by commercial auditing organizations were very high, so, with an eye to both the credibility and the affordability of the programme, two specialized independent auditors with the necessary professional qualifications were contracted. More recently, the number of auditors has been expanded through a partnership with state tourism organizations providing training for a small number of staff.

By November 2005, a total of 157 product audits had been completed (Charters, 2005a). Emphasizing the effectiveness of the auditing process, Charters (2005a) reported that, of these 157 audited products, 4% had been delisted, 41% were required to make minor changes and 55% completed the audit process with no changes required. Many of the non-compliance issues related to operators not displaying the EcoCertification logo appropriately as required by their certification, and thus not putting the brand in the marketplace.

The auditing process requires a prearranged on-site visit to an operator's office with access to facilities and documentation, but does not require auditors to participate in tour products to receive the full experience, including interpretation. This raises the question of how the quality of a product can be assessed without it being experienced. Is ecotourism auditing more than the assessment of technical criteria? For example, is it enough to have an interpretation plan, or should the presentation of interpretation be considered? The Great Barrier Reef Marine Park Authority, an important partner and stakeholder in the EcoCertification programme, has raised this issue, and the current thinking is that the scope of audits needs to be expanded (S. Pahl, personal communication, 31 January 2006), incorporating a comprehensive analysis of the operation, talking to staff and participating in tours.

All these changes to the programme could be seen as improvements introduced as a result of the experience of implementing and managing it. The experience of NEAP/EcoCertification may be that the 'ideal' is rarely possible as a balance is sought between bureaucracy, complexity, credibility and affordability. For example, the introduction of a regular auditing programme or expanding the scope of auditing would add substantially to the cost of the programme (financial sustainability is considered later in this chapter). Some of the improved management practices or systems would not have been possible to implement in the early stages of the programme and have only become possible with the increased financial and administrative capacity that comes with the maturing and growth of the programme and acceptance within the marketplace.

Partnerships

Another issue of some importance to the EcoCertification programme is that of its relationship with other organizations, particularly government agencies. All three levels of government in Australia (federal, state and local) have some responsibility for land and environmental management and tourism development, planning and promotion. Ecotourism Australia has sought to promote the benefits of certification to agencies, particularly at state and federal level, as a complementary programme to support their own efforts to achieve objectives in land management and tourism development. A number of partnerships have been formed, such as with Conservation and Land Management in Western Australia (see Ingram, Chapter 15, this volume) and the Great Barrier Reef Marine Park Authority in Queensland, which both provide access to extended licences for EcoCertified operators. These partnerships have also contributed to strengthening the certification programme with support in the review of criteria that are specifically relevant to certain activities, such as marine tourism operators. Ecotourism Australia has made ongoing efforts to establish and expand such partnerships, and is considering the addition of further criteria specific to certain groups of operators, such as in relation to marine safety, or working in particular locations where strict management practices need to be enforced (S. Pahl, personal communication, 31 January 2006). Chapter 15 in this volume deals with this issue of partnerships, but it is worthwhile recognizing that these partnerships offer benefits to operators, but also wider benefits by providing a strong incentive for operators to become certified and thus to consider the sustainability implications of their practices and potential improvements.

Some Issues Arising from Implementation of NEAP II

A number of observations can be made arising from operator feedback and the experience of implementing NEAP I and II. Documented sources of operator feedback include: results of a survey of 32 operator members of EAA in 1998, half of whom were certified under NEAP I (Fleming, 1998); Tourism Queensland research in 2000, in which 93 of the 99 certified operators at the time were interviewed on their satisfaction with and expectations of NEAP (Enhance Management, 2000a); and, in 2002, an Ecotourism Australia market survey, which received responses from 54% of the 133 certified operators and focused on perspectives on future directions of NEAP, rebranding the programme and willingness to pay for increased audits and marketing (EA, 2002).

The first observation relates to the difficulty faced by operators in completing the application form correctly. The application document in all versions of NEAP/EcoCertification to date has been sizeable and complex, with a large number of different criteria. Some operators find certain criteria difficult to understand, and the process to be intimidating, presenting a disincentive for them to complete the application. Fleming (1998) notes that the most commonly expressed negative aspect of the programme was that the documentation was too involved, too time-consuming and too daunting. There may be many sources of confusion and frustration for operators, and these would contribute to the likelihood of documents being incompletely or incorrectly filled in (and thus extra time and frustration for the assessor) or of the application being put aside. As all operators complete the same document, many criteria will be irrelevant for a particular product or operation, thus contributing to operator confusion or frustration.

One of the greatest challenges is in developing 'measurable' criteria that reflect the principles and are unambiguous. However, the criteria do not always cater for all situations and their meaning is not always clear. Under NEAP II, the Assessment Group worked to achieve consistency and transparency in their decisions, but were often faced with having to make policy decisions on interpretation of a particular criterion in relation to underlying principles. This required discussions with the Management Group and was time-consuming and frustrating for all parties, including operators awaiting an outcome on their application.

As the programme has grown in the marketplace, competitive pressures or agency benefits and incentives (see Ingram, Chapter 15, this volume) may have resulted in some operators with lesser commitment to, or understanding of, the principles of sustainability seeking certification. As some of these operators may not fit the 'mould' of operators for which criteria were designed, their applications may reflect a different understanding or interpretation of the criteria, thus adding new challenges to the assessor. Such applications were very often incomplete.

These difficulties are, of course, an expected aspect of the ongoing evolution of a programme where criteria may be ambiguous or where new applications challenge existing understanding or criteria. The experience of NEAP II resulted in numerous refinements presented in EcoCertification, which was designed to clarify unclear or ambiguous criteria (Charters, 2003). Despite this, the document remains long and complex, containing many criteria that are not relevant to every product. In late 2005, the EcoCertification Management Committee announced that development of an online application form was under way. Such a form will make the programme more accessible, allowing applicants to be presented only with criteria relevant to the type of product and activities nominated.

A further concern relating to the capacity of operators to complete the application correctly relates to the size of operations. Large operators may be able to assign an employee (often with responsibility for environmental management) specifically to deal with the application. But most operators within the nature-based tourism and ecotourism sectors are not large and do not have employees with this specific portfolio of responsibility. The smallest operators often face the most difficult challenges, as commonly a single person is responsible for all aspects of the operation. If the process becomes too time-consuming, confusing or difficult, it may be put aside or left altogether.

The issue of affordability is also critical to small operators, as highlighted in the NEAP market survey (EA, 2002), which asked questions about increased costs for marketing and for on-site verification. Respondents raised concerns regarding both level of marketing and need for on-site verification, but strong views were also expressed on the issue of raised fees. Examples of comments include:

> For small operators the costs are becoming uneconomic!
>
> [Increasing fees are] a real disincentive for many [small operators] to belong to and be accredited by NEAP.
>
> As the goal is to encourage more businesses to meet NEAP standards, we need to be very careful NEAP remains affordable to small businesses.
>
> We don't want it to be something only affordable to big operators.

In recent years, with the explosion of compulsory public liability insurance costs for tourism operators in Australia, particularly adventure tourism operators, and increasing regulatory and licensing demands, some operators are finding that the additional time and financial cost of voluntary certification is beyond the capacity of the business.

A final point worth recognizing here is the role of the certification process as an educational tool. The *NEAP Industry Survey* (Enhance Management, 2000a) found that only 10% of operators identified education as an initial motivation to become certified, well below the desire to self-evaluate (26%), seek formal recognition (22%) or access marketing opportunities (22%). However, once engaged in the certification process, 48% of operators identified education (as increased awareness or implementation of environmentally sustainable practices) as the most important impact of NEAP, well ahead of impacts such as competitive advantage (30%), assurance of quality (24%) or marketing opportunities (24%). The process of completing the application document results in an educational outcome for operators; however, some operators need assistance to complete the application. One source of assistance is from programme personnel, such as administration or assessors. During NEAP II, assessors regularly contacted operators for additional information, only to find that the operators would then seek further information or support from them, making the assessment an interactive and hands-on process, contributing directly to the operator's capacity to achieve certification. In developing and promoting a certification scheme, the opportunity for the scheme to provide education, to raise awareness and change practices and to improve products should be recognized and actively promoted.

Issues Arising from the Introduction of EcoCertification

NEAP has always offered a scaled fee system, based on gross annual turnover, to ensure affordability to small operators, but just how equitable is this system? While affordability will always be an individual judgement of each operation in relation to funds available and perceived benefits, the fees associated with NEAP/EcoCertification increased dramatically in late 2003 (Table 22.3). A new fee system was introduced under NEAP II from 1 July 2003, which involved substantial increases, but included within the annual fee was membership of Ecotourism Australia. With the launch of EcoCertification, the base-level fees were reduced (but remained substantially higher than they had been prior to July 2003). An additional option, 'EcoCertification Plus', was also introduced, offering EA membership and its associated benefits in the organization, including web page listings and promotion and marketing.

Table 22.3 highlights the level of increase in fees over a period of less than 1 year (June 2003 to January 2004). Proportionately, the increase in fees is far greater for small operators with a low turnover. Also, annualized total fee rate for each turnover bracket as a proportion of gross turnover decreases considerably with larger operators. That is, an operator in the smallest turnover category, earning AU$100,000, pays about 0.4% of their total annual turnover. For an operator with gross turnover just under AU$10 million, annualized total fee would be a little over 0.01% of gross turnover. So, in this sense, certification is almost 40 times more expensive for the smaller operator than the larger. (An across-the-board CPI-based fee increase was introduced in November 2005, with operators advised via their annual renewal notice.)

Recent discussions with the CEO of EA nevertheless indicated that there was no signficant negative reaction from operators to the increase in fees in 2003 (S. Pahl, personal communication, 31 January 2006). On the contrary, to his knowledge, no operator withdrew from the programme because of the fee increases, and the continued growth of the programme is testament to its acceptance in the marketplace. In fact, Stephen Pahl indicated that fees prior to 2003 were not realistic in relation to running a viable programme, and fees are considered by operators to be very affordable. A few points are worth making here. The first would be that willingness to pay fees would clearly relate to the relative value that operators consider they are getting from the programme. Stephen Pahl is of the view that, with the growth in the programme, the efforts to improve programme credibility through changed assessment and auditing processes, the considerable efforts to increase market awareness with the rebranded EcoCertification programme, and expanded commitment from state agencies to the programme, operators perceive

Table 22.3. Operator fee changes from NEAP II to NEAP III/EcoCertification.

Operator annual turnover (AU$)	Fee type	NEAP II		EcoCert. from Jan. 2004	Increase: Pre-1/7/03 to Jan. 2004	EcoCert. % max. turnover
		Pre-1/7/03	Post-1/7/03			
Less than $100,000	Application	176	198	200		
	Annual	110	320[a]	220		
	EcoCertification Plus			115[a]		
	Total cost 3 years	506	1158	860	70%	0.29%
	Total cost 3 years incl. EcoCert. Plus			1205	138%	0.40%
$100,000 to $250,000	Application	203.5	260	260		
	Annual	165	400[a]	280		
	EcoCertification Plus			115[a]		
	Total cost 3 years	698.5	1460	1100	57%	0.15%
	Total cost 3 years incl. EcoCert. Plus			1445	107%	0.19%
$250,000 to $1 million	Application	286	330	330		
	Annual	330	580[a]	460		
	EcoCertification Plus			165[a]		
	Total cost 3 years	1276	2070	1710	34%	0.06%
	Total cost 3 years incl. EcoCert. Plus			2205	73%	0.07%
$1 million to $3 million (2002)	Application	368.5	430	430		
	Annual	550	840[a]	680		
	EcoCertification Plus			225[a]		
$1 million to $5 million (2003 on)	Total cost 3 years	2018.5	2950	2470	22%	0.02%
	Total cost 3 years incl. EcoCert. Plus			3145	56%	0.02%
Over $3 million (2002)	Application	583.5	530	530		
	Annual	825	1100[a]	840		
	EcoCertification Plus			375[a]		
$5 million to $10 million (2003 on)	Total cost 3 years	3058.5	3830	3050	(0%)	0.01%
	Total cost 3 years incl. EcoCert. Plus			4175	37%	0.01%
Over $10 million (2003 on)	Application	583.5	730	730		
	Annual	825	1500[a]	940		
	EcoCertification Plus			750[a]		
	Total cost 3 years	3058.5	5230	3550	16%	
	Total cost 3 years incl. EcoCert. Plus			5800	90%	

[a] Includes annual EA membership.

considerably better value in the programme now than prior to the introduction of EcoCertification. The other point would be that the EA office is likely to be getting feedback from operators who are involved in the programme. That is, the information is not coming from a truly representative sample of operators since those who choose not to be a part of the programme, whether through genuine unwillingness/inability to pay for the services offered or for other reasons, are less likely to be communicating with the EA office, so their views are less likely to be understood or considered.

Approximately half of the certified operators have chosen to take up the EcoCertification Plus option, including membership (S. Pahl, personal communication, 31 January 2006). This more expensive option has tended to be taken up by larger operators, smaller operators preferring to remain on the base certification rate. EcoCertification Plus thus creates a two-tier system of operators, those paying for extra services including promotion and those not paying, and thus the potential to create an inequity between the presentation and promotion of large versus small operators.

Certification as a Competitive Advantage (Fig. 22.2)

Research undertaken on behalf of Tourism Queensland (Enhance Management, 2000a) identified strong concern amongst operators regarding low public awareness of NEAP. This was generally attributed to a lack of marketing or the inefficiency of marketing initiatives and was frequently identified by operators as the reason for NEAP's failure to provide a competitive advantage to their business. While some operators described a competitive advantage and increase in business, many did not see this outcome. Some operators appear to describe their NEAP experience in largely economic terms, that is, balancing the costs incurred in fees against the benefits experienced (or not) in increased business. Many operators recognize (and seek) a wider range of benefits, but may still feel frustration with the lack of direct benefit through increased business.

> The economic cost of involvement must relate closely to the benefits of participation. To date we have been unable to attribute very much in terms of market advantage.
>
> NEAP must provide more business to members than if it didn't exist . . . why would we spend more money on certification if it doesn't attract more business?
>
> (Unpublished operator comments in responses to NEAP market survey, EA, 2002)

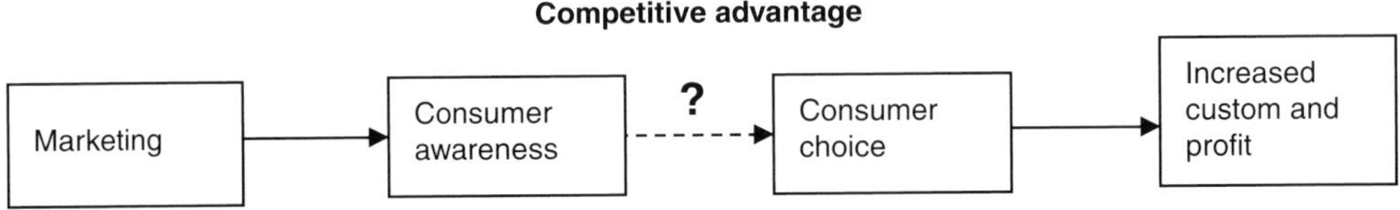

Fig. 22.2. Competitive advantage.

Competitive advantage has often been identified as a potential benefit of certification programmes. The EcoCertification application document lists 'competitive advantage in marketing' as the first of six benefits to operators. Identified benefits to consumers include that the programme provides a recognized means of identifying genuine nature tourism and ecotourism products (EA, 2003). There is an implicit assumption here that tourists are interested in whether a product adopts genuine sustainability practices in nature and ecotourism, and thus that tourists are likely to respond to altruistic consideration of environmental issues and make decisions based on environmental performance indicated by certification status. This assumption is supported by a consumer survey of visitors to NEAP-certified operations (Enhance Management, 2000b), which found that, after being given a description of NEAP, the majority of visitors would be more likely to select a certified operator in the future and would be willing to pay more for a certified product.

It is not the intention of this chapter to explore the issue of consumer response and behaviour in detail. It should, however, be noted that, while consumers often report a willingness to make an altruistic decision based on environmental factors, even to pay more for doing so, there is also ample evidence to indicate that consumer behaviour does not always follow declared preference or intention. Sharpley (2000), for instance, challenges the assumption that environmental awareness converts into consumer choice, particularly in the context of tourism, where motivations are focused very much on personal needs and 'outward looking environmental concern is likely to have a low priority' (p. 51). In fact, he considers that the claimed environmental values of consumers and their actual behaviour are often contradictory.

If there is a question over the link between consumer awareness and consumer choice, then this must challenge the logic of competitive advantage. Given that many operators have also questioned the approach to marketing NEAP/EcoCertification, and have suggested that not enough effort has gone into promoting the brand direct to tourists as consumers, it is perhaps not surprising that some operators are not experiencing the competitive advantage that they might have expected.

Taylor *et al.* (2000) investigated operator responses to three tourism business certification programmes in Australia (not including NEAP), finding that, though operators had a high expectation of benefit derived from consumer awareness of certification, concern was expressed about low levels of consumer awareness. Taylor *et al.* (2000: 18) concluded that 'where businesses have been proactive in promoting their accredited status, some benefit has been derived'.

There is a clear message from this for EcoCertification. Promoting a competitive advantage from certification is risky. If this is the primary reason that operators choose to be certified, then they may well be dissatisfied with the programme if they do not see a direct increase in customers related to their certification status. To avoid dissatisfaction with EcoCertification and alienation of the operator base, it is important that the programme should stimulate in operators a realistic expectation of consumer behaviour and economic benefit. On the other hand, encouraging operators to be more proactive themselves by promoting their certification status and what this means may well provide a positive impact for their businesses as well as assisting in the broader promotion of the certification programme and raising of consumer awareness. In all its versions, NEAP/EcoCertification has provided information to support operators in promoting the certification programme and product certification status. In fact, under the 'responsible marketing' principle, for any product to achieve certification, core criteria require:

- At least one of the marketing methods in continual circulation will define nature and/or ecotourism.
- At least one of the most widely used marketing methods will include the EcoCertification logo alongside certified products (EA, 2003).

Although the competitive advantage of certification remains the first listed benefit in the application document, it seems that Ecotourism Australia recognizes the difficulty in this. The Chief Executive indicated that, at operator certification workshops around Australia, increased profit is not sold as the primary benefit.

> We want people to be committed to sustainable operations, to make a commitment to continuous improvement. The program provides a framework for best practice sustainable operations and stimulates continuous improvement. If operators are not prepared to come into the program within that framework (but just seeking profit), then it is just a waste of time.
>
> (S. Pahl, personal communication, 31 January 2006)

So the 'internal' benefits of the programme to an operation (including the 'educational' aspect of the programme mentioned previously) should be considered as the primary benefit to operations. At the same time, according to Stephen Pahl (personal communication, 31 January 2006), the 'external' benefits of the programme, the awareness and perception within the marketplace, are important, and the EA has made major efforts to raise the profile and awareness of the EcoCertification brand.

Current Status and Success of EcoCertification

Over the years, many questions have been raised about the sustainability of the NEAP/EcoCertification programme, particularly in relation to the dependence on volunteer input, the level of fees and consumer buy-in ('consumers' as operators choosing to become certified, but also as tourists choosing to buy certified products). Changes to the programme have generally been evolutionary, building on the experience of implementation through modification, rather than revolutionary, though each of the relaunched programmes (NEAP II and EcoCertification) have introduced substantial changes. Each year, a report on progress has been presented at the Ecotourism Australia Annual General Meeting, which provides an opportunity for those outside the management committee to hear of the achievements of the programme over the past year. The annual programme report presented in November 2005 outlined a number of positive achievements (Charters, 2005a). These include the following (the sections from Growth to Engagement are adapted from Charters, 2005a).

Growth

Currently there are 225 EcoCertified operators with over 520 products and the programme is growing consistently at 20% per annum (Fig. 22.3).

Distribution

The programme is a truly seamless national certification programme and has strong and growing representation across all states of Australia (Fig. 22.3). (We shall have to accept that there is growth across all states: Fig. 22.3 actually highlights the challenge for EcoCertification of becoming more relevant and accepted outside Queensland.)

Impact

While ecotourism and nature-based tourism make up about 25% of the tourism industry, and only about 6% of ecotourism operators hold EcoCertification, EcoCertified operators are having a significant impact on the industry, as indicated by their representation in the Australian Tourism Awards. For example, 75% of award winners in the ecotourism category and over 60% of award winners in the adventure tourism category are EcoCertified.

Acceptance

EcoCertification is accepted under the national Tourism Accreditation Australia programme, allowing EcoCertified operators to also be certified under the national programme and display the national green tick logo.

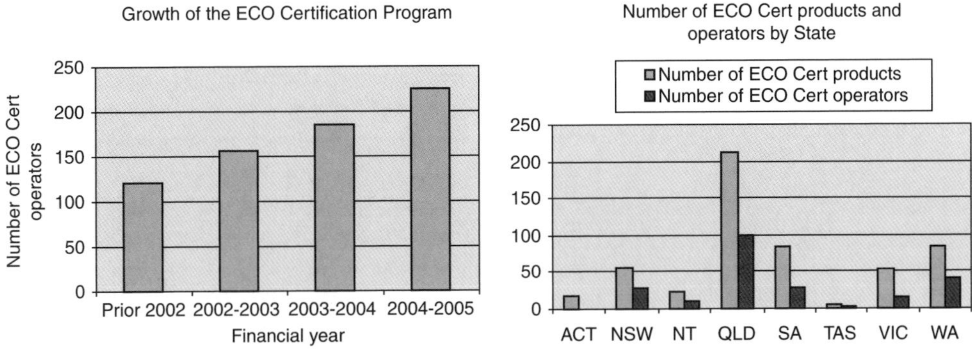

Fig. 22.3. Growth of EcoCertification programme and number of certified products and operators by state (from Charters, 2005a).

EcoCertification is included in the Australian government's 'Accreditation Portal' initiative, allowing applications to go online, saving time and reducing costs for both administration of the programme and for operators, and providing an opportunity for regular alterations and updates to the programme rather than having to wait for the 3-year review.

Partnerships with agencies, such as those with the Great Barrier Reef Marine Park Authority in Queensland and Conservation and Land Management in Western Australia (see Ingram, Chapter 15, this volume), allow EcoCertified operators to qualify for extended operating permits.

Verification

Assessment processes have improved, becoming more efficient, and the audit programme has continued, with 72 operators and 157 products being audited across Australia.

Engagement

Throughout 2004/05, 19 workshops have been held in different parts of Australia to assist operators with the application process. The exposure of EcoCertified products has also been increased by EA attending tourism trade events in Australia, Germany and Japan (Charters, 2005a).

These listed achievements indicate an admirable performance by the programme, particularly given its volunteer-driven roots and need to be self-supporting from the beginning. The outcomes are perhaps particularly important for sustainability of the programme, with the ongoing expansion of numbers of operators and products despite the substantial increase in fees from late 2003.

Other possible measures of success of the programme, not discussed by Charters (2005a), include assessment of operator satisfaction or attrition numbers, monitoring of consumer recognition and, of course, financial performance of the programme.

The operator experience and attrition

The three reports presenting operator views mentioned above (Fleming, 1998; Enhance Management, 2000a; EA, 2002) raised enough issues of concern to suggest that some ongoing process of monitoring the operator experience is needed. In NEAP II, a feedback form dealing with the application criteria and structure was included as part of the application document. As an additional component of the already long and complex application form, this was often not completed, though responses were considered in the programme review process. Under EcoCertification, the application document contains no survey, but an annual survey of operator members is conducted through the EA office. This survey has a wider focus than the NEAP II feedback, covering not only the programme itself, but also its administration, efficiency and delivery of service. While the survey outcomes have not been made publicly available, results are collated and contribute to the ongoing process of programme review.

Without publication of operator responses to these recent surveys, it is impossible for those outside the programme to understand what information is being used in the development or review of the programme. Experience over many years of dealing directly with operators and considering previous surveys does raise the question of operator satisfaction. Operator members regularly express dissatisfaction with the outcomes from the programme, particularly in relation to direct economic benefit from membership. Some operators have questioned whether they will continue with NEAP/EcoCertification.

> At this stage we receive no measurable benefit from being EAA Advanced Eco accredited. If the fees increase, it is doubtful we will continue. We support the concept and ethics but in the long run it must generate a financial return.
>
> We are considering pulling out of NEAP/EAA as we see little value while believing it a good idea.
>
> (Unpublished operator comments in responses to NEAP market survey, EA, 2002)

Recognizing that many changes have been made to the programme since these comments were made, and that other more positive views were expressed, the comments do raise an issue that has not been covered in any annual report for NEAP/EcoCertification – the rate of attrition. A searchable database of EcoCertified operators is available on the EA web site (www.ecotourism.org.au). Searches of all operators were conducted in April 2004 and again in December 2005. While there may be problems with the database (accuracy and currency), these two searches allow for a quick comparison of both growth and attrition of operators/products.

Table 22.4 indicates a considerable growth in the aggregate number of certified operators (39%) and products (48%) over little more than a year and a half. On 25 April 2004, the database contained records of 164 operators

Table 22.4. Aggregate numbers of certified products and operators.

Product type		25/4/04	31/12/05	Net increase	New	Attrition
Tour	Operator	105	145	41 (39%)	54	14
	Product	271	407	136 (50%)		
Accomm.	Operator	44	50	6 (14%)	11	5
	Product	49	53	4 (8%)		
Attraction	Operator	15	31	16 (107%)	17	1
	Product	18	41	23 (128%)		
Total	Operator	164	226	62 (38%)	82	20
	Product	338	501	163 (48%)		

offering 338 products over the three product types. On 31 December 2005, this had increased to 226 operators and 501 products. By cross-checking the database records, these figures can be broken down into actual new operators and operators lost to the system. This shows an increase of 82 new operators (or exactly 50% increase on the number in April 2004), but a corresponding attrition of 20 operators (or 12% of the original number). While the growth rate is extraordinary, the attrition rate should be of some concern, and may reinforce the need for systematic monitoring of the operator experience, including some kind of exit survey to understand the factors influencing attrition. Such an exit survey may also aid in developing a wider understanding of the industry response to the programme, avoiding the bias inherent in gathering information from a sample that is not representative (as mentioned in the discussion of fees above).

Financial viability

One of the great challenges for a certification programme is to be affordable and yet viable. NEAP began by minimizing its operating costs, depending heavily on volunteer commitment to get a programme functioning. The maturing of the programme has seen a move away from what was an unsustainable dependence on volunteers and low-cost options to a more professional programme, but clearly this comes at a cost.

While the great achievements in growth of the programme outlined above indicate a positive future, what of the financial sustainability of the programme? The introduction of auditing under EcoCertification has clearly added considerably to the cost of managing the programme, and expanding the scope of audits will further increase the cost. A direct budget allocation is made by EA to the auditing process each year, but the cost of auditing has been supplemented by contributions from Tourism Queensland and the South Australian Tourism Commission (S. Pahl, personal communication, 31 January 2006). EcoCertification is wholly owned by Ecotourism Australia, and separate budget details are not published. Annual financial details for the EA include income and expenditure items against EcoCertification, and on this basis the programme would seem to be functioning at a considerable profit, with income approximately double expenditure. But many costs, including some auditing costs, office management, communications and administration, are not included in these items, but are integrated into other budget items. Despite this, the EA CEO believes that the programme is 'most definitely paying for itself'.

Despite the constraint of a self-funding model, the programme has gradually expanded and built a reputation amongst operators and government agencies in under a decade to get to the stage where it can provide certification of products, including a professional auditing component, anywhere in Australia. On this basis, the programme would have to be considered a financial success. However, every decision made, every change introduced, offers new opportunity for improvement, but also potentially the seeds of failure if the stakeholders – operators, state agencies and ultimately tourists – disagree with the directions taken or the previously mentioned balance of characteristics, such as bureaucracy, complexity, credibility and affordability, tips in the wrong direction.

Some Questions and Challenges for EcoCertification

A question of market differentiation

The idea of market differentiation, which is so often promoted as a benefit of certification, is based on the expectation that only the best operators, those adopting the best practices, will achieve certification. Part of the attraction to these operators is that certification can assist them to differentiate themselves as genuine 'eco' operators from the 'eco-cowboys', the 'greenwashing' and the 'ecotourism lite' (Honey and Stewart, 2002).

At the same time, Honey and Stewart (2002) argue that certification will help ecotourism to achieve its potential by providing a set of tools, standards and criteria to move from conceptualization to codification (p. 3), and that, by charting a new direction, the principles and practices of ecotourism can infuse and ultimately transform the entire tourism industry (p. 8). The reach and influence of EcoCertification across the industry, via such aspects as expansion of the programme membership and representation of certified operators in tourism awards, have been previously referred to as a great achievement for the programme. Partnerships with protected area agencies are resulting in larger numbers of operators seeking certification, and benefits to those protected area managers are maximized if all operators gain EcoCertification.

The notion of influencing sustainable practices across an entire industry is admirable and desirable. Yet the idea of transforming the social and environmental practices across the industry through the tool of certification introduces a fundamental contradiction. How can an operator gain a marketing benefit if all (or even a large proportion of) operators are certified?

One answer might be that we cannot have it both ways, that marketing benefits from product differentiation and selling certification as a preferred approach for licensing in protected areas are mutually exclusive. One implies that a relatively small number of operators are certified, the best operators, self-motivated to achieve excellence in sustainability performance. The other implies a move away from certification being a 'voluntary' system to some form of 'regulation' encouraging all operators to adopt improved practices.

The answer, of course, is that NEAP/EcoCertification does seek to have it both ways, with three different levels of certification with progressively more stringent requirements placed on each. However, for competitive advantage to be maintained for higher levels of certification, it is crucial that the highest level of certification is rewarding the very highest level of performance and practice (recognizing the elite products), that the certification levels are recognizably different to consumers, and that progressively higher levels of certification are differentiated in the benefits available to them, such as gaining better access to certain promotional opportunities. On the first point, the question must be asked whether the highest level has become too easy, with 58% of certified products achieving 'Advanced EcoCertification' level, 28% achieving 'Ecotourism' level and 14% certified at 'Nature Tourism' level (Charters, 2005b). (Should this be seen as a positive, that so many products have achieved the highest level of practice, or a negative, that the highest certification level available does not adequately differentiate the elite products? Could it be that the programme is still largely attracting the elite products, the operators who are the 'true believers' of sustainability?)

On the second point, there must be adequate differentiation in the marketplace to promote the excellence achieved by operators certified at Advanced Ecotourism level above the minimum level achieved by some other operators. Based on promotional programmes, consumer awareness of EcoCertification and the existing logos for the three levels of certification (Fig. 22.4), questions have been raised regarding the recognizable differentiation benefit for operators with higher levels of certification. Seeing any one of these logos in isolation may tell the consumer that the product is certified, but not the level of achievement relative to other products/certification levels.

On the third point, regarding promotional benefits, EcoCertification Plus offers greater benefit to those who are willing to pay for it, rather than a merit-based system of certification level. The promotion of operators and products via the EcoCertification web site lists all operators and products in the same way. The only differentiation of certification level on the EcoCertification web site is on the basis of the logo assigned to the operator, which, of course, depends on viewers recognizing the difference between the logos and the implication of those differences.

The certification landscape

Within Australia, there is increasing coordination of the various state-based tourism business certification schemes, with Tourism Accreditation Australia (TAA) licensing programmes in Victoria, South Australia, Tasmania, Northern

Fig. 22.4. EcoCertification logos.

Territory and Western Australia under the National Tourism Accreditation Program label. A large number of operators are certified in some states under these schemes, and enjoying the benefits of their membership, such as discounted access to state marketing campaigns. EcoCertification has now also been endorsed by TAA with its expansion to cover business management and ethics principles, suggesting that, rather than being a complementary programme, EcoCertification is a direct competitor in the territory of existing business certification schemes. At the same time, some mainstream tourism certification programmes have moved towards the addition of 'green' components to their packages. In late 2003, a Green Star rating scheme for accommodation was launched by AAA Tourism, the national tourism body of Australian motoring organizations, in conjunction with Green Globe. There is a danger that, rather than seeing a rationalization of certification, there will be a proliferation of competing schemes, leading to a dilution of the market and confusion of customers (Honey and Stewart, 2002; Toth, 2002). Operators too must make a choice between schemes. Some may choose to join more than one scheme, but many will consider the relative costs and benefits of different schemes and select only one.

EcoCertification was initially viewed by some state-based tourism business certification schemes as a competitor. More recently, the various organizations have worked with Ecotourism Australia to seek synergies and beneficial outcomes. As the required content of the National Tourism Accreditation Program is contained within Chapters 1 and 2 of the EcoCertification document, EcoCertified operators are deemed to have met the requirements of state-based tourism business certification schemes, so they can display the state-based certification logo as well as the EcoCertification logo. In some states, Ecotourism Australia has negotiated for EcoCertified operators to receive all the benefits of state-based tourism certification, including discounts on state marketing campaigns. This means that EcoCertified operators do not have to be members of the state-based scheme as well to gain these benefits. The cooperation has gone further to include the training of a small number of state tourism organization employees in environmental management system auditing and their registration as professional auditors for the EcoCertification programme, allowing for cost efficiencies in delivery of auditing EcoCertified products. Rather than functioning in competition, this cooperation between organizations and certification schemes has helped in the move towards a cohesive certification landscape across Australia that is efficient for operators and recognizable to consumers.

Equity and accessibility

Honey and Stewart (2002: 22) identify two contradictory cross-currents within the tourism industry: one towards the consolidation of big players into fewer, larger corporations, based mainly in the global North and catering largely to the mass tourism market; and the other towards a proliferation and decentralization of businesses, many in host countries in the global

South and based on the principles of ecotourism. Honey and Stewart (2002: 23) go on to consider the debate over the 'North–South' divide:

> whether tourism certification is simply another technique for strengthening the hand of powerful and largely foreign owned corporations at the expense of businesses, communities, and countries in the South or whether certification can be shaped into a tool for setting standards and criteria that promote and protect the interests and welfare of those in the South.

This debate has relevance to the situation of ecotourism certification in Australia. If we replace 'North' with large corporations and 'South' with the small operations and local communities, then we can see the potential for the same issues to arise. In Australia, the ecotourism industry includes many small operators, but also a number of large corporations provide products that meet the requirements of NEAP/EcoCertification. Given the complex and demanding nature of the NEAP application process, consideration must be given to whether small operators are discriminated against by the process, and whether, as a result, larger companies are being strengthened by their capacity to achieve high-level certification. This is not to say that small operators cannot, or do not, achieve Advanced Ecotourism certification. However, with the capacity of operators in mind, NEAP was originally designed to be affordable for all operators, practical for operators in remote areas without access to higher education institutions and consultants, simple to complete with straightforward documentation and non-technical and inclusive (Charters, 2000). Given these realities and intentions, the difficulties faced by small operators need to be considered to ensure that those operators are not being excluded by the very nature of the certification process, but that their interests and welfare are being promoted and protected.

Questions have also been asked in this chapter about the equity of fee scales for EcoCertification and capacity of smaller operators to fund certification, as well as the potential inequities in benefits introduced by 'EcoCertification Plus'. The move to an online application form will undoubtedly simplify and streamline the process, which should make achieving certification simpler for those operators with access. It is also possible that some operators may not have the skill, the technology or the access to enable them to use this online environment, so hard-copy applications will still need to be provided (again, leaving the process more difficult for those less able or in more isolated environments). With all these factors in mind, EcoCertification will need to remain vigilant to ensure that it does not become the preserve of the bigger, more affluent (more powerful?) operators, but that the profile of certified operators is a reasonable reflection of the broader ecotourism and nature tourism industry.

Conclusion

NEAP/EcoCertification is clearly a success story. It was the first national ecotourism certification programme, and is often heralded as a successful model to build on and learn from. NEAP began as a low-cost programme, designed to be practical but achievable, affordable and accessible, and from the beginning was driven by volunteers. Ensuring credibility of the certification brand presents a range of problems and has required ongoing change to the programme assessment and auditing. The administration and assessment of a programme are always going to be a challenge to get right, as exemplified by the apparent contradiction between the 'independence' of the assessment process and efficiency in implementing criteria. Challenges must also be faced in moving from a small volunteer-driven programme to a more 'professional' one. NEAP has always managed to remain essentially self-funded, quite an achievement in the world of certification. While external funds have been needed for special projects, including supporting development of the auditing programme, the basic operations of the programme have been covered by operator registrations. As the programme has expanded, the expense of its operation has increased, but so has the capacity to meet costs of programme improvements, such as the introduction of paid professional assessors and independent third-party auditors.

EcoCertification will continue to build partnerships to achieve better coverage in the market and produce greater benefits for operators. Partnerships with state protected area management agencies are a good example, where the agencies, operators and the EcoCertification programme can all benefit from a constructive relationship. But expansion of such partnerships will continue to attract operators with little previous knowledge of, or interest in, sustainability to seek EcoCertification. While exposing these operators to new ideas and providing incentives to improve practices, this will also create new challenges for the programme.

NEAP/EcoCertification has continued to grow and expand. But it is relatively easy to count the numbers and think everything is going well. It is always more difficult to consider what we should really be measuring to monitor success: who is missing out, or whether the programme is really identifying and rewarding genuine quality in ecotourism and nature tourism.

The evolution of the programme will continue. In July 2006 the fourth generation of NEAP/EcoCertification was released simultaneously with the launch of the online application form. While this new version contains minor modifications to wording and criteria, the online application environment provides benefits to applicants and programme administrators, in particular by allowing real-time modifications to be made where necessary, and as applicants can now be channelled only to relevant sections of the document, allowing information and criteria to be developed that are specific to activities and locations. Further changes will be made in the move to continue to improve the programme, to encourage continuous improvement in operator practices and to make the programme more efficient, effective and accessible. Not all changes will work or be positive for all stakeholders, so it is important that the programme undertakes regular reviews, monitors various criteria of success, including the operator experience, and is engaged with external stakeholders and opinion. Critical to this is the consideration of 'negative' criteria, such as attrition rates or exit surveys. The transparency of the programme is also an issue to consider. Across the community, Eco-Certification has many stakeholders with an interest in the directions that the programme takes and how decisions are made. External questioning should be considered as a healthy aspect of the ongoing development of the programme, but, for these questions to be relevant, they must be informed. Perhaps there is not only a need for EA to investigate the 'negative' aspects of the programme, but also to be transparent and publish the outcomes of those investigations. Asking questions and facing challenges openly will be an important means for EcoCertification to further its success and to continue to provide a model from which other programmes can learn.

The fundamental objective of promoting sustainable practice and quality in nature-based and ecotourism must not be lost in the ongoing drive for accessibility, professionalism, credibility and efficiency in the programme. Perhaps the Mount Everest of challenges for EcoCertification remains the building of consumer awareness, the recognition of the logo and creating real market advantage for certified members.

Acknowledgements

Many people have contributed to my understanding of the NEAP/EcoCertification programme, including many past and present staff and board members of Ecotourism Australia. For support, stimulating discussions and commitment to the goals of a successful and credible certification programme, I am indebted to members of the NEAP Assessment Panel, particularly Stuart Toplis, Matt Whitting, Jenny Nichol and Sandra Taylor. My thanks go to Alice Crabtree for her comments on an earlier version of this chapter drawn from years of experience in working with the NEAP and IES, and to the anonymous reviewers, who provided valuable comments. I would also like to thank the CEO of Ecotourism Australia, Stephen Pahl, for his generosity with time and information in helping me understand some of the policy directions and the experience of implementing EcoCertification.

References

Charters, T. (2000) Nature and Ecotourism Accreditation Program. In: Charters, T. and Law, K. (eds) *Best Practice Ecotourism in Queensland.* Tourism Queensland, Brisbane, pp. 33–53.

Charters, T. (2003) NEAP Management Committee Report. *ECOnews: The Newsletter of Ecotourism Australia*, Ecotourism Australia, Brisbane, November–December, 2003/04.

Charters, T. (2005a) ECOCertified Tourism Report. In: *Ecotourism Australia Limited Annual Review 2005.* Ecotourism Australia, Brisbane, pp. 2–3.

Charters, T. (2005b) Sustaining unforgettable natural experiences. Keynote presentation to Ecotourism Australia National Conference, Friday, 2 December 2005, Hobart, Tasmania.

Chester, G. and Crabtree, A. (2002) Australia: the Nature and Ecotourism Accreditation Program. In: Honey, M. (ed.) *Ecotourism and Certification: Setting Standards in Practice.* Island Press, Washington, DC, pp. 161–185.

Commonwealth of Australia (1992) *National Strategy for Ecologically Sustainable Development.* Australian Government Publishing Service, Canberra.

Commonwealth of Australia (1994) *National Ecotourism Strategy.* Commonwealth Department of Tourism, Canberra.

Commonwealth of Australia (1995) *Two-way Track. Biodiversity, Conservation and Ecotourism: An Investigation of Linkages, Mutual Benefits and Future Opportunities.* Department of Environment, Sports and Territories, Canberra.

Commonwealth of Australia (2003) *Tourism White Paper: A Medium to Long term Strategy for Tourism.* Australian Government, Canberra.

Ecotourism Association of Australia (EAA) (2000) *NEAP: Nature and Ecotourism Accreditation Program. Second Edition.* Ecotourism Association of Australia, Brisbane.

Ecotourism Association of Australia (EAA) (2001) NEAP corporate governance. Unpublished internal document, Ecotourism Association of Australia, October.

Ecotourism Australia (EA) (2002) Feedack results on NEAP survey. Unpublished internal report, prepared by Lene Fallstrom Andersen and Keith Williams for Ecotourism Australia. Ecotourism Australia.

Ecotourism Australia (EA) (2003) *EcoCertification: A Certification Program for the Australian Nature and Ecotourism Industry.* Third Edition. Ecotourism Australia, Brisbane.

Enhance Management (2000a) *NEAP Industry Survey.* Tourism Queensland, Brisbane.

Enhance Management (2000b) *NEAP Consumer Survey.* Tourism Queensland, Brisbane.

Fennell, D. (2003) *Ecotourism: An Introduction,* 2nd edn. Routledge, London, UK.

Fleming, S. (1998) Evaluating the National Ecotourism Accreditation Program. Graduating seminar report, Bachelor of Business in Tourism, School of Tourism and Hospitality Management, Southern Cross University.

Honey, M. (ed.) (2002) *Ecotourism and Certification: Setting Standards in Practice.* Island Press, Washington, DC.

Honey, M. and Rome, A. (2001) *Protecting Paradise: Certification Programs for Sustainable Tourism and Ecotourism.* Institute for Policy Studies, Washington, DC.

Honey, M. and Stewart, E. (2002) Introduction. In: Honey, M. (ed.) *Ecotourism and Certification: Setting Standards in Practice.* Island Press, Washington, DC, pp. 1–29.

Sharpley, R. (2000) The consumer behaviour context of ecolabelling. In: Font, X. and Buckley, R.C. (eds) *Tourism Ecolabelling: Certification and Promotion of Sustainable Management.* CAB International, Wallingford, UK.

TAA (Tourism Accreditation Australia) (2005) TAA History. Available at: www.tourismaccreditation.org.au/about.asp?about=history (viewed 20 December 2005).

Taylor, D., Rosemann, I. and Prosser, G. (2000) *The Effect of Accreditation on Tourism Business Performance: An Evaluation.* Occasional Paper Number 3, Centre for Regional Tourism Research, Southern Cross University, Lismore.

Toth, R. (2002) Exploring the concepts underlying certification. In: Honey, M. (ed.) *Ecotourism and Certification: Setting Standards in Practice.* Island Press, Washington, DC, pp. 73–101.

23 Creating Regional Networks of Sustainable Tourism Stakeholders: Europe's Voluntary Initiatives for Sustainability in Tourism (VISIT) and the Sustainable Tourism Certification Network of the Americas

HERBERT HAMELE,[1] NAUT KUSTERS,[2] RONALD SANABRIA[3] AND ELIZABETH SKINNER[4]

[1]*ECOTRANS, Germany;* [2]*ECEAT, The Netherlands;* [3]*Rainforest Alliance, Costa Rica;* [4]*Columbia University, USA*

Chapter Profile

More than 100 voluntary initiatives for sustainable tourism exist around the world. Many of these initiatives are making positive contributions to environmental and social issues; however, there are issues associated with the numbers of different programmes, the lack of reciprocity and mutual recognition between programmes, the financial viability of programmes and the limited consumer recognition and penetration of the programmes. One option that can assist in addressing some of these issues is the development of regional networks of sustainable tourism stakeholders. This chapter describes the development and implementation of two regional networks, the VISIT network in Europe and the Sustainable Tourism Network of the Americas, and highlights the benefits and challenges of this approach. Regional networks such as these can provide opportunities for harmonization of standards, which could lead to the establishment of an accreditation system for certification programmes, building consensus for developing, promoting and implementing best management practices, sharing information and building demand for an accreditation body. Opportunities also exist for joint collaboration and marketing strategies.

Introduction

In 2000/01, the World Tourism Organization (WTO) commissioned the European Network for Sustainable Tourism Development (ECOTRANS) to conduct a global study on voluntary initiatives for sustainable tourism (WTO, 2001). More than 100 voluntary initiatives were found, ranging from voluntary efforts, charters, codes of conduct and award programmes for the recognition of excellent innovation to formal systems of ecolabelling and certification. While many initiatives were making positive contributions to environmental and social issues, the sheer number of programmes (with more on the way), the lack of reciprocity and mutual recognition among them and the relatively limited penetration of these voluntary schemes indicated an urgent need for consolidation and harmonization. In addition, other studies (Honey and Rome, 2000; Rainforest Alliance, 2003) found that many certification programmes were struggling to survive financially and were unable to reach consumers and measurable demonstrations of improved sustainability were elusive.

The sheer numbers of certification programmes mean that both consumers and the travel industry face confusion when they attempt to weigh the comparative benefits of various tourism certification schemes and labels. The lack of common baseline standards or generic criteria makes differentiation between valid certification labels that 'guarantee' environmentally friendly (above all, certificates in Europe) or genuine ecotourism (above all, certificates in the Americas or Australia) and programmes that are simply 'greenwashing' almost impossible.

One potential solution is the development of an accreditation system that creates an international standard by which to evaluate these different schemes. Schemes that meet the standard would be accredited by the international system and receive technical and marketing support. This approach has been embraced by the forestry sector (the Forest Stewardship Council), the organic movement (IFOAM) and other industries. The Sustainable Tourism Stewardship Council (STSC) feasibility study (Rainforest Alliance, 2003) spent more than 2 years in public consultation (during the regional preparatory meetings for the 2002 International Year of Ecotourism and the UN World Ecotourism Summit) exploring the possibility of developing an international accreditation body for sustainable tourism, and found support for its development.

The consultation process identified a strong need for the development of regional networks of certification schemes, NGOs, governments, industry and others working towards sustainable tourism in their regions. Stakeholders felt strongly that they needed regional support in the form of information sharing, regional baseline standards, marketing, technical assistance and training of small and medium-size enterprises in sustainable practices. They stressed that the development of regional networks should be a first step towards the development of an international body such as the Sustainable Tourism Stewardship Council.

The STSC feasibility study (Rainforest Alliance, 2001) demonstrated that, ultimately, an international accreditation agency will be needed to help monitor, manage and market the myriad programmes around the globe, and help improve the benefits that certification delivers. However, it was also clear that there is a need for an intermediate stage to strengthening certification programmes before an STSC could be established. Even with an established STSC, there is likely to be a need for support and coordination with other agencies and organizations in helping countries and tourism operations ready themselves to access accredited certification programmes and for certification programmes to become STSC-ready (i.e. comply with STSC rules).

One of the key conclusions of the STSC study was that efforts to harmonize international standards and address some of the challenges cited would best be started through an inclusive participatory mechanism. This logically suggests an intermediary step that would facilitate inter-regional exchange – such as consolidation of programmes into regional networks.

In response to these findings, tourism leaders around the world began to develop regional networks. The two most developed are VISIT in Europe and the Sustainable Tourism Certification Network of the Americas, but there are fledgling efforts in Asia–Pacific and Africa.

Sustainable Tourism Certification Network of the Americas

In Latin America and the Caribbean the existence of and the potential for future establishment of unsustainable tourism ventures threatens both impoverished people and important biodiverse and sensitive ecosystems. Sustainable tourism is being considered as a genuine alternative that will help foster the well-being of local communities and help alleviate poverty not only by fostering environmental conservation and social responsibility but also by helping activate the delivery of local products and services by small and medium-size enterprises (SMEs) and community-based operations. This region has the largest number of sustainable tourism certification programmes already operating in developing nations, and many new programmes are expected to be launched in the future (including programmes in Brazil, Chile, Costa Rica, Cuba, the Dominican Republic, Ecuador, Guatemala, Mexico, Peru, Uruguay and Venezuela). National and local certification programmes in this region are at very different levels of development but most are less than 5 years old. The newness of these programmes and the lack of entrenched processes facilitate the potential to implement changes in systems and criteria that will help empower local people and protect natural areas. The Rainforest Alliance helped organize a certification network in Latin America as an outcome of the research undertaken as a part of its STSC feasibility study.

The Sustainable Tourism Certification Network of the Americas was launched in September 2003 at the Regional Conference of the Americas on Sustainability Certification of Tourism Activities in Bahia, Brazil, organized by the World Tourism Organization (WTO), and hosted by the Hospitality Institute and the Brazilian government (WTO *et al.*, 2003).[1] This Network constitutes one of the components of the international partnership effort led by UNEP/DTIE, TIES, CESD and the Rainforest Alliance to promote integration of sustainability into tourism policies and higher environmental and social standards for tourism. The launch of this Network brought together representatives from leading certification programmes in the region and other supporting organizations. Experiences related to certification were exchanged, and common objectives were defined at this meeting. Due to the interest generated among representatives from the USA, Canada and the Caribbean islands and the fact that North America represents an important market for tourism operations in the Caribbean and Latin America, it was decided that the geographical scope of the network should be expanded to include certification programmes in North America and the Caribbean. Certification programmes (as of January 2006) participating in the Sustainable Tourism Certification Network of the Americas include: Green Globe, Blue Flag and QTC (the Caribbean islands); Certification for Sustainable Tourism, CST (Costa Rica); Green Deal (Guatemala); National Program of Certification for Sustainable Tourism in Peru, CSTP (Peru); Programa de Certificação em Turismo Sustentável, PCTS (Brazil); SmartVoyager (Ecuador); and Sustainable Tourism Eco-certification Program, STEP (USA).

The Sustainable Tourism Certification Network of the Americas is intended to encourage dialogue among these various participants and to act as a regional clearing house for certification information and technical assistance. Participants at the Network launch defined their vision as follows: 'The Network is the reference for sustainable tourism certification in the Americas, its initiatives are well-known in the market, have credibility and generate benefits for conservation, local communities and competitiveness for the tourism industry.' The participants also agreed that the mission of the Network is to:

> promote sustainable tourism in the region, through the strengthening of certification initiatives, based on mutual respect and recognition, joint efforts, harmonisation [balancing] of systems, and the sharing of information and experiences. Through the recognition and respect of the environmental and socio-cultural diversity, the Sustainable Tourism Certification Network of the Americas, will work with: integrity and ethics, transparency, participation, efficiency and effectiveness.
>
> (Turismo & Conservación Consultores, 2003)

The Rainforest Alliance has served as the initial Secretariat for this Network since its launch. Through National Liaisons, the Network encourages participation of representatives from a variety of stakeholder groups and welcomes all initiatives that are managing certification programmes in the region.

The Network functions with the following bodies:

- General Assembly: made up of countries represented by their National Liaison and Certification Programmes, plus the Founding Member class.

- Technical Secretariat: provides the General Assembly with technical support, and attends the General Assembly with the right to provide input but without voting rights. The Secretariat coordinates Network operations and will assist in the National Forum development process.
- National Forum: represents a multiparty national complex. It represents country interests and has representatives from the different sectors involved in the nation's sustainable tourism.
- National Liaisons: have the following functions per agreement:

1. They are the national representatives from the country members of the Network of the Americas in the General Assembly, the National Forum and the Network Secretariat.
2. These bodies bring their country's perspectives to the General Assembly.
3. The National Liaisons play a proactive role in meeting Network objectives and coordinate actions and mechanisms to make sure that the National Forum performs the activities entrusted to it (lobbying, certification support, Network sustainability financing and project management).

To become National Liaisons, organizations must meet the following criteria:

1. Be democratically elected by National Forum members.
2. Be working, supporting and/or fostering sustainable tourism certification initiatives.
3. Have at least 2 years of experience and track record in sustainable tourism.
4. Be entities operating for 2 years and have management capacity (to take on the above-mentioned responsibilities).
5. Have stated commitment to the Network vision, mission, values and objectives by subscribing to a Memorandum of Understanding with the Network Secretariat.
6. Ensure adequate representation of their country's or region's different stakeholders.
7. Have time availability to work on Network activities.
8. Guarantee information dissemination in their countries or regions using communication channels and mechanisms established by the Network.
9. Be committed to holding transparent, representative and participatory communications with the different sectors.
10. Certification Programmes will be able to represent their countries as National Liaisons, provided they prove that their election took place through a participatory process and that said participation is still active in the National Forum.

Examples of National Liaisons are Plan 21 in Argentina, Belize's Programme for Belize and the Chilean Eko-Support.

- The Network has three kinds of members that represent different actors involved in sustainable tourism in the region: Certification Programmes, Founding Members and Associated Members.

The Network of the Americas focuses on seven objectives:

- To consolidate the Network: identify and structure the involvement of the relevant stakeholders.
- To establish effective communication: establish communication channels and information exchange among stakeholders.
- To develop common work tools: compile and harmonize sustainable tourism best practices and standards and develop a common baseline.
- To increase participation by SMEs: actively encourage and support SMEs in implementing best practices and certification processes.
- To develop a marketing strategy: establish common marketing strategies.
- To support and strengthen certification programmes: strengthen programmes though training, technical assistance and institutional development.
- To establish sustainable financing mechanisms: seek resources (technical, economic and financial) to contribute to the achievement of the mission and specific objectives of the Network.

Baseline standard development

One of the most challenging objectives of the Network of the Americas was to move towards the identification of a common baseline standard. The objectives for developing this baseline standard were to:

1. Facilitate communication among programmes.
2. Establish the basis for a monitoring and assessment system that will, in the future, allow measurement of the general impact of the member programmes.
3. Identify the points of coincidence and consensus among the member programmes that will allow development of a joint marketing strategy for certified enterprises on the basis of those points with which they already comply.
4. Serve as the cornerstone for countries that are just initiating their certification programmes and for other similar initiatives.

Each organization within the Sustainable Tourism Certification Network of the Americas is focused on using tourism as a tool to support community development, biodiversity conservation and other environmental, sociocultural and economic improvements. By actively collaborating with one another and sharing information and experience through the Network, members are beginning to strengthen both their individual and collective efforts. Participating in the Network of the Americas has been a benefit for its members, affording them an opportunity to further integrate regionally and nationally accepted sustainable tourism standards into their own certification initiative (S. Blanco, Guatemala, electronic communication, 2004; B. Mullis, Colorado, electronic communication, 2004).

The first step in developing a baseline standard was to research and analyse relevant national and international standards being implemented in the Americas region. The participating certification programmes, with support from the Secretariat, focused on the geographical region of the Network, and included the different regional, national and international standards that are applied by certification programmes in this region.

The standards reviewed in the first round (as of August 2004) included ten existing certification programmes, ranging from Certification for Sustainable Tourism (CST) Costa Rica, Green Deal, Guatemala Green Globe Company Standard, Green Globe International Ecotourism Standard and SmartVoyager Standard for Tourism Boats in the Galapagos Islands, Ecuador.

In the initial analysis of these certification standards, the member certification programmes identified a series of common factors (indicators or standards) present in the majority of programmes. With this information, an initial document was generated in which basic criteria were classified in an access database. The database captured information on each standard at three different grouping levels:

- Level 1 corresponds to the three macro-areas of concern in sustainable tourism certification:
    - Environmental
    - Sociocultural
    - Economic
- Level 2 includes ten subcategories of principles or descriptors on which the standard will be analysed, such as:
    - Level 1: Environment
        - Level 2: 1.1 Water
1.2 Energy
- Level 3 includes the detail on subcategories of principles or descriptors. An example would be:
    - Level 1: Environment
    - Level 2: 1.1 Water
    - Level 3: 1.1.1 Water consumption is measured continuously and there exists a register of the results

In September 2005, staff representing certification programmes and the National Liaisons ratified their adherence to the draft common baseline standard. This standard includes criteria relating to issues such as water and energy consumption, soil pollution, impacts on wildlife, provision of visitor information, use of local staff, building design, pest control and compliance with laws, standards and regulations. This document has also been used by other programmes, such as the Milieubarometer in The Netherlands, to compare its compatibility with certification standards being used in the Americas. During 2006, this common baseline standard served as the basis for discussion and has been circulated to all interested parties.

Pilot groundwork to facilitate access to certification

A significant challenge for sustainable tourism is the need to facilitate access to technical assistance, training and funding for small and micro-businesses to implement good practices and enter certification processes. Thus, the activities of the Sustainable Tourism Certification Network of the Americas have been supported by a technical assistance component to address some of the challenges at the national level on a pilot basis in four countries: Belize, Costa Rica, Ecuador and Guatemala. A complete training and technical assistance programme on best practices and certification will be executed over 4 years, starting in August 2003, by four partner organizations: Programme for Belize, Rainforest Alliance – Costa Rica (Alianza para Bosques), Alianza Verde in Guatemala and the Ecuadorean Ecotourism Association (ASEC) with support from the Inter-American Development Bank and several other funding agencies.[2] The purpose of these activities is to reach out to all kinds of operations, including community-based operations that usually have no access to technical assistance and training programmes. This effort is creating a window of opportunity for tourism operations that would voluntarily like to participate in the implementation of best practices and enter a certification programme.

These training and technical assistance activities are aimed at managers of community-based, small and medium-sized tourism enterprises, who will attend workshops and receive assistance in business management practices (BMP), sustainable tourism certification, monitoring and evaluation of impacts and marketing, so that they will have the information and tools needed to succeed in a highly competitive tourism industry. Initially, the project partners will work with existing BMP and certification initiatives in the four participating countries, and will coordinate efforts with certification initiatives in Brazil. Thereafter, the project will work with trained tourism operations in the pilot countries, to implement the BMP guidelines.

The technical assistance component has been complemented by the development of marketing activities to support certification programmes that participate in the Network. These activities will directly benefit SMEs that have implemented the baseline standard. As of December 2005, this initiative has been able to provide training for 79 trainers and 812 community and private entrepreneurs and more than 1236 people have been introduced to sustainable tourism best practices through seminars.

An important marketing effort has been encouraging tour operators to sign cooperative agreements with the Rainforest Alliance, the purpose of which is to motivate their affiliated business enterprises to join them in conserving biodiversity and reducing tourism's negative impacts. The tour operators commit to organizing training events and recruiting participants to join the BMP programme, and then give priority to hotels and lodges that adopt best practices when designing their tour packages. These affiliated businesses are then eligible to receive technical assistance, marketing support and staff training related to effective business management practices, providing they meet specific requirements. In this manner, the initiative guarantees sustainability in the entire supply chain, as well as responding also to the need for providing credibility and variety for tourists interested in vacations that promote positive development for the areas they visit and not those who leave a negative impact on their biodiversity or communities.

Other key marketing activities have been the development and ongoing distribution of the Catalogue of Certified Products and the Eco-Index for Sustainable Tourism, an online resource that went live in 2006. Targeted as a resource for tour operators, the catalogue includes details and contact information for the 141 hotels, restaurants and other tourism businesses that are certified by one of the existing programmes in Latin America and the Caribbean. The Eco-Index is housed on the Rainforest Alliance web site for the use of tour operators and travellers, featuring a searchable database that includes a description of sustainable tourism businesses and their contact information. If a business is not certified, it may still participate in the Eco-Index if it can prove it has the backing of a relevant organization that verifies its social or environmental sustainability.

Future steps to consolidate the Network of the Americas

Research to address key common challenges

One of the objectives of the Sustainable Tourism Certification Network of the Americas is to develop common tools that members can use to strengthen their capacity to offer certification services, to move towards a common baseline standard and to address four key common concerns:

- Ensuring access to certification programmes and expertise by small and community-based tourism businesses.
- Investigating how best to market certification programmes to businesses and end-users.
- Developing methods for monitoring and evaluating the results of certification.
- Replicating successful models of the financial sustainability of certification programmes.

These challenges were identified during the consultation workshops held in the framework of the STSC feasibility study, and confirmation on the need to work jointly in these areas was reached at the first international meeting of the Network of the Americas in September 2003. Under the auspices of the MIF/IDB, the Ford Foundation and others, the Network of the Americas is working with TIES, which is undertaking research to help address these challenges. This research is needed to fortify the work being done at the national, regional and international levels. The results of these projects will address four of the main challenges formulated by Network members. The majority of the research will focus on Latin America, to coincide with the geographical concentration of the certification activities of the Network. In addition, existing certification programmes in other regions, Asia, Africa and Europe are being studied; governments, industry, NGOs and consumer groups consulted; new certification programmes monitored and assisted; and, gradually, other networks developed to parallel the ones in Europe and the Americas. By addressing these challenges, certification programmes can better contribute to the quality of sustainable tourism operations.

A principal vehicle for consultation, education and organization has been regional and international conferences, where TIES, with support from other organizations, has conducted workshops, consultations and surveys around these and other research topics. These projects will run over 4 years, beginning October 2003, and centre on facilitating SME access to certification programmes. While this research will be most immediately utilized in Latin America, all of these topics are central to the global advancement of tourism certification work. Four research projects are being conducted by TIES and other organizations in the next few years (TIES, 2003).

The first research project will focus on identifying strategies to engage SME- and community-based operations in certification. This project examines several certification programmes specially designed to target SMEs and determine the main technical and financial challenges that these operations face in fulfilling certification requirements. TIES is responsible for assembling already existing best practices, codes of conduct and other criteria designed to both protect the rights and respect the culture of indigenous and local communities involved in tourism, and it will develop a directory of organizations around the world that are involved in local/indigenous communities and tourism, as well as a bibliography of relevant literature. TIES is also examining the need for technical advice and financial assistance for small tourism businesses that are seeking certification, describing the most common technical and skill needs facing community tourism projects and discussing possible funding mechanisms.

For these purposes, TIES has used online discussion forums and obtained information from ongoing studies on community-based tourism operations. At least one workshop was held in 2005 in each of the target countries (Costa Rica, Belize, Guatemala, Ecuador and Brazil), tailored to indigenous and community-based operations, to finalize the assessment of the challenges of accessing certification processes.

With this information, TIES will develop and field-test, in coordination with its NGO partners and the members of the Sustainable Tourism Certification Network of the Americas, a set of sustainability criteria through consultations with indigenous organizations in Latin America and key countries in other regions. The main purpose of this research is to recommend to certification programmes strategies to foster SME participation in certification processes.

The second research project entails the development of market analysis and recommendations for the increasing demand for certified products from both industry and consumers. During 2004 and early 2005, TIES developed market analyses in target countries (Costa Rica, Belize, Guatemala, Ecuador and Brazil) to identify the most appropriate market opportunities for sustainable tourism and ecotourism. These studies examined the commercialization chain (local, regional and international) and tourists' preferences for environmentally and socially responsible businesses and certified tourism products. This effort was also aimed at identifying the most effective communication and marketing targets.

Simultaneously, TIES surveyed current marketing strategies and capacities of leading tourism certification programmes and the main vehicles (web sites, guidebooks, travel magazines and outbound tour operators, as well as university, museum and environmental NGO travel programmes) for promoting the use of certified operations. An examination of how other industries (wood, organic foods, coffee, etc.) have built consumer demand was also conducted.

To complement this research, TIES undertook a consultation with consumer demand experts and consumer advocacy organizations in the USA and Europe (as the major outbound markets for sustainable and ecotourism) as well as focus groups drawn from the tourism industry (particularly outbound operators) and tourism media (particularly magazines and guidebooks). TIES examined the range of benefits currently being offered to businesses, additional incentives desired by businesses and current industry support for certification, and developed a list of possible incentives that governments and certification programmes could offer to attract businesses to becoming certified. It also conducted one-on-one interviews with business leaders as well as several focus groups to discuss what businesses seek from certification and the range of alternatives that could be offered by government, trade associations, international organizations, the travel media and outbound operators.

TIES (2005) produced a report that documents the current consumer demand for ecolabels, the methodology and recommended techniques and incentives for creating demand within the industry for certification and the preparation of a draft strategy for building consumer demand for certified products within the tourism industry.

The third research project is aimed at developing monitoring and evaluation indicators and systems for certification programmes. One of the key challenges of current certification programmes is the quantification of the environmental, social and economic impacts of certification activities, which, in turn, increases the difficulty of communicating accomplishments and the benefits of getting certified, supporting certification or using certification as a tool for sustainable tourism development. The members of the Network of the Americas are aware of this challenge and, with support from TIES, are developing a framework that would include creating a set of goals, objectives and indicators that would measure the impacts of certification. Some examples will be drawn from the criteria outlined in the Mohonk Agreement for Sustainable and Ecotourism Certification Programs (Honey and Rome, 2000), and social, environmental and economic indicators are being included.

The development of a monitoring and evaluation (M&E) system and protocols to track results and train personnel involved in certification programmes in its use is greatly needed. Field-testing of this system took place in Guatemala, Costa Rica, Brazil, Belize and Ecuador in 2005. The objective is to examine if these initiatives are meeting the requirements for ensuring sustainability, i.e. protecting and providing tangible benefits for both the local environment and local communities around tourism businesses. The findings of this research, which include a guide and training modules for the use of the M&E system, became available in 2006.

The final research project will analyse the financial sustainability of certification programmes. During 2006, TIES developed a strategy for giving recommendations for certification programmes' sustainability and produced a report outlining a range of viable options that can be used to finance certification programmes. To undertake this activity, TIES will develop questionnaires for government officials, representatives of international agencies, certification experts and tourism businesses. It will analyse the financial structure of leading tourism certification programmes, how leading 'green' certification programmes within the tourism industry as well as other industries (wood, coffee, organic foods, etc.) are financed, how much they cost to create and run annually, what individual businesses pay to go through the certification process and what additional funding mechanisms are under discussion. With this information, it will be possible for certification programmes in the Americas, and hopefully in other parts of the world, to better develop a range of possibilities for future financial sustainability, define recommendations for the types of incentives that can be provided by governments and international organizations, and define mechanisms to raise funds from businesses being certified that take into account their financial size and capacity.

The preliminary results of these four research projects, which aim to address some of the common challenges outlined in this chapter, have been available online at TIES and the Rainforest Alliance's web sites since 2006.

Strengthening the Sustainable Tourism Certification Network of the Americas

Apart from finalizing the research projects outlined above, the Network of the Americas will continue to consolidate the Network by reaching out to other certification programmes in the region, by inviting other organizations not necessarily managing certification programmes to take part in Network activities, continue the development of technical assistance activities in pilot countries, participate in the international exchange of knowledge and experience via an international newsletter in partnership with Rainforest Alliance and ECOTRANS and finally seek resources to begin cross-regional exchanges with VISIT, a sister regional network in Europe, which will be discussed in the following section of this chapter. Modest outreach will be undertaken in Africa and Asia Pacific, where other groups are already actively engaged in certification efforts, such as the Ecotourism Association of Kenya, the Australian EcoCertification programme (formerly known as NEAP), Thai GreenLeaf Program and others.

The VISIT Network in Europe

In contrast to Latin America, sustainable tourism certification in Europe has focused more on the use of natural resources and pollution-related matters and has more 'green' tourism certification programmes than any other region of the world. Tourism ecolabelling started in Europe in the 1980s (Hamele, 1996). In 2005, there were more than 50 environmental certificates and awards in Europe, covering all types of tourism suppliers, including accommodation, beaches, marinas, protected areas, restaurants, handicrafts, golf courses, tour packages and various other tourism-related activities. More than 30 schemes certify accommodation services: hotels with or without restaurants, camping sites, youth hostels, farmhouses, alpine huts, holiday houses, guest houses and bed and breakfast lodgings (http://destinet.ewindows.eu.org/instruments/voluntaryinstruments/voluntary certification).

VISIT was established as a regional network of ecolabelling programmes and complementary initiatives to address the challenges of the lack of coordination among these programmes. In 2004, in accordance with the recommendations of the STSC feasibility study, VISIT members formally launched their Association, the first of its kind in the world. The establishment of VISIT represented the culmination of ongoing liaison and cooperation among more than a dozen leading tourism ecolabels. Seven of these labels founded VISIT, together with ECEAT projects and ECOTRANS as initiators and ECOCAMPING as the leading environmental management certificate for camping sites in Europe. The seven ecolabels are based in The Netherlands, Italy, Denmark, Latvia, the UK, Switzerland and Luxembourg and represent over 1500 participating tourism enterprises. They include (as of January 2006): Legambiente Turismo (Italy); the Milieubarometer (The Netherlands); Ecolabel Luxembourg (Luxembourg); Green Tourism Business Scheme (UK); Steinbock Label (Switzerland); Green Certificate (Latvia); and the Green Key (international). The primary goal of VISIT is to ensure that ecolabelling in tourism is successful, practical and responsible.

Membership of VISIT is either as a full member or as an associate. Full membership with right of vote is open to type I tourism ecolabels (third-party certification) that already have certified products. Associate membership is open to certificates under development and other voluntary initiatives for sustainable tourism. Full members with certificates from the Association are required to comply with the VISIT Standard and to be prepared to recognize other full members as legitimate ecolabels, cooperate with them and work towards common objectives.

VISIT accomplishments

The VISIT Association has established itself as the European platform for tourism ecolabels, is widely accepted and collaborates with other initiatives and networks. Currently a dozen ecolabels participate. The organization has developed and tested a European set of sustainable development indicators and is assessing the global situation of ecolabelling in tourism by using the 50+ existing certificates to analyse differences, strengths and needs. Twenty-one key requirements were assessed by VISIT-certified programmes and interested ecolabels, leading to an agreement on a set of common standards for type I tourism ecolabels, derived from the international ISO 14020 standards with which 12 programmes complied (the 'VISIT ecolabels'). The VISIT brand and slogan ('Caring for the environment – is caring for the visitor') was developed and combined with a comprehensive international promotional campaign complementing the ecolabels' individual activities.

A number of online resources were launched, including the free VISIT Holiday Guide online, www.yourvisit.info, promoting more than 1500 certified tourism businesses plus 2700 beaches and marinas; www.eco-tip.org, with information on the 50+ environmental certificates for European tourism and examples of best practices; and Green Travel Market online (www.greentravelmarket.info), educating over 1000 tour operators and assessing 180 exemplary tour packages. Since 2006, these and other information services have been available on the DestiNet portal for quality-assessed sustainable tourism information, hosted by the European Environment Agency (http://destinet.ewindows.eu.org).

VISIT has received recognition in Europe as a key initiative, has been invited to give presentations at more than 30 national and international conferences, tourism fairs and workshops of main stakeholders' associations, and has reached more than 4 million consumers and professionals with over 100 dissemination activities in collaboration with print and Internet media. It has actively publicized the benefits of certification, such as reduced consumption (energy, water, chemicals) and waste, and will continue to identify a list of further requirements and proposals to make ecolabelling tourism a success (see: www.ecotrans.org/nav_frame_en.htm, VISIT project).

The VISIT standard

The alliance between the ecolabels within VISIT is based on mutual understanding and recognition and agreement to adopt a common standard: the VISIT standard for tourism ecolabels in Europe.

VISIT aims to promote those ecolabels, which guarantee a high level of environmental quality of their products in their respective countries. Therefore, a common standard for tourism ecolabels in Europe is required to recognize those ecolabels that are highly demanding and reliable. According to International Standards Organization (ISO) terminology, this means fulfilling the requirements for so-called 'type I' third-party-verified certificates. This ensures that ecolabelled products do not mislead consumers or make erroneous claims regarding their environmental quality.

In 2001/02 a partnership with ten regional, national and international ecolabelling schemes was established within the VISIT project. Together with ECOTRANS, as independent coordinator, these labels based their work on the internationally recognized ISO 14024 standard for type I ecolabels. Step by step, all ISO requirements were discussed and adapted to the needs of tourism services in Europe. The knowledge and experience of the different circumstances in the countries involved and the daily work experience of the experts resulted in the VISIT standard for tourism ecolabels in Europe.

By the end of 2002, the participating ecolabelling organizations recognized this standard for their own schemes. The core baseline consists of 21 key requirements. The recognition of the VISIT standard and compliance with its requirements were accepted as a precondition for any later promotion as 'VISIT ecolabels'.

To assess compliance with the VISIT standard, the following documents from each ecolabel were provided for and checked by ECOTRANS in 2002 and 2003:

- A signed declaration on compliance with each of the 21 requirements, together with a list of documents to show evidence.
- A complete list of environmental performance and management criteria for each label.
- A detailed description of the application, verification and certification procedure.
- A full, up-to-date list of certified tourism products in Europe.
- Additional printed material and information on the ecolabels' web sites.

The following seven questions allow a quick check to determine if a tourism ecolabel is likely to comply with the VISIT standard:

1. Does the ecolabel aim to contribute to sustainability and service quality?
2. Do the criteria include performance and limit consumption requirements in most relevant environmental fields and along the 'life cycle' (purchase – service – waste)?
3. Do the criteria go beyond legislation?
4. Must the labelled businesses monitor their consumption of energy and water and production of waste?
5. Does the verification procedure include independent on-site audits?
6. Is the period to use the label limited to 3 years?
7. Are the criteria and the list of certified tourism services available to the public?

The common standard VISIT members are required to meet is summarized in Box 23.1. In addition to their compliance with the VISIT standard, participating certification programmes have individual special strengths: each has unique criteria with a different focus related to regional legislation, climate issues, environmental problems or the level of technical and management standards their products have achieved. Such individual strengths are justification for their long-term existence, besides international certificates. They have flexibility, can consider the national technical standard and legislation

Box 23.1. The VISIT common standard.

A VISIT ecolabel for tourism services:

1. Aims to contribute to sustainable tourism development in Europe and as far as possible verify those products with advanced performance in terms of environmental qualities.
2. Aims to contribute to maintaining and enhancing service quality in tourism in Europe.
3. Recognizes other ecolabels meeting the VISIT standard.
4. Has considered product life-cycle issues when setting product environmental criteria.
5. Requires attainable levels and gives consideration to relative environmental impacts ('per unit'), measurement capability and accuracy.
6. Is based on sound scientific, engineering, management and social principles. The criteria are derived from data that support the claim of environmental preferability (high environmental benefit and/or efficiency).
7. Takes into account during the process of establishing the criteria relevant local, regional and global environmental issues, available technology and economic and social issues, avoiding compromising service quality.
8. Reviews the criteria and product functional requirements within a predefined period.
9. Declares that compliance with environmental and other relevant legislation is a precondition for the applicant to be awarded and to maintain the label.
10. Selects product environmental criteria that are expressed in terms of impacts on the environment and natural resources or emissions to the environment. Such performance criteria shall be expressed in absolute (numbers) or relative (%) figures and measure units (e.g. kWh, litre, volume, weight per product, room, bed, overnight stay, m^2) and may also recommend the exclusion/non-use of special materials or substances.
11. Requires criteria in the following environmental fields as far as relevant in its area of operation and as far as relevant for the specific product group: purchasing, transport and mobility, energy, water, waste, chemical substances, air, noise, nature/landscape.
12. Requires that accommodation has the following management criteria that complement other environmental management systems: environmental commitment, environmental coordinator, communication with and training of guests, staff and public; monitoring regularly energy, water and waste consumption/overnight.
13. Is able to demonstrate transparency through the following stages of its development and operation: product categories, product environmental criteria, period of validity of criteria, testing and verification methods, certification and award procedures, compliance verification procedure and complaints procedure.
14. Legally protects the ecolabel (i.e. the certification mark/logotype) in order to prevent unauthorized use and to maintain public confidence in the programme.
15. Is voluntary in nature.

(*continued*)

Box 23.1. (Continued).

16. Is open to all potential applicants of the predefined product group in the area of operation. All applicants who fulfil the product environmental criteria and the other programme requirements are entitled to be granted a licence and authorized to use the label.
17. Guarantees that all the elements in the product environmental criteria and product function characteristics are verifiable by the ecolabelling body.
18. Has a verification procedure that guarantees a high level of reliability. This includes on-site visits at least every 3 years (accommodation: once per certification period).
19. Has general rules guiding the overall operation of the programme. These general rules control the general conditions for the awarding of the licence and the use of the label.
20. Issues awards on business performance against criteria that apply to the site for a predefined period of not more than 3 years.
21. Maintains a publicly available list of products that have been awarded the label.

when updating their criteria and can develop their schemes for new product groups along the tourism supply chain.

The VISIT network has allowed members to demonstrate best practice in the various countries and product groups, raise consumer awareness of and increase demand for ecolabelled and environmentally friendly products, provide orientation for governments on difficulties with legislation and on opportunities or needs to improve laws, green the tourism supply chain and make connections with green activities in destinations.

TourBench – a tool to measure the impacts of ecolabels in a tourism business

All certificates for environmental quality need to demonstrate their effectiveness. For example, the VISIT standard requires ecolabels for accommodation to 'monitor regularly energy, water, waste consumption/overnight' (overnight stay) (VISIT requirement no. 12). With this in mind, the VISIT partners and participating ecolabels tested the monitoring of environmental consumption data.

As a result, a new initiative was launched to develop TourBench, an online benchmarking system for the measurement of environmental consumption. Since 2005, TourBench has been ready to use in nine languages. Non-certified accommodation businesses can check whether their activity is sufficient to obtain a relevant ecolabel. When a basic set of data is put into the system, it shows the user (e.g. any accommodation business) its own energy and water consumption, use of chemicals and production of waste and compares it with other businesses. A list of recommendations generated by the system, including return on investment calculations, helps businesses to make the right decisions; a list of available certificates with direct links invites them to prepare and apply for an ecolabel, preferably one that fulfils the VISIT standard. By checking their environmental consumption, existing certified accommodation businesses can fulfil one of the most important requirements of the certification system. Registration and use of the web site is free of charge (www.tourbench.info). Those ecolabels that recommend TourBench to their certified members receive the benchmarks and average consumption of their businesses and can compare the results with other ecolabels or with non-certified businesses in the same country.

VISIT Holiday Guide: the European guide with a plus in environmental quality

To move the market towards sustainability, consumers need easy access to ecolabel products and services. As part of the VISIT initiative, two database-powered web sites have been established to offer consumers and tour operators full and free access to all accommodation and other tourism services certified by the VISIT ecolabels: the VISIT Holiday Guide and the Green Travel Market.

The VISIT Holiday Guide, launched in 2003 under the motto 'Your visit makes the difference', is available online in English, German and Dutch and provides a detailed and structured description of more than 1000 hotels, bed and breakfasts, guest houses, youth hostels, campsites and restaurants, combined with attractive pictures. This Guide allows consumers to find appropriate environmentally friendly accommodation by clicking on holiday destinations on the map of Europe: www.yourvisit.info/visit holiday guide/search accommodation

The VISIT ecolabels in Austria, France, Scotland, Denmark, Sweden, The Netherlands, Switzerland, Luxembourg, Italy, Catalunya and Latvia guarantee that their awarded businesses conform to high standards in all important environmental aspects, and these are checked on site by independent auditors. In addition, the VISIT Holiday Guide promotes more than 2000 beaches and 700 marinas certified by Blue Flag International (www. yourvisit.info/visit holiday guide/search beaches and marinas).

Green Travel Market: promoting certified tourism products to tour operators

The Green Travel Market (available at www.greentravelmarket.info) is an online business-to-business service for tour operators, journalists and other professionals. It gives up-to-date and reliable information on existing ecolabelled and Fair Trade tourism products around the world. All sustainable products presented on this virtual marketplace have been screened for quality and sustainability aspects. Different types of sustainable tourism products along the tourism supply chain participate in the Green Travel Market: destinations, protected areas, accommodation networks, individual accommodation, community-based tourism networks, visitor attractions and activities, excursions and tours, incoming tour operators and transport services. The Green Travel Market offers a wide array of services to help tour operators to integrate sustainable products into their packages. A team of professional matchmakers from different countries is currently assisting interested tour operators in finding reliable partners and creating highly sustainable and exciting tour packages. Registration is free and provides access to a growing database with attractive sustainable tourism products from all over the world.

The certified VISIT products will be further promoted among European and US-based tour operators as part of a new project, Travelife (travelife.eu), which promotes a sustainable tour operator supply chain. In this project, with financial support from the European Union (EU) LIFE programme, tour operators and European certification schemes work together to:

- Promote the development of European-wide standards for tour operator sustainable supply-chain management methodologies.
- Introduce a standard among all members of the Dutch ANVR tour operator association and the UK Federation of Tour Operators (FTO), and European dissemination and implementation among other interested tour operator associations, such as the German Forum Anders Reisen, the Belgium ABTO and the Italian ASTOI tour operator associations.
- Develop an international online tour operator training and action planning system, supporting key personnel, to introduce the supply-chain management systems and create awareness of sustainable tourism and the benefits of sustainable tourism certification programmes.
- Harmonize checklists and codes of conduct used by tour operators to assess their suppliers (e.g. hotels, guides) on sustainability issues and sector-wide implementation through an online suppliers assessment system.
- Create strategic partnerships between groups of tour operators and certification schemes in order to increase the number of certified hotels in pilot destinations: Catalunya, Austria and Costa Rica.
- Create a global overview of certified products and inform European and North American tour operators about them by directly and actively approaching 1000 tour operators.

Strengthening the VISIT Association

From 2006, VISIT intends to recruit more tourism certification schemes, consolidate their network and establish various activities and services. These may include: connecting the participating ecolabels through a web site, undertaking market research and message development, developing promotional campaigns with national and international tour operators, piloting a verification system, developing technical tools such as a performance evaluation (e.g. TourBench monitoring and benchmarking tool) and maintaining and enhancing the partnerships among ecolabelling activities based on cooperation and collaboration within the VISIT Association and with other international initiatives, such as the EU Flower and the STSC initiative.

Potential for harmonization: VISIT ecolabels and EU Flower

Parallel to the development of the VISIT initiative, the European Commission developed the European Ecolabel for Tourism, which was created to reward tourist accommodation services and tourists that respect the environment. In 2004, the European Commission also established criteria for campsite services and, since 2005, these services can apply for the European Ecolabel. This ecolabel identifies good environmental performance as an added quality value when consumers are choosing a resort. Businesses displaying the EU Flower logo have officially been recognized as environmentally friendly (http://www.ecolabel_tourism.com).

Any hotel or camping site in Europe can now apply for this official European-wide-acknowledged certificate. To avoid consumer confusion, the EU Flower and the national ecolabels need to harmonize their messages to the consumer. For example, the EU Flower represents the European standard and national ecolabels represent the national standards that exceed the European standard. In the case of the Austrian ecolabel, the criteria were revised for accommodation businesses. The next step is for VISIT to harmonize the criteria and verification procedures of the two schemes. In terms of the criteria, there is already a significant overlap between the leading national ecolabels in Europe and the EU Flower scheme. Nine out of 11 VISIT ecolabels plus the EU Flower for accommodation already require the same or similar criteria for 23 different environmental issues. This overlap of criteria allows the VISIT ecolabels and the EU Flower to work together on joint targets for the next revision of their criteria, with the aim of having, for example, in 2007 a set of 20 mandatory criteria for more than 1000 certified hotels and campsites in Europe. This common environmental quality level could then be communicated as added value by the tour operators and international information services.

The existing verification procedure for the VISIT standard requires an on-site visit at least every 3 years; however, the degree of detail differs from scheme to scheme. The EU Flower scheme has not yet made an on-site visit obligatory, but recommends on-site audits by the national accreditation bodies responsible for verification. Until the end of 2005, all certified accommodation businesses in 11 countries received an on-site audit and some were certified with both the EU Flower and the national ecolabel scheme, e.g. Austria and Switzerland. Their experiences will provide some important lessons for the further development of a European baseline standard.

It is anticipated that agreement on a common baseline standard may serve as a way of limiting the scope of audits to the most important and generic criteria and help reduce costs associated with auditing. There is potential at the national level for the organizations responsible for the EU Flower scheme to collaborate with the VISIT ecolabels so that there is only one site audit for both schemes. For applicants, this would mean reduced costs and time and a two-for-one deal. Currently, each ecolabel has its own promotional and marketing approach; however, if a set of common criteria for accommodation services is developed, opportunities exist for joint promotion between the VISIT and EU Flower schemes, which will be mutually beneficial.

Initial Networking Efforts in Asia–Pacific

While the development of regional networks is well progressed in the Americas and Europe, fledgling networks are emerging in the Asia–Pacific region. The Asia–Pacific region has a few well-developed certification programmes, for example, the EcoCertification programme (previously known as NEAP) in Australia (see Chapter 22), which is a sustainable nature and ecotourism-specific certification programme for the accommodation, tour and attraction sectors, and the Green Leaf Program in Thailand, which is a sustainable tourism certification programme for the accommodation sector. Green Globe, now based in Australia, has a small but growing influence in the region. With significant promotion, there is growing support for its range of schemes, including the Green Globe Company Standard and the Green Globe International Ecotourism Standard. The former scheme is a global standard for all sectors of the sustainable tourism industry and has government support in New Zealand, Bali, China, Fiji and Australia; has certified businesses in Australia, Fiji, India, Indonesia, Maldives, Sri Lanka and Vietnam; and has companies going through the certification process in Laos, Thailand and East Timor. The latter scheme is a global standard specifically for the ecotourism industry in the product sectors of accommodation, tours and attractions. This standard is derived from a marriage of the NEAP programme with the GG Company Standard and is licensed to Green Globe for distribution everywhere except Australia (see Chapter 6). Tour operations are currently going through the certification process in China, Fiji and New Zealand, with the only two GG International Ecotourism Standard training courses to date having been run in China and Australia.

Currently, there are many isolated and fragmented attempts to develop more sustainable forms of tourism that provide genuine returns for local communities, help alleviate poverty and provide for the conservation of wildlife, ecosystems and cultural heritage. These programmes are often supported by conservation NGOs, such as SNV, WWF, Conservation International and Flora Fauna International, which have been most active in the Asia–Pacific region. However, there is also growing regional interest in developing sustainable tourism. Local governments are keen to maximize the potential of tourism as means of generating revenue (ecotourism especially is perceived as a high-end niche market), as well as implementing more sustainable practices. Sustainable tourism or ecotourism certification programmes are presently being discussed or in the process of development in Vietnam, Bhutan, Nepal, Philippines, India, Vanuatu, Malaysia, regional areas of China and New Zealand and possibly other countries.

To help provide support for ecotourism development and networking between these relatively isolated initiatives, the International Ecotourism Society (TIES) has appointed a regional director in Australia with principal funding by the Ford Foundation and additional support provided by an Asia–Pacific desk in Washington, DC, funded by the Freeman Foundation, to help coordinate communication between these programmes. A bimonthly newsletter (currently available only in English) has been launched that provides a communication network between these largely isolated and fragmented efforts. This network not only is designed to support sustainable and ecotourism initiatives and encourage more sustainable development, but is also expected to eventually evolve into a more formal regional certification network that will parallel the VISIT Initiative in Europe or the Network of the Americas.

Conclusions: the Future for Regional Networks for Sustainable Tourism

The findings of recent research conducted by organizations such as the WTO, Rainforest Alliance, ECOTRANS, TIES and others have identified some current and future trends in sustainable tourism and certification and the need to consolidate regional networks of certification programmes. Many countries value the potential of sustainable tourism and regard certification as one valuable tool in defining, conserving and promoting sustainable tourism as an asset and an industry. Today, many sustainable tourism projects in Central America include certification or verification in their design. For instance, the recently approved USAID-funded initiatives in Guatemala, Nicaragua and Honduras and the Protected Areas and Environmentally Sound Products component of the Central American Environmental Regional Project (PROARCA) have included a component on sustainable tourism certification as one of the competitiveness tools to be implemented in the process of developing sustainable tourism operations in Central America.

While many different national and regional certification standards and programmes have developed over the years, interest exists in collaborating and communicating on ways to address the challenges facing sustainable tourism and certification. Much of this communication and collaboration is happening at a regional level, as evidenced through the networks launched in Europe (VISIT) and in the Americas, which in turn can help foster more changes on the ground towards sustainability. The potential and benefits of regional networks were well summed up by Brian Mullis (Colorado, electronic communication, 2004) who stated:

> Sustainability, like beauty, may always be in the eye of the beholder no matter how many tools we provide. Regardless, there is no question that the

> Sustainable Tourism Certification Network of the Americas and other networks will be instrumental in helping the travel and tourism industry to maintain cultural integrity, essential ecological processes, biological diversity and life support systems throughout the Americas and beyond.

Participation in these networks has already resulted in benefits in terms of positioning and national recognition, particularly for smaller certification programmes. For example, the establishment of the Network of the Americas has provided important support for the Guatemalan Green Deal programme; according to Saul Blanco (S. Blanco, Guatemala, electronic communication, 2004), 'the support and perception from private and public entities has positively changed since we became network members and this will ease our chase for a more responsible tourism industry'.

The same benefits of networks have also been identified by the larger consolidated programmes and their representatives. According to Deirdre Shurland (D. Shurland, Puerto Rico, electronic communication, 2004) of the Caribbean Alliance for Sustainable Tourism (CAST) programme:

> CAST regards the Sustainable Tourism Certification Network of the Americas as an important network for facilitating exchanges of information between Network members on their sustainable tourism certification programmes . . . The Network's resources are being used for efficient transfer of information and for strengthening of the various participating programmes, which would otherwise be a very costly effort for CAST.

Other benefits she mentioned included the ability of the network to raise the profile and importance of tourism certification as a method for improving standards of performance among travel and tourism businesses, especially destination quality and authenticity and the health and safety of visitors.

Nevertheless, there is a recognition that, for the small and medium-size enterprises (SMEs) to participate in certification and in the industry at a regional and international level, there is a need for in-country technical assistance to be developed and offered. Good case studies are provided by the detailed process of how certification is encouraged through VISIT and the Network of the Americas' work and research, demonstrating that, even if the final outcome is not to certify all products, training and technical assistance efforts provided for SMEs in the implementation of good practices are occurring, and these are helping to improve the quality of sustainable tourism operations. The impact that certification programmes are having cannot be measured only by the number of certified businesses, but rather by the number of businesses, associations, NGOs and governments using certification standards as a capacity-building tool that affects real sustainable actions.

For consumers to have any confidence in sustainable tourism certification, an internationally recognized accreditation system that can accommodate regional differences needs to be in place. The regional networks are taking the first steps in trying to create standards harmonization, which could then lead to developing an accreditation system. VISIT and the Network of the Americas represent a potential vehicle for tourism certification programmes to build trust and to take ownership of the systems proposed in the STSC feasibility study. This will allow for building consensus around the components that must be part of all certification programmes, such as developing, promoting and implementing best management practices, sharing information, building demand for an accreditation body and encouraging certification programmes to take a more active role in supporting a future STSC. These initiatives have focused more on being catalysts and facilitators rather than attempting to establish a centralized, comprehensive, full-service accreditation outlet from day one.

With appropriate collaboration and communication, the regional networks can develop a joint communication and marketing strategy, which will raise the effectiveness of marketing and promotion to consumers and will minimize costs.

These networking efforts address the need to create communication mechanisms among programmes. The support of private foundations and multilateral funding agencies is vital for providing the technical assistance needed to support successful uptake of best practices and voluntary programmes such as certification and others. An example is provided by the work now being carried out in several Latin American countries, which will supply important information from pilot operations, together with the research being done by TIES.

Regional networks in the Americas, Europe, Asia–Pacific, Africa and other regions can benefit from collaboration and discussions with each other. It is only with this joint cooperation that a global forum and accreditation body for sustainable tourism certification can succeed.

Notes

[1] For complete minutes from the 2003 Regional Conference of the Americas on Sustainability Certification of Tourism Activities, visit WTO's web site (www.world-tourism.org/sustainable/conf/cert-brasil/esp.htm).

[2] Initial funding was provided by a USAID-funded PROARCA initiative in Central America for the development of training tools and the testing of training modules. This work was later completed with the support from MIF/IDB. Additional resources are being provided by the executing organizations, the Ford Foundation, the Dutch Royal Tropical Institute (KIT) and Fundecooperación for work in Costa Rica, the Tinker Foundation for work in Guatemala and the Overbrook Foundation for work in Ecuador.

References

ECOTRANS/ECEAT projects (2004) The VISIT Initiative: tourism eco-labelling in Europe – moving the market toward sustainability. Available at: www.ecotrans.org/nav_frame_en.htm (VISIT project).

ECOTRANS: ECO-TIP Information service online: eco-labels worldwide. Available at: http://www.eco-tip.org

Hamele, H. (1996) *The Book of Environmental Seals and Eco-labels, an International Overview of Current Developments.* A study commissioned by the Federal Ministry for the Environment, Berlin.

Honey, M. and Rome, A. (2000) *Mohonk Agreement.* Institute for Policy Studies, Washington, DC. Available at: http://www.ips-dc.org

Rainforest Alliance (2001) *A Proposal from the Rainforest Alliance as Coordinator of the Feasibility Study, Organizational Blueprint and Implementation Plan for a Global Sustainable Tourism Stewardship Council (STSC): An Accreditation Body for Sustainable Tourism Certifiers.* Rainforest Alliance, New York.

Rainforest Alliance (2003) *Sustainable Tourism Stewardship Council: Raising the Standards and Benefits of Sustainable Tourism and Ecotourism Certification.* Rainforest Alliance, New York.

Rainforest Alliance and Turismo & Conservación Consultores (2002) *Diagnósticos de Sitio para el Golfo de Honduras, Golfo de Fonseca, La Mosquitia Nicaragüense, la Mosquitia Hondureña y Cahuita-Bocas del Toro.* Rainforest Alliance, San Jose.

Sanabria, R. (1999) *Exploring Ecotourism Certification: Creating a Conceptual Framework for the Rainforest Alliance, Summary, Final Report.* JP Morgan Internship, Rainforest Alliance, New York.

TIES (2003) *Summary of Certification Research Projects.* TIES, Washington, DC.

TIES (2005) *Consumer Demand and Operator Support for Socially and Environmentally Responsible Tourism.* TIES, Washington, DC.

TIES, IPS, UNEP and Rainforest Alliance (2002) *Partnership for Effective Implementation of Tools for Monitoring Ecotourism and Sustainable Tourism: A Concept Paper.* TIES, Washington, DC.

TIES, IPS, UNEP, Rainforest Alliance and WTO (2003) Press release: partnership for effective implementation of tools for monitoring ecotourism and sustainable tourism. Rainforest Alliance, New York, p. 1.

Turismo & Conservación Consultores (2003) *Primera Reunión de la Red de Certificación de Turismo Sostenible delas Américas.* Memoria, Turismo & Conservación Consultores, San Jose.

United Nations Environment Program (UNEP) *Eco-labels in the Tourism Industry.* Industry and Environment Technical Report No. 29, Industry and Environment, UNEP, Paris.

World Tourism Organization (2001) *Voluntary Initiatives for Sustainable Tourism, Worldwide Inventory and Comparative Analysis of 104 Eco-labels, Awards and Self-Commitments.* WTO, Madrid.

World Tourism Organization *et al.* (2003) *Regional Conference of the Americas on Sustainability Certification of Tourism Activities. Proceedings.* WTO, Madrid.

24 Conclusion: Challenges and Issues for Quality in Ecotourism

ALICE CRABTREE[1] AND ROSEMARY BLACK[2]

[1]*Ecotourism Consultant, Cairns, Queensland, Australia;* [2]*Charles Sturt University, Albury, NSW, Australia*

This volume presents some of the issues, challenges and initiatives that can help improve our understanding of quality in ecotourism. We hope that by looking at the spectrum of quality assurance mechanisms currently available, and presenting the perspectives and viewpoints of a range of stakeholders and the lessons learnt from other related areas of the tourism industry (e.g. Fair Trade), we have provided clues and pointers on how to convert the potential and promises ecotourism makes into reality. We feel that this volume presents a collection of previously unheard voices and interesting perspectives on quality in ecotourism that will allow a greater understanding of what is required, but also an appreciation of the challenges of delivering quality ecotourism.

Gaining a Consensus on the Principles of Ecotourism

One of the issues that (re-)emerges with regularity in ecotourism is the problems associated with the lack of a definitive and universally accepted 'statement' on ecotourism (see Chapter 1 in this volume). This issue appears to provide not only the genuinely ignorant, but also the genuinely mindful but deceitful, with an excuse or a pretext for either distorting ecotourism with greenwash and a thin veneer of environmental and sociocultural practices (lite practices) or dismissing ecotourism as nothing more than a mythical beast. This is compounded by the mindful (but disillusioned) – who, rather than supporting the term ecotourism and the general consensus on ecotourism's key principles, abandon it to its fate and instead invent new terms (Fennell, 2001). This situation is also compounded by the mindful but selfish – who think that repackaging ecotourism with subtle variations or points of differences and calling it something new will gain them credence, new followers and a greater market share. Green tourism, endemic tourism, ethical tourism, responsible tourism, geotourism, hybrids of ACE (adventure, cultural and ecotourism) and NEAT (nature, ecotourism and adventure tourism), variations go on, and ecotourism gets hurt (Buckley, 2000). The only winners are the greenwashers and the cynics. This is not a startling new discovery, but it does have important implications for trying to get a handle on quality in ecotourism.

The startling differences that exist in ecotourism definitions and the lack of clear dividing lines between ecotourism and other forms of nature-based tourism are used as an excuse for the lack of consistency in ecotourism product. While understanding that there are still debate and surprisingly fierce arguments over the exact wording or semantics of the definition of ecotourism, this hiatus is not necessary. There is clear consensus on the key principles and the tenets and philosophy of ecotourism – a natural area focus, ecological sustainability, provision of interpretation or education, returns to the local environment (conservation) and community and cultural sensitivity (see Chapter 1). The intent of ecotourism is clear – to minimize the negative effects of tourism whilst maximizing the positive impacts so that there is a net positive benefit to the physical and social environments. It is the embodiment of a triple bottom line – a win for the environment, a win for the community and a win for economic returns.

Notwithstanding the clear consensus on the key principles of ecotourism, the way in which the intent of ecotourism is operationalized varies. This is inevitable, given the spectrum of sectors inherent in all tourism product (e.g. accommodation (see Mehta, Chapter 21 in this volume), touring, attractions, transport, etc.), the location (national and regional variations in technology, resources, environmental capacity, legislative framework) and stakeholders involved (all with distinct interests, motivations and needs). It is not surprising, therefore, that the actual emphasis or the particular mix of key ecotourism principles that go to make up an ecotourism product can differ. This leads to the argument that, rather than trying to clarify and identify, with precision, the individual elements that make up quality ecotourism, we look instead at the outcomes. If quality ecotourism is simply that there is a net positive benefit to the environment (encompassing here the human social dimension as well as the natural environment), the exact way in which this is achieved can, and probably should, vary in response to local circumstances and environments. This suggests that legitimate expressions of ecotourism might then appear fundamentally different.

Conundrums: Hard versus Soft Ecotourism

This logic, however, leads to another conundrum – for, if defining quality ecotourism relies on the outputs in terms of a measurable increase in sustainability performance, the paradox arises whereby a product at the hard end of the ecotourism spectrum (Orams, 2001; see also Chapter 1 in this volume) should be deemed of lesser quality than a product at the soft end of ecotourism. This apparent contradiction occurs because hard ecotourism product tends to 'preach to the converted' (Beaumont, 1999) and effects small, if any, changes in visitors' environmental ethics. Hard ecotourism involves direct, personal experiences (and hence small groups), gravitates towards physical challenge and favours remote and exotic 'untouched' locations. This form of ecotourism means that the participants are restricted to the fit and the wealthy, with little ability to effect significant change for better sustainability, simply because the numbers involved are so small.

In fact, hard ecotourism has been accused of having a tendency to actually pose a significant, if unintentional, threat to the most precious of environments. Hard ecotourism has a propensity towards remote, true wilderness and areas of high conservation significance, as well as authentic, rather than staged or mediated, contact with, for example, indigenous cultures. Once the economic juggernaut that tourism spawns starts rolling, it is very hard to control – and ecotourism may pave or open the way for mainstream tourism, with little emphasis on sustainability and little regard for conservation, to follow. The good intentions of ecotourism may be crushed under the wheels of copycat enterprises without the same ethics or principles.

Soft ecotourism, in contrast, may actually have greater success in effecting measurable and significant increases in environmental sustainability, because small shifts in tourist behaviour or consumption in a large number of participants add up to a significant shift overall. This, combined with the fact that soft ecotourism usually takes place in less pristine, less fragile or sensitive natural and cultural environments, means that there is often actually less potential for significant damage. The fact that soft ecotourism is often part of a multidimensional trip, of short duration, mediated by guides or intermediaries, less physically challenging (not an immersion experience) and often includes larger groups, with staged rather than truly authentic experiences, does minimize the potential for significant damage. This paradox creates the absurdity that a product that does not necessary represent the very best in terms of a quality ecotourism experience could be considered better-quality ecotourism. Unfortunately, soft ecotourism often becomes so contrived that it metamorphoses into the mainstream, with little emphasis on ecotourism principles – losing the sense of place or empathy with the environment, regard for conservation and returns to the community.

In looking at quality in ecotourism, how do we come to terms with the fact that high-quality ecotourism experiences may be elitist and probably ineffectual in generating significant increases in sustainability, whereas soft ecotourism may be so superficial that, to all intents and purposes, its ability to generate passion or drive a significant sustainability change is stifled? Unfortunately, this is not the only challenge or issue that exploring quality in ecotourism presented us with.

Measuring Quality in Ecotourism: Some Challenges

In trying to evaluate and measure quality ecotourism, one of the first tasks in developing this volume was to break down various descriptions and definitions of ecotourism into key principles. Throughout this volume we have looked at some of the individual principles and components of ecotourism in greater depth by presenting case studies that illustrate how these factors were incorporated into various programmes or initiatives. However, although close examination of the principles as stand-alone components (see Chapter 1 in this volume) has merits in exploring the ingredients, it soon becomes apparent that quality ecotourism does not rely on assembling the 'best' of each, but on a special mix of ingredients that best expresses the overall intent of ecotourism (win–win–win) in that particular environment.

Despite this dictum, there are many that insist on focusing on one of the ingredients of ecotourism, often to the exclusion of others. The quintessential example of this is the general focus on ecotourism interpreted as 'tourism in a green place'; that is, tourism is defined by its location rather than its principles or management practices. As is argued in Chapter 1, and eloquently examined by Weaver (2001a), whilst ecotourism should be regarded as a subset of nature tourism, not all nature tourism is ecotourism. Those who insist on confusing and interchanging ecotourism (or insist on hybridization) with adventure tourism (e.g. skiing, snowboarding, all-terrain vehicles, horse riding, mountain biking, rafting, etc.) because it also predominantly uses natural settings are wrong, even though considerable overlap between these sectors does exist (Kutay, 1990; Buckley, 2006). Adventure tourism takes place *in* natural settings but is distinguished from ecotourism by the focus on providing (perceived) risk and physical challenges and utilizing specialized equipment and skills, rather than epitomizing environmental sustainability and providing tangible returns for both conservation and local communities.

Perhaps more understandable is the confusion with wildlife tourism, also nature-based, albeit with generally passive (and probably less destructive) access mechanisms and oft-included interpretive opportunities. However, wildlife tourism's main focus is *about* nature. Ecotourism's firm focus is *for* nature, and quality ecotourism has to address this – whether it is in a high-quality natural environment such as a World Heritage Site or a degraded site that is being rehabilitated. The for-nature component does not equate to ecotourism alone unless a mix of the other ingredients (key principles) is added in. So, although it can be seen that deconstructing ecotourism leads to some interesting diversions, it does little to help ease the identification of quality ecotourism.

Equally problematic is the fact that some of the principles of ecotourism are difficult to measure, evaluate or even consistently deliver. How do you capture the 'wow' factor of fabulous interpretation, or the serendipity of the right mix of clients, nature performing and a picture-postcard-perfect day that leads to tourists leaving with a firm sense of place and empathy for the environment? Can we really attribute (let alone measure) a significant change of behaviour and pro-environmental attitudes solely to an ecotourism experience (Ham and Weiler, 2001)? Heritage interpreters are often passionate about their subject, and there is no doubt intuitively that conservation ideals are likely to be generated through inspiring interpretive experiences. However, to date it has proved difficult to assess long-term behavioural and attitudinal changes as a result of an ecotourism experience (Haig, 1997;

Beaumont, 1999). Given that any ecotourism product should include interpretation or education, presumably quality ecotourism should excel in this area. However, few quality assurance mechanisms for ecotourism incorporate interpretation performance measures. This may reflect some neglect or the undeniable difficulty in assessing the effectiveness of interpretation. Still, a few certification programmes, such as the Australian EcoCertification programme, have attempted to develop and incorporate interpretation criteria (see Chapter 22 in this volume), but these only prescribe that interpretation should be included and planned and that guides should have appropriate knowledge and skills. However, the increasing numbers of quality assurance mechanisms and training programmes specifically targeted at guides (see Chapters 17, 18 and 19 in this volume) suggest that there is increasing recognition of the pivotal role they occupy in delivering quality ecotourism.

These difficulties in evaluating, measuring and monitoring components of ecotourism do constrain our ability to accurately delineate quality ecotourism. The majority of indicators, quality assurance tools and overwhelming number of criteria in ecotourism-specific certification programmes focus on specific environmental criteria, such as waste and energy management, potable water or minimal impact guidelines for specific environments. This concentration on environmental criteria is, hopefully, not because the other key principles are considered any less important, but because these elements are relatively easy to quantify. Energy consumption and other environmental criteria lend themselves to hard science – clear and unambiguous measures of amounts used that can be benchmarked. There is now an increasing range of sophisticated monitoring and evaluation tools that indicate whether or not sustainable performance in a number of environmental criteria is met: for example, TourBench (2006), which is an online benchmarking system for measuring environmental consumption (www.tourbench.info) and Earthcheck (2006), which has developed a system of indicators to allow a wide range of industries to systematically benchmark their environmental performance (www.earthcheck.org).

However, the lack of significant sociocultural criteria in certification programmes (Synergy, 2000; Font and Buckley, 2001; WTO, 2002) is probably partly because there are few clear and unambiguous measures for social and cultural health and/or sustainability. Some may feel that the concentration on environmental issues rather than on sociocultural components is to be expected amongst commercial enterprise. The former provide 'eco'-savings while the sociocultural components tend to demand expenditure, such as fair wages, improved employment conditions and addressing human rights. On the other hand, this disproportionate focus on environmental issues may reflect the fact that many of the quality assurance tools for sustainable tourism have been developed in Europe (for instance, 78% of the ecolabels according to a WTO, 2002, report). This region has relatively high economic performance, coupled with strong labour protection rights, and perhaps this evident environmental degradation spawns this priority. Developing countries, in contrast, tend to use ecotourism as a sustainable development, an alternative livelihood or for poverty alleviation.

Defining Ecotourism Quality: Moving On from the Environment

Whatever the underlying reason for this undue focus on environmental issues, more attention is now being focused on quality assurance tools to encourage, stimulate, address and measure socio-economic sustainability. This trend will hopefully lead to more equitable distribution of economic benefits of tourism. This change of focus from environmental performance to ensuring that benefits of tourism are more widely distributed is a moral imperative. The ethics are simple – ensuring that the people who bear the main costs of tourism in terms of environmental impacts and sociocultural change should reap at least some of the economic gains (see Chapter 12). Unfortunately, putting this into practice is not quite as simple. The majority of ecotourism quality assurance tools do incorporate a basic demand for returns to local communities through prescribing elements such as local employment, use and consumption of local products and even occasionally a demand for training, professional development and donations.

However, tourism enterprises run a business, and the realities of obtaining consistent supplies of local goods, price differentials and difficulties in obtaining quality products mean that there can be no concise rule that dictates percentages purchased or number of local people employed. If there is a settlement close by, can you obtain the skills you need in the labour force? If not, can you train them? What is a fair wage? What if the local people do not want to be involved? How can you provide appropriate donations for the local community? The circumstances vary: each tourism enterprise is unique and flexibility is needed in what is relevant and appropriate in different circumstances. This very flexibility is often a downfall, for, with no prescribed standard, the results are often relatively superficial practices that put a veneer of responsible, ethical behaviour over continuing inequalities and inadequate returns to the local community. The injustices range from the inadvertent, those who do not know how to ensure corporate social responsibility, to the deliberate, and they have given rise to an advocacy industry that exposes unethical tourism enterprises and practices, for example, the UK-based NGO Tourism Concern (2006) (www.tourismconcern.org.uk).

If simple measures for evaluating a principle of quality ecotourism, such as the amounts of goods purchased locally or the number of local people employed, are difficult to apply, the move to incorporate or address more demanding sociocultural criteria that include measures to protect the integrity of local communities' social structures is fraught with difficulty. How do you prescribe a tool to evaluate components that are important, such as the appropriateness of land acquisition or mechanisms to ensure that the rights and aspirations of indigenous peoples are being met? There are many who would say that these are not elements that tourism enterprises have control over, or can influence, but sometimes they are, and sometimes they can. It is in this area of ensuring returns to the local communities and social integrity that ecotourism and ecotourism quality assurance mechanisms most clearly display the immaturity of the industry.

However, there are some excellent role models and mentors, such as Fair Trade in Tourism South Africa (see Chapter 14 in this volume), which has pushed the boundaries to show that non-exploitative labour arrangements are feasible and viable. The improvement in tourism standards and certification programmes also presents opportunities for indigenous communities to replace histories of exploitation and marginalization by the tourism industry (see Chapter 13). However, if indigenous involvement is considered desirable, it will be necessary to create flexible and customized frameworks and programmes, as well as standards and concepts of quality to reflect the diversity of communities. The development of programmes such as Aboriginal Tourism Australia's Respect Our Culture Certification Program (2006) (www.rocprogram.com) demonstrates how to address cultural protocols, and interestingly proclaims the use of the quality assurance tool of certification as a business development, rather than an evaluation tool.

There is a trend towards more people-centred models of tourism development, with new terms and 'movements' being promoted, such as community-based tourism, Pro-Poor Tourism, Tourism for Poverty Alleviation and Tourism for Peace. Most of these models have an emphasis on social issues and often participatory community development. There are obvious overlaps between these newer models and some of ecotourism's basic tenets, and in examining quality ecotourism there is a lot to learn from these movements. There is certainly a need to really push the boundaries of ecotourism beyond environmental initiatives and gain a better understanding of how to address some of the sociocultural issues, and have a more balanced or holistic approach. However, although quality ecotourism is a judicious mix of elements that address all of the key principles of ecotourism, the primary focus of ecotourism remains on natural areas and biodiversity conservation.

Achieving Quality in Ecotourism: Tools in the Toolbox

In Part One of this volume, the spectrum of quality assurance tools that have been developed and applied in the ecotourism industry to address and improve quality were discussed. In Chapter 2, we discussed the toolbox of quality assurance mechanisms, with a focus on voluntary initiatives currently being used to achieve quality ecotourism. We included a spectrum from awards to codes of conduct, to certification and accreditation, as well as some of the evaluation and monitoring mechanisms, such as benchmarking, audits and indicators. Chapter 3 focused specifically on awards of excellence and Chapter 4 discussed the benefits and challenges of using codes of conduct. Two examples of certification programmes that have been developed for application at different spatial levels were then reviewed. The Smart Voyager Program based in the Galápagos Islands is an area-specific programme (see Chapter 5), whereas Green Globe is a global programme (see Chapter 6) The final two chapters in Part One of this volume examined indicators as tools to benchmark, monitor and potentially promote quality ecotourism (see Chapters 7 and 8). As with any spectrum, however, there is a merging at the edges between the different initiatives – with awards blurring into pseudo-certification at one end, and certification blurring almost into regulation at the other. In the future, it is likely that we shall see a stronger shift in this spectrum, with governments more strongly supporting voluntary initiatives because of their potential to dictate quality best practices rather than minimal acceptable standards. The 'carrot' of tangible benefits that certification can deliver to ensure sustainable practices rather than the 'stick' of regulation, fines and penalties may be a better and possibly more cost-effective strategy.

Stakeholders' Perspectives on Quality in Ecotourism

As discussed in Part Two of this volume and specifically Chapter 9, there are many stakeholders involved in ecotourism and each has their own interests, motivations and needs. Quality ecotourism can serve many purposes, including conservation, poverty alleviation, community empowerment and reputation building. For national and regional governments, ecotourism may offer a more sustainable approach to tourism that provides significant benefits, including good foreign exchange earnings, long-term economic stability and economic diversification, stemming offshore leakage and encouraging regional growth and decentralization. For many NGOs, ecotourism offers an opportunity to protect and manage natural areas, through financing or actively contributing with labour, research or in-kind donations, additionally empowering local people to become involved in conservation.

The fact that ecotourism promises 'so much to so many' presents significant challenges in meeting all the stakeholders' expectations. However, all stakeholders have vested but different interests in ensuring that products and services that promote themselves as ecotourism are fulfilling the key principles. The quest for quality ecotourism assurance sometimes spawns partnerships between different stakeholder groups, such as education NGOs and conservation NGOs (see Chapter 18), private enterprise and conservation NGOs, public land managers and tourism enterprises (see Chapters 15 and 16) and government and indigenous communities (see Chapters 13 and 14). The challenges, benefits and opportunities for partnerships for protected area managers are explored in Chapters 15 and 16. The experiences of one protected area manager with certification programmes are discussed in Chapter 15 and the case study of PAN Parks provides an example of a certification programme for European wilderness areas in Chapter 16. Despite the different demands these groups place on ecotourism, they all need to ensure that the ecotourism experiences are genuine, the products and operators are ethically sound, the industry is environmentally and culturally sensitive and local communities are gaining some benefits and not being exploited.

Towards Quality in Ecotourism: a Focus on Certification Programmes

Although we have looked at a spectrum of voluntary tools, many of the chapters have focused on certification programmes. This emphasis reflects the increase in number of sustainable tourism or ecotourism-specific certification programmes over the last 10–15 years, and more are coming on line (as of 2006 there are 80 programmes worldwide). This plethora of sustainable tourism and ecotourism certification programmes mirrors the growing importance of the use of these initiatives to address quality issues and improve industry standards above regulatory minima mandated by legal frameworks (Fennell, 2003). The growth in the number of certification programmes also suggests increasing societal pressure for environmental and sociocultural sustainability, while avoiding government regulation.

This strong trend towards certification programmes reflects attempts to provide an assurance, a guarantee of quality. In comparison, codes of practice, guidelines and awards serve a valuable function as awareness-raising instruments, and indicators serve to monitor and provide snapshot information that warns if the system is out of balance. Certification involves many stakeholders (see Chapter 9 in this volume), and is multidimensional. It has the capacity to add value to ecotourism enterprises and also benefit a number of different consumers – both primary and secondary. Certification programmes, if well developed and implemented, may provide some of the following benefits:

- Provide tourists with environmentally and socially responsible choices/brands.
- Provide a benchmark that evaluates environmental, social and economic sustainability and hence provides secondary consumers (communities, indigenous people, NGOs, governments, protected area managers) with a method to filter and/or choose appropriate tourism.
- Help raise awareness of responsible business practices for the public.
- Provide a blueprint for or help educate businesses on sustainable practices (industry operators).
- Provide cost reductions through eco-savings for operators.
- Protect the environment (for conservationists) and resource base (operators).
- Provide an effective alternative to legislation or regulation by government.
- Improve public relations (operators, government, indigenous people).
- Provide a marketing advantage for certified operators.

This last point is often promoted by certification programmes, but current evidence suggests that such an advantage is negligible to non-existent (see Chapter 10 in this volume). However, as some of the chapters in this volume demonstrate, not all certification programmes are able to achieve some or all of these benefits. As the case studies of programmes demonstrate (see, for example, Chapters 5, 6, 16 and 22), there are still some significant problems and challenges that certification programmes need to overcome if they are going to be valuable tools that permeate the ecotourism industry and help redress greenwashing and ecotourism lite with credibility and legitimacy.

The diversity in what is measured in ecotourism-specific, rather than just sustainable tourism, certification programmes can be startling and causes significant challenges (see Bien, 2004). Most certification programmes, especially those that are more general sustainable certification programmes, or ecolabels have a disproportionate emphasis on environmental criteria, as previously discussed. Include the need to be flexible regarding sociocultural components and the difficulty in assessing performance in this area.

The popularity of certification programmes, expressed by the number of existing programmes and the increasing numbers of both local and national programmes in development (Font and Buckley, 2001; WTO, 2002; Chapter 23 in this volume), is partly to blame for the current lack of success of certification programmes as a serious mechanism to raise quality in ecotourism. This situation needs to be addressed by a range of stakeholders, including funding bodies of proposed programmes, programme managers and the ecotourism industry. As outlined in Chapter 23, opportunities exist to consolidate programmes into regional networks. The challenges of a significant lack of consumer recognition and buy-in (especially of their primary consumers, the tourists) and confusion as to what sustainable tourism or ecotourism certification programmes mean and measure are serious problems (see Chapter 11). This is compounded by the number of certification programmes on the market and the lack of consistency between them. Combined with perceptions of high costs and the lack of equitable access for small, medium and micro-enterprises and for developing countries, this means that certification programmes are not yet a significant force in delivering quality ecotourism. As Chapter 20 demonstrates, many ecotourism operators view investment in environmental certification as an ineffective use of limited human and/or financial resources, and further research is needed to explore the barriers to certification of ecotourism businesses.

Certification, like any tool, has its limitations and is not the panacea to solve all the problems associated with tourism. Certification cannot subsitute for good business practices or improve a poor location or product. Clients will not visit places that are inaccessible, too highly priced, unsafe or unhealthy, no matter how sustainable or 'eco-friendly'. However, the number of quality assurance tools available to assist the ecotourism industry is a positive development, and all of the tools covered in this volume have the capacity to encourage the industry to improve its performance.

Concluding Remarks

This volume presents the current state of play on quality in ecotourism, including both theoretical and practical (industry) points of view. The chapters in this volume discuss some of the challenges associated with planning and implementing quality ecotourism and provide numerous international case studies from a range of authors. The book considers a range of quality control mechanisms or tools, including certification programmes, from a variety of ecotourism and sustainable tourism stakeholders. Most of the chapters in this volume look at quality in ecotourism from a variety of stakeholders' perspectives: the tourist/consumer, community, ecotour guide and operator, non-government organizations and certification programme managers and protected area managers.

To break the cycles and clichés of 'tourism sowing the seeds of its own destruction' and 'loving areas to death', it is necessary for quality strategies to be endorsed and embraced, not just by the enlightened few but mainstreamed into all types of tourism. Quality ecotourism has a significant role to play in mentoring and leading mainstream tourism to achieve more sustainable outcomes.

We hope this volume adds to a better understanding of quality ecotourism, with the investigation of tools to monitor, measure and assure genuine ecotourism exploration.

References

Beaumont, N.K. (1999) Ecotourism: the contribution of educational nature experiences to environmental knowledge, attitudes and behaviours. Unpublished doctoral thesis, Australian School of Environmental Studies, Griffith University, Nathan, Queensland.

Bien, A. (2004) *A Simple User's Guide to Certification for Sustainable Tourism and Ecotourism.* The International Ecotourism Society, Washington, DC.

Buckley, R. (2000) Neat trends: current issues in nature, eco- and adventure tourism. *International Journal of Tourism Research* 2(6), 437–444.

Buckley, R. (2006) *Adventure Tourism.* CAB International, Wallingford, UK.

Earthcheck (2006) Available at: www.earthcheck.org. (accessed 18 September 2006).

Fennell, D.A. (2001) Areas and needs in ecotourism research. In: Weaver, D. (ed.) *The Encyclopedia of Ecotourism.* CAB International, Wallingford, UK, pp. 639–656.

Fennell, D.A. (2003) *Ecotourism.* Routledge, London, UK.

Font, X. and Buckley, R. (eds) (2001) *Tourism Ecolabelling: Certification and Promotion of Sustainable Management.* CAB International, Wallingford, UK.

Haig, I. (1997) Viewing nature: can a guide make a difference? Master of Arts thesis in Outdoor Education, Department of Outdoor Education, Griffith University, Brisbane, Queensland.

Ham, S.H. and Weiler, B. (2001) 100,000 beating bird hearts: tourism, wildlife and interpretation. Paper presented to the National Wildlife Tourism Conference, Hobart, Tasmania, 28–30 October 2001.

Kutay, K. (1990) Ecotourism: travel's new wave. *Vis à Vis*, July, 34–80.

Orams, M.B. (2001) Types of ecotourism. In: Weaver, D. (ed.) *The Encyclopedia of Ecotourism.* CAB International, Wallingford, UK, pp. 23–36.

Respect Our Culture (ROC)(2006) Available at: www.rocprogram.com (accessed 18 September 2006).

Synergy (2000) *Tourism Certification: An Analysis of Green Globe 21 and Other Tourism Certification Programs.* WWF-UK, London, UK.

TourBench (2006) Available at: www.tourbench.info (accessed 15 September 2006).

Tourism Concern (2006) Available at: www.tourismconcern.org.uk (accessed 15 September 2006).

Weaver, D.B. (2001a) Ecotourism in the context of other tourism types. In: Weaver, D. (ed.) *The Encyclopedia of Ecotourism.* CAB International, Wallingford, UK, pp. 73–84.

World Tourism Organization (WTO) (2002) V*oluntary Initiatives for Sustainable Tourism: Worldwide Inventory and Comparative Analysis of 104 Eco-Labels, Awards and Self-Commitments.* WTO, Madrid, Spain.

Glossary

Accreditation. A procedure by which an authoritative body formally recognizes that a certifier or certification programme is competent to carry out specific tasks (i.e. it certifies the certifier or demonstrates they are doing the job properly). This procedure can be qualifying, endorsing and licensing entities that perform certification of businesses, products, processes or services. In Australia, New Zealand, Canada, Fiji and some other countries, accreditation has been used synonymously with certification (Honey, 2002).

Accreditation body. Accreditation bodies 'certify the certifiers' and their capacity to certify companies or products. At present, there is a proposal for the creation of a Sustainable Tourism Stewardship Council that would become a tourism accreditation body.

Adventure tourism. Tourism that incorporates an element of risk, higher levels of physical exertion and a need for specialized skills to enable successful participation. The concept is subjective in that perceptions of risk and thresholds of physical exertion vary from person to person (Weaver, 2001).

Assessment. The process of examining, measuring, testing or otherwise determining conformity with requirements specified in an applicable standard (Toth, 2000).

Assessment, site or diagnostic visit. Process of examining conformity with requirements by visiting a site or organization. A site visit comprises a variety of assessment methods such as site observation, impact testing, desk review of measurements and management documentation, and staff interviews to cross-examine findings.

Assessor. A person who officially considers and examines an organization's performance or a process.

Audit. A systematic and objective evaluation that compares performance against a set of standards or criteria.

Auditor. A person who officially considers and examines an organization's performance or a process.

Backstage. A coping mechanism wherein an area within a local community is formally or informally designated for the retention of the culture in a non-commercialized form for the community's own use. Tourism is entirely or mostly excluded from such areas, although hard ecotourists or allocentric tourists may seek access to such areas in order to attain an 'authentic' tourism experience (Weaver, 2001).

Benchmark. A given value of some phenomenon against which the performance of an operation or destination can be judged. For example, a benchmark of 2% might be regarded as the desirable standard of growth in visitor intake that a certain ecotourism destination can sustain (Weaver, 2001).

Benchmarking. The process of comparing performances and processes within an industry to assess relative position either against a set industry standard or against those that are 'best in class'. Benchmarking is not synonymous with baselining, which establishes the existing level of performance within an operation (Synergy, 2000).

Best management practice(s). Series of principles and concrete recommendations that can be implemented by different land-use sectors. These practices are based on the outcomes of impact assessments, scientific research, pilot testing projects, adaptation to local realities and multi-stakeholder discussions. These best management practices can be used as the basis for the development of policies, codes of conduct and public awareness materials, and for the implementation of technical assistance, training and certification.

Best practice. An industry standard of the most advanced practice in respect of particular criteria, such as the energy-efficient operation of an ecolodge or effective interpretation techniques. Best practice is often used as the standard against which benchmarking is undertaken (Weaver, 2001).

Biodiversity. The variety of live forms, i.e. the different plants, animals and microorganisms, the genes they contain and the ecosystems they form. Biodiversity is usually considered at four levels: genetic diversity, species diversity, community diversity and ecosystem diversity.

Certification. A voluntary procedure that sets, assesses, monitors and gives written assurance that a product, process, service or management system conforms to specified requirements and norms. A certification/awarding body gives written assurance to the consumer and the industry in general. The outcome of certification is a certificate and usually the use of an ecolabel.

Certification programme. A complete system containing all the requirements needed to obtain a certification award or ecolabel. A certification programme will be managed by a certification body, but the programme is larger that the certification body or an individual certifier.

Codes of conduct. Itemized lists of recommended behaviour towards achieving sustainability that can apply to operators or tourists. These rudimentary quality control mechanisms are often criticized for their vagueness and self-regulation, but are also supported for providing moral advice for adherents and for providing broad directives for operators in an unthreatening manner (Weaver, 2001).

Community. People living in one place, district, state or country (NEAP, 2000).

Conformity assessment. A process that involves a product, service or system being evaluated for conformity against a standard.

Corporate social responsibility. A company's obligation to be accountable to all its stakeholders in all its operations and activities with the aim of achieving sustainable development, not only in the economic dimension but also in the social and environmental dimensions.

Criteria. Set of principles used as a means of judging. See standards.

Cultural tourism. Travel for the purpose of learning about cultures or aspects of cultures (Honey and Rome, 2001).

Ecolabelling. A scheme in which a product, company, service or destination may be awarded an ecological label on the basis of its 'acceptable' level of environmental impact. The acceptable level of environmental impact may be determined by consideration of a single environmental hurdle or after undertaking an assessment of its overall impacts (Synergy, 2000). Ecolabelling sometimes refers to the natural environment only; sometimes it takes into account social and cultural environments as well. An eco-quality label marks the state of the environmental quality, such as water quality for beaches or quality of wildlife in national parks (Honey, 2002).

Ecolodges. A specialized type of ecotourism accommodation that is usually located in or near a protected area or other ecotourism venue, and is managed in an environmentally and socioculturally sustainable fashion. Although having a high profile within the ecotourism sector, ecolodges globally account for only a very small proportion of all ecotourist visitor nights (Weaver, 2001).

Ecotourism. 'Responsible tourism to natural areas that conserves the environment and improves the welfare of local people', according to the International Ecotourism Society. A more comprehensive definition is:

> travel to fragile, pristine, and usually protected areas that strives to be low impact and (usually) small scale. It helps educate the traveller; provides funds for conservation; directly benefits the economic development and political empowerment of local communities; and fosters respect for different cultures and for human rights.
>
> (Honey, 2002)

Ecotourism certification programmes. Programmes that cover business, services and products that describe themselves as involved in ecotourism. They focus on individual or site-specific businesses, have standards that are tailored to local conditions and are largely or totally performance-based (Honey and Rome, 2001).

Ecotourism lite. This involves a business adopting sensible but small, cosmetic and often cost-saving practices that are typically marketed as major innovations (Honey, 2002).

Ecotourist. A tourist who participates in ecotourism activities. Ecotourists are commonly segmented into hard and soft ideal types and are mainly from more developed regions such as North America, Western Europe, Australia and New Zealand (Weaver, 2001).

Environmental impact assessment (EIA). The process of predicting and evaluating the impacts of specific developments or actions on the environment. The EIA process involves: (i) reviewing the existing state of the environment and the characteristics of the proposed development; (ii) predicting the state of the future environment with and without the development; (iii) considering the methods for reducing or eliminating any negative impacts; (iv) producing the environmental impact statement for public consultation that discusses these points; and (v) making a decision about whether the development should proceed in the proposed site, along with a list of relevant mitigation measures (Synergy, 2000).

Environmental impact statement. The report resulting from an environmental impact assessment.

Environmental management system (EMS). This is the part of the overall management system that includes the organizational structure, responsibilities, practices, procedures, processes and resources for determining and implementing the environmental policy. An environmental management system includes tools such as environmental impact assessment, environmental auditing and strategic environmental assessment (Synergy, 2000).

Fair Trade. A movement that aims to address imbalances in international trade in agricultural commodities like coffee, tea and fruit, through trading partnerships and labelling of goods exported by developing countries, usually for consumption in high-income countries located in the 'North'. Fair Trade is based on the premise that socially informed consumers will pay a premium price in exchange for a reliable guarantee that certain social, labour and environmental standards have been met during the production process (Kocken, 2003).

Green consumer. A consumer whose behaviour (including purchasing) is influenced by considerations of the environmental implications of their actions. The growth in the non-superficial green consumer market is an indicator of the emergence of the green paradigm (Weaver, 2001).

Greenwashing (veneer environmentalism). A term used to describe businesses, services or products that promote themselves as environmentally friendly when they are not.

Guidelines. A set of principles put forward to establish standards or determine a course of action (HarperCollins, 1999).

Hard ecotourist. An ecotourist market segment that is strongly biocentric and characterized as an ideal type by the desire for deep and meaningful interaction with natural settings, minimal services, orientation towards enhancement sustainability, FIT, physically and mentally challenging experiences and specialized travel. Hard ecotourists constitute only a very small proportion of the ecotourist market (Weaver, 2001).

Indicator. In the context of certification, an indicator is a measurable element of the criteria that the verification process will assess.

Indigenous people. Generally referring to the original inhabitants of an area.

Indigenous tourism. Tourism that respects and accommodates local traditions where there is substantial community or local control over the social and natural resources involved in tourism (see Vivanco, Chapter 13 in this volume).

International Organization for Standardization (ISO). A world federation based in Geneva to develop voluntary standards designed to facilitate international manufacturing, trade and communications (Honey, 2002).

Interpretation. A means of communicating ideas and feelings that help people enrich their understanding and appreciation of their world and their role within it.

ISO 9000. The international series of standards for quality management systems.

ISO 14001. The international standard for environmental management systems.

Licence. A certificate or document giving official permission to undertake an activity on public land or to drive a vehicle.

Life-cycle assessment. This is a variant of an EMS that tracks a product, process or activity from 'cradle to grave'. In the tourism industry, it assesses the use of resources and social and environmental impact during three phases: (i) departure and return travel; (ii) stay at the destination; and (iii) activities at the destination. For accommodations, the three-phase life cycle can be analysed as: (i) construction; (ii) operation; and (iii) demolition (Honey and Rome, 2001).

Limits of acceptable change (LAC). A land management philosophy that identifies specific indicators of environmental quality and tourism impacts and defines thesholds within which the conservation goals of a protected area are met (Weaver, 2001).

Mass or mainstream tourism. Commonly used term for large-scale tourism, implying participation by the mass or bulk of a society's population. The term is usually used in reference to the post-Second World War era of exponential tourism growth (Weaver, 2001).

Mohonk Agreement. A document containing a set of general principles and elements that should be part of any sound ecotourism and sustainable tourism certification programmes. Adopted at an international workshop held at Mohonk Mountain House, New Paltz, New York, 17–19 November 2000.

Monitoring. The continued measurement and evaluation of environmental impacts to compare an organization's environmental performance with agreed environmental targets. Monitoring in certification programmes usually refers to the process of ensuring that the applicant meets the criteria throughout the period of validity of the certificate/ecolabel.

Nature tourism/nature-based tourism. Any type of tourism that relies mainly on attractions directly related to the natural environment. Ecotourism and 3S tourism are both types of nature-based tourism (Weaver, 2001).

Network. An interconnected group or system of ecolabel or certification schemes.

Permit. A certificate or document giving official permission to undertake an activity, such as public land permits to undertake specific recreational activities, and workplace health and safety permits.

Protected area. An area of land and/or sea especially dedicated to the protection and maintenance of biological diversity and of natural and associated cultural resources, and managed through legal or other effective means. Protected areas (high-order protected areas such as national parks in particular) are the most popular ecotourism setting (Weaver, 2001).

Quality. This is a subjective concept. It refers to excellence, superiority, class, eminence, value and worth, but what is quality for one person may not be quality to the next (Polovitz Nickerson, 2006).

Quality ecotourism. Ecotourism products, services and experiences that meet the key principles of ecotourism, which are: a natural area focus, environmentally sustainable, some component of interpretation or education, provides returns for the environment and returns for local communities and is culturally sensitive.

Quality system. A formal set of internationally recognized procedures and standards that indicates conformity to industry best practice. These are not currently evident in ecotourism, though many argue that their adaptation is the next logical step in the ongoing professionalism of the sector (Weaver, 2001).

Regulation. A rule, principle or condition that governs procedure or behaviour as required by official rules (HarperCollins, 1999).

Small and medium-sized enterprises (SMEs). These are generally companies that employ more than ten but fewer than 250 individuals. Companies employing fewer than ten people are generally referred to as micro-enterprises (Honey, 2002).

Soft ecotourist. An ecotourist market segment that is more anthropocentric in perspective, and prefers short-term and diversionary contact with the natural environment. This preferably occurs in a well-serviced and mediated setting, such as a sacrificial space within a high-order protected area. Soft ecotourists are often the same as mass tourists and constitute the overwhelming majority of the ecotourist market (Weaver, 2001).

Stakeholders. All parties having an interest in a particular tourism project or certification programme (Honey and Rome, 2001). They may include environmentalists, protected area managers, tourism industry representatives, consumers, host countries, host communities, funders and financiers, and others who have an interest in a particular tourism project or certification programme.

Standard. A document approved by a recognized body that provides for common and repeated use of a prescribed set of rules, conditions or requirements (Honey, 2002).

Standards, difference between standards and criteria. Criteria are established means to verify if performance or process has reached the quality of the standards required.

Standards, performance-based. Level of quality set according to the ability of applicants to meet a minimum performance on a series of indicators. Minimum performances are based on benchmarks for that specific indicator against the average performance within the sector.

Standards, process-based. Level of quality set according to the ability of applicants to produce evidence of actions taken to make a positive contribution towards or achieve the goals of the certification programme.

Star ratings. A rating system used to designate quality, such as the Automobile Association's star rating system for hotels.

Stewardship councils. These are multi-stakeholder partnerships designed to provide a forum in which various actors with different interests in the targeted sectors can engage in collaborative solution-oriented dialogue to their mutual advantage and can create market-based incentives to stimulate the production and consumption of certified sustainable products. Stewardship councils accredit certifiers based on their performance and help ensure that the certification is being conducted through objective and transparent mechanisms (Honey, 2002).

Sustainable development. A term popularized by the Brundtland Report in the late 1980s as development that meets the needs of the present generation without compromising the ability of future generations to meet their needs (Weaver, 2001).

Sustainable tourism. According to the World Tourism Organization, 'envisaged as leading to management of all resources in such a way that economic, social and aesthetic needs can be fulfilled while maintaining cultural integrity, essential ecological processes, biological diversity, and life support systems' (Honey, 2002).

Sustainable tourism certification programmes. Programmes that measure a range of environmental, sociocultural and economic equity issues both internally (within the business, service, or product) and externally (with regard to the surrounding community and physical environment) (Honey and Rome, 2001).

3S tourism. 'Sea, sand and sun' or beach resort tourism. 3S tourism can be included in other types of tourism, but is usually associated with mass tourism (Weaver, 2001).

Tourism. The activities of persons travelling to and staying in places outside their usual environment for more than 1 day and less than 1 continuous year for leisure, business and other purposes.

Voluntary initiatives (agreements). These are agreements in the tourism industry that are not legally required or binding and are usually focused on achieving environmental benefits beyond what the law requires (Honey, 2002).

World Tourism Organization (WTO). A UN institution based in Madrid that collects data on tourism and lobbies on behalf of the industry. Founded in 1975, its members include 134 national governments and more than 325 affiliates, representing tourism-related businesses (http://european-fair-trade-association.org/Efta/Doc/History.pdf).

References

HarperCollins (1999) *Concise Dictionary*, 4th edn. HarperCollins Publishers, Glasgow, UK.

Honey, M. (ed.) (2002) *Ecotourism and Certification: Setting Standards in Practice*. Island Press, Washington, DC.

Honey, M. and Rome, A. (2001) *Protecting Paradise: Certification Programs for Sustainable Tourism and Ecotourism*. Institute for Policy Studies, Washington, DC, USA.

Kocken, M. (2003) *Fifty Years of Fair Trade – A Brief History of the Fair Trade Movement*.

NEAP (2000) *Nature and Ecotourism Accreditation Program, Second Edition*. NEAP, Brisbane, Australia.

Polovitz Nickerson, N. (2006) Some reflections on quality tourism experiences. In: Jennings, G. and Polovitz Nickerson, N. (eds) *Quality Tourism Experiences*. Elsevier Butterworth-Heinemann, Oxford, UK, pp. 227–235.

Synergy (2000) *Tourism Certification: An Analysis of Green Globe 21 and Other Tourism Certification Programs*. WWF-UK, London, UK.

Toth, R.B. (2000) *Implementing a Worldwide Sustainable Tourism Certification System*. R.B. Toth and Associates, Alexandria, Virginia.

Weaver, D. (2001) *Ecotourism*. John Wiley and Sons Australia, Milton, Queensland.

Index